HANDBOOK OF INNOVATION IN

Handbook of Innovation in Public Services

Edited by

Stephen P. Osborne

University of Edinburgh, UK

Louise Brown

University of Bath, UK

Edward Elgar
Cheltenham, UK • Northampton, MA, USA

Published by
Edward Elgar Publishing Limited
The Lypiatts
15 Lansdown Road
Cheltenham
Glos GL50 2JA
UK

Edward Elgar Publishing, Inc.
William Pratt House
9 Dewey Court
Northampton
Massachusetts 01060
USA

A catalogue record for this book
is available from the British Library

Library of Congress Control Number: 2012943184

This book is available electronically in the ElgarOnline.com
Social and Political Science Subject Collection, E-ISBN 978 1 84980 975 7

ISBN 978 1 84980 974 0 (cased)

Typeset by Servis Filmsetting Ltd, Stockport, Cheshire
Printed and bound by MPG Books Group, UK

Contents

About the editors

Stephen P. Osborne is Professor of International Public Management and Director of the Centre for Public Services Research at the University of Edinburgh Business School, Scotland. He specialises in public management reform, innovation and change, and the role of the third sector in public services provision. He is editor of *Public Management Review* and President of the International Research Society for Public Management.

Louise Brown is Reader in Social Work at the Department of Social and Policy Sciences, University of Bath, England. Her research interests are in implementing innovation in public sector services, particularly social care; managing risk and scaling up innovation. She is an editorial board member of *Public Management Review* and a Fellow at the National Institute for Clinical Excellence in Health (NICE).

Contributors

Damon Alexander is a Research Fellow in the School of Social and Political Sciences at the University of Melbourne, Australia.

Rhys Andrews is a Reader in Public Management at Cardiff Business School, Wales.

Sue Baines is a Reader at Manchester Metropolitan University, England, where she works on issues of the mixed economy of welfare and social care and its effects on service users, carers, households and organisations.

James Barlow holds a Chair in Technology and Innovation Management at Imperial College Business School, England, specialising in healthcare services and infrastructure.

Cathy Barton-Sweeney is a Researcher and Honorary Lecturer in the Centre for Primary Care and Public Health, Barts and the London School of Medicine and Dentistry, England.

Victor Bekkers is Professor of Public Administration and Public Policy at Erasmus University Rotterdam, The Netherlands.

George A. Boyne is Professor of Public Sector Management and Dean of Cardiff Business School, Cardiff University, Wales.

Kerry Brown holds the Mulpha Chair in Tourism Asset Management and is the Director of the Research Centre for Tourism, Leisure and Work at Southern Cross University, Australia.

John M. Bryson is McKnight Presidential Professor of Planning and Public Affairs in the Hubert H. Humphrey School of Public Affairs at the University of Minnesota, USA.

Mike Carter has extensive experience at senior management level in the private and public sectors and is a Fellow at the Universities of Bath and Exeter. He is also the former Director of Executive Development, the Centre for Leadership Studies, University of Exeter Business School, and has taught leadership, sensemaking and organizational change on a variety of MBA and executive development programmes.

Celine Chew is Senior Lecturer at Cardiff University, Wales, and Associate of the Centre for Business Responsibility Accountability, Sustainability and Society (BRASS) funded by the Economic and Social Research Council (ESRC), UK. She is an editorial board member of *Public Management Review* and *Marketing Intelligence and Planning*.

Ian Colville is Senior Lecturer in the School of Management, University of Bath, UK where he is also Director of the Change Management Forum. The purpose of the forum is to provide a place which brings practitioners and academics together, such that organisational change theory meets organisational practice to their mutual benefit. He is an editorial board member of *Human Relations and Organization Studies*.

Mark Considine is Professor and Dean of the Faculty of Arts at the University of Melbourne, Australia.

Barbara C. Crosby is an Associate Professor specialising in leadership studies in the Hubert H. Humphrey School of Public Affairs at the University of Minnesota, USA.

Paul Cunningham is Director and Senior Research Fellow in the Manchester Institute of Innovation Research at the University of Manchester. He has over 25 years' experience in the study of the governance and impact of Science, Technology and Innovation policies, both in the UK and internationally.

Jakob Edler is Professor of Innovation Policy and Strategy and Executive Director of the Manchester Institute of Innovation Research, MBS, University of Manchester, England. His main research areas in recent years have been demand-side innovation policy and the role of public procurement to spur innovation; governance of science and innovation with a focus on internationalisation; and the development of evaluation concepts for policy and programmes.

Michelle Farr is a Research Officer and Teaching Fellow in the Department of Social and Policy Sciences at the University of Bath, England.

Shaun Goldfinch is an Associate Professor at Nottingham University Business School, England.

Trisha Greenhalgh is a London GP and Professor of Primary Health Care, Queen Mary University of London, England.

Jean Hartley is Professor of Organisational Analysis at Warwick Business School, England, with research interests in innovation and organisational change, and in public leadership.

Gill Harvey is Reader in Health Management at Manchester Business School, England. She has a professional background in nursing and previously worked for the Royal College of Nursing, England, where she was Director of the Quality Improvement Programme. She has researched and published widely on the implementation of evidence and facilitating quality improvement in practice.

Brian W. Head is Professorial Research Fellow, Institute for Social Science Research, University of Queensland, Australia. His research interests include collaboration to address major social issues, early intervention approaches, evidence-based policy capacities, service delivery, community consultation and governance issues.

Birgit Jæger is Professor of Science Technology and Society at Roskilde University Department of Society and Globalisation, Denmark. She is currently working on a study on 'Collaborative Innovation in the Public Sector'.

Andrew Johnston is currently Principal Lecturer in International Business at Sheffield Business School, Sheffield Hallam University, England. His research interests focus primarily on the regional economic development process, specifically innovation and entrepreneurship in both public and private sector contexts, university–industry collaboration, knowledge flows and inter-organisational networks.

Paul Joyce is Director of Liverpool Business School at Liverpool John Moores University, England. He has worked on various projects in the UK and internationally on strategic management, innovation and reform in the public services.

Robyn Keast is an Associate Professor in the School of Management, Queensland University of Technology, Australia. Her research focus centres on the structural and micro-processes of networks and collaborative arrangements providing public and voluntary sector service delivery and innovation.

Tony Kinder is Senior Lecturer in Management and works on service innovation in the Business School at the University of Edinburgh, Scotland.

Jenny M. Lewis is Professor of Public Administration and Public Policy at Roskilde University, Denmark and the University of Melbourne, Australia.

Carrick Longley is an active duty Marine Corps Captain and doctoral student in Information Sciences at the Naval Postgraduate School in Monterey, USA.

Laurence E. Lynn, Jr. is Sid Richardson Research Professor at the Lyndon B. Johnson School of Public Affairs, University of Texas at Austin, USA.

Fergus Lyon is Professor of Enterprise and Organisations in the Centre for Enterprise and Economic Development Research, Middlesex University, England. He is currently Associate Director (Social Enterprise) of the ESRC-funded Third Sector Research Centre.

Michael Macaulay is Professor in Public Management at Teesside University, England, and has published extensively in the fields of public ethics, integrity and anti-corruption, particularly within the context of local government.

Fraser Macfarlane is a Senior Research Fellow in the Centre for Primary Care and Public Health, Barts and the London School of Medicine and Dentistry, England.

Kate McLaughlin was Senior Lecturer in Public Management in INLOGOV at the University of Birmingham, England. She has now retired.

Myrna P. Mandell is Professor Emeritus at California State University, USA and an Adjunct Faculty at Southern Cross University, Australia, and is recognised as a scholar and researcher in the field of networks and network management.

Mike Martin is a Visiting Professor at Newcastle University, England. His research interests are in issues of information sharing and the information economy.

Valentina Mele is Assistant Professor in the Department of Policy Analysis and Public Management, Bocconi University, Italy.

Ian Miles is Professor of Technological Innovation and Social Change at Manchester Institute of Innovation Research, Manchester Business School, England, and also Head of the Laboratory of Economics of Innovation at ISSEK, Higher School of Economics, Russia. In addition to research on service innovation and knowledge-intensive business services, his work has encompassed foresight and futures studies, information technology innovation and social indicators.

Hannah Noke is an Associate Professor in Entrepreneurship and Innovation at Nottingham University Business School, England. Her research focuses on the transformation of organisations through the implementation of innovation, particularly within the public sector context.

David Norris is Senior Lecturer in Marketing at Teesside University Business School, England. His research interests lie in the field of innovation, particularly looking at how innovation can be used to enhance organisations.

Zoe Radnor is a Professor of Operations Management at Cardiff Business School, Wales. Her area of interest is in performance and process improvement and management in public services. She has led research projects for the Scottish Executive, HM Revenue and Customs, HM Court Services, HealthCare, and Local Government and Higher Education organisations which have evaluated how 'lean' techniques are and could be used in the public sector.

Mary Lee Rhodes is an Assistant Professor of Public Management at Trinity College, Republic of Ireland.

Nancy C. Roberts is a Professor of Defense Analysis in the School of Operational and Information Sciences at the Naval Postgraduate School in Monterey, USA.

Kirsty Strokosch is a Research Associate of the Centre for Public Services Research at the University of Edinburgh Business School, Scotland. She is interested in the co-production of public services at the individual and organisational levels.

James H. Svara is Professor of Public Affairs and Director of the Center for Urban Innovation at Arizona State University, USA.

Jacob Torfing is a Professor in Politics and Institutions at the Department of Society and Globalisation, Roskilde University, Denmark, and Director of the Centre for Democratic Network Governance, Roskilde University, Denmark.

Elvira Uyarra is a Research Fellow at the Manchester Institute of Innovation Research, University of Manchester, England. Her current research interests centre on the areas of regional science and innovation policy; the geography of knowledge and innovation; evolutionary approaches to public policy; and the innovation impact of public procurement.

Richard M. Walker is Professor of Public Management and Policy in the Department of Public and Social Administration at City University of Hong Kong, Hong Kong, SAR. His research examines performance in public organisations and questions of innovation, strategic management, red tape and so on, together with sustainable development.

Joe Wallis is a Professor and Head of the Department of Management at the American University of Sharjah, United Arab Emirates. His research interests mainly focus on the political economy of reform, leadership and public sector economics. He has co-authored five books, including the *International Handbook of Public Management Reform*, and has written over 70 articles, including some that have appeared in *Public Administration*, *Public Management Review*, *Public Money and Management*, *Governance*, *World Development* and the *Australian Journal of Public Administration*.

Jennifer Waterhouse is a Senior Lecturer in the Newcastle Business School at the University of Newcastle, Australia.

Rob Wilson is a Senior Lecturer at Newcastle University, England, where he works in the Business School. His research interests are in the exploration of the challenges of information and innovation in the mixed economy of public services.

Paul Windrum is Associate Professor in Strategy at University of Nottingham Business School, England, and Visiting Professor at Max Plank Institute for Economics, Germany. He is an expert on innovation in public and private sector services. Publications include *Innovation in Public Services: Entrepreneurship, Creativity and Management*.

Acknowledgements

The editors acknowledge the invaluable contributions of Matthew Pitman, at Edward Elgar, and Isobel Speedman, at the University of Edinburgh. This volume would have been impossible without them.

Introduction: innovation in public services
Stephen P. Osborne and Louise Brown[1]

INTRODUCTION

> The general topic of innovation has inspired vast amounts of research, theorizing, speculation, and wishful thinking . . . Innovation is advocated . . . by sundry philosophers, journalists, politicians, industrialists and social reformers. (Kimberly 1981, p. 84)

Kimberly's judgement on the pre-eminence of innovation as a concept reflected no doubt the results of two decades of tectonic societal change throughout the 1960s and 1970s. Yet it resonates also with the place that innovation currently occupies in public policy and public services management in the early twenty-first century (Aldbury 2005). Since the early 1980s, it has become one of the key 'buzzwords' beloved by policy makers and practitioners around the world (Borins 2001; Eshima et al. 2001) – leading one commentator to dismiss it as 'policy chic' (Behn 1997). Indeed, it has an appeal that seems hard to argue with. It combines a determination to reform and improve the delivery of public services with a whiff of 'state of the art' business practice. Surely no one can disagree with such a heady cocktail?

In the UK, for example, the growing dominion of innovation as an influential concept in public policy can be traced back to the early 1980s and it has continued ever since. In 2008 the Cabinet Office exhorted that 'government must embrace a new culture that celebrates local innovation' (Cabinet Office 2008, p. 7). Likewise the highly influential White Paper *Innovation Nation* asserted that innovation in public services 'will be essential to meet the economic and social challenges of the 21st century' (Department of Innovation, Universities and Skills (DIUS) 2008a, p. 8; see also Audit Commission 2007).

What is curious is that this pre-eminence has developed over the past three decades despite the absence of an evidence base. Until recently, comparatively little was known of the contingencies, processes and impact of innovation in public services (Osborne and Brown 2011). As a consequence both public policy and academic research have been predicated upon a diffuse view of the nature and process of innovation in relation to public services, despite repeated calls for evidence-based (or at least, evidence-influenced) public policy (e.g. Nutley et al. 2007). The effect of this has been to leave policy makers and public service managers with little guidance upon how to manage the challenging process of innovating in service delivery; the UK *Innovation Hub* report published in 2008 going so far as to state that it is 'too early to be prescriptive about managing innovation' (DIUS 2008b, p. 19). Whilst there may indeed still be gaps in our knowledge, this book aims to provide a framework for understanding and supporting innovation in public services. For the first time, it brings together research on innovation in public services from around the globe.

This introductory chapter is intended to provide a guide to the remainder of the book. It will begin by exploring the challenges that we face in understanding innovation and argue that there are several key issues that need to be addressed in developing further this understanding. The second part will then provide an overview to the rest of the volume and the key issues that it addresses.

INNOVATION IN PUBLIC SERVICES: THREE FLAWS

Our initial premise is that there are three flaws that have undermined our understanding of innovation in public services. These are:

- a flawed understanding of the nature of innovation;
- the positioning of innovation as a normative 'good' in public policy and resultant prescriptive policy making; and
- the adoption of an inappropriate model of innovation from the manufacturing, rather than the services, sector.

The first two of these flaws are addressed here whilst the third is the subject of a separate chapter.[2]

A Flawed Understanding of the Nature of Innovation

The study and practice of innovation in public services were beset over the latter half of the twentieth century by persistent misunderstandings of its nature. In the UK, for example, it has been subjected to mistaken characterisations from two perspectives. First, the Conservative government of the 1980s drew upon Porter's theory of 'competitive advantage' (Porter 1985) as the central mechanism through which to drive improvement in public services delivery. This mechanism placed innovation at the heart of the effective workings of the market in order to achieve precisely such 'competitive advantage' (Nelson 1993). However, like much of the New Public Management movement, this approach drew upon management experience and theory derived from the manufacturing sector, with a concentration upon the development of finite products in a stable market environment and 'based upon assumptions drawn from manufacturing industry' – services as such were considered by Porter to be 'fragmented industries' and received scant attention in the model (Nankervis 2005, p. 111). This led to an approach to the development and support of innovation in public services by central government that subsequently concentrated upon the design of 'innovation products' rather than 'service processes'. This is explored further below.[3]

The policies of the subsequent UK Labour government of 1997–2010 were affected by a different problem, however. The place of innovation in the public policy debate has never disappeared – indeed, 'innovation' was at the core of that Labour government's agenda since the publication of the *Modernising Government* White Paper (Cabinet Office 1999). This describes innovation as a process of the '*continuous improvement* in central government policy making and [public] service delivery' (para. 4.9, our emphasis) – a characterisation contained in a series of subsequent policy documents – for example, House of Commons Select Committee of Public Accounts (2003), Audit Commission (2007), Cabinet Office (2008) and DIUS (2008a).

This formulation is at odds with the extant innovation research literature which situates not continuous improvement but rather 'newness' or *discontinuous change* at the heart of the innovation process (e.g. Tushman and Anderson 1985; Herbig 1991; de Brentani 2001; Johannessen et al. 2001) – and that this is what differentiates its managerial challenges from those of incremental organisational change or service development. This view of innovation is clearly at odds with that employed within the current UK policy framework and elsewhere, notwithstanding the guidance of the academic advisors to the UK government who have continued to emphasise both the complexity of innovation and the centrality of discontinuous change to it as a process (e.g. Mulgan and Albury 2003; Hartley 2006).

Such a re-conceptualisation, we argue, is an injustice to the intricacy of managing both innovative and incremental service development. Both are essential for reforming and improving public services – but both require different approaches to their facilitation and sustenance. Public policy does an injustice to both by conflating them together. Even the work of Mulgan and Albury (2003) continues to conflate incremental innovation (discussed further below) with incremental service development and organisational change. This is a fatal flaw. It misunderstands the differing challenges that service development and service innovation pose. It is a quite different task, for example, to support staff in developing their existing skills than to tell them that these skills have been made redundant and that they need to re-train to retain their post (if it has not been made redundant too, of course). The distinctive nature, and challenges, of innovation, as opposed to service development or change (such as the management of risk, uncertainty and failure), become lost in such sophistry.

This has two implications for public policy. First, we need to know whether the public service reform process is based upon incremental development or upon innovation because it helps us understand the trajectory of this reform and to evaluate its strengths and limitations. Secondly, it matters at a very fundamental level to the public service managers and staff embroiled within the reform process. The management of innovation is an entirely different task from the management of developmental change, as suggested above. If public service managers and staff (whether they are situated in the public, private or third sector) are to be provided with the requisite managerial tools to carry out their roles effectively, then it is essential that public policy is based upon an accurate understanding of the innovation process, rather than conflating it with the rather different, if as important, process of developmental change.

Innovation as a Normative Good

Recent UK papers for Society for Local Authority Chief Executives (SOLACE) (Thomas 2008) and for the Innovation Unit (Horne 2008) have urged the normative need for innovation – yet with no clear statement of what this means, beyond 'the need to improve existing services' (Horne 2008, p. 6). In a similar vein Westall, focusing on the role of social enterprise in innovation, describes innovation as 'changes in products, services and processes . . . to meet new needs in new ways' (Westall 2007, p. 4).

Contained within this discourse has been the enduring assumption that any particular innovation must, *a priori*, be 'a good thing' – because the overall process of innovation is 'a good thing'. Yet these are statements of an entirely different order. One can agree that 'innovation' as a process is essential for the improvement of public services – but that is not the same as asserting that any specific innovation must therefore be positive, simply because it is 'an innovation'.

This conceptualisation of innovation as a normative good can also be found embedded in the dialogue about 'social innovation'. Harris and Albury (2009) situate this as innovation 'for the social and public *good*' (p. 16, our emphasis), compounding the assumption that innovation must always be a positive boon. Social innovation, it seems, can only ever be such a boon and so any opposition to it must therefore be reactionary and somehow 'not' in the public good (for a more detailed exploration of the nature of 'social innovation' see Phills et al. 2008 and Murray et al. 2010).

However, as Hartley (2005) has noted, whilst innovation and improvement have often been assumed to be synonymous this is by no means always the case. Consider briefly the innovative technology that has allowed the development of biometric identity cards. This is clearly both a technical and social innovation. Yet where does that leave the large numbers of citizens complaining that this innovation is not so much a normative good as an infringement of their civil liberties and another step in the creation of a 'big brother' society – or even those scientists who argue that the technology itself is flawed and easy to circumnavigate (Lips et al. 2009)? Similarly the 'pin-down' and 'regression therapy' approaches to residential social care for young people in the 1990s were undoubtedly innovative in their nature – yet few would not argue that they breached fundamental human rights and as such had no place in the repertoire of social work, no matter how 'innovative' they might have been (Levy and Kahan 1991; Kirkwood 1993; Kendrick 1998).

Such over-reaching assertions about innovation do little to facilitate appropriate innovation in public services, nor do they acknowledge the potential for negative effects of innovation, or the challenges that this poses for its support and management. Van de Ven (1988) has made this important point more broadly: the way in which innovation and success have become seen as interchangeable. Noting that innovation 'is often viewed as a good thing because the new idea must be useful' he argues that innovations that do not produce such a normative improvement are subsequently redefined – '[they] are not normally called innovations, they are usually called mistakes' (1988, p. 105). The difficulty with such normative assumptions is that they do nothing for our understanding of the innovation process in public services – and potentially hinder the guidance that can be offered to policy makers and practitioners about the promotion, support and management of appropriate and effective innovation in public services. Innovation is vital to the provision of effective and responsive public services. However, its support and management require a nuanced approach that acknowledges that not all positive change is always innovative and that not all innovative change is always beneficial. We will now present a framework that we argue offers precisely such a nuanced and engaged approach to understanding innovation in public services.

UNDERSTANDING INNOVATION IN PUBLIC SERVICES

The Nature of Innovation

The appraisal of UK public policy around innovation and public services above noted that there was a lack of precision about what is actually meant by innovation and that there was a normative tendency that assumed innovative activity must be a positive – and that this approach was also part of a somewhat circular definition of an innovation. Both these limitations can also be found in the research literature. Membretti (2007) and Meeuwisse (2008), for example, both evaluate innovation in public services without any clear definition of what is meant by 'innovation'. The European Union PUBLIN programme on innovation in public services (Koch and Hauknes 2005) includes impressive reviews of the private and public sector innovation literature (e.g. Halvorsen et al. 2005; Roste 2005), yet the programme is also disappointing in its conceptualisation of innovation. Halvorsen et al. (2005), for example, initially define it simply as 'changes in behaviour' (p. 2), later refining this to the 'implementation of a conscious programme of change to gain certain effects or results' (p. 63) – a definition subsequently adopted by the programme as a whole. The problem with such a broad definition of innovation is two-fold. First, it assumes that innovation must be a conscious process, yet this is often not the case. The commercial development of 'Post-It Notes', for example, was certainly an innovation, but it was entirely an accidental by-product of a search for another product (Peters and Waterman 1982). Just as with change more generally, innovation can be an emergent as well as a planned process – and for many public services, change and/or innovation can be thrust upon them by political decisions or by 'accidental invention' as much as a conscious determination to address a 'performance gap' (Golden 1990). Secondly, it falls prey to the conflation of innovation and incremental development identified earlier, with similar results.

There is, however, a substantial literature that explores the nature of innovation – and that could provide an important input into the policy process. Contemporary innovation theory thus differentiates between four modes of change to products and services – three innovative modes and one developmental (Garcia and Calantone 2002). The first is *radical innovation* – a comparatively rare event that transforms the entire societal paradigm of production (classic examples being the replacement of canals by the railways in the industrial revolution and the creation of the World Wide Web). The second type is *architectural innovation*. This results in changes to both organisational skills and competencies and to the market/needs that an innovation is addressing – but within the existing production paradigm (Henderson and Clark 1990). The third type of innovation is often called *incremental innovation*. The term 'incremental' here is slightly misleading. Such innovation still involves discontinuous change to products or services. However, it takes place within the existing production paradigm and affects either organisational skills and competencies or the market/needs that the innovation is addressing, not both (Garcia and Calantone 2002). The fourth type of change is *product or service development*, that builds upon existing skills or markets/needs and may well involve significant organisational learning – but that does not involve any element of 'newness' or discontinuity (Sundbo 1997).

In differentiating these four types of change it is important not to fall victim to the above flaw of assuming any normative element to the discussion. Over time a series of non-innovative developments can be as significant for a service as one incident of innovation, whilst incremental innovations may be more significant or enduring than architectural ones. The central issue here is to understand the different policy contexts and approaches to their management that different types of change and innovation require. One size does not 'fit all'.

This approach to understanding innovation has been explored within the public services literature also. Osborne (1998)[4] has developed this approach to understanding innovation in public services. Whilst not including the 'radical' innovation category above, it differentiates between total (architectural) innovation and two types of incremental innovation (expansionary and evolutionary) – as well as differentiating innovation '*per se*' from gradual service development. Such an approach, we believe, offers a more effective framework for conceptualising innovation in public services and for driving forward both meaningful research and evidence-influenced public policy making and public services management.

The Source of Innovation

The traditional model of innovation has long argued in favour of individual agency as the source of innovation – the 'hero innovator' model popularised by Peters and Waterman (1982) or the assertions of management guru Drucker (1985) that '[e]ntrepreneurs innovate'. Roberts and King (1996) developed this approach in the context of public sector organisations (PSOs). Based upon extensive psychological testing they developed a model of the 'public entrepreneur' as tenacious and goal driven, working long hours, willing to take risks, confident and skilled in using political connections. More sophisticated versions of this approach have moved beyond 'simple' individual agency to explore the interaction between the individual and his or her organisation (Jelinek and Schoonhoven 1990) – and there are also a number of such studies in relation to public services (e.g. Barlett and Dibben 2002; Windrum 2008).

Useful though these individual approaches are, they often lack an organisational or institutional context for public services (Praill and Baldwin 1988). In this context, two areas of research on public services innovation are important. On the one hand, both Ferlie et al. (1989) and Baldock and Evers (1991) have emphasised the importance of the organisational locus of innovation: top-down innovation is primarily concerned with organisational and service efficiency whilst bottom-up innovation is primarily concerned with organisational and service effectiveness. On the other hand, the work of Borins (2001) and Crosby and Bryson (2005) has emphasised the importance not only of individual agency but also of the 'innovation sponsor' who (at the political and/or organisational level) provides the mandate and space for innovative activity, including the risks that it involves. In such a context the sponsorship of senior managers and/or politicians is an essential pre-condition of innovation. They may not need to sanction each individual project but a mandate and culture of innovation must exist to permit staff to engage in the risks (and likelihood of failure) that innovation invariably involves.

Latterly, research and theory upon the sources of innovation has also shifted from the organisational locus to that of the environment. Increasingly research has emphasised the importance of an open systems and institutional understanding of the sources of innovation. In relation to services, this explicitly acknowledges the importance of organisational and institutional environmental sensitivity (Tether 2003); the need to work across horizontal networks in services provision rather than maintain a closed organisational boundary (Ahuja 2000; Brown and Duguid 2000; Chesbrough 2003); and the centrality of service users as a prime source of innovation (Alam 2006; Von Hippel 2007). This has led to models of innovation facilitation that are embedded precisely in this open systems orientation and that look outward from the organisation or service rather than internally (e.g. Santonen et al. 2007).

Such approaches can also be identified in research upon public services innovation. A major contribution of the PUBLIN programme on public services innovation has been to draw attention to this open systems and institutional context of innovation (e.g. Roste 2005). Osborne et al. (2008) have also emphasised the importance of the institutional context for the innovative capacity of third sector organisations, whilst Windrum and Garcia-Goni (2008), Considine et al. (2009) and Van Buuren and Loorbach (2009) have all explored the importance of organisational, environmental and policy networks for innovation. Brown (2007) has also examined the significance of the regional clustering of public service innovations for their sustainability. Finally, Walker (2007) has brought the environmental and organisational perspectives together for PSOs through use of the concept of 'organisational–environmental configuration'.

This research provides us with a more sophisticated understanding of the sources of innovation and their contingencies than has been found in public policy and public services delivery to date. These ideas are explored further in this volume. Overall, it offers us a more sophisticated view of the role and management of innovation in public services delivery than has hitherto been the case. Such a view is, we argue, vital to researchers and students of public policy making and public services delivery, as well as to policy makers, civil servants and the managers of public services themselves.

A GUIDE TO READING THIS BOOK

This book is intended both for the inquisitive student and practitioner and for the researcher. A systematic reading will provide an overview of the key issues in innovation in public services and a multi-disciplinary approach to their examination. Alternatively the book can be treated as a resource. Each chapter is self-contained in its contribution and can be read in its own right to provide a novel perspective on innovation in public services. The choice of approach is, as they say, yours.

The book is structured in six parts, followed by a concluding chapter. Part I examines the context for innovation in public services and situates it within trajectories of public service reform. The opening chapter of Joe Wallis and Shaun Goldfinch presents a global perspective upon this, and Laurence E. Lynn, Jr then teases out some of the linkages, and contradictions, in the relationship between public services reform and innovation in public services. Jean Hartley then moves on in this contextual section to explore the state of our knowledge about innovation in public services. In particular she unravels the complexities of the relationship between innovation in the public and private sectors. Stephen Osborne and Ian Miles conclude this section with two chapters exploring the contribution of services theory to understanding innovation in public services.

Part II then goes on to explore the change management challenges that innovation presents for public services. Ian Colville and Mike Carter provide an over-arching framework for understanding organisational change and its management, whilst Kerry Brown and Jennifer Waterhouse provide a 'state-of-the-art' review of current approaches to change management. John Bryson and Barbara Crosby conclude this part of the book by exploring what to do 'when stakeholders matter' and the complexities of stakeholder engagement in the innovation process.

Part III moves on to examine the core managerial challenges that innovation presents for public services. Brian Head starts by tackling the issue of evidence-based policy making and its implications for innovation in public services, whilst Osborne and Brown raise some key issues about the governance of risk in innovation in public services – they argue for a holistic and transparent approach rather than a technocratic one. There are then four chapters that look at the strategic, entrepreneurial, leadership and strategic roles. Both Zoe Radnor and her colleagues and Roberts and Longley explore the role that entrepreneurship and individual agency can play in public service innovation, whilst James Svara explores the role of leadership in successful innovations in local government in the US. Paul Joyce takes a more rational view of the issue, exploring strategic planning approaches to innovation and their impact upon public services. Part III concludes with two chapters reviewing distinct but important issues. Edler and Uyarra examine the public procurement process and the extent to which it can inhibit or enable innovation in public services. Finally, Macaulay and Norris engage with the difficult issue of the ethics of innovation in public services.

Part IV then moves to review the specific issue of information and communications technology (ICT) and e-government – both as innovations in public services in their own right and as enablers of other innovative developments in public services. Victor Bekkers reviews the potential of ICT as a source of innovation, Valentina Mele analyses the public policy context of innovation and its import for public services, and Rob Wilson and his colleagues examine a specific case where ICT-enabled services were an innovation in their own right, in the context of services for older people.

Part V next engages with the important issues of collaboration, networks and the co-production of innovation in public services, both with service users and third sector organisations. Jacob Torfing provides an important conceptual framework to understand 'collaborative innovation' and Tony Kinder looks at the inter-organisational dynamics of innovation in a collaborative context. Mary-Lee Rhodes then offers a complex systems view of innovation before Myrna Mandell and Robyn Keast and Jenny Lewis and her colleagues present network-based approaches to innovation – in the context of public service delivery and public policy making respectively. This part concludes with a group of chapters looking at third sector and user involvement in public services innovation. Kirsty Strokosch presents an important framework to understand the roles of both of these groups in innovation. The dynamics of third sector involvement are then considered in three chapters by Osborne and his colleagues, Paul Windrum, and Celine Chew and Fergus Lyon. Finally, the role of users and citizens in innovation in public services is approached by two important chapters by Birgit Jæger and by Michelle Farr.

Part VI contains six case studies of innovation in practice, all examining different issues. First, Gill Harvey returns to the issue of evidence-based policy making and considers what it might mean in practice; Paul Cunningham engages with the process of innovation in the context of the health service and Richard Walker explores the impact of organisational factors upon the innovative capacity of local governments. This part ends with three final case studies – of the challenges of structural innovations in the context of local government by Rhys Andrews and George Boyne, and two perspectives upon the crucial issue of the diffusion of innovations in public services and their sustainability in the context of the UK health service, by James Barlow and by Trisha Greenhalgh and her colleagues.

The book closes with a concluding chapter by the editors, reviewing what we know, and what we still need to know, about innovation in public services.

NOTES

1. The first part of this chapter has been abridged and developed from Osborne and Brown (2011).
2. See chapter 4.
3. See note 2, above.
4. See also chapter 26.

REFERENCES

Ahuja, G. (2000). Collaborative networks, structural holes and innovation: a longitudinal study. *Administrative Science Quarterly*, 45, 425–455.

Alam, I. (2006). Removing the fuzziness from the front-end of service innovations through customer interactions. *Industrial Marketing Management*, 35, 468–480.

Aldbury, D. (2005). Fostering innovation in public services. *Public Money and Management*, 25(1), 51–56.

Audit Commission (2007). *Seeing the Light: Innovation in Local Public Services*. London: Audit Commission.

Baldock, J. and Evers, A. (1991). On social innovation – an introduction. In R. Kraan and Associates (ed.), *Care for the Elderly: Significant Innovations in Three European Countries*. Frankfurt: Campus Verlag, pp. 87–92.

Bartlett, D. and Dibben, P. (2002). Public sector innovation and entrepreneurship: case studies from local government. *Local Government Studies*, 28(4), 107–121.

Behn, R. (1997). Why innovate? In A. Altchuler and R. Behn (eds), *Innovation in American Government*. Washington, DC: Brookings Institute.

Borins, S. (2001). *The Challenge of Innovating in Government*. Washington, DC: IBM Center for the Business of Government.

Brown, J. and Duguid, P. (2000). *The Social Life of Innovation*. Boston, MA: Harvard Business School Press.

Brown, L. (2007). The adoption and implementation of a service innovation in a social work setting – a case study of family group conferencing in the UK. *Social Policy and Society*, 6(3), 321–332.

Cabinet Office (1999). *Modernising Government*. London: HMSO.

Cabinet Office (2008). *Excellence and Fairness: Achieving World Class Public Services*. London: Cabinet Office.

CCAF–FCVI (2010). *Innovation, Risk and Control*. Ottawa: CCAF–FCVI.

Chesbrough, H. (2003). The era of open innovation. *Sloane Management Review*, Summer, 35–41.

Considine, M., Lewis, J. and Alexander, D. (2009). *Networks, Innovation and Public Policy*. Basingstoke: Palgrave.

Crosby, B. and Bryson, J. (2005). *Leadership for the Common Good*. San Francisco, CA: Jossey Bass.

de Brentani, U. (2001). Innovative versus incremental new business services: different keys for achieving success. *Journal of Product Innovation Management*, 18, 169–187.

Department of Innovation, Universities and Skills (DIUS) (2008a). *Innovation Nation*. London: DIUS.

Department of Innovation, Universities and Skills (DIUS) (2008b). *The Whitehall Innovation Hub*. London: DIUS.

Drucker, P. (1985). *Innovation and Entrepreneurship*. London: Heinemann.

Eshima, Y., Katayama, T. and Ohno, T. (2001). Public management innovation in Japan: its characteristics and challenges. *International Review of Administrative Sciences*, 67(4), 699–714.

Ferlie, E., Challis, D. and Davies, B. (1989). *Efficiency Improving Innovations in the Care of the Elderly*. Aldershot: Gower.

Garcia, R. and Calantone, R. (2002). A critical look at technological innovation typology and innovativeness terminology: a literature review. *Journal of Product Innovation Management*, 19, 110–132.

Golden, O. (1990). Innovation in public sector human service programs: the implications of innovation by 'groping along'. *Journal of Policy Analysis and Management*, 9(2), 219–248.

Halvorsen, T., Hauknes, J., Miles, I. and Roste, R. (2005). *On the Differences between Public and Private Sector Innovation*. Oslo: NIFU STEP.

Harris, M. and Albury, D. (2009). *The Innovation Imperative*. London: NESTA.

Hartley, J. (2005). Innovation in governance and public services: past and present. *Public Money and Management*, 25(1), 27–34.

Hartley, J. (2006). *Innovation and Its Contribution to Improvement*. London: Department for Communities and Local Government.

Henderson, R. and Clark, K. (1990). Architectural innovation: the reconfiguration of existing product technologies and the failure of established firms. *Administrative Science Quarterly*, 35(1), 9–30.

Herbig, P. (1991). A cusp catastrophe model of the adoption of industrial innovation. *Journal of Product Innovation Management*, 8(2), 127–137.

Horne, M. (2008). *Honest Brokers: Brokering Innovation in Public Services*. London: Innovation Unit.

House of Commons Select Committee of Public Accounts (2003). *Improving Public Services Through Innovation: The Invest to Save Budget. Sixteenth Report of Session 2002–03*. London: House of Commons.

Jelinek, M. and Schoonhoven, C. (1990). *The Innovation Marathon*. Oxford: Blackwell.

Johannessen, J.-A., Olsen, B. and Lumpkin, G. (2001). Innovation as newness: what is new, how new, and new to whom? *European Journal of Innovation Management*, 4(1), 20–31.

Kendrick, A. (1998). *'Who Do We Trust?' The Abuse of Children Living Away from Home in the United Kingdom*. Paper presented to the 1998 Conference of the International Society for the Prevention of Child Abuse, Neglect and Harm, Auckland, September.

Kimberly, J. (1981). Managerial Innovation. In P. Nystrom and W. Starbuck (eds), *Handbook of Organizational Design*. Oxford: Oxford University Press, pp. 84–104.

Kirkwood, A. (1993). *The Leicestershire Inquiry 1992*. Leicester: Leicestershire County Council.

Koch, P. and Hauknes, J. (2005). *On Innovation in the Public Sector*. Oslo: NIFU STEP.

Levy, A. and Kahan, B. (1991). *The Pindown Experience and the Protection of Children: The Report of the Staffordshire Child Care Inquiry*. Stafford: Staffordshire County Council.

Lips, A.M., Taylor, J. and Organ, J. (2009). Managing citizen identity information in e-government service relationships in the UK: the emergence of a surveillance state or a service state? *Public Management Review*, 11(6), 833–856.

Meeuwisse, A. (2008). Organizational innovation in the Swedish welfare state. *Critical Social Policy*, 28, 187–205.

Membretti, A. (2007). Building citizenship as an innovative service. *European Urban and Regional Studies*, 14, 252–263.

Mulgan, G. and Albury, D. (2003). *Innovation in the Public Sector*. London: Cabinet Office.

Murray, R., Grice, J. and Mulgan, G. (2010). *The Open Book of Social Innovation*. London: NESTA.

Nankervis, A. (2005). *Managing Services*. Melbourne: Cambridge University Press.

National Audit Office (2000). *Supporting Innovation: Managing Risk in Government Departments*. London: National Audit Office.

Nelson, R. (1993). Technological innovation: the role of non-profit organizations. In D. Hammock and D. Young (eds), *Nonprofit Organizations in a Mixed Economy*. Ann Arbor, MI: University of Michigan Press, pp. 363–377.

Nutley, S., Walter, I. and Davies, H. (2007). *Using Evidence: How Research Can Inform Public Services*. Bristol: Policy Press.

Osborne, S. (1998). Naming the beast: defining and classifying service innovations in social policy. *Human Relations*, 51(9), 1133–1154.

Osborne, S. and Brown, K. (2005). *Managing Change and Innovation in Public Service Organizations*. London: Routledge.

Osborne, S. and Brown, L. (2011). Innovation, public policy and public services delivery in the UK: the word that would be king? *Public Administration*, 69(4), 1335–1350.

Osborne, S., McLaughlin, K. and Chew, C. (2008). The once and future pioneers? The innovative capacity of voluntary organizations and the provision of public services: a longitudinal approach. *Public Management Review*, 10(1), 51–70.

Peters, T. and Waterman, R. (1982). *In Search of Excellence*. New York: Harper and Row.

Phills J., Jr., Deiglmeier, K. and Miller, D. (2008). Rediscovering social innovation. *Stanford Social Innovation Review*, 6(4), 34–43.

Porter, M. (1985). *Competitive Advantage*. New York: Free Press.

Praill, T. and Baldwin, S. (1988). Beyond hero-innovation: real change in unreal systems. *Behavioural Psychotherapy*, 16(1), 1–14.

Roberts, N. and King, P. (1996). *Transforming Public Policy*. Cambridge, MA: Ballinger.

Roste, R. (2005). *Studies of Innovation in the Public Sector*. Oslo: NIFU STEP.

Santonen, T., Kaivo-oja, J. and Suomala, J. (2007). *Introduction to National Open Innovation System (NOIS) Paradigms*. Turku: Finland Futures Research Centre, Turku School of Economics.

Sundbo, J. (1997). Management of innovation in services. *Service Industries Journal*, 17(3), 432–455.

Tether, B. (2003). The sources and aims of innovation in services. *Economics of Innovation and New Technology*, 12(6), 841–855.

Thomas, E. (ed.) (2008). *Innovation by Design in Public Services*. London: SOLACE Foundation.

Tushman, M. and Anderson, P. (1985). Technological discontinuities and organizational environments. *Administrative Science Quarterly*, 31, 439–465.

Van Buuren, A. and Loorbach, D. (2009). Policy innovation in isolation? Conditions for policy renewal by transition arenas and pilot projects. *Public Management Review*, 11(3), 375–392.

Van de Ven, A. (1988). Central problems in the management of innovation. In M. Tushman and W. Moore (eds), *Readings in the Management of Innovation*. Cambridge, MA: Ballinger, pp. 103–122.

Von Hippel, E. (2007). Horizontal innovation networks – by and for users. *Industrial and Corporate Change*, 16(2), 1–23.

Walker, R. (2007). An empirical evaluation of innovation types and organizational and environmental characteristics: towards a configuration approach. *Journal of Public Administration Research and Theory*, 18, 591–615.

Westall, A. (2007). *How Can Innovation in Social Enterprise Be Understood, Encouraged and Enabled?* London: Office of the Third Sector.

Windrum, P. (2008). Innovation and entrepreneurship in public services. In P. Windrum and P. Koch (eds), *Innovation in Public Sector Services*. Cheltenham and Northampton, MA: Edward Elgar, pp. 3–20.

Windrum, P.P. and Garcia-Goni, M. (2008). A neo-Schumpeterian model of health services innovation. *Research Policy*, 37, 649–672.

PART I

THE CONTEXT OF INNOVATION IN PUBLIC SERVICES

1. Explaining patterns of public management reform diffusion

Joe Wallis and Shaun Goldfinch

INTRODUCTION

The diffusion of substantively similar reforms in significantly diverse settings is a subject of considerable interest in the field of public policy and public administration. This is reflected in the volume of literature that has developed over the last 25 years on the diffusion of New Public Management (NPM) prescriptions.

Different scholars have suggested different criteria for determining their substantive similarity. For example, Hood (1991) finds a commonality in their tendency to privilege 'efficiency' over both 'fairness' and 'safety' values while Dunleavy et al. (2006) find integrating NPM themes in processes of 'disaggregation', 'competition' and 'individualisation'. In this chapter we propose that the overarching common theme of NPM is the adoption of putative market and private sector business practices into the management of the public sector. Examples of this (from Hood 1991, 1998; Boston et al. 1996; Goldfinch 1998; Dunleavy et al. 2006) include:

- A focus on 'efficiency' and 'doing more with less'.
- Decentralised structures with smaller, multiple and often single-purpose agencies and putatively flexible and innovative staff replacing highly centralised bureaucracies. Related to this were a number of policy/operations and funder/provider splits.
- Motivation of public servants based on financial incentives rather than professional ethos or duty, with contracts, particularly written ones, being a key part of this process.
- Adoption of a 'managerialism' where management is seen as a generic, 'rational' and 'scientific', but also innovative and creative, discipline with similar demands and practices across both public and private sectors.
- Greater autonomy to agency managers including decision-making power on human resources and information technology (IT) and other operational matters.
- Internal and external market or quasi-market mechanisms to imitate market competition, including the widespread use of competitive mechanisms, written contracts, 'contracting-out' and ultimately privatisation.
- A move from input reporting to 'output', outcome or results reporting.
- A 'customer focus', sometimes defined primarily in market terms, for the provision of public services.
- Adoption of corporate-type accrual accounting systems and fiscal transparency mechanisms.
- Professional, union and operational group influence severely curtailed, with such

groups often characterised as 'rent seeking' interests to be excluded from decision making.

- Politicians taking a back-seat with respect to 'operations', setting the broad parameters of 'policy' or 'strategy' and leaving day-to-day business to professional managers.

It should be pointed out that, to a varying degree, these measures involve *discontinuous change* and an element of *public service innovation* in the sense defined by Osborne and Browne (2005) that 'what had been acceptable or adequate for the provision of public services will no longer be so – their provision will require new structures or skills that mark a break with this past experience' (p. 5). The study of their diffusion can therefore be approached in an analogous way to the study of technological diffusion. We would argue that such an approach can make a contribution to comparative studies of the spread of NPM.

These have tended to be more empirically than theoretically oriented, focussing little on the causal mechanisms that drive diffusion. An exception is Pollitt and Bouckaert's (2004) proposition that NPM reforms tend to be adopted in countries where political leaders face either fiscal problems or legitimacy problems and advance their own rationally determined political interests by adopting NPM so as to 'distance themselves as politicians from the system of administration and law and then blame that system for either the expenditure problem and/or the legitimacy problem' (p. 184). These scholars go on to suggest that institutional factors may affect the type of NPM measures that politicians may select in order to achieve this distancing and blaming goal. For example, they observed that: (i) countries with a *Rechtsstaat* tradition such as Germany tend to select measures that advance a 'maintaining' strategy of squeezing resources employed in the public sector without altering the way it is administered; (ii) countries with 'a general disposition toward consensual, often meso-corporatist styles of governance' (e.g. Finland, Netherlands, Sweden) select those that advance a 'modernising' strategy deploying techniques imported from the private sector, that seek to underline the need for public provision and serve to 'strengthen rather than dilute the state' (2004, p. 187); while (iii) Anglo-Saxon countries have, at some times, followed a 'marketising' approach of placing public services under more pressure to be efficient by increasing competition within the public sector and between public organisations and private firms while, on other occasions, they have emphasised 'minimising' the role of the state by transferring public finance and/or provision functions to the private sector through privatisation and contracting out.

Implicit in Pollitt and Bouckaert's study are certain key features of a rational interest explanation of reform diffusion. First, whatever pressure or influence domestic decision-makers face from external actors, they nevertheless have discretion to choose those approaches that best fit their country's functional needs. Secondly, this choice can be made on the basis of a cost–benefit analysis that takes into account the impact of institutional factors on the costs of adoption and the private benefits political leaders derive from blame avoidance.

A number of puzzles nevertheless remain for this type of rational interest-based explanation of NPM adoption. Why did countries (such as Ireland) adopt NPM prescriptions during the period from the mid-1990s to 2008 when sustained economic growth turned the fiscal situation around from one where politicians would even need to consider 'distancing and blaming' options (Connaughton 2010)? Why has the NPM agenda advanced substantively in the last 10 years in previous 'laggards' such as Japan (Yamamoto 2009) and been 'revived' in others such as the Netherlands (Boer et al. 2007), while 'stalling' and, in some respects, 'retreating' over the same period in previous 'exemplars' such as New Zealand, Australia and the UK (Hood and Peters 2004; Dunleavy et al. 2006; Chapman and Duncan 2007)? Why have there been differences between the scope and rate of diffusion of NPM 'ideas', 'rhetoric', 'policy decisions' and 'practices' (Pollitt 2001; Goldfinch and Wallis 2010)?

This chapter seeks to go beyond a rational interest approach in explaining the motivation and predicting the pattern of NPM diffusion. In doing this it acknowledges that, as a form of innovation, the adoption of NPM can be *emergent* as well as *planned* since it *'derives from the political context of public services'* (Osborne and Brown 2005, p. 7).

The chapter is structured into the following sections. The first evaluates alternative external pressure, normative imitation and Kuhnian paradigm shift explanations of reform diffusion. The second goes on to argue that an observed 'wave-like' pattern can best be explained in terms of a cognitive–psychological model that takes into account the effect that the parallel development of insider enthusiasm and outsider scepticism can have on this trajectory. It also considers whether this approach can also explain and predict the diffusion of an emerging set of 'post-NPM' measures. The third, and concluding, section suggests how the preceding analysis can be drawn on to evaluate the relationship between leadership and scepticism in the decision processes surrounding reform adoption.

ALTERNATIVE EXPLANATIONS OF NPM DIFFUSION

External Pressure

Perhaps the simplest explanation for the diffusion of substantively similar reform measures is that it is a response to the incentives and sanctions provided by powerful external actors such as international organisations (IOs). There are, however, a number of problems with this explanation of the diffusion of NPM:

- There is no evidence that even during the late 1980s and early 1990s when institutions such as the International Monetary Fund and World Bank appeared to have reached agreement on the broad micro and macro elements of an appropriate economic strategy that this 'Washington Consensus' extended to encompass explicit public management reform prescriptions (see Williamson 1994).
- Even if pressure to adopt NPM had been effectively exerted behind the scenes then it would surely have resulted in a pattern of diffusion that was both more rapid and global in its scope than the observed 'linguistic clustering' and laggard behaviour by countries that remained wedded to more traditional administrative systems despite seeking to advance the main stabilisation and liberalisation components of the Washington strategy.

Normative Imitation

A more plausible explanation of the influential role IOs can play in the diffusion of generic organisational and reform recipes can be found in a normative imitation model in terms of which they promote their implementation in 'exemplar' countries as 'benchmarks' for others to follow. Political leaders in these countries do so, not because the reform recipes effectively address functional needs or emerging policy issues in their countries, but because they enhance their legitimacy, allowing these leaders to present themselves as 'arch modernisers' on a quest to overcome the forces of tradition in order to reshape their administrations according to state-of-the-art principles of best practice. A normative imitation model would thus predict that NPM, like other fads or fashions, would 'spread like wildfire . . . much faster than a cost–benefit analysis would suggest' (Weyland 2005, p. 275).

This would seem to be at odds with the observed reticence many countries displayed in adopting NPM recipes despite their international promotion during the early 1990s. A case in point is the contractualist version of NPM implemented in New Zealand between 1988 and 1991. Despite the fact that it was heralded by IOs, showcased at conferences and observed at first hand by visiting teams of public servants, its diffusion was very limited (perhaps only to the State of Victoria in Australia) and it remained more a source of fascination than emulation (Schick 1998).

In general the normative imitation model would seem to better explain the diffusion of NPM rhetoric than policy decisions to adopt NPM or the process of embedding new measures in practice. The gap between the rhetoric and reality of its diffusion is a recurrent theme in comparative studies of public management reform. Examples of 'reform laggards' which have nevertheless at times espoused NPM rhetoric include both France, where the Chirac 'Quality Agenda' and intermittent initiatives to delegate greater autonomy to field services appear to have had minimal impact (Jones and Cole 2009), and Germany, where NPM rhetoric is reflected in a 'New Steering Model' that has failed to effect a comprehensive shift away from a Weberian bureaucracy (Kuhlmann et al. 2008).

Kuhnian Model of Paradigmatic Change

It did not take long after the adoption of NPM in Anglo-Saxon countries in the late 1980s for this to be hailed as the start of a global process whereby administrative systems based on the Progressive Public Administration (PPA) 'paradigm' would be reformed according to principles derived from this new paradigm (Aucoin 1990; Hood 1994). According to a Kuhnian model, a process of paradigmatic change could potentially go through three phases (Hall 1993).

There would be a relatively long period of paradigm stability (such as PPA enjoyed in many countries through much of the twentieth century) during which the authority of the reigning paradigm would gradually be eroded as it increasingly failed to make sense of policy dilemmas in a changing environment. This process of erosion could eventually culminate in a period of paradigmatic fragmentation during which a number of alternative and incommensurable models or paradigms would be pushed forward for consideration.

Peters (1996) characterised the field of public administration as being in this state of flux, with the authority of the long-standing bureaucratic model giving way to 'four emerging models': a 'market model' based on competition between single-purpose agency-type providers; a 'participative model' based on engaging employers and citizens in decision making; a 'flexible model' that invokes an 'adapt or die' approach with regard to existing organisations; and a 'deregulated model' that seeks to empower managers through the removal of bureaucratic rules and red tape.

Finally, during the third stage, a reformist advocacy coalition (see Sabatier and Jenkins-Smith 1999) would bring some aspects of these models together to forge a purportedly coherent policy paradigm and exercise the collective policy leadership required to overcome various sources of resistance encountered at veto points in the policy process and ensure its embodiment in concrete policy decisions that come to be embedded in the operating routines, structures, systems and cultures that shape the behaviour of public organisations.

There are a number of problems with this model insofar as it is applied to explain and predict the diffusion of NPM. First, while it might explain how similar ideas about public management and public servant motivation might well become shared across countries, albeit at different levels of abstraction, this does not necessarily translate to similar policies and techniques being agreed upon or adopted. Moreover, the same models and theories can sometimes be drawn on to justify policy design; and to critique the same design. For example, new institutional economics (NIE) was often cited, sometimes by policy-makers themselves, as a key influence on what was to be called NPM (Scott et al. 1990). However, aspects of NIE, particularly transaction cost analysis, also provided a useful critique of a state sector overly decentralised under NPM.

Secondly, the coherence of the policy paradigm that came to be identified as NPM is open to debate. It seems to encompass at least some aspects of the competing models identified by Peters, suggesting to its critics that it can possibly mean all things to all (Hood 1991; Boston et al. 1996), with the shifting edges of NPM making it possible to fit almost any type of reform within its barriers (Rhodes and Weller 2003). Reforms with tenuous links to NPM are often cited as examples of its diffusion. As Jorgen Christensen (2009) notes, in Denmark some of what was later termed the NPM agenda was implemented in the 1960s and 1970s – well before any talk of NPM – and justified in particularly Danish ways. Reform has continued, although Christensen plays down the intellectual coherence of the reforms and their derivation from overseas experience, instead seeing their evolution through complex interactions between ideas, interests and actors. In Hong Kong, modernisation patterns that would later be observed as typical of NPM were introduced in the 1970s and subsequent reforms evolved on this base, rather than simply aping international NPM agendas (Cheung 2009).

Aspects of NPM can seem contradictory and possibly incoherent. Despite its association with the call to let 'managers manage', its implementation has often been characterised by the introduction of more central and highly specified controls through contracting out, performance evaluation and accountability mechanisms, which in some cases limit managerial autonomy – or at least make it highly problematic (Gregory 2009; Wegrich 2009). The veracity of the de-bureaucratisation and 'post-bureaucracy' claims of NPM are doubtful, with simply the form of bureaucracy being changed and NPM initiatives being layered (Thelen 2003) upon existing structures. For example, despite the rhetoric, input and procedural controls still maintain a hold in some Asian systems such as Japan (Yamamoto 2009), in other parliamentary systems such as New Zealand and the UK, and in Western European systems such as Germany. They are now supplemented by a 'new red tape' of output, outcome and other measures, invasive and time-consuming account-ability and evaluation controls, limits on professional autonomy and self-regulation, and so on.

Thirdly, the proposition that variations in the scope and rate of diffusion of NPM can be related to the magnitude of reform obstacles and effectiveness of policy leadership deployed to overcome them in particular countries is largely unfalsifiable. It is moreover based on the view that leadership effectiveness is related to its capacity to overcome resist-ance. This is, of course, at odds with democratic, learning-oriented perspectives on lead-ership that question the equation of 'dissent' with 'resistance' and relate the quality of leadership, not to an intransigent type of conviction or advocacy politics, but to its capac-ity to listen and learn from objections raised not only by powerful opponents but also by sceptics who often speak from the periphery of the policy process (Senge 1990; Piderit 2000).

In the next section, we will seek to turn the leadership proposition on its head by arguing that the failure to provide democratic learning-oriented leadership provides the essential condition for the diffusion process to be driven by waves of insider enthusiasm in which the biases and distortions predicted by cognitive–psychological models fuel a mounting outsider scepticism that can be drawn upon to support a pendulum swing away from the measures being prescribed.

COGNITIVE–PSYCHOLOGICAL FACTORS AND INSIDER ENTHUSIASM IN THE DIFFUSION OF NPM

A cognitive–psychological model can be used to explain three observed features of the diffusion of NPM policy decisions: (i) the wave-like pattern they follow over time – starting slowly, gathering momentum and then tapering off, possibly to be followed by a new wave of substantively different reforms; (ii) their tendency to intermittently break out in geographic and linguistic clusters; so that (iii) viewed over a long period of more than 20 years, researchers such as Gualmini (2008) can discern a global impact of NPM on public sector decision making with substantively similar reform measures being adopted in diverse settings. According to this type of model, decision-makers cope with the uncertainty and limits of information processing by following certain heuristics or inferential shortcuts. The three most commonly cited in the literature on bounded ration-ality are the *availability*, *anchoring* and *representativeness* heuristics (Thaler 2000; Gilovich et al. 2002).

The availability heuristic comes into play when decision-makers focus on the most striking and immediate information. Policy innovations in countries they are 'close' to geographically, linguistically or historically tend to capture their attention more than developments in more 'distant' countries. Once their attention is captured by a striking innovation it will tend to anchor the process of considering other options so that they devote less time and resources to exploring adaptation possibilities or searching for alternatives. Both processes can explain the clustered pattern of substantively similar NPM-type reforms.

However, their wave-like diffusion over time can be explained in terms of the deployment of a representativeness heuristic that 'induces people to draw excessively clear, confident, and firm inferences from a precarious base of data' (Weyland 2005, p. 284). The promotion of what Goldfinch and Wallis (2010) call 'convergence myths' is an example of the application of this heuristic.

Goldfinch and Wallis note the enthusiasm with which the advocates of NPM hailed its adoption in certain exemplar countries as signalling a global paradigm shift that would reach its conclusion when public management structures around the world came to converge around its distinctive set of prescriptions. However, they point out that this is mirrored by the enthusiasm with which the 'death of NPM' has been proclaimed by some writers who have discerned significant commonality in diversity in some 'post-NPM' reform trends – in countries including Australia, New Zealand, the UK, and the Netherlands – including moves to introduce 'networks', 'joined-up government' and 'whole-of-government' perspectives, the reintegration of public sector values, assertion of central control over agencies, and 'third generation' reforms (Andresani and Ferlie 2006; Chapman and Duncan 2007; Christensen and Lægreid 2007; Halligan 2007). Some writers have enthusiastically portrayed these events as a *'paradigmatic change* which attempts to redefine how we think about the state, its purpose and . . . ways of functioning' (O'Flynn 2007, p. 353; emphasis added). Others have raised the possibility that the diffusion of NPM may eventually come to be viewed as the transitional stage in the emergence of a 'New Public Governance' (NPG) that will become consolidated as the true paradigmatic successor to PPA (Osborne 2010, p. 1).

Goldfinch and Wallis (2010, p. 1099) argue that claims of a global convergence on either an NPM or NPG paradigm constitute a policy myth that can have 'an existence and function above and beyond an empirical "reality"' since it is 'useful' to the in-groups who promote it by providing them with greater potential access to the power, consultancies and financial benefits that insider status entails.

Here we extend this argument by proposing that the in-group enthusiasm that underlies the perpetuation of policy myths requires a breakdown in the processes of *deliberative rationality* which provide some check against the distortions associated with bounded rationality. Unlike bounded rationality, which is a characteristic of individual decision making, deliberative rationality is an institutional norm that can govern *processes* of collective decision making. For example, it can promote and preserve the free internal expression of scepticism to counter and balance the biases, distortions and propensity to enthusiasm of boundedly rational policy actors who find common cause in advocating the adoption of particular policy innovations.

Such scepticism can be seen as a barrier to reform diffusion. By pouring 'cold water' on reform proposals, it can also be perceived as weakening commitment to advance the reform process. The distinction Falbe and Yukl (1992) made between commitment, compliance and resistance is salient in this regard, particularly since the OECD (2001) applied this distinction in delineating the key features of an effective 'Public Sector Leadership for the Twenty First Century'.

A policy decision to adopt a public management reform measure can be seen as setting in motion a top-down process that can induce three types of response from actors expected to implement the decision: *resistance, compliance* or *commitment*. It can provoke *resistance* when some actors oppose the requested action and try to 'avoid doing it by refusing, arguing, delaying, or seeking to have the request nullified' (Falbe and Yukl 1992, p. 640). However, from this perspective, the effectiveness of top-down leadership should not just be evaluated according to whether it 'overcomes' or circumvents such resistance and sets in place a mix of rewards and sanctions that are sufficient to assure compliance from the type of actor who 'carries out the requested action but is apathetic about it rather than enthusiastic, makes only a minimal or average effort, and does not show any initiative' (Falbe and Yukl 1992; pp. 639–640). Rather, to be effective, leadership must both overcome resistance and induce the commitment that can be said to occur when a team member agrees internally with the request, 'is enthusiastic about it and is likely to exercise initiative and demonstrate unusual effort' in seeking to carry it out (Falbe and Yukl 1992, pp. 639–640).

This type of commitment can probably best be fostered in cohesive teams that use member enthusiasm as a selection mechanism, marginalising and excluding sceptics by effectively treating the voicing of scepticism as an expression of resistance. Interaction within such in-groups could thus pass the 'threshold of boundedness' that Collins (1993) suggests is necessary for the 'emotional energy' or enthusiasm of members to be enhanced through processes of mutual stimulation and reinforcement.

When the advocacy and implementation of reform diffusion is left within the hands of enthusiastic in-groups, it is quite possible that the resulting gain in cohesion and commitment may be achieved with a corresponding loss in deliberative rationality and exacerbation of the biases and distortions associated with bounded rationality. Weyland's (2005) observations with regard to the diffusion of pension privatisation schemes in Latin America could thus just as easily apply to the diffusion of either NPM or NPG reform measures:

> Most ... reforms ... were elaborated by small teams that gained increasing cohesion as members who rejected privatisation quit or were forced out. The limited size and relative homogeneity of the reform teams allowed the problematic inferences and judgments that various members derived through cognitive heuristics to reinforce rather than counterbalance each other. Thus the closed decision-making process often led to a cumulation of distortions, not a mutual correction of individual deviations from full rationality, which collective decision making could in principle produce. By contrast where for specific institutional reasons an unusually wide range of experts participated in the discussion on ... reform ... cognitive heuristics held less sway at the aggregate level. (pp. 282–283)

From this perspective, the marginalisation and exclusion of reform sceptics may be viewed not as a recipe for greater leadership effectiveness but as a symptom of *leadership failure* or even *misleadership*. Including sceptics, giving them a voice in the decision process, not only enhances the deliberative rationality of the decision process but also fulfils the moral responsibility of leadership to engage followers in a quest to continually evaluate prevailing definitions of reality (Van Heerden 2010).

Indeed, the advisory role of senior public servants was often traditionally understood as providing a sceptical reality check to the enthusiastic tendencies of activist political leadership. Operating behind a deliberative veil, they would be careful not to make their scepticism public, but would, at the same time, consider it completely appropriate to express it where necessary in free and frank 'private conversations' with ministers (Hood and Lodge 2006). In this regard they would see themselves as ethical guardians of the public interest understood as ensuring a number of 'process considerations' were followed, including 'regard for the law, regard for principles of natural justice, consideration of the long as well as the short term, acknowledgment of previous commitments [and] avoidance of both the substance and appearance of personal or agency interest' (Martin 1991, p. 382). This view is congruent with the self-understanding that Aberbach et al. (1981) reported senior public servants had of their being a source of 'equilibrium' rather than 'energy' in the policy process and possessing a competence that was essentially dispassionate, politically neutral and value-free. Such a self-understanding has tended to break down as NPM-type reforms have encouraged a more visible leadership characterised by public advocacy of a departmental line in the name of enhancing the managerial accountability of these actors.

Sceptics, of course, do not go away, even in a policy environment that marginalises them in the interests of strengthening cohesive team leadership. They often continue to snipe from the sidelines. One symptom of their marginalisation from the policy process is that democratic discourse can become impoverished and assume the type of 'intransigent' pattern observed in different historical contexts by Hirschman (1991).

On the one side, Hirschman argues that sceptics will resort to three basic 'reactionary' arguments against reform. The first is the 'futility thesis' – that the reforms will fail to make any significant difference to actual behaviour. The frequent reference in the comparative literature on public management reform to instances where policy rhetoric has failed to be translated into policy decisions or where 'implementation gaps' have arisen after decisions have been made to undertake particular reforms suggests the importance of this thesis to critiques of both NPM- and NPG-type reforms. The second is the 'perversity thesis' – that the reforms are generating unintended, perverse outcomes. An example is the argument that reformer efforts to enhance managerial discretion and accountability may have had the opposite 'perverse' effect of increasing the complexities of achieving accountability and increasing the incentive to avoid responsibility (Gregory 2009). Thirdly, there is the 'jeopardy thesis' – that the reforms could jeopardise or damage an unappreciated historical achievement. The concerns critics of NPM had that reforms could weaken a public service ethos and critics of NPG had that calls for public servants to exercise 'public value-seeking leadership' could jeopardise trust relationships with ministers in Cabinet systems of governance (Rhodes and Wanna 2007) are examples of this type of argument. All three not only seek to demythologise reformistic rhetoric but allude to the hidden agendas and private self-seeking motives that underlie the perpetuation of these myths (Goldfinch and Wallis 2010).

On the other side, according to Hirschman (1991), reform enthusiasts typically advance three counterarguments. The 'futility of resistance' thesis is a variant of the convergence myth – if the whole world is converging on a set of reform prescriptions, then it becomes increasingly unreasonable to preserve 'outdated' institutions. Similarly, the case for reform is made even more compelling by the 'desperate predicament' thesis that amplifies the 'rotten-ness' and pervasive systemic failure of existing structures and the 'imminent danger' thesis that highlights the risks of delaying reform. All three seek to decontest the policy agenda by framing any expression of reform scepticism as inherently unreasonable within the context in which reforms are being pursued.

At this juncture, we make two propositions about the relative political strength of reform enthusiasm and reform scepticism. First, reform enthusiasm is likely to produce greater group cohesion than reform scepticism. Enthusiasts are more likely to be drawn to interact with one another and strive together to advance a common reform cause while at the same time finding it difficult to interact with sceptics. By contrast, scepticism itself does not have the same drawing power. Sceptics have a greater propensity to voice their concerns as independent actors or 'lone dissenters'. In the absence of effective learning-centred leadership that seeks to preserve deliberative rationality by holding enthusiasts and sceptics together, the corresponding exclusion and scattering of sceptics and concentration of enthusiasm in powerful in-groups may provide the impetus behind the rapid diffusion of reform innovations that can follow an initial period of cautious assessment and limited experimentation.

However, our second proposition is that reform scepticism may be a more sustainable position than reform enthusiasm. If the breakdown of deliberative rationality gives reform enthusiasts the opportunity to drive the reform process forward, their tendency to ignore the 'blind spots' and 'fatal flaws' in the reform recipes they are striving to implement (Hood 1998) may generate an accumulation of disappointments that can both cause their enthusiasm to wane and give increasing ammunition to sceptics, either operating on the periphery of the policy process or 'silently' within the organisations they are seeking to transform. But can or should sceptics continue to sit on the sidelines if policy entrepreneurs seek to reassemble their critiques into a reform agenda that can capture the enthusiasm of a new 'advocacy coalition' committed to redirect or reverse the reform trajectory?

This situation faced critics of NPM reforms in the UK and New Zealand in the late 1990s. Incoming Labour governments had promised to address a range of state sector problems, including scandals and 'sleaze', possible misuse of public funds, and concerns over state capacity, policy coordination and longer-term focus (Goldfinch 2009). There was an opportunity for a 'post-NPM' advocacy coalition to be mobilised with these problems being framed as being the unintended, but nevertheless predictable, consequences of NPM reforms implemented during the previous decade and with proposals being made to shift the direction of reform from, *inter alia*: (i) 'agentification' towards a more 'joined up' or integrated public service that encouraged networked collaboration rather than competition between government organisations; (ii) enhancing managerial autonomy towards establishing state-wide guidelines on certain issues (such as ethical standards, IT procurement and employment procedures – see Goldfinch 2009); (iii) a short-term focus on outputs to a long-term focus on 'outcomes' and inter-agency coordination and cooperation to address wicked issues (Campbell 2007); (iv) a focus on users of services as 'clients' to an engagement with them as citizens and partners in decision making (Kelly 2007); and (v) motivation through financial incentives to engagement and empowerment through public value-seeking leadership (Moore 1995).

The question facing those actors who had taken a sceptical position with regard to NPM was how they should interpret this change in reform direction, particularly since it appeared to give structure to some of their critiques and solutions. They could, of course, simply maintain the integrity of their sceptical position. Some did this, drawing attention to gaps between the rhetoric and reality of reform (Campbell 2007; Gauld and Goldfinch 2006). A new twist on the 'futility thesis' was, for example, advanced in New Zealand, where scholars such as Gregory (2006) and Ellwood and Newberry (2007) argued that some key aspects of NPM, such as the rules governing fiscal responsibility, accrual accounting and capital charges, had become so institutionalised that attempts to increase collaborative efforts between agencies were largely unavailing since they ran up against logics contained in the existing output and purchasing system. Others joined with scholars such as Christensen and Lagried (2007) and Hood and Peters (2004) in suggesting that the above-mentioned themes constituted an adaptation rather than a reversal of NPM. There was also the possibility that they simply defined a 'Third Way', social democratic position on public management reform and that another ideological shift and changes of government could see NPM revived and reinvigorated even in the regimes where it is supposed to have died. The demise of Labour governments in New Zealand and the UK in elections following the 2008 global financial crisis certainly provides a context in which this proposition can be explored although it could also be argued that any reform shift can be attributed more to the pendulum shift from capacity building during periods of fiscal surplus to expenditure control during periods of fiscal stringency. Finally, there would be those who would abandon their previous scepticism and take the opportunity to assume insider status by enthusiastically promoting a new convergence myth based on the eventual replacement of the 'old' NPM paradigm with a new one based on the principles of NPG.

The externalisation of scepticism may thus produce a pendulum-like pattern of policy succession in which one reform enthusiasm succeeds another. Should this only be viewed negatively? Moran (2003) has argued that institutional reform in Britain has been characterised by 'hyper-innovation' since the Thatcher and Major governments broke up an established 'club' style of government and opened up the trajectory for further reform. This suggests that while the de-institutionalisation of policy scepticism inherent in the advisory role of the public service weakened deliberative rationality and increased the risk of avoidable policy errors, it may also (probably unintentionally) have created a more dynamic reform environment that placed public organisations under greater pressure to enhance their innovative capacity. At the very least, public managers would have had to assume a more visible leadership role in mobilising enthusiasm to drive change processes forward. Sceptics could argue that this could be either an exercise in 'impression management' (Wallis and McLoughlin 2010) or the pursuit of 'change for the sake of change'. However, to be credible it should be reflected in a break up of 'silos', 'established routines' and 'entrenched interests' (Vermuelen et al. 2010) that create space for a greater internal enthusiasm for innovation that, according to 'contingency theorists', may provide the necessary internal response to external pressures to innovate (Osborne and Browne 2005, p. 136).

We conclude by suggesting some of the general implications that can be drawn from the relationship between leadership and scepticism that we have sought to explore.

CONCLUSION

Reform has sometimes been characterised from a sceptical perspective as a process of adopting different fashionable and changing rhetorics, or perhaps a ritual or semantic game (Goldfinch 2006). As Noordegraaf (2009, p. 267) notes, in the Netherlands reform was to some extent a process of 'verbal renewal' where 'linguistically, Dutch administrators turned into "managers" in the 1980s; managers became "strategists" and "public entrepreneurs" in the 1990s; and they turned into "leaders" around the turn of the century'.

The rhetorical turn to 'leadership talk' does, however, raise the question of the relationship between leadership and scepticism in the reform process. The understandings of leadership applied by IOs such as the OECD (2001) in promoting its development at every level of the public sector appear to have been derived from the literature on transformational leadership and 'change management' (Bass 1990; Kotter 1995). In essence this conceives leadership as a process of stimulating and focusing waves of enthusiasm that drive processes of cultural change deep within and widely across organisations. This process of horizontal and vertical diffusion of a 'strategic change vision' implicitly seeks to marginalise and exclude sceptical voices from the decision-making process, treating them as expressions of 'resistance' that need to be 'overcome'. In sum, effective leadership is an enthusiastic leadership that makes an enemy of scepticism.

An alternative learning-oriented view of leadership (Senge 1990; Piderit 2000) has come more to the fore since 2008 as the global crisis has exposed the hubris of those who have previously purported to practise transformational leadership (Rawlinson 2009). From this perspective, the harnessing of enthusiasm and silencing or banishing of scepticism is a symptom more of a misleadership that weakens deliberative rationality and enhances 'groupthink' and the biases and distortions associated with bounded rationality. The cycles of enthusiasm, pendulum swings and 'hyper-innovation' observed in the trajectory of public management reform in some countries are thus not inevitable but predictable when the need to balance scepticism with enthusiasm in collective decision making is ignored. However, whatever weakening in deliberative rationality this entails should be balanced against the space it creates for public organisations to enhance their innovative capacity.

REFERENCES

Aberbach, J., Putnam, R. and Rockman, B. (1981). *Bureaucrats and Politicians in Western Democracies*. Cambridge, MA: Harvard University Press.
Andresani, G. and Ferlie, E. (2006). Studying governance within the British public sector and without – theoretical and methodological issues. *Public Management Review*, 8(3), 415–431.
Aucoin, P. (1990). Administrative reform in public management: paradigms, principles, paradoxes and pendulums. *Governance*, 3(1), 115–137.
Bass, B.M. (1990). *Bass and Stogdill's Handbook of Leadership*. New York: Free Press.
Boer, H., Enders, J. and Leisyte, L. (2007). Public sector reform in Dutch higher education: the organizational transformation of the university. *Public Administration*, 85(1), 27–46.
Boston, J., Martin, J., Pallot, J. and Walsh, P. (1996). *Public Management: The New Zealand Model*. Auckland: Oxford University Press.
Campbell, C. (2007). Spontaneous adaptation in public management: an overview. *Governance*, 20(3), 377–400.
Chapman, J. and Duncan, G. (2007). Is there now a new 'New Zealand' model? *Public Management Review*, 9(1), 1–25.
Cheung, A. (2009). Public management reform in Hong Kong. In S. Goldfinch and J. Wallis (eds), *International Handbook of Public Management Reform*. Cheltenham and Northampton, MA: Edward Elgar, pp. 317–335.
Christensen, J. (2009). Danish public management reform before and after NPM. In S. Goldfinch and J. Wallis (eds), *International Handbook of Public Management Reform*. Cheltenham and Northampton, MA: Edward Elgar, pp. 279–299.
Christensen, T. and Lægreid, P. (2007). The whole-of-government approach to public sector reform. *Public Administration Review*, 67(6), 1059–1066.

Collins, R. (1993). Emotional energy as the common denominator of rational social action. *Rationality and Society*, 5(2), 203–220.

Connaughton, B. (2010). Reticent or robust reform? Charting the development of the central bureaucracy in Ireland. *Limerick Papers in Politics and Public Administration*, No. 2.

Dunleavy, P., Margetts, H., Bastow, S. and Tinkler, J. (2006). New Public Management is dead – long live Digital-Era Governance. *Journal of Public Administration Research and Theory*, 16(3), 467–494.

Ellwood, S. and Newberry, S. (2007). Public sector accrual accounting: institutionalising neo-liberal principles. *Accounting, Auditing and Accountability Journal*, 20(4), 549–573.

Falbe, C. and Yukl, G. (1992). Consequences for managers of using single influence tactics and combinations of tactics. *Academy of Management Journal*, 35(3), 638–665.

Gauld, R. and Goldfinch, S. (2006). *Dangerous Enthusiasms: E-government, Computer Failure and Information System Development*. Dunedin: Otago University Press.

Gilovich, T., Griffin, D. and Kahneman, D. (2002). *Heuristics and Biases: The Psychology of Intuitive Judgment*. Cambridge: Cambridge University Press.

Goldfinch, S. (1998). Evaluating public sector reform in New Zealand: have the benefits been oversold? *Asian Journal of Public Administration*, 20, 203–232.

Goldfinch, S. (2006). Rituals of reform, policy transfer, and the national university corporation reforms of Japan. *Governance – An International Journal of Policy and Administration*, 19(4), 585–604.

Goldfinch, S. (2009). New Zealand: reforming an NPM exemplar? In S. Goldfinch and J. Wallis (eds), *International Handbook of Public Management Reform*. Cheltenham and Northampton, MA: Edward Elgar, pp. 155–172.

Goldfinch, S. and Wallis, J. (2010). Two myths of reform convergence. *Public Administration*, 88(4), 1099–1115.

Gregory, R. (2006). Theoretical faith and practical works: de-autonomizing and joining-up in the New Zealand state sector. In T. Christensen and P. Lægreid (eds), *Autonomy and Regulation: Coping with Agencies in the Modern State*. Cheltenham and Northampton, MA: Edward Elgar.

Gregory, R. (2009). New Public Management and the politics of accountability. In Shaun Goldfinch and Joe Wallis (eds), *International Handbook of Public Sector Reform*. Cheltenham and Northampton, MA: Edward Elgar, pp. 66–87.

Gualmini, E. (2008). Restructuring Weberian bureaucracy: comparing managerial reforms in Europe and the United States. *Public Administration*, 86(1), 75–94.

Hall, P. (1993). Policy paradigms, social learning and the state: the case of economic policymaking in Britain. *Comparative Politics*, 25(3), 275–296.

Halligan, J. (2007). Reintegrating government in third generation reforms of Australia and New Zealand. *Public Policy and Administration*, 22(2), 217–238.

Hirschman, A. (1991). *The Rhetoric of Reaction: Perversity, Futility, Jeopardy*. Cambridge, MA: Harvard University Press.

Hood, C. (1991). A public management for all seasons. *Public Administration*, 69(1), 3–19.

Hood, C. (1994). *Explaining Economic Policy Reversals*. Buckingham: Open University Press.

Hood, C. (1998). *The Art of the State: Culture, Rhetoric, and Public Management*. Oxford: The Clarendon Press.

Hood, C. and Lodge, M. (2006). *The Politics of Public Service Bargains*. Oxford: Oxford University Press.

Hood, C. and Peters, G. (2004). The middle aging of New Public Management: into the age of paradox? *Journal of Public Administration Research and Theory*, 14(3), 267–282.

Jones, G. and Cole, A. (2009). French administrative reform: change and resistance. In S. Goldfinch and J. Wallis (eds), *International Handbook of Public Management Reform*. Cheltenham and Northampton, MA: Edward Elgar, pp. 220–234.

Kelly, J. (2007). Reforming public services in the UK: bringing in the third sector. *Public Administration*, 85(4), 1003–1022.

Kotter, R. (1995). Why transformation efforts fail. *Harvard Business Review*, 20(4), 55–67.

Kuhlmann, S., Bogumil, J. and Grohs, S. (2008). Evaluating administrative modernization in German local governments: success or failure of the 'New Steering Model'? *Public Administration Review*, 68(5), 851–863.

Martin, J. (1991). Ethics. In J. Boston (ed.), *Reshaping the State: New Zealand's Bureaucratic Revolution*. Oxford: Oxford University Press.

Moore, M. (1995). *Creating Public Value: Strategic Management in Government*. Cambridge, MA: Harvard University Press.

Moran, M. (2003). *The British Regulatory State: High Modernism and Hyper Innovation*. Oxford: Oxford University Press.

Naschold, F. (1995). *The Modernization of the Public Sector in Europe: A Comparative Perspective on the Scandinavian Experience*. Helsinki: Ministry of Labour.

Noordegraaf, Mirko (2009). Dynamic conservatism: the rise and evolution of public management reforms. In Shaun Goldfinch and Joe Wallis (eds), *International Handbook of Public Sector Reform*. Cheltenham and Northampton, MA: Edward Elgar, pp. 262–278.

OECD (2001). *Public Sector Leadership for the 21st Century*. Paris: Organization for Economic Co-operation and Development.

O'Flynn, J. (2007). From New Public Management to public value: paradigmatic change and managerial implications. *Australian Journal of Public Administration*, 66(3), 353–366.

Osborne, S. (ed.) (2010). *The New Public Governance: Emerging Perspectives From the Theory and Practice of Public Governance*. London: Routledge.

Osborne, S. and Browne, K. (2005). *Managing Change and Innovation in Public Service Organizations*. London: Routledge.

Peters, B.G. (1996). *The Future of Governing: Four Emerging Models*. Lawrence, KS: University Press of Kansas.

Piderit, S.K. (2000). Rethinking resistance and recognizing ambivalence: a multidimensional view of attitudes toward an organizational change. *Academy of Management Review*, 25(4), 783–794.

Pollitt, C. (2001). Convergence: the useful myth? *Public Administration*, 79(4), 933–947.

Pollitt, C. and Bouckaert, G. (2004). *Public Management Reform: A Comparative Analysis* (2nd edition). Oxford: Oxford University Press.

Premfors, R. (1998). Reshaping the democratic state: Swedish experiences in a comparative perspective. *Public Administration*, 76(1), 141–159.

Rawlinson, R. (2009). *Leadership Lessons and the Economic Crisis: Where We've Come From and Where We're Headed*. Frankfurt: Booz and Co.

Rhodes, R. and Wanna, J. (2007). The limits to public value, or rescuing responsible government from the Platonic guardians. *Australian Journal of Public Administration*, 66(4), 406–421.

Rhodes, R.A.W. and Weller, P. (2003). Localism and exceptionalism: comparing public sector reforms in European and Westminster systems. In T. Butcher and A. Massey (eds), *Modernizing Civil Services*. Cheltenham and Northampton, MA: Edward Elgar, pp. 16–36.

Sabatier, P. and Jenkins-Smith, H. (1999). The advocacy coalition framework: an assessment. In P. Sabatier (ed.), *Theories of the Policy Process*. Boulder, CO: Westview Press, pp. 117–166.

Schick, A. (1998). Why most developing countries should not try New Zealand's reforms. *World Bank Research Observer*, 13(1), 123–131.

Scott, G., Bushnell, P. and Nikitin, S. (1990). Reform of the core public sector: the New Zealand experience. *Governance*, 3(2), 138–167.

Senge, P.M. (1990). *The Fifth Discipline: The Art and Practice of the Learning Organisation*. New York: Doubleday.

Thaler, R. (2000). From Homo Economicus to Homo Sapiens. *Journal of Economic Perspectives*, 14, 45–61.

Thelen, K. (2003). How institutions evolve. In J. Mahoney and D. Rueschmeyer (eds), *Comparative Historical Analysis in the Social Sciences*. Cambridge: Cambridge University Press, pp. 208–241.

Van Heerden, A. (2010). *Leaders and Misleaders: The Art of Leading Like You Mean It*. Auckland: Maruki Press.

Vermuelen, F., Puranam, P. and Gulati, R. (2010). Change for change's sake. *Harvard Business Review*, June, 71–76.

Wallis, J.L. and McLoughlin, L. (2010). A modernisation myth: public management reform and leadership behaviour in the Irish public service. *International Journal for Public Administration*, 33(8), 441–450.

Wegrich, K. (2009). Public management reform in the United Kingdom: great leaps, small steps and policies as their own cause. In Shaun Goldfinch and Joe Wallis (eds), *International Handbook of Public Sector Reform*. Cheltenham and Northampton, MA: Edward Elgar, pp. 137–154.

Weyland, K. (2005). Theories of policy diffusion. *World Politics*, 57, 262–295.

Williamson, J. (1994). *The Political Economy of Policy Reform*. Washington, DC: Institute for International Economics.

Yamamoto, K. (2009). Public sector management reform in Japan. In S. Goldfinch and J. Wallis (eds), *International Handbook of Public Management Reform*. Cheltenham and Northampton, MA: Edward Elgar, pp. 336–350.

2. Innovation and reform in public administration: one subject or two?
Laurence E. Lynn, Jr.

INTRODUCTION

Unlike the last Osborne volume to which I contributed, *The New Public Governance: Emerging Perspectives on the Theory and Practice of Public Governance* (Osborne 2010), 'innovation' and 'reform' in public administration' are not new. No New Public Innovation will be celebrated here. Innovation and reform in public administration and management have been written about for decades.

Q: Really? What do people write about?

A: Well, here's a book. The review says that it's 'filled with crisp stories about heroic managers who battle against the odds to bring innovation forth often from hostile organizations' (Light 1996, p. 121).

Q: Um, is it all 'over-the-top' like that?

A: No. Some of it never makes it out of base camp. Take mind mapping ... but I digress. We mavens of these subjects write about many things. We write about what innovation and reform are. How to do them. When to do them. Or not. Where and when they have occurred and the results. How to evaluate them. What the profession needs to know about innovation and reform. Some of it's pretty good, like my 1993 paper ...

Q: Aren't 'innovation' and 'reform' pretty much the same thing?

A: Certainly not. I mean, of course they're related, maybe like ...

Q: What's the difference, then?

A: Um, you may want to consult other mavens on this important question. But *do not try and think about this at home!* You will need professional assistance. So, let me ...

Q: I think you're pulling my leg.

A: Sorry. Seriously, this is interesting stuff. Let me convince you. First, I'll discuss definitions, first of reform, then of innovation. But I'll spare you a tedious summary of all the academic literature on reform and innovation. Instead, I'll show you how systematic research of all kinds is distilled into medium-proof how-to-do-it lessons and guidance for practitioners. Then – here you must pay particular attention – I'll explain the logic of how reform and innovation are logically related, with a cool chart. Finally, I'll take up the question, 'Is innovation as important in the public sector as it is in the for-profit sector?' The answer is, 'No, but, if undertaken, reform and innovation in government are inseparable: innovation without reform is like Hamlet without the Prince of Denmark.

Q: Wow!

A: Thank you. Now, lend me your ears.

PUBLIC SECTOR REFORM

Begin with an image of public bureaucracies – or public administration in general – as sluggish, rule-bound, rigidly hierarchical, performing far less effectively than they should or could. Public bureaucracies should be more efficient and adopt new technologies, better treatments, best practices from both private and public sectors. What is needed is critical thinking about the status quo, some we-can-do-better leadership. In other words, it is time for reform.

A wave of such reforms originating in Great Britain, Australia, and New Zealand beginning in the 1970s became known worldwide as New Public Management (NPM). The central idea was that public management should mimic corporate management in its emphasis on measured performance and competition to promote efficiency. Rather than relying on large bureaucratic agencies (and, as in Europe, nationalized industries), government should be disaggregated into smaller operating agencies linked to policymakers by performance contracts.[1]

What does 'reform' mean?[2] In their book on the subject, Christopher Pollitt and Geert Bouckaert (2004, p. 8) define public management reform as 'deliberate changes to the structures and processes of public sector organizations with the objective of getting them (in some sense) to run better'. NPM provides quintessential examples. Because they are given significant publicity, reform initiatives, whether generated by legislators or administrators, are the most visible of the many kinds of changes in public administration policies and practices that regularly occur at all levels of government.

Focusing on whole-of-government, one-size-fits-all reform initiatives like NPM can be misleading, however. Michael Barzelay (1997)[3] argues that:

> A focus on initiatives is less helpful in comprehending what governments are actually doing . . . [S]ome changes in public management policy happen without being included in an initiative . . . [And] focusing on initiatives often permits only a vague understanding of policy content. A clearer understanding requires an effort to specify either the policy instruments or programs of action involved, or both.

Adoption of new tools of action, forms of organization, ways to perform governmental functions such as budgeting, budget execution and personnel administration, techniques of communication and coordination, and managerial strategies for improving organizational performance often reflect the efforts of officials operating well below the political radar on behalf of specific organizational, programmatic, or personal goals. Seemingly quotidian changes can be cumulatively more significant than the more politically visible but often less successful initiatives. 'The bulk of the improvements in government efficiency that have taken place in recent years,' wrote George Downs and Patrick Larkey (1986, p. 259), 'have resulted not so much from overt, grandiose reform schemes as from a host of modest, tactical reforms.' That assessment still holds.

Pollitt has studied public sector reforms generally associated with NPM. He summarizes the intended results as follows (2000, pp. 185–186):

● savings (reduced budget appropriations);
● improved processes (faster, more accessible complaints procedures, quicker

turn-around times for repairs or the processing of licenses, 'one-stop' service locations, and the like);

- improved efficiency (better input/output ratios, such as more students graduating per full-time equivalent number of staff, the same number of drivers' licenses issued with 20 percent fewer staff);
- greater effectiveness (less crime, poverty, functional illiteracy, homelessness, drug abuse, gender or ethnic inequality; more new jobs created, more contented and trusting citizens); and
- an increase in the overall capacity/flexibility/resilience of the administrative system as a whole (through the recruitment and training of more skilled, more committed public servants).

Pollitt and Bouckaert have also identified four types of results from reform initiatives: operational results, process results, improvements in organizational/institutional capacity, and progress toward a goal (Pollitt and Bouckaert, 2004).

In competitive electoral regimes, reform proposals are politicians' way of demonstrating commitment to 'good government'. Herbert Simon has said that 'The Power to innovate . . . is probably the principal power of the bureaucracy in the realm of policy and value' (Simon 1967, p. 106). Thus, as Ian Thynne shows, both politicians and administrators are '"drivers" and/or "supporters" of reform, as influenced by their policy roles and contributions, along with electoral politics and government–legislature alignments' (Thynne 2003, p. 449). As Thynne, Pollitt and Bouckaert, Walter Kickert, and others have argued, however, differences in these roles, in governing institutions, and in national beliefs and traditions mean that path dependence will characterize reform trajectories which, therefore, will inevitably differ across countries.

PUBLIC SECTOR INNOVATION

The concept of public sector innovation has evolved on a separate track from public sector reform. Unlike reform (as in 'reform school'), innovation is sexy and fun.

Over the past half century, innovation and cognate fields such as creative problem solving have become the focus of research, consultancies, and management development and training programs. Innovation has achieved the status of what Pollitt and Peter Hupe (2011) have called 'magic concepts' (others include 'participation', 'accountability', and 'governance'). 'A high degree of abstraction, a strongly positive normative charge, a seeming ability to dissolve previous dilemmas and binary oppositions and a mobility across domains, give them their "magic" character' (2011, p. 641). In other words, merely invoking a magic concept like innovation creates the impression that 'we are embarking on a noble cause' without further (tedious) justification. But, say Pollitt and Hupe, 'Limitations are also identified. Magic concepts are useful, but potentially seductive. They should not be stretched to purposes for which they are not fitted' (2011, p. 641).

Innovation might be thought of as simply an improvement in government operations originating with a new, bright idea. The problem would be to elicit ideas, insights, and possible solutions that are far from obvious and that require imagination, or that appear to be at variance with 'the right way to do things'. Exhorting colleagues and subordinates to 'think outside the box' and rewarding promising results for doing so might help. So, too, might bringing in people known to be creative, to be (constructive) contrarians, or to have considerable imagination and the ability to think in a nonlinear, what-if-we-look-at-it-this-way manner that makes heretofore hidden solutions emerge. The high failure rate (or short half life) of innovations in both public and private sectors, however, and the fact that innovative efforts are usually never made, suggest that public sector innovation is more difficult than simply eliciting new ideas.

A more widely accepted definition of innovation is 'the intentional introduction and application within a role, group, or organization, of ideas, processes, products or procedures, new to the relevant unit of adoption, designed to significantly benefit the individual, the group, or wider society' (West, 1990, quoted in Omachonu and Einspruch 2010, p. 3; cf. Anderson et al. 2004). It captures 'three important characteristics of innovation: (a) novelty; (b) an application component; and (c) an intended benefit' (Omachonu and Einspruch 2010, p. 4; cf. Lansisalmi et al. 2006). Note that what is new about an innovation in this definition is the location of its application; innovation can be old wine in a new bottle, the diffusion to new settings of an idea originating elsewhere.

Examples of innovation in health care that reflect this definition include

> an electronic Personal Health Record solution (ePHR) to enable consumers to record and selectively share healthcare information about themselves and their loved ones in a secure manner . . . an electronic Clinician Health Record solution (eCHR) to enable physicians and other healthcare providers to securely access healthcare information collated from any number of trusted sources relating to an individual patient in a structured and easily accessible way . . . a healthcare informatics platform to enable all healthcare data to be stored and accessed via the ePHR and eCHR solutions. The platform is based on industry-standard technologies and data models [and . . .] the use of robots in rehabilitation therapy for victims of stroke. Robots being built by a team at MIT are able to help deliver therapy with the promise of reducing elbow and shoulder impairments in stroke victims. (Omachonu and Einspruch 2010, pp. 7–8)

An even bolder definition of innovation has been termed 'disruptive', 'radical', 'transformational', or 'revolutionary' innovation (Hage and Hollingsworth 2000). These are 'innovations that disorder old systems, create new players and new markets while marginalizing old ones, and deliver dramatic value to stakeholders who successfully implement and adapt to the innovation' (Omachonu and Einspruch 2010, p. 4). Laurence Lynn (1997) asserts: 'Innovation [in government] is properly defined as an original, disruptive, and fundamental transformation of an organization's core tasks. Innovation changes deep structures and changes them permanently.' This definition implies that the other definitions might be termed 'innovation lite', which is indistinguishable from ordinary change.

An example of radical innovation is the widely publicized CompStat program which transformed the New York Police Department from a reactive into a proactive crime-fighting force.[4] The entrepreneurial innovators included the Chief of Police and his key deputies, who devised a series of specific steps:

- make precinct commanders provide briefings to command staff on the weekly numbers, maintain up-to-date pin maps, and prepare acetate overlays;
- bring borough commanders and precinct commanders together on a regular basis to discuss the numbers, and address detailed questions;

- set an ambitious goal on which all personnel would focus: reduce crime by 10 percent;
- institutionalize the weekly meetings: the maps were computerized and became the basis for the discussions, and the name CompStat was coined, referring to computerized comparison crime statistics;
- establish a tradition of tough, unsentimental interactions, resembling interrogations, between command staff and precinct commanders;
- encourage the process to trickle down, so that precinct commanders and tour commanders began using the process; and, as experience was gained,
- refine the model, focusing on: accurate and timely intelligence on crime; rapid deployment of policing resources; effective tactics for addressing problems; and relentless follow-up and assessment.

These basic features of CompStat have been widely replicated in police departments, other service delivery departments, and even entire cities (e.g. Baltimore), across the United States. Rarely replicated, however, is the internal restructuring which was essential to the success of this system and which qualifies it as a true innovation. As criminal justice scholar Paul O'Connell (2001, p. 9), puts it,

> An emphasis was placed upon the realignment of organizational resources. An ambitious reengineering effort shifted the department from being a centralized, functional organization to a decentralized, geographic organization. A number of centralized, functional units were broken up with their functions (and personnel) redistributed to new geographically decentralized units (precincts). Functional specialists were placed under the command of newly defined geographic managers, thereby moving decision making down the organizational hierarchy.

Failure to grasp the importance of the reorganization and 'reengineering' that supported CompStat accounts for the limited success of attempts to replicate it elsewhere. In such replications, the data-driven meetings became merely an add-on to previous bureaucratic routines and produced little change in operations or improvements in outcomes. As will be argued below, properly understood, innovation and reform are inseparable.

PLAYBOOKS, FIELDBOOKS, CHECKLISTS, AND LESSONS

A large literature is concerned with innovation in the corporate, nonprofit, and public sectors. Often, the applicability to practice of theoretical and theory-based empirical research is obscure. As the intended audience for findings includes practitioners, significant effort is devoted to distilling the findings of systematic investigation by scholars and practitioners into artifacts such as playbooks, fieldbooks, checklists, and lessons. For these research artifacts to be useful rather than superficial requires striking a balance between their generality (so that they are useful in many contexts) and their concreteness (so that they resonate with contextual realities). As practitioners tend to learn from each other rather than from academic journals and monographs, examples of such artifacts provide insights into how reform and innovation are understood in practice.

Guidance for Reformers

An early effort at lessons for large-scale administrative reform was an ex post listing of a dozen factors that affected the 1960s implementation of the Planning–Programming–Budgeting System (PPBS) in the U.S. government. These could serve as a checklist for future implementers of similar one-size-fits-all administrative reforms (Harper et al. 1969, pp. 631–632):

1. The extent of the participation in system and process design of officials most concerned with the effects that the system may have on programs.
2. Identification of common areas of interest and a process which focuses on these areas.
3. Performance of studies which demonstrate the usefulness of analysis and the publicizing of such studies.
4. The attitude of the congressional committees responsible for an agency's substantive activity and its appropriations.
5. The attitude of the major clientele groups affected by the agency's programs.
6. The attitude of the examining group within the Bureau of the Budget responsible for reviewing and evaluating the agency program.
7. The age of the agency and/or its programs.
8. The extent to which the agency has an already developed analytic capability and the nature of the process through which those activities are incorporated into decision making.
9. The susceptibility of the agency mission to analytic effort, notably the difficulty in designing benefit measures for the evaluation of programs.
10. The difficulty of, or the extent to which, appropriate data and accounting systems have been developed.
11. The degree of congruity between the analytic program structure and the agency's organization structure.
12. As an outgrowth of the previous two factors, the difficulty associated with translating cost and other information from the basic appropriations accounts in which the budget is prepared to the program structure in which it is examined and in which programs are evaluated.

This checklist strikes a good balance between generality and concreteness.

Decades later, a retrospective analysis of PPBS implementation led to another list: of 'lessons for change agents' which constitutes a 'playbook' for reformers (Lynn forthcoming). Note that these admonitions are more general than the above list but concrete enough to be useful:

1. Before launching a government reform initiative, find out where the government has been and where it is now – and why.
2. Real change agents go 'all in' [that is, seek full, not partial, implementation].
3. Work through existing institutions, not ad hoc arrangements.
4. Change agents must be absolutely clear about the concept, its rationale, and the steps needed to implement it.

5. Craft a sound argument for any reform initiative that is easily comprehended by supporters and critics alike.
6. Reform needs champions; fill key subcabinet positions with people who care about it.
7. Don't forget: Government is politics, not economics.
8. Reforms that are oversold invite skepticism and will eventually be perceived to have failed.
9. Reform takes time; it will begin to become meaningful in a second term.
10. To survive transitions, reforms themselves must be institutionalized.

A final example of such artifacts is derived from evaluating the administrative reforms implemented by the Clinton and George W. Bush administrations in the U.S. (Bruel and Kamensky 2008).

Put Management Issues on the Front Burner Early . . .
Clearly Define the Scope of the Effort in Advance . . .
Come to Agreement on an Initiative Development and Selection Process . . .
Invest in Implementation and Follow Through . . .

Though brief and concise, considerable elaboration was associated with each lesson so that they would be useful enough to avoid the epithet 'bromides'.

Guidance for Innovators

Although early innovation research was conducted primarily by scholars of the private sector, the field of public administration took notice. Of the previously discussed PPBS, implemented in the 1960s, a contemporary observer said: '[PPBS encourages] *innovation* by making the consequences of action more visible and subject to evaluation, rather than by destroying the control features of bureaucracy' (Lyden 1969, p. 85, italics added). In addition, the International City and County Management Association began formally recognizing outstanding innovators. Now, public innovators have a substantial literature devoted to their concerns, including a journal, *The Innovation Journal: The Public Sector Innovation Journal*, which began publication in 1995.

An early (1976) how-to-do-it guide for innovators, including those in the public sector, was *Promoting Innovation and Change in Organizations and Communities*, by Jack Rothman, John Erlich, and Joseph Teresa. Begin with organizational goals, they say, and program objectives, easy to overlook by innovators. Next, identify actors who are powerful in goal setting. Then formulate a strategy to cope with or enlist the support of those powerful actors. Finally, undertake detailed operational analysis of specific objectives, facilitating and limiting factors of the change agents, clients, and other actors and entities in the environment, gauging participants' reactions to change strategies. The results, alas, are more likely to be incremental than fundamental, but then public entrepreneurs and agencies are not like Steven Jobs and Apple, Inc. As a Harvard Business School Professor once summarized the problem of public management, 'The private manager's enabling resources – structure, finances, people – are the public manager's constraint', substantially beyond the public administrator's control.

Fast forward through the era of 'Reinventing Government' and New Public

Management, which accelerated effort on behalf of public sector innovation. Now, public administrators have *The Public Innovator's Playbook: Nurturing Bold Ideas in Government* (Eggers and Singh 2009). This well-produced book describes (italics added) '*The* Innovation Cycle', '*The* Five Strategies for Innovation', and '*The* Innovation Organization'. It has as well 'Good Sources on Innovation' that include books on government innovation, business innovation, idea generation, networks and innovation plus resource publications, organizations, and Web sites.

In a nutshell, according to this playbook, the organization's structure must support the innovation cycle – idea generation, idea selection, idea implementation, and idea diffusion – and the five innovation strategies – cultivate, replicate, partner, network, and open source. *The Public Innovator's Playbook* largely ignores the political environment, however. It helpfully suggests that public sector innovators 'get support' from unions and politicians, but political and legal constraints do not loom large.

There are appropriate resources for public sector innovators elsewhere, however. The Government Innovators Network, maintained by the Kennedy School of Government's Ash Center for Democratic Governance and Innovation at Harvard University, is a forum for public administrators at all levels of government to share their insights and lessons learned. The Center's 'Innovation in Government Awards' program promotes innovation in government (CompStat received an award) and provides a useful source of information on public sector innovation, which is particularly important as public officials tend to trust other public officials more than they do more codified academic literature (Lynn 1997).

Throughout the awards cycle for the Innovations in Government Award, each applicant is rated according to the following criteria, actually a checklist, implicitly endorsing a transformational definition of innovation:

- Its *novelty*, the degree to which the program demonstrates a leap in creativity.
  - Does the program represent a fundamental change in the governance, management, direction, or policy approach of a particular jurisdiction?
  - Does the program represent a significant improvement in the process by which a service is delivered?
  - Does the program introduce a substantially new technology or service concept?
- Its *effectiveness*, the degree to which the program has achieved tangible results.
  - Does the program respond to the needs of a well-defined group of clients?
  - Does the program demonstrate its effectiveness in meeting its stated goals and objectives quantitatively and qualitatively?
  - Does the program produce unanticipated benefits for its clients?
  - Does the program present evidence of already completed, independent evaluation?
- Its *significance*, the degree to which the program successfully addresses an important problem of public concern.
  - To what degree does the program address a problem of national import and scope?
  - To what degree does the program make substantial progress in diminishing the problem within its jurisdiction?

   ○   To what degree does the program change the organizational culture or the traditional approach to management or problem solving?
- Its *transferability*, the degree to which the program, or aspects of it, shows promise of inspiring successful replication by other governmental entities.
  - ○   To what extent can this program be replicated in other jurisdictions?
  - ○   To what extent can this program serve as a model that other jurisdictions will seek to replicate?
  - ○   To what extent are program components, concepts, principles, or insights transferable to other disciplines or policy areas?

Novelty, listed first, features 'a leap in creativity', a notion reinforced by linking effectiveness with 'unanticipated benefits', significance with 'a problem of national import and scope', and transferability with being a 'model'. Mere replication would not seem to be enough. It is important to note, however, that political challenges are not mentioned; these are innovations whose entrepreneurial sponsors claim to have already succeeded or be on the road to success.

There are many other sources for codified guidance from scholars including Robert Behn, Sandford Borins, David Osborne, and Nancy Roberts. According to Borins (2002, p. 467), for example: 'Political leaders and agency heads can create a supportive climate for bottom-up innovation by consulting staff, instituting formal awards and informal recognition for innovators, promoting innovators, protecting innovators from control-oriented central agencies, and publicly championing bottom-up innovations that have proven successful and have popular appeal.'

In the final analysis, cautions Behn (1995, p. 232), 'Creating an innovative public agency is itself a task of innovation. Each innovative organization will be different. It will be pursuing different purposes. Or it will be pursuing them in a different organizational context, within a different political environment, or within different legal constraints. There is no recipe for replicating an innovation.' The occupational hazard of innovation scholarship is offering unqualified advice that is never wrong.

REFORM AND INNOVATION: JOINED AT THE HIP

What remains unclear is whether there is any conceptual relationship between 'reform' and 'innovation'. Although that relationship has already been implied by references in the preceding section to the interrelationships between organizational structures and innovation, a multi-decade intellectual journey will clarify it.

Innovation, Economic Growth, and Social Improvement

A logic relating innovation and social improvement originated with Joseph A. Schumpeter, in his 1934 book, *The Theory of Economic Development* (Sweezy 1943). In it he argues that economic change originates with an innovation that results in a process of economic development leading to social improvement. 'Innovation,' he claimed, 'is the activity or function of a particular set of individuals called entrepreneurs . . . [who] must . . . have . . . qualities of leadership' (Sweezy 1943, pp. 93–94). This causal account is supported, said Paul Sweezy, by 'an overwhelming mass of obvious and indisputable facts' (1943, p. 96).

The decades after World War II saw the beginnings of an enduring academic interest in innovation and organizational change – predominantly technological change at first – as a characteristic of capitalism and of specific industries and firms. Distinctions were drawn between invention, innovation, and imitation (Brozen 1951). Innovation research became popular in the study of business management and organization, and most research on innovation and innovation adoption still focuses on the private sector (Damanpour and Schneider 2009; Moore and Hartley 2010).

An intellectual bridge from Schumpeterian logic to innovation in government is the effort to distinguish between 'managers' and 'entrepreneurs' wherein the Schumpeterian view of entrepreneurs as innovators is replaced by 'the Weberian notion of entrepreneurs as sources of formal authority in an organization (Hartmann 1959). Thompson (1965, p. 1) took yet another step by establishing a relationship between formal authority and innovation. The goal of the entrepreneur should be to alter bureaucratic structures so as 'to increase innovativeness, such as, increased professionalization, a looser and more untidy structure, decentralization, freer communications, project organization when possible, rotation of assignments, greater reliance on group processes, attempts at continual restructuring, modification of the incentive system, and changes in many management practices'. Thompson (1965, p. 1) suggested (presciently for 1965) that 'bureaucratic organizations are actually evolving in this direction'.

One more logical step and a useful insight emerges. In *The Free Market Innovation Machine: Analyzing the Growth Miracle of Capitalism* (2002), economist William J. Baumol argues that it is not cost-reducing price competition that is the driving force behind economic growth but innovations within firms which must be matched by competitors and which can lead to collaborations among firms in the creation of new innovations. Putting these logics together, we see that firms, in other words, compete by reforming (restructuring) themselves to become and remain innovative. Reform and innovation are endemic to capitalism.

Reform, Innovation, and Government Efficiency

How, neoliberals in particular have asked, can the public sector be infused with the innovative dynamism of the private sector? That question, long a staple of American discourse, was raised by neoliberal regimes of the fiscally constrained 1970s. New Public Management became the term associated with the private sector-mimicking reforms that would awaken moribund bureaucracies by confronting them with the need to compete for resources and to achieve performance targets. The goal was not 'growth' of the public sector, however, but its opposite: leaner, innovative public agencies performing their service delivery missions more efficiently and effectively.

By the logic set forth above, public management *reform* can produce organizational *innovation* if reformers employ two distinct levers – entrepreneurial strategies and changes in organizational structures – on behalf of efficiency and service improvement.

Does this linking of reform and innovation make practical sense? Paul Light (1996) thinks so. He distinguishes between individual entrepreneurs generating good ideas that

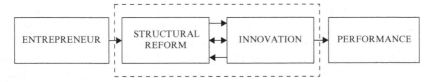

Figure 2.1   How entrepreneurs improve government performance

lead to innovation, and 'organizational reform', which is about 'the less visible, but perhaps more important work [of building] organizations in which innovation comes more naturally [by] redesigning public agencies, flattening organization charts, creating and using market pressure, or building learning systems' (Light 1996, p. 122).

The paradigmatic logic is shown in Figure 2.1. The process might be regarded as a theory, as the causal arrows suggest. The dotted line isolates the key operational process wherein structural changes enable or facilitate innovation. It is initiated by an entrepreneur or team of entrepreneurs at a strategic location in a system or organization. The result is a positive, perhaps measurable, improvement in performance – in effectiveness, efficiency, innovativeness or, as Pollitt suggested, in other dimensions of governing. Its intended use, however, is less as a theory than as a heuristic or an analytic framework that informs the design and interpretation of innovation research to four interrelated elements of innovation.

Conundrums of Change

This framework necessarily oversimplifies both the means and ends, and even the causal logic, of system or organizational change. Listing some familiar terms of art in the study and practice of change illustrates their variety: transformation, organizational development, organizational learning, best practices, creativity/creative problem solving, performance management, evidence-based policy, entrepreneurship, leadership, change agents, champions, reinvention, re-engineering, diffusion. All are concerned with the who, what, why, and how of change. The processes whereby public entrepreneurs identify and transform opportunities for, as Mark Moore (1995) has put it, 'creating public value' into actual performance vary widely and inevitably reflect individual managers' distinctive types and perceptions, from systematic and analytic to intuitive and experiential. In other words, 'reform' and 'innovation' are 'talked about' in many different languages and pursued in many different ways.

The causal relationship between structural reform and innovation, moreover, may be led by innovation – such as a new technology requiring reorganization – or by reform – such as the creation of more fluid communication and reporting channels within the organization – or be simultaneous – as with CompStat (discussed above). Innovation may not require system/organizational reform (new treatment procedures for front-line personnel), and reform may not require innovation (simplified reporting or monitoring procedures). In other words, the analytic framework depicted in Figure 2.1 is consistent with many different theories of the change process, with units of analysis ranging from whole governments to specific programs and locations to a particular treatment modality.

Finally, though one may observe what are considered successful cases of performance improvement associated with reform and innovation, the blooms of change may be annuals rather than perennials. The half life of a performance improvement, whether it be in specific outputs and outcomes or in organizational capacity and process efficiency, may be longer if it involves a permanent change in technology; shorter if changes in personnel – the entrepreneur leaves – or ordinary bureaucratic forces tend to weaken or undermine earlier results.

These considerations notwithstanding, when we talk about 'innovation' and 'reform' in public administration, we are talking about processes of change, occurring over intervals of time which may be short or long, which may reflect patterns of path dependence within given political jurisdictions, which tend to emphasize the role of causal agents, and whose prospects for diffusion and longevity are enhanced by structural and cultural change.

MUST GOVERNMENT INNOVATE?

In the private sector, when markets are competitive in price, quality, and access, innovative firms are more likely to survive and prosper. Surely government must *change* because its political environment is constantly changing. But is there in the public sector a need to innovate?

Although Simon (1967) saw innovation as a source of bureaucratic power, acquiring and using such power can threaten agency autonomy or resources if it fails or if other values are jeopardized. Osborne and Gaebler (1992) argue that when public officials get their operating funds from legislatures, their incentives to invest in innovation by decentralizing decision making and empowering employees are weak; to attempt innovation and fail is worse. Public agencies are mission-, needs-, and mandate-driven. The political incentive to avoid duplication and waste tends to produce monopoly power in ministries and departments. The priorities, often outweighing efficiency, are reliability, equitable access, effectiveness, and the satisfaction of stakeholders ranging from taxpayers to client advocates to individual legislators. Even with NPM, reliability may trump creativity as a bureaucratic imperative.

Efforts to innovate should and will be ongoing, however. What should innovators know?

For one thing, the kind of change in public operations governed by the rule of law warranting the label 'innovation' or 'reform' necessarily involves all of the difficulties associated with arranging cooperative collective action in politics: conflict, defection, asymmetric information, and assessment and assignment of risks (Lynn 1997). The avoidance of conflict and controversy by would-be change agents is likely to be why change efforts fail. Don't avoid conflict.

Creativity is difficult to program. It is individual, a product of passion and intellect, the natural inclination of iconoclasts who thrive on taking risks and challenging the status quo. Group-think all too often stifles the bright ideas of such people. Moreover, as Figure 2.1 emphasizes, organizational structures can restrain or enable innovation. An innovative organization is flexible to the point of being a bit chaotic. The ambitious, clever entrepreneur thrives in such a milieu. There is intellectual energy; the environment is contentious and exciting. Tolerate the chaos.

Paradoxically, however, innovation also requires a leader with the authority to make decisions and enforce agreements without abusing that authority. A leader/entrepreneur is more effective if a bit of charisma is combined with a lot of good judgment, tolerance of ambiguity, and a love of argument, passion, risks, and action. Leave your door, and your mind, open.

Above all, accept that innovation typically requires cultural change, and change agents must be willing to invest considerable time and effort in translating structural changes into durable changes in how agencies do their work. In the public sector, cultural change is intensely political. Change agents must always be mindful of *who* gets what, when, and how. Effort devoted to creating conceptual distinctions between 'innovation' and 'reform' or laboring over such definitions is probably a waste of time. The challenge is the deliberate promotion of significant improvement in government operations and performance however measured or defined. Skill and determination, not magic words, are what is needed to justify and achieve such far-reaching changes in any government in the world. Spend time learning how to do it, then stay with it.

AFTERWORD

Q: You said earlier that 'innovation' and 'reform' were not the same thing, didn't you?
A: That was a long time ago.
Q: It was an hour ago!
A: 'Do what I do, not what I say.'
Q: That's a cliché! You said . . .
A: To innovation and reform mavens, it is wisdom. *The Public Innovators' Playbook* says, 'creativity is thinking up new things, innovation is *doing* new things'. Stop thinking. Go *do* something.
Q: What I should do is talk to someone else.
A: Talk to my fellow maven, Christopher Pollitt. He's very good on subjects like this.

NOTES

1.   Such reform concepts did not produce the frisson in America that they did in much of the rest of the world, however, because most, if not all, of their features had already become widely used 'tools of government' following World War II.
2.   The following discussion adapts material from Hill and Lynn (2008) and Lynn (2006).
3.   Quoted by Hill and Lynn (2008, p. 338).
4.   The following discussion is adapted from Hill and Lynn (2008), pp. 367–374.

REFERENCES

Anderson, N., De Dreu, C. and Nijstad, B.A. (2004). The routinization of innovation research: a constructively critical view of the state-of-the-science. *Journal of Organizational Behavior*, 25, 147–173.
Anthony, Scott D. (2009). *The Silver Lining: An Innovation Playbook for Uncertain Times*. Boston, MA: Harvard Business Review Press.

Anthony, Scott D. (2011). Seize the silver lining: a checklist for innovation. HBR Blog Network, 8 June. Available at: http://blogs.hbr.org/anthony/2009/06/seize_the_silver_lining_a_chec.html.

Barzelay, Michael (1997). Politics of public management reform in OECD countries. Paper presented at the II International Congress of CLAD on State and Public Administration Reform, Margarita Island, Venezuela, 14–18 October.

Baumol, William J. (2002). *The Free Market Innovation Machine: Analyzing the Growth Miracle of Capitalism*. Princeton, NJ: Princeton University Press.

Behn, Robert D. (1995). Creating an innovative organization: ten hints for involving frontline workers. *State and Local Government Review*, 27(3), 221–234.

Borins, Sandford (2002). Leadership and innovation in the public sector. *Leadership and Organization Development Journal*, 23(8), 467–476.

Brozen, Yale (1951). Invention, innovation, and imitation. *American Economic Review*, 41(2), 239–257.

Bruel, Jonathan D. and Kamensky, John M. (2008). Federal Government reform: lessons from Clinton's 'Reinventing Government' and Bush's 'Management Agenda' initiatives. *Public Administration Review*, 68(6), 1009–1026.

Damanpour, Fariborz and Schneider, Marguerite (2009). Characteristics of innovation and innovation adoption in public organizations: assessing the role of managers. *Journal of Public Administration Research and Theory*, 19, 495–522.

Downs, George W. and Larkey, Patrick D. (1986). *The Search for Government Efficiency: From Hubris to Helplessness*. New York: Random House.

Eggers, William D. and Singh, Shalabh Kumar (2009). *The Public Innovator's Playbook: Nurturing Bold Ideas in Government*. Deloitte Research. Available at: http://www.deloitte.com/assets/DconGlobal/Local%20 Assets/Documents/dit_ps_innpvatprs[;aubppl_100409.pdf.

Elkin, Stephen L. (1983). Towards a contextual theory of innovation. *Policy Sciences*, 15(4), 367–387.

Hage, J. and Hollingsworth, R.A. (2000). A strategy for analysis of idea innovation networks and institutions. *Organizational Studies*, 21, 971–1004.

Harper, E.L., Kramer, F.A. and Rouse, A.M. (1969). Implementation and use of PPB in sixteen Federal agencies. *Public Administration Review*, 29(6), 623–632.

Hartmann, Heinz (1959). Managers and entrepreneurs: a useful distinction? *Administrative Science Quarterly*, 3(4), 429–451.

Hill, Carolyn J. and Lynn, Laurence E., Jr. (2008). *Public Management: A Three-Dimensional Approach*. Washington, DC: CQ Press.

Lansisalmi, H., Kivimaki, M., Aalto, P. and Ruoranen, R. (2006). Innovation in healthcare: a systematic review of recent research. *Nursing Science Quarterly*, 19, 66–72.

Light, Paul (1996). Book review. *Journal of Policy Analysis and Management*, 15(1), 121–124.

Lundvall, Bengt-Åke (ed.) (2010). *National Systems of Innovation: Toward a Theory of Innovation and Interactive Learning*. London and New York: Anthem Press.

Lyden, Fremont J. (1969). Innovation in bureaucracy? *Public Administration Review*, 29(1), 84–85.

Lynn, Laurence E., Jr. (1997). Innovation and the public interest: insights from the private sector. In Alan A. Altshuler and Robert D. Behn (eds), *Innovations in American Government: Opportunities, Challenges, and Dilemmas*. Washington, DC: The Brookings Institution, pp. 84–103.

Lynn, Laurence E., Jr. (2006). *Public Management: Old and New*. London: Routledge.

Lynn, Laurence E., Jr. (forthcoming). Reform of the Federal Government: lessons for change agents. In Robert Wilson, Norman Glickman and Laurence E. Lynn, Jr., *Reshaping the Federal Government: The Policy and Management Legacies of the Johnson Years*. Austin, TX: University of Texas Press.

Moore, Mark H. (1995). *Creating Public Value: Strategic Management in Government*. Cambridge, MA: Harvard University Press.

Moore, Mark and Hartley, Jean (2010). Innovations in governance. In Stephen P. Osborne (ed.), *The New Public Governance: Emerging Perspectives on the Theory and Practice of Public Governance*. London: Routledge, pp. 52–71.

O'Connell, Paul E. (2001). Using performance data for accountability: the New York City Police Department's CompStat model of police management. In Mark A. Abramson and John M. Kamensky (eds), *Managing for Results 2002*. Lanham, MD: Rowman and Littlefield, pp. 179–224.

Omachonu, Vincent K. and Einspruch, Norman G. (2010). Innovation in health care delivery systems: a conceptual framework. *The Innovation Journal*, 15(1), Article 2, 1–20.

Osborne, David and Gaebler, Ted (1992). *Reinventing Government: How the Entrepreneurial Spirit is Transforming the Public Sector*. Reading, MA: Addison-Wesley.

Ouchi, William G. and Wilkins, Alan L. (1985). Organizational culture. *Annual Review of Sociology*, 11, 457–483.

Pollitt, Christopher (2000). Is the emperor in his underwear? An analysis of the impacts of public management reform. *Public Management*, 2, 181–199.

Pollitt, Christopher and Bouckaert, Geert (2004). *Public Management Reform: A Comparative Analysis.* Oxford: Oxford University Press.

Pollitt, Christopher and Hupe, Peter (2011). Talking about government: the role of magic concepts. *Public Management Review*, 13(5), 641–658.

Rothman, Jack, Erlich, John L. and Teresa, Joseph G. (1976). *Promoting Innovation and Change in Organizations and Communities: A Planning Manual.* New York: John Wiley and Sons, Inc.

Simon, Herbert A. (1967). The changing theory and changing practice of public administration. In Ithiel de Sola Pool (ed.), *Contemporary Political Science: Toward Empirical Theory.* New York: McGraw-Hill, pp. 86–120.

Sweezy, Paul M. (1943). Professor Schumpeter's theory of innovation. *Review of Economics and Statistics*, 25(1), 93–96.

Thompson, Victor A. (1965). Bureaucracy and innovation. *Administrative Science Quarterly*, 10(1), 1–20.

Thynne, Ian (2003). Public management reform: 'drivers and supporters' in comparative perspective. *Public Management Review*, 5(3), 449–459.

West, M.A. (1990). The social psychology of innovation in groups. In M.A. West and J.L. Farr (eds), *Innovation and Creativity at Work: Psychological and Organizational Strategies.* Chichester: Wiley, pp. 309–334.

3. Public and private features of innovation
Jean Hartley

INTRODUCTION

This chapter has two main purposes. The first is to outline key themes and questions relevant to innovation in public services, as an analytical framework against which to consider the principles of innovation theory in general. The second is to examine what can be learnt from the extensive research into innovation in the private sector and what must be reconceptualised to take account of the particular goals, purposes and contexts which characterise public organisations. This is important whether the public sector innovates on its own or collaboratively with other sectors.

The discourse about public services innovation is full of myths, assertions and assumptions. It suffers from having projected onto it the prejudices, the hopes and fears, the frustrations and ambitions of management theorists, policy-makers and practitioners. A senior manager whose role was 'Head of Public Sector Innovation' for a private company commented that people polarised in their assumptions about his job, believing either that the job was overwhelming in size and scope or that it was tiny. Add to that the paucity of innovation research in public management theory, with relatively few researchers working in the area, and also the neglect of the public sector in innovation theory, and one has a heady cocktail of ignorance, lack of evidence, and unexamined and untested assumptions.

On the other hand, this creates a rich field for researchers who are willing to pioneer new thinking, provide new evidence about innovation, and create theory about innovation in government and in public service organisations.

Given the varied meanings which are given to innovation in public policy (Osborne and Brown 2011) and in academic writing (Lynn 1997; Osborne 1998; Hartley 2005), I offer a brief working definition of innovation here. Altshuler and Zegans (1997) define it as 'novelty in action' and Bessant (2005) distinguishes between invention – having a bright idea – and innovation – translating the idea into implementation and use. So innovation is something which is put into practice. Many writers preserve the notion of innovation for 'radical' or 'breakthrough' novelty and others concur in arguing that innovation is disruptive, involving step-change not incremental improvements (e.g. Osborne and Brown 2005; Lynn 1997). It is therefore very different from continuous improvement (Hartley 2011; Osborne and Brown 2011). Inevitably, the extent of innovation is socially constructed (Greenhalgh et al. 2004). Innovation may or may not be successful (Moore 2005).

PUBLIC AND PRIVATE

It is important to examine what can be derived from the large literature on innovation in the private sector. First, there is a common (though I will argue, mistaken) view that the private sector is 'better' at innovation than the public sector. It is valuable to examine the evidence for this view, and to understand what this might tell us about innovation processes and outcomes, across and by sector.

Second, there is an assumption that the public sector will improve its success in innovation if it adopts more of the strategies and practices used by the private sector. In this way, the private sector is used as a benchmark against which the public sector is compared in terms of innovation – and divergence is taken to mean that the public sector is deficient and needs to adopt more methods from the private sector. For example, part of the argument for introducing more competition in the UK national health service is the assumption that competition will drive up standards and will enhance innovation. This is not a proven point (see below).

Third, it is striking how much of the innovation literature is derived from the private sector, a point noted by several scholars (Altshuler and Behn 1997; Albury 2005; Hartley 2005; Moore 2005; Osborne and Brown 2011). Indeed, until recently, the literature was primarily from manufacturing (e.g. automobile design, electronics, scientific equipment). It is only in the last two decades that a literature based on service industries has been emerging (Miles 2000; Gallouj 2002). Much innovation theory has derived from new product development, where an innovation in technology can be observed and broadly recorded, even if its full implications are not initially known. There are important technological developments in public services, for example e-government technologies and new health equipment, but there are difficulties in applying concepts derived from *product* innovation to *service* and *organisational* innovation (Alänge et al. 1998). Service innovations typically have high levels of ambiguity and uncertainty since they are affected by the variability of the human characteristics of both service giver and service receiver (the latter, in some cases, as a co-producer). The innovation is often not a physical artefact at all, but a change in service (which implies a change in the relationships between service providers and their users), and many features are intangible, with high levels of tacit knowledge.

Finally, not only is the academic literature on innovation largely based on the private sector, but often there is little awareness that it is. Some literature is 'context-blind' and thereby over-generalises from the private sector. For example, it is not unusual to have an article on innovation start with a statement about the necessity of innovation for gaining or maintaining an edge over competitors in 'the market'. Innovation is seen as critical for 'the firm', helping to attract 'customers' and to 'make a profit from' a new product or process. Given this sector-blindness, there is a need to sift the literature on innovation carefully to ensure that insights and evidence are relevant and applicable to public organisations.

Understanding the limits and possibilities of learning across and between sectors is critical if public services organisations are to avoid the fads and fashions of the management field (Abrahamson 1991) and avoid 'over-adoption' of innovations or innovation processes (Rogers 2003).

Graham Allison (1983) famously argued that the public and private sectors were 'alike in all unimportant respects' – there are similarities but there are also fundamental differences. This is not an easy area to navigate because the boundaries between public and private sectors are 'neither clear nor permanent' (Flynn 2007, p. 1) and, in addition, the field is burdened with a number of assertions, assumptions and prejudices (Rainey and

Chun 2005). Academic disciplines vary in their emphases on particular features of public and private and therefore whether they emphasise similarity or difference. Here, I focus on the issues relevant to innovation processes and outcomes for public service organisations.

Any simple division between 'public' and 'private' is neither theoretically nor empirically feasible. First, there are a number of inter-relationships and inter-dependencies between sectors (Bozeman 1987; Bozeman and Moulton 2011), including, for example, firms operating under regulatory frameworks devised by the state, privatised and contracted-out public services, commissioned services, the increasing prevalence of hybrid organisations, and collaborative governance.

Second, there are substantial variations within sectors which mean that simple binary comparisons are not sufficient to explain different organisational processes and outcomes. The public/private dimension may be one factor, but also important will be size, task or function and industry characteristics (Rainey 2009), and each of these may influence the approach to innovation. This highlights the need to examine innovation not solely in terms of public/private but in terms of a set of organisational characteristics, where there may be more commonality across than within sectors.

Third, Bozeman (1987) argues that all organisations have some degree of publicness (e.g. all private firms work under state legislation and regulation to some extent). To clarify differences across sectors and across organisations he outlines two key dimensions – which he calls economic authority and political authority – which together create a number of combinations. Economic authority concerns the degree to which the organisation has control over its revenues and assets. Political authority is derived from the legitimacy conferred by citizens, and legislative and governmental bodies, and enables the organisation to act on behalf of those institutions and to make binding decisions for them. Both of these dimensions are valuable to consider in relation to innovation in public service organisations, and we will argue that the second (political authority) is particularly salient in considering public services innovation.

Hartley and Skelcher (2008) argue that one of the distinctive elements of public management is that it operates within a democratic and political context, with governance by politicians and accountability to the electorate. Rainey and Chun (2005) note that differences between sectors are most salient where the organisation has to interact with its external environment. Thus, the distinctive elements of public organisations are their purposes (goals and values), their stakeholders and the impact of their external environment, including the institutional field and degree to which it operates in a market environment (Feldman 2005; Pettigrew 2005). The similarities are more to be found in relation to certain managerial processes internal to the organisation.

INNOVATION PHASES AS AN ANALYTICAL DEVICE

It is common in the management literature to find innovation being considered in terms of stages or phases, though the number of phases and their description may vary (e.g. Rogers 2003;Tidd and Bessant 2009). Although these management stages appear linear and rational, innovation can be chaotic, emergent and unpredictable (van de Ven et al. 1999) and interconnected (Rickards 1996). Van de Ven (1986) likens the process to a

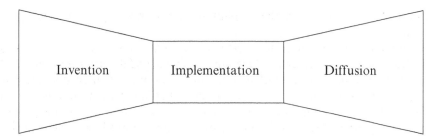

Figure 3.1   Three phases in a process view of innovation

hologram not a linear process, while Bason (2010) comments that the process can seem more like a half-rolled-up yarn of wool than a smooth innovation funnel. In public services, a policy announcement about innovation may reverse the phases (Hartley 2005).

Nevertheless, analysing phases or stages can be valuable, and here we use phases derived from viewing innovation as a process, with three main elements (Osborne and Brown 2005): invention, implementation and diffusion. These are shown in Figure 3.1.

The first phase, invention, is the creativity and ideas phase, corresponding to Tidd and Bessant's (2009) searching and selecting stages. It covers the processes of inventing, finding or harvesting ideas, or recognising needs and opportunities, which have potential as the starting point of innovation. Phase 2, implementation, is about turning those ideas into concrete changes for the organisation or service – it is about making the idea happen and working out whether and how it needs adjustment in the shift from idea to action, and how it will fit with other organisational processes (Denis et al. 2002). The final phase, analytically, is the diffusion of innovation, which, it will be argued, is a particularly crucial element of innovation for public services.

Bearing in mind my earlier caveats about both over-simplification and over-generalisation from the private sector literature on innovation, we turn to use this analytical device to examine some key features of innovation actors, processes and outcomes. Of course, there will be exceptions to many of the observations below – a case where a private firm acts in the same way as a public one, or where a public organisation functions like a private one. The aim is not to create a clear delineation, but to show differences in emphasis in order to highlight some aspects of the innovation process which may have been neglected by the context-blind literature, and which provides a research agenda for public service innovations.

INVENTION

Dimensions of Innovation

There are a number of typologies of innovation but I argue that it is more helpful to conceptualise innovation as dimensions rather than types, because any innovation may involve more than one type. For example, a new piece of medical equipment (a product innovation) may also entail new ways of providing the service (service and process innovation) and may also enable the hospital to cater for new types of patient (position innovation).

For both public and private sectors, many dimensions are similar – product, service, process, strategic, position (Hartley 2005) and business model (Birkinshaw et al. 2008). However, there are three aspects of innovation which are not often discussed in the private sector literature but which appear in the public innovation literature. Political scientists point to the existence of policy innovations – the adoption of new policies by governments (e.g. Berry 1994). Scholars also discuss innovations in governance (Hartley 2005; Voss 2007; Moore and Hartley 2008), by which they mean new procedures and institutions to make decisions about policies and resources for the public sphere. Finally, Hartley (2005) identifies rhetorical innovation – new language and new concepts which are used to mobilise support from the public or other significant stakeholders. These three aspects of innovation are not discussed in the generic or private sector literature about innovation. Innovations in policy, governance and rhetoric each signal the salience of the political context for public service organisations. In this sense, innovations taking place in public organisations always need to consider the wider policy context and the public sphere, not just the innovation's relevance for a specific organisation.

The Unit of Analysis

In the literature about private sector innovation, the firm is the primary unit of analysis (e.g. Dougherty 2006) and innovation is considered as important to the extent that it helps a firm develop, keep or revive a competitive edge (e.g. Kim and Mauborgne 1999) or gain markets and market share. There is also growing interest in how innovation is achieved through strategic alliances and collaborative networks of organisations (e.g. Belussi and Arcangeli 1998), whether this is innovation generated through supply chains, through formal business groups and associations, through communities of practice (Powell et al. 1996) or through open innovation with members of society (Chesbrough 2003). There is, additionally, a large literature in economics and economic sociology about industrial sector clusters to support innovation (e.g. Crouch and Voelzkow 2009), where the level of analysis is the industry or sector rather than the firm. However, much of this discussion still centres on the advantages of these innovation practices to the individual firm.

A focus on the individual organisation can be helpful in understanding public services innovation and a number of studies have used this unit of analysis (e.g. Newman et al. 2001; Walker et al. 2011). There is also a focus in some studies on what can be described as an 'industrial sector', such as schools or healthcare (e.g. Greenhalgh et al. 2004). Beyond that, the focus of analysis is sometimes on an organisational field. Scott (2007) defines this as those organisations operating in the same domain (as indicated by the similarity of their services), along with other organisations that critically influence their performance (e.g. funders, contractors, partners). An organisational field for a public organisation will include government (sometimes at more than one level), audit and inspection, and other regulatory agencies. This reinforces the issue of political authority and influence which is often present for public service organisations. Some innovations only make sense at the organisational field level, in collaborative innovations. For example, the policy and practice innovation in the UK government programme 'Total Place' was a 'whole area' approach to creating a step-change in the ways in which particular services are designed and provided, across a range of organisations. In the Leicestershire county locality, all key public and voluntary organisations (health, police, local authorities, fire and the voluntary sector) worked collaboratively to address the complex, cross-cutting problems associated with drug and alcohol misuse (Benington and Hartley 2009).

There are thus differences in emphasis in the literature about the unit of analysis for the public and private sectors, though theoretically each of these levels of analysis is appropriate across both sectors. The greater emphasis for management scholars (excluding economists here) on innovation across the organisational field in the public services sector underscores the importance and influence of the external societal environment on the public services sector.

The Environmental Drivers of Innovation

For private firms, and for the market economy, competition is seen to be an important driver of innovation, and innovation a key driver of economic change and development. Schumpeter (1950) is often taken to be a key writer in this regard.

It has sometimes been assumed that the corollary of this is that since public services do not (usually) operate in competitive markets, innovation is low in the public sector.

However, a number of writers challenge the assumption that competition is the primary driver of innovation, arguing that different mechanisms operate in the public sector. There is substantial empirical evidence of considerable innovation in the public sector (Albury 2005; Hartley 2005) and that many of the key innovations of the last few decades originated in the public sector – not least the internet. These writers argue that innovation is a crucial element of public policy and management in a dynamic society, where needs and aspirations are shifting. Innovation is also seen to be a critical method for improving the performance of government, and enhancing government's legitimacy with citizens (Moore and Hartley 2008).

The Catalysts of Innovation

People in a number of different roles may contribute to the initiation, design, development and diffusion of an innovation. The literature, until recently, focused primarily on the creativity of managers and employees within the organisation and how to enhance their capacity to come up with creative ideas, to recognise needs in the market or society, and to use 'recombinant' innovation (taking an innovation which works in one area and using it in a quite different application through knowledge brokering) (Hargadon 2002). This is still an important source of invention and many organisations manage the flow of ideas strategically and structurally, using for example R and D departments or knowledge-brokering groups. In the public sector, work by Borins (1998) showed that managers and employees are a significant source of ideas. In thinking about managers and staff as catalysts, there are considerable similarities between sectors, and much to learn between them about the strategies of both creating and harvesting ideas and of developing proposals and prototypes which have innovation potential.

Networks are also an important source of invention (and also of diffusion) in both sectors, whether these are supply chains, communities of practice, business associations or professional networks (e.g. Birkinshaw et al. 2007; Hartley and Downe 2007). Again, one can find similarities across sectors, though there are known to be differences in the degree of learning and knowledge transfer in collaborative compared with competitive networks (Inkpen and Crossan 1995).

A third catalyst of innovation is the users of products and services. Von Hippel (1988) noted that many innovations are developed or improved by 'lead users' who are familiar with the product or service through regular use and who communicate and collaborate with the producing organisation to develop the innovation. Chesbrough (2003) and von Hippel (2005) have analysed the burgeoning phenomenon called 'open innovation'. Open innovation occurs where individuals or groups in society co-produce innovations. Increasingly, firms invite the participation of users to help them design new products and services (Nokia, Lego and Goldcorp are recent examples). They may also employ staff to actively search for and co-opt ideas from the public.

In the public sector, there is less use, as yet, of open innovation (which is very different from public consultation on existing proposals), though some organisations are starting to become involved; for example the expert patient initiative in some healthcare or engaging with citizens to create and implement new ideas (Bason 2010). Interestingly, while the processes of open innovation could be similar across sectors, public service leaders have to maintain awareness of who is involved. Open innovation ought not to take place solely with customers or users, because of the wider public nature of the organisational goals and values in the public sector. Some users may have ideas for innovation which cut across the needs of other groups. Some stakeholders may be more articulate, or hold access to power and influence compared with others; and so open innovation in the public services has to take account of different motivations, needs and consequences.

The fourth key catalyst of public service innovation is elected politicians. Both national and local politicians, along with their advisors, have a central role in innovation. They can be engaged in developing new policy frameworks (Albury 2005; Considine et al. 2009); announcing innovation intentions (Hartley 2005); using rhetorical innovation to mobilise support among the public for the innovation (Moore and Hartley 2008); helping to create an organisational climate receptive to innovation and fostering support inside the organisation (Newman et al. 2001; Rashman et al. 2005; Borins 2012). Even where innovations are initiated by managers and staff, political support will, in some cases, contribute to the nurturing and continuation of the innovation (Rashman et al. 2005). Sometimes policy initiatives can lead to large-scale, universal and radical innovations across a whole nation (Albury 2005), such as happened in the setting up of the NHS in the 1940s and now its commercialisation in the 2010s. Top-down innovation through policy announcements by politicians creates a different challenge and climate for innovation compared with innovations which originate from within the organisation.

This consideration of the roles which catalyse innovations shows a sharp difference between the public and private sectors. While both sectors use managers, staff, networks and users to create and/or harvest innovations, there are two major differences in the public sector – the need to think about citizens not just users, and the role of elected politicians in initiating and pushing forward innovation. These again relate to the wider democratic and policy context.

The key themes discussed in this section of the chapter are summarised in Table 3.1.

Table 3.1   The invention phase: public and private sector approaches to innovation: similarities and differences in emphasis

	Private sector emphasis	Public sector emphasis
Dimensions of innovation	Product, service, process, market/ position, strategic, business model, management innovation	As for private sector but also policy, governance and rhetorical innovation
The unit of analysis for innovation	Firm, and sometimes its strategic partners and supply chain. Also industrial sectors and clusters	Individual organisation, industrial sectors and institutional fields
The environmental drivers of innovation	Competition	Changing needs and aspirations of society
The catalysts of innovation	Managers and staff Networks Open innovation with customers and users	Managers and staff Networks Open innovation with citizens, users and advocates Elected politicians and policy advisors

IMPLEMENTATION

Turning ideas into practical changes in the organisation, and in services to the public, happens in the implementation phase, and it is here, perhaps, that we see more similarities between public and private sectors. Some elements covered under invention continue to be important in this section (e.g. politicians as catalysts, environmental drivers, etc.) but will not be repeated here. Similarities and differences with a particular focus on implementation are shown in Table 3.2.

Table 3.2   The implementation phase: public and private sector approaches to innovation: similarities and differences in emphasis

	Private sector emphasis	Public sector emphasis
Organisational design (e.g. bureaucratic structure, size, innovation culture)	Size fosters innovation at different phases Bureaucracy reduces innovation Culture supports innovation	Size fosters innovation at different phases Bureaucracy reduces innovation Culture supports innovation
Criteria of success	Profits Market position and market share	Improvement in service to the public Public value
Accountability	To the firm	To the public

Organisational Design

Much of the implementation of innovation takes place within organisational settings, as managers and staff work out the practicalities of the new initiative and try to ensure that it is embedded with other practices and processes, in both sectors. Some implementation occurs in inter-organisational collaboration (e.g. Moore and Hartley 2008; Tidd and Bessant 2009) and in processes of co-production (von Hippel 2005) in both sectors. Collaborative innovation still involves paying attention to organisational structures, cultures and processes as well as partnership working. It is not possible here to address all organisational features which foster or hinder innovation, but sufficient to examine the case in relation to publicness.

Some characteristics of the organisation appear to foster or dampen down innovation (both in the invention and implementation phases). Different organisational characteristics also help or hinder in different phases of innovation. For example, small organisational size tends to be conducive in the invention phase, but large organisational size makes it easier to allocate funds to implementation and to embed the innovation in organisational processes (Hage and Aiken 1967). Organisational size varies across both sectors so one would expect variation within sectors. Large organisations, contrary to common opinion, tend to be better at exploiting innovation and taking it through all stages to completion (Damanpour 1992).

Potentially also relevant is the role of bureaucratic structures (taken here to mean a particular form of organisation with hierarchy, division of labour, rules and prescribed roles) compared with more organic structures. The literature suggests that innovation is harder to foster in a bureaucracy (Burns and Stalker 1961; Thompson 1965) and there is some evidence that public managers face greater degrees of formalisation and centralisation (Rainey 2009). However, Rainey and Chun (2005) conclude that there is mixed evidence as to whether public or private organisations are more bureaucratic, and that where differences between sectors are found they are not that large.

It is known that having a strong innovation culture – one which is positive towards new ideas, is supportive of challenges to existing ways of doing things, and which searches for promising practices outside the organisation – is very valuable in supporting innovation (Rickards 1996) while some cultures suppress innovation (Kanter 1984). Culture refers to the shared norms, values and assumptions which are typical of the organisation or work group. At the level of employees, surveys have found that private and public managers express similar levels of receptivity to innovation, and to reform and organisational change (e.g. Rainey 1983; Elliot and Tevavichulada 1999). Employees also perceive similar levels of risk taking across the sectors (Bozeman and Kingsley 1998). It is often assumed that public service organisations have a poor climate for innovation but the evidence, to the extent that it exists, suggests that there are no clear differences between sectors. This may be a factor which has more variation within than across sectors.

Criteria of Success

In some of the academic and policy literature, innovation is treated as though it has inherent value – as though any innovation is, by definition, good for a firm, an organisation or for society, and essential as a means for firms to be competitive and successful (e.g. Chesbrough 2003; Tidd and Bessant 2009).

This is rarely the case for the public service sector. Some innovations, for example medical equipment, are commercially exploitable but these tend to be exceptions. Innovation is mainly seen to be justifiable to the extent that it increases the quality, efficiency or fitness for purpose of services; where it improves the ways in which decisions about services are made; or where it addresses a performance gap (Walker and Damanpour 2011).

The criteria of successful public innovation are not only about organisational performance metrics but are about the contribution of the innovation to the public sphere (Hartley 2011). Innovation in the public sector needs to be analysed not only in terms of improvement of service or process (e.g. faster, cheaper, more reliable, higher quality, greater reach) but also in terms of public value, which consists both of what the public values and what adds value to the public sphere (Benington, 2011).

'Public value' has to be created without the benefit of hindsight (given that innovation by virtue of being new is inherently risky and uncertain) and it sometimes requires political and managerial judgement as to whether a particular policy or strategy will achieve the sought-after outcomes. Therefore, the question 'how can public value be measured' can never be fully and finally answered – there may be different assessments according to context and organisational capacity, according to short-term and longer-term perspectives, according to whether this reinforces particular strengths and weaknesses of the organisation – quite apart from the different judgements, values and priorities that varied stakeholders may place on the innovation. Thus, right at the heart of any public innovation is the existence of a tension, not only about what the public values compared with adding value to the public sphere, but also about who judges public value and on what basis.

Accountability and Transparency

Innovation, by definition, is uncertain in both process and outcome. It is new and it is discontinuous with previous products, processes and/or services, so there is a risk that it will fail. The estimate for the private sector is that 30–45 per cent of innovation projects fail and that half overrun their budgets or timeline (Tidd and Bessant 2009). So there are risks as well as benefits with innovation. Decisions about the costs, the benefits, the risks and the rewards are central to innovation processes (though that does not necessarily mean that they are evidence based, because power-influenced and reputational decisions occur in both sectors).

In navigating these uncertainties, organisations may try to manage risk by using a set of decision-making processes as an innovation funnel leading from initial conception through to wide and full implementation, such as stage/gate processes, or constructive challenge meetings, or search strategies about promising practices in other organisations. In these elements of managing evidence and decision processes, there is a lot to learn between the public and private sectors.

But accountability differs between the sectors, and may affect the ways in which innovation is driven and decisions evaluated. In the private sector, innovation is sometimes restricted to those directly involved in design and development, whether internally to the company or as part of a strategic alliance. If competitive edge is advanced by innovation, then the organisation may try to keep it under wraps for as long as possible. The classic examples are the unveiling of a new concept car at a motor show, or the Apple iPad. Of course, some innovations are created through open innovation, and the decision whether to be secretive or open lies with the organisation. Accountability for the innovation resides in the firm or strategic alliance, with shareholders as the justification for this. Transparency (or not) is a strategic choice.

By contrast, most public services, at least in theory (and barring security services perhaps), develop innovations in ways which enable greater access to both the ideas and the decision making by the public, and sometimes in the full glare of media publicity. Some innovations may be scrutinised in Parliament or local councils; the political opposition may attack the proposed innovation; the public may be consulted about the ideas or comment vociferously; the media may comment on the innovation and its implied costs and consequences; evaluation data may be published. Accountability is not just within the organisation but also to elected representatives and the public. There is a presumption of transparency for many innovations. Furthermore, given that services in the public sphere are often contested in terms of value and priorities, there may be considerable public debate as to whether a particular innovative effort should be prioritised or not, with what amount of resources, and with awareness that an innovation which improves the service for a certain type of user or citizen may make it worse for another.

I am not aware of evidence about the impact of accountability and transparency on the ways in which innovation is conceived, designed, developed, argued against and adopted in an organisational setting. But one can imagine that a tight R and D team, working in the private sector comfort of restricted access to scrutiny, can develop a level of trust and constructive challenge that may be more difficult where there are many voices and opinions from various publics about the desirability, credibility and worthiness of the innovation. Again, this brief analysis suggests that developing innovation in a democratic context may carry different pressures.

DIFFUSION

Diffusion, sometimes called dissemination, describes the spread of ideas and practices over time among members of a social system (e.g. Rogers 2003; Greenhalgh et al. 2004). Here, we focus on diffusion among organisations rather than by individuals and we do not address the characteristics of the innovation itself which may aid diffusion (Rogers 2003). There is a large though fragmented literature on diffusion and it is not feasible here to cover all aspects though key elements are shown in Table 3.3.

Motivation of Innovator to Diffuse

The motivation to engage in the sharing of promising practices has a different normative bias in the public compared with the private sector. In the latter, given that innovation is often a driver to maintain competitive position or to gain first-mover advantage, there are often intense pressures to keep the innovation confidential within the organisation or within a very tight circle of collaborators. This may involve the use of patents, copyright,

Table 3.3   The diffusion phase: public and private sector approaches to innovation: similarities and differences in emphasis

	Private sector emphasis	Public sector emphasis
Motivation of innovator to diffuse	Restrict diffusion in order to exploit commercial advantage, through patents etc.	Extend diffusion to other organisations in order to improve public services
Motivation of adopter to take on the innovation	Incentive to learn from competitors	Lack of incentive to learn from others in same field

design rights and so on, to keep intellectual property, or at least delay replication by competitors. In the public sector, certain innovations of value to the private sector can be commercialised through patents and so on, but mainly there is a public value imperative for an innovating organisation to share ideas and practices across the organisational field for societal benefit. An innovation in treating cancer, or helping the unemployed back into regular work, is useful to the extent that it is widely adopted or adapted across similar organisations, not that one organisation has a clear lead over another. An innovation which originates in one public service may also have value when it is adopted in other services. Some innovation award schemes have been set up at least in part to support the spread of promising practices across public services (Hartley and Downe 2007; Borins 2008). Diffusion also, interestingly, serves a particular function for public service organisations in managing risk, in that the uncertainties, including political risk, of innovation implementation are ameliorated by adapting what another organisation has done rather than inventing from scratch (Hartley and Benington 2006).

Motivation of Adopter to Take Up the Innovation

On the other hand, there may be different pressures on the adopting organisation between public and private sectors. Organisations do vary across both sectors in their preparedness and their ability to engage with promising practice, to engage in search for promising ideas, to notice and take on board, to learn from and adapt ideas into a particular organisational setting (Zahra and George 2002) and it is possible to find organisations in both sectors which are relatively inert to innovation. However, there is an interesting research agenda to explore whether there are differences in motivation and process in the adoption of innovation between sectors. Where a private sector organisation is not inert, there are likely to be pressures to try to obtain knowledge of the innovation which is providing a competitor with a market lead and to try to 'reverse engineer' the innovation in order to understand it, replicate it or improve it (e.g. the 'Japanisation' of the motor industry or the tablet computer in the computer industry).

Enthusiasm and drive to adopt promising practices are evident in parts of the public services (Rashman et al. 2005) but there is also a literature looking at why diffusion can be difficult to achieve (e.g. Buchanan et al. 2006). Some of the reason for this may be the dimensions of innovation involved – service and organisational innovations are often harder to diffuse than product innovations (Walker et al. 2011) and the public services have a high proportion of such innovations, which require a high degree of tacit knowledge (Alänge et al. 1998). However, in addition, the public service sector sometimes lacks the incentives associated with competition, and given the public context of account-ability and transparency noted earlier, may face public criticism where an innovation is introduced. Interestingly, both political and managerial leadership are particularly important in creating a climate for public service organisations to enable diffusion to take place (Greenhalgh et al. 2004; Hartley and Rashman 2007).

Overall, in considering diffusion, there is wide variation within and across sectors, but again the obligation on public service organisations to create wider public value means that diffusion is more central to the innovation endeavour than it often is for the private sector. This relates to the point about the unit of analysis being the firm/alliance or the organisational field. Again, this underscores the importance of understanding the political and environmental context in which innovations take place.

CONCLUSIONS

This chapter set out to address two aims. The first was to analyse public services innova-tion as a lens through which to explore innovation theory. The second was to explore where the public and private sectors converge or diverge in their approach to innovation, and what this tells us about public services innovation.

The chapter has viewed innovation as a process which is partly led and managed. I have used phases as an analytical device to explore different aspects of innovation. This is to enable key questions to be asked about who is involved in innovation, in what ways, with what intentions and with what outcomes. Many of the analytical points examined relate to more than one phase of innovation (e.g. catalysts operate in all phases of innovation).

The comparison between the private and public sectors is undertaken at an organisa-tional and field level and provides some interesting insights into how innovation comes about and is developed and diffused in public service organisations, particularly in areas and processes which have been under-studied due to the dominance of private sector perspectives on innovation. The caveats are manifold – there is no hard and fast distinc-tion between public and private, and organisations vary in the degree to which they are influenced by the wider political and policy context. So, there is considerable variation within, as well as across, sectors. I have focused on emphases within sectors rather than rigid distinctions. It would be easy for a reader to point out exceptions to the broad gen-eralisations made. But that would miss the point of my analysis, which is to make clear when, where and why the public features of innovation have an impact on innovation processes and outcomes.

There is a lot to learn between the public and private sectors, but given the context-blindness of the innovation literature, the highlighting of the public features of innova-tion is particularly instructive, revealing important processes, values and priorities for public service organisations.

Whether the focus is on the dimensions of innovations, the environmental drivers of innovation, the unit of analysis of innovation, or the roles played by different catalysts, one finds an insistent presence of the formal political environment, and of the role of users not just as customers but as citizens. In the phase of managing the implementation of innovations (using stage-gate processes or sifting ideas in the innovation funnel) there may be a number of managerial similarities across sectors, but even here managers have to operate within a wider field of actors, including citizens and politicians. And the outcomes being sought are often different, with public service organisations seeking to achieve not organisational gain alone but to add public value. (Of course, private firms can create public value but that is not their primary task, whereas it is for public organisations.) And diffusion may well vary across sectors since there is a normative duty on innovative organisations to share their ideas and practices with others in their sector to extend the quality, efficiency and effectiveness of the service across a society. So, 'publicness' (Bozeman 1987) in the innovation field seems to matter, and matter very substantially.

Managers may use managerial and organisational practices, tools and techniques across sectors, but the context in which they occur and the purposes and aims of their work are likely to be different. Zan et al. (1993) noted that 'context is not just a stimulus environment but a nested arrangement of structures and processes where the subjective interpretations of actors perceiving, comprehending, learning and remembering help shape process' (p. 270). In other words, context is not just the 'wrap-around' in which to set theory and research – it fundamentally affects aims, behaviours and understanding. Other factors such as organisational size, function, type of service, absorptive capacity and management processes matter too, and in some situations are more important or interact. However, unless innovation research takes sufficient account of the wider political and policy context in which innovation takes place it will miss key ways in which to theorise, explain and understand innovation. Additionally, unless some of the broad differences in purpose, actors and processes between public and private sectors are understood, then collaboration between sectors will be more difficult or will be inadequately theorised.

REFERENCES

Abrahamson, E. (1991). Managerial fads and fashion: the diffusion and rejection of innovations. *Academy of Management Review*, 16, 588–612.

Alänge, S., Jacobsson, S. and Jarnehammar, A. (1998). Some aspects of an analytical framework for studying the diffusion of organizational innovations. *Technology Analysis and Strategic Management*, 10(1), 3–21.

Albury, D. (2005). Fostering innovation in public services. *Public Money and Management*, 2, 51–56.

Allison, G. (1983). Public and private management: are they fundamentally alike in all unimportant respects? In J. Shafritz and A. Hyde (eds), *Classics of Public Administration*. Belmont: Wadsworth.

Altshuler, A. and Behn, R. (1997). *Innovation in American Government*. Washington, DC: Brookings Institution.

Altshuler, A. and Zegans, M. (1997). Innovation and public management: notes from the state house and city hall. In A. Altshuler and R. Behn (eds), *Innovation in American Government*. Washington, DC: Brookings Institution, pp. 68–82.

Bason, C. (2010). *Leading Public Sector Innovation*. Bristol: Policy Press.

Belussi, F. and Arcangeli, F. (1998). A typology of networks. *Research Policy*, 27, 415–428.

Benington, J. (2011). From private choice to public value? In J. Benington and M. Moore (eds), *Public Value: Theory and Practice*. Basingstoke: Macmillan, pp. 31–51.

Benington, J. and Hartley, J. (2009). *Whole Systems Go! Leadership Across the Whole Public Service System*. London: National School of Government.

Berry, F. (1994). Sizing up state policy innovation research. *Policy Studies Journal*, 22(3), 442–456.

Bessant, J. (2005). Enabling continuous and discontinuous innovation: learning from the private sector. *Public Money and Management*, 25(1), 35–42.

Birkinshaw, J., Bessant, J. and Delbridge, R. (2007). Finding, forming and performing: creating networks for discontinuous innovation. *California Management Review*, 49(3), 67–83.

Birkinshaw, J., Hamel, G. and Mol, M. (2008). Management innovation. *Academy of Management Journal*, 33(4), 825–845.

Borins, S. (1998). *Innovating with Integrity*. Washington, DC: Georgetown University Press.

Borins, S. (ed.) (2008). *Innovations in Government: Research, Recognition and Replications*. Washington, DC: Brookings Institution, pp. 138–158.

Borins, S. (2012). Making narrative count: a narratological approach to public management innovation. *Journal of Public Administration Research and Theory*, 22(1), 143–164.

Bozeman, B. (1987). *All Organizations are Public*. San Francisco, CA: Jossey Bass.

Bozeman, B. and Kingsley, G. (1998). Risk culture in public and private organizations. *Public Administration Review*, 58, 109–118.

Bozeman, B. and Moulton, S. (2011). Integrative publicness: a framework for public management strategy and performance. *Journal of Public Administration Research and Theory*, 21(suppl. 3), 363–380.

Buchanan, D., Fitzgerald, L. and Ketley, D. (2006). *The Sustainability and Spread of Organizational Change*. Abingdon: Routledge.

Burns, T. and Stalker, G. (1961). *The Management of Innovation*. London: Tavistock.

Chesbrough, H. (2003). *Open Innovation*. Boston, MA: Harvard Business School Press.

Considine, M., Lewis, J. and Alexander, D. (2009). *Networks, Innovation and Public Policy*. Basingstoke: Palgrave Macmillan.

Crouch, C. and Voelzkow, H. (2009). *Innovation in Local Economies*. Oxford: Oxford University Press.

Damanpour, F. (1992). Organizational size and innovation. *Organization Studies*, 13, 375–402.

Damanpour, F. and Gopalakrishnan, S. (1998). Theories of organizational structure and innovation adoption: the role of environmental change. *Journal of Engineering and Technology Management*, 15(1), 1–24.

Denis, J-L., Hebert, Y., Langley, A., Lozeau, D. and Trottier, L. (2002). Explaining diffusion patterns for complex health care innovations. *Health Care Management Review*, 27, 60–73.

Dougherty, D. (2006). Innovation in the twenty-first century. In S. Clegg, C. Hardy, T. Lawrence and W. Nord (eds), *The Sage Handbook of Organization Studies*. London: Sage, pp. 598–617.

Elliot, R. and Tevavichulada, S. (1999). Computer literacy and human resource management: a public/private sector comparison. *Public Personnel Management*, 28, 259–274.

Feldman, M. (2005). Management and public management. *Academy of Management Journal*, 48(6), 958–960.

Flynn, N. (2007). *Public Sector Management*. London: Sage.

Gallouj, F. (2002). *Innovation in the Service Economy*. Cheltenham: Edward Elgar.

Greenhalgh, T., Robert, G., Macfarlane, F., Bate, P., Kyriakidou, O. and Peacock, R. (2004). Diffusion of innovations in service organisations: systematic literature review and recommendations for future research. *Milbank Quarterly*, 82, 581–629.

Hage, J. and Aiken, M. (1967). Program change and organizational properties. *American Journal of Sociology*, 72(2), 503–519.

Hargadon, A. (2002). Brokering knowledge: linking learning and innovation. *Research in Organizational Behavior*, 24, 41–86.

Hartley, J. (2005). Innovation in governance and public services: past and present. *Public Money and Management*, 25(1), 27–34.

Hartley, J. (2011). Public value through innovation and improvement. In J. Benington and M. Moore (eds), *Public Value: Theory and Practice*. Basingstoke: Palgrave, pp. 171–184.

Hartley, J. and Benington, J. (2006). Copy and paste, or graft and transplant? Knowledge sharing in inter-organizational networks. *Public Money and Management*, 26(2), 101–108.

Hartley, J. and Downe, J. (2007). The shining lights? Public service awards as an approach to service improvement. *Public Administration*, 85(2), 329–353.

Hartley, J. and Rashman, L. (2007). How is knowledge transferred between organizations involved in change? In M. Wallace, M. Fertig and E. Schneller (eds), *Managing Change in the Public Services*. Oxford: Blackwell, pp. 173–192.

Hartley, J. and Skelcher, C. (2008). The agenda for public service improvement. In J. Hartley, C. Donaldson, C. Skelcher and M. Wallace (eds), *Managing to Improve Public Services*. Cambridge: Cambridge University Press, pp. 3–23.

Inkpen, A. and Crossan, M. (1995). Believing is seeing: joint ventures and organization learning. *Journal of Management Studies*, 32(5), 595–618.

Kanter, R. (1984). *The Change Masters*. London: Unwin.

Kim, W. and Mauborgne, R. (1999). Creating new market space. *Harvard Business Review*, 77(1), 83–93.

Lynn, L. (1997). Innovation and the public interest: insights from the private sector. In A. Altshuler and R. Behn (eds), *Innovation in American Government*. Washington, DC: Brookings Institution, pp. 83–103.

Miles, I. (2000). Innovation in services. In J. Fagerberg, D. Mowery and R. Nelson (eds), *The Oxford Handbook of Innovation*. Oxford: Oxford University Press, pp. 433–458.

Moore, M.H. (2005). Break-through innovations and continuous improvement: two different models of innovative processes in the public sector. *Public Money and Management*, 25(1), 43–50.

Moore, M. and Hartley, J. (2008). Innovations in governance. *Public Management Review*, 10(1), 3–20.

Moore, M.H., Sparrow, M. and Spelman, W. (1997). Innovation in policing: from production line to jobs shops. In A. Altshuler and R. Behn (eds), *Innovation in American Government*. Washington, DC: Brookings Institution, pp. 274–298.

Mulgan, G. and Albury, D. (2003). *Innovations in the Public Sector*. London: Cabinet Office.

Newman, J., Raine, J. and Skelcher, C. (2001). Transforming local government: innovation and modernisation. *Public Money and Management*, 21(2), 61–68.

Osborne, S. (1998). Naming the beast: delivering and classifying service innovations in social policy. *Human Relations*, 51, 1133–1154.

Osborne, S. and Brown, K. (2005). *Managing Change and Innovation in Public Service Organizations*. London: Routledge.

Osborne, S. and Brown, L. (2011). Innovation, public policy and public services delivery: the word that would be king? *Public Administration*, 89(4), 1335–1350

Pettigrew, A. (2005). The character and significance of management research on the public services. *Academy of Management Journal*, 48, 973–977.

Powell, W., Koput, W. and Smith-Doerr, L. (1996). Interorganizational collaboration and the locus of innovation: networks of learning in biotechnology. *Administrative Science Quarterly*, 41(1), 116–130.

Rainey, H. (1983). Public agencies and private firms: incentive structures, goals and individual roles. *Administration and Society*, 15, 207–242.

Rainey, H. (2009). *Understanding and Managing Public Organizations*. San Francisco, CA: Jossey Bass.

Rainey, H. and Chun, Y. (2005). Public and private management compared. In E. Ferlie, L. Lynn and C. Pollitt (eds), *Oxford Handbook of Public Management*. Oxford: Oxford University Press, pp. 72–102.

Rashman, L., Downe, J. and Hartley, J. (2005). Knowledge creation and transfer in the Beacon Scheme: improving services through sharing good practice. *Local Government Studies*, 31(5), 683–700.

Rickards, T. (1996). The management of innovation: recasting the role of creativity. *European Journal of Work and Organizational Psychology*, 5(1), 13–27.

Rogers, E. (2003). *Diffusion of Innovations* (5th edn). New York: Free Press.

Schumpeter, J. (1950). *Capitalism, Socialism and Democracy*. New York: Harper and Row.

Scott, W.R. (2007). *Institutions and Organizations* (3rd edn). London: Sage Publications.

Thompson, V. (1965). Bureaucracy and innovation. *Administrative Science Quarterly*, 10, 1–20.

Tidd, J. and Bessant, J. (2009). *Managing Innovation*. Chichester: Wiley.

Van de Ven, A. (1986). Central problems in the management of innovation. *Management Science*, 32, 590–607.

Van de Ven, A., Polley, D., Garud, R. and Venkataraman, S. (1999). *The Innovation Journey*. New York: Oxford University Press.

Von Hippel, E. (1988). *The Sources of Innovation*. Cambridge, MA: MIT Press.

Von Hippel, E. (2005). *Democratizing Innovation*. Cambridge, MA: MIT Press.

Voss, J-P. (2007). Innovation processes in governance: the development of 'emissions trading' as a new policy. *Science and Public Policy*, 34(5), 329–344.

Walker, R., Damanpour, F. and Devece, C. (2011). Management innovation and organizational performance: the mediating effect of performance management. *Journal of Public Administration Research and Theory*, 21(2), 367–386.

Zahra, A. and George, G. (2002). Absorptive capacity: a review, reconceptualisation and extension. *Academy of Management Review*, 27, 185–203.

Zan, L., Stephano, S. and Pettigrew, A. (1993). *Perspectives on Strategic Change*. Berlin: Springer.

4.   A services-influenced approach to public service innovation?[1]
Stephen P. Osborne

INTRODUCTION

As has been well documented elsewhere (for example, Mischra 1984), the late twentieth century neo-liberal revolution in approaches to the management of public services delivery included an inherent assumption in the supremacy of private sector business management methods over those traditionally found within public administration (often referred to in shorthand as the 'New Public Management', or NPM (Hood 1991)). In the UK, a key influence in this process was undoubtedly the New Right think-tanks of the 1980s, such as the Adam Smith Institute (for example, Pirie 1988). These bodies articulated the model of 'competitive advantage' (Porter 1985) as the central mechanism through which to drive improvement in public services delivery. This mechanism placed innovation at the heart of the effective workings of the market in order to achieve precisely such 'competitive advantage'.

The then Conservative UK government subsequently adopted a model of public services reform predicated upon the assumption that the introduction of competition and market disciplines to public services would lead to both greater economy and greater efficiency in public services delivery (Wistow et al. 1994). Drawing upon Porter's theory of competitive advantage above, it was argued that the rigours of competition would require public service providers to innovate in order to maintain an advantage over their competitors – and that this process of innovation would thence lead to the improved efficiency and effectiveness in public services delivery.

However, a key element of Porter's model was its explicit roots in manufacturing industries, with a concentration upon the development of finite products in a stable market environment and 'based upon assumptions drawn from manufacturing industry' – services as such were considered by Porter to be 'fragmented industries and received scant attention in the model' (Nankervis 2005, p. 111). This led to an approach to the development and support of innovation in public services by central government that subsequently concentrated upon the design of 'innovation products' rather than 'service processes'.

Yet, as other authors have argued (for example, Spohrer et al. 2008; Droege et al. 2009), the roots of this model explicitly within the experience of the manufacturing sector of the economy limit its applicability to the service sector, and particularly in times of economic turbulence and rapid change. It does not acknowledge or reflect the nature of *services* (including public services) as a distinctive sector. There is now, however, a substantial literature that identifies the core elements of services as a distinctive sector from that of manufacturing. These characteristics, discussed in more detail below, make the innovation process a profoundly different one for services (Sundbo 1997). Further, a key element of the services approach to the management of innovation is the importance of an *open systems* orientation that explicitly acknowledges the importance of the organizational and institutional environments (Tether 2003). This important point is also returned to below.

This chapter addresses this contention head on. First it will outline briefly a critique of the prevailing theoretical model of public management, as outlined above, developing further our critique of its fundamental flaw in its manufacturing, or goods-dominant, bias and its increasing irrelevance to the contemporary world of public policy and public services delivery. Secondly it will explore the potential of services theory to generate new theoretical insights and frameworks for public management that are more 'fit for purpose' for contemporary public services delivery. Finally, following on from this, it will explore the implications of such an approach for innovation in public services.

THE LIMITATIONS OF TRADITIONAL PUBLIC MANAGEMENT THEORY

Contemporary public management theory is broadly encapsulated within the NPM paradigm (McLaughlin et al. 2002). The classic formulation of the NPM was in Hood's (1991) seminal paper, which drew attention to the growth of a distinctly managerial, as opposed to administrative, approach to public services delivery. The key elements of the NPM, as outlined in that paper, are:

- the adoption of a consciously managerial, as opposed to administrative or professional, approach to public services delivery;
- the dis-aggregation of service entities to their component units, and a focus on their unit costs;
- a pre-occupation with performance management and output control;
- the growth of the use of markets and competition as a means to allocate resources; and
- an attention to the lessons from private sector management for the delivery of public services (Hood 1991).

This seminal paper, and others, led subsequently to important debates both about the appropriateness of the managerial, as opposed to administrative and/or professional, model for public services delivery and about its impact upon this delivery (*inter alia*, Metcalfe and Richards 1991; Kickert 1997; Flynn 2002; Pollitt and Bouckaert 2004). Predating this discussion has been a further dialogue about the comparable nature of private and public sector management: are they indeed, to use the classic formulation of Allison, 'alike in all unimportant aspects' (Allison 1983)? These critiques have led to several significant attempts to challenge the hegemony of the NPM as the over-arching framework for our understanding of public services delivery – including new public administration (Frederickson 1996),[2] public value (Benington and Moore 2011), digital governance (Dunleavy 2006) and the new public governance (Osborne 2010). Despite this debate, though, NPM has nonetheless endured as a (if no longer 'the') pre-eminent theoretical framework for our understanding of contemporary public services delivery

– as witnessed by the recent publication of a major new handbook devoted to its analysis (Christensen and Laegreid 2011).

What has been remarkable in this debate has been the implicit assumption of a unified and integrated body of management theory derived from private sector experience and upon which to ground public management. This is far from the case. In fact, the concepts and evidence upon which current public management theory is based have been drawn from a body of private sector theory based upon the experience of manufacturing and industry – such as Porter's influential work on competitive advantage (Porter 1985). This body of theory assumes a number of core elements of the production process – that production and consumption are discrete processes that are ruled by different logics; that consequently the costs of production and consumption are distinguishable and separable; that marketing is a distinct function related to the selling of pre-produced products; and that consumers are largely passive in this process (Lusch and Vargo 2006).

Over the past three decades, however, there has developed an alternative body of theory and research about the management of *services*. Originating initially in a discussion about the marketing of services (Gronroos 1978), this has now evolved into a substantive theory of services management in its own right (for example, Normann 2002; Lovelock and Wirtz 2004; Gronroos 2007).

SERVICES-DOMINANT MANAGEMENT THEORY: KEY TENETS

At its most basic level, manufacturing theory relates to activities that physically change materials to produce saleable goods whilst services theory relates to activities concerned with the transaction of intangible benefits (Normann 2002). Whilst there are numerous statements of the characteristics of such services, three core characteristics are agreed upon. First, that whilst a product is invariably concrete (such as a washing machine) *a service is intangible – it is a process* (staying at a hotel is not simply about the quality of the room that you rent, it is also about the overall process/experience of your stay). This is not to say that the content of a service (its purpose) is irrelevant. This is nonsense. Of course a service (whether a healthcare or lifestyle service) must deliver its intended benefits. However, service users invariably judge that service not simply upon such delivery but also upon their experience of the process of service delivery. In turn, the value of the service depends both on its core business (its content) and all accessory characteristics that complement the process of its delivery (Normann 2002). Research consistently suggests that service users expect their service to be 'fit for purpose', but base their judgement of its performance upon their expectations and experience of the process of service delivery rather than upon outcomes (Gronroos 2007). This means that influencing and understanding the customer's perceptions of a service is fundamental to his or her experience of, and satisfaction with, that service. This is in part about shaping customer expectations and in part about managing the interaction between service staff and a customer at the point of delivery. Gronroos has argued persuasively that a common failing of services management is attempting to provide a 'missing product' rather than concentrating upon the process of service delivery (Gronroos 1998). Moreover, consumers invariably adopt the same criteria to rate their service experience, regardless of the service industry (Palmer

1994). This point calls for two reflections: that the core characteristics of the *service delivery process* play a dominant part in determining the perceived value of a service, and that the expectations that a user will have in accessing a public service are similar to those that s/he might place upon any other type of service. This is pursued further below.

The second core concept of services theory is that there is different production logic for manufactured goods and services. For the former, production, selling and consumption occur separately (as with the above example of a washing machine). With services however, *production and consumption occur simultaneously*. The production of a sporting event takes place at exactly the same time as its consumption, for example, as do the production and consumption of residential care. Because production and consumption are not separable for services, this implies entirely different business logic for them from manufactured goods (Prahalad and Ramaswamy 2004; Edvardsson et al. 2005). It is quite possible to reduce the unit costs of a manufacturing good, for example, by reducing labour costs in order to increase the efficiency of production (perhaps through automation). To a certain extent, changes to production staff do not affect the sale of that good in the market or the experience of that good by its consumers. However, for a service, reducing its unit costs by changing staffing levels or experience directly affects the experience of that service by its users. This implies an entirely different logic from the management of manufacturing goods, as opposed to services (Vargo et al. 2008). Because the production and consumption of services take place contemporaneously the production process directly affects consumption rather than having an articulated relationship to it. At an extreme, it matters little to a user if the production staff for their washing machine are dressed only in their underpants, as long as the washing machine itself is fit for purpose. Yet this scenario would be wholly different in the case of the staff in a restaurant or hotel, for example!

Finally, the role of the consumer is different for manufactured goods and services. In the former case of manufactured goods they are 'simply' their purchasers and consumers. However, for services, *the consumer is also a co-producer of the service*.[3] At the most extreme, no service is ever produced identically to two consumers – a meal in a restaurant is as much a product of the interaction between the customer and the waiter as it is of the quality of the food, whilst a surgical procedure is influenced just as much by the individual pathology of a patient as by the skills of the doctor. At a fundamental level, therefore, co-production is not an 'add-on' to services but a core feature of them (Strokosch and Osborne 2009).

The implications of these features for public services are impossible to do justice to in this short chapter, and indeed are beyond its remit. However, two are especially significant. First, that the performance of a (public) service is not solely about its design to be 'fit for purpose' but is, at least, equally about the subjective experience of that service by its users. This is made up of the confluence of their expectations of the service and their perceptions of the service delivery process. Secondly, that this processual experience is created at what Normann (2002) has called the 'moment of truth', when the service user and a specific staff member (be it professional, receptionist or car park attendant) of the service organization interact. According to Normann, services

> are the result of social acts which take place in direct contact between the customer and representatives of the service company. To take a metaphor from bullfighting ... the perceived

[service] quality is realized at the moment of truth, when the service provider and the service customer confront one another in the arena. At that moment they are very much on their own ... It is the skill, motivation and the tools employed by the form's representative and the expectations and behaviour of the client which will together create the *service delivery process.* (Normann 2002 pp. 20–21; my emphasis)

Hence the key to successful public services management does not lie solely in the design of effective public services – this is a necessary but not sufficient condition. Rather it also requires both governing and responding to the service expectations of service users, and training and motivating the service delivery workforce to interact positively with the users. The process of service delivery affects service outcomes as much as service design.

It is important of course not to reduce the array of service experiences to sophistry. Clearly the above characteristics are a continuum not a steady state. There is a world of difference between hospitality services, the creative industries and financial services, for example – the latter may limit consumer co-production purely to the completion of forms with personal data whilst the former require far more inter-personal interaction (Maddern et al. 2007). Further, the increasing use of web-based and electronic media to provide financial and retail services, in particular, has a whole logic and experience of its own that is challenging many of the assumptions of the last two decades about the process of service delivery (Bitner et al. 2000).

Even the proponents of a distinct body of services theory have questioned the universality of these characteristics. On the one hand, some have argued that the basics of services theory can be applied to manufactured goods in order to add value, so that services management becomes the dominant business logic – an approach known as 'servitization' (Baines et al. 2009). On the other hand, others have argued that the above characteristics are actually second-level characteristics of services and that the core differentiation between goods and services resides in ownership: ownership of a good is transferred when a manufactured product is sold but not when a service is consumed (Lovelock and Wirtz 2004). This school of thought has reached its zenith in the work of Stephen Vargo and his colleagues (Lusch and Vargo 2006), who talk about *service-dominant* rather than *services-dominant* theory. They argue against the idea of a body of 'services management' theory discrete from manufactured. Turning the traditional argument on its head they argue that 'service' is a core feature of both services and manufacturing management in modern day markets – it is the only way to add genuine value to any good or service. They argue that service has 'always characterized the essence of economic activity' (Vargo and Lusch 2006, p. 17) and that in the modern knowledge-based society this has become even more so: production is actually a process of knowledge transformation rather than of tangibility, whilst genuine added value for any good or service comes from its co-production with the consumer.

This holistic approach has its critics from both manufacturing and services scholars as being a 'bridge too far' (for example, Achrol and Kotler 2006). Nonetheless it does draw attention to the centrality of process and additionality in the delivery of effective services rather than solely their design. The implications of a service-dominant approach for both theory and practice are still under review by the research community. For the purposes of this chapter a more cautious line will be taken that concentrates upon public services as 'services'.

A SERVICES-DOMINANT APPROACH TO INNOVATION IN PUBLIC SERVICES

It is important in this argument not to overstate our case. As argued further below, public services have distinctive characteristics that mean any services-dominant approach cannot simply be a mechanistic transfer of insights from private sector service experience. This would be sophistry and is a legitimate critique of the simplistic 'consumerist' approaches to public services delivery that seek to privilege the consumer perspective but without a broader grounding in services business logic (Jung 2010; Powell et al. 2010). However, a genuinely services-dominant approach to innovation in public services is predicated upon the role that co-production plays in services delivery. This chapter therefore explores this concept in more detail before examining its import for innovation in public services.

Understanding Co-production[4]

There is a substantial literature within the public administration and public management field concerned with 'co-production' in the implementation of public policy and the design and delivery of public services (*inter alia*, Brudney and England 1983; Ostrom 1996; Alford 1998; Evers 2006; Bason 2011). Whilst this literature includes a continuum of perspectives on co-production, its focus is upon user and/or citizen[5] participation in service delivery, particularly during planning, delivery or evaluation at the operational level of service production. In particular it has often set the co-production of public services apart – as a variation on the 'traditional' model of public service delivery where 'public officials are exclusively charged with responsibility for designing and providing services to citizens, who in turn *only* demand, consume and evaluate them' (Pestoff 2006, p. 506; my emphasis). Thus it discusses the ways in which user and/or citizen involvement can be 'added into' the operational process of service production (and as opposed to the higher, more strategic level of policy making). Such a mode of co-production, I would argue, has more in common with manufacturing production logic as discussed above, where production and consumption are separated as different and discrete processes. Thus public services are conceptualized as goods to be designed and produced by public policy makers and service professionals and consumed (relatively) passively by service users – co-production can only occur at the behest of, and controlled by, service professionals. This last point is highlighted most clearly within healthcare, where it has been argued that, as professional bodies and clinicians control both the diagnosis and treatment of health-related needs, then they can generate and control demand to ensure supply utilization (Stickley 2006).

From this perspective, co-production is often seen as a normative, voluntary good that can be an 'add-on' to the public service production process, rather than be intrinsic to it. Such additionality has been associated conventionally with efforts to achieve broader societal objectives, such as to enhance democracy, by placing service users at the heart of service delivery decision-making processes (Alford 2002; Bovaird 2007). However, its negative aspects have also been discussed in the public administration literature (for example, Levine and Fisher 1984).[6]

In contrast to this literature, the services literature offers a very different perspective upon co-production. This is as a core, inalienable, element of the service delivery process. Services management theory situates co-production as one of the core characteristics of service delivery – an essential and intrinsic process of interaction between any service organization and the consumer at the point of production of a service (Gronroos 2007). The question thus is not how to 'add in' co-production to public services but rather how to manage and work with its implications for effective public service delivery.

As discussed above, Normann (2002) has termed this 'the moment of truth' in services provision. The experience, and impact, of a service process is shaped as much by the subjective expectations of the user and by his or her active role in the service delivery process as by service staff themselves. Service organizations can only 'promise' a certain process or experience – the actuality is dependent on such co-production. A classic example of this would be the co-produced experience of residential care by the interaction of staff and service users in a residential home for the elderly. In reality, of course, co-production is more of a continuum than a steady state. Public services such as residential care and education are clearly instances where it is high, owing to the fact that consumption and production take place at the same point in time and with direct face-to-face contact between the service user and the service provider (in the care home or the classroom respectively). By contrast, they are rather lower for electronic public services (such as paying your local taxes through a web portal) that do not have the inter-personal immediacy of face-to-face contact between the service provider and the service user. Yet even such services do still exhibit co-production from a services management perspective – even if the co-production of such 'e-services' is essentially passive (inputting financial data on yourself or choosing from a list of pre-set options).

A particularly significant contribution from such a conceptualization of co-production to public management is in the area of innovation in public services (Osborne and Brown 2011). The characteristics of services, discussed above, make the innovation process a profoundly different one for services than for manufacturing (Gallouj 2002; Drejer 2004; Pires et al. 2008) – yet this perspective is notable by its absence in the discussion of innovation in public services. The services management literature above, for example, has long emphasized that innovation in services is a question of a co-produced process, rather than of discrete product design – yet public policy persists in a product design approach to innovation (for example, Lekhi 2007; Thomas 2008; Horne 2009).

A core element of a services-dominant approach to innovation in public services is thus that service users are central to the co-production of innovation in services. Kirsty Strokosch pursues this argument further, in her chapter later in this book.

Kristensson et al. (2008) differentiate between two types of relationships that can exist between consumers and service organizations in such innovation: customization and co-creation. *Customization* is where the customer's role is at the end of the process, where he or she suggests changes to a near finalized prototype. *Co-creation*, on the other hand, is where the customer actively contributes from the beginning of this process. It seeks to unlock the tacit, or 'sticky', knowledge that service users possess in order to improve existing or develop new services (Von Hippel 1994, 2005). Here, the service organization is proactively seeking to uncover, understand and satisfy 'latent (or future) needs', rather than simply reacting to existing expressed needs. The mechanisms through which customers are involved in such co-creation include brainstorming, interviews, mock service delivery exercises, innovation labs and team meetings (Alam 2006). Those customers who co-create during this process are likely to be selected by the organization on the basis of their knowledge and capabilities ('lead users') or their close relationship with the service managers (Kristensson et al. 2008). Needless to say, as well as exploring the benefits of co-production for service innovation, this literature also highlights some of its draw-backs, not least the cost implications of an over-customization (Alam 2006), itself implicit in the critiques of the consumerist approaches to public services of the last two decades (Powell et al. 2010).

Such an approach is one that can only enrich our understanding of innovation in public services from a services-dominant perspective that emphasizes the centrality of the service user to the process. However, it is also important, in concluding, to delineate some of the limitations and challenges that must be faced in adapting services-dominant theory from a business to a public services context. There are nuances that are required in the applica-tion of services-dominant theory to public services. Six issues, I would argue, are espe-cially important. First, when considering the application of any body of research and theory from business experience, the distinctiveness of public services needs to be remem-bered. Whilst public services have increasingly adopted models and insights from busi-ness practice, it is not a simple or mechanistic task and not all models or insights are always appropriate. Innovation in a commercial service to make a profit is somewhat different from innovation in a public one to meet a social or economic need and where consumer satisfaction, alone, is not an adequate measure of public service performance. This was the central flaw of the consumerist approaches to public services that were early partial and imperfect attempts to apply discrete elements of services theory to public services – but without a full understanding of services logic in the rounds (an excellent critique of these approaches is in Powell et al. 2010).

Secondly, there can be practical obstacles to be overcome in adapting a services-dominant approach to innovation in public services delivery. Whilst not absolute limita-tions, these obstacles have to be negotiated in reframing the public service innovation process as a services-dominant process. These obstacles include professional opposition to user-led services (Bovaird and Loeffler 2003) and passive, partial and/or tokenistic applications of services-dominant approaches (Sinclair 2004).

Thirdly, one would not want to replace the role of the surgeon by that of the patient in the 'co-production' of innovations in oncology or other health services – the former's professional expertise is vital and irreplaceable, but needs to be integrated with the 'sticky' or tacit knowledge that Von Hippel argues service users possess. It is important therefore not to have a reductive approach that reduces the undertaking to mere sophistry.

Fourthly, the development of information and communication technologies (ICT) poses new challenges for services management, in both business and public services. In general many of the traditional 'caveats' about the nature of the service encounter have been challenged over the last decade by the rise of e-services (Surjadjaja et al. 2003). In terms of public services innovation, the progress has been variable, with some arguing that it has been either 'chaotic' or an opportunity missed for genuine transformation (Layne and Lee 2001; West 2004). Others, though, have argued that 'digital governance' has the potential to generate innovation through genuine user and citizen engagement with public service delivery (Margetts 2006) – and indeed sometimes irrespective of whether public service managers or politicians would want it (Bekkers et al. 2011). In this sense digital governance and a services-dominant approach that privileges co-production may well go hand in hand with public services innovation in the early twenty-first century.

Fifthly, there are inevitable cases where the user of a public service is an unwilling or coerced user. The prison service is a classic example here. In this context the professionals of the prison service have a custodial function that is hard to co-produce or even to conceptualize as a service (for the prisoners, at least), even though it is. Even here, however, it has been argued that the electronic tagging of convicted criminals within the community is a genuinely innovative form of co-produced custody that transforms the nature of the service (Corcoran 2011). Margetts (2009) goes further with this argument, too, suggesting that ICT and web-enabled technologies may be an innovative approach to the co-production of public services – again suggesting that community-based custodial options may be one area ripe for such innovation. Fagan and Davies (2000) also have inverted this argument. They contend that coercion in the delivery of law and order services is not a limitation upon co-production – but rather that such coercion 'raises concerns about the legitimacy of law [and] threatens to weaken citizen participation' and that co-production is consequently a legitimate and innovative response to such service failure that can maintain 'the broader social norms of contemporary policing'.

Finally, a services-dominant and co-production approach is particularly fraught where public services, as is often the case, have multiple and/or conflictual users. In the above case of custodial prison services, for example, it is a moot point who the actual service user is – the convicted criminals themselves, or the court, victims of crime, or society more broadly. This dilemma is highlighted particularly by Bovaird (2005): not only are there multiple potential users of public services in such cases, but their needs can be contradictory and sometimes diffuse – a substantive challenge for services theory that will require genuine development to encompass. Yet such contestation is not a reason to delimit a services-dominant approach to innovation in public services but rather is a reason to acknowledge its greater complexity in public services than in the business sector.

Tools to negotiate such multiple and conflictual situations in public services do exist, such as stakeholder approaches (as developed in Chapter 8 by Crosby and Bryson) and would be highly appropriate for application to co-production and innovation in public services. Certainly an active, services-cognizant, approach is required for such complex situations, rather than one that is simply concerned with compliance with administrative arrangements (Foo et al. 2011). It is because of, rather than in spite of, these issues that I would argue for a services-dominant approach to innovation in public services. Such an approach can only enrich our theoretical and practical understanding of its challenges by placing them in a framework based upon the actuality of service delivery rather than a misunderstanding of them as discrete goods produced in a wholly transactional fashion.

NOTES

1.   A much extended and developed argument, that explores the contribution of services-dominant theory to public management as a whole, is published as S. Osborne, Z. Radnor and G. Nasi (2013). A new theory for public services management? Moving beyond consumerism to a services-dominant approach? *American Review of Public Administration*, in press.

2. Admittedly this concept also has a longer lineage in the US – see Frederickson (1976) for a more detailed discussion.
3. This does not imply any active willingness to co-produce upon behalf of the customer – simply that it is impossible to use a service without, in some way, contributing to its co-production (Korkman 2006). This might be at a minimal level (by co-producing an insurance policy by inputting your personal details) or more holistically (by co-producing a vacation experience through your needs, desires and involvement in 'your' holiday).
4. The concept of 'co-production' is explored more extensively elsewhere in this volume, in the chapters by Jaeger, Strokosch and Farr.
5. Indeed, sometimes these two quite distinct terms are conflated together – for example Rosentraub and Warren (1987).
6. These limitations are discussed further in the chapter by Strokosch, below.

REFERENCES

Achrol, R. and Kotler, P. (2006). The service-dominant logic for marketing: a critique. In R. Lusch and S. Vargo (eds), *The Service-Dominant Logic of Marketing*. New York: M.E. Sharpe, pp. 320–334.
Alam, I. (2006). Removing the fuzziness from the fuzzy front-end of service innovations through customer interactions. *Industrial Marketing Management*, 35, 468–480.
Alford, J. (1998). A public management road less travelled: clients as co-producers of public services. *Australian Journal of Public Administration*, 57(4), 128–137.
Alford, J. (2002). Why do public-sector clients coproduce? *Administration and Society*, 34(1), 32–56.
Allison, G. (1983). Public and private management: are they fundamentally alike in all unimportant respects? In J. Perry and K. Kraemer (eds), *Public Management: Public and Private Perspectives*. Palo Alto, CA: Mayfield.
Baines, T., Lightfoot, H., Benedettini, O. and Kay, J. (2009). The servitization of manufacturing: a review of literature and reflection on future challenges. *Journal of Manufacturing Technology Management*, 20(5), 547–567.
Bason, C. (2011). *Leading Public Sector Innovation*. Bristol: Policy Press.
Bekkers, V., Edwards, A., Moody, R. and Beunders, H. (2011). Caught by surprise? Micro-mobilization, new media and the management of strategic surprises. *Public Management Review*, 13(7), 1003–1021.
Benington, J. and Moore, M. (2011). *Public Value: Theory and Practice*. Basingstoke: Palgrave.
Bitner, M., Brown, S. and Meuter, M. (2000). Technology infusion in service encounters. *Journal of the Academy of Marketing Sciences*, 28(1), 138–149.
Bovaird, T. (2005). Public governance: balancing stakeholder power in a network society. *International Review of Administrative Sciences*, 71(2), 217–228.
Bovaird, T. (2007). Beyond engagement and participation – user and community co-production of public services. *Public Administration Review*, 67, 846–860.
Bovaird, T. and Loffler, E. (2003). Understanding public management and governance. In T. Bovaird and E. Loffler (eds), *Public Management and Governance*. London: Routledge.
Brudney J. and England, R. (1983). Toward a definition of the coproduction concept. *Public Administration Review*, January/February, 59–65.
Christensen, T. and Laegreid, P. (eds) (2011). *Ashgate Research Companion to New Public Management*. Farnham: Ashgate.
Corcoran, M. (2011). Dilemmas of institutionalization in the penal voluntary sector. *Critical Social Policy*, 31(1), 30–52.
Drejer, I. (2004). Identifying innovation in surveys of services: a Schumpeterian perspective. *Research Policy*, 33, 551–562.
Droege, H., Hildebrand, D. and Forcada, M. (2009). Innovation in services: present findings and pathways. *Journal of Service Management*, 20(2), 131–155.
Dunleavy, P. (2006). *Digital Era Governance*. Oxford: Oxford University Press.
Edvardsson, B., Gustafsson, A. and Roos, I. (2005). Service portraits in service research: a critical review. *International Journal of Service Industry Management*, 16(1), 107–121.
Evers, A. (2006). *Current Strands in Debating User Involvement in Social Services*. Strasbourg: Council of Europe.
Fagan, J. and Davies, G. (2000). Street stops and broken windows: *Terry*, race and disorder in New York City. *Fordham Urban Law Review*, 28, 457–504.
Flynn, N. (2002). *Public Sector Management*. London: Prentice Hall.

Foo, L.-M., Asenova, D., Bailey, S. and Hood, J. (2011). Stakeholder engagement and compliance culture. An empirical study of Scottish Private Finance Initiative projects. *Public Management Review*, 13(5), 707–729.

Frederickson, G. (1976). The lineage of New Public Administration. *Administration and Society*, 8(2), 149–174.

Frederickson, G. (1996). Comparing the reinventing government movement with the New Public Administration. *Public Administration Review*, 56(3), 263–270.

Gallouj, F. (2002). *Innovation in the Service Economy*. Cheltenham and Northampton, MA: Edward Elgar.

Gronroos, C. (1978). A service-oriented approach to marketing of services. *European Journal of Marketing*, 12(8), 588–601.

Gronroos, C. (1998). Marketing services: the case of a missing product. *Journal of Business and Industrial Marketing*, 13(4/5), 322–338.

Gronroos, C. (2007). *Service Management and Marketing*. Chichester: John Wiley and Sons.

Hood, C. (1991). A public management for all seasons? *Public Administration*, 69, 3–19.

Horne, M. (2008). *Honest Brokers: Brokering Innovation in Public Services*. London: Innovation Unit.

Jung, T. (2010). Citizens, co-producers, customers, clients, captives? A critical review of consumerism and public services. *Public Management Review*, 12(3), 439–447.

Kickert, W. (1997). Public governance in the Netherlands: an alternative to Anglo-American 'managerialism'. *Public Administration*, 75(4), 731–752.

Korkman, O. (2006). *Customer Value Formation in Practice: A Practice-Theoretical Approach*. Report A155. Helsinki: Hanken Swedish School of Economics.

Kristensson, P., Matthing, J. and Johansson, N. (2008). Key strategies for the successful involvement of customers in the co-creation of new technology-based services. *International Journal of Service Industry Management*, 19(4), 474–491.

Layne, K. and Lee, J. (2001). Developing fully functional e-government: a four stage model. *Government Information Quarterly*, 18(2), 122–136.

Lekhi, R. (2007). *Public Service Innovation*. Manchester: The Work Foundation.

Levine, C. and Fisher, G. (1984). Citizenship and service delivery: the promise of co-production. *Public Administration Review*, 44, 178–189.

Lovelock, C. and Wirtz, J. (2004). *Services Marketing: People, Technology, Strategy*. London: Pearson Educational.

Lusch, R. and Vargo, S. (eds) (2006). *The Service-Dominant Logic of Marketing*. New York: M.E. Sharpe.

Maddern, M., Maull, R. and Smart, A. (2007). Customer satisfaction and service quality in UK financial services. *International Journal of Production and Operations Management*, 27(9/10), 998–1019.

Margetts, H. (2006). E-government in Britain: a decade on. *Parliamentary Affairs*, 59(2), 250–265.

Margetts, H. (2009). The Internet and public policy. *Policy and Internet*, 1, 1–21.

McLaughlin, K., Osborne, S. and Ferlie, E. (eds) (2002). *The New Public Management*. London: Routledge.

Metcalfe, L. and Richards, S. (1991). *Improving Public Management*. London: Sage.

Mischra, R. (1984). *The Welfare State in Crisis*. Brighton: Wheatsheaf.

Nankervis, A. (2005). *Managing Services*. Melbourne: Cambridge University Press.

Normann, R. (2002). *Service Management*. New York: John Wiley.

Osborne, S. (ed.) (2010). *The New Public Governance?* London: Routledge.

Osborne, S. and Brown, L. (2011). Innovation, public policy and public services: the word that would be king? *Public Administration*, 89(4), 1335–1350.

Osborne, S., Radnor, Z. and Nasi, G. (2013). A new theory for public services management? Moving beyond consumerism to a services-dominant approach? *American Review of Public Administration*, in press.

Ostrom, E. (1996). Crossing the great divide: coproduction, synergy and development. *World Development*, 24(6), 1073–1087.

Palmer, A. (1994). *Principles of Services Marketing*. London: McGraw Hill.

Pestoff, V. (2006). Citizens and co-production of welfare services. *Public Management Review*, 8(4), 503–519.

Pires, C., Sarkar, S. and Carvelho, L. (2008). Innovation in services – how different from manufacturing? *Services Industries Journal*, 28(9/10), 1337–1354.

Pirie, M. (1988). *Privatisation*. Aldershot: Wildwood House.

Pollitt, C. and Bouckaert, G. (2004). *Public Management Reform – A Comparative Analysis*. Oxford: Oxford University Press.

Porter, M. (1985). *Competitive Advantage*. New York: Free Press.

Powell, M., Greener, I., Szmigin, I., Doheny, S. and Mills, N. (2010). Broadening the focus of public service consumerism. *Public Management Review*, 12(3), 323–339.

Prahalad, C. and Ramaswamy, V. (2004). *The Future of Competition: Co-Creating Unique Value with Customers*. Boston, MA: Harvard Business School Press.

Rosentraub, M. and Warren, R. (1987). Citizen participation in the production of urban services. *Public Productivity Review*, 10(3), 75–89.

Sinclair, R. (2004). Participation in practice: making it meaningful, effective and sustainable. *Children and Society*, 18, 106–118.

Spohrer, J., Vargo, S., Caswell, N. and Maglio, P. (2008). *The Service System is the Basic Abstraction of Service Science*. Proceedings of the 41st Hawaii International Conference on System Sciences, Hawaii.

Stickley, T. (2006). Should service user involvement be consigned to history? A critical realist perspective. *Journal of Psychiatric and Mental Health Nursing*, 13(5), 570–577.

Strokosch, K. and Osborne, S. (2009). *Understanding the Co-production of Public Services: A New Approach and Its Implications for Public Services Delivery*. Paper presented at the Conference of the British Academy of Management, Brighton, September.

Sundbo, J. (1997). Management of innovation in services. *Service Industries Journal*, 17(3), 432–455.

Surjadjaja, H., Ghosh, S. and Antony, J. (2003). Determining and assessing the determinants of e-service operations. *Managing Service Quality*, 13(1), 39–53.

Tether, B. (2003). The sources and aims of innovation in services. *Economics of Innovation and New Technology*, 12(6), 841–855.

Thomas, E. (ed.) (2008). *Innovation by Design in Public Services*. London: SOLACE Foundation.

Vargo, S. and Lusch, R. (2006). Evolving a new dominant logic for marketing. In R. Lusch and S. Vargo (eds), *The Service-Dominant Logic of Marketing*. New York: M.E. Sharpe, pp. 3–28.

Vargo, S., Maglio, P. and Akaka, M. (2008). On value and value creation: a service systems and service logic perspective. *European Management Journal*, 26, 145–152.

Von Hippel, E. (1994). 'Sticky Information' and the locus of problem solving: implications for innovation. *Management Science*, 40(4), 429–439.

Von Hippel, E. (2005). *Democratizing Innovation*. Cambridge, MA: MIT Press.

West, D. (2004). E-government and the transformation of service delivery and citizen attitudes. *Public Administration Review*, 64(1), 15–27.

Wistow, G., Knapp, M., Hardy, B. and Allen, C. (1994). *Social Care in a Mixed Economy*. Buckingham: Open University Press.

5. Public service innovation: what messages from the collision of innovation studies and services research?

Ian Miles[1]

INTRODUCTION: INNOVATION STUDIES

Innovation studies grew rapidly as an area of research over the last quarter of the twentieth century, as detailed by authors such as Fagerberg (2004) and Godin (2010), and as reflected in handbooks giving overviews of the field (Dodgson and Rothwell 1994; Fagerberg et al. 2004). Research was long dominated by a focus on manufacturing industry, and in particular on 'high-tech' industries such as aerospace, the automotive industry and pharmaceuticals. Service innovation had gained substantial attention by the first years of the twenty-first century (cf. Miles 2000), to the point that a *Handbook of Innovation and Services* was published in 2010 (Gallouj and Djellal 2010). But innovation in the public sector has been even more neglected in the mainstream of innovation studies. Even in the Gallouj and Djellal *Handbook* there are only a handful of index references to public services; one chapter is devoted to public health care, but this is mainly an account of one case study (concerning UK diabetes education). With public services constituting a substantial fraction of the services sectors, it is important to put more effort into exploring the scope for fruitful integration of work on public service innovation with innovation studies more generally.

TYPES OF INNOVATION

The term 'innovation' itself is used both to refer to the process of innovation and the outcome of innovation as a new product. It also has broader and narrower senses, with innovation studies broadly covering:

- *Invention*: the process whereby new ideas are generated, or the new idea itself, whether as just a concept or as a working model or prototype. The 'research' element of research and development (R&D) is often involved in invention of technological devices, though new ideas can also be generated from creativity drawing on experience with design or production. Recent years have seen increased attention to links between creativity and innovation.
- *Innovation*: the process whereby inventions are translated into commercialised or applicable approaches and products, or these approaches and products themselves. Some managers insist that innovations should only refer to the successful introduction of the new ideas into markets or industrial activity, though the definition of success then becomes debated – some technical successes fail to gain market

acceptance, for example. Tidd et al. (1997, p. 66) suggest that 'innovation is a process of turning opportunity into ideas and putting these into widely used practice'. There is a tendency in innovation studies to focus on technological innovations, where we will often be concerned with the 'applied development' ends of R&D. But it is widely accepted that innovations may involve more organisational developments, such as new marketing methods or methods of arranging supply chains and work flows.

- *Diffusion and adoption*: the innovation's roll-out within organisations, or dissemination in markets, so that it is implemented by increasing numbers of users. There is often a process of 'reinvention', whereby users develop new applications of the innovation, create new complementary products to increase its functionality, and so on; some authors use ideas such as 'innofusion' to refer to the active development of new configurations and practices by users of innovations (Fleck 1993).

Numerous distinctions are drawn between different types of innovation: a prominent example is that between *product* and *process* innovation (e.g. Johnson 2001). Product innovation involves new or improved goods or services organisations supply to their consumers or clients; process innovation (not the same as 'innovation process'!) involves new or improved ways of producing and delivering goods and services. In practice, it is not always easy to differentiate between the two types of innovation, even in manufacturing industry – new products often require new processes, and change in processes may well involve some change in product characteristics.

Another standard distinction is between *incremental* and *radical* innovation (Freeman 1982). The former involves a small modification in a product or process – it requires little change in the skills needed to use it, but (typically) delivers better performance (or lower cost). Radical innovation usually provides much improved or different functionality, from the application of substantially new underlying knowledge; it usually requires more adaptation on the part of users and producers. Freeman (1982) also discusses revolutionary innovations – developments with massive implications across the economy, where breakthroughs in fundamental knowledge allow for new products and processes to be introduced pervasively. New information technology (IT) is identified as a prime example of such revolutionary innovations.

Henderson and Clark (1990), who noted that innovation may involve limited components or whole systems, add to radical and incremental innovation the ideas of *modular* and *architectural* innovation. In modular innovation, a new conception of the core configuration is established but the key linkages are retained; for example, the replacement of analogue telephones with digital. In architectural innovation, new linkages are required between components in the configuration, creating a new product (such as online bank services) but maintaining the core framework. Such innovation is often triggered by change in a component but the core design concept is essentially unchanged.

Another popular idea is Christensen's (1997) *disruptive* innovation, which focuses on the market effects of innovation, rather than on the novelty of the product or process from the innovator's perspective. Disruptive innovations involve very new and usually unexpected ways of doing things, and threaten existing markets and industry structures by competing on the basis of new markets or functionalities (an example is music downloads). (In contrast, a *sustaining* innovation has little effect on existing markets or industry structures.) A disruptive product innovation may reach markets (as did budget airlines) or provide functions (as did digital cameras) that the established products cannot. The new product may be better quality, lower priced or meet a different set of user needs.

STAGES OF INNOVATION

Innovation, understood as a process, unfolds through time. Diffusion studies explore how populations adopt new ideas or products, and the characteristics of 'early adopters' and 'laggards'; researchers plot diffusion curves representing the spread of the innovation through potential user populations. The diffusion trends of successful innovations typically take the form of S-shaped curves: the incidence of adoption is initially low, accelerates to a period of 'take-off' from which it continues at a high level, and eventually declines as the market becomes saturated. Early adopters are typically described as being more aware of innovations and more capable of taking the risk of acquiring unfamiliar and perhaps untested products; as being younger, more affluent, more exposed to media carrying technical information, and more technically experienced; as having higher status and better linkages into social networks.

Diffusion trends often diverge from the ideal S-shape. They may be disrupted by such perturbations as seasonal fluctuations in expenditure, or longer-term events such as wars and business cycles. Adoption may be thwarted by the rapid emergence of successful competitor products, because of changing social needs or market demands; or because the products do not do their job well or cheaply enough for most of the target users. Rogers (1994), the most prominent diffusion researcher, sees adoption as influenced by critical features of the product: relative advantage (substantial benefits relative to costs, as compared with current ways of doing things); compatibility (with existing or planned equipment or services); complexity (the amount of learning required by users); reliability (expected availability for use, ease and cost of repair and maintenance, etc.); and observability (ease of gaining knowledge about the innovation).

Diffusion is the evolution of the user base; but the innovation and the innovation process evolve in tandem. Through the 'product life cycle', the innovation is typically seen as developing from being expensive and hard to use, to being cheap and less demanding of advanced skills – rendering it more attractive for adoption by mass markets. Abernathy and Utterback (1978) suggest that when a new product is introduced into the market, its features are liable to be unstable, but as understanding of user requirements grows, the innovation becomes 'mature'. The focus of innovation shifts – from improving the product and stabilising its design (adapting the product to users), to emphasis on increasing production efficiency and cost reduction (making mass production possible). Finally, both product and process have become mature, and innovation may focus on product differentiation and customisation.

The ways in which innovation is managed and conducted also evolve. Rothwell (1994) outlined five generations of (thinking about) industrial innovation management[2] – from simplistic linear technology-push models through to more complex processes, with cross-functional integration and collaboration with external partners, suppliers and customers; and now with use of new IT to create internal and external linkages and collaborate in innovation through joint ventures, strategic alliances, and the like. This latter model corresponds to Chesbrough's (2003) popular notion of *open innovation*. A firm with too much internal focus may miss numerous opportunities, since many ideas appear to be outside the organisation's current business or would require external capabilities or assets to realise their potential. But with open innovation, firms commercialise external innovations – from other firms as well as their own internal ideas – through developing and deploying external (as well as in-house) pathways to the market. Many companies have been developing new strategies to exploit open innovation, by exploring the ways in which external ideas and technologies can fill the gaps in their current business – while ensuring that they can capture sufficient of the value created.

Various open innovation strategies have been distinguished, and there has been an upsurge of interest in applying social networking tools such as innovation competitions and crowdsourcing. It should also be noted that new technologies are being applied in the course of innovation management – computer-aided design and simulation, coordination of virtual R&D teams, and so on.

More generally, innovation studies emphasise 'systems of innovation' more than single innovators and inventors. The original 'national systems of innovation' framework was used for understanding how it was that some countries apparently performed much better than others in translating new knowledge into commercial success. Regional and sectoral systems of innovation have also been brought into focus (Edquist (2004) reviews such systems thinking). Different stakeholders involved directly in the innovation process (e.g. funding development, helping to effect relevant regulations, procuring new equipment) and less directly (e.g. those responsible for education and training) have varying interests and capabilities, and are related together dynamically. The alignment of interests and flows of information and knowledge across these groups can shape the development and diffusion of innovations. Other studies focus on specific innovations and innovation programmes, and explore the nature of the constituencies involved and the sets of stakeholders who have to be aligned – and aligned to the nature of the knowledge and technological practice itself – in order for the project to take off (e.g. Molina's (1997) 'sociotechnical constituency' approach).

In addition to the focus on technological innovation, and on innovation in manufacturing sectors, it should also be noted that many innovation studies take it for granted that the main driver of innovative activity is the pressure of competition across private firms. Fundamental new knowledge may arise from research in the public sector (genomics from universities, the Web from CERN, etc.), but private enterprise is seen as driving the rapid development and adoption of innovations. While some studies point out such factors as the search for aesthetic tidiness on the part of engineers, and the role of fashions and fads in the adoption of new products (by consumers and managers alike), much of the literature has an economistic tendency to treat individuals and firms as rational and seeking to maximise easily understood benefits (such as profits). Even so, innovation studies challenge the assumptions of mainstream economics, stressing instead the heterogeneity of firms, imperfect information, efforts to disrupt markets, and the like. Thus innovation studies form an important part of the backbone of what is variously known as evolutionary and neoSchumpeterian economics. Yet even while recognising the limitations of mainstream economic appraisal, there is still a marked tendency to focus on the private sector and competitive pressure as at the heart of innovation.

SERVICES AND INNOVATION STUDIES

Traditionally, innovation has been identified with technological innovations, which were mainly seen as flowing from manufacturing industries. Service industries at best adopted these innovations. Even exceptional services like railways and telecommunications, where there might be some R&D, were largely 'supplier driven', as Pavitt (1984) located them in an influential taxonomy of sectoral innovation characteristics. Soete and Miozzo (1989) demonstrated that Pavitt's taxonomy, with slight adaptation, could be applied to differentiate among service industries. They see some services sectors – personal services (food and drink, repair businesses, hairdressers, etc.), most retail trade – as largely *supplier dominated*. In contrast, *production-intensive, scale-intensive sectors* feature large-scale back-office administrative tasks that are often amenable to some automation through application of new IT. *Network sectors* are also large scale, and are dependent on extensive networks – these may be physical (e.g. transport and travel services, wholesale trade and distribution) or informational (e.g. banks, insurance, broadcasting and telecommunications). Such services are important in shaping IT networks, and play a major role in defining and specifying innovations. Another category is *specialised technology suppliers and science-based sectors* – software and specialised business services, laboratory and design services – where the main source of technology is the businesses' own innovative activity and the innovations tend to be 'user dominated'.

Soete and Miozzo located public or collective services (education, health care, administration) within the supplier-dominated category. Certainly these sectors procure large volumes of technologies from outside sources – all apply IT extensively, while health in particular makes use of many specialised innovations such as those in pharmaceuticals, surgical equipment, and the like. But these are also services with considerable resemblance to the large network service organisations in the private sector – there are obvious analogies between surgeries, hospitals, schools, colleges, employment and social security centres, and the like, and the branches of banks, supermarkets and other such bodies. There are also striking dissimilarities in that health and education services, at least, have very 'knowledge intensive' workforces – at least assessed by high shares of graduates among their employees. (Miles (2008) uses educational credentials as a basis for one of a series of statistical contrasts across service sectors.) Public services are liable to vary among themselves (and over time); some quite possibly feature resemblances to scale and network-intensive sectors, and to knowledge-intensive patterns, rather than simply following supplier-driven or external innovation patterns.

A German analysis of firm-level innovation survey data (only featuring private sector firms) resulted in similar classifications. Hipp and Grupp (2005) identified distinctive *external innovation-intensive, network-intensive, scale-intensive* and *knowledge-intensive* patterns – but warned against identifying service sectors with service innovation patterns. There are correlations – for example, the knowledge-intensive pattern was particularly common in technical KIBS (Knowledge-Intensive Business Services), the network-based pattern in banking and the supplier-dominated pattern in other financial services – but all sectors featured several of the patterns. Companies that nominally belong to the same sector can have quite different innovation patterns, which will no doubt prove to be the case for public service organisations.

APPROACHES TO SERVICE INNOVATION

Much research on service innovation is better described as being about 'innovation in services (industries)'. The unit of analysis is often the innovating firm, and the sorts of innovation considered are often fairly standard technological innovations. Many studies exploring differences among service sectors, or between service and manufacturing industries, are based on large-scale innovation surveys. These surveys rarely include public services in their samples, though there are now efforts to develop instruments suitable for public sector organisations (Innobarometer 2011; Hughes et al. 2011).

Coombs and Miles (2000), following in the footsteps of Gallouj and Weinstein (1997), saw the majority of studies as taking one of two approaches. The *assimilation approach* sees innovation in services as raising few new issues compared with those addressed in studies of manufacturing. Similarly, economists discussing services trade or productivity commonly portray most economic attributes of services as fundamentally similar to those found in manufacturing. Apparent differences tend to be matters of degree, rather than substantial qualitative divides: services just happen to have intangible products rather than producing physical goods and raw materials. The implication is that theories, concepts and statistical tools, developed in manufacturing contexts, readily apply to services.

Such an approach is taken up by some innovation researchers who turned to study services after having focused on manufacturing sectors. Thus many of the earlier statistical studies of innovation in services, deploying data produced in innovation surveys, stress the points of similarity between services and manufacturers. The assumption – and often the conclusion – of such work is that existing instruments will work effectively to describe the service economy. If there are differences in productivity and innovation, these will simply mean that services are lagging behind other sectors. This could be explained by various factors – for example, many sectors are dominated by small firms and low-skill labour, which would be expected to reduce service industries' propensity to innovate. And public sector services are burdened with bureaucracy and lacking competition.

Gallouj and Weinstein (1997), pointing out that many studies tend to focus on new technologies (especially IT) as the critical form of innovation in services, had identified a *technologistic approach*, which Gallouj and Savona (2010) see as identical with the assimilation approach. (Droege et al. (2009) disagree.) But while assimilationists tend to stress familiar types of technological innovation, a technologistic approach could still see technological innovation as taking distinctive forms in service industries. Thus Barras (1986, 1990) proposed that service organisations follow a 'reverse product cycle', in contrast to manufacturers. They begin with use of new technology (in back offices) to render production of services more efficient, culminating in the creation of new services (at the customer interface or front office). Barras saw IT as a twentieth century technological revolution in service industries, analogous to the transformation of nineteenth century manufacturing by new power systems. Service organisations were becoming technology intensive; learning about new ways to accomplish their goals by applying IT, they could set off on trajectories of service innovation based on this use. But would these be distinctive trajectories, or do they conform to the standard product cycle model as they become experienced technology users?

Coombs and Miles' second perspective, the *demarcation approach*, stresses the distinctiveness of services activities and industries. This approach is displayed in many case studies of services activities, often by researchers from service management, marketing and quality research traditions; there are also discussions of particular problems in assessing service productivity in conventional terms (e.g. Gadrey 2002; Grönroosa and Ojasalo 2004).

The distinctiveness means that services and service innovation often require novel theories and instruments. For instance, most services conduct little R&D, rendering R&D intensity a poor indicator for identifying 'high-tech' or 'knowledge intensive' services; new approaches are required (perhaps workforce skill profiles?). Or again, the analysis of innovative patterns of services 'trade' has to pay more attention to investment, franchising and partnerships rather than conventional exports. Research on New Service Development (NSD) has emphasised emerging issues connected with the features of services. Johne and Storey (1998), in an early review of studies of this topic, stressed the challenges for marketing new services that are associated with coproduction and interactivity. The cooperation of users is critical in shaping the quality of the service outcome and the effectiveness of service innovation. Studies focusing on factors facilitating successful introduction of new services (e.g. Martin and Horne (1995)) typically see the NSD process as requiring more attention to customer features and roles, and to their expectations and experiences. Alongside the users themselves, employees are often vital: their interaction with customers in coproducing the service is central, their insights about customers and service processes may stimulate innovative ideas, and innovation may require them to acquire skills and knowledge. It is rare for successful NSD to be achieved by a few experts; much innovation emerges from ad-hoc, on-the-job experimentation, and it is fairly common for large-scale service innovation to be organised through transitory project management structures.

While many aspects of services differ from those typifying manufacturing, much of this distinctiveness relates to two common characteristics of services: interactivity in the service relationship and intangibility of the service product.

THE SERVICE RELATIONSHIP: INTERACTIVITY

The relationship between supplier and user of the service, unlike that typical between the producer and user of goods, often involves contact extending over a long period of time. Thus service designers talk about the 'service journey' or 'pathway', addressing not just economic exchanges but also the changing states of the service user, and the physical and symbolic environments of service provision (the 'servicescape' of Bitner 1992).

The user or customer has not only to be physically present, but also often has to contribute more actively to the creation of the service. This interaction between supplier and user for service production is described as 'consumer-intensivity' (Gartner and Reissman 1974) and as 'servuction' (Belleflamme et al. 1986; Eiglier and Langeard 1987), though the term 'coproduction' has now come to the fore. The amount and type of effort that is put in by the partners vary from service to service – compare, for example, cinema attendance, a taxi journey, treatment at the dentists', getting an appraisal of business practices from a consultant . . . Often, the quality of the user inputs is critical for the quality of the final service. Clients may also interact with each other while on service journeys, affecting the quality of their service experiences. Other users' behaviour can make the difference between great and terrible experiences. Innovation may be directed at widening or reducing the scope for interaction among customers, at allowing users to choose what sort of interaction they may desire, and the like.

The service relationship is bound to have substantial influence on service innovation – indeed, it can be the focus of innovation efforts, aimed at introducing new roles, new channels and new forms of interaction. Much recent innovation has concerned self-service systems and online service delivery; requiring learning and behavioural change on the part of the user as well as the service supplier. Innovations involving the client interface and service interactivity need not be technological: for example, the introduction of new 'scripts' for service staff, enabling them to quickly deal with individual customers in ways that match their characteristics; nurses performing triage in hospital entry procedures; helpline operators dealing with problems that customers are experiencing; employment bureaux using standardised systems to capture and communicate details of potential employees. Many 'self-services' shift tasks more to the user, who helps him- or herself to select and carry goods in a supermarket, food in a restaurant, and so on (see Gershuny and Miles (1983) for early discussion of this trend). This reduces labour costs for the service organisation – and sometimes improves the quality of the experience for the customer. Such innovations require creation of a mutually acceptable framework for identifying and accessing the objects of the service. Goods may have to be weighed and packaged in standard ways, for example; shopping trolleys or trays must be provided; the sales relationship may be reconfigured around a till. Of course, IT is often used in support of self-services, with ATMs and online bank accounts replacing counter staff in banks and self-service check-outs now coming into use in supermarkets, for example.

Interactivity necessarily involves information exchanges between parties, creating huge scope for application of IT. Thus beyond IT use in the administrative and organisational functions of back offices, and in online services, IT applications include visual aids to support presentations and teaching, new media for information exchange, monitoring and sensing systems for health and security, and automated and semi-automated equipment for many service activities.

FROM INTERACTIVITY TO INTANGIBILITY

Service products are more to do with relationships and (coproduction) processes than they are about creating tangible physical goods. We can see service activities as about *doing* things rather than *making* things. Service activities, of course, generally use physical artefacts in the course of production of their benefits, and some produce tangible changes in the state of people (new dentures and hairstyles) or artefacts (repair and maintenance services). But intangibility is a common characteristic of service activities and products, and affects service innovation and innovation processes. For example, it is hard to protect service innovations with the IPR arrangements (patents) deployed for innovation in material goods; patents may be a poor measure of innovation outputs for service firms (patenting can happen in the service industries – see FhG-ISI (2003)). Service firms also undertake R&D, though typically to a lesser extent than manufacturers; there are many reasons for this, but one issue may be that R&D tax credits systems rule out support for R&D on social and managerial issues (see Miles (2007)) – just one way in which policy support for innovation may discriminate against service activities.

Intangibility is associated with other features of service products – for example, many are difficult to store, transport or demonstrate in advance of purchase. Service innovation often seeks to address these features, for example finding ways to add tangibility to estab-lished or new services (e.g. loyalty cards), to deliver them to remote customers (e.g. through the Internet), to provide evidence of quality (trials, quality standard accredita-tion, etc.). These 'information asymmetries' of service exchanges have led to regulation of many services, and create challenges for service suppliers in convincing customers about the novelty and/or superiority of their innovative services.

Some studies indicate that service firms may put more stress on organisational innova-tion as compared with technological innovation. Howells and Tether (2004) found a substantial share of services firms claiming that their main innovative activities were *solely* organisational, while it was uncommon for manufacturing firms to do so. Kanerva et al. (2006) report that services firms (especially in the financial and wholesale sectors) are more prone to initiate organisational change; Schmidt and Rammer (2006) and Miles (2008) report that manufacturers and IT service sectors feature firms tending to report more technology-based innovations, while most service sectors report more organisa-tional innovation. But firms that are innovators of one sort also tend to adopt other sorts of innovation, so that while there are differences of the sort demarcationists would anticipate, they are not as clear-cut as claimed.

A SYNTHESIS?

The demarcation perspective makes a persuasive case that some features of service innovation – nontechnological dimensions, innovation in the service relationship, and so on – are particularly pronounced, if not uniquely distinctive. The demarcation approach has highlighted important features of services and service innovation. But at least some of these are features of innovation that are present in many manufacturing firms – though they have been neglected in most accounts of manufacturing innovation. In many respects there is convergence between manufacturing and service sectors (Miles 1993). Many manufacturing firms more resemble the traditional view of services; and many service industries are becoming more like traditional (or at least post-Fordist) manufac-turing. There is a case for transcending the assimilation/demarcation divide through the development of a *synthesis approach*. As well as being more elegant to have a single approach than a multiplicity of ways of tackling processes that sometimes overlap and intertwine, and that often share some similar features, this would enable us to argue for integrated training, comprehensive innovation policies, and the like. It should also better reflect important phenomena in modern economies which the partial approaches might overlook. It should form the basis for more adequate indicators to enrich understanding of innovation right across the economy. It will help account for variations within and across goods and service innovation, and help address the service activities of manufacturing firms and the goods-producing activities of service organisations.

One effort to synthesise approaches stems from service marketing, where scholars and practitioners had found that services could not rely on the methods used for marketing goods. 'Service-dominant logic' (Vargo and Lusch 2006; Lusch et al. 2008) can be seen as a synthesis approach in which service is the end result of all economic activity, whether through a service firm supplying services to a consumer, or a manufacturing firm supplying goods for consumers to produce their own services. *Service* is seen as a process and relationship, rather than just as an 'intangible good'. All economic activity can be seen in this perspective as an exchange of services, involving a *coproduction* process, where both 'supplier' and 'client' contribute resources to create and achieve benefits. The service-dominant logic proposes a new framework for marketing and other analysis that should apply to all sectors. Thus the focus moves away from describing the particular features of service products and industries to examining service as a pervasive economic phenomenon. The emphasis is on service (the coproduction relationship) rather than on services (which we might consider to be the benefits that are supplied to the users). In terms of innovation, this approach suggests we should attend to changes in the resources the partners bring to the coproduction relationship; in the benefits they receive from it, and in the way they act and interact in this relationship.

Some researchers propose characterising (service) innovations in a multidimensional fashion. Thus, rather than simply classifying innovations as belonging to one or other type – drawing strict boundaries between, for example, technological and organisational innovation, product and process innovation, and so on – den Hertog et al. (2010) identify fields of activity, that characterise different service innovations. These are not specific types of innovation, since in practice many innovations involve simultaneous changes across several of the six dimensions:

1. *New service concept*: the value created by the service provider (or coproduced with the customer). The innovation may be a new way of solving a customer's problem or meeting a customer's need, perhaps by combining existing service elements in a new configuration.
2. *New customer interaction* focuses on innovation in the interaction process between the provider and the customer, and thus on the role customers are playing in the creation of value. The client may be an important source of innovative ideas, coproducing innovation as well as the service!
3. *New value systems* (chains and clusters): new sets of business partners involved in jointly coproducing a service (and often a new service). This is a point where discussion of open innovation and service innovation coincide. Important new services can be developed in large communities linked through platforms and networks of businesses.
4. *New revenue models*: the distribution of costs and revenues needs to be aligned, especially where multiple actors are involved. The shift to charging for a service rather than selling a good could be seen as a new revenue model, as could shifts between subscription and advertising-based models for online services.
5. *Personnel, organisation, culture elements of a new delivery system*: these involve alignment of management and organisation so as to enable service workers to perform new jobs, and to develop and offer innovative services. 'Soft' elements of the service delivery system can allow firms to differentiate themselves from the competition. This may require new organisational structures and team skills, for example, and can

be a focus for innovation as well as a necessary complement for innovations that are centred on the other dimensions.

6.   *Technological elements of a new service delivery system*: application of new technology (predominantly, but not exclusively, IT) to allow for improved production and use of services by allowing for new interfaces and ways of delivering services or service elements.

Many innovations involve change on several dimensions; the success of innovation will usually require that these are mutually coherent. Den Hertog et al. (2010) go on to examine the six 'dynamic service innovation capabilities' required to effectively support service innovation processes: (1) signalling user needs and technological options; (2) conceptualising; (3) capabilities in bundling and unbundling; (4) coproducing and orchestrating; (5) scaling and stretching; and (6) learning and adapting. They argue that successful service innovators (including manufacturing firms that are servicising) are liable to be those that outperform their competitors in at least some of these capabilities.

A synthesis approach should be a fruitful basis for management and policy action, and for exploring future prospects for service innovation. So far, though, empirical research has mainly focused on mapping out some of the main varieties of service innovation processes, and of innovation in service firms – where we have the advantage of access to large-scale survey studies that allow us to examine firms classified into major sectors (but not to explore specific innovations).

DIVERSITY WITHIN SERVICES

The diversity of service industries and firms means that practically anything we might assert about their common or distinctive features will immediately bring to mind counterexamples – are the products intangible? Is production coterminous with consumption? Is there a high level of customisation and/or human contact? and so on.

Much service innovation research has stressed the variation of practices across distinctive firms and sectors. In addition to the many survey studies published in recent years, there are now some very substantial overviews of service innovation and innovation in services – including several chapters in the Gallouj and Djellal (2010) *Handbook*. Major findings of such studies include:

- Some technology-related services – mainly business services in areas such as engineering, computer, R&D services, and so on – are similar to high-tech manufacturing firms in terms of their propensity to innovate, devotion of resources to innovation, and organisation innovation efforts (with established R&D departments and a focus on technological rather than organisational innovation).
- Many other services sectors have fewer firms actively introducing innovations, typically devote lower levels of resources to innovation efforts and are not strongly inclined towards R&D. Innovation is often 'on the job' and ad hoc, or else organised through project management or new product development teams set up for particular innovation efforts.
- New IT is an enabling technology, and sometimes a trigger, for many innovations

in information-based services, and in informational components of many services and back-office processes. Many service organisations are extremely heavy users of new IT, though some more traditional services are less so. The heavy users include services that themselves deal with IT use (computer and telecommunications services) as well as services with high levels of professional staff, and large-scale 'network' organisations; relatively low users include many small enterprises in trade and personal services.

- Innovation in service delivery need not rely so heavily on IT, however. From the pizza delivery by motorbike, to the self-service model of acquisition of services from organisations of many types, from the development of detailed scripts for service personnel to use in negotiations with clients, to the design of more efficient or pleasant 'servicescapes'; much attention has been given to features of the service encounter that are not readily definable as either product or process innovation.

- The organisation of innovation in service organisations is found to often diverge from the R&D management model characteristic of manufacturing (at least, high-tech manufacturing). Technical KIBS and some large service organisations may feature specialised R&D departments (and dedicated R&D managers and staff), conducting research of a strategic nature. But these are exceptions. And as the synthesis approach suggests, too, firms are likely to apply more than one method of managing innovation across their range of innovative activities. R&D activity may be directed at the main products and industrial processes, for example, but not at web presence, distribution and retail activities, or at other product-related services.

Sundbo and Gallouj (2000) described a number of broad patterns of innovation management seen in different organisations. They noted alongside the *classic R&D* pattern (found mainly in large and/or technology-based firms) six other ways of organising innovation. The *services professional* pattern is based on professionals generating ad-hoc and highly customised solutions for clients; thus innovations rely on employees' professional skills, and innovation intelligence may flow through professional networks and associations or other communities of practice. This pattern often applies in KIBS such as consultancy firms, and in 'creative industries' (e.g. advertising and design). A major challenge for these firms is 'capturing' and replicating innovations that are made in practice by professionals, and much attention in knowledge management is directed to this. A second model, the *neo-industrial* pattern, combines the two outlined above: much distributed innovation in the course of professional practice takes place, alongside a specialised R&D or innovation department. This characterises some large consultancies – and also some health services. A third model is the *organised strategic innovation* pattern encountered in large service firms, such as airlines, hotel chains and retailers, where innovation is organised in the form of projects that are directed by more or less transitory cross-functional teams, working through distinct steps of project management, and often with strong leadership from marketing groups. The *entrepreneurial* pattern characterises start-up firms, offering innovative services based on new technologies or business models: typically such firms later move on to one of the other innovation modes. An *artisanal* pattern characterises classic supplier-driven sectors, where major innovations are imported from other sectors, though innovation may also be driven by regulations and demand, and from practice (employees and managers may be sources of incremental innovation). This is found in many smaller-scale and low-tech physical ('operational') services, such as cleaning and catering. Finally, the *network* pattern involves a network of firms acting together, and adopting common standards or operating procedures. There are technology-related initiatives, such as adoption of common mobile phone or e-commerce standards and platforms; there are business model and service initiatives, as in franchises in sectors such as fast food and hotels, and also in some professional sectors.

Whether we see public services as quite distinctive, as following one or other of these patterns, or as hybrids – as is suggested above for health services – it is apparent that they can have approaches to organising innovation that are more or less like those found in the private sector. Even if there are distinctive features – such as scrambling to implement new practices that have been politically imposed from on high – it should be possible to draw further analogies and explore key features in the light of these. For instance, it is not uncommon for public services to feature several sorts of R&D-like systems: the National Health Service in the UK has its own R&D programme,[3] and most government departments have their own research programmes and sometimes feature agencies which are themselves research intensive (the Environment Agency is a case in the UK). Though much research is contracted out to universities, consultants and private firms, so it could be argued that much new knowledge comes from outside the organisation. Private firms are celebrated for 'open innovation' – in other words, sourcing innovative ideas from outside their own boundaries (Chesbrough 1994). So this outsourcing of research by the public sector (often to other parts of the public sector) need not imply that they are passive adopters of ideas that are created by other parties.

Practitioners also document new approaches to service innovation and its management, and the emergence of *service design* frameworks practice is striking. Alongside established techniques such as service blueprinting (Bitner et al. 2008 provide a recent account), methods such as storyboarding (from the creative industries), interface and interaction design (from informatics), and research and assessment methods such as ethnography and the use of virtual reality, are being used to model and design complicated services. They address such features as multiple service encounters and relationships extended over long periods of time and multiple venues – not only in private services like airports and theme parks, but also in public health, education and the like. (For reviews of the field see Moritz (2005), Saco and Goncalves (2008), Macintyre et al. (2011) and specialised journals such as *Touchpoint*, launched in 2009.)

IMPLICATIONS FOR PUBLIC SERVICES

The awakening of interest in service innovation means that there is a wealth of material about innovation in private services that can be drawn upon. There have been a few attempts to relate such analyses to public service innovation, notably in the European projects PUBLIN and SERVPPIN.[4] Several analyses in these projects point to the scope for applying, and extending, ideas from innovation studies in this way. Thus Windrum and his colleagues (Windrum and Garcia-Goni 2008; Windrum et al. 2010) explore the aligning of interests across multiple stakeholders, and the prominence of interactions between public and private sector actors in many of these innovations. Another important recent development is attention focused on the notion of 'social innovation' – in fact a rather disputed concept, with some authors using it to cover nontechnological innovation, some to describe innovations coming from civil society, and some simply examining innovations that are largely developed in pursuit of social rather than just commercial objectives. Here we see a parallel to the idea of disruptive innovation – 'transformational innovation', depicted by Mulgan (2007).

Public service innovation may well often be characterised by top-down initiatives, where 'roll-out' is seen as the order of the day rather than more conventional diffusion – though often professionals and the public have some independence in adoption decisions, in which case diffusion analysis can provide useful insights. Innovation management processes may be weighted towards these top-down initiatives, and the observation that bottom-up innovations may be slow and hard to reproduce more widely suggests that other modes of innovation management should be considered. Open innovation may be a particularly useful rallying call.

Additionally, the idea that innovations are likely to evolve through a life cycle should be given serious consideration; the assumption that authorities can envisage and dictate the final form of a service is problematic. Experience from practitioners and end-users may well need to be embedded as innovations are stabilised. Both competing and complementary innovations (from other public services and countries, from the private sector, from civil society) may shape the trajectory of uptake and impact of innovations. The need for engagement of a wide range of stakeholders and expertise in service design processes is even more important for the public sector than for private sector innovations.

Finally, it cannot be assumed that simply trying to make public services more like the private sector – as in much New Public Management advocacy – will automatically lead to more, and more effective, public service innovation. Innovation practices and management processes need to be actively fostered. This has been recognised in recent years in a barrage of initiatives designed to support innovation in UK public services – public sector reform alone was not delivering sufficiently rapidly on this front. It remains to be seen whether this momentum will be retained during the present wave of financial stringency and rhetoric against public service managers.

NOTES

1. The research reported in the present study was implemented in the framework of the Programme of Fundamental Studies of the Higher School of Economics (HSE) in 2011–12.
2. First and second generations feature rather simple linear models, where innovation is developed as a result of need pull or technology push, through a set of stages from the laboratory to the final commercial product or process. The linear model came under increasing criticism as linkages between the various stages were noted (e.g. between R&D and marketing) so a third generation recognised the interaction and feedback across various steps in the innovation process. The fourth generation, sometimes seen as the 'Parallel Model', sees yet more emphasis on linkages and alliances, with better integration of activities within the firm and increasingly also with upstream suppliers and downstream customers. Finally, for Rothwell, the fifth generation features yet more integration and networking across the value chain and with other external knowledge sources, with innovation a more continuous activity, and now with use of new IT to create internal and external linkages and collaborate in innovation through joint ventures, strategic alliances, and the like.
3. The National Institute for Health Research (NIHR) (see the website at http://www.nihr.ac.uk/research/

Pages/default.aspx – accessed 21 July 2011) and note also the Department of Health Policy Research Programme, and the Medical Research Council (websites at, respectively, http://www.dh.gov.uk/en/ Aboutus/Researchanddevelopment/Policyresearchprogramme/index.htm, and http://www.mrc.ac.uk/ index.htm – accessed 21 July 2011).
4. As of 30 August 2011 relevant documentation can be obtained from the PUBLIN website at http://www. step.no/publin/ and that of SERVPPIN at http://www.servppin.com/. Another valuable source on public service innovation is the *Innovation Journal* (http://www.innovation.cc/), while NESTA's work on public services can be accessed at http://www.nesta.org.uk/assets/documents/ready_or_not.

BIBLIOGRAPHY

Abernathy, W.J. and Utterback, J.M. (1978). Patterns of innovation in technology. *Technology Review*, 80(7), 40–47.
Barras, R. (1986). Towards a theory of innovation in services. *Research Policy*, 15(4), 161–173.
Barras, R. (1990). Interactive innovation in financial and business services: the vanguard of the service revolution. *Research Policy*, 19(3), 215–237.
Belleflamme, C., Houard, J. and Michaux, B. (1986). *Innovation and Research and Development Process Analysis in Service Activities*, Brussels, EC, FAST Programme. Occasional Papers no. 116.
Bitner, M.J. (1992). Servicescapes: the impact of physical surroundings on customers and employees. *Journal of Marketing*, 56(2), 57–71.
Bitner, M.J., Ostrom, A. and Morgan, F. (2008). Service blueprinting: a practical technique for service innovation. *California Management Review*, 50(3), 66–94.
Chesbrough, H. (2003). *Open Innovation: The New Imperative for Creating and Profiting from Technology*. Boston, MA: Harvard Business School Press.
Christensen, C. (1997). *The Innovator's Dilemma: When New Technologies Cause Great Firms to Fail.* Cambridge, MA: Harvard Business School Press.
Coombs, R. and Miles, I. (2000). Innovation, measurement and services: the new problematique. In J.S. Metcalfe and I. Miles (eds), *Innovation Systems in the Service Economy*. Dordrecht: Kluwer, pp. 83–102.
den Hertog, P., van der Aa, W. and de Jong, M.W. (2010). Capabilities for managing service innovation: towards a conceptual framework. *Journal of Service Management*, 21(4), 490–514.
Dodgson, M. and Rothwell, R. (eds) (1994). *Handbook of Innovation*. Cheltenham and Northampton, MA: Edward Elgar.
Droege, H., Hildebrand, D. and Heras Forcada, M.A. (2009). Innovation in services: present findings, and future pathways. *Journal of Service Management*, 20(2), 131–155.
Edquist, C. (2004). Systems of innovation – perspectives and challenges. In J. Fagerberg, D. Mowery and R. Nelson (eds), *The Oxford Handbook of Innovation*. Oxford: Oxford University Press, pp. 181–208.
Eiglier, P. and Langeard, E. (1987). *Servuction*. Paris: McGraw-Hill.
Fagerberg, J. (2004). Innovation: a guide to the literature. In J. Fagerberg, D. Mowery and R. Nelson (eds), *The Oxford Handbook of Innovation*. Oxford: Oxford University Press, pp. 1–26.
Fagerberg, J., Mowery, D. and Nelson, R. (eds) (2004). *The Oxford Handbook of Innovation*. Oxford: Oxford University Press.
FhG-ISI (2003). *Patents in the Service Industries*, Karlsruhe, FhG-ISI, March 2003. EC Contract No. ERBHPV2-CT-1999-06. Available at: ftp://ftp.cordis.lu/pub/indicators/docs/ind_report_fraunhofer1.pdf (accessed 5 September 2012).
Fleck, J. (1993). Innofusion: feedback in the innovation process. In S.A. Stowell, D. West and J.G. Howell (eds), *Systems Science: Addressing Global Issues*. Dordrecht: Kluwer Academic/Plenum Publishers, pp. 181–208.
Freeman, C. (1982). *The Economics of Industrial Innovation*. Aldershot: Frances Pinter.
Gadrey, J. (2002). The misuse of productivity concepts in services: lessons from a comparison between France and the United States. In J. Gadrey and F. Gallouj (eds), *Productivity, Innovation and Knowledge in Services: New Economic and Socio-Economic Approaches*. Cheltenham and Northampton, MA: Edward Elgar.
Gallouj, F. and Djellal, F. (eds) (2010). *The Handbook of Innovation and Services*. Cheltenham and Northampton, MA: Edward Elgar.
Gallouj, F. and Savona, M. (2010). Towards a theory of innovation in services. In F. Gallouj and F. Djellal (eds), *The Handbook of Innovation and Services*. Cheltenham and Northampton, MA: Edward Elgar, pp. 27–48.
Gallouj, F. and Weinstein, O. (1997). Innovation in services. *Research Policy*, 26, 537–556.
Gartner, A. and Reissman, F. (1974). *The Service Society and the New Consumer Vanguard*. New York: Harper and Row.

Gershuny, J. and Miles, I. (1983). *The New Service Economy*. London: Frances Pinter.
Godin, B. (2010). *'Innovation Studies': The Invention of a Specialty (Parts 1 and 2)*. Working Papers No. 7 and 8, Project on the Intellectual History of Innovation. Montreal: Institut national de la recherche scientifique (INRS). Available at: http://www.csiic.ca/innovation.html (accessed 24 August 2011).
Grönroosa, C. and Ojasalo, K. (2004). Service productivity: towards a conceptualization of the transformation of inputs into economic results in services. *Journal of Business Research*, 57, 414–423.
Henderson, R.M. and Clark, K.B. (1990). Architectural innovation: the reconfiguration of existing product technologies and the failure of established firms. *Administrative Science Quarterly*, 35, 9–30.
Hipp, C. and Grupp, H. (2005). Innovation in the service sector: the demand for service-specific innovation measurement concepts and typologies. *Research Policy*, 34(4), 517–535.
Howells, J. and Tether, B. (2004). *Innovation in Services: Issues at Stake and Trends* Inno Studies Programme (ENTR-C/2001). Brussels: Commission of the European Communities. Available at: http://www.isi.fraunhofer.de/isi-media/docs/isi-publ/2004/isi04b25/inno-3.pdf (accessed 24 August 2010).
Hughes, A., Moore, K. and Kataria, N. (2011). *Innovation in Public Sector Organisations: A Pilot Survey for Measuring Innovation across the Public Sector*. London: NESTA. Available at: http://www.nesta.org.uk/library/documents/Innovation_in_public_sector_organisations_v9.pdf (accessed 25 August 2011).
Innobarometer (2011). *Innobarometer 2010: Analytical Report on Innovation in Public Administration* (prepared by Gallup). Brussels: Pro-Inno Europe. Available at: http://www.proinno-europe.eu/page/innobarometer (accessed 25 August 2011).
Johne, A. and Storey, C. (1998). New service development: a review of literature and annotated bibliography. *European Journal of Marketing*, 32(3/4), 184–251.
Johnson, D. (2001). What is innovation and entrepreneurship – lessons for larger organisations. *Industrial and Commercial Training*, 33(4), 135–140.
Kanerva, M., Hollanders, H. and Arundel, A. (2006). *Can We Measure and Compare Innovation in Services?* Luxembourg: European TrendChart on Innovation. 2006 TrendChart report available at http://archive.europe-innova.eu/servlet/Doc?cid=6373&lg=EN (accessed 31 August 2010).
Lusch, R.F., Vargo, S. and Wessels, G. (2008). Toward a conceptual foundation for service science: contributions from service-dominant logic. *IBM Systems Journal*, 47(1), 5–14.
Macintyre, M., Parry, G. and Angelis, J. (eds) (2011). *Service Design and Delivery*. Berlin and New York: Springer.
Martin, C.R. and Horne, D.A. (1995). Level of success inputs for service innovations in the same firm. *International Journal of Service Industry Management*, 6(4), 40–56.
Miles, I. (1993). Services in the new industrial economy. *Futures*, 25(6), 653–672.
Miles, I. (2000). Services innovation: coming of age in the knowledge-based economy. *International Journal of Innovation Management*, 4(4), 371–390.
Miles, I. (2007). R&D beyond manufacturing: the strange case of services' R&D. *R&D Management*, 37(3), 249–268.
Miles, I. (2008). Patterns of innovation in service industries. *IBM Systems Journal*, 47(1), 115–128. Available at http://www.research.ibm.com/journal/sj/471/miles.html (accessed 21 July 2011).
Molina, A. (1997). Insights into the nature of technology diffusion and implementation: the perspective of sociotechnical alignment. *Technovation*, 17(11/12), 601–626.
Moritz, S. (2005). *Service Design: Practical Access to an Evolving Field*. Koln: Koln International School of Design. Available at: http://stefan-moritz.com/welcome/Service_Design_files/Practical%20Access%20to%20Service%20Design.pdf (accessed 24 August 2011).
Mulgan, G. (2007). *Ready or Not? Taking Innovation in the Public Sector Seriously*. London: NESTA (National Endowment for Science, Technology and the Arts). Available at: http://www.nesta.org.uk/publications/provocations/assets/features/ready_or_not_taking_innovation_in_the_public_sector_seriously (accessed 20 September 2012).
Pavitt, K. (1984). Sectoral patterns of technical change: towards a theory and a taxonomy. *Research Policy*, 13, 343–373.
Rogers, E. (1994). *Diffusion of Innovations*. New York: Free Press (original edition 1972).
Rothwell, R. (1994). Towards the fifth-generation innovation process. *International Marketing Review*, 11(1), 7–31.
Saco, R.M. and Goncalves, A.P. (2008). Service design: an appraisal. *Design Management Review*, 19(1), 10–19.
Schmidt, T. and Rammer, C. (2006). *The Determinants and Effects of Technological and Nontechnological Innovations – Evidence from the German CIS IV*. Mimeo, Centre for European Economic Research (ZEW), Department of Industrial Economics and International Management, Mannheim, Germany.
Soete, L. and Miozzo, M. (1989). *Trade and Development in Services: A Technological Perspective*. MERIT Working Paper No. 89-031. Maastricht: MERIT.
Sundbo, J. and Gallouj, F. (2000). Innovation as a loosely coupled system in services. In J.S. Metcalfe and I. Miles (eds), *Innovation Systems in the Service Economy*. Dordrecht: Kluwer.

Tidd, J., Bessant, J. and Pavitt, K. (1997). *Managing Innovation: Integrating Technological, Market and Organisational Change*. Chichester: John Wiley & Sons Inc.

Vargo, S. and Lusch, R.F. (2006). Service-dominant logic: what it is, what it is not, what it might be. In R.F. Lusch and S. Vargo (eds), *The Service-Dominant Logic of Marketing: Dialog, Debate, and Directions*. Armonk, New York: M.E. Sharpe, pp. 43–56.

Windrum, P. and Garcia-Goni, M. (2008). A neo-Schumpeterian model of health services innovation. *Research Policy*, 37, 649–672.

Windrum, P., Garcia-Goni, M. and Fairhurst, E. (2010). Innovation in public health care: diabetes education in the UK. In F. Gallouj and F. Djellal (eds), *The Handbook of Innovation and Services*. Cheltenham and Northampton, MA: Edward Elgar, pp. 129–152.

PART II

INNOVATION AND CHANGE IN PUBLIC SERVICES

6.   Innovation as the practice of change in the public sector
Ian Colville and Mike Carter

> Progress, far from consisting in change, depends on retentiveness. When change is absolute there remains no being to improve and no direction is set for possible improvement: and when experience is not retained, as among savages, infancy is perpetual. Those who cannot remember the past are condemned to repeat it.
>
> George Santayana (1905/2006, p. 284)

Whether it be the banking collapse in 2008, riots in English cities during the summer of 2011 or the continuing machinations in the contemporary Euro crisis which have almost inconceivable implications for the world financial system, events seem to be less predictable, more complex and more dynamic than has been represented in previous generations of organizational theory (Farjoun, 2010). As a consequence, organizations are increasingly surprised by what they have to deal with, either because there is a break in expectations that come from situations that are not anticipated or situations do not advance as planned (Bechky and Okhuysen, 2011; Cunha et al. 2006). Either way, managers struggle to make sense of them (Weick 2009). Organizations increasingly have to be capable of 'managing the unexpected' by engaging in innovation through organizational change (Poole and Van de Ven 2004; Weick and Sutcliffe 2007). Against such a background managers are exhorted to innovate in order to stay abreast of what is happening and to engage in the practice of change management. So what are the implications of this for academics and practitioners, not least for developing relevant compass bearings to find direction in this contemporary landscape?

The aim of this chapter is to draw on the literature of change and innovation for thinking about and providing such a direction for change, in particular enabling innovation in the public sector. The formation of the UK coalition government in 2010 and the need to address a huge budgetary deficit provided the impetus for public sector reform across the whole sector. Previous approaches to public sector reform had reached their limits (Leadbeater 2004), suggesting a need for radical transformation and a new approach that went far beyond prior experience. Because change is contextually understood and driven, there are no universal recipes and no one can tell you exactly how it should be done. However, as summed up by Lewin (1952, p. 169), 'there is nothing so practical as a good theory'; that is, good theory informs and enhances good practice. With this in mind, we shall address Santayana's (1905/2006) two assertions: that progress depends as much on continuity as change; and the inherent dialectic, that we should hold the past as both guide and warning to the future.

We postulate that innovation is not merely a set of ideas that can be borrowed from different organizational contexts and superimposed on passive actors. Rather, it is the complement to organization change theory articulated through the practice of management and the engagement of staff. In so doing, we find that the disjuncture of differentiation and integration in developing innovative organizations can be ameliorated by more effective management – the linchpin that provides utility to practice and also fuels further academic sensemaking. We illustrate our analysis through an exemplar of innovative change in a public sector organization, the Counter Terrorism (CT) unit within the Metropolitan Police Service (MPS). This organization is charged with extraordinary responsibilities for protecting the public, in which failure to stay abreast of changing patterns of terrorist threat through organizational innovation and change can lead to life-threatening situations and possible catastrophe.

This chapter is structured in four sections. The first is entitled integrating innovation and change, where we offer a review of literature which underpins our approach and theorizing. The second outlines our case example and the context in which practice gains meaning, and elaborates the background and methodology associated with the case. Thirdly, we discuss our findings and their implications for both theory and practice, before drawing to a close with our final section in which we conclude that increasing dynamic complexity requires new understandings and practice of organizational change and innovation.

INTEGRATING INNOVATION AND CHANGE

The literature of both organizational change and innovation is voluminous, such that a comprehensive review lies outside the confines of this chapter. However, there are some authors, such as Lewin, Van de Ven and Weick, whose work persists and underpins others' theorizing and provides the foundations on which we develop our understanding. The history of organizational change literature effectively begins with Kurt Lewin (1952), who theorized that the status quo is maintained in a dynamic equilibrium where the forces driving for change are balanced by the restraining forces. The equilibrium is disturbed where the driving forces overwhelm the restraining forces and the organization is ready for change. Lewin used the analogy of ice to suggest that first the organization becomes unfrozen, leading to a phase during which change takes place, before being refrozen, solidifying the change in the organization. This model of unfreeze/change/refreeze has endured in one form or another for so long and become so pervasive in the literature that, as Hendry (1996, p. 624) noted, 'Scratch any account of creating and managing change and the idea that change is a three stage process which begins with a process of unfreezing will not be far below the surface. Indeed it has been said that the whole theory of change is reducible to this one idea of Kurt Lewin's.' Our contention is that there is more to change theory than Lewin: there are other ways of conceptualizing change. Furthermore, we propose that in contemporary environments characterized by unpredictability and complexity, they are possibly more relevant to practice than Lewin's concerns.

Some of these themes are echoed in innovation research where, for example, Bessant and Maher (2009) propose that service transformation can be delivered through radical innovation. Innovation in the public sector lacks the compelling, driving concepts of (tangible) product and profit. So whilst there might be good reasons for change (reduction in public expenditure and service improvement), there is often little vested interest for organizations which lack the competitive imperative that can be a spur to radical

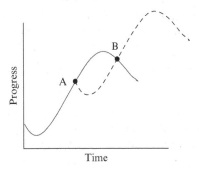

Figure 6.1   Handy's (1994) Sigmoid Curve

change. Bessant and Maher (2009, p.558) advocate a 'smart strategy' that positions organizations at the centre of the innovation search space where they are able to pick up on and amplify early trends and responses that emerge in difficult-to-predict, complex environments replete with multiple stakeholders and influencers. This suggests organizational actors able to flex within broad behavioural parameters from 'business as usual' emergent change to 'edge of chaos' new-to-the-world innovation.

In one sense, all organizational change is innovative in that it is a difference in form, quality or state over time in the management activities of the organization (Van de Ven and Poole 1995). However, in a more restricted sense, management innovation represents a particular form of organizational change, where the change is a novel or unprecedented departure from the past (Hargrave and Van de Ven 2006; Birkinshaw et al. 2008, p.826). This is certainly in keeping with Bessant and Maher's (2009) position in terms of a radical transformation. While we do not wish to lose the connection with novel change and innovation, we hold that in looking for an 'unprecedented departure from the past', there is a tendency to confirm Lewinian change. This biases managers' chances against seeing 'small departures from the past' or, in Bessant and Maher's (2009) terms, picking up on 'early trends' that can add up to novelty over time. This alerts us to the need for a non-Lewinian approach to understanding change, and also highlights the extent to which innovation of management and organization practices (rather than technical/engineering innovation) and organizational change are, on occasions, treated synonymously. Hence what we require is a means of comparing and contrasting different theories of change and, by implication, innovation.

Change and the Sigmoid Curve

Handy's (1994) concept of the Sigmoid Curve (see Figure 6.1) offers a helpful way of achieving this, in his life cycle model of change which, as he puts it, captures the story of life; that is, we are born, we wax and we wane. In order to intervene positively to prevent the inevitable decline, he asks, where is the right place to start change to start the second upward curve? Should this start at point A or point B? The answer, Handy says, is:

> at point A where there is time, as well as the resources and energy, to get the new curve through its initial explorations and the floundering before the first curve begins to

dip downwards . . . That would seem obvious, were it not for the fact that at point A all the messages coming through to the individual or the institution are that everything is going fine, that it would be folly to change when the current recipes are working so well. All that we know of change, be it personal change or change in organizations, tells that the real energy for change only comes when you are looking disaster in the face, at point B on the first curve. (Handy 1994, p. 51)

The idea that we *should* change at point A but actually only *do* change at point B captures the history of organizational change theory and its practice. It also points to the dilemma that is facing contemporary organizations, which is that if you wait until point B before you begin to change in our complex and dynamic world, you are likely to be too late. As we have seen, for Lewin (1952) the status quo is maintained where the forces driving for change are balanced by the restraining forces in a dynamic equilibrium. Point B is, in effect, where the driving forces overwhelm the restraining forces and the organization is unfrozen. In elaborating Lewin's model of change, Schein (1996) considers unfreezing, or point B, as the stage where 'survival anxiety' comes to be acknowledged in the organization. That is, the feeling that if we do not change, we will fail to meet our needs or fail to achieve some goals or ideals we have set ourselves. Staring disaster in the face then leads to survival anxiety that in turn generates a sense of urgency (Kotter 1995) that makes it very plain that the organization needs to change if it is to continue. A popular way of expressing this idea that people only change when they 'feel the heat' is found in the expression 'the burning platform', a phrase much used by consultants and oft-repeated by senior civil servants. Again, this is consistent with Lewin (1952), who talked of the need for 'an emotional stir-up' as a means of disturbing the equilibrium of the status quo. That is, to get change started you have to overcome inertia, defined as the inability of the organization to change as rapidly as the environment (Pfeffer 1997, p. 163). In essence, an inertial understanding of change says that until a gap becomes apparent between the organization and the environment, that is sufficiently wide to generate a sense of urgency/burning platform, there is little or no motivation to change. In terms of the aphorism, 'If it ain't broke, don't fix it.'

In brief, Lewin's theory of change accords with Handy's point B. But what of the possibility of change at point A? How has this been theorized and why has it not been considered significant? This dualism between change at point A or point B runs through the literature of organizational change. Watzlawick et al. (1974) made the distinction between first order and second order change. First order change was continuous and incremental while second order change was discontinuous and revolutionary. First order change never amounted to substantive change because, in this conceptualization, it generated change within the given system which itself remained unchanged; that is, there was changeability in process but invariance in outcome. The lack of potency of first order change was captured in the French witticism quoted by Watzlawick et al. (1974): 'plus ça change, plus c'est la meme chose' – the more things change, the more they stay the same. This definition of first order change has proved to be pervasive and it effectively means that substantial change is restricted to second order change, in line with the Lewinian perspective.

In their influential review of organizational change literature, Weick and Quinn (1999) adopt this dualism as an organizing framework. They use the term 'episodic change' to group together organizational changes that tend to be infrequent, discontinuous and intentional; that is, second order or point B. The link with Lewin (1952) is clear in that change is understood in terms of unfreeze/change/refreeze. In comparison, continuous change is ongoing, evolving and incremental; that is, first order or point A. The point of difference with Watzlawick et al.'s (1974) understanding of first order change is that while these changes are small, they are cumulative. They add up over time to change that is substantive.

Thus there are two types of change, which each posit different processes and triggers for bringing about change. Historically, episodic change, or second order change, has dominated and it is brought about by a growing realization, or gap with the environment, usually in the form of lapses in performance that trigger radical, second order thinking and change. This is reactive change and the risk is that in complex, dynamic and unpredictable environments there will not be time available to catch up with the environment – to close the gap – before failure. The other type of change is continuous or first order: it happens in anticipation of events, is motivated by curiosity and sensemaking, rather than inertia, and involves incremental innovative changes that are cumulative. First order change can be viewed as taking place within the same set of organizational assumptions, for example health care reforms have typically vested executive authority to non-clinical bureaucracies such as UK National Health Service (NHS) Strategic Health Authorities, maintaining the assumption that the work of clinicians will be controlled by professional managers. Second order change can be viewed as actually changing the organizational assumptions, such as illustrated recently by the British Government's proposal to restructure the NHS through establishing GP Commissioning Consortia.[1] The assumptions in this reform rest upon clinicians taking responsibility for the strategic commissioning and procurement of services in collaboration with other GP practices through consortia and non-clinical service providers within a tightly defined, governance-orientated structure that they lead as clinicians, rather than as professional managers.

A 'smart strategy' for sustained innovation, that bridges first and second order change, therefore needs more than good design; it requires active disturbance at a strategic level that builds behavioural repertoires to maintain active search (Starbuck 1993) and flexible response over a sustained period of time. We propose that such behavioural repertoires can best be considered in terms of the blend of investment in and expectation of people – that is, their employees – so they and the organization are enabled to deliver commitment, enthusiasm and achievement through high performance (see Figure 6.2). Definitions of expectation and investment vary from organization to organization but too much or too little of either, for too long, causes an imbalance for which there are consequences. A typical example in the UK is Marks & Spencer (a long-established, major retail company): it found life too easy, failed to initiate change and flipped from a state of complacency to anxiety as record profit gave way to redundancies and loss of shareholder confidence with all the forced changes in behaviour this engendered.

Maintaining an appropriate mix of expectation and investment in people is an active process. It needs to operate at all levels of an organization, and be contextualized to local need. This is effectively reflected in the linkage of organization values and behaviours through the discipline of formal policy and performance practice – it is simply too important to leave to chance (Colville and Murphy 2006), albeit a difficult balance to achieve and maintain.

Where such equilibrium is achieved, the organization can avoid the either/or

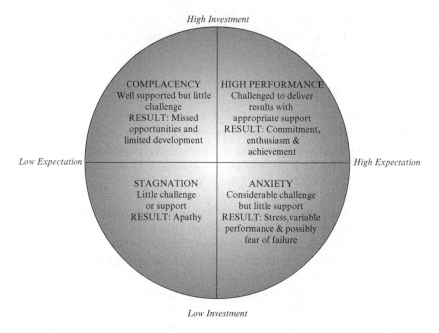

Figure 6.2   Expectation of and investment in people

polarization of slow emergent change or transformative change born out of crisis that is articulated by Weick and Quinn (1999, pp. 365–375) as episodic 'infrequent, discontinuous and intentional' or continuous change that 'tends to be ongoing, evolving and cumulative'. In their longitudinal study of large commercial organizations Johnson et al. (2007) identified a tendency towards 'operational drift'. This research identified many examples of organizational actors who identified and supplied needs or latent needs by innovating goods or services in line with market demands and tuning their organizations to deliver those goods or services in a competitive and timely manner. However, in the longer term (over a period of decades), very few were able to match changes in their business context with appropriate change in their organizations. A bias developed for maintaining custom and practice at the expense of innovation and development. Ultimately such organizations were so far adrift from their business context that they became unsustainable and either transformed or expired.

Sustainable organizational change requires convergent periods where structure, systems, controls and resources are directed towards increased alignment (Romanelli and Tushman 1994). However, organizational change without innovation is sustainability without purpose (long-term failure). Innovation requires 'action persistence' (Weick 1993), commitment that ensures the plausibility of alternatives. Conversely, innovation without change is expediency without sustainability (short-term wins). Thus, these forces appear entirely non-rational and yet they define the dichotomy inherent in Santayana's warning and provide the challenge to managers in the public sector for whom political imperative adds to an already complex environment.

We propose that the literatures of organizational innovation and organizational

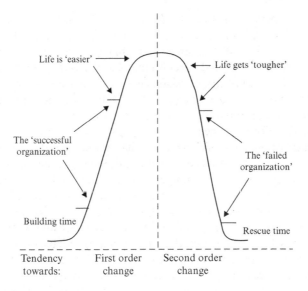

Life is 'easier' ⟶   ⟵ Life gets 'tougher'

The 'successful
organization'

The 'failed
organization'

Building time

Rescue time

Tendency   First order   Second order
towards: change   change

Figure 6.3   Organizational life cycle

change can best be integrated through a sensemaking perspective (Weick 1995). Change is not defined by en*think*ment but rather en*act*ment, we literally act our way into situations (Weick 1979). This process of innovating and changing across time in effect draws attention to the process of moving from how things are currently done to what has to happen for them to be done differently in the future; that is, change and innovation. Building on Handy's (1994) Sigmoid Curve we propose a more exaggerated model that draws together Johnson et al.'s (2007) longitudinal research with tendencies towards first order and second order change taking place at different phases of the organizational life cycle, as depicted in Figure 6.3.

A 'smart strategy' for innovation, as suggested by Bessant and Maher (2009), would include options for first and second order change, but by choice rather than default or financial imperative. Handy (1994) suggests that organizations need to change before they become too comfortable or complacent with success: they need to maintain an edge that keeps them alive to new opportunities. To do this, managers may need to pause, try out new ideas, improvise and innovate, possibly at the expense of sacrificing short-term gains or even popularity to achieve sustained long-term growth. We suggest that smart leaders enable 'smart strategy' by creating the innovation space necessary for long-term success by an active engagement in managing change. They keep their organizations current and their people on their toes – complacency is regarded as an anathema to be sought out and banished; it is a cost that simply cannot be afforded (Conner 1998).

However, a problem may reside in success, to the extent that organizations that experience success for too long, resulting in immutable policies and practices, become increasingly resistant to internal and external pressures for change. They only 'believe it when they see it' – and that is often too late in the way events are unfolding. For example, EMI Recorded Music was unable to recognize the emergent nature of the internet until technology companies rather than music companies controlled content delivery.

It is when an organization is out of balance, out of joint with its environment, that changes need to take place in organization design and associated behaviours. This is especially difficult for successful organizations that have ritualized success by building structures and behaviours designed to retain that success, but by distancing the executive from the customer base and creating resistance through patterns of internal communication. Thus many are not so much caught out by, but caught up in their organizations. Hence such issues are not apparent (why change a winning formula?) because they are not believed, and therefore not seen.

Perhaps not surprisingly, few organizations change ahead of the curve and before they become over-reliant on existing success, as it requires exceptional, innovative managing and organizing to even think about change on the left-hand side of the Sigmoid curve, let alone to pull it off. This gives rise to the need for leaders to consider an alternative to the aphorism: 'if it ain't broke, don't fix it' might instead become 'if it ain't broke, fix it – it's the only time you've got'. This proposition is problematic because, without the benefit of hindsight, knowing where you are on the curve remains indeterminate. Using foresight rather than hindsight means leaders need to use all the resources available to them, and this means the intelligence and ability of their people through whose talents opportunities and threats can be identified, communicated and acted upon. Knowing what and when it is right to change is the holy grail of managers the world over. In the following section, we present an example from the public sector which demonstrated these attributes in the form of the CT unit from within New Scotland Yard (NSY).

CONTEXT AND CASE

Efficiency as a synonym for change has a long history in the public sector, particularly in terms of Whitehall. The term 'efficiency' entered the mainstream lexicon of public sector management in the early years of the Thatcher government. Nevertheless the term is not associated exclusively with one political party, as successive administrations have promoted major change initiatives including: the Financial Management Initiative (1982),[2] Modernising Government (1999),[3] Next Steps (2002)[4] and the Gershon Review (2004).[5] A more recent major initiative, the 2010 Comprehensive Spending Review, is the HM Treasury-led process that allocates public expenditure. In contrast to its predecessors, rather than defining a process of change to achieve efficiency it defines a policy of change (i.e. restraint and cut-backs in public expenditure to re-balance the national debt following the banking collapse in 2007/08 and subsequent recession) across all other reforms.[6]

In May 1997, the Labour Party in the UK was elected to government on a manifesto of change and investment in public services. 'Britain can and must be better: better schools, better hospitals, better ways of tackling crime, of building a modern welfare state, of equipping ourselves for a new world economy.'[7] In May 2010 the newly formed coalition government published its programme of policies and set forth an agenda for reforming public services. The implications of this are that the days of big government are over and that centralization and top-down control have proved a failure.[8]

Hence the UK is in the early stages of still defining further reform of its public services. Previous initiatives highlighted the need for better value for money as a means of driving public sector organizations towards higher levels of efficiency through innovative change to strategy and practice. Now the demand is to create better value whilst also cutting cost and taking people out of public employment: there is little equivocality; money *will* be taken out of the system. And whilst the thrust has been on reducing costs we propose that such efficiencies are born out of new behaviours. Thus change from inefficiency to efficiency needs to be moderated by balancing the actions of people before the balancing of budgets.

Fieldwork

Both authors have conducted research into change and innovation in a variety of both public and private sector organizations over a number of years, working both individually and sometimes jointly on a sum total of 27 investigations. In so doing we have seen that the private sector imperative to make profit or close ensures a bias for action to deliver innovation and change because standing still is not an option: those that do, fail. Many of our research participants in the public sector cite extreme difficulties in delivering change and innovation, including rigid policy and practice, lack of available incentives and poor systems to work with, all resulting in under-performance and too many short-term government reforms that are changed before they are fully implemented and established.

Our public sector research has been conducted in different fields, including central government (such as HM Customs and Excise, HM Foreign Office and HM Home Office), local government and Police Authorities. In this chapter, we draw on a recent example which has arisen from our work in HM Home Office, researching the Counter Terrorism Unit, SO15, of NSY. Over a 6-month period, we conducted semi-structured interviews with the Deputy Assistant Commissioner (DAC) around our core research question of 'how does this organization work to counter terrorism?' He has a lifetime's career experience of working in the police service and CT units, latterly culminating in executive responsibility over the MPS CT unit. Researching in such a secure environment required us to have Home Office security clearance at DV (developed vetting) level. In addition, it meant that collecting and revealing data were more difficult than might be the case in most other organization studies. However, we were allowed to record 12 interviews with the DAC, each lasting between 1.5 and 2 hours, which were transcribed by a security-cleared transcriber. We were also given sight of significant documentary evidence and allowed to gather anecdotal evidence from key personnel within the unit. Data analysis was conducted by both researchers using classic qualitative interview strategies and practices (Miles and Huberman 1994; Silverman 2001; Corbin and Strauss 2008) and shared back with participants. This has also enabled us to cross-check the veracity of our analysis. In the context of this chapter, direct quotation is considered neither necessary nor appropriate for elaborating our findings and analysis with regards to innovation and change. The next section goes on to elaborate our case findings and implications for both theory and practice.

DISCUSSION

There is, inevitably, a gap between theory and practice. Here we seek to bridge it by reference to our case example and further developing theoretical understanding to capture the

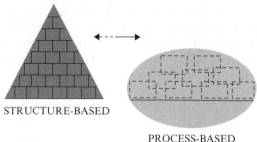

STRUCTURE-BASED

PROCESS-BASED

Figure 6.4   Forms of organizing

complexities of this discussion. In so doing, we offer a simple, but not simplistic, alternative to interpretations inherent to the, now apparently false, aphorisms to which we referred in the first section: 'I'll believe it when I see it' and 'If it ain't broke don't fix it'.

Until 2005, the lead UK police response to the growing threat of international terrorism (the 1993 bombing of the World Trade Centre; the Twin Towers' New York attack in 2001, known as 9/11; the Madrid train bombs of 2005; and the London 7/7 bombings, also in 2005) was coordinated through the CT Branch of the MPS. These attacks increasingly relied upon a specific and, to Western populations, novel form of terrorism (suicide bombing) based upon religious belief rather than political ideology. This phenomenon led to a change of thinking for law enforcement agencies in Western countries, more comfortable with traditional forms of deterrence and criminal intelligence gathering as seen in the republican and loyalist inspired attacks in Northern Ireland through the latter part of the 20th century. The advent of suicide bombing over recent years has its origins and continuance in the social and religious environment of various regions of the world. It is in every sense a tactic that causes maximum anxiety for societies subject to attack. 'Whilst it can be used for strategic outcomes, it is basically a tactic designed for psychological warfare or targeted assassination' (Hutchinson 2007, p. 191).

The question of what strategies may deter risk-taking actors who willingly commit suicide is not only challenging for policy makers but also of significant importance to those who have to carry out those policies as 'terrorists employ asymmetric methods against adversaries they cannot match militarily' (Malet 2008, p. 723). Put another way, by changing the pattern of attack, the terrorist organization seeks to stay one step ahead of the organization which is trying to counter and, hence, nullify each new move. Change and novelty, such as the advent of suicide bombing, have to be met with a changed and novel counter-response. However, that is difficult to achieve in a public sector bureaucracy.

The broad structure and mandate of the police service in the UK can be traced to the formation of the MPS in 1829. It was, and remains, a largely uniformed organization regulated internally by a code of discipline that formalizes relationships between different ranks within hierarchical boundaries. It fits comfortably within our structure-based graphic (see Figure 6.4), evidenced by a job for life (or at least until pensionable service has been reached),[9] information flows along vertical lines, tightly regulated behaviour and many levels of responsibility, each clearly denoted by formal badges of rank that mirror those of the British Army. This is a classic Weberian bureaucracy which provides

Table 6.1   Characteristic behaviours associated with different forms of organizing

Behaviour characteristic of structure-based organizing	Behaviour characteristic of process-based organizing
• Individual position/job as basic unit of organization	• Team as basic unit
• Relations with environment handled by specialist boundary-spanners	• Densely networked with environment
• Vertical flows of information	• Horizontal and vertical flows of information
• Decisions come down, information flows up	• Decisions made where information resides
• Tall (many layers of management)	• Flat (few layers of management)
• Emphasis on structures	• Emphasis on processes
• Emphasis on rules and standard procedures	• Emphasis on results and outcomes
• Career paths upward, linear	• Career paths horizontal, non-linear
• Single strong culture with strong expectations of behaviour	• Diversity of viewpoints and behaviours

Source: Adapted from Ancona et al. (2005).

the organizational structural template on which many public sector organizations are based. They are designed for efficiency through the standardization of work processes and find it difficult to adjust or change (Mintzberg 1992). When they do change, it tends to be driven by inertia, taking place episodically and in line with the Lewin model (point B in Figure 6.1). This kind of structural analysis also fails to reflect that it is people who embody organization, not structures.

By the 1980s, it had become apparent that increasingly complex structural forms that had enabled organizations to grow had come at a cost: 'As their label clearly warns, divisions divide. The divisional model fragmented companies' resources; it created vertical communication channels that insulated business units and prevented them from sharing their strengths with one another' (Ghoshal and Bartlett 1995, p. 88). Most organizational change in recent times reflects a shift along the continuum from left to right in Figure 6.4, as the shape of the future transforms, regardless of sector, from one of mass production and structure-based bureaucracy to mass innovation and process-driven efficiency. Behaviours associated with both forms of change *in* organizations are indicated in Table 6.1. The structure-based form and characteristic behaviours tend to reflect the attitude which has 'seen it all before' and, as a consequence, has established routines and recipes for dealing with situations. They are often associated with bureaucratic organizations. The problem is that this organizational form has difficulty seeing change in the environment. Often, as we have suggested, it is only seen when it is too late, or events, sometimes tragically, reveal that the assumptions on which the organization was acting no longer hold.

In the realm of CT, the 9/11 Commission Report (2004, p. 348) says: 'The terrorism fostered by bin Laden and al Qaeda was different from anything the government had faced before . . . Its crimes were on a scale approaching acts of war, but they were committed by a loose, far-flung, nebulous conspiracy, with no territories or citizens or assets that could be readily threatened, overwhelmed, or destroyed.' Thus CT agencies were prepared for and on the alert for signs of the past: unprepared for and unaware of signals of an emerging, changing present. The Commission concluded that the attacks of 9/11 revealed four kinds of failure – in imagination, policy, capabilities and management (2004, p. 339) – reserving its most stinging criticism for a failure in organizational rather than individual imagination. Such imagination – that is, an organizational form and culture which facilitate innovation – is not a gift usually associated with bureaucracies. Nevertheless, the Commission noted: 'it is crucial to find ways of routinizing even bureaucratizing the exercise of imagination' (2004, p. 334).

One way to do this is to create an organizational form that is based more on process than structure, as illustrated in Figure 6.4, and which has the characteristic behaviours denoted in Table 6.1. As the nature of the terrorist threat changed, this is effectively what took place inside NSY and outside, as it became more densely networked with security and intelligence services throughout the world. This had the effect of shifting traditional roles and assumptions to become more attuned to working in complex and fast-moving contexts. The innovation is to create an organization that is capable of seeing and responding to changes in the environment in a timely manner. However, creating the structure is not sufficient to enable this to happen. The DAC sought to encourage his staff to experience novel events and to learn how to accommodate to them swiftly and effectively. We found three particularly illustrative examples of this in our data:

- In the early hours of Sunday 31 August 1997, the Assistant Commissioner for Special Operations at MPS telephoned and woke his senior CT team and informed them of the death of the Princess of Wales in Paris. He instructed them to deal with the international focus on the UK and public response to the death. He did not know what that would entail but, correctly, anticipated a huge media response that would drive the nature and scale of the subsequent events.
- Within 24 hours of the Bali night club bombings of 2002, CT officers flew to Indonesia where they worked with the intelligence services of the USA and Australia to support the Indonesian authorities in coordinating the hunt for the bombers and securing evidence from the devastated crime scene.
- Immediately following the Indian Ocean earthquake and tsunami in 2004, CT officers were deployed to South East Asia where they played a vital role in victim identification, often using advanced forensic techniques.

It is now normal routine for UK SO15 CT officers to attend significant global events, whether or not linked to terrorist activity. They go to share expertise as part of a responsible international response but they also go to learn from and experience complex environments. In so doing they have extended their behavioural repertoire to the more adroit behaviours that we might expect to be found in our process-orientated model (see Figure 6.4).

Indeed, as our case illustrates, people were, individually and collectively, encouraged to develop behaviours more characteristic of process-based organizing at every level. For example, the Assistant Commissioner showed clearly that he expected high levels of commitment from his officers, was intolerant of what he regarded as sloppy behaviours, and insisted that boundaries were challenged if they got in the way of effective policing. In return, he always supported his officers by providing them with opportunities to learn and grow, he challenged them to be the best they could be and provided a supportive environment to ensure that this was possible.

Thus CT officers give consideration to unknown challenges yet to come and develop actions that ensure a continuous search for new trends and network opportunities. They deliberately engage in messy, poorly defined environments, not always knowing what they may learn or add but always knowing that such insight may benefit their responsibilities, even if it is not immediately apparent. They understand the cost of engaging in novel situations but they also appreciate the benefits to long-term sustainable innovation.

Our case demonstrates an organization in which people were anticipating rather than reacting to change and, as such, were driven not by inertia but by curiosity. This is the type of change that takes place at point A on the Sigmoid Curve and is supported by more process-orientated organization, as depicted in the circle form in Figure 6.4 – a form of organization in which 'change never starts because it never stops' (Weick and Quinn 1999, p. 381). If, as we have suggested, the environment will be increasingly typified by dynamic complexity (Farjoun 2010), then organizations which wait for inertia to trigger change will be too late to change. Thus we conclude that to adapt to future environmental circumstances, organizations will have to become innovative in how they carry out *continuous change*. At the same time, theorizing change will also have to innovate to account for the practice of continuous change rather than episodic change (see, for example, Tsoukas and Chia (2002) for the beginnings of such a reappraisal).

Here then is a tightly regulated public sector organization providing an example of innovative change. A common aim was identified: the protection from terrorism of UK citizens wherever they resided, during a period of sustained and growing threat that could, had it not been met robustly, have led to a succession of increasingly violent attacks. Organizational members were encouraged to challenge their own thinking and that of others; they were often deployed into situations far outside their comfort zones but were then expected to bring new learning to colleagues. A process of creative disturbance, in effect innovating and changing, was encouraged. People felt challenged but also supported.

Organizations tend to be a blend, transcending a simple either/or model. It is, however, possible to recognize, and indeed influence, the routine behaviour or bias that, on the left, might be suited to a more stable environment and, on the right, a more dynamic environment. As with any bias, there are tradeoffs – stability for adroitness, focus for flexibility, simplicity for complexity, and so on. It therefore follows that the nature of the organization needs to reflect the environment in which it operates if it is to thrive. The key lies in finding the balance between flexibility and stability. Complex environments cannot be fully engaged and understood by holding faith with established routines and meanings as they require requisite variety and active discrediting (Weick 1979), meeting complex situations with complex thinking. This necessitates enabling an environment where such behaviours can thrive. Hence organizations need managers who reflect this through the organizing of their visions and work practices, whilst also recognizing the need to provide adequate support for their people.

Birkinshaw et al. (2008, p. 826) argue that management innovation is a particular form of organizational change that involves 'a novel or unprecedented departure from the past'. We demur not from the spirit of this definition but instead, the letter. SO15 had to deal with novelty, or requisite variety, and introduced management practice that was an unprecedented departure from the past. In this case, wholeheartedly adopting Birkinshaw et al.'s (2008) definition could 'bias' our theorizing about change, and consequently management innovation, away from a processual understanding of continuous change towards a Lewinian view. However, through the analysis we have developed and expounded in this section, we are theoretically equipped to see innovation in the form of change at point A which helps dovetail innovation and change. From this, we conclude that a future research agenda for this field of interest should develop further an understanding of the interrelationship between innovation and change by exploring more closely the way in which individuals interpret, act and ascribe meaning to the world, in making sense of this complex, social, organizational process (McCabe, quoted in Birkinshaw et al., 2008, p. 829). In other words, this is how, as theorists and practitioners of organizational change and innovation, we stay abreast of events and make sense of the world.

CONCLUSION

In sum, how SO15 organizes itself through continuous change and innovation stands as an example and a challenge to both theory and practice. It stands as an example of the type of organizational form that is fitted to environments that are suffused by dynamic complexity and which we suggest will be the contexts in which all organizations will have to contend. It also illustrates the type of change that will be called for and the motors for change that will be required. Continuous changing driven by imagination and curiosity will have to predominate over episodic change driven by inertia and anxiety for the simple reason that dynamic complexity will mean that change driven by inertial lag will create a gap that will be beyond most organizations' ability to close in time.

   This is as much of a challenge to theories of organizational change and innovation as it is to the skills of those leading and managing change in practice. Innovation involves not just thinking differently but also doing differently. This is why innovation is bound up with the practice of change management. As the public sector comes under increasing and continuous pressure to innovate, the ability to manage change becomes a core skill. We have argued in this chapter that organizations will have to move towards forms that can cope with increasing levels of environmental complexity and dynamism. A number of models and heuristics have been outlined which aid our understanding of what is involved in the practice of change management and how it can be accomplished. To this we have added a more detailed analysis, from which we develop the notion of continuous innovatory change. We conclude that this offers heuristics for the 'doing' rather than a recipe of how to do it: there is no recipe for change management or innovation. As such, they function more as compass bearings providing direction rather than a map. Maps help in known worlds – worlds that have been chartered before. However, here we are dealing with a 'brave new world' (i.e. challenging), the shape and direction of which are still emerging. Amidst this dynamic complexity, we conclude that effective innovation and change management require skilful ability to remember the past without being a slave to it whilst being open to the shock of a new order.

NOTES

1. *Equity and Excellence: Liberating the NHS: Commissioning for Patients.* DoH 2010.
2. The Financial Management Initiative (*Efficiency and Effectiveness in the Civil Service*) was launched in September 1982 as an umbrella for the efficiency scrutiny programme and with a wider focus on corporate planning, efficiency and objective setting.
3. *Modernising Government White Paper* (1999): This White Paper sets out an agenda for modernising government which is predominantly based on the assumption that all policy making should be 'evidence-based'.
4. *Delivering the NHS Plan: next steps on investment, next steps on reform.* In this document the Secretary of State for Health presented a progress report on the NHS Plan. He detailed what had been achieved to date and the programme of changes yet to come. Achievements to this point and planned changes to the programme were detailed.
5. On 14 July 2004 HM Treasury published what is known as the 'Gershon report' (*Releasing Resources to the Front Line - Independent Review of Public Sector Efficiency*). The report identifies efficiency measures which by 2008 will produce annual savings of some £21b.
6. As an indicator of the extreme nature of UK public sector debt, in 2010 the UK Government spent £43 billion (i.e. £120 million per day) on interest charges on its debts.
7. *New Labour because Britain deserves better.* Labour Party manifesto 1997, p. 3.
8. *The Coalition: our programme for government.* Programme for policy between the Conservative and Liberal Democrat parties coalition government, 2010.
9. All warranted police officers in the UK are servants of the Crown and once they have completed 2 years' probationary service they cannot be dismissed, or made redundant unless in breach of the disciplinary code.

REFERENCES

9/11 Commission Report (2004). *The Full Final Report of the National Commission on Terrorist Attacks upon the United States.* Boston: W.W. Norton and Co.

Ancona, D., Kochan, T., Scully, J., Van Maanen, J. and Westley, F. (2005). *Managing for the Future: Organizational Behavior and Processes,* 4th ed. Cincinatti, OH: South-Western, Division of Thomson Learning.

Bechky, B.A. and Okhuysen, G.A. (2011). Expecting the unexpected? How swat officers and film crews handle surprises. *Academy of Management Journal,* 54, 239–261.

Bessant, J. and Maher, L. (2009). Developing radical service innovations in healthcare – the role of design methods. *International Journal of Innovation Management,* 13(4), 555–568.

Birkinshaw, J.M., Hamel, G. and Mol, M. (2008). Management innovation. *Academy of Management Review,* 33(4), 825–845.

Colville, I.D. and Murphy, A.J. (2006). Leadership as the enabler of strategizing and organizing. *Long Range Planning,* 39, 663–677.

Conner, D.R. (1998). *Leading at the Edge of Chaos: How to Create the Nimble Organization.* London: John Wiley and Sons.

Corbin, J. and Strauss, A. (2008). *The Basics of Qualitative Research,* 4th ed. London: Sage.

Cuhna, M.P., Clegg, S.R. and Kamoche, K. (2006). Surprises in management and organization: concept, sources and a typology. *British Journal of Management,* 17, 316–329.

Delivering the NHS Plan: Next Steps on Investment, Next Steps on Reform (2000). London: HM Department of Health, Cm 5503.

Farjoun, M. (2010). Beyond dualism: stability and change as a duality. *Academy of Management Review,* 35, 202–225.

Financial Management Initiative Efficiency and Effectiveness in the Civil Service (1982). London: Her Majesty's Home Civil Service, Cmnd 8616.

Gershon Review: Releasing Resources to the Front Line – Independent Review of Public Sector *Efficiency.* (2004), London: HM Treasury. Available at: http://www.nao.org.uk/publications/0506/improving_government_efficienc.aspx

Ghoshal, S. and Bartlett, C.A. (1995). Changing the role of top management: beyond structure to process. *Harvard Business Review,* Jan–Feb., 86–96.

Handy, C. (1994). *The Empty Raincoat.* London: Hutchinson.

Hargrave, T. and Van de Ven, A.H. (2006). A collective model of organizational innovation. *Academy of Management Review,* 31, 864–888.

Hendry, C. (1996). Understanding and creating whole organizational change through learning theory. *Human Relations*, 49, 621–641.

Hutchinson, W. (2007). The systemic roots of suicide bombing. *Systems Research and Behavioral Science* 24(2), 191–200.

Johnson, G., Scholes, K. and Whittington, R. (2007). *Exploring Corporate Strategy*. London: Prentice Hall.

Kotter, J.P. (1995). Leading change: why transformation change efforts fail. *Harvard Business Review*, March–April, 59–66.

Leadbeater, C. (2004). *Personalisation Through Participation*. London: Demos.

Lewin, K. (1952). *Field Theory in Social Science: Selected Theoretical Papers by Kurt Lewin*. New York: Harper and Row.

Malet, D. (2008). Faith in the system: conceptualizing grand strategy in the post 9/11 world order. *Studies in Conflict and Terrorism*, 31(8), 723–735.

Miles, M.B. and Huberman, M. (1994). *Qualitative Data Analysis,* 2nd ed. London: Sage.

Mintzberg, H. (1992). *Structure in Fives: Designing Effective Organizations*. Englewood Cliffs, NJ: Prentice-Hall.

Modernising Government (1999). London: HM Cabinet Office, Cm 4310.

Pfeffer, J. (1997). *New Directions for Organizational Theory: Problems and Prospects.* Oxford: Oxford University Press.

Poole, M.A. and Van de Ven, A.H. (eds) (2004). *The Handbook of Organizational Change and Innovation.* Oxford: Oxford University Press.

Romanelli, E. and Tushman, M. (1994). Transformation as punctuated equilibrium. *Academy of Management Journal*, 37, 1141–1158.

Santayana, G. (1905/2006). *The Life of Reason, Vol. 1*. New York: Charles Scribner Publishing.

Schein, E.H. (1996). *Organizational Leadership and Change*. London: Sage.

Silverman, D. (2001). *Interpreting Qualitative Data: Methods for Analysing Talk, Text and Interaction*, 2nd ed. London: Sage.

Starbuck, W.H. (1993). Strategizing in the real world. *International Journal of Technology Management*, 8, 77–85.

Tsoukas, H. and Chia, R. (2002). Organizational becoming: rethinking organizational change. *Organization Science*, 13, 567–582.

Van de Ven, A.N. and Poole, M.S. (1995). Explaining development in organizations. *Academy of Management Review*, 31, 864–888.

Watzlawick, P., Weakland, J.H. and Fisch, R. (1974). *Change: Principles of Problem Formation and Problem Resolution.* New York: W.W. Norton and Co.

Weick, K.E. (1979). *The Social Psychology of Organizing*, 2nd ed. Reading: Addison-Wesley.

Weick, K.E. (1993). Sensemaking in organizations: small structures with large consequences. In J.K. Murningham (ed.), *Social Psychology in Organizations*. Englewood Cliffs, NJ: Prentice Hall, pp. 10–37.

Weick, K.E. (1995). *Sensemaking in Organizations.* London: Sage.

Weick, K.E. (2001). *Making Sense of the Organization*. Oxford: Blackwell.

Weick, K.E. (2009). *Making Sense of the Organization, Vol. 2.* Oxford: Blackwell.

Weick, K.E. and Quinn, R.E. (1999). Organizational change and development. *Annual Review of Psychology*, 50, 361–386.

Weick, K.E. and Sutcliffe, K.M. (2007). *Managing the Unexpected*. San Francisco, CA: Jossey-Bass.

7. Managing the change process: the state of the art
Kerry Brown and Jennifer Waterhouse

INTRODUCTION

The change management processes involved in providing a coherent framework to enable implementation of innovation in the public sector reflect both contemporary trends in organisational change management and changes to public service organisations. Managing the change process and implementing appropriate change programmes require understanding of the operating environment of modern public services, as these do not remain stable but undergo flux according to new influences and structures. State of the art change management programmes may then align with the latest operating frameworks and modes or seek to create new or hybrid contexts for public services.

Further, the public sector context is challenging for implementing change management initiatives as the bureaucratic governance framework of public services may work against change and communication about change, resulting in change fatigue (Frahm and Brown 2007). The public services context, while capable of delivering highly innovative initiatives, however, may be particularly resistant to change (Brown and Keast 2005). A critical warning for organisations contemplating undergoing organisational change is that organisational change management programmes are prone to high failure rates (Beer and Nohria 2000).

This chapter considers the drivers for change and examines consequent public services structures and management to deliver the new agenda. It outlines change initiatives within these structures and examines the ways in which public services have implemented change. The outcomes and implications for practice are discussed and assessed. Early work by Dunphy and Stace (1990) supports the link between the ability of an organisation to innovate and adapt to change, and its overall effectiveness and continued viability. The policy and practice for public services also maintain a stance that the purpose of change management is to develop an attitude or context in which innovation may be developed. Change management in the public sector is an important adaptation faculty to develop the path to a new desired alternative and also achieve effectiveness and a climate of innovation. Innovation and change are critical and interlinked phenomena in contemporary public services.

CHANGES IN PUBLIC SERVICES

Understanding organisational change in public services requires analysing key change imperatives and characteristics. These feature first a shift from an internal to an external public service orientation. Traditional public service organisational structures were characterised by internally focused institutional arrangements such as internal labour markets, a career service built on promotion by seniority and functional silos to allow specialisation (Caiden 1999; Brown 2008). These conventional frames have been transformed through an externalisation of public services in implementing contractual arrangements for workers and service delivery, macro-level policy and service initiatives broadly formed into 'joined up' action and networked governance arrangements.

'Collaboration' is a term frequently used by Canadian, Australian and UK governments and foreshadows one of the most significant changes in public service orientation and operation (Waterhouse et al. 2011). Moreover, emergent arrangements represent a move to a new framework that marks a distinct shift from prior adversarial, contractual and market-oriented approaches to one that is focused on sharing risk and reward, operating on relational principles, getting the services delivered or complex project completed without a narrow focus on the bottom line, and managing through personal relationships rather than designated authority or legal specification (Ryan et al. 2005; Keast et al. 2006).

The chapter outlines and analyses these shifts. It also explores the different change management approaches. The effect on public service delivery, public policy making and the future of the 'public-ness' of services is considered.

THEORIES OF CHANGE

Theories of change in the public sector are argued to be premised on organisational transformation comprising large-scale, planned administrative change (Fernandez and Rainey 2006). However, DiMaggio and Powell's (1983) seminal work on institutional isomorphism is a common theoretical basis for change being directed at creating organisations that are similar by adopting and replicating one organisation's or sector's structures, practices and processes into another organisation or sector. Isomorphism, then, is the way that new approaches are diffused throughout a social arena or across the globe, with one organisation adopting a novel model and others copying each new element or application as it becomes public knowledge.

Ashworth et al. (2007) also put forward that institutional theory may provide critical theoretical insights into change management and conclude that the objective of change is not necessarily better organisational performance outcomes but greater legitimacy, particularly through *compliance* to stakeholder expectations. Building new institutional arrangements in response to change management programmes is not a new phenomenon; however, the use of compliance regimes for change, especially in response to stakeholders, provides a new orientation to change management approaches. This theoretical proposition starts to align changes to bureaucratic intention but from the perspective of external influences and relations.

Gersick (1991) developed an early response to understanding a new ethos of change within organisations as a shift from incrementalism to the theory of punctuated equilibrium states that following a long period of stability, change is sudden and complete, moving from one paradigm to another. These models of change have implications for understanding programmes for managing change. Gersick (1991) alerts us to the possibility that change is achieved by fundamentally altering organisations and their underpinning values and operational bases swiftly and dramatically. Accepting the punctuated equilibrium model of change for public services, then, would align change management programmes with this framework. The implication is that change management pro-grammes should not simply adopt a rational planning approach but a strategic outlook that allows for ambiguity and adaptability to volatile contexts after a long period of stability.

The underpinning frameworks of these different theories of change according to Fernandez and Rainey (2006) affect the capacity of managers to bring about change in organisations. Change may be internally or externally generated, or effected from top down or bottom up within organisations. The ability of managerial-level organisational members to develop and implement successful change programmes will be contingent on these different elements. Significant theoretical development and empirical research has examined various change models. However, Van de Ven and Poole (1995) identify that no single model sufficiently explains the complex reality of organisational change and there remains little understanding of how different change drivers combine to bring about change.

THE DRIVERS FOR CHANGE MANAGEMENT IN PUBLIC SERVICES

While economic pressures and the search for greater market efficiency are well-recognised drivers for change in public services, Wise (2002) contended that other values also drive change to public sector operation and services provision. Citing evidence from a cross-national comparison of public sector change, Wise (2002) suggested that demands for social equity, democratisation and empowerment, and an emphasis on quality of working life and engagement were also drivers of change in public services. Since that time, market efficiency drivers have given way to cross-sectoral arrangements between government and private and non-profit or community sectors although economic stress remains a critical driver of change. This focus from Wise (2002), however, consolidated the stand-point that other social and human-centred considerations apart from fiscal prescriptions for understanding public sector change could be derived.

Considerable changes have occurred in public sectors globally in that most have moved from New Public Management (NPM) to models that adopt a network approach and associated governance framework (Kettl 2000; Dunleavy et al. 2005). Dunleavy et al. (2005) specifically refer to digital era governance and the adoption of new principles of reintegration, needs-based holism such as exemplified in 'one stop shops'. This approach foreshadows the advent of both the digital era of e-government and of greater collabora-tive mechanisms for public service provision. Kelman (2007) offered that inter-organisational collaboration between both the non-profit and for-profit sectors, and the public sector is one of the key changes facing public services. Drivers for change, then, are pressures to operate across different sectors in collaborative frameworks.

Further, however, at the same time there has been a critical path to develop innovation capacity within public sectors. The drive to collaboration is identified not only by linking sectors, but is a key plank in the innovation agenda. Change management programmes are also identified as important ways of developing a culture of innovation.

The identified studies undertaken in the mid-2000s pointed to the beginning of cross-sector engagement, followed by policy prescription and programmatic intent for change management to achieve this engagement, and heralded an emergent paradigm developed under the rubric of collaboration. While NPM remained the dominant framework for most of the decade and traces of NPM were evident into the next decade, the shift to externalisation of public service activity altered significantly the underpinning principles of public service operation. It is argued that this trend has come to be one of the most significant changes in culture and organisation for public services. Gersick's (1991) contention that the applicable theory underpinning public sector change may be closer to the theory of punctuated equilibrium rather than bureaucratic stability or the theory of isomorphism may provide a critical standpoint here.

In a speech to the Canadian Public Sector Conference in November 2011, the Executive Director of the Administrative Services Review within the Privy Council Office, Wilma Vreeswijk, cited *multiple, sequential and simultaneous* change as significantly impacting the delivery of public services in Canada (Vreeswijk, 2011). The multiplexity of change in public services, then, requires change models that can deal with this level of complexity.

The pace, scale and scope of change programmes in public services and public service organisations are important but under-researched elements of the way in which public services change may be conceptualised and implemented. It has been argued that empirical evidence of the impact of change pace is lacking (Amis et al. 2004). Issues of the scale of change are pertinent in public services, and change efforts range from large-scale or disruptive *transformational* change to small-scale and step-wise *incremental* change models (Osborne and Brown 2005).

Transformational Change

Transformational change is contended to be radical and innovative and to demonstrate a deep and significant departure from accepted ways of organisational operation and management (Kleiner and Walter 1989). Nutt and Backoff (1997), in their study of facilitation of organisational change, contend that the scale and scope of change required to manage modern organisations result in a requirement for large-scale change to fundamentally shift an organisation. This 'fundamental shift' is at the base of transformational change.

Incremental Change

As outlined by Ashworth et al. (2007) incremental models of change suggest that change should be implemented in a gradual, 'step-wise' manner. Nutt (1992) conceptualises *deep change* as transformational change that creates new knowledge and ways of acting and interacting. This framework is contrasted with incremental change, which is argued to be change that is processual, easily reversed and does not afford lasting or immutable change.

While large-scale transformational change is a common goal of organisational change management efforts, research findings indicate that incremental change is the usual outcome of change initiatives (Pettigrew et al. 2001). This finding suggests that change efforts concentrating on transformational change models may underestimate the enormity of the task or fail to achieve the large-scale change required. Van de Ven and Poole (1995) offer research findings on process theories of organisational change that introduce the concept of multiple change processes happening simultaneously, or variously embedded within each other, and put forward a model of continuous change. Change models that are episodic, one-off change events may not capture and resolve the required change complexity or address issues relating to the enduring nature of change.

CHANGING CHANGE MODELS

Lewin's (1952) early model of change in organisations relied on the presumption that successful organisational change proceeds in three steps: 'unfreezing', 'moving' and 'freezing'. Locking in the change was considered an important aspect of change action. Many contemporary change models operate on the basis of this three step process (Waddell et al. 2004). Kotter (1998) also offers a form of planned change, with identified processes to guide change. However, the complexity of the change may create difficulty for ensuring the time required for Lewin's (1952) third step of 'refreezing' is undertaken to embed the change within an organisation.

Changing organisational structures may provide some critical avenues to understand and enact organisational change in public sector organisations. However, we argue that the deeper change at the level of culture provides a surer and strengthened organisational response to change. Organisational culture is a slippery concept but is generally thought of as 'the way we do things around here', as suggested by Deal and Kennedy (1982). Addressing culture is critical when organisations seek to transform or reinvent themselves to address major changes in their environment.

Brown et al. 2003, in a study of organisational change, outline an intermediate change programme that follows a hybrid model. The approach is based on aligning with government priorities as a political risk mitigation strategy, retaining some bureaucratic aspects such as conforming to existing rules and regulations. However, it also introduces relational elements of community and stakeholder engagement along with new forms of communicative competencies such as organisational storytelling (Brown et al. 2003). This hybrid mix of planned change and bureaucratic observance of changing rules within prescribed guidelines with novel and less-well-defined relational and stakeholder change approaches provided a middle way to approach change management.

While collaboration across public service organisations and with other sectors has been a clear new direction in services delivery that has implications for the content and format of change management within public services, collaboration first requires new collaborative competencies to initiate and implement requisite structures and governance arrangements. The impetus for setting up collaborative approaches centres on the potential for developing innovation or innovative responses to demands on public services to be responsive, reduce costs and deliver goods and services that resolve complex problems. That new forms of governance are required is outlined by Bingham et al. (2005), who noted that new processes and structures aligning with collaboration were required. New types of interaction identified by Bingham et al. (2005) were deliberative democracy, e-democracy, public conversations, budgets set through participatory processes, citizen juries, collaborative policy making and other types of dialogue-driven activities.

Wheatley's (1994) research into new types of organisations examined how organisational life could be characterised as organic, self-organising systems. Wheatley (1994) contended that core organisational competencies for dealing with complex situations should focus on relationship building and networking, and in teams to build trust and quality relationships. Further, the skills for advancing a change agenda in a chaotic, volatile environment are an ability to plan for an unknown future, to develop and promote conversation and storytelling capabilities, and establish meaningful intra-organisational relationships (Wheatley 1994). Ashworth et al.'s (2007) study of Best Value in the UK indicated that structural isomorphism is the critical approach to diffusion of change in the public sector.

In summary, genuine organisational change is described as transformation involving:

- The creation of new organisational forms at a collective level.
- The creation of new roles at an organisational level.
- The reconfiguration of power relations, especially the formation of new leadership groups, and the creation of a new culture, ideology and organisational meaning.

Public sector organisations adopt different types of change as managers develop different ideas about how to undergo change processes. Many enact change from the top but others draw on the experiences of those at the lower organisational ranks to become involved in change programmes. Many changes are simply 'organic' in that change has emerged slowly as a result of the passage of time or as a result of contextual changes in the broader political, social and business environment over which public service organisations exert little or no control.

DIFFUSION OF CHANGE

Change studies have evidenced a number of different strategies that can be adopted when undertaking change. We suggest there is a suite of 'mix and match' elements that can be considered when undertaking change. Table 7.1 outlines these different elements to demonstrate that all the different aspects can be offered as part of a programme of change, depending on change objectives. Not all change is transformational; that is, not all change has a clear strategic direction and works in a planned, 'event-like' manner towards the achievement of that goal. Indeed, change in organisations generally goes through short periods of transformational, rapid change followed by periods of greater stability where there is some low-level change occurring. This mode of change aligns with

Table 7.1   Mix and match change elements

Leadership style	Change drivers	Pace of change	View of change	Scope
Transformational	Top down Coercive Inspirational	Slow	As an event	Individual unit
Transactional	Bottom up Participative	Rapid	As ongoing and continuous	Large division Organisation wide

Gersick's (1991) proposition that punctuated equilibrium is an appropriate theory to understand change in public services.

While change is a clear imperative for organisations and there are many change programmes underway for public services, successful change management is less evident. The reasons for this problematic relationship between change management programmes and their successful conclusion is next discussed.

BARRIERS TO CHANGE

There are many reasons for the inability of change management programmes to be implemented successfully. Apart from inadequately implemented change programmes, participants may experience change fatigue, namely large-scale change occurring simultaneously with multiple small-change events (Frahm and Brown 2007). The ongoing nature of change often results in limited success as there is 'no end' to the change process together with the over-communication and over-management of change. Failure to realise change objectives then has a negative effect on employees' ability to accept proposed future changes. Over-communication of small-change events was identified as counter-productive to encouraging employees to participate in and embrace change, being tiresome for organisational members (Bokeno and Gantt 2000; Brown et al. 2003). In their case study of public sector change, Frahm and Brown (2007) found that work groups were not accepting of the term 'continuous change' as the framework for their change management programmes and reframed the concept, preferring 'continuous improvement' instead.

Doyle et al. (2000) argue that public service organisations experience greater difficulty than the private sector in implementing change due to the unique nature of the public service operating without recourse to the profit motive and requiring impartial, consistent outcomes.

ISSUES IN SUCCESSFULLY MANAGING CHANGE IN PUBLIC SERVICES

Common factors identified by the Queensland Public Service Commission (no date) for successful change management are:

- Planning and identifying objectives for the change.
- Governance in place to support the altered arrangements.
- Committed leadership to guide the change.
- Informed stakeholders by consultative communication to participate and commit to the change.
- Aligned workforce to ensure the new structures match workplace arrangements for employees.

These factors are common to many change agendas, especially identifying objectives, leadership, informed stakeholders and 'thick' communication. New elements include the alignment of change with new structures and processes and change governance. The change management governance arrangements offer an important and often neglected aspect of change management. The suggested governance arrangements are aimed at establishing the requisite rules, responsibilities and structures within the organisations undergoing change to oversee the change. Suggestions of a steering committee, change sponsor, change agent and 'work stream owners' offer a hierarchical structure for change governance, and while these roles may have utility for successful change programmes, the framework is purposefully built on a system of hierarchical authority. Further, the principles of change outlined by the Queensland public sector remain focused on a sequential mode of operating to develop a change approach.

PROSCI is a planned system of change that relies on set steps and processes to bring about change (http://www.change-management.com/). It has been used across public sectors including state government departments. A fundamental part of the change process in PROSCI is the people element of change and a key strategy has been to teach staff how to implement changes themselves. Similar to the steps outlined by the Queensland Public Service Commission (no date) for successful change management programmes, this programme is a planned programme of change that has been utilised by public sector agencies.

Successful change management programmes are increasingly examined in terms of the ability to address complex and cross-cutting issues and cross-sectoral arrangements. Moreover, innovation in public services has been identified as the key to developing a standpoint or perspective that assists public services to meet the challenges of tight budgets, greater participation by citizens and the requirement for novel ways of services provision, especially in relation to e-government and technology.

THE WAY OF THE FUTURE FROM THE PRESENT: CHANGE MANAGEMENT IN PUBLIC SERVICES

Change management in public services has been consciously articulated to cross-sectoral approaches and acknowledged to be reliant on cooperation with other sectors for success. Prescriptions for change are embedded in the innovation stances of public services, and change and innovation are both driven by central agencies within the public sector. The 'state of the art' of change management indicates a focus on collaboration ability and implementing new forms of interaction by citizens with public services.

The European Innovation Union is an example of the new thinking in innovation and the way in which innovative change management can support innovation. Instituted in October 2010, as part of the Europe 2020 programme to build economic growth and jobs through innovation, the European Innovation Union also has an objective of building better relationships between different sectors, as it relies on public sector and private interaction to develop an innovation framework.

The United Kingdom is an acknowledged leader in public sector innovation. The British government established the Better Regulation Executive that seeks to improve regulation by offering a web portal that citizens, public sector employees, non-profit organisational members and the private sector can use to respond to innovative ideas to reduce impacts or improve regulations (http:www.betterregulation.gov.uk). Issues are logged and addressed through the web portal. This initiative links to engendering change through information technology and was foreshadowed by authors such as Dunleavy et al. (2005) and West (2004).

The Australian government has spent considerable effort on the necessary change management approaches and programmes for innovation. Priority 1 of the *Powering Ideas* agenda (Commonwealth of Australia 2009) establishes a principle that supports high-quality research, and the second and third priorities focus on skills development and commercialisation of research. However, priorities 5, 6 and 7 of the Australian Innovation System focus on cross-sector, cross-institutional collaboration to deliver innovation (Commonwealth of Australia 2009). The developed *Innovation Action Plan for the Australian Public Sector* (Department of Industry, Innovation, Science and Research, 2011) following the Cutler Report on Innovation (Cutler 2008), *Powering Ideas* (Commonwealth of Australia 2009) and *Empowering Change* (Management Advisory Board, 2010) offers collaboration, experimentation and an ongoing learning approach as well as new technologies to support innovation. These are also the embedded change management approaches to deliver innovation. However, change management to deliver innovation is recognised by the Management Advisory Board (2010) as inherently risky due to its experimental approach, its perceived lack of adherence to principles of good public administration and its anti-hierarchical operational standpoint. The challenge is to develop a culture of innovation through change management programmes that are open to the possibilities of innovation as set out by the Management Advisory Board (2010) to improve productivity in a context of declining government expenditure.

CONCLUSIONS

The state of the art in managing the change processes of public services combines prior understanding of successful change management as residing in change actors and processes that align to public services structures and institutions, following from the work of Ashworth et al. (2007) and Gersick (1991). Some change programmes implemented within the public sector still rely on the precepts of Lewin's change model with modern updates. The existence of these underpinning principles for the programmes testifies to the durability of the model but may suggest a limited ability to align new change models to changes occurring within public services.

Within the logic of change programmes it is often assumed that there is embedded a rational and strategic response to the changing environment. However, political and contextual factors often play a significant part in the adoption of particular types of change agendas and the ability to adapt to changing circumstances is an important feature of public service organisations.

The range of research on change management confirms critical components of successful implementation of change programmes are organisational vision, deep or thick communication, strategic leadership, and combining the broader issue of deliberative positioning of the organisation to ensure organisational members are motivated to advance the change agenda. These 'lists' of characteristics of good change management programmes belie the complexity of changing the overarching frames that apply to public services, however.

Achieving successful organisational change in public services is not easy, as organisational change programmes are often found to fail. Outcome measurement and evaluation of change programmes for public services are confounded by the inability to develop performance indicators that rely on demonstrated difference in activity such as greater levels of profits or increased outputs (Osborne and Brown 2005). Transition to governance approaches has re-ordered the prior certainties of public service organisations undergoing planned, rational change management programmes that are set to move the organisation from one path to a different but knowable path from the outset. The call to produce innovation or innovation capabilities in public services offers a more uncertain path to change management and change outcomes. However, the new approach also recognises the current challenges that befall the modern public sector, requiring cross-cutting responses that bring diverse groups together to resolve complex issues. Collaboration is the watchword in this context and has been put forward as a comprehensive way to instil change in public services. Change management programmes based on developing collaboration competencies and assisting in understanding what the requisite leadership, management and organisational governance approaches might comprise are at issue. Certainly, collaboration, while a worthy aspiration, is difficult to achieve and it takes trust, new kinds of leadership and alternative arrangements and structures to start to develop a comprehensive response to the agenda. The multiplex and diverse interests and stakeholders relating to public purpose also point to the greater complexity and nuances demanded of managers and organisational members in implementing public service change initiatives.

REFERENCES

Amis, J., Slack, T. and Hinings, C.R. (2004). The pace, sequence and linearity of radical Change. *Academy of Management Journal*, 47(1), 15–39.

Ashworth, R., Boyne, G. and Delbridge, R. (2007). Escape from the iron cage: organizational change and isomorphic pressures in the public sector. *Journal of Public Administration Research and Theory*, 19(1), 165–187.

Beer, M. and Nohria, N. (2000). *Breaking the Code of Change*. Boston, MA: HBS Press.

Bingham, L., Nabatchi, T. and O'Leary, R. (2005). The new governance: practices and processes for citizen participation. *Public Administration Review*, 65(5), 547–558.

Bokeno, R.M. and Gantt, V.W. (2000). Dialogic mentoring. *Management Communication Quarterly: MCQ*, 14, 237–270.

Brown, K. (2008). Human resource management in the public sector. In R.S. Beattie and S.P. Osborne (eds), *Human Resource Management in the Public Sector*. Abingdon: Routledge.

Brown, K. and Keast, R. (2005). Social services policy and delivery in Australia: centre–periphery mixes. *Policy and Politics*, 33(3), 505–518.

Brown, K., Waterhouse, J. and Flynn, C. (2003). Change management practices: is a hybrid model a better alternative for public sector agencies? *International Journal of Public Sector Management*, 16(3), 230–241.

Caiden, G.E. (1999). Administrative reform: proceed with caution. *International Journal of Public Administration*, 22(6), 815–832.

Commonwealth of Australia (2009). *Powering Ideas: An Innovation Agenda for the 21st Century*. Canberra: Commonwealth of Australia.

Cutler, T. (2008). *Venturous Australia: Building Strength in Innovation*. Canberra: Commonwealth of Australia.

Deal, T.E. and Kennedy, A.A. (1982). *Corporate Cultures: The Rites and Rituals of Corporate Life*. Harmondsworth: Penguin Books.

Department of Industry, Innovation, Science and Research (2011). *Innovation Action Plan for* the Australian Public Sector, Canberra: Commonwealth of Australia.

Doyle, M., Claydon, T. and Buchanan, D. (2000). Mixed results, lousy process: the management experience of organizational change. *British Journal of Management*, 11(Special Issue), S59–S80.

Dunleavy, P., Margetts, H., Bastow, S. and Tinkler, J. (2005). New Public Management is dead – long live digital-era governance. *Journal of Public Administration Research and Theory*, 16, 467–494.

Dunphy, D. (1996). Organizational change in corporate settings. *Human Relations*, 48(5), 541–552.

Dunphy, D. and Stace, D. (1990). *Under New Management: Australian Organisations in Transition*. Sydney: McGraw-Hill.

Fernandez, S. and Rainey, H. (2006). Managing successful organizational change on the public sector. *Public Administration Review*, 66(2), 168–176.

Frahm, J. and Brown, K. (2006). Developing communicative competencies for a learning organization. *Journal of Management Development*, 25(3), 201–212.

Frahm, J. and Brown, K. (2007). First steps: linking change communication to change receptivity. *Journal of Organizational Change Management*, 20(3), 370–387.

Gersick, C. (1991). Revolutionary change theories: a multi-level exploration of punctuated equilibrium paradigm. *Academy of Management Review*, 16(1), 10–36.

Hill, C. and Jones, G. (1998). *Strategic Management: An Integrated Approach*. Boston, MA: Houghton Mifflin.

Keast, R. and Brown, K. (2006). Adjusting to new ways of working: experiments in service delivery in the public sector. *Australian Journal of Public Administration*, 65(4), 41–53.

Keast, R., Mandell, M. and Brown, K. (2006). Mixing state, market and network governance modes: the role of government in 'crowded' policy domains. *International Journal of Organization Theory and Behavior*, 1(9), 27–50.

Kelman, S. (2007). Public administration and organization studies. *Academy of Management Annals*, 1(1), 225–267.

Kettl, D.F. (2000). The transformation of governance: globalization, devolution, and the role of government. *Public Administration Review*, 60(6), 488–497.

Kleiner, B. and Walter, W. (1989). Understanding organisational change. *Leadership & Organization Development Journal*, 10(3), 25–31.

Kotter, J. (1998). Leading change: why transformation efforts fail. *Harvard Business Review*, 73(2), 59–67.

Lewin, K. (1952). *Field Theory in Social Science*. London: Tavistock Publications.

Management Advisory Board (2010). *Empowering Change: Fostering Innovation in the Australian Public Service*. Canberra: Attorney General's Department.

Morgan, G. (1997). *Images of Organization*, 2nd edn. Thousand Oaks, CA: Sage.

Nutt, P. (1992). *Managing Planned Change*. New York: Macmillan.

Nutt, P.C. and Backoff, R.W. (1997). Facilitating transformational change. *Journal of Applied Behavioral Science*, 33(4), 490–508.

Orlikowski, W.J. (1996). Improvising organizational transformation over time: a situated change perspective. *Information Systems Research*, 7(1), 63–92.

Osborne, S. and Brown, K. (2005). *Managing Change and Innovation in Public Service Organizations*. London: Routledge.

Pettigrew, A.M., Woodman, R.W. and Cameron, K.S. (2001). Studying organizational change and development challenges for future research. *Academy of Management Journal*, 44(4), 697–713.

Queensland Public Service Commission (no date). *Change Management Best Practices Guide: Five Key Factors Common to Success in Managing Organisational Change*. Brisbane: Queensland Government.

Ryan, N., Furneaux, C., Pink, A. and Brown, K. (2005). Public sector contracting: an Australian study of changing work conditions. *Management Revue*, 16(4), 438–457.

Van den Ven, A. and Poole, M. (1995). Explaining development and change in organizations. *Academy of Management Review*, 20(3), 510–540.

Vreeswijk, V. (2011). *Using Fiscal Restraint to Drive Transformation, Innovation and Collaboration*. Public Sector Transformation 2011: Complexity, Cost Control and Change conference, 28 November, Ottawa.

Waddell, D., Cummings, T.G. and Worley, C.G. (2004). *Organisation Development and Change*. Melbourne: South-Western Thompson Learning.

Waterhouse, J., Keast, R. and Brown, K. (2011). *Negotiating the Business Environment: Theory and Practice for All Governance Styles*. Melbourne: Tilde Press.

West, D. (2004). E-government and the transformation of service delivery and citizen attitudes. *Public Administration Review*, 64(1), 15–27.

Wheatley, M. (1994). *Leadership and the New Science: Learning about Organizations from an Orderly Universe*. San Francisco, CA: Berret-Koehler.

Wise, L. (2002). Public management reform: competing drivers of change. *Public Management Review*, 62(5), 555–567.

8. Managing stakeholders in the change and innovation process
John M. Bryson and Barbara C. Crosby

INTRODUCTION

This chapter focuses on how and why public managers might go about using stakeholder identification and analysis techniques in order to help their organizations effectively manage change processes. A range of stakeholder identification and analysis techniques is reviewed. The techniques cover: organizing participation; problem or opportunity formulation and direction setting; solution search; building a winning coalition around proposal development, review, and adoption; and implementing, monitoring, and evaluating strategic interventions. The chapter argues that wise use of stakeholder analyses can help frame issues that are solvable in ways that are technically and administratively feasible and politically acceptable and that advance the common good. Conversely, failure to attend to stakeholder interests, resources, and influence can stymie efforts to help organizations innovate to deal with or anticipate changes in their environment. Moreover, stakeholder involvement can help public managers improve innovation designs that may look good on paper but not be sufficiently attuned to conditions on the ground or to political forces.

The chapter concludes with a number of recommendations for management research, education, and practice. It draws heavily on Bryson (2004, 2011), Bryson and Patton (2010), and Bryson et al. (2011).

The decision about how to define stakeholders is consequential, as it affects *who* and *what* counts (Mitchell et al. 1997). In this chapter stakeholders are defined broadly as 'any person, group or organization that can place a claim on an organization's (or other entity's) attention, resources, or output, or is affected by that output' (Bryson 2011, p. 48). Taking a more inclusive view of who counts as a stakeholder is compatible with typical approaches to democracy and social justice, in which the interests of the nominally powerless must be given weight (Lewis and Gilman 2005). While specific stakeholder definitions vary, the literature is clear that stakeholder support is needed to create and sustain winning coalitions; to ensure the long-term viability of policies, plans, and programs; and to ensure long-term viability of organizations. Key stakeholders must be satisfied, at least minimally, or public policies, organizations, communities, or even countries and civilizations will fail.

WHY STAKEHOLDER ANALYSES HAVE BECOME SO IMPORTANT

It has now become a truism that we live in a shared-power, no one-wholly-in-charge world. When it comes to major public problems, no single organization 'contains' the problem (Kettl 2002). Instead many individuals, groups, and organizations are involved or affected or have some partial responsibility to act. What is true inter-organizationally is also increasingly true intra-organizationally. Figuring out what the problem is and what solutions might work is actually part of the problem, and taking stakeholders into account is a crucial aspect of problem solving (Crosby and Bryson 2005; Bardach 2008). Effective change management becomes in large part the effective management of stakeholder relationships (Hill and Lynn 2009; Ackermann and Eden 2011). Said differently, we are moving into an era when networks of stakeholders are becoming at least as important as, if not more important than, markets and hierarchies (Powell 1990; O'Leary and Bingham 2009).

In networked situations, attention to stakeholders is important throughout a change process because 'success' for public organizations – and certainly survival – depends on satisfying key stakeholders according to their definition of what is valuable (Moore 1995; Bryson 2011). (Note that 'key stakeholders' also include 'insiders' such as public managers and employees, as well as 'outsiders' such as political overseers and funders.) If key stakeholders are not satisfied, at least minimally, according to their criteria for satisfaction, the normal expectation should be that something will change – for example, the change effort will fail, budgets will be cut, elected or appointed officials will lose their jobs, new initiatives will be undermined, and so on.

Attention to stakeholders is also needed to assess and enhance political feasibility (Ackermann and Eden 2011), especially when it comes to articulating and achieving the common good (Bryson et al. 2002). Finally, attention to stakeholders is important to satisfy those involved or affected that requirements for procedural justice, procedural rationality, and legitimacy have been met (Suchman 1995; Ackermann and Eden 2011). Note that what is being said does *not* imply that all possible stakeholders should be satisfied, or involved, or otherwise wholly taken into account; only that the *key* stakeholders must be, and that the choice of which stakeholders are key is inherently political (Stone 2002), has ethical consequences (Lewis and Gilman 2005), and involves judgment. Note, too, that political feasibility does not mean that innovative solutions will be substantively rational (Simon 1996), but absent political feasibility, substantively rational innovations are unlikely to be implemented.

Because attention to stakeholders is so important, stakeholder analyses become important and can help public organizations better manage their change efforts. The underlying assumption is that *change processes that employ a reasonable number of competently done stakeholder analyses are more likely to be successful than those that do not*. The techniques covered in this chapter should all be considered for use. At a minimum, stakeholder analyses should help public managers figure out who the key stakeholders are and what would satisfy them. Ideally, the analyses will help reveal how satisfying those key stakeholders will create more effective change processes that create public value and advance the common good. The next section discusses a number of stakeholder identification and analysis techniques. Table 8.1 shows how the stakeholder identification and analysis techniques fit with a standard phased, purposeful action, or teleological change management process (Poole et al. 2000; Demers 2007). See Table 8.1 for a summary of this section.

Table 8.1 Change management stakeholder identification, analysis, and engagement techniques

Change management phase	Technique	Purpose	Reveals	Figure
1. Organizing participation	List change stakeholders	To develop initial list of stakeholders and begin to conduct an iterative process of narrowing the field of key stakeholders	Broad list of stakeholders	
	Basic stakeholder analysis technique	To identify the interests of individual stakeholders	Key change management issues, including clues about purposes of the change effort	
	Power versus interest grids	To determine which players' interests and power issues must be considered	Players, context setters, subjects, and crowd Clues about: • Common ground for all or subsets of stakeholders • Possible coalitions of support and/or opposition • Strategies for changing views of stakeholders • Ways to advance the interests of the powerless	Figure 8.1
	Stakeholder influence diagrams	To identify how stakeholders influence one another	Who influences whom among the stakeholders Who the most influential stakeholders are	
	Bases of power – directions of interest diagram	To identify the sources of a stakeholder's power To clarify a stakeholder's interests or stakes To help planning team identify common ground across all stakeholder groups	The goals the stakeholder seeks to achieve or the interests they seek to serve, as well as the power base on which the stakeholder can draw to pursue those interests	Figure 8.2

Phase	Technique	Purpose	Output	Table
2. Problem or opportunity formulation and direction setting	Finding the common good and the structure of a winning argument	To indicate what the 'common good' is for a group of stakeholders and to indicate how arguments will need to be structured to build a winning coalition	The goals likely to unite a significant number of stakeholders and to enable formation of a winning coalition	
	Purpose network or hierarchy	To engage the change management team in identifying purposes beyond the initial purpose and establishing the primary purpose of the change management effort	Causal network or hierarchy of purposes indicating which purposes are prerequisite to or help achieve other purposes Primary purpose of change effort	
	Participation planning matrix	To indicate probable level of stakeholder participation and relationship of change effort and change managers to stakeholders	Possible overall strategy for engagement and likely action plans	Table 8.2
3. Solution search	Stakeholder role plays	To understand how different stakeholders respond to different aspects of the change and change management process	Insights into how other stakeholders think	
4. Building a winning coalition around proposal development, review, and adoption	Proposal support versus opposition grids	To identify which stakeholders are likely to support which recommendations and which are likely to oppose them	Recommendations that have a strong coalition of support Recommendations that may need to be changed in order to garner support	
	Recommendation attractiveness versus stakeholder capability grid	To identify recommendations that are likely to be implemented due to stakeholder capacity and those that will fail due to lack of capacity	Recommendations that have strong stakeholder capacity to be implemented	
5. Implementing, Monitoring and Evaluating Strategic Interventions	Recommendation implementation strategy development grid	To help stakeholders gain a clear picture of what will be required for implementation and help develop action plans that will tap stakeholder interests and resources	Resources and strategies for successful implementation	Table 8.3

AN ARRAY OF TECHNIQUES

This section presents 12 stakeholder identification and analysis techniques in enough detail for readers to get a good idea of what is involved in using them. (Additional techniques will be found in Bryson 2011 and Bryson et al. 2011.) The techniques are grouped into five categories: organizing participation; problem or opportunity formulation and direction setting; solution search; building a winning coalition around proposal development, review, and adoption; and implementing, monitoring, and evaluating strategic interventions. All of the techniques are fairly simple in concept and rely on standard facilitation materials such as flipcharts, marking pens, tape, colored stick-on dots, and so on. All it takes to do them is a group willing to devote some time and effort to doing so – an expenditure of resources that typically is miniscule when compared with the opportunity costs of less than adequate performance, or even disaster, that typically follow in the wake of failing to attend to key stakeholders, their interests, and their information.

Phase 1 – Organizing Participation

Stakeholder analyses are undertaken for a purpose and that purpose should be articulated as clearly as it can be before the analyses begin – while also understanding that purposes may change over time. The purpose should guide the choices concerning who should be involved in the analyses and how. Typically, stakeholder analyses are undertaken as part of policy, plan, or strategy change exercises; or organizational development efforts. Different analyses will be needed at different stages in these processes.

Deciding who should be involved, how, and when in doing stakeholder analyses is a key strategic choice. In general, people should be involved if they have information that cannot be gained otherwise, or if their participation is necessary to assure successful implementation of initiatives built on the analyses (Thomas 1995). Organizers of change processes often want to know what is the optimal level of stakeholder involvement. The specific answer depends on the situation. There very well may be important trade-offs between early and later participation in analyses and one or more of the following: representation, accountability, analysis quality, analysis credibility, analysis legitimacy, the ability to act based on the analyses, or other factors, and these will need to be thought through. Fortunately, 'the choice' actually can be approached as a sequence of choices, in which first an individual or small planning group begins the effort, and then others are added later as the advisability of doing so becomes apparent.

Five stakeholder identification and analysis techniques are particularly relevant to helping organize participation: list stakeholders; the basic stakeholder analysis technique; power versus interest grids; stakeholder influence diagrams; and the bases of power–directions of interest diagram.

List stakeholders
This technique begins when an individual or group connected to a proposed change effort brainstorms the list of individuals or groups who care about or are affected by the change. Those doing the brainstorming should realize that other stakeholders may emerge

subsequently. Next, the stakeholders should be ranked according to their importance to the change effort. When doing so, consider the stakeholder's power, legitimacy, and attention-getting capacity (Mitchell et al,. 1997).

This step is typically 'back room' work. Necessary additional information inputs may be garnered through the use of interviews, questionnaires, focus groups, or other targeted information-gathering techniques in this and subsequent steps. In this step it is important to make sure stakeholders are identified at the right level of aggregation, meaning at a level that makes sense from a strategic perspective (Ackermann and Eden 2011). For example, usually 'the government' is not a stakeholder, but some parts of it might be, such as the city council (or particular members of it) or the police force (or some part of it). You should be able to find the 'voice' of each stakeholder that is identified, be it an actual individual or a representative of the group.

The basic stakeholder analysis technique

The basic analysis technique is described in Bryson (2011, pp. 133–137). It offers a quick and useful way of: identifying stakeholders and their interests, clarifying stakeholders' views of a focal organization (or other entity), identifying some key strategic issues, and beginning the process of identifying coalitions of support and opposition. Bryson describes how this technique was used to bring about major change in a state department of natural resources in the United States, because it showed participants how existing strategies ignored important stakeholders – who refused to be ignored – as well as what might be done to satisfy the stakeholders.

The technique involves several steps. If a large group is involved, the steps typically are undertaken in a sequence beginning with small-group exercises followed by large-group plenary discussions:

- Brainstorm the list of potential stakeholders.
- Prepare a separate flipchart sheet for each stakeholder.
- Place a stakeholder's name at the top of each sheet.
- Create a narrow column down the right side of each sheet and leave the column blank.
- For each stakeholder, in the area to the left of the narrow column, list the criteria the stakeholder would use to judge the organization's (or other entity's) performance (or list what the stakeholder's expectations are of the organization).
- Decide how well you think the stakeholder thinks the organization is doing from the stakeholder's point of view. Use colored dots to indicate a stakeholder judgment of *good* (green), *fair* (yellow), or *poor* (red).
- Identify and record what can be done quickly to satisfy each stakeholder.
- Identify and record longer-term issues with individual stakeholders and with stakeholders as a group.

Additional steps might be included such as:

- Specify how each stakeholder influences the organization.
- Decide what the organization needs from each stakeholder.
- Rank the stakeholders according to their importance to the organization. When

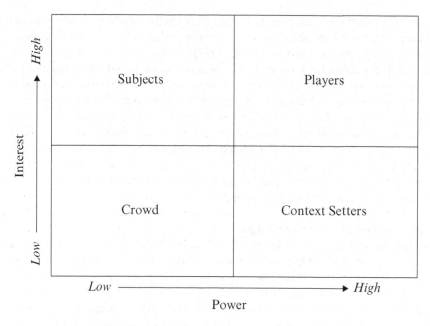

Source: Eden and Ackermann (1998, p. 122).

Figure 8.1   Power versus interest grid

doing so consider the stakeholder's power, legitimacy, and attention-getting capacity (Mitchell et al. 1997).

Power versus interest grids
Power versus interest grids are described in detail by Eden and Ackermann (1998, pp. 121–125, 344–346; see also Bryson 2011, pp. 407–409) (see Figure 8.1). These grids array stakeholders on a two-by-two matrix where the dimensions are the stakeholder's interest (in a political sense as opposed to simple inquisitiveness) in the organization or issue at hand, and the stakeholder's power to affect the organization's or issue's future. Four categories of stakeholders result: *Players*, who have both an interest and significant power; *subjects*, who have an interest but little power; *context setters*, who have power but little direct interest; and the *crowd*, which consists of stakeholders with little interest or power.

Power versus interest grids typically help determine which players' interests and power bases *must* be taken into account in order to address the problem or issue at hand. They also help highlight coalitions to be encouraged or discouraged, what behavior should be fostered, and whose 'buy in' should be sought or who should be 'co-opted'. Finally, they provide some information on how to convince stakeholders to change their views. Interestingly, the knowledge gained from the use of such a grid can be used to help advance the interests of the relatively powerless (Bryson et al. 2002).

A power versus interest grid is constructed as follows:

- Tape four flipchart sheets to a wall to form a single surface two sheets high and two sheets wide.
- Draw the two axes on the surface using a marker pen. The vertical axis is labeled *interest* from low to high; while the horizontal axis is labeled *power* from low to high.
- Planning team members brainstorm the names of stakeholders by writing the names of different stakeholders as they come to mind on a 1.5" × 2" (2.5 cm × 5 cm) self-adhesive label, one stakeholder per label. Alternatively, if the basic analysis technique has been performed, the names should be taken from that list.
- Guided by the deliberations and judgments of the planning group members, a facilitator should place each label in the appropriate spot on the grid. Labels should be collected in round-robin fashion, one label per group member, until all labels (other than duplicates) are placed on the grid or eliminated for some reason.
- Labels should be moved around until all group members are satisfied with the *relative* location of each stakeholder on the grid.
- The group should discuss the implications of the resulting stakeholder placements.

Stakeholder influence diagrams

Stakeholder influence diagrams indicate how the stakeholders on a power versus interest grid influence one another. The technique is taken from Eden and Ackermann (1998, pp. 349–350; see also Bryson et al. 2002) and begins with a power versus interest grid. The steps in developing such a diagram are as follows:

- The planning team should start with a power versus interest grid and then for each stakeholder on the grid suggest lines of influence from one stakeholder to another.
- A facilitator should draw in the lines with a soft-lead pencil.
- Two-way influences are possible, but an attempt should be made to identify the primary direction in which influence flows between stakeholders. If there are two-way influences, make each direction of influence a separate arrow and label the nature of what the influence is.
- Engage in a dialogue about which influence relationships exist, which are most important, and what the primary direction of influence is.
- Once final agreement is reached the pencil lines should be made permanent with a marker pen.
- The results and implications of the resulting diagram should be discussed, including identifying who the most influential or central stakeholders are.

Bases of power – directions of interest diagrams

This technique builds on the power versus interest grid and stakeholder influence diagram, and involves looking more closely at each of the stakeholder groups, including the most influential or central stakeholders. A bases of power – directions of interest diagram can be created for each stakeholder. The technique is an adaptation of Eden and Ackermann's 'star diagrams' (1998, pp. 126–128, 346–349; see also Bryson et al. 2002).

A diagram of this kind indicates the sources of power available to the stakeholder, as well as the goals or interests the stakeholder seeks to achieve or serve (see Figure 8.2).

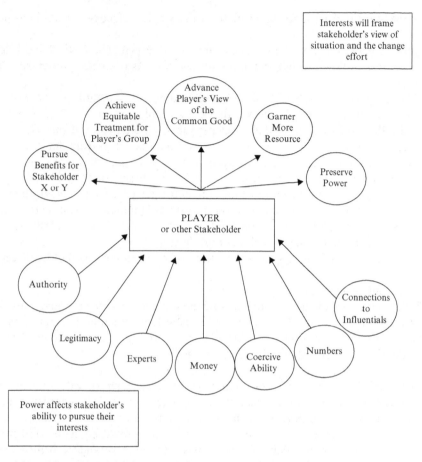

Source: Adapted from Eden and Ackermann (1998, p. 127) and Bryson et al. (2002).

Figure 8.2   Bases of power – directions of interest diagram, with examples of power bases and interests

Power can come from access to or control over various support mechanisms, such as money and votes, or from access to or control over various sanctions, such as regulatory authority or votes of no confidence (Eden and Ackermann 1998, pp. 126–127). Directions of interest indicate the aspirations or concerns of the stakeholder. Typically the diagrams focus on the stakeholder's bases of power and directions of interest in relation to a focal organization's purposes or goals; that is, they seek to identify the powers that might affect achievement of the focal organization's purposes.

There are two reasons for constructing the diagrams. The first is to help the planning team find the common ground – especially in terms of interest – across all of the stakeholder groups. After exploring the power bases and interests of each stakeholder, the planning group will be in a position to identify commonalities across the stakeholders as a whole, or across particular subgroups. This search will allow the group to find the *common good and the structure of a winning argument* (see next technique). Secondly, the diagrams are intended to provide background information on each stakeholder in order to know how to tap into their interests (see also below) or make use of their power to advance the common good. For example, background information can be used in stakeholder role plays (see also below) to further understand stakeholder reactions to specific issues or proposals for change.

A bases of power – directions of interest diagram may be constructed as follows:

- Attach a flipchart to a wall. Write the stakeholder's name in the middle of the sheet.
- The planning team then brainstorms possible bases of power for the stakeholder and the facilitator writes these on the bottom half of the sheet.
- Based on discussion within the group, arrows are drawn on the diagram from the power base to the stakeholder, and between power bases to indicate how one power base is linked to another.
- The planning team then brainstorms goals or interests they believe the stakeholder has. The facilitator writes these on the top half of the sheet. Arrows are drawn from the stakeholder to the goals or interests. Arrows are also used to link goals and interests when appropriate.
- A thorough discussion of each diagram and its implications should occur.

Phase 2 – Problem or Opportunity Formulation and Direction Setting

Problem or opportunity formulation often is best managed via a two-step process (Crosby and Bryson 2005, pp. 228–236). The first step involves conducting exploratory research into stakeholders and their views and the nature, causes, and consequences of the problem or opportunity. The second step involves more detailed research. It is important to give adequate attention to the first step, because without it important aspects of the problem or opportunity and its impact on stakeholders may be ignored. The stakeholder analyses suggested in this phase build on those discussed earlier and are mostly intended to facilitate direction setting and the assurance of political feasibility down the line. Effective problem or opportunity formulation, in other words, depends on clearly understanding stakeholders and their interests, both separately and in relation to each other, so that problems can be formulated in such a way that they have a chance of being solved in practice. Three additional techniques are particularly relevant: finding the common good and the structure of a winning argument, the purpose network diagram, and participation planning matrix.

Finding the common good and the structure of a winning argument
Bryson et al. (2002) created this technique and used it successfully to help develop a viable political strategy for producing better outcomes for young African American men in a large county in the United States. The technique builds on the bases of power – directions of interest technique. Bases of power – directions of interest diagrams can be explored in depth to determine which interests or themes appear to garner support from a significant number of stakeholders. Members of the planning team will need to search for these common themes, which are called *supra-interests*. For each theme, the team should construct a label that appears to capture or integrate the specific interests that comprise it. The identification of common themes is a subjective exercise calling for creativity,

discernment, and judgment. After identifying these themes, the team should distribute the labels on a flipchart and draw arrows to indicate how themes are linked to each other. The resulting diagram, or map, will thus represent the supra-interests that tie together the individual stakeholders' interests as well as what the relationships among the supra-interests appear to be.

The map is called 'the common good and the structure of a winning argument' because it indicates – at least in part – what the common good is for this group of stakeholders, as well as how arguments will probably need to be structured to tap into the interests of enough stakeholders to create a winning coalition. In other words, if persuasive arguments can be created that show how support for specific changes will further the interests of a significant number of important stakeholders, then it should be possible to forge the coalition needed to adopt and implement the changes. Being relatively clear about goals or interests – while not always necessary – does help when it comes to producing success-ful programs and projects (Nutt 2002). Difficulties can thus focus on means to achieve specific goals, rather than on conflicts over those ends. Conflicts over means can be resolved through interest-based bargaining and through the creation of pilot projects or small experiments to identify the most effective approaches. In addition, the structure of a winning argument outlines a viable political rhetoric around which a community of interests can mobilize, coalesce, and co-align to further the common good (Majone 1989; Stone 2002).

Purpose network diagram

Stakeholder analyses and involvements as part of a change process should be undertaken for a clear purpose and that purpose (or purposes) should be articulated as clearly and as early as possible in the process – while also understanding that purposes may change over time. The purpose network diagram can be very helpful in this regard. The technique is adapted from Bryson et al. (2007).

A purpose network (or hierarchy) diagram indicates the various inter-related purposes that the proposed changes might serve. These ideally will include the overarching pur-poses, or mission; major subordinate purposes, or goals; and purposes subordinate to but supportive of goals, that typically would be referred to as objectives. Note that the change effort's purpose must mesh at least in part with the interests of key stakeholders or the process will not get off the ground; or, if it does, will not get very far. The other techniques discussed in this chapter can help assure a co-alignment of key stakeholder interests and change effort purposes. Of particular use in this regard is the bases of power – directions of interest diagram.

The following steps are used to create a purpose network diagram:

- Tape four flipchart sheets to a wall to form a single surface two sheets high and two sheets wide with one-inch overlaps where they join.
- The analysis group then brainstorms a list of possible purposes (i.e. the potential set of goals, aims, outcome indicators, aspirations, mandated requirements, and critical success factors) for the change effort and places each on a 3″ by 5″ (approx-imately 7.5 cm by 12.5 cm) self-adhesive label. Purpose statements should begin with a verb (get, produce, create, show, demonstrate, etc.) and include only a single purpose (i.e. they should not include 'and' or 'or' or 'in order to' in the statement).

- The labels are then attached to the flipchart-covered surface.
- The group should then rearrange the labels as needed to construct a causal network (or hierarchy) indicating how purposes are linked by inserting arrows to indicate the direction of causation (or influence or support). Arrows indicate how fulfilling one purpose helps fulfill a subsequent purpose(s); in other words, the arrows go from a means to an end, or an action to an outcome, in the form of links in a chain. Arrows should be made with a soft-lead pencil so that the group can move labels around, erase arrows, or otherwise change its mind.
- Once the network (or hierarchy) is created, the group should decide which purposes are the actual primary intended and subsidiary purpose(s) of the change effort. Note that the primary intended purpose may end up being different from what group members or other stakeholders originally thought. It is also possible – perhaps even likely – that the purpose(s) may be changed somewhat based on further stakeholder analyses.

Participation planning matrix

In a sense, all of the techniques considered so far are relevant to planning for stakeholder participation. The participation planning matrix, however, is specifically designed for this purpose. The matrix adapts contributions from the International Association for Public Participation (http://www.iap2.org/associations/4748/files/IAP2%20Spectrum_vertical.pdf (accessed 6 September 2012)), specifically the notion of a spectrum of levels of public participation, and from the change process phases used in this chapter to organize techniques. The levels of participation range from ignoring stakeholders through to empowerment in which the stakeholders or some subset of them are given final decision-making authority. Each level has a different goal and makes a different kind of promise – implicitly if not explicitly (see Table 8.2).

The matrix prompts planners to think about responding to or engaging different stakeholders in different ways over the course of a change effort. As a result, the benefits of taking stakeholders seriously may be gained while avoiding the perils of inappropriately responding to or engaging stakeholders. The process for filling out the matrix is as follows:

- Begin using this matrix relatively early in any change effort.
- Fill out the matrix with stakeholders' names in the appropriate boxes and then develop action plans for how to follow through with each stakeholder.
- Revise the matrix as the change effort unfolds.

Phase 3 – Solution Search

Solution search is often best managed via a three-step process (Crosby and Bryson 2005, pp. 252–255). The first step involves a broad scan within and outside normal search channels, to gain an understanding of the possible territory within which solutions might be found. The second step employs a narrow-gauge search within the most promising territories to find specific solution components likely to be effective, ethical, and acceptable to key stakeholders. And finally, detailed exploration follows of identified solution components. Some subset of these components will provide the basis for

Table 8.2   Participation planning matrix: differing levels of participation and accompanying promises from the change managers to the stakeholder

Phases in change process	Types of involvement	Do not engage	Engage as data source	Inform	Consult	Involve	Collaborate	Empower
	Promise change managers make:		We will honor human subjects protocols and treat you and the data with respect	We will keep you informed of the change effort's progress and findings	We will keep you informed, listen to you, and provide feedback on how your input influenced the change process	We will work with you to ensure your concerns are considered and reflected in options considered, make sure you get to review and comment on options, and provide feedback on how your input is used in the change process	We will incorporate your advice and suggestions to the greatest extent possible, and give you meaningful opportunities to be part of the change management decision-making process	This is your change management effort. We will offer options to inform your decisions. You will decide and we will support and facilitate implementing of what you decide
	Those engaged are especially important and useful for...		Providing needed data	Disseminating information and creating interest in the effort	Anticipating issues, identifying landmines, suggesting priorities, and enhancing the credibility	Affirming the importance, appropriateness and utility of the change effort, attracting attention to results, and establishing	Serving as primary intended users or beneficiaries of changes because of their high interest, interpersonal	Capacity development, using the change effort to build their capacity to engage in further possible change efforts

	of the change effort	credibility	style, availability, influential positions and/ or connections, and sense of ownership of the effort
Phase 1 – Organizing Participation			
Phase 2 – Problem of Opportunity Formulation and Direction Setting			
STEP 3 – Solution Search			
STEP 4 – Building a Winning Coalition			
STEP 5 – Decision Making and Implementation			

- Fill out the matrix by placing stakeholders' names in the boxes that best signify their best level of involvement. Then develop action plans for how to follow through with each stakeholder.
- Cycle back and revise the matrix as the evaluation design and methods unfold.

Source: Adapted from Bryson (2011, p. 412–413; and Bryson, Patton, and Bowman, 2011, p. 8) and from the International Association for Public Participation's Public Participation Spectrum of levels of public participation (http://www.iaps.org/practionertools/Spectrum.html)

a solution to identified problems or opportunities. Solutions are likely to be a recombination of existing components, rather than a wholly new mutation (Kingdon 2002; Latour 2005).

Stakeholder role plays
As the work of assembling components into possible solution packages proceeds, stakeholder role plays can be very useful for assessing possible stakeholder reactions. They are also extremely useful in the next phase of building a coalition around particular proposals. Eden and Ackermann (1998, pp. 133–134) show how role plays, in which different members of the planning group play the roles of different stakeholders, can be used to develop proposals that are likely to address stakeholder interests, effectively build a supportive coalition, and ensure effective implementation. Role plays have the special benefit of enhancing the planning group's capacity to understand how other stakeholders think. Role plays build on the information revealed by other analyses, perhaps especially by bases of power – directions of interest diagrams.

A stakeholder role play involves the following steps:

● Each member of the planning team reviews any other relevant stakeholder analyses that have been done.
● Each member of the planning team assumes the role of a different stakeholder.
● With the stakeholder's bases of power – directions of interest diagram as a guide, each team member should answer two questions about any proposal from the stakeholder's point of view:
  ● How would I react to this option?
  ● What would be done that would increase my support or decrease my opposition?
● Use flipchart sheets to record the responses.
● Do the exercise more than once and keep modifying proposals to increase their robustness and political viability.

Once stakeholders and their interests have been identified and understood, it is typically still advisable to do additional analyses in order to develop proposals that can garner adequate support in the next phase.

Phase 4 – Building a Winning Coalition Around Proposal Development, Review, and Adoption

Two techniques will be considered here: stakeholder support versus opposition grids, and proposal attractiveness versus stakeholder capability grids. The first helps assess whether the necessary coalition has formed in support of proposed changes, while the second assesses whether key stakeholders are capable of implementing proposed changes.

Stakeholder support versus opposition grid
Nutt and Backoff (1992) developed the technique. The following steps may be followed to construct a support versus opposition grid:

- Tape four flipchart sheets to a wall to form a single surface two sheets high and two sheets wide.
- Draw a two-by-two matrix on the surface using a marker pen. The entire vertical axis on the left is labeled *support and opposition for proposed changes*. The part of the vertical axis above the horizontal midline is labeled *support* from *low* at the horizontal line to *high* at the top of the axis. The vertical axis on the left below the horizontal midline is labeled *opposition* from *low* at the horizontal line to *high* at the bottom of the axis. The horizontal axis across the bottom is labeled *power* from *low* on the left hand side to *high* on the right hand side.
- On a different set of flipchart sheets the planning group should brainstorm the list of potential stakeholders likely to be implicated by the proposed changes. Alternatively, if the basic analysis technique has been performed, the names should be taken from that list.

Stakeholders' names should then be placed on 1" × 1.5" (approximately 2.5 cm × 3.75 cm) self-adhesive labels, one stakeholder per label.

- Guided by the deliberations and judgments of the planning group members, a facilitator should place each label in the appropriate spot on the grid.
- Labels should be moved around until all group members are satisfied with the *relative* location of each stakeholder on the grid.
- The group should discuss the implications of the resulting stakeholder placements. Particular attention should be given to the stakeholders who appear in the right-hand quadrants. In other words, attention should be devoted to the more powerful stakeholders.
- The group should figure out whether the necessary coalition in support of the proposed changes can be formed. If not, conversation should focus on what might need to be done to increase the supportive coalition and to decrease the number and power of opponents.

A serious question concerns how large a winning coalition should be. The political science literature on policy adoption tends to emphasize the idea of a *minimum* winning coalition, since creating a larger coalition is likely to entail having to make so many concessions or trades that the proposal becomes so watered down it cannot achieve its original purpose (Riker 1962, 1986). On the other hand, the literature on collaborative planning argues that a larger coalition probably should be pursued, since sustained implementation requires broad-scale support and the minimum winning coalition may not provide it (Innes and Booher 2010). Obviously, in any specific case a thoughtful discussion should focus on answering this question.

Proposal attractiveness versus stakeholder capability grid
This type of grid is discussed in Bryson et al. (1986, pp. 73–76; see also Bryson 2011, pp. 423–425) and involves assessing the attractiveness of proposals against stakeholder capacities to implement them. The grid indicates proposals that are likely to be implemented successfully, because they match stakeholder capacities, and those that are likely to fail because of lack of capacity. The technique is therefore especially useful in

shared-power, no-one-in-charge situations where planners are necessarily led to focus on the proposals that are likely to be implemented successfully. Proposals that are high in attractiveness and capacity certainly should be pursued. Proposals that are otherwise attractive but do not match up well with stakeholder capacities will require a substantial build-up of stakeholder capabilities in order to be implemented. Where to find the resources for the build-up should be explored and discussed during the proposal development, review, and adoption process. Low-attractiveness proposals are best discarded.

The process for constructing one of these grids is:

- Construct a two-by-two attractiveness versus capability grid on flipchart(s). The axes representing attractiveness and capability can each range from low to high.
- Develop criteria to assess the attractiveness of proposals from low to high (in terms of mission, goals, results, outcomes, or stakeholder-related criteria) and capabilities necessary for successful implementation from low to high.
- Have a list of proposals and a list of stakeholders ready.
- Write proposals on self-adhesive labels of one color, one proposal per label, and place on the grid in the appropriate position after considering both the proposal's attractiveness and the various stakeholders' capacities to implement it.
- Discuss results and any implications for building necessary capacity among stakeholders, or for getting unattractive proposals off the agenda.
- Record results of the discussion on flipchart sheets.

Phase 5 – Implementing, Monitoring and Evaluating Strategic Interventions

In a sense, all of the techniques considered so far are relevant to implementation, since they are concerned with helping develop proposals likely to garner significant stakeholder support, but managers should still focus directly on stakeholders during implementation (Nutt 2002; Crosby and Bryson 2005; Bryson 2011). Developing an implementation strategy development grid can help planners and decision makers gain a clearer picture of what will be required for implementation and help them develop action plans that will tap stakeholder interests and resources. The technique is adapted from Meltsner (1972), Coplin and O'Leary (1976), Kaufman (1986), and Christensen (1993) and builds on information revealed by previously created bases of power – directions of interest diagrams, stakeholder support versus opposition grids, stakeholder role plays, and policy attractiveness versus stakeholder capability grids (see Table 8.3).

The process for filling out one of the grids is fairly simple:

- Create a grid either on a single flipchart sheet or flipchart sheet-covered wall.
- Assemble the results of previously done bases of power – directions of interest diagrams, stakeholder support versus opposition grids, stakeholder role plays, and policy attractiveness versus stakeholder capability grids.
- Fill out the policy implementation strategy grid.
- Discuss next steps and prepare action plans

This completes the discussion of specific stakeholder analysis techniques. As can be seen, a wide variety of techniques is available to perform the basic functions of strategic

Table 8.3   Change implementation strategy development grid

Stakeholders	Stake or interest	Re-sources	Action channels open to stake-holder	Probability of partici-pation and manner of doing so	Influence – as a product of resources and partici-pation	Implications for implemen-tation strategy	Action plan elements
Supportive stakeholders							
Opposing stakeholders							

Source: Bryson (2011, p. 425); adapted from Meltsner (1972), Coplin and O'Leary (1976), Kaufman (1986), and Christensen (1993).

change management. Each technique provides a different kind of information that can at times be of tremendous assistance.

BEYOND TECHNIQUES

Examples abound of how careful stakeholder analysis and involvement have contributed to successful innovation in public and nonprofit enterprises. We will mention three examples prominent in our own research.

The African American Men Project, Hennepin County, Minnesota

The county planning director and supportive county commissioners launched this project in 1999 to discover and remedy the causes of extremely poor outcomes for young African American males in Hennepin County, which contains Minneapolis, the largest city in Minnesota. The planning director knew that several stakeholders were key: the men themselves; local African Americans who had attained considerable power in business, government, or nonprofit organizations; government officials (especially county commissioners); and scholars who had studied causes and consequences of structural discrimination against African American men and of intergenerational poverty. The planning director organized a steering committee that drew these stakeholders into multiple planning sessions, in which many of the techniques described in this chapter were employed. The power versus interest grid, stakeholder influence diagrams, and the supra-interest maps were especially influential in helping participants realize that neither a social justice frame nor a social service framing of the central issue would produce enough support for changing systems and behaviors that all too often left African American men poorly educated, unemployed, and in and out of the criminal justice system. Construction of the supra-interest map showed that many key stakeholders, from the business community to government officials to the men themselves, wanted full employment, healthy families, strong communities, and the like. The map led participants to develop the theme 'What's good for African American men is good for Hennepin County'. This theme infused the project's final report and helped persuade the full Hennepin County Board of Commissioners to authorize and fund an ambitious extension of the project that produced many solid accomplishments (Bryson et al. 2002).

MetroGIS, Minneapolis–St. Paul Metropolitan Area

MetroGIS was initiated with conversations beginning in 1995 and has grown into an award-winning geographic information system (GIS) serving the seven-county Minneapolis–St. Paul metropolitan area. MetroGIS is coordinated and staffed by the Metropolitan Council (MC), the regional government, but is perhaps most usefully viewed as a voluntary collaboration – and what interviewees call a 'virtual organization' – involving over 300 local and regional governments, partners in the state and federal governments, and academic institutions, nonprofit organizations, and businesses.

The MC staff member who was assigned the task of exploring the possibility of launching a regional GIS developed multi-stakeholder forums to reveal the needs of potential contributors to and users of such a system. Especially important was a strategic planning workshop in which 22 technical experts, local government planners, elected officials, and others developed a statement of intent (including basic elements of the mission and goals) and strategic issues to be addressed. The event also resulted in creation of a Coordinating Committee to help guide subsequent efforts and provided the seeds of a set of 'guiding principles' that have steered the development of MetroGIS ever since. In subsequent years, the staff member, who became MetroGIS coordinator, showed keen sensitivity to the power and interests of key stakeholders. He has made sure that stakeholders have a number of ongoing ways to be involved in shaping the system and helping it evolve to meet user and citizen needs (Bryson et al. 2009; Crosby and Bryson 2010).

Heading Home Hennepin

In 2006 the coordinator of a nonprofit homeless shelter in Minneapolis collaborated with a Hennepin County commissioner and the Minneapolis mayor to launch an ambitious campaign to end homelessness, an innovative antidote to the conventional approach of responding to homelessness with ever-expanding shelters and reliance on detox, jail, and emergency services. They invited a carefully selected group of clergy, business leaders, elected officials, government executives, service providers, people from foundations, and people experiencing homelessness to serve on a Commission to End Homelessness. These organizers sought to include an array of stakeholders, but especially wanted some powerful people who could make decisions that would make a difference in this area of concern. In keeping with their attentiveness to the power and interests of these stakeholders, the organizers promised them that they would be done with their work in 100 days. The Commission also received reports from several committees that involved 200 community members and focused on different aspects of homelessness: families, singles, youth, and financing (Crosby and Bryson 2007).

The result was a plan to end homelessness in Hennepin County in 10 years. The plan was approved by the Minneapolis City Council and the Hennepin County Board in 2006 and began implementation in 2007. A small staff was assembled and based in county government. Despite the effects of the recession, the initiative has had many successes:

- Funding was secured from the State Legislature, the business community, and federal agencies.
- Staff worked with police to develop responses other than arrest and jail time for people who are panhandling or intoxicated.
- Staff worked with landlords to guarantee rents for people who might be high-risk tenants.
- Many teenagers coming out of foster care have made housing plans.
- Case managers were designated to help people who have been homeless for many years.
- Businesses and congregations have provided volunteers for Project Homeless Connect, a massive event that occurs several times a year and brings services together in one place for individuals and families experiencing homelessness.
- About 2000 affordable housing units have been created.

Throughout this effort, the organizers have focused on the specific ways in which different stakeholders are connected to the overarching shared interest in eliminating homelessness. For example, they have involved downtown business people in two main ways: through their congregations, where they have a moral impulse to assist people in need, and through their interest in the character of downtown spaces, which they want to keep attractive for workers and visitors.

These three cases demonstrate in brief the utility of thinking strategically about which stakeholders must be involved in understanding the need for social innovation and developing ideas and agreements that respond to the need. They also highlight the importance of workshops, committee meetings, working group sessions, and other forums in which large and small groups of stakeholders can employ the techniques described in this chapter and work on specific aspects of the innovation challenge.

CONCLUSIONS

In his classic work on policy analysis, the late Aaron Wildavsky (1979, pp. 5–19) argued that one of the keys to effective policy change was 'creating problems that could be solved'. In other words, policy analysis is a kind of art in which problems must be solvable, at least tentatively or in principle, in order to be understood and addressed effectively. 'Solvable' means both that good ideas worth implementing have been found or created *and* there is likely political support for implementing them. To be really useful, policy analysis thus requires linking *substantive rationality* with *political feasibility* in order to 'mobilize support for substance' (Wildavsky 1979, p. 1). A number of authors have argued that stakeholder analyses are a key to identifying problems that can and should be solved (e.g. Freeman 1984; Ackermann and Eden 2011; Bryson 2011) – particularly in situations where no one is wholly in charge but many are involved, affected, or have some partial responsibility to act (e.g. Crosby and Bryson 2005). Each stakeholder analysis technique presented in this chapter is designed to help public and nonprofit managers or groups think and act strategically over the course of a change effort in such a way that good ideas worth implementing can be found *and* implemented.

Some might argue that stakeholder analyses involve a lot of rigmarole that produces not too surprising results. For example, Mintzberg et al. (2009, p. 426) put little faith in them, although their criticism seems to be based on a very limited understanding of the full range of available stakeholder analysis techniques. On the other hand, we have Nutt's (2002) masterful study of 400 strategic decisions that indicates that a failure to attend carefully to stakeholder interests and information can easily lead to disaster. Given Nutt's evidence, and given how relatively simple and cheap the technology is, doing stakeholder analyses certainly would appear to be a clear candidate for what Bardach (1998) calls a 'smart practice'. We would go further and assert that *not* doing stakeholder analyses would often appear to be a 'dumb practice'.

Whether the practice really is smart depends on which techniques are used for what purposes, when, where, how, by whom, and with what results. Each of the techniques has a different purpose and reveals some things while hiding, or at least not highlighting, others. Like any other technique designed to aid strategic thinking and acting, stakeholder analyses must be undertaken skillfully and thoughtfully, with a willingness to learn and revise along the way (Bardach 1998; Hill and Lynn 2009). For some small change efforts, a one-time use of one or two techniques may be all that is necessary; for larger change efforts, a whole range of techniques will be needed at various points throughout the process. Hybrid techniques or new techniques may need to be invented along the way. The key point is the importance of thinking strategically about why, when, where, how, and with whom the analyses are to be undertaken, and how to change direction when needed.

It is also worth noting that stakeholder analyses can be used to advance causes that many people would believe do not serve the common good or create public value. Stakeholder analyses should never be seen as substitutes for virtuous and ethical practice, although they may be a part of promoting such practices (Lewis and Gilman 2005). Conceivably, one way to avoid outcomes that do not create public value is to begin with an inclusive definition of stakeholders, so that the net of considerations about who and what counts is cast widely to begin with. Another step appears to be undertaking enough stakeholder analyses to prompt the kind of 'strategic conversation' (Van der Heijden 2005) needed to discover a morally and ethically sound version of the common good to pursue. In the end, the analyses certainly do not guarantee that public value will be created, but they may provide information that helps.

Finally, there is quite an agenda for research, education, and practice around stakeholder identification and analysis. Very little research has been published on which techniques work best under which circumstances and why. Indeed, critics might argue with considerable justification that at present there is no overwhelming body of evidence indicating that stakeholder analyses *do* help produce desirable outcomes.

In terms of education, stakeholder analyses are either not taught, or else are taught in a very limited way, in schools of public policy, administration, and planning. Students should be introduced to the range and uses of the various techniques. Practitioners, meanwhile, often have a more limited knowledge of stakeholder identification and analysis techniques than they should. They, too, should be introduced to the range and uses of the various techniques. In sum, a variety of stakeholder analyses appear to be very useful tools for improving public and nonprofit management, fostering innovation that creates public value, and advancing the common good. However, there is a great deal of work to be done in terms of research and education before that promise is fully understood and realized in practice.

REFERENCES

Ackermann, F. and Eden, C. (2011). *Making Strategy: Mapping Out Strategic Success*. Thousand Oaks, CA: Sage.
Bardach, E. (1998). *Getting Agencies to Work Together*. Washington, DC: Brookings Institution Press.
Bardach, E. (2008). *A Practical Guide to Policy Analysis*, 3rd edn. Washington, DC: CQ Press.
Bryson, J.M. (2004). What to do when stakeholders matter: stakeholder identification and analysis techniques. *Public Management Review*, 6(1) 21–53.
Bryson, J.M. (2011). *Strategic Planning for Public and Nonprofit Organizations*, 4th edn. San Francisco, CA: Jossey-Bass.
Bryson, J.M. and Patton, M.Q. (2010). Analyzing and engaging stakeholders. In Joseph S. Wholey, Harry P. Hatry and Kathryn E. Newcomer (eds), *The Handbook of Practical Program Evaluation*, 3rd edn. San Francisco, CA: Jossey-Bass, pp. 30–54.
Bryson, J.M., Ackermann, F. and Eden, C. (2007). Putting the resource-based view of strategy and distinctive competencies to work in public organizations. *Public Administration Review*, 67(4), 702–717.
Bryson, J.M., Crosby, B.C. and Bryson, J.K. (2009). Understanding strategic planning and the formulation and implementation of strategic plans as a way of knowing: the contributions of actor-network theory. *International Journal of Public Management*, 12(2), 172–207, with supplemental materials available through the publisher's website.
Bryson, J.M., Cunningham, G. and Lokkesmoe, K. (2002). What to do when stakeholders matter: the case of problem formulation for the African American Men Project of Hennepin County Minnesota. *Public Administration Review*, 62(5), 568–584.
Bryson, J.M., Freeman, R.E. and Roering, W. (1986). Strategic planning in the public sector: approaches and directions. In B. Checkoway (ed.), *Strategic Perspectives on Planning Practice*. Lexington, MA: Lexington Books, pp. 65–85.
Bryson, J.M., Patton, M.Q. and Bowman, R.B. (2011). Working with evaluation stakeholders: a rationale, step-wise approach, and toolkit. *Evaluation and Program Planning*, 34, 1–12.
Christensen, K. (1993). Teaching savvy. *Journal of Planning Education and Research*, 12, 2–12.
Coplin, W. and O'Leary, M. (1976). *Everyman's Prince: A Guide to Understanding Your Political Problem*. Boston, MA: Duxbury Press.
Crosby, B. and Bryson, J.M. (2005). *Leadership for the Common Good: Tackling Public Problems in a Shared Power World*. San Francisco, CA: Jossey-Bass.
Crosby, B.C. and Bryson, J.M. (2007). Leadership for the common good: creating regimes of mutual gain. In R. Morse, M. Kinghorn and T. Buss (eds), *Transforming Public Leadership for the 21st Century*. Washington, DC and New York: National Academy of Public Administration and M.E. Sharpe, pp. 185–202.
Crosby, B.C. and Bryson, J.M. (2010). Integrative leadership and the creation and maintenance of cross-sector collaboration. *Leadership Quarterly*, 21, 211–230.
Demers, C. (2007). *Organizational Change Theories: A Synthesis*. Thousand Oaks, CA: Sage.
Eden, C. and Ackermann, F. (1998). *Making Strategy: The Journey of Strategic Management*. London: Sage Publications.
Freeman, R.E. (1984). *Strategic Management: A Stakeholder Approach*. Boston, MA: Pitman.
Hill, C. and Lynn, L. (2009). *Public Management*. Washington, DC: CQ Press.
Innes, J. and Booher, D. (2010). *Planning with Complexity*. New York: Routledge.
International Association for Public Participation IAP2 Public Participation Spectrum. Available

at: http://www.iap2.org/associations/4748/files/IAP2%20Spectrum_vertical.pdf (accessed 6 September 2012).

Kaufman, J. (1986). Making planners more effective strategists. In B. Checkoway (ed.), *Strategic Perspectives on Planning Practice*. Lexington, MA: Lexington Books, pp. 87–104.

Kettl, D. (2002). *The Transformation of Governance: Public Administration for Twenty-first Century America*. Baltimore, MD: Johns Hopkins University Press.

Kingdon, J. (2002). *Agendas, Alternatives, and Public Policies*. New York: Longman.

Latour, B. (2005). *Reassembling the Social*. New York: Oxford University Press.

Lewis, C. and Gilman, S.C. (2005). *The Ethics Challenge in Public Service: A Problem-Solving Guide*, 2nd edn. San Francisco, CA: Jossey-Bass.

Majone, G. (1989). *Argument, Evidence and Persuasion in the Policy Process*. New Haven, CT: Yale University Press.

Margerum, R. (2002). Collaborative planning: building consensus and a distinct model of practice. *Journal of Planning Education and Research*, 21, 237–253.

Meltsner, A. (1972). Political feasibility and policy analysis. *Public Administration Review*, 32, 859 867.

Mintzberg, H., Ahlstrand, B. and Lampel J. (2009). *Strategy Safari: A Guided Tour Through the Wilds of Strategic Management*, 2nd edn. London: FT Press.

Mitchell, R.K., Agle, B.R. and Wood, D.J. (1997). Toward a theory of stakeholder identification and salience: defining the principle of who and what really counts. *Academy of Management Review*, 22(4), 853–886.

Moore, M. (1995). *Creating Public Value*. Cambridge, MA: Harvard University Press.

Nutt, P. (1992). *Managing Planned Change*. New York: Prentice-Hall.

Nutt, P. (2002). *Why Decisions Fail: Avoiding the Blunders and Traps That Lead to Debacles*. San Francisco, CA: Berrett-Koehler Publishers Inc.

Nutt, P. and Backoff, R. (1992). *Strategic Management of Public and Third Sector Organizations: A Handbook for Leaders*. San Francisco, CA: Jossey-Bass.

O'Leary, R. and Bingham, L. (2009). *The Collaborative Public Manager*. Washington, DC: Georgetown University Press.

Poole, M.S., Van de Ven, A.H., Dooley, K. and Holmes, M.E. (2000). *Organizational Change and Innovation Processes: Theory and Methods for Research*. New York: Oxford University Press.

Powell, W. (1990). Neither market nor hierarchy: network forms of organization. In B. Staw and L. Cummings (eds), *Research in Organizational Behavior*. Greenwich, CT: JAI Press, pp. 295–336.

Rainey, H. (1997). *Understanding and Managing Public Organizations*, 4th edn. San Francisco, CA: Jossey-Bass.

Riker, W. (1962). *The Theory of Political Coalitions*. New Haven, CT: Yale University Press.

Riker, W. (1986). *The Art of Political Manipulation*. New Haven, CT: Yale University Press.

Simon, H.A. (1996). *Sciences of the Artificial*, 3rd edn. Cambridge, MA: MIT Press.

Stone, D. (2002). *Policy Paradox and Political Reason*, 2nd edn. New York: W.W. Norton.

Suchman, M. (1995). Managing legitimacy: strategic and institutional approaches. *Academy of Management Review*, 20(3), 571–610.

Thomas, J.C. (1995). *Public Participation in Public Decisions*. San Francisco, CA: Jossey-Bass.

Thompson, L. (2001). *The Mind and Heart of the Negotiator*, 2nd edn. Upper Saddle River, NJ: Prentice-Hall.

Tuchman, B. (1984). *The March of Folly: From Troy to Vietnam*. New York: Knopf.

Van der Heijden, K. (2005). *Scenarios: The Art of Strategic Conversation*, 2nd edn. Chichester: John Wiley & Sons.

Wildavsky, A. (1979). *Speaking Truth to Power: The Art and Craft of Policy Analysis*. Boston, MA: Little, Brown.

PART III

KEY MANAGERIAL ISSUES IN INNOVATION IN PUBLIC SERVICES

9. Evidence-based policy-making for innovation
Brian W. Head

INTRODUCTION

The use of reliable evidence as an input for policy development and for the improvement of service delivery is widely agreed to be vital. Indeed, high-quality decision-making seems improbable without sound evidence and thorough debate about options and outcomes. Sound evidence is a necessary condition for developing close links between service goals, implementation actions, and good outcomes for clients and citizens. The benefits of well-informed decision processes include increased capacity for effective policy design, more effective programme implementation, better monitoring of performance, and thus improved outcomes for clients and citizens.

Innovation for improvement in public policy and public services is generally seen to depend on knowledge and evidence, even for those issues where the level of scientific certainty is modest. Innovation is generally seen as a desirable feature of policy systems, and the 'diffusion' of innovation through new programmes and professional practices is central to the success of innovation. However, 'change for its own sake' has negative effects, undermining morale and capabilities; organizational restructuring often exhibits some of these negative features. This discussion is therefore concerned only with reforms or innovations aimed at policy/programme improvements which are socially valued, and overlooks the negative examples of managerial change based on ideology rather than evidence. Among many possible examples of innovation in public services, we highlight cases where relevant evidence has been mobilized to assist in decision-making.

Decisions and choices are made in the context of ideas, expertise, interests, values and institutions. In this context, rigorous research-based knowledge is seldom positioned at the centre of decision-making. That is why evidence-*informed* policy advice and management practice is a more realistic goal for public sector managers than evidence-based policy. Nevertheless, within this more realistic scope, there are enormous benefits from using best available information. In settled and slowly moving policy areas, the findings of systematic research are able to be considered, with programmes adjusted incrementally as new knowledge and experience provide a basis for improvement; whereas in fast-moving and future-oriented policy areas, the best available knowledge might come from the pooling of expert judgements and from scenario analysis.

This chapter outlines some of the background to the debate on 'evidence-based' vs 'evidence-informed' policy; raises questions about how various forms of innovation are dependent on different types of evidence and expertise; notes some reasons why the public sector context offers substantial constraints, as well as opportunities, especially through partnering; and discusses some examples of evidence being utilized to facilitate public service innovation. The links between innovation and evidence-based approaches are seen to be important, but highly variable.

EVIDENCE AND POLICY

The recent history of attempts by government agencies, researchers and practitioners to establish a stronger evidence base for policy and programme decision-making is well known (Davies, Nutley and Smith 2000; Bochel and Duncan 2007; Nutley, Walter and Davies 2007; Boaz et al. 2008; Head 2008a; Head 2010). The underlying motivations for these attempted improvements in the evidence base are varied – managerial concerns with efficiency and cost-effectiveness, professional concerns with the quality of services, and political concerns about implementing promised changes or improvements. The debate has moved along from an initial concern to make a rational case for increased investment in data collection and analytical capacities in public organizations, to a more recent focus on the production and evaluation of guidance materials on how to implement evidence-based policy and professional practice (e.g. Halladay and Bero 2000; Dopson and Fitzgerald 2005; UK Treasury 2007). What are the knowledge bases for change and innovation in public services?

In reality, many key issues remain unresolved, including fundamental matters such as:

1. Rigorous research findings are not yet available in many areas for informing policy and programme decisions. As knowledge grows, the gaps and limitations may become even more evident. Thus the desire to move rapidly from a focus on improving the knowledge base (understanding the problem) to taking decisive action (fixing the problem) may be less secure in some areas than others.
2. The availability of reliable research does not ensure its subsequent uptake, influence and impact (Lavis et al. 2003; Boaz, Fitzpatrick and Shaw 2008). Hence the policy process is evidence-informed rather than evidence-based. Policy-makers, whether civil servants or political leaders, are influenced by many factors in addition to research evidence (Head 2008a). Policy managers are motivated by perceptions about external coordination and support (stakeholders and partner organizations) as well as the systematic evidence base. Political leaders are often preoccupied with maintaining support among allies, responding to media commentary and managing political risks.
3. The translation and accessibility of research knowledge are often inadequate for the needs of decision-makers (Bochel and Duncan 2007). There may be a poor 'fit' between how information has been assembled by researchers (e.g. scientific reports) and the practical needs of policy and programme managers. Researchers themselves are seldom adept at packaging and communicating their findings, and many prefer to adopt a low profile in public debates on 'hot' issues.
4. There are several forms of relevant knowledge, ranging from experimental science, systematic reviews and evaluation studies, through to the professional judgements of managers and service providers, and the experiences of stakeholders and clients. How should policy-makers and service providers weigh the relative merits of these forms of knowledge, and can they be sensibly combined (Pawson 2006; Cherney and Head 2010)? Are some forms of evidence more useful for innovation and improvement projects than others?
5. Evidence-informed approaches to policy innovation and programme improvement

operate across a range of policy and service domains. The scale of change required may be narrow or extensive, with one or several levels of organizational complexity. Some issues are handled through technical–administrative techniques, illustrated by the top-down waves of public sector reform through New Public Management (NPM) undertaken in the name of efficiency and accountability since the 1980s. On the other hand, many areas of social policy involve large numbers of stakeholders who need to be engaged or consulted, requiring network and partnership approaches to achieve shared purposes (Goldsmith and Kettl 2009). These variable contexts have different implications for knowledge and innovation. For example, complex connections between inter-related social issues will increase the knowledge, coordination and innovation challenges at every step of the policy and implementation cycle.

6. The degree of policy controversy associated with an issue makes the evidence base appear to be less certain and less objective. Thus, in controversial or turbulent policy fields, 'evidence' is contested and arguments tend to become politicized. Policy discussion in such contexts may lack the rational, evolutionary and deliberative characteristics that are most conducive to developing agreed bodies of research evidence about 'what works'. Over time, some of these areas may settle into a more stable paradigm for discussion and assessment.

7. The 'what works' literature is largely based on evaluation and audit studies that look retrospectively at whether stated targets are being achieved in current programmes. Such studies may be conducted for a range of different purposes (Behn 2003), but are often designed primarily to demonstrate accountability for expenditures rather than designed as opportunities for mutual learning and further exploration of alternative thinking (Edelenbos and Van Buuren 2005). The 'what works' evaluation and audit literature, in other words, is not oriented to provide a sufficient base for selecting valuable future innovations. Indeed, the processes which are most likely to *generate* and embed innovation are seldom raised within the evaluation literature, and are more typically discussed in the literatures concerned with 'new governance', partnership and social innovation.

INCREMENTAL CHANGE, LEARNING AND INNOVATION

In seeking to use best available information for policy and programme improvement, there is a fundamental distinction between two scales of innovation – fine-tuning (adjustment orientation) and major reform (paradigm-shift or transformational orientation). *Incremental* change and adjustment occurs on a daily basis in modern public services. An extensive array of performance-reporting information is used to fine-tune service system performance. Service systems data are the foundation for 'continuous improvement', based on quality-management principles and business-process efficiency principles that have been developed over several decades. The evidence base for 'continuous improvement' comprises the information base concerning service cost, efficiency and service quality that allows managers to track progress against key performance indicators and targets. This performance management approach has become extensive and detailed (Van Dooren, Bouckaert and Halligan 2010), especially in large service sectors with standardized activities and unit-costing for service delivery. By its nature, this 'continuous improvement' approach enables managers to oversee efforts to fine-tune their existing systems, with a focus on product and process enhancements. It can be argued that, in most cases, these internal management performance systems tend to engage in 'single-loop' learning (Argyris 1976) rather than question the underlying framework of policy strategies and key actions. The search for productivity improvements occurs within an existing preferred paradigm. Given this background, where are the sources of wider thinking about innovative reform?

One possibility is that external assessment of public services could offer a more robust lens for inquiry into best practice and for identifying opportunities for substantial improvement (Walshe, Harvey and Jas 2010). Such assessments can operate at all organizational levels, from macro (whole system) to micro (individual organizations). Inspectorates, auditors and commissioned evaluations take a systematic approach to data quality and data analysis, and might be expected to exhibit high levels of objectivity and detachment in their assessments. Most projects that are subject to external evaluation are judged within the existing framework of agreed standards and actions, rather than provide a new basis for reconsidering key underlying assumptions ('double-loop' learning). This is to be expected in stable policy areas, where there is less incentive to think 'outside the box' because the existing services framework seems both adequate and legitimate. But where there have been major problems, and the legitimacy of the current paradigm has been questioned, the findings of external assessors might provide a basis for arguments that new departures are warranted.

A further source of substantive change has been information technology (IT), and especially the development of electronic data bases since the 1980s, which have revolutionized organizational management and financial accounting. The initial focus was on improving business systems, utilizing the greatly expanded options for data processing and analysis. After these initial improvements to organizational systems, the focus shifted to redesigning service systems to take advantage of enhanced information and communication channels (Henman 2010). The continuing waves of change in communications technology are opening new opportunities for much more extensive consultation with clients and citizens, and dialogue-based engagement with stakeholders.

Another source of broader thinking is the scope and quality of political debate on public affairs, including the leadership roles and problem-solving capacities of decision-makers themselves (Heifetz 1994; Moore 1995). As noted below, the public service context is generally risk-averse and wedded to established routines. New ideas are therefore more likely to gain traction outside government departments, sponsored by policy entrepreneurs in non-governmental organizations (NGOs), think-tanks, research networks, the media and business associations. Political leaders may engage with such ideas as they enter into social, economic and environmental debates, and some new ideas may be adopted and modified by political leaders, whether in government or in opposition parties. Policy promises made by leaders can provide significant opportunities for seeking new approaches to deal with newly recognized problems and for tackling ongoing problems in new ways.

CONSTRAINTS AND OPPORTUNITIES FOR MAJOR CHANGE

The constraints on public sector managers who might wish to engage in innovation and risk taking are well known. Public officials are heavily constrained by government priorities and commitments, administrative routines, probity and accountability frameworks, professional/organizational culture, the detailed requirements of financial and human resource management, and the endless reporting and briefing cycles. There are strong strands of political science research pointing not only to the institutional constraints and inertia of governmental organizations and accountability systems, but also to the political contingencies and non-rational elements that underlie policy decisions and the selection of policy instruments (e.g. Hall and Taylor 1996; Peters 2005).

Senior public sector managers must deal with the complex demands of managing upwards (meeting the needs and expectations of Ministers and agency chiefs), downwards (ensuring their own work units are operating efficiently) and outwards (working with stakeholders, partners and clients outside government: Moore 1995: p. 17; O'Toole, Meier and Nicholson-Crotty 2005). The key issue for public officials supporting innovation is likely to be the balance between the positive incentives and the negative sanctions attached to initiatives that potentially challenge the status quo and its many vested interests, both inside and outside the government sector. In routine management of public programmes, officials do not have political or legal authorizations to engage in negotiations or debates that question established systems. Predictability and accountability requirements reinforce a risk-averse organizational culture. Research findings are generally not thoroughly utilized by government agencies (Landry, Amara and Lamari 2001), and the capacity of government agencies to identify and 'absorb' internally and externally generated knowledge is highly variable (Ouimet et al. 2009; Harvey et al. 2010). Qualitative research suggests many public managers tacitly use evidence that reinforces rather than queries existing policy stances (Stevens 2011).

And yet, important innovations occur in and through the public sector (Albury 2005; Moore 2005). Transformative innovation in the public sector can be internally or externally focused. The first type (*internal* transformation of public organizations) is concerned with *processes* for restructuring public sector organizations and managerial processes to achieve greater efficiencies and capabilities. Major examples at a macro level include the wide range of top-down reforms associated with NPM since the 1980s; in many cases this reform movement was accelerated by market-based instruments such as contracting out the provision of products and services (Pollitt and Bouckaert 2004). Public sector reform movements such as NPM have been generated and diffused as much by political–economic preferences as by evidence-based assessments. Reforms of this type have a very uneven history in terms of producing enduring and valued improvements in effectiveness. However, to the extent that NPM sometimes allows flexibility for public sector managers to select various methods to achieve agreed goals, the foundations for other important service-oriented innovations might be constructed.

The second type of transformation (*externally* focused major innovation) is concerned with service design and delivery. Here, the focus is on developing new means to improve outcomes for citizens and service-users. One important and highly visible strand in the last 20 years has been the creation of interactive and accessible information channels, using the internet to provide accurate and detailed information and communication services, and to better connect government agencies with citizens and clients. Technology-enabled improvements in service systems (e.g. in social-care, health-care or public transport) focus on accessible service information for citizens and performance-monitoring information for officials. A second, and more fundamental, basis for improving human services is evidence-informed innovation in policy design and corresponding innovations in programme delivery. Policy design work is at the centre of public policy and management, and policy innovation is often driven politically from a high level. Paradigm shifts in policy require high-level political authorization and direction; this is rarely available to public officials, and is usually associated with a change of government or an ideological change in preferred policy instruments. A third basis for change is regulatory innovation (Ayres and Braithwaite 1992; Black, Lodge and Thatcher 2005; OECD 2011). The key issues for designers of regulatory regimes are how to generate effective and economical compliance with standards and principles. Here, new evidence concerning the motives of actors, and their responses to various incentives and sanctions, has assisted regulation analysts to develop new and more effective approaches to social, environmental and business regulation.

Osborne and Gaebler (1992) had championed the role of local-level public sector entrepreneurship to improve services and focus on results. The US federal government 'Re-invention' movement during the Clinton Presidency subsequently focused on streamlining and energizing the bureaucracy (Borins 1998; Kettl 1998). In the UK, the service improvement programmes for local authorities devised by central government encouraged better outcomes based on performance metrics, with differential rewards and sanctions. Given the important role of local authorities in service delivery, decentralized initiatives can become major sources of service innovation. However, if services are seriously under-funded and if local knowledge and discretion are overwhelmed by rigid central requirements, the likelihood of innovative services is greatly diminished (Sullivan, Barnes and Matka 2006).

Political leadership sets the priorities and directions for public policy in a democracy, and public sector innovation should seek to achieve better outcomes within this broad framework set by government. The values and commitments of political leaders, the mobilization of stakeholder interests and media representations of public opinion all play very large roles in how policy is interpreted and adjusted. The role of ideas and arguments is crucial (Majone 1989; Hajer and Wagenaar 2003). The political context, such as a crisis or a regime change, sometimes allows new problems to be identified and new solutions to be canvassed (Kingdon 1995). Evidence-based analyses can contribute to shaping these alternatives.

Despite the generally risk-averse organizational climate of public sector culture, there are two important foundations for valuable innovation that can be developed and legitimated by public managers. The first is to develop the evidence base that can underpin constructive change and the second is to develop partnerships and collaborative approaches with NGOs for tackling complex problems.

EVIDENCE SYSTEMS TO SUPPORT INNOVATION

In considering the appropriate evidence base for assessing and guiding service improvement, the relevant information is much broader than official statistics. There is a wide spectrum of insights and contributions to knowledge available from experts, stakeholders and clients. These contributions vary by discipline (e.g. IT, economics, sociology, management, public health, etc.); by occupation-based skills within relevant organizations (e.g. services professionals, contract managers, policy advisors, programme evaluators); and by the various groupings of stakeholders and clients.

Investing in the evidence base to support public sector innovation requires a systematic commitment to programme evaluation and community engagement. Establishing and developing an evaluation culture are the key to generating valuable forms of innovation. Building evaluation capability in the public sector requires several elements: investment in skills training, investment in multi-level data collection, analysis of current performance data, consideration of longer-term trends and contingencies, comparative analysis across regions and national boundaries, investment in the regular evaluation of programmes, and willingness to publish both the data and the evaluation findings to encourage discussion. However, these rational–analytical elements operate in a political environment shaped by government policy commitments, stakeholder support for various options, and ideological preferences. The availability of good data and analytical skills is an important foundation but not a sufficient basis for evidence-informed policy design. Innovative solutions emerge in the context of debate, not simply from technocratic expertise. A sound policy process requires analysis, consultation and deliberative debate.

Decisions about policy and programmes in the real world are always taken with available knowledge from diverse sources, rather than waiting for comprehensive and rigorous findings from evaluation studies. Indeed, there would be few examples of valuable innovation if decision-makers had to wait for a high level of scientific certainty to emerge from evaluation research. Rigorous scientific methods for programme evaluation, with systematic data analysis and controlled trials as recommended by the Campbell Collaboration (www.campbellcollaboration.org), have been mandated for some social programmes by legislators in the USA. However, while it is important to recognize differences in the quality of research studies, based on the level of methodological rigour used to design and interpret field studies, the claim that randomized controlled trials (RCTs) as pioneered in medical research should be generally applied in the social sciences is misleading. The alternative position turns on the difficulty of implementing RCTs in sensitive areas of social policy; the difficulty of transplanting quasi-experimental results to large-scale programmes; and the tendency of RCTs to downplay the knowledge and experience of professionals with field experience (Schorr and Auspos 2003; Pawson 2006). Moreover, decision-makers, policy managers, scientists and service-users may have very different perspectives on what kinds of evidence are most trustworthy. A helpful understanding of causes and consequences may emerge from 'systematic reviews' of all available research (Petticrew and Roberts 2005), taking into account the rigour of the methods followed, but the practical knowledge of professionals should not be discounted.

PREVENTION PROGRAMMES AS SOCIAL EXPERIMENTS

Innovative approaches to address social problems have gradually emerged in recent decades, through various processes of advocacy, lobbying, experimentation and diffusion. For example, 'preventative' approaches towards improving individual and community well-being have become increasingly common. The policy rationale for the prevention approach to social problems is to take early action to anticipate, prepare for, and intervene to mitigate the likely effects of social harm. In the fields of health, education and social development, for example, the emphasis is on ensuring that every child receives the care required in their early years for healthy physical, emotional and cognitive development. This universal objective (primary prevention) is complemented by targeted strategies to assist more vulnerable children and families with high risk-factors, who are less able to avoid poor outcomes (secondary prevention). The evidence base for these dual strategies is substantial – for example, studies establishing the developmental significance of the early years (Shonkoff and Phillips 2000); studies identifying higher-risk social groups for additional services (France and Homel 2007); cost–benefit analyses of mainstream and targeted strategies (Heckman 2006); and so on. These policy and programme ideas have been translated into major social policy interventions (Coote, Allen and Woodhead 2004), such as Head-Start and Harlem Children's Zone in the USA, Sure-Start and Every Child Matters in the UK, and Communities for Children in Australia. Progress is likely to be slow in developing models that work under specific conditions, and diffusion of 'silver bullet' solutions is unlikely (Brooks-Gunn 2003).

Prevention programmes cannot aim to reduce all sources of harm in a comprehensive sense. Rather, they take an evidence-informed approach to identifying likely sources of harm and identifying cost-effective methods to mitigate the onset or the worsening of poor outcomes for individuals and groups. Often the intention is to improve the capacities and skills of the vulnerable groups (e.g. financial literacy, parenting skills) rather than simply increasing the direct services provided by others on their behalf. The evidence of community benefits does not speak for itself; there are major educational and political challenges in communicating the overarching aims and benefits of prevention, in identifying the roles and responsibilities of government, NGOs and families, and in acknowledging the practical limits on government's ability to manage risks for every social group. It is important to foster informed debate on the distinctive features of prevention approaches, and find ways to re-balance public spending between prevention services and emergency responses to problem-cases. Benefits demonstrated by evaluation studies generally take years to emerge, and funding decisions are therefore made on the likelihood rather than certainty of good outcomes. In this sense, interventions *are* experiments, engaged in a process of controlled experimentation backed up by the ongoing evaluation of innovations (Campbell 1969, 1998).

In practice, adjustments need to be made as programmes evolve, for example to clarify roles in coordination and delivery. The downside of pragmatic adjustment is that programme 'fidelity' (adherence to core testable propositions defined in the original programme logic) may be weakened and the results of evaluation would thus also be weakened (Fixsen et al. 2005). However, there is arguably an inherent difference between the central knowledge typically used for programme design and the detailed contextual knowledge used for managing field situations, where general goals and procedures need to be tailored for local conditions.

One way of dealing with this dilemma is to make greater use of devolved governance arrangements with community-based NGOs. This involves a paradigm shift away from central government control and towards greater empowerment of local bodies with strong grassroots connections. In programmes funded by central bodies but largely implemented at local and regional levels, accountability and effectiveness issues often hinge on how the trade-off between central rules and local flexibility has been determined. In many cases the central controls appear to undermine the achievement of optimal outcomes at local level because local contexts are not given the legitimacy they deserve (Geddes 2006; Sullivan, Barnes and Matka 2006; Geddes, Davie and Fuller 2007). This represents a major challenge for effective learning about best practice at the local level. It also complicates analysis of whether and how local successes could be 'scaled up' or mainstreamed into becoming general programmes at national level.

THE COMPLEX COORDINATION CHALLENGE

The appropriate governance frameworks for facilitating innovation and complex problem-solving are strongly contested. With the recent displacement of traditional state-centred approaches to innovation and coordination, the two key governance approaches are neo-liberal economics and networked governance. They exhibit different approaches to the innovation and coordination challenges. The neo-liberal preference is for governments to step back from a directive role and to rely instead on market-based mechanisms to achieve effective outcomes. In choosing instruments for intervention, neo-liberals prefer price-based incentives as an alternative to the previous orthodoxies of expanding government-provided services and more detailed regulation. The relevant *evidence* base would focus on how markets and incentives work in these domains. For example, homelessness could be tackled through rent assistance in the private rental market; green energy choices could be supported through price incentives; and welfare payments could be conditional on job-seeking efforts by parents and regular school-attendance by children. This neo-liberal approach is seen as less cumbersome than state-centred interventions, which are claimed to require heavy investments in staffing, reporting, accountability, coordination and compliance.

However, it is important to note that neo-liberal policy solutions still require excellence in public sector governance, especially the framework of rules and the skills, knowledge, integrity and coordination capabilities of public managers and their political masters. Every policy domain is shaped by public authority, including those where neo-liberal preferences for market structures, rules and instruments are strongly entrenched (Bell and Hindmoor 2009). This steering role for government provides opportunities for evaluation research to inform decision-makers' judgements about effectiveness, for example the conditions under which these market-based innovations actually produce good outcomes.

The alternative approach to innovation in complex policy areas is networked governance (Moore and Hartley 2008; Goldsmith and Kettl 2009; Osborne 2010). The strategic assumptions here are that the knowledge base for addressing complex issues (whether social, economic or environmental) is always incomplete; that complex issues are inter-related and constantly changing; that drawing on the knowledge and experience of experts and stakeholders across various sectors (government, business, community, research, etc.) helps develop a shared understanding of problems and challenges; and that evidence-informed pathways emerge from collaborative processes of debate. Collaboration through partnerships and dialogue may be more time-consuming, but the willingness of decision-makers to interact with stakeholders in addressing difficult issues will generally produce more robust options and outcomes (Bommert 2010).

Recent studies suggest that public/private innovation in services does not emerge simply through top-down planning, but emerges through the actual processes of working across organizational boundaries, and that network relationships are crucial (Considine and Lewis 2007; Bommert 2010). In this approach, the focus may include encouraging capacity-building in NGOs (or in joint public/NGO partnerships) as a basis for innovative practice in service delivery. While the main focus may be the efficient management of current problems, there is also potential for developing 'prospective' understanding of how issues may unfold, how contingencies may be anticipated, and how new solutions can be constructed through shared problem-solving.

In multi-level political systems the evidence base for evaluating programme success is complex (Bache and Flinders 2004; Geddes 2006), and local/regional scales are vitally important for testing the efficacy of programmes with national scope. For evaluators, this multi-scalar dimension complicates the task of programme evaluation (Spicer and Smith 2008); that is, the problem of establishing the parameters of 'what works for whom under what conditions' in a context where there are multiple actors and levels. For programme managers, the structural rigidities of inter-governmental roles need to be tackled, with new emphasis on the effective management of collaborative networks to negotiate and energize beneficial collective outcomes (Koppenjan and Klijn 2004).

Such networks call for new kinds of strategic and operational skills. For example, relationship management skills are fundamental for the governance of collaborations and partnerships, but are not envisaged in the business model of NPM. Roles and responsibilities for networks and partnerships need to be freshly negotiated, and performance expectations clarified for each initiative. For policy managers located in different agencies, there are major challenges in developing an integrated policy approach across the diverse issues that may contribute to programme outcomes. Effective coordination is vital, both for strategy development and for programme implementation (O'Toole and Montjoy 1984). Implementation managers have additional problems in implementing joint activities in a coordinated manner, including both service delivery and performance monitoring. Agencies require specific incentives for collaborative action; collaborative intent and collaborative capacity cannot be assumed, and have to be developed over time (Sullivan, Barnes and Matka 2006). Inter-organizational work requires special skills, persistence over time, and structured commitment to learning from current and past experience. This requirement for 'joined up' collaborative effort may be especially difficult for agencies whose organizational culture has not embraced previous experiences of successful collaborations (Bardach 1998; Ling 2002; Bogdanor 2005).

CONCLUSIONS: REFORM AND INNOVATION IN TURBULENT TIMES

The government sector is not (and probably never was) a well-ordered and predictable system where detailed evidence about effective performance is a central input into policy development and decisions about adjusting and improving programmes. Evidence-rich policy systems are most securely grounded in those areas of social, health, educational and environmental policy where it is possible to monitor and assess underlying trends and causal patterns on a routine basis. This understanding of baseline information provides a foundation for understanding the impacts of specific interventions and ongoing adjustments. By contrast, evidence-based approaches seem to have less standing and influence in those areas where the issues are turbulent, 'wicked' and subject to rapid change (Head 2008b; Byrne 2011). Evidence is deployed under very different conditions in turbulent policy fields marked by value conflict, rapid change and high risk. Evidence is used for partisan purposes by proponents in various policy arguments, undermining the conditions for a consensual and methodical approach to evidence formation.

There are two distinct types of knowledge challenge in these circumstances. One is the *knowledge uncertainty* arising from complex and rapid change, where there are many 'known unknowns' and research gaps. Here, the main lines of new thinking focus on sharing expert knowledge from diverse sources and developing joint research agendas. The second is the problem of *stakeholder conflict* over values, risk perceptions and appropriate actions (Schon and Rein 1994). Here, the main pathways tend to be dialogue-based engagement processes where empirical and normative issues can be debated and moderated. Use of future scenarios, allowing stakeholders to focus on desired outcomes and strategic risk management, can sometimes assist in creating more alignment of thinking across groups. However, governments are seldom able to create the deliberative spaces for addressing such problems. Thus, policy issues which are complex, contested and turbulent are often identified as matters where social innovation processes outside government might be more likely to generate new thinking (Mulgan 2006, 2009; Kohli and Mulgan 2010). Governments then have the option of adopting, adapting or partnering to support the outcomes of such innovative thinking.

A recent public sector attempt to consider these challenges through cross-sectoral engagement is the New Synthesis Project initiated in Canada (Bourgon 2007), which has evolved into an international network (Bourgon and Milley 2010). The underlying philosophy is that the 'public space' needs to be expanded by bringing citizens and stakeholders into the value-creation process. Of course, 'co-production' of services is already a reality in several service areas (Alford 2009), but the New Synthesis approach goes further in envisaging robust engagement processes for tackling unresolved and fast-changing problems.

In conclusion, despite two decades of structural reforms and performance measurement, innovation has not generally become the hallmark of public sector behaviour. Better training for public managers in leadership and problem-solving skills has assisted in encouraging innovation, but the structural impediments have remained. While some agencies have undoubtedly engaged in innovation, and have spent considerable efforts implementing mandated reforms within their organizational processes, it has not proved possible to mandate public sector innovative behaviour beyond niche process areas (such as the adoption of IT-enabled customer service). Indeed, the culture of the public service in almost every nation tends to be risk-averse and procedural, owing to administrative requirements for accountability, procedural fairness and predictability.

The most recent waves of innovation have come from two directions: (i) the encouragement of NGOs to provide innovation leadership, while continuing to work in partnerships with government and business; and (ii) the widespread development of specialized roles for knowledge-brokering and bridge-building between organizations (Ward et al. 2010) – this development is based on ideas drawn from the knowledge diffusion and knowledge translation literatures (e.g. Bammer, Michaux and Sanson 2010). More generally, working through networks and partnerships is increasingly identified as a crucial approach for adding value in many fields of public policy and service planning (Goldsmith and Eggers 2004).

Further research is warranted to improve the evidence base for understanding cases where robust and well-grounded innovation occurs, and especially where public officials and resources can encourage the success of others. Public service leaders and agencies can invest in better information, and better leadership skills for managing change processes; but the key outward-looking factors promoting innovation are likely to be network engagement and linkage supports.

REFERENCES

Albury, D. (2005). Fostering innovation in public services. *Public Money and Management*, 25(1), 51–56.

Alford, J. (2009). *Engaging Public Sector Clients: From Service-Delivery to Co-production*. Houndmills: Palgrave Macmillan.

Argyris, C. (1976). Single-loop and double-loop models in research on decision making. *Administrative Science Quarterly*, 21(3), 363–375.

Ayres, I. and Braithwaite, J. (1992). *Responsive Regulation: Transcending the Deregulation Debate*. Oxford: Oxford University Press.

Bache, I. and Flinders, M. (eds) (2004). *Multi-level Governance*. Oxford: Oxford University Press.

Bammer, G., Michaux, A. and Sanson, A. (eds) (2010). *Bridging the Know–Do Gap: Knowledge Brokering to Improve Child Wellbeing*. Canberra: ANU e-Press.

Bardach, E. (1998). *Getting Agencies to Work Together: The Practice and Theory of Managerial Craftsmanship*. Washington, DC: Brookings Institution Press.

Behn, R.D. (2003). Why measure performance? *Public Administration Review*, 63(5), 586–606.

Bell, S. and Hindmoor, A. (2009). *Rethinking Governance*. Cambridge: Cambridge University Press.

Black, J., Lodge, M. and Thatcher, M. (eds) (2005). *Regulatory Innovation: A Comparative Analysis*. Cheltenham and Northampton, MA: Edward Elgar.

Boaz, A., Fitzpatrick, S. and Shaw, B. (2008). *Assessing the Impact of Research on Policy: A Review of the Literature*. London: King's College and Policy Studies Institute.

Boaz, A., Grayson, L., Levitt, R. and Solebury, W. (2008). Does evidence-based policy work? Learning from the UK experience. *Evidence and Policy*, 4(2), 233–253.

Bochel, H. and Duncan, S. (eds) (2007). *Making Policy in Theory and Practice*. Bristol: Policy Press.

Bogdanor, V. (ed.) (2005). *Joined-Up Government*. Oxford: Oxford University Press.

Bommert, B. (2010). Collaborative innovation in the public sector. *International Public Management Review*, 11(1), 15–33.

Borins, S.F. (1998). *Innovating with Integrity*. Washington, DC: Georgetown University Press.

Borins, S.F. (ed.) (2008). *Innovations in Government*. Washington, DC: Brookings Institution.

Bourgon, J. (2007). Responsive, responsible and respected government: towards a new public administration theory. *International Review of Administrative Sciences*, 73(1), 7–26.

Bourgon, J. and Milley, P. (2010). *The Frontiers of Public Administration: The New Synthesis Project*. Available at: http://www.ns6newsynthesis.com/documents/new_frontiers.pdf (accessed 30 July 2012).

Brooks-Gunn, J. (2003). Do you believe in magic? What we can expect from early childhood intervention programmes. *Social Policy Report*, 17(1), 1–14.

Byrne, D. (2011). *Applying Social Science: The Role of Social Research in Politics, Policy and Practice*. Bristol: Policy Press.

Campbell, D.T. (1969). Reforms as experiments. *American Psychologist*, 24(4), 409–429.

Campbell, D.T. (1998). The experimenting society. In W.N. Dunn (ed.), *The Experimenting Society: Essays in Honor of Donald T. Campbell*. New Brunswick, NJ: Transaction Publishers, pp. 35–68.

Cherney, A. and Head, B.W. (2010). Evidence-based policy and practice: key challenges for improvement. *Australian Journal of Social Issues*, 45(4), 509–526.

Considine, M. and Lewis, J.M. (2007). Innovation and innovators inside government: from institutions to networks. *Governance*, 20(4), 581–607.

Coote, A., Allen, J. and Woodhead, D. (2004). *Finding Out What Works: Building Knowledge about Complex Community-Based Initiatives*. London: King's Fund.

Davies, H.T., Nutley, S.M. and Smith, P.C. (eds) (2000). *What Works? Evidence-Based Policy and Practice in Public Services*. Bristol: Policy Press.

Dopson, S. and Fitzgerald, L. (eds) (2005). *Knowledge to Action? Evidence-Based Health Care in Context*. Oxford: Oxford University Press.

Edelenbos, J. and Van Buuren, A. (2005). The learning evaluation: a theoretical and empirical exploration. *Evaluation Review*, 29(6), 591–612.

Ferlie, E., Fitzgerald, L., Wood, M. and Hawkins, C. (2005). The non-spread of innovations: the mediating role of professional groups. *Academy of Management Journal*, 48(1), 117–134.

Fixsen, D., Naoom, S., Blase, K., Friedman, R. and Wallace, F. (2005). *Implementation Research: A Synthesis of the Literature*. Tampa, FL: University of South Florida.

France, A. and Homel, R. (eds) (2007). *Pathways and Crime Prevention*. Abingdon: Willan Publishing.

Geddes, M. (2006). Partnership and the limits to local governance in England. *International Journal of Urban and Regional Research*, 30(1), 76–97.

Geddes, M., Davie, J. and Fuller, C. (2007). Evaluating local strategic partnerships. *Local Government Studies*, 33(1), 97–116.

Goldsmith, S. and Eggers, W. (2004). *Governing by Network: The New Shape of the Public Sector*. Washington, DC: Brookings Institution Press.

Goldsmith, S. and Kettl, D. (eds) (2009). *Unlocking the Power of Networks: Keys to High Performance Government*. Washington, DC: Brookings Institution Press.

Hajer, M.A. and Wagenaar, H. (eds) (2003). *Deliberative Policy Analysis: Understanding Governance in the Network Society*. Cambridge: Cambridge University Press.

Hall, P.A. and Taylor, R. (1996). Political science and the three new institutionalisms. *Political Studies*, 44(5), 936–957.

Halladay, M. and Bero, L. (2000). Getting research into practice: implementing evidence-based practice in health care. *Public Money & Management*, 20(4), 43–50.

Hartley, J. (2005). Innovation in governance and public services: past and present. *Public Money and Management*, 25(1), 27–34.

Harvey, G., Skelcher, C., Spencer, E., Jas, P. and Walshe, K. (2010). Absorptive capacity in a non-market environment. *Public Management Review*, 12(1), 77–97.

Head, B.W. (2008a). Three lenses of evidence based policy. *Australian Journal of Public Administration*, 67(1), 1–11.

Head, B.W. (2008b). Wicked problems in public policy. *Public Policy*, 3(2), 101–118.

Head, B.W. (2010). Reconsidering evidence-based policy: key issues and challenges. *Policy and Society: An Interdisciplinary Journal of Policy Research*, 29(2), 77–94.

Heckman, J.J. (2006). Skill formation and the economics of investing in disadvantaged children. *Science*, 312 (5782, 30 June), 1900–1902.

Heifetz, R.A. (1994). *Leadership Without Easy Answers*. Cambridge, MA: Harvard University Press.

Henman, P. (2010). *Governing Electronically: E-Government and the Reconfiguration of Public Administration, Policy and Power*. Houndmills: Palgrave Macmillan.

Kettl, D.F. (1998). *Reinventing Government: A Fifth-Year Report Card*. Washington, DC: Brookings Institution.

Kingdon, J. (1995). *Agendas, Alternatives and Public Policies*, 2nd edn. New York: HarperCollins.

Kohli, J. and Mulgan, G. (2010). *Capital Ideas: How to Generate Innovation in the Public Sector*. Young Foundation and Center for American Progress.

Koppenjan, J. and Klijn, E.-H. (2004). *Managing Uncertainties in Networks*. London: Routledge.

Landry, R., Amara, N. and Lamari, M. (2001). Utilization of social science research knowledge in Canada. *Research Policy*, 30(2), 333–349.

Lavis, J.N., Robertson, D., Woodside, J., McLeod, C. and Abelson, J. (2003). How can research organizations more effectively transfer research knowledge to decision makers? *Milbank Quarterly*, 81(2), 221–248.

Ling, T. (2002). Delivering joined-up government in the UK. *Public Administration*, 80(4), 615–642.

Majone, G. (1989). *Evidence, Argument, and Persuasion in the Policy Process*. New Haven, CT: Yale University Press.

Moore, M.H. (1995). *Creating Public Value*. Cambridge, MA: Harvard University Press.

Moore, M.H. (2005). Break-through innovations and continuous improvement: two different models of innovative processes in the public sector. *Public Money and Management*, 25(1), 43–50.

Moore, M.H. and Hartley, J. (2008). Innovation in governance. *Public Management Review*, 10(1), 3–20.

Mulgan, G. (2006). The process of social innovation. *Innovations*, 1(2), 145–162.

Mulgan, G. (2009). *The Art of Public Strategy: Mobilizing Power and Knowledge for the Common Good*. Oxford: Oxford University Press.

Nutley, S., Walter, I. and Davies, H. (2007). *Using Evidence: How Research can Inform Public Services*. Bristol: Policy Press.

OECD (Organization for Economic Cooperation and Development) (2011). *Regulatory Policy and Governance*. Paris: OECD.

Osborne, S.P. (ed.) (2010). *The New Public Governance? Emerging Perspectives on the Theory and Practice of Public Governance*. London: Routledge.

Osborne, S.P. and Brown, K. (2005). *Managing Change and Innovation in Public Service Organizations*. London: Routledge.

Osborne, D. and Gaebler, T. (1992). *Reinventing Government: How the Entrepreneurial Spirit is Transforming the Public Sector*. Reading, MA: Addison-Wesley.

O'Toole, L.J. and Montjoy, R.S. (1984). Interorganizational policy implementation: a theoretical perspective. *Public Administration Review*, 44(6), 491–503.

O'Toole, L.J., Meier, K. and Nicholson-Crotty, S. (2005). Managing upward, downward and outward. *Public Management Review*, 7(1), 45–68.

Ouimet, M., Landry, R., Ziam, S. and Bedard, P.O. (2009). The absorption of research knowledge by public civil servants. *Evidence and Policy*, 5(4), 331–350.

Pawson, R. (2006). *Evidence-Based Policy: A Realist Perspective*. London: Sage.

Peters, B.G. (2005). *Institutional Theory in Political Science*, 2nd edn. New York: Continuum.

Petticrew, M. and Roberts, H. (2005). *Systematic Reviews in the Social Sciences*. Oxford: Blackwells.

Pollitt, C. and Bouckaert, G. (2004). *Public Management Reform: A Comparative Analysis*, 2nd edn. Oxford: Oxford University Press.

Schon, D.A. and Rein, M. (1994). *Frame Reflection: Toward the Resolution of Intractable Policy Controversies*. New York: Basic Books.

Schorr, L.B. and Auspos, P. (2003). Usable information about what works: building a broader and deeper knowledge base. *Journal of Policy Analysis and Management*, 22(4), 669–676.

Shonkoff, J.P. and Phillips, D.A. (2000). *From Neurons to Neighborhoods: The Science of Early Childhood Development*. Washington, DC: National Academy Press.

Spicer, N. and Smith, P. (2008). Evaluating complex area-based initiatives in a context of change. *Evaluation*, 14(1), 75–90.

Stevens, A. (2011). Telling policy stories: an ethnographic study of the use of evidence in policy-making in the UK. *Journal of Social Policy*, 40(2), 237–255.

Sullivan, H., Barnes, M. and Matka, E. (2006). Collaborative capacity and strategies in area-based initiatives. *Public Administration*, 84(2), 289–310.

UK Cabinet Office (2008). *Think Research: Using Research Evidence to Inform Service Development for Vulnerable Groups*. London: Social Exclusion Taskforce, Cabinet Office.

UK Treasury (2007). *Analysis for Policy: Evidence-Based Policy in Practice*. London: Government Social Research Unit, Treasury.

Van Dooren, W., Bouckaert, G. and Halligan, J. (2010). *Performance Management in the Public Sector*. London: Routledge.

Walshe, K., Harvey, G. and Jas, P. (eds) (2010). *Connecting Knowledge and Performance in Public Services: From Knowing to Doing*. Cambridge: Cambridge University Press.

Ward, V., Smith, S., Carruthers, S., Hamer, S. and House, A. (2010). *Knowledge Brokering: Exploring the Process of Transferring Knowledge into Action*. Leeds: University of Leeds, Leeds Institute of Health Sciences.

10. Innovation in public services: engaging with risk[1]
Stephen P. Osborne and Louise Brown

INTRODUCTION

The policy trajectory privileging innovation as a means to improve the efficiency and effectiveness of public services in the UK has been moving at pace. Referred to recently by NESTA (the National Endowment for Science, Technology, and the Arts) as 'the innovation imperative' (Harris and Albury 2009) and enshrined within the UK government White Paper *Innovation Nation* (Department of Innovation, Universities and Skills (DIUS) 2008), the desire to use innovation to reform public services is strong. This commitment has increased as the extent of the economic recession and its impact on public expenditure have been exposed (Patterson et al. 2009, p. 12). However, the same research also identified that this economic climate may lead to a focus upon less risky types of innovation, irrespective of comparative levels of need.

Within this policy context, one issue that we argue has received less attention than it deserves is that of the role of risk in innovation (Osborne 1998; Brown 2010; Osborne and Brown 2011).[2] Often within the public service context, risk is presented as a negative phenomenon – at best as something to be minimised if not avoided. Yet writers on innovation in both the business and public sectors have emphasised the centrality of risk to successful innovation (e.g. Singh 1986; Borins 2001). This chapter argues that current public service frameworks do not facilitate the successful negotiation and management of risk within the innovation process and argues for an alternative based upon *negotiated risk governance* rather than minimisation.

MANAGING INNOVATION AND RISK IN A PUBLIC POLICY CONTEXT

In the broader management literature, much of the literature associated with managing risk derives from either the corporate financial sector (e.g. Stulz 1996) or the health and safety industry (Rasmussen 1997). In both these contexts, definitions of risk are couched in negative terms: '[r]isk is the probability of a particular adverse event occurring during a stated period of time . . . the likelihood of some specific negative event' (Breakwell 2007, p. 2). A further recurrent theme in the literature is the differentiation of 'risk' and 'uncertainty' – risk being decision making in the context of known options and their likely outcomes and uncertainty being decision making in the context of unknown options and outcomes (e.g. Tversky and Fox 1995).

In public services, extant public policy in the UK does offer guidance at the broadest level of risk management (e.g. HM Treasury 2004; National Audit Office 2004). Yet this guidance makes no reference to the often contested nature of public services and their benefits or the challenges of balancing risks and benefits in the innovation process. The

Audit Commission (2007) has also acknowledged the importance of risk in the innovation process – but again offers little in the way of guidance beyond exhortations that risk
management is 'critical in keeping innovative projects on track' and that local authorities
believe that it is 'making an increasing contribution to the delivery of innovative projects'
(p. 40). Similarly, the important recent White Paper *Innovation Nation* (DIUS 2008)
noted that current public policy could create a 'heightened aversion to risk' in public
services (p. 72) – but with no detailed guidance on responding to this. The Public
Management Risk Association (ALARM) acknowledges the contested risks in public
services – but once more adopts an explicit *risk minimisation* approach, on the basis that
risk incurs an un-necessary financial burden on public services (Williams 2009). In
Scotland, the recent strategic framework for innovation (Scottish Government 2009)
worryingly makes no mention at all of the management of risk in relation to innovation
in public services.

Within the public service research literature, there is also a small, if unsatisfactory,
literature on risk and risk management. *Inter alia*, Hood (2002) has argued that risk
management is primarily concerned with blame attribution rather than safety; Vincent
(1996) has contended that the public scrutiny of public services makes it more difficult
than in the private sector; and Harman (1994) has maintained that it has actually lessened
the accountability of public services and opened up more opportunities for fraud.

It is clear from Vincent's review, too, that much of this existing public sector literature
is concerned with (insurable) personal/organisational liability for service decisions within
a decentralised state, rather than the more specific case of risk in service decisions. When
the latter is explored, he argues, it is invariably within a professional context (such as in
social care (Munro 2009) or research (Leung and Isaacs 2008)) rather than within public
and social policy. Where public and social policy does explore risk, Vincent concludes,
and bringing the argument back to Hood, is where public organisations seek to '"cover"
themselves from public scrutiny and accountability'. The ability of this literature to offer
meaningful guidance or understanding of innovation in public services is, we argue,
limited in the extreme. Indeed, one recent major, and generally thorough, textbook on
risk management in public services (Drennan and McConnell 2007) made only three
passing references to risk and innovation in public services, all along the lines that
'innovation brings with it some degree of risk' (p. 43).

The broader risk management literature is also problematic for public services, with
their associated contestability. Often the approach taken is a technocratic one, based
upon the 'objective' assessment of risk on scientific grounds (e.g. Pender 2001). Such an
approach is not appropriate in areas where the nature of risks and their potential benefits
are contested. One approach that does go beyond this is that of Renn (2008). He argues
that both risk and acceptable levels of risk are socially constructed phenomena. Thus risk
management requires not just the application of scientific knowledge but also a political
(in its broadest sense) process of negotiation. It requires social values to be integrated
with evidence of risk levels and outcomes. As such *risk governance* (as opposed to management) requires an inclusive process with a premium upon broad political debate about
acceptable levels of risk for identified innovations, inter-personal and inter-organisational
negotiation, and a commitment to ongoing communication about risk and comprehensive participation in its governance. The question at the core of these processes, he argues,
is not 'how safe is safe', but rather 'how much uncertainty and ignorance [about real or

potential risks] are the main actors willing to accept in exchange for some given benefit?' (Renn 2008, p. 277).

Such a negotiated approach to risk management has much to offer to public policy, we believe, and is being developed further by these authors (Brown and Osborne 2013). It lays bare the contested nature of innovations in public services and their outcomes, and provides a framework within which to negotiate levels of risk in such innovation – in societal, organisational, service user and workforce professional terms. It puts a premium upon communication and participation (remembering that much innovation in services comes precisely from service user co-production – Alam 2006). As such, a framework for risk governance in innovation in public services is surely an essential pre-requisite for the future and a step-change improvement from the mechanistic and technocratic approaches to risk management currently found in public policy.

NOTES

1. This chapter was first printed as an article of the same title in *Public Money & Management*, 31(1), 4–6. This work is also currently being developed further and an extended and developed framework will be published as L. Brown and S. Osborne (2013). Risk and innovation: towards a framework for risk governance in public services. *Public Management Review*, 14(1).
2. Significantly, a recent, and otherwise excellent, ESRC publication on risk and public services (Hood and Miller 2009) made no mention of risk in relation to innovation in public services.

REFERENCES

Alam, I. (2006). Removing the fuzziness from the front-end of service innovations through customer interactions. *Industrial Marketing Management*, (35), 468–480.

Audit Commission (2007). *Seeing the Light: Innovation in Local Public Services*. London: Audit Commission.

Borins, S. (2001). *The Challenge of Innovating in Government*. Washington, DC: IBM Center for the Business of Government.

Breakwell, G.M. (2007). *The Psychology of Risk*. Cambridge: Cambridge University Press.

Brown, L. (2010). Balancing risk and innovation to improve social work practice. *British Journal of Social Work*, 40(4), 1211–1228.

Brown, L. and Osborne, S. (2013). Risk and innovation: towards a framework for risk governance in public services. *Public Management Review*, 14(1).

Department of Innovation, Universities and Skills (DIUS) (2008). *Innovation Nation*. London: DIUS.

Drennan, L. and McConnell, A. (2007). *Risk and Crisis Management in the Public Sector*. London: Routledge.

Harman, E. (1994). Accountability and challenges for Australian Governments. *Australian Journal of Political Science*, 29(1), 1–17.

Harris, M. and Albury, D. (2009). *The Innovation Imperative*. London: NESTA.

HM Treasury (2004). *The Risk Programme: Improving Government's Risk Handling. Final Report to the Prime Minister*. London: HM Treasury.

Hood, C. (2002). The risk game and the blame game. *Government and Opposition*, 37(1), 15–37.

Hood, C. and Miller, P. (2009). *Risk and Public Services*. Oxford: ESRC Public Services Programme.

Leung, F. and Isaacs, F. (2008). Risk management in public sector research: approach and lessons learned at a national research organization. *R & D Management*, 38, 510–519.

Munro, E. (2009). Managing societal and institutional risk in child protection. *Risk Analysis*, 29(7), 1015–1023.

National Audit Office (2004). *Managing Risks to Improve Public Services*. London: NAO.

Osborne, S. (1998). The innovative capacity of voluntary organizations: implications for local government. *Local Government Studies*, 24(1), 19–40.

Osborne, S. and Brown, L. (2011). Innovation, public policy and public services delivery in the UK: the word that would be king? *Public Administration*, 89(40), 1335–1350.

Patterson, F., Kerrin, M., Gatto-Roissard, G. and Coan, P. (2009). *Everyday Innovation: How to Enhance Innovative Working in Employees and Organisations*. London: NESTA.

Pender, S. (2001). Managing incomplete knowledge: why risk management is not sufficient. *International Journal of Project Management*, 19, 79–87.

Rasmussen, J. (1997). Risk management in a dynamic society: a modelling problem. *Safety Science*, 27(2/3), 183–223.

Renn, O. (2008). *Risk Governance: Coping with Uncertainty in a Complex World*. London: Earthscan.

Scottish Government (2009). *Innovation for Scotland: A Strategic Framework for Innovation in Scotland*. Edinburgh: Scottish Government.

Singh, J. (1986). Performance, slack, and risk taking in organizational decision making. *Academy of Management Journal*, 29(3), 562–585.

Stulz, R. (1996). Rethinking risk management. *Journal of Applied Corporate Finance*, Autumn, 8–24.

Tversky, A. and Fox, R. (1995). Weighing risk and uncertainty. *Psychological Review*, 102(2), 269–283.

Vincent, J. (1996). Managing risk in public services: a review of the international literature. *International Journal of Public Sector Management*, 9(2), 57–64.

Williams, G. (2009). *Applying Management of Risk (M_o_R) for Public Services*. Sidmouth: ALARM.

11. Entrepreneur or entrepreneurship in public services?

Zoe Radnor, Hannah Noke and Andrew Johnston

INTRODUCTION

As a consequence of reforms in the public sector to improve effectiveness and efficiency and to raise responsiveness to citizens' needs, a search for alternative frameworks to manage and guide the management of public sector organisations has been called for (Zampetakis and Moustakis 2007). Recent changes in society have meant that public sector organisations are expected to provide better value (Cripps 2002), often by adopting private sector standards commonly found in areas such as hospitality and banking (Currie et al. 2008). The impact of these changes has left the public sector struggling to re-orientate and searching for new ways to manage itself, which has increased the call for the public sector to turn towards entrepreneurship and innovation (Caruana et al. 2002). This is especially true in the case of the UK, where the Coalition Government elected in 2010 has set out a comprehensive plan of spending cuts to reduce the budget deficit (HM Treasury 2010), forcing public sector organisations to rethink, reorganise, maintain and even improve service provision with fewer resources (Radnor 2010).

The term 'public sector entrepreneurship' has been developed by theorists who have turned their attention to examining the need for creative, opportunity-seeking and innovative behaviours associated with entrepreneurship in the context of public service activities (e.g. Ramamurti 1986; Doig and Hargrove 1987; Bellone and Goerl 1992). Entrepreneurship has been viewed by some as a panacea for transforming the public sector through driving innovative practices (Eisinger 1988; Osborne and Gaebler 1993). Another stream of research suggests that entrepreneurship represents an effective strategic response to environmental turbulence, suggesting that when discontinuities in the environment threaten existing modes of operation this creates numerous opportunities for innovative behaviour (Covin and Slevin 1991). This is summarised well by Mack et al. (2008, p. 233), who state: 'along with efficiency and creativity, innovation has been advocated as a means for public bureaucracies, governmental [departments] . . . to transfer themselves into flexible, more responsive units that work more efficiently and serve their constituencies (and taxpayers) more effectively'.

The focus of this chapter is to understand the role of entrepreneurship in the public sector, and in particular to understand if public sector entrepreneurs can drive innovation within public services. It will outline an example from a UK Local Government organisation to explore some of the tensions and barriers facing an individual entrepreneur attempting to drive radical service transformation change through the organisation. The case study illustrates that, despite considerable external support (including Central Government and Academics), failure to engage and gain internal support resulted in a reduction of power. This led to less than full implementation of a key change programme together with loss of support for the entrepreneur, which in turn reduced the sustainability of both the activity and the individual within the organisation.

ENTREPRENEURSHIP

Entrepreneurship is not a simple concept, and is one that has multiple meanings (Acs 2006), yet the differences between these various meanings can be subtle. In fact, defining the concept is regarded as one of the most difficult aspects in studying it, albeit a crucial one (Casson 1982). Although there is widespread use of the terms 'entrepreneur' and 'entrepreneurship', misconceptions are still commonplace (Hebert and Link 1989). Whilst most individuals could name an entrepreneur, citing examples such as Richard Branson and James Dyson, this refers to just one facet of entrepreneurship; that is, the 'occupational notion' of entrepreneurship; the act of owning and managing one's own business (Sternberg and Wennekers 2005). In contrast is the 'behavioural notion' of entrepreneurship, which refers to the seizing of opportunities and is not necessarily linked to the notion of ownership (Sternberg and Wennekers 2005). This is commonly referred to in the literature as 'corporate entrepreneurship' and can include firm-level entrepreneurship, such as innovators or pioneers, as well as individuals in organisations (Covin and Slevin 1991). Focusing on the 'behavioural notion' of entrepreneurship allows us to understand actions, rather than the occupational element of creating and/or running a business, thus divorcing the process of entrepreneurship from the individual entrepreneur (Atherton 2004).

Entrepreneurship in the Public Sector?

Conflicting evidence exists regarding the applicability of entrepreneurship to the public sector. Some argue it is dependent on one individual, citing the example of military leaders (Doig and Hargrove 1987). Others focus on the personal and situational attributes of entrepreneurship that allow innovation to flourish (Mack et al. 2008). These attributes include encouraging participation, inclusive decision making, coalition building and engendering trust (Mack et al. 2008). It is, however, the concepts of ownership, risk taking and profit that are the most contentious in relation to the public sector. Boyett (1996, p. 37) argues that entrepreneurship's 'relevance to the public sector may be questionable, where the leaders are neither the owners of their institution, nor are they expected to be profit motivated in their management'.

   Some debate focuses on the aspect of risk taking which, according to Covin and Slevin (1991), relates to the burden of risk by the individual in risking some of their own capital in order to start their own business. This situation obviously does not exist for the public sector and so, together with the higher degree of bureaucracy, it is argued by some that often public services are risk adverse, which prohibits innovation (Borins 1998). Other challenges for entrepreneurial behaviour in public services relate to the management structures and systems which can become a barrier, as for entrepreneurship to flourish the existing structures and systems within an organisation should not be allowed to erode 'flexibility, intuition, flair [or] creativity' (Thompson 1999, p. 210). The situation is further compounded by the nature of the public sector's statutory responsibilities and the use of public money, holding public sector managers to account (Currie et al. 2008) and placing them under greater scrutiny (Bozeman and Kingsley 1998). As a result the public sector institutional set-up has a significant bearing on the ability of agents within those organisations to act entrepreneurially (Battilana et al. 2009).

The concept of profit is often argued not to be relevant to the public sector, as these organisations do not function simply to generate profit but to provide public or quasi-public goods, merit goods or correct market failures. Unlike private organisations, where profit levels determine how competitive or successful an organisation is, public sector organisations are pushed and pulled in many different directions (Boyne 2002). It is due to this lack of a clear profit motive for action that scholars have questioned the relevance of entrepreneurship to the public sector and its transferability to contexts where profit is not the main objective (Hughes 1998).

In reality much of the discussion deals with semantics, especially when defining risk. In many cases, when risk is related to entrepreneurship it is defined in financial terms. Yet, if we consider Baird and Thomas's (1985) definition – 'venturing into the unknown' – we can focus on the non-financial definitions of risk, many of which are discussed in the entrepreneurship literature, such as personal risk, social risk and psychological risk (Gasse 1982). Therefore, if we consider risk more broadly it provides us with the leverage to argue that risk taking can be a valid part of public entrepreneurship and not be at odds with the overall statutory responsibilities to citizens.

Timmons (1994, p. 7) defined an entrepreneur as someone who 'pursues an opportunity, regardless of the resources they control'. Importantly, managers that display tendencies of proactiveness and opportunity recognition are key as relates to the growth of firms because they provide the vision and imagination necessary to engage in opportunistic expansion – attributes that are probably required in public organisations when considering the pressures of achieving efficiency and delivery of appropriate levels of service. Innovativeness is also linked to the concept of corporate entrepreneurship and is considered an important factor for characterising entrepreneurship. Innovativeness reflects a firm's tendency to spot opportunities and act upon them. According to Sadler (2000) those opportunities may not be commercially advantageous but can be transformed into a 'new value'. They do not have to be defined solely in terms of the pursuit of profit but can also relate to advancement and improvement.

The public sector entrepreneur can have a number of similarities with the institutional entrepreneur, the most important being that their aim is to transform an organisation in some way (DiMaggio 1988). This focus on transformation suggests that the public sector entrepreneur can be considered to be a change agent, as in the case of the institutional entrepreneur (Battilana et al. 2009). However, separating the individual from the organisation has proved to be difficult (Battilana 2006); this 'paradox of embedded agency' suggests that for an individual to change an organisation they must first free themselves of the environment in which they exist (Seo and Creed 2002). Given the structures of the public sector, some of which have been outlined above, the ability to separate the individual within the organisation may be challenging.

Public sector entrepreneurship research offers little evidence of the most suitable way of encouraging and implementing entrepreneurship within public organisations. Borins (1998) highlights that public sector innovation frequently arises from 'holistic' integration of cross-agency initiatives. This is further supported by Boyett's (1996) observation that entrepreneurship in the public sector does not rely upon individual characteristics; rather the change can be achieved through a group desire. This evidence suggests that the main initiators of entrepreneurship within public organisations do not need to be organisational leaders or politicians but can be career public servants; that is, middle-level managers and frontline staff. This, however, leaves us with a contradiction with the public sector entrepreneurship literature itself, as Boyett's (1996) definition of the public sector entrepreneur would only include senior managers.

This chapter will illustrate the attempts of one middle manager to introduce radical innovative service transformational change into a Local Government organisation in line with policy development and meeting the needs of the citizen. It will explore how the key challenges of being an entrepreneur willing to take ownership and risk impacted on the sustainability, legitimacy and power of the manager as an individual and then on the change programme. The case study will illustrate the challenges and difficulties discussed through the literature of sustaining, allowing or encouraging public sector entrepreneurship.

CASE STUDY: CRANLEIGH METROPOLITAN BOROUGH COUNCIL[1]

This case study follows the journey of Antonio Smyth during his time at Cranleigh Metropolitan Borough Council (CMBC) implementing Cranleigh Centre Plus (CC Plus) as part of a radical Service Transformation programme. Antonio became responsible for the Customer Access To Services (CATS) team, which had to facilitate the transfer of services from the various Directorates into a planned customer call centre – CC Plus. The vision was that it would be the first point of contact and 'a one-stop-shop' for citizens when dealing with the Council. The initiative, CC Plus, was initially driven from the top by the Leader and Chief Executive but Antonio was appointed to oversee its implementation. Understanding the potential of the agenda to include a wide set of services through a business process review approach which involved identifying, mapping, understanding and implementing improved services into CC Plus, Antonio embarked on his entrepreneurial journey within Cranleigh. This radical innovation was an attempt to lead Service Transformation and ensure that CMBC remained a leading Council. The initiative was also aimed to achieve larger efficiency savings across the organisation than could be gained from single-department initiatives. Furthermore it responded to the agenda of customer value, through greater customer satisfaction, enabling access through whatever means and methods they chose, through the delivery of an integrated service offering. At the time of the case study CMBC was one of only very few Councils attempting such innovation of implementing a one stop shop.

A case study approach was taken to capture the initiatives that have been introduced within CMBC. Within the organisation the case study was to provide a useful evaluation through an objective critical review of the process of Service Transformation. Part of the evaluative process was to derive key learning points to: a) aid CMBC in the future in its development of Service Transformation; b) for the Cabinet Office to develop a case study for Service Transformation documentation; and c) so the Cabinet Office could inform

Table 11.1   Summary of data collection

	Number of people	Occurrence
Semi-structured interviews	8	1
Longitudinal interviews with Antonio	–	7
Corporate Board workshop	20	1
Observations of meeting	–	4

other Local Authorities undertaking similar work how they may learn from CMBC's experience.

The case study was achieved through carrying out semi-structured interviews with key individuals within CMBC (see Table 11.1). A further key information source was the observation of key events between the Cabinet Office and CMBC by the research team. The formal observation of key meetings was supplemented with various other methods of data collection such as gathering formal feedback from participants through short feedback forms at a Corporate Board workshop. Principally the feedback form was designed to capture and understand the perceptions of the participants of the implementation process. This enabled a perceptions gap analysis to be conducted to ascertain current awareness of the transformation process. Research interviews were completed with the two principal stakeholders of the project from the Cabinet Office as well as a number of formal and informal discussions with Antonio and his team from CMBC. The purpose of the interviews was to clarify understanding of the project from different perspectives to ascertain if the objectives were shared as well as perceived barriers and challenges to the project's completion. Further evaluative research was undertaken for CC Plus which resulted in two reports being produced to support the findings from the evaluative research.

The data were analysed using an analytic proposal devised by Radnor (2002) allowing for rigorous coding and classification. The technique follows six key steps: 1) topic ordering; 2) constructing categories; 3) reading for content; 4) completing coded sheets; 5) generating coded transcripts; and 6) analysis to interpretation. This technique ensures a logical coding of data and marshalling of evidence, avoiding the dangers of inaccuracy which might have arisen from an over-mechanistic approach. However, once the data were coded, the approach sought to maximise the degree and speed with which they could be analysed and reanalysed through the use of an integrated suite of Windows Office computer software and all the benefits this can bring to the data interpretation process. Through using this method of analysis of qualitative data a level of sensitivity to detail and context was enabled, as well as accurate access to information. This method of analysis and interpretation enabled rigorous searching for patterns, building of theories or explanations and grounding them in data, allowing the key themes from this research study to emerge from the data to build a coherent understanding.

The sections below describe the background to CC Plus, the actions Antonio took to develop legitimacy in what he was doing by drawing on external policy, knowledge and expertise, and the internal challenges and barriers that were evident within the organisation.

Background to CMBC

CMBC serves a local population of over 350,000 and employs around 14,000 members of staff within seven directorates (departments): Chief Executive's Office, Children's Services, Education and Community Services, Housing, Urban Environment, Law and Property, and Finance. CMBC was amongst the top-performing local authorities in England, yet the Chief Executive was keen to improve the service it provided. She explained the opportunity she saw:

> CMBC provides several hundred services for our customers, all of which have many different access points, in different buildings with different opening times and using different systems. For example, Housing Services are in one building, Finance, where you pay your bills, in another and benefit payments (part of Finance) in three others. So anyone wanting, as many people do, to access several services at once have to trail around the city, only then to get referred to another department somewhere else. We also have over 100 different telephone numbers – how is a customer meant to know which is the right one? We have decided we want to create one point of contact, a one-stop-shop, where we can bring all our services together and do as much for the customer at the first point of contact. This will make things much better for the customer and should also create important efficiency savings for CMBC.

As a result, the Chief Executive and Leader of the Council, recognising the challenge of Service Transformation, recruited management consultants to assess the feasibility of the concept. They set out a 'Road Map' and were involved in the initial phase for the introduction of CC Plus. Further support for the initiative was provided through the appointment of Antonio.

Cranleigh Centre Plus

In Spring 2008, two years after the recognition of the need, CC Plus was opened as a convenient and accessible customer contact point for many of the Council's services. Residents could, for example, pay their tax bills, report faulty street lights or missed bin collections, report abandoned vehicles, pay housing bills, and even register births and deaths. It also provided access to other services such as Age Concern, Citizens' Advice Bureau, and other public sector and community agencies such as Tourist Information, CENTRO (the local transport provider) and Box Office services, selling tickets to events held at Council venues. CC Plus had long opening hours and was accessible by phone, email or by walking into the first CC Plus contact centre in Cranleigh town centre.[2] The walk-in centre was a large, spacious, modern building with large glass doors leading towards a reception area. Cash machines were available for paying Council bills, private rooms for conversations with advisors, and computers providing free internet access. The centre employed around 50 FTEs (full-time equivalents), including the Customer Service Manager, customer advisors, team managers and an IT technician. The five teams of advisors rotated between face-to-face and phone channels.

This was a radical change in the way that services were delivered. The centre provided efficiency gains by bringing services together and sharing information. More importantly, customers received a better service, as Antonio Smyth describes:

> We have created a customer-focused service organisation that can provide a wide range of services at first point of contact by whichever channel the customers choose to use. At the moment this includes face-to-face, telephone, email or web. We've got information on every service that the Council provides at our fingertips and we've got around 120 services that could be delivered through CC Plus. The Council provides about 700 services but some services are not appropriate to CC Plus and will not go in.

However, this meant that the future started to become uncertain for the development of CC Plus because, 'by the summer we were moving towards a crisis point for the CATS team because we were still not getting very far at integrating services into the contact centre' (Antonio Smyth). At this time CC Plus was not operating at full capacity and there was staff complacency because not many services had been transferred. As Antonio pointed out: 'At this stage some would say we had a white elephant. A beautiful big building but dealing with only fourteen services out of seven hundred. It looked like a disaster to some.' However, in November 2008 there was a potential turning point in the implementation when Antonio's role was promoted to senior management level, providing him with the necessary position to have the authority to drive key decisions. He started with a mission to target four service areas: the Banking Hall, Planning and Development Control, Housing Services, and Benefits and Revenue telephone enquiry. These four major pieces of work would be in the customers' interest and help make CC Plus financially sustainable.

The Banking Hall service was transferred to CC Plus but there were some challenges with the other service areas. These three services, Planning and Development Control, Housing Services, and Benefits and Revenues, held telephone call/contact centres. Compared with CC Plus the three Directorates offered a reduced service, operating restricted opening hours and dealing with customers by phone or email. Amongst these three call/contact centres there was a feeling that any transfer of their services to CC Plus would not be beneficial, with a belief that CC Plus could only act as a messaging service rather than delivering services to meet customer needs. As one call centre manager reported:

> It would be very disappointing if our calls have to be dealt with at CC Plus. This would lead to a reduction of service to our customers because they would still have to be transferred on to us so there would be delays and a lot more double handling.

This view obviously conflicted with the original concept of reducing the number of telephone numbers to ring for Council services and the creation of CC Plus as a 'one stop shop'. However, Housing Services was largely transferred, with the exception of Housing Repairs, which dealt solely with tenants' repairs enquiries. Benefits and Revenue call centres were allowed to continue, with none of their services transferred to CC Plus. Planning and Development Control transferred over a period of time through Antonio and his team building a good relationship with the Planning Department.

Antonio as a Public Sector Entrepreneur

Antonio was not the original visionary of bringing the services together but what he was able to visualise was how the plan had to be implemented. In addition, Antonio did not own or necessarily control the resources needed to effect the change; both these observations would suggest that he is not an entrepreneur. However, what happened was that Antonio observed the resistance to the changes within the organisation and set about an active process of sharing, learning, encouraging, and coalition building in order to transform it. The fact that Antonio was not the original visionary may have helped avoid the problem of embedded agency; he was charged with being a change agent. In order to legitimise the activities Antonio involved external partners in the implementation process; these included the Cabinet Office and Warwick University Business School. There were a number of elements that identified Antonio's behaviour and activity as entrepreneurial, including: he was prepared to take a risk; prepared to challenge current practices; had a clear focus of the concept and model of the new innovative way of working (the one stop shop); and a strong drive for performance and improvement. However, the structures, systems and organisational design became challenges for Antonio in a number of ways that are explored below. They raise the question whether there can be a 'public sector entrepreneur'.

Legitimacy
At the time of the research, especially near the beginning, Antonio often stated that the only risk he perceived was not delivering the programme (setting up CC Plus). He often articulated surprise when his vision and ideas, which he perceived would be engaged within the organisation, were not wholly supported. In order to highlight the importance and relevance of the programme and his ideas he sought legitimacy from a number of sources.

Around the time of the development of CC Plus the UK Government through the Cabinet Office developed an agenda for change focused around Service Transformation. During the same period many Local Authorities engaged with ideas of Service Transformation, either within the Authority or supported by guidance of Central Government departments including the Cabinet Office, Department of Communities and Local Government (CLG) and the Audit Commission. The aim of transformational government was to identify further savings to government, citizens and businesses by focusing on the channels through which services were delivered and how they could be made more responsive to citizen and business needs. Service Transformation was focused on delivering improved experiences and outcomes for citizens and businesses at a lower cost (Varney 2006, p. 7).

Antonio leveraged the support and involvement of the Cabinet Office to provide legitimacy for the implementation of CC Plus. The Cabinet Office was keen to understand the implementation process of transformational government in Local Government in order to make further recommendations in terms of 'good practice'. Cranleigh was one of a number of Local Authorities that were working with the Cabinet Office. Antonio hoped this would provide him with external support that could make it difficult for the internal powers to resist. The impetus for change would then become an external force, so Antonio hoped this would give him the legitimacy to push the changes through within the organisation. Thus, it could be noted that Antonio sought legitimacy as a change agent from outside the organisation.

Antonio sought further legitimacy through the involvement of Warwick Business School, through the evaluation of the multi call centres in relation to their performance measurement and management systems, and through a case study write-up of the development of CC Plus. He hoped that the evaluation of the multi call centre would highlight and identify the overlap, lack of service, lack of customer focus and multi expense and repeat of activities, and so on. He hoped the evaluation would legitimise the one stop shop as the first point of contact for the citizen.

Another form of legitimacy was sought through the sharing of learning with other Councils. This was achieved by developing an understanding of activities and processes when CMBC staff visited other organisations and other personnel came to CMBC.

> We have been very open because I want their feedback and their ideas. For example I like what is being done with customer insight in Hammersmith and Fulham because we haven't done any of that but I would like to get to a point where we can start pulling that data automatically. We are seeing all sorts of things that will allow us to change direction and build on it. (Antonio Smyth)

It was felt that working with other Councils was an easy process, as they were open in showing CMBC what they had done and achieved and CMBC was the same. Working with and being supported by the Cabinet Office also brought advantages, as it provided help and reassurance through the changes that were being implemented. Also, tenacity, drive and clarity of purpose in some individuals who were interested in the programme provided much required support. However, in the end these sources of legitimacy were not enough. As discussed below, CC Plus never reached its original aim and Antonio, due to his drive, focus and ultimately his belief in the programme, became the scapegoat for its 'failure'.

Challenges Antonio Faced

There were a number of issues and challenges both for the development of CC Plus and for Antonio as an entrepreneur.

Leadership

Initially the Chief Executive and Leader had strong involvement, predominantly leading the organisation and setting up the original vision for the programme. Their appointment of Antonio's role was to ensure that Service Transformation had some degree of corporate ownership and was politically accepted. Antonio's role was to champion the change and motivate others to engage in the innovation of CC Plus. However, for the Service Transformation and creation of CC Plus to be successful, as with many change processes, it was important to have constant and sustainable political and managerial support. The case shows a lack of corporate leadership, commitment and governance reflected by the lack of support and encouragement needed to enable the transfer of services to CC Plus from the Directorates which held on to their call centres. Leading from the top through a strong corporate board was required to support the Service Transformation process. However, leadership from the Chief Executive was only relevant to a point. After this other layers of management in the organisation needed to become leaders.

> [CE support is] very good for getting it sorted and getting people to take an interest in the concept but once it's up and running the time invested from the CE is less, therefore it's the quality of the management below the CE that is important. (CATs team leader)

The leadership within CMBC was considered to be lacking in the necessary drive at times. 'They have signed up with their heads but not with their hearts' was a comment mentioned in the interviews. Therefore, in progressing the change it was suggested that a more emergent approach, allowing key and engaged individuals to lead small pockets of change, may have eventually gained momentum and support.

The issue of senior management buy-in was also compounded by inadequate budget and resources allocated to the work, which gave a message that the Service Transformation work was not that important. This was underlined at times by a lack of shared corporate commitment, with in-fighting within the senior management team and the cabinet (political leadership). This was particularly apparent when the evaluation of the multi call centres – which presented significant evidence of the downside of having them – was ignored. The report actually became a weapon to expose Antonio further.

Staff engagement

It was important to link the changes with improved job satisfaction and rise in motivation. It was evident that, in terms of job satisfaction, the outcomes meant that people took interest in their job rather than feeling sidelined into 'I am a trading standards person and that is all I will be able to do.' The Service Transformation changes meant CMBC could engage with staff to identify and build capacity for the processes delivering the services. However, it was recognised that, to support Service Transformation, it was important to engage staff more widely and corporately through training on customer care beyond individual services. People automatically assumed that it was someone else that should change and not their service:

> However, it's not been easy bringing about change. Obviously we [CAT team] have to spend a lot of time with the people who are directly affected by what we come up with and it takes a lot of time and patience to get them on board, especially when their jobs are affected. Even when the transfer is seen as a good idea and the Directorate work with us in partnership mode, it can still be quite painful dealing with all the issues. We have to rely on our soft skills. And it's not becoming easier either. In fact as we start to move into some of the areas which really don't want to be part of this, it will become more difficult. So far we have only worked with areas that have been more receptive. (Antonio Smyth)

The motivation for Antonio and the CAT team was to improve the service to customers. However, some staff had not internalised and committed to that aim, and often focused on 'What's in it for me?' rather than 'What's in it for the customer?' This often led to an attitude of, 'this is a good thing for the customer but you can't do it because you can't touch us because we're precious'. Essentially, some staff did not believe that the existing service was worse than the new service being offered and so saw no reason to change: 'some powerful Directors are used to having their own way'.

Perception of change

Antonio encountered resistance to the change he was driving and implementing when attempting to encourage individual services to understand that Service Transformation applied to them and all services. In many of the Directorates there was no perceived need to change as CMBC was seen as a well-performing Council, meaning the current performance did not create questions around work practices. This illustrates the paradox of embedded agency: individuals within the organisation perceive it to be well run and do not see the need for change. Therefore there is no incentive or motive to enact any changes. In this environment any individual not sharing these views risks being perceived as an outsider; the change agent, in this case Antonio, can be viewed with suspicion or as a loose cannon (Borins 1998). There was a need to get everyone to buy into the concept that understanding and satisfying the customer would be better served by changing the service processes and operations through the implementation of CC Plus.

DISCUSSION

The situation within CMBC is that CC Plus still exists, with the majority of services identified as appropriate now within CC Plus. However, the services that resisted the implementation programme (Benefits, Revenues and some of Housing) remain outside of CC Plus.

What happened to Antonio? The support for the transformation programme remained elusive from several Directorates. The conclusion was that Antonio could no longer sustain the vision and was eventually asked to leave CMBC along with the CEO. The Service Transformation programme was perceived by many to be a risky and radical strategy in a Council that did not need to change. This was especially the case for those Directors that retained 'power' and prevented their Directorates from being incorporated in CC Plus. Clearly, this culture of inertia and the lack of leadership support ultimately weakened Antonio's position. His legitimacy was externally generated and top-down in nature, in that it came from Central Government. Whilst this enabled Antonio to circumvent the institutional environment he was attempting to change and provided him with the agency to undertake these measures, it ultimately left him exposed. Through Antonio's case we have witnessed the application of public sector entrepreneurship, where individuals inside organisations pursue opportunities independent of the resources they currently control (Stevenson and Jarillo 1990), partake in new things and depart from the customary to pursue opportunities (Vesper 1990), and attempt to develop a spirit of entrepreneurship within the existing organisation (Hisrich and Peters 2007).

Jennings and Lumpkin (1989) found that entrepreneurial organisations tend not to penalise managers if risky projects fail. For an organisation whose statutory obligation is to offer accountability to its stakeholders this is somewhat of a dilemma and is linked to the discussion around risk taking. If entrepreneurship is to flourish then managers must perceive an environment that encourages calculated risk taking whilst maintaining reasonable tolerance for failure (Jennings and Lumpkin 1989). Within CMBC the complacency regarding its performance left it without the desire to take risks; rather, it wished to maintain the status quo. The current performance level left the organisation without the desire to be innovative, leaving those that perceived the need to change in a position of isolation.

The entrepreneur typically is characterised by a narrow focus and an unwillingness to follow rules and stay within boundaries. This describes Antonio and his vision, although he would argue that he was attempting to make the changes to bring increased performance to the Council and value to its citizens. In reality Antonio was attempting to break down empires but ultimately, although he was 'championing' the innovation, due to his lack of power and his position in the organisation, he was unable to motivate all the Directors in order to carry out the task of transfering all the services to CC Plus. Antonio's background did not stem from the Council – he was appointed from an educational setting, whereas many of the Directors of Services had been in place within the Council for many years. This barrier of social cohesion perhaps had an influence and in the end was too much to overcome by Antonio and his team.

As Drucker (1985) argues, entrepreneurship is as much a public sector as a private sector phenomenon, largely due to the processes involved in the systematic search for and analysis of opportunities which have the potential to generate innovation. Whilst the opportunities are not the same as those sought to gain profit in the private sector, the benefit in the public sector is to the group of individuals that public organisations serve in offering 'value'. This is the important point to remember and without this recognition new innovative opportunities within public services will not move forward. It is this motivation of those acting entrepreneurially within the public sector that is the desirable characteristic. Furthermore, Ramamurti (1986, p. 143) argues that, as with their private counterpart, the public sector entrepreneur is the 'highly creative, self confident person with many innovative ideas, who works doggedly to translate his ideas into reality'. Although most people would argue that a person like this would be an asset to any organisation, this case study has illustrated that such an individual or the opportunity he was attempting to drive was not recognised.

We must acknowledge that the characteristics used to define entrepreneurship are largely associated with economists' point of view (Ramamurti 1986) and do not always lend themselves to the public sector context. For this reason entrepreneurship in the public sector has to be viewed in different terms, but this is not to say that it is not appropriate – rather, it has differences that must be acknowledged. It is through accepting and acknowledging the similarities and differences compared with its private sector counterpart that public sector entrepreneurship can be defined as 'the process of creating value for citizens by bringing together unique combinations of public and/or private resources to exploit social opportunities' (Morris and Jones 1999, p. 74).

One caveat remains: that to simply accept that the concept of entrepreneurship can be applied to the public sector would be wrong; to assume the models and frameworks from the private sector are applicable to the public sector context without little thought of adaptation to the specific context would also be wrong. Like other change and transformation approaches entrepreneurship needs to be considered as context dependent (Radnor et al. 2011). As this case study has clearly illustrated, the role of the entrepreneur within a public sector organisation needs to be defined, and supported very differently.

CONCLUSION

This chapter sought to understand the role of entrepreneurship within the public sector context. Through reviewing the literature and a case study in a local government organisation key differences of the public sector context that prevent the traditional characteristics of entrepreneurship being simply transferred to this different setting were presented.

Instead it calls for us to look at some of the characteristics differently and understand what they mean within the public sector context. One key example discussed related to risk: traditionally entrepreneurship associates risk with financial risk; that is, the entrepreneur risking their own funds in setting up a new venture. However, if we examine risk through a different lens then risk can actually be interpreted from different positions. In the case of Antonio the risk related to personal risk, social risk and psychological risk in relation to him and his team.

Through following the story of Antonio's vision for the implementation of CC Plus, it is apparent that entrepreneurship can occur within the public sector context. Antonio exhibited characteristics of entrepreneurship through recognising the opportunity of delivering more 'value' to the citizen, having a clear vision, being willing to take risk, and drawing on external organisations to provide legitimacy to the Service Transformation programme.

However, the issue that was observed in the case study was that of sustainability and power. It is not enough to act entrepreneurially or be a champion. As this case study clearly shows, there needs to be ongoing sustainable power, directly or indirectly, that can be enacted – the power to enable and motivate change. Antonio was willing to take ownership and risk but the organisation did not support him; this led eventually to his downfall and the non-completion of the Service Transformation programme. Boyett's (1996) definition of public sector entrepreneurs refers only to senior managers as entrepreneurs but many studies in public services have found public entrepreneurship to be associated with career public workers who are often middle managers. Due to the nature of the public sector structure and bureaucracy this disconnect may be a key barrier, and so unless senior management buy-in is achieved real change and innovation opportunities will be missed. Interestingly, initially Antonio was a middle manager, which may have been a position he was perceived to hold (and the leadership did not seek to correct) even after his promotion, thus possibly not allowing him the power he hoped for.

Our contribution highlights that entrepreneurship can take place within the public sector, but due to its idiosyncratic nature, first we have to redefine entrepreneurship and what that means to the public sector. Secondly, entrepreneurship does occur, but individuals exhibiting the characteristics associated with being an entrepreneur are not enough to create change – especially when senior management do not perceive the need for change. This has implications for the future, where the impetus for change needs to understand the role of the corporate public sector entrepreneur in effecting change. There must be recognition that for innovation and change to take place entrepreneurial characteristics are required, but these cannot reside in an individual; rather, the approach has to be holistic and all encompassing. In other words, entrepreneurship in the public sector may be about organisational or corporate entrepreneurship rather than the development of public sector entrepreneurs.

NOTES

1. The names of the Council and the individuals concerned have been changed.
2. More were planned throughout the Borough but these had been put on hold.

REFERENCES

Acs, Z. (2006). How is entrepreneurship good for economic growth? *Innovations*, Winter, 97–107.

Atherton, A. (2004). Unbundling enterprise and entrepreneurship: from perceptions and preconceptions to concept and practice. *International Journal of Entrepreneurship and Innovation*, 10(2), 121–127.

Baird, I.S. and Thomas, H. (1985). Toward a contingency model of strategic risk taking. *Academy of Management Review*, 10(2), 230–243.

Battilana, J. (2006). Agency and institutions: the enabling role of individuals' social position. *Organization*, 13(5), 653–676.

Battilana, J., Leca, B. and Boxenbaum, E. (2009). How actors change institutions. *Academy of Management Annals*, 3(1), 65–107.

Bellone, C.J. and Goerl, G.F. (1992). Reconciling public entrepreneurship and democracy. *Public Administration Review*, 52(2), 130–134.

Borins, S. (1998). *Innovating with Integrity: How Local Heroes are Transforming American Government*. Washington, DC: Georgetown Washington Press.

Boyett, I. (1996). The public sector entrepreneur – a definition. *International Journal of Public Sector Management*, 9(2), 36–51.

Boyne, G.A. (2002). Public and private management: what's the difference? *Journal of Management Studies*, 39(1), 97–122.

Bozeman, B. and Kingsley, G. (1998). Risk culture in public and private organizations. *Public Administration*, 58, 109–118.

Caruana, A., Ewing, M.T. and Ramaseshan, B. (2002). Effects of some environmental challenges and centralization on the entrepreneurial orientation and performance of public sector entities. *Service Industries Journal*, 22(2), 43–58.

Casson, M. (1982). *The Entrepreneur: An Economic Theory*. Oxford: Martin Robertson.

Covin, J.G. and Slevin, D.P. (1991). A conceptual model of entrepreneurship as firm behaviour. *Entrepreneurship Theory and Practice*, 16, 7–25.

Cripps, S. (2002). *Further Education, Government's Discourse Policy and Practice*. Aldershot: Ashgate.

Currie, G.H., Humphreys, M., Ucbasaran, D. and McManus, S. (2008). Entrepreneurial leadership in the English public sector: paradox or possibility? *Public Administration*, 86(4), 987–1008.

DiMaggio, P.J. (1988). Interest and agency in institutional theory. In L.G. Zucker (ed.), *Institutional Patterns and Organizations*. Cambridge, MA: Ballinger, pp. 3–22.

Doig, J. and Hargrove, E. (eds) (1987). *Leadership and Innovation: A Biographical Perspective on Entrepreneurs in Government*. Baltimore, MD: Johns Hopkins University Press.

Drucker, P. (1985). *Innovation and Entrepreneurship*. London: Heinemann.

Eisinger, P.K. (1988). *The Rise of the Entrepreneurial State: State and Local Economic Development Policy in the United States*. Madison, WI: University of Wisconsin Press.

Gasse, Y. (1982). *Elaborations on the Psychology of the Entrepreneur: Encyclopaedia of Entrepreneurship*. C.A. Kent, D.L. Sexton and K.H. Vesper. Englewood Cliffs, NJ: Prentice-Hall, pp. 58–71.

Hebert, R.F. and Link, A. (1989). In search of the meaning of entrepreneurship. *Small Business Economics*, 1(1), 39–49.

Hisrich, R.D. and Peters, M.P. (2007). *Entrepreneurship: Starting, Developing and Managing a New Enterprise*. Chicago, IL: Irwin.

HM Treasury (2010). *Budget 2010*. London: The Stationery Office.

Hughes, O.E. (1998). *Australian Politics*, 3rd edn. Melbourne: Macmillan.

Jennings, D.F. and Lumpkin, J.L. (1989). Functionally modelling corporate entrepreneurship: an empirical integrative analysis. *Journal of Management*, 15(3), 485–503.

Mack, W.R., Green, D. and Vedlitz, A. (2008). Innovation and implementation in the public sector: an examination of public entrepreneurship. *Review of Policy Research*, 25(3), 233–252.

Morris, M.H. and Jones, F.F. (1999). Entrepreneurship in established organizations: the case of the public sector. *Entrepreneurship Theory and Practice*, 24(1), 71–91.

Osborne, D. and Gaebler, T. (1993). *Reinventing Government: How Entrepreneurial Spirit is Transforming the Public Sector*. Reading, MA: Addison-Wesley.

Radnor, H. (2002). *Researching your Own Professional Practice: Doing Interpretive Research*. Buckingham: Oxford University Press.

Radnor, Z.J. (2010). Transferring lean into government. *Journal of Manufacturing Technology Management*, 21(3), 411–428.

Radnor, Z.J., Holweg, H. and Waring, J. (2011). Lean in healthcare: the unfilled promise? *Social Science and Medicine*, 74(3), 411–428.

Ramamurti, R. (1986). Public entrepreneurs: who they are and how they operate. *California Management Review*, 28(3), 142–158.

Sadler, R.J. (2000). Corporate entrepreneurship in the public sector: the dance of the chameleon. *Australian Journal of Public Administration*, 59(2), 25–43.

Seo, M. and Creed, W. (2002). Institutional contradictions, praxis, and institutional change: a dialectical perspective. *Academy of Management Review*, 27(2), 222–247.

Sternberg, R. and Wennekers, S. (2005). Determinants and effects of new business creation using Global Entrepreneurship Monitor data. *Small Business Economics*, 24(3), 193–203.

Stevenson, H.H. and Jarillo, J.C. (1990). A paradigm of entrepreneurship: entrepreneurial management. *Strategic Management Journal*, 11, 17–27.

Thompson, J.L. (1999). The world of the entrepreneur – a new perspective. *Journal of Workplace Learning: Employee Counseling Today*, 11(6), 209–224.

Timmons, J.A. (1994). *New Venture Creation: Entrepreneurship in the 21st Century*. Burr Ridge, IL: Irwin.

Varney, D. (2006). *Service Transformation: A Better Service for Citizens and Businesses, a Better Deal for the Taxpayer*. London: Cabinet Office.

Vesper, K. (1990). *New Venture Strategies*. Englewood Cliffs, NJ: Prentice-Hall.

Zampetakis, L.A. and Moustakis, V. (2007). Fostering corporate entrepreneurship through internal marketing. *European Journal of Innovation Management*, 10(4), 413–433.

12. Against all odds: bottom-up entrepreneurship and innovation in the Department of Defense
Nancy C. Roberts and Carrick Longley

INTRODUCTION

How does an entrepreneur in a large military bureau innovate from the bottom up in a context that is change resistant, and even when change does occur, it tends to be top-down driven and rewarded (Spulak 2010)? What does it take to push a new idea forward to ensure a successful innovation in this context? These questions form the backdrop to our case study of Lighthouse – a new tool and technology for military data collection and analysis. Our goal is to document the entrepreneurial and innovation processes that enabled a university student to launch what some are calling a 'game changer' in how the military collects and analyzes data in its field-based operations.

From an organizational perspective, these questions are important for several reasons. Virtually all studies of military innovation point to the difficulty of innovating in organizations that are 'intrinsically inflexible, prone to stagnation, and fearful of change' (Grissom 2006, p.919). As Stephen Rosen (1991) notes, not only are large military bureaucracies difficult to change, 'they are *designed not to change*' (p.2, emphasis added). To ensure civilian control and coordination of national security policy, all major innovation models in the military have been found to follow a similar pattern. All assume innovation requires pressure from external authority, and when initiated they are kick-started from the top down (Grissom 2006; Spulak 2010).[1]

Yet there are empirical cases of innovations from the bottom up, although not widely acknowledged as such. For example, the Marine Corps' innovative small wars doctrine is considered the result of a bottom-up process that occurred outside formal channels through an informal discourse among a small number of middle-ranking and junior officers in the Corps' schools and journals to advance a new doctrinal focus – the Advanced Base Mission (Grissom 2006). This case and others have led Adam Grissom of Rand to suggest the beginning of a 'Kuhnian moment', where the apparent anomalies of bottom-up innovations are growing and rendering the field's prevailing assumptions and frameworks about top-down military innovation inadequate to describe empirical reality. Thus he sees a conceptual and theoretical void to be filled, but foresees two challenges that must be addressed for the effort to be successful. First, researchers need to build an empirical foundation of bottom-up innovation on which models and hypotheses can be developed for comparison and testing. And secondly, they must develop conceptual models of military innovation that identify the necessary and sufficient conditions for bottom-up innovation to occur.

We take up these challenges by presenting an empirical study of bottom-up military innovation – the case of Lighthouse, an innovative idea developed by Captain Carrick Longley, the second author of this chapter. The study is unique on two counts. As an example of reflexive writing, the inclusion of the entrepreneur as author allows us to combine his personal accounts and observations for a more complete analysis of the innovation experience. At the same time, his participation as both observer and subject challenged us to question how his perceptions might be impacting our view of the case and its analysis. Attentive to these concerns, Longley took primary responsibility for the case write-up and Roberts took primary responsibility for the analysis, while each served as critical evaluator of the other's contributions. The study is also unique as an example of *process* research (Mohr 1982) – uncommon in the innovation literature[2] and even more so in the military literature. Process studies focus on *how* innovation occurs rather than on *what* determines innovation outcomes. Examples of process studies that do exist tend to be retrospective and reliant on archival data. In this instance, we have first-hand reports and observations of an on-going process as it evolves through the initiation and design phases of the innovation process. From this vantage point, we believe we are well positioned to identify the necessary and sufficient conditions for bottom-up innovation to occur.

The first section of the chapter introduces our conceptual framework in which we embed this study of entrepreneurship and innovation. It draws on both the private and public sector literature and lays the foundation for the case in the next section. The case analysis follows in the third section. Here we identify the basic elements of what we believe are necessary and sufficient conditions for bottom-up entrepreneurship and innovation to be successful in large bureaucratic, military organizations. The chapter concludes with some implications for future research and practice.

CONCEPTUAL FRAMEWORK

Entrepreneurship has a long lineage. A well-established concept in business and government, it has appeared in many guises in its 150-year history. Despite the multiplicity of definitions, there is general agreement that those who start up new, innovative organizations in the private sector are business entrepreneurs (Schumpeter 1951; Drucker 2006). Those in the public sector who establish new public organizations are considered executive entrepreneurs (Lewis 1980; Roberts 1992; Roberts and King 1996) and those who craft new ideas and implement them as innovative public policy are referred to as policy entrepreneurs (Kingdon 1984; Roberts 1992; Roberts and King 1996).

A fundamental understanding of entrepreneurship, whether in business or the public sector, begins with the innovation process. Innovation is the translation of a new idea from its initial state to its actualization in practice as a full-blown innovation (Schroeder et al. 1989). The innovation process begins with a new idea. The idea can be a new technology, service, product, or even an administrative procedure or process (Daft and Becker 1978). Classification of an idea as 'new' depends on its context. An idea is considered to be new if it is perceived to be new by the relevant unit of adoption (Zaltman et al. 1973, p. 10). Sometimes new ideas originate in a particular setting. In other instances, a new idea is adapted or even borrowed from another setting and then applied in the entrepreneur's unique context (Peltz and Munson 1982).

The development of the new idea and the association of the idea with some need, problem, or concern mark the first phase of the innovation process, often referred to as

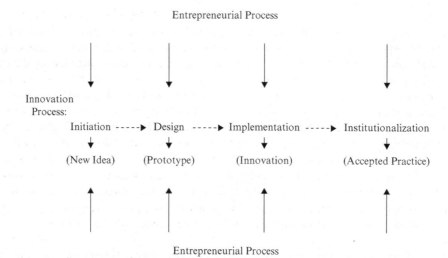

Source: Figure adapted from Roberts and King (1996), p. 225.

Figure 12.1   Interactive processes of entrepreneurship and innovation

initiation or creation (Polsby 1984; Roberts 1992; Roberts and King 1996). Initiation is followed by the design phase that translates the idea into a more concrete and tangible form (such as a prototype, model, or position paper). Completion of the design phase requires the approval of powerholders and gatekeepers whose resources and support are necessary to proclaim the new idea as *invention, law, statute, policy,* or *program*. Implementation follows the design phase when the new idea is tested in practice to ascertain how well it functions. New ideas that survive implementation are described as innovations; ideas that do not survive are considered to be failed ideas (Roberts 1992; Roberts and King 1996). Institutionalization is the final phase, when the new idea becomes accepted practice. Thus we can think of the innovation process as consisting of a series of hurdles or transformations that move the new idea from its initial to its final state. The horizontal dimension in Figure 12.1 represents the process graphically.[3]

The vertical dimension in Figure 12.1 represents the entrepreneurial process. Entrepreneurs are the creators and drivers of the innovative idea as it moves through time. In order to push their ideas forward, they engage in a set of activities to protect their ideas and give them shape and form. The range of their activities can be extensive depending on how well known the idea is, how much resistance there is to it, and the level of support it attracts. One way to think of the vertical dimension is to view it as representing an entrepreneurial activity structure. Previous research on policy entrepreneurs who advocated radical policy change grouped their activities into four basic categories: creative and intellectual activities; strategic activities; mobilization and execution activities; and administrative and evaluative activities (Roberts 1992). Taken as a whole, the activities resulted in a relational field of entrepreneurial energy to protect the new idea, defend it against its detractors, and nurture it through the vagaries of the innovation process.[4]

The idea vector and the entrepreneurial vector are interrelated. They work in tandem to produce innovation. The idea vector tracks the various manifestations of the new idea (idea, prototype, innovation, accepted practice) as it moves through the processes of initiation, design, implementation, and institutionalization. The unit of analysis of the innovation process is the new idea. The entrepreneurial vector tracks the agents of change who galvanize support for and counter resistance to the innovative idea as it moves through time. The unit of analysis for the entrepreneurial process is the entrepreneur and the relational network of activities he/she develops in support of the innovative idea (Roberts 1992; Roberts and King 1996; Roberts 2007).

This model provides several conceptual advantages over others (e.g. Eggers and Singh 2009; Sorensen and Torfing 2011). First, it enables us to distinguish between entrepreneurship and innovation that, although related, are best treated as two separate processes. Entrepreneurs are a necessary but not sufficient element for innovation to occur. Their creativity and initiative spark the development of new ideas. They are the catalysts that propel the innovative idea forward and mold and shape it through the innovation process. At the same time, entrepreneurs fail or succeed to the extent their ideas attract support and resources from others. At some point, the innovative idea takes on a life of its own and has to be treated as separate from the entrepreneur who gave it life. In fact, the ideal situation is when others begin to call the innovative idea their own. Thus the entrepreneur and the innovative idea need to be treated as two related but conceptually distinct entities (Roberts 1992; Roberts and King 1996).

The entrepreneurship–innovation model also enables us to make finer-grained distinctions between individual and collective forms of entrepreneurship. Individual entrepreneurship relies on the exploits of a single individual who works through all phases of the innovation process. Acting independently, she generates a new idea, creates its design, and oversees its translation and implementation into practice. In contrast, collective entrepreneurship draws on multiple people to husband and shape an idea through initiation, design, and implementation into a full-blown innovation. Probing collective entrepreneurship more deeply, we find its expression can take one of two forms: *team entrepreneurship* or *functional entrepreneurship* (Roberts 1992; Roberts and King 1996; Roberts 2007). Team entrepreneurship occurs when multiple entrepreneurs join forces and work together to push an idea through *all* phases of the innovation process. Although each person is an entrepreneur in his own right, all decide it is more advantageous to pool their resources and act in concert. Functional entrepreneurship, on the other hand, occurs without the presence of a single entrepreneur. It occurs when experts from different functional areas of expertise coordinate their efforts and resources in order to push a new idea into practice (Roberts 1992; Roberts and King 1996; Roberts 2007).

CASE STUDY: BUILDING LIGHTHOUSE – A FIELD-BASED DATA COLLECTION AND ANALYSIS SYSTEM

Introduction

In 2007 Captain Longley led an Operational Control Element of Signals Intelligence Marines in Ramadi, Iraq. The Anbar Awakening had occurred earlier in the year and resulted in a major de-escalation of the violence. The de-escalation gave U.S. security forces a greater opportunity to assist Iraqis in rebuilding their lives and to shift from targeting operations and the direct use of military force to non-kinetic operations that emphasize tribal engagements, governance, economics, information gathering, and analysis of the socio-political context.

The U.S. military's ability to conduct non-kinetic operations presented significant challenges. The biggest of these was the ability to understand the needs of the local population. Despite a decade engaged in overseas operations, the U.S. military had difficulties in understanding the socio-political landscape, or the 'human terrain' as it is called. So, over the course of 24 months, Captain Longley embarked on a journey that would lead to multiple iterations, tests, and redesigns of a new idea – a technical system and methodology that could enable the war fighter to better understand the socio-cultural environment.

In its most recent iteration, the innovative idea is best described as a smart phone application that permits the systematic collection of structured and socio-culturally relevant field data. Once collected, the data are immediately uploaded to a server and analyzed using various software packages to map social networks and their locations. From early 2008 until mid 2011, several prototypes emerged in the search for a better, cheaper, and more comprehensive solution to the problems of field-based data collection and analysis. In the process, the new idea would undergo four name changes; two platform redesigns; a partnership and subsequent dissolution with a commercial vendor; the demonstration and test of the project throughout Southeast Asia, the U.S., and Afghanistan; and the presentation of the system to nearly 40 senior executives and general officers throughout the Department of Defense (DoD) and foreign militaries.[5] To date, the innovative idea is in the design phase of the innovation process and moving toward field implementation.

The Context and New Ideas

Captain Longley arrived at the Naval Postgraduate School (NPS) in April 2008 and spent his first nine months completing prerequisites (e.g. calculus, physics, and computer science) in the Information Warfare Systems Engineering curriculum. Invited to attend field experiments later in the year at Camp Roberts just outside Paso Robles, California, he came away with a new idea for his thesis research – the creation of a hybrid communication network that would integrate small tactical radios with commercial off-the-shelf cellular phones. His idea came from his frustrations in Iraq in 2007 where field personnel had difficulty sending very short situation reports from positions only a few kilometers apart to the command and control center at Camp Ramadi. He thought it might be possible to create an integrated communication system using radios and advanced information technology that would link up outlying posts and their command centers. 'Rudder checks' with fellow officers, however, suggested his initial idea was unlikely to be successful.

Searching for ways to address the military's communication and information management problems, a second idea soon followed – the use of smart phones for collecting and transmitting information in the field. While in Iraq, Captain Longley had witnessed very capable Marines spending an inordinate amount of time cleaning and processing data to get it into the appropriate format for analysis. Analysts spent nearly 80 percent of their

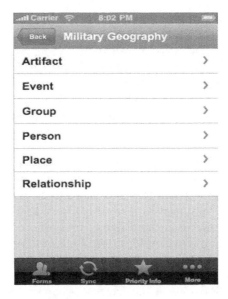

Figure 12.2   Mock-up of the HTACS Military Geography form

time (or more) manipulating and formatting data and approximately 20 percent of their time actually doing the analysis. Deeming it to be 'a huge waste of time' that severely limited the efficiency of the unit, he proposed to design a system to collect, process, and structure socio-cultural data that would streamline data preparation and expedite analysis. He named it the Human Terrain Analysis and Collection System (HTACS).

HTACS
To create the system, Captain Longley linked up with Chief Warrant Officer 3 Chad Machiela, a student in the Defense Analysis Department. Machiela had spent a considerable amount of time deployed at the small-unit level and shared Longley's frustrations about information management in the field. Longley also teamed up with another student who provided the programming support for HTACS. The first task for the team was to develop a mock-up of how data could be collected. Built from a framework Chief Warrant Officer Machiela had developed in a course on the Anthropology of Conflict, they created a unit called 'military geography', seen in Figure 12.2. Waiting until units returned to base, trying to make sense of hand-written field notes, and putting them into a format (which was never consistent across the operators) was time consuming and error prone, and made work in the units more difficult. The point of the mock-up was to illustrate how, using a mobile application, data could be gathered and formatted during field operations in a more systematic way.

The team's next step was to get funding. The Information Warfare curriculum came up with money for the purchase of several iPod touches (as cell phones were too expensive) and a laptop to be used to code the software. Preparations for field experiments were next. Another mock-up demonstration was readied for Thailand which would be part of an exercise called Crimson Viper.[6] During Crimson Viper in the spring of 2009, Captain

Longley set up a booth to attract attention and support for his idea. Although HTACS was only a mock-up at this point, the team was searching for a future demonstration site and testing ground. They generated interest from several organizations, especially the Marine Corps. Colonel De Guzman, the Marine Force Pacific Operations Officer, was receptive but advised a name change from HTACS to something more 'vanilla'. The notion of collecting data on humans did not sit well with many people, so following Crimson Viper, HTACS became the Multi-modal Information Support Tool (MIST).

MIST

In search of a sponsor for the new idea, now renamed MIST, the team traveled to the Office of Naval Research Global in Tokyo, the Office of Defense Cooperation in Cambodia, and set up meetings with U.S. and Thai agencies in Thailand. Still without a functioning system, they continued to rely on briefs and mock-ups to sell their idea. Although they activated strong demand signals everywhere they briefed, no sponsor surfaced who would agree to move the idea from concept to prototype.

Back in Monterey in the summer and autumn of 2009, Longley continued his master's curriculum. After completing courses in geospatial analysis and network analysis offered through the CORE Lab in the Defense Analysis Department, he began to understand that MIST had potential beyond its use as a data collection tool. Advanced analytic methods such as geospatial and social network analysis would be possible in field settings if MIST's systematic procedures reduced data collection time and simultaneously yielded more reliable and valid data. Longley thus pressed forward in designing and architecting MIST as a system with both data collection and data analytic capabilities. Although MIST was more than a simple mock-up at this point, much more had to be done to produce a prototype. Longley had to learn programming when his partnership with a fellow student dissolved. He and Machiela had to maintain a heavy briefing schedule on campus and a travel schedule throughout the U.S. and abroad to attract interest in his idea. He briefed senior military leaders such as the Commander of Special Operations Command, Admiral Eric Olson, and senior executives in Special Operations Pacific (SOCPAC), a command very interested in getting a working prototype of MIST.

As with many unsponsored projects, finding resources to develop the prototype took a considerable effort. Two possibilities opened up. SOCPAC began searching for appropriate funding within the DoD, first with the Navy Irregular Warfare group at the Office of the Secretary of Defense and then with the Counter Narcotics Technology Program Office in Dahlgren, Virginia. In late 2009, Colonel Dave Maxwell, the strategic advisor group lead for the U.S. Army Special Operations Command (USASOC), invited Longley and Machiela to fly out to Fort Bragg, North Carolina in February 2010. He arranged a briefing to the Commanding General of USASOC, Lieutenant General John Mulholland. LTG Mulholland immediately saw the potential of MIST and directed his staff to start the process for incorporating it into the Special Forces training pipeline. To kick off the effort, he wanted a prototype to be part of ROBIN SAGE, the last exercise in the Special Forces training course. Upon returning to Monterey, Longley and Machiela continued work on MIST and explored ways to introduce it to USASOC and SOCPAC. Both initiatives represented funding and testing opportunities for a prototype. But there was one nagging concern – there was no prototype to test.

Figure 12.3   ODK Collect menus

From Idea to Prototype

In early spring 2010, Longley came across the Open Data Kit (ODK) software set – an open-source[7] data collection and repository system developed at the University of Washington. Quickly reading up on the ODK suite, he found he could deploy the military geography framework on an Android phone (the main screen can be seen in Figure 12.3), transmit the data to an aggregation server, and display the data visually in Google Earth. By late spring he had a functioning MIST prototype just in time for the upcoming exercise in Thailand[8] where he planned to field test it.

Just before the exercise, MIST went through another name change. Unfortunately, MIST referred to several organizations already in place, so the name was confusing to many. On the advice of his co-advisor, Jim Ehlert, Longley changed the name to the Field Information Support Tool (FIST), a name that held for the remainder of 2010.

FIST
Captain Longley went to the Sattahip Naval Base in Thailand during CARAT Thailand 10 in May 2010. His purpose was to collect data for a notional humanitarian disaster. Specifically, he wanted to demonstrate how he could use FIST to geo-locate several hospitals, pharmacies, and medical clinics on a map. He called the demonstration prototype FIST-Light (since it was not a fully functioning prototype at this point). The demonstration was a success. He had his proof of concept – the ODK worked as a data collection tool for the first time in a field environment. On the heels of CARAT Thailand, FIST was featured in the Naval Postgraduate School newsletter that circulated a massive monthly situation report within the DoD. Longley began receiving daily emails about FIST with suggestions of applications from humanitarian assistance to combat operations in Iraq and Afghanistan. He also received very good news – the

Marine Corps approved his request for a two-year extension to continue working on FIST.

Longley continued to refine the FIST ODK collection system and prepare for its next operational demonstration – the Multinational Communications Interoperability Program Pacific Endeavor (PE) to be held in Singapore in August 2010. For PE10, Longley picked up another FIST team member – Captain Derek Snyder, a U.S. Marine Corps student at NPS, who traveled with him to Manila where they collected notional disaster data. They sent their data and reports through a cellular network to the Changi Command and Control Center in Singapore. Again, they demonstrated the utility of FIST. The write-up of its success circulated widely throughout the Department of Defense.

Shortly after PE10, USASOC sponsored a test of FIST in Afghanistan with Chief Warrant Officer Machiela leading the efforts on the ground. The goal was to demonstrate FIST's viability and utility in support of the Village Stability Operations in and around Kandahar. For three months, Machiela took a handful of phones to Afghanistan to demonstrate the use of FIST as a data collection tool and then as an analytic tool that gave immediate feedback to counter insurgency operations on the ground. The three month effort gave FIST even greater exposure and validated its use at the tactical level. Once the news of these pilot tests circulated, requests for assistance poured into the CORE Lab that taught the advanced methodology courses.

After Machiela returned from Afghanistan, he and Longley learned that SOCPAC had been successful in getting funding from the Counter Narcotics Technology Program Office in Dahlgren, Virginia. This was one of the two funding initiatives they were pursuing. The contract was awarded in November 2010 and work was to begin immediately. However, there was a complication. In the time between the funding request and its approval, the research sponsored by SOCPAC in the Pacific, supported by Jim Elhert and the Kestrel Technology Group, had morphed into the development of a comprehensive information and knowledge management system, although they still wanted FIST subsumed into their system. Research sponsored by the CORE Lab and USASOC continued to view FIST in more limited terms as a socio-cultural data collection and analysis system.

To keep the two funding and program initiatives separate, Longley changed the name of his prototype to OpenFist to differentiate it from FIST, the version Kestrel was promoting in the Pacific. The openness underscored what he believed to be his prototype's value-added contribution – the use of commercial off-the-shelf and open-source technologies (e.g. ODK) in combination with CORE Lab's research methodologies. It had the additional advantage of being entirely government owned and operated which, when fielded, would make it a very low cost innovation for the operational needs of the Special Operations and Marine Corps communities.

OpenFIST

OpenFIST was the fourth name change and it triggered considerable consternation among the various communities involved. But Longley felt it was imperative to keep the two versions of his prototype separate since they each had different goals. Moreover, he learned that the Kestrel Technology Group had filed for trademark rights to FIST. As a contractor, the company ultimately expected to sell its product to the government and obviously make a profit. Longley did not see this arrangement as providing the best value for the DoD. He certainly would have found it difficult to explain to the Marine Corps that he was working on a system owned by a private company that would then turn around and charge the Marine Corps large sums of money for its use. And since by this time he had other funding and field test options in Afghanistan and elsewhere, he and the CORE Lab decided to pursue a separate path, despite the funding that SOCPAC offered.

Early in 2011, Captain Longley continued development on OpenFIST. He adopted a new series of commercial and open-source software platforms that provided a more comprehensive, flexible data collection and processing system compared with the FIST-Light or FIST-Kestrel products. In addition, he moved from the Android platform back to the iOS platform and integrated newer technology that was more secure, flexible, and dynamic than the previous iterations. But given the consternation over the name change and continued fallout – some not-so-veiled threats of lawsuits – Longley thought it prudent to again change the prototype's name.

Lighthouse
Longley needed to rebrand his prototype. The renaming of OpenFIST to Lighthouse was done to highlight the open-source data collection tools he had integrated and to signal their broader applications. To him Lighthouse represented an integrated data collection system working in concert with the analytic methodology espoused by the CORE Lab. He thought the symbol of a lighthouse conveyed an important image – illuminating social networks to enable the troops to understand and navigate in the human terrain.

Longley's team continues to analyze every component and process of the Lighthouse prototype to determine new and better ways to design an effective system for collecting, processing, and analyzing data and ultimately helping ground-level troops to deal with the complex socio-cultural environment in which they operate. Lighthouse is on tap to redeploy to Afghanistan on a much larger scale. Initiatives are underway in California to use Lighthouse for a counter-gang initiative in concert with the Department of Homeland Security. Longley expects the prototype to continue to evolve as its design matures, but he is pressured for time. Given the frequent rotation of service members, he has less than a year left before he returns to operations. In that time frame, Lighthouse has to be developed into a stable system that can be implemented in the field. Although Longley has designed the majority of the technical work, Lighthouse still needs a team of engineers with the technical prowess and passion to guide it through the complex organization we know as the DoD. Without dedicated oversight, it risks falling by the wayside before it achieves ultimate success as a fully developed innovation.

CASE ANALYSIS

In the study of Lighthouse to date, we have found six necessary conditions for bottom-up entrepreneurship and innovation in large military bureaus: entrepreneurial problem solvers; new ideas; collective entrepreneurship; start-up resources; incubators of innovation; and idea champions. *Entrepreneurial problem solvers* begin the innovation process.[9] They focus on things that aren't working and try to fix them. When simple solutions elude them, they launch a search process for better ways of doing things. The search can take them in many different directions. In this case, it took Captain Longley to a graduate program in Information Systems, where he started the search for solutions to the information management problems he saw in the field. Problem solvers also are determined. We see evidence of this determination when Longley had to learn calculus, physics, and computer science as part of his program requirements and then computer programming when his first partner dropped out of the project. As inveterate problem solvers, what others might call 'roadblocks' entrepreneurs see as things to get over, around, and past in the search for a solution to a problem that they think needs to be solved.

Entrepreneurial problem solvers also are ideas people. *New ideas* are identified and sorted based on their potential to solve the problem. This is where the creativity characteristic of entrepreneurs comes in. When one new idea doesn't pan out – for example, integrating small-level tactical radios with commercial off-the-shelf cellular phones in an attempt to create a 'hybrid' communications network – then another takes its place – for example, collecting and transmitting information in the field using smart phones, and ultimately settling on the idea of collecting and analyzing field data with sophisticated methodologies. Constantly scanning the environment and ever alert for new opportunities, Longley easily transitioned away from a proprietary information management system when he found the ODK, an open-source technology that was cheaper and easier to use to build his prototype.

The sole entrepreneur working by himself against all odds is a heroic notion, but not a very realistic one in large, complex military bureaus. Entrepreneurial tasks and activities are wide ranging and require a broad base of expertise, as Roberts (1992) found in her studies of policy entrepreneurs. Others need to participate. Thus we find *collective entrepreneurship* more likely when engaged in bottom-up innovation.[10] In this case, the team included Chad Machiela, who helped develop the cell phone application menus informed by his understanding of Anthropology, along with his extensive experience in social network analysis and geospatial analysis. Derek Snyder signed on to evaluate the innovative idea during the demonstrations and field tests. His feedback provided important guidance for prototype redesigns. The programmers also played an important role, as Longley was pulled away to conduct field tests and market to gatekeepers whose approvals would be required to move his prototype up the chain of command.

No innovation, bottom up or top down, occurs without *critical start-up resources*. Two were particularly significant in this case: time and seed money. Time is important in the military since personnel have short rotations before they are on to their next assignments. Longley only had two years in his master's program before he was expected to leave for his next unit. Two years is very little time to complete a rigorous curriculum, in addition to moving a new idea through initiation, design, and implementation in a very large, complex bureau. Fortunately, he was able to extend his program of study, which gave him another two years in the hope of working through at least the design phase of the innovation process. Seed money was also important. Although his innovative idea was not expensive compared with large-scale military projects, it did require funds for travel and equipment. Luckily, Longley connected with organizations and units that had slack resources to invest in him and his ideas.

As *incubators of innovation*, three organizational entities provided Longley with funding and intellectual support. He landed at the Naval Postgraduate School in Monterey, California, a military university whose mission, in part, was defined as a hub for technological innovation. This context offered a receptive and inviting space to test his ideas in on-going field demonstrations and exercises that were regular features of campus activities. The Defense Analysis Department, populated by an interdisciplinary group of scholars in wide-ranging fields from Economics to History, was a fertile ground for inquiry. Known for its innovative thinking in counter insurgency, the department attracted a group of students and faculty who saw themselves as a counterweight to the military's traditional ways of thinking. Chad Machiela had just graduated from this program when he met Longley and, as was noted earlier, he played a key role in developing modules for data collection, as illustrated in Figure 12.2. In addition, through his methodological training, honed through his exposure to the CORE Lab courses, Machiela expertly demonstrated what could be done in the field when new data collection and management tools were paired with the CORE Lab's analytic techniques. Thus the third entity in the trifecta of incubators was the CORE Lab, a recent start-up founded by two entrepreneurial faculty members – Doug Borer and Nancy Roberts – who understood the need for new methods and technology to support field operations. The Lab served as a hub of innovation within the Defense Analysis Department and attracted students from other departments around campus who, like Longley, were looking for safe havens to test their ideas and develop their analytic skills.

And, last but not least, bottom-up entrepreneurship and innovation needs *idea champions* whose job it is to run interference for the entrepreneur and his idea as they wend their way through the maze of hierarchical checkpoints and gatekeepers. Many served in this role: Mr. Jim Elhert and Dr. Nancy Roberts signed on as Longley's thesis advisors and helped him give shape to his ideas and designs; Brigadier General Vincent Stewart and Major General Melvin Spiese provided 'top cover' and high-level support when Longley requested an unheard of two year extension at NPS; from his vantage point of strategic advisor group lead for USASOC, Col. Dave Maxwell pulled Carrick's new idea from obscurity onto the decision agenda, where it came to the attention of Lieutenant General John Mulholland, whose extensive field experience enabled him to immediately see its value and import. Idea champions in turn were useful in forging a network of participants who field tested Lighthouse, generating a growing base of support among ground commanders.

In the study of Lighthouse to date, we have found six sufficient conditions for bottom-up entrepreneurship and innovation to be successful: the management of the idea's identity and meaning; the management of attention; the management of resistance and conflict; the management of the network; the management of organizational interfaces; and the management of tensions. The intellectual and conceptual challenges of *managing the idea's identity and meaning* emerged early in the process. Problem definitions and solutions (the new idea) can be framed in numerous ways, but Longley understood this framing had to fit the context in which both would be embedded. He was fully aware that data collection and information management had been a source of consternation among the troops. A chorus of complaints had been growing and the 'solutions' offered were not found to be workable. They were heavy, expensive, and relied on proprietary technology that took long periods of time to vet in a complex web of DoD stakeholders whose sign-off was required to make any innovation 'field ready'. The troops wanted something light, easy to use, inexpensive, and, most importantly, built using the latest information technology. If they could use cell phones to communicate and exchange information at home why not in the field they asked? This sensitivity to context presents a strategic challenge to the entrepreneur. New ideas need to be enveloped with contextual nuances, explanations, and details or they will not resonate with the potential community of interest. The name changes for the innovative idea and prototypes, while puzzling at first, can be understood in this light. Names do matter; they are signaling devices to attract interest, support, and resources. Longley understood it was important to position the idea within the larger DoD community, and hence Lighthouse, after four attempts, finally was able to establish its brand identity.

Management of attention is a day-to-day struggle. A new idea competes in a sea of ideas, some old, some new, some from inside the organization, and some from the outside. Idea competition requires the entrepreneur to differentiate his new idea from others and to help the potential users understand what value-added contributions his ideas offer that others do not. To capture attention and educate the end users requires constant information dissemination, marketing, and mobilization activities such as briefings and site visits. Getting the idea on people's 'radar screen' and keeping it there can be a full-time effort. Media support from NPS helped, but it was a double-edged sword. With media attention comes greater interest, greater interest generates requests for briefings, and with briefings come more requests for information and site visits. It is a vicious cycle that threatens to overwhelm the entrepreneur and his team and drain them of the time and energy they need to focus on idea development and design.

Management of resistance and conflict is essential in bottom-up entrepreneurship and innovation and requires some careful thought and finely tuned political skills. Longley, for example, anticipated resistance regarding his new idea in terms of security – the 'information on the phones would not be secure', the 'phones could be lost or stolen', and so on. He was prepared to answer these challenges from competitors and others who were just unclear about what was being proposed. The entrepreneur also should be able to gauge the level of resistance and conflict the new idea is likely to generate and prepare for it. Research indicates that people tend to be relatively willing to try new ideas when they view them as offering a clear advantage over the status quo; as having characteristics best described as compatibility, trialability, observability, and simplicity (Rogers and Kim 1985, p. 88). Since Longley judged Lighthouse to be simple, compatible with current systems, and easy to submit to field trials and generate results, he defended it as a clear advantage over alternatives. He was not well prepared, however, to do battle with contractors who viewed him as an upstart, threatening their products already approved as programs of record; nor was he prepared for the challenges from his former advisor Jim Elhert and his advisor's partner, the contractor Kestrel, who were pushing a competing alternative to Lighthouse. Kestrel had filed a trademark for FIST and OpenFIST, even though neither FIST nor OpenFist had been part of the cooperative research agreement (CRADA) Kestrel had signed with the university. NPS lawyers, administrators, multiple commands, and the entrepreneurial team got dragged into deliberations over what to do next. After months of wasted time and effort, Longley changed his prototype's name to Lighthouse and let Jim Elhert and Kestrel retain the names of FIST and OpenFIST. The battle over the names was not worth their continued threats and disruptions. In retrospect, Longley and his team should have anticipated this level of conflict, especially with vendors who stood to lose a great deal of money if he were successful. Stakeholder audits (Roberts and King 1989) and stakeholder management (Bryson 2004) might have been helpful to at least identify future competitors and those who saw his ideas as a threat to their contracts and livelihoods and to prepare some strategies to deal with them.

Bottom-up entrepreneurship and innovation in large military bureaus not only requires collective entrepreneurship, it also requires the *management of a complex network* of participants (Kickert et al. 1997; Koppenjan and Klijn 2004), preferably using collaboration (Sorensen and Torfing 2011) rather than political maneuvering. The core of the network is the project team. Longley had to find people to join the project and engage them in tasks that needed to be done (e.g. programming, drop-down menus for data collection). He needed to maintain their commitment with constant explanations of what they were doing, why it was important, and how it would benefit them and their organizations. The administrative nuts and bolts of project management were essential: communication with team members (special software systems to facilitate information sharing and coordination); face-to-face meetings when the situation required it; proposal writing to keep money flowing to support the innovative idea and its design; and project evaluation (does our new idea work and what are we going to do if it doesn't?). Longley also had an extended network of supporters, champions, advisors, and potential users with whom he collaborated. They had to be kept abreast of the latest developments. He had to decide how much information and what level of detail needed to be shared, and how to incorporate the network into the development efforts. Email communications facilitated these exchanges, but they also generated hundreds of emails that had to be answered and tracked over time. As his network grew, more and more of his attention had to be devoted to its management.

Management of organizational interfaces is a particularly nettlesome issue for Lighthouse. We know that context matters for innovation success (Walker 2007). Ideas like Lighthouse are always embedded in larger systems, but the question is how the hand-off from one system to another should build on mutual capabilities and minimize areas of difference. Stand-alone projects tend not to survive, especially those reliant on soft-ware. What will be the connection between Lighthouse and the other systems it feeds? How will data transfer occur and in what format? Where will data be housed and by whom? Beyond these technical issues, implementation also involves the long-term viability and compatibility of Lighthouse within a complex maze of organizations known as the DoD, each of which has its own data collection and analysis capabilities. As one of the world's largest organizations dedicated to U.S. national security, it remains to be seen whether a subset of stakeholders will find enough areas of agreement to push for Lighthouse adoption and whether their collective efforts will enable it to become a program of record built into the Program Objective Memorandum (POM) that recommends programming and resource allocations. These issues have yet to be settled. If and when they are, and the prototype survives into practice, only then will the idea become a full-blown innovation.

If Captain Longley manages to find a pathway through the minefield of challenges above, it suggests he has been able to *manage the tensions* inherent in DoD innovation and entrepreneurship and somehow strike a balance among all of them. There are the tensions in the entrepreneur's personal life – how to manage the competing demands of entrepreneurship and those of his home and family. There are the professional issues of a student entrepreneur who has to satisfy the degree requirements of a Master of Science and a PhD and at the same time single-mindedly drive an innovative idea forward. There are the exigencies of entrepreneurship which require intense focus and dedication to the innovative idea while responding to the institutional pressures and demands of the chain of command which requires deference to authority and willingness to put collective requirements above personal desires. There is the necessity for integrated, coordinated information systems across DoD, suggesting a top-down approach to change, while at the same time there is the bottom-up approach which attempts to respond to the demands of field-level operators for information technology that meets their unique and specialized needs.

CONCLUSION

Lighthouse, a new innovative idea and system for military field-based data collection and analysis, has had a circuitous path through the initiation and design phases of the innovation process. All indicators suggest we are at the end of the design phase and moving toward implementation. Yet we know that new technologies can surface and force a recycling back into idea generation and design, as happened in earlier iterations of Lighthouse. We also are aware that design can be truncated at any point. Serious budgetary cutbacks are underway throughout the DoD. Retrenchment can choke off seed money and, most importantly, the time needed for new idea development and design. Lighthouse does have the advantage in this regard since in an economic downturn it is hard to argue against an innovative idea that utilizes low-cost, off-the-shelf technology and gathers enthusiastic support from the field, not only in military communities, but in those working in other agencies such as U.S. Aid and the Department of Agriculture. Still, implementation is the point of failure of many innovations and until this idea is accepted into practice, a declaration of success is premature (Klein and Sorra 1996; Piening 2011).[11]

At this juncture, we offer our conceptual framework of bottom-up entrepreneurship and innovation in the DoD as a work in progress, that while not yet complete, lays out what we believe are the necessary and sufficient conditions for success, at least through the initiation and design phases. It is our hope that these twin pillars of theory construction will move us closer to filling the conceptual and theoretical void in the literature. In the meantime, we leave readers with a metaphor which we believe aptly describes the processes we have been tracking. The entrepreneur and his innovative idea are just two elements in a web of relationships in a large *complex adaptive system* known as the DoD. They provide opportunities for experimentation and learning that enable the DoD as a whole to adapt and change. But similar to other complex adaptive systems, the DoD system is likely to be highly sensitive to initial conditions, so the relationships among all the interdependent system parts are expected to be nonlinear, their final trajectory impossible to predict (Czerwinski 1998). At this point we do not know if the collective, emergent behavior of the system elements will give rise to the innovation of Lighthouse. At the same time, we view these 'nonlinear and multidirectional relationships as a source of inspiration, not contradiction' (Brown and Katz 2009, pp. 85–86). They teach us to 'embrace the mess,' and 'allow complexity to exist . . . because complexity is the more reliable source of creative opportunities' (p. 86). It opens the door to 'the systematic approach to the invention of possibilities' (Buchanan 1992, p. 13).

NOTES

1. Examples of public sector bottom-up innovations are growing in number (e.g. Borins 2001; Bartlett and Dibben 2002), but they are still rare in military organizations.
2. See Roberts and King (1996) as an example.
3. Innovation phases do not imply a sequential logic in the idea's trajectory. We know for example that the more novel an innovative idea, the more overlap there tends to be among the phases. What this means in practice is that when entrepreneurs work on highly original, innovative ideas, they may be engaged in both initiation and design or design and implementation at the same time.
4. The phases of the innovation process describe innovation in global terms, stating the necessary conditions for innovation to occur. If a new idea is not created, designed, and implemented, it will not be able to attain the developed status we attribute to an innovation. In contrast, public entrepreneurs can go through a much messier process that follows no predetermined set of activities. As Kingdon reminds us, 'events do not proceed neatly in stages, steps, or phases . . . Participants do not first identify problems and then seek solutions for them; indeed, advocacy of solutions often precedes the highlighting of problems to which they become attached' (Kingdon 1984, p. 215). In fact, some would advocate this messiness, by encouraging public entrepreneurs to work implementation issues while they are creating and designing new policy (Pressman and Wildavsky 1973).
5. This burst of activity around a new idea and its offshoots is consistent with what has been found in the business literature, for example Schroeder et al. (1989).
6. Crimson Viper would be the technology precursor to an even later exercise called COBRA GOLD. COBRA GOLD is an annual bilateral military exercise held between the Royal Thai Armed Forces and the U.S. military.
7. 'Open source' refers to information that is freely available on the Web without charge to users.
8. The exercise was called Combined Operations Afloat and Readiness Training (CARAT).
9. There are many terms in the literature to describe creative, innovative people in the public arena: public entrepreneurs; policy entrepreneurs; executive entrepreneurs; bureaucratic entrepreneurs; and political entrepreneurs. Bureaucratic entrepreneurs are in formal positions in the bureaucracy but they are not in executive positions. Although considered to be a leader in the Marine Corps, Captain Longley commands units within the larger organization so the term that best describes his activities is bureaucratic entrepreneur. Were he to serve in an executive position and run a separate, stand-alone organization, he would be called an executive entrepreneur. For a fuller description of the different types of public entrepreneurs see Roberts (1992) and Mack et al. (2008).
10. See Roberts and King (1996) for a discussion of the different types of collective entrepreneurship, especially pages 10–18 and Chapter 7. See also Borins (2001) and Csikszentmihalyi (1996).
11. It is important to point out that from a process perspective, 'success' should not be interpreted to mean that the innovation is the 'correct response to a performance gap in the field,' or even that it was 'the culmination of a set of actors pursuing their own ends'. These 'frames' as well as others could be utilized to 'explain' the outcomes in the innovation process to date. Our use of the term simply acknowledges that for an innovative idea to be a success, it has survived through initiation, design and implementation to become accepted practice; it has met the necessary and sufficient conditions for innovation to occur. Our interests were in charting *how* the idea moved through time in a large public bureau, not in identifying *what* the determinants of its success were and how it might be compared with other alternatives. These are issues for future consideration.

REFERENCES

Bartlett, D. and Dibben, P. (2002). Public sector innovation and entrepreneurship: case studies from local government. *Local Government Studies*, 28(1), 1–24.

Borins, S. (2001). Encouraging innovation in the public sector. *Journal of Intellectual Capital*, 2(3), 310–319.

Brown, T. and Katz, T. (2009). *Change by Design: How Design Thinking Transforms Organizations and Inspires Innovation*. New York: HarperCollins.

Bryson, J.M. (2004). What to do when stakeholders matter. *Public Management Review*, 6(1), 21–53.

Buchanan, R. (1992). Wicked problems in design thinking. *Design Issues*, 8(2), 5–21.

Csikszentmihaly, M. (1996). *Creativity: Flow and the Psychology of Discovery and Invention*. New York: HarperCollins.

Czerwinski, T. (1998). *Coping with the Bounds: Speculations on Nonlinearity in Military Affairs*. Washington, DC: National Defense University.

Daft, R. and Becker, S. (1978). *Innovations in Organizations.* New York: Elsevier Science.

Drucker, P.R. (2006). *Innovation and Entrepreneurship.* New York: Harper Paperbacks.

Eggers, B. and Singh, S. (2009). *The Public Innovator's Playbook.* Washington, DC: Deloitte Research.

Grissom, A. (2006). The future of military innovation studies. *Journal of Strategic Studies,* 29(5), 905–934.

Kickert, W.J.M., Klijn, E.-H. and Koppenhan, J. (eds) (1997). *Managing Complex Networks.* London: Sage.

Kingdon, J.W. (1984). *Agendas, Alternatives, and Public Policies.* New York: Little, Brown.

Klein, K.J. and Sorra, J.S. (1996). The challenge of innovation implementation. *Academy of Management Review,* 21(4), 1055–1080.

Koppenjan, J. and Klijn, E.-H. (2004). *Managing Uncertainties in Networks.* London: Routledge.

Lewis, E. (1980). *Public Entrepreneurship: Toward a Theory of Bureaucratic Political Power.* Bloomington, IN: Indiana University Press.

Mack, W.R., Green, D. and Vedlitz, A. (2008). Innovation and implementation in the public sector: an examination of public entrepreneurship. *Review of Policy Research,* 25(3), 233–252.

Mohr, L.B. (1982). *Explaining Organizational Behavior: The Limits and Possibilities of Research.* San Francisco, CA: Jossey-Bass.

Peltz, D.C. and Munson, F.C. (1982). Originality level and the innovating process in organizations. *Human Systems Management,* 3, 173–187.

Piening, E.P. (2011). Insights into the process dynamics of innovation implementation. *Public Management Review,* 13(1), 127–157.

Polsby, N.W. (1984). *Political Innovation in America: The Politics of Policy Initiation.* New Haven, CT: Yale University Press.

Pressman, J. and Wildavsky, A. (1973). *Implementation.* Berkeley, CA: University of California Press.

Roberts, N.C. (1992). Public entrepreneurship and innovation. *Policy Studies Review,* 11(1), 55–74.

Roberts, N.C. (2007). Public entrepreneurship as social creativity. *World Futures,* 63(1), 595–609.

Roberts, N.C. and King, P.J. (1989). The stakeholder audit goes public. *Organizational Dynamics,* Winter, 63–79.

Roberts, N.C. and King, P.J. (1996). *Transforming Public Policy: Dynamics of Policy Entrepreneurship and Innovation.* San Francisco, CA: Jossey-Bass.

Rogers, E.M. and Kim, J.-I. (1985). Diffusion of innovations in public sector organizations. In R.L. Merritt and A.J. Merritt (eds), *Innovation in the Public Sector.* Beverly Hills, CA: Sage, pp. 85–105.

Rosen, S.P. (1991). *Winning the Next War: Innovation and the Modern Military.* Ithaca, NY: Cornell University Press.

Schroeder, R.G., Van de Ven, A.H., Scudder, G.D. and Polley, D. (1989). The development of innovative ideas. In A.H. Van de Ven, H.L. Angle and M.S. Poole (eds), *Research on the Management of Innovation: The Minnesota Studies.* New York: Harper & Row, pp. 107–134.

Schumpeter, J.A. (1951). *Essays: On Entrepreneurs, Innovation, Business Cycles, and the Evolution of Capitalism.* Edited by Richard V. Clemence. Boston, MA: Addison-Wesley Publishing.

Sorensen, E. and Torfing, J. (2011). Enhancing collaborative innovation in the public sector. Unpublished paper.

Spulak, R.G. (2010). *Innovate or Die: Innovation and Technology for Special Operations.* McDill Air Force Base, FL: The JSOU Press.

Walker, R.M. (2007). An empirical evaluation of innovation types and organizational and environmental characteristics: towards a configuration framework. *Journal of Public Administration Research and Theory,* 18, 591–615.

Zaltman, G., Duncan, R. and Holbek, J. (1973). *Innovations and Organizations.* New York: Wiley.

13. Leading successful innovation in local public services
James H. Svara

In order to address new policy challenges, improve productivity, better serve and more fully engage a changing citizenry, local governments have the option of becoming more innovative. The questions that have not been fully answered in the research on local government innovation are – how and why do they do it? This chapter addresses the fundamental questions of whether government organizations are capable of innovation and renewal, what kinds of innovations occur in local governments, and what characteristics are associated with innovative organizations with special attention to the role of leaders.

In popular views and some academic critiques, governmental organizations are seen as reactive and resistant to change, at worst, or constrained by circumstances that make some capable of innovation and others not. Local governments have divergent characteristics regarding the likelihood of being innovative. On the one hand, they are close to the publics they serve and have both the opportunity and the pressure from their populations to develop new approaches that address local needs. On the other hand, local governments often have limited resources and wide variation in the capability and inclination of government officials to develop or adopt new approaches. There can be resistance to change that limits the spread of new approaches from one local government to another. Despite the importance of innovation in local government, scholarly understanding of the types, level and impact of innovation in government and the organizational features associated with variation in innovation is limited. We still know little about the scope of innovation in an organization or how innovations are sequenced over time or reinforce each other. It is not clear the extent to which innovations are developed within the organization or borrowed from others. There is virtually no guidance for how to promote innovation. How should governments organize staff to develop or identify new approaches? What role should the leader play to stimulate innovation without stifling creativity? How do organizations broaden the participation of staff members in generating and supporting new ideas?

The objectives of this chapter are to review the measurement of innovation in city governments and the factors associated with it. From this evidence, drawn from existing research, some ideas are advanced regarding the innovation process in city governments that achieve high levels of sustained change and high innovation and the factors that advance or impede these conditions.

THE NATURE OF INNOVATION

The term 'innovation' refers to the introduction of new or alteration of existing practices with the intention of producing positive results – the standard definition used in local government research (Damanpour and Evans 1984). The two forms of innovation are: (a) adoption of 'standard' or 'leading' new approaches from outside the organization, such as e-government techniques, and (b) invention of new approaches or substantial modification of methods or practices from other organizations to create new approaches, that is, 'reinvention' (Rogers 2003, p. 17). New approaches originate in organizations that are pioneers and early adopters, and may diffuse through other organizations over time. Given their importance in generating the process of change that other governments follow, it is especially important to understand the characteristics of innovation leaders that are creative, willing to experiment and give early credibility to novel approaches.

Scope and Characteristics of Innovations

There are two major approaches in research on organizational innovation in the public sector that correspond to the adoption–invention distinction. The first examines diffusion and adoption of new ideas and practices, such as the utilization of techniques of 'reinventing government' or e-government, based on surveys of a large number of cities, and identifies the organizational and jurisdictional correlates of variation in adoption (Kearney, Feldman and Scavo 2000; Moon and deLeon 2001; Damanpour and Schneider 2006; Kwon, Berry and Feiock 2009; Jun and Weare 2011; Nelson and Svara 2012). The second approach examines the creation of new methods and practices within organizations. This research focuses on specific examples of change, such as Borins' (2000) examination of new ideas that received the Ford Foundation/Kennedy School of Government innovation award, or case studies of how individual organizations develop new approaches.

An important theme in diffusion studies is the drivers that incline some organizations to adopt new approaches. DiMaggio and Powell (1983) suggest a distinction between coercive, mimetic and normative processes as the primary causal logic behind the diffusion process. In coercive processes, the innovation is adopted because the organization is forced to do so; for example, as a result of new legislation. In mimetic processes, the innovation is adopted because the organization finds it appropriate or practical to copy the practice of other organizations considered to be successful and influential based on images of innovativeness or high efficiency (Abrahamson 1991; Berry and Berry 2007). Competition between similar organizations may also generate mimicry (Strang and Soule 1998, p. 274). In normative processes, the innovation is adopted because the organization seeks to meet aspirational goals, such as those supported by the shared values of professional associations. These drivers do not explain, however, why certain governments launch new initiatives or have a strong tendency to develop new approaches or be early adopters.

The scope and timing of innovations may be related to the way that public organizations search for new approaches. Building on Cyert and March (1963), Greve (2003) stresses the importance of three types of search processes that organizations use in the innovation process: problemistic search, institutionalized search and slack search. *Problemistic search*, prompted by crisis or a shortfall in performance (Kelman 2008), may be narrowly focused on addressing the perceived problem. In contrast, *institutionalized search* reflects an organizational commitment to finding new approaches, such as units involved in strategic planning, research and development, marketing or innovation. A variety of new approaches are being taken in local governments to assemble teams of creative problem solvers rather than relying exclusively on a specialized administrative unit (Thoreson and Svara 2011), and some governments choose to share the search process with other governments informally, on a regional basis, or through a formal network.[1] *Slack search* comes from staff members who have the time and motivation to look for different and better ways to do things. Slack search is most likely to proceed in an unstructured way. Using team approaches, quality circles or employee reward programs that recognize staff members who propose constructive new approaches are focused ways to get staff members to consider new and better policies, services or processes. Understanding the search process requires examination of behavior of leaders and individual staff members and how they network as well as exploring organizational commitment and search processes.

Patterns of Diffusion

It is common to assume that the spread of an innovation will approximate a bell-shaped curve when measuring the number of persons or organizations that adopt a new approach at different points in time. As Rogers (2003) has observed in a wide range of settings, there is a small number of pioneers and a modestly larger number of early adopters – normally about one in six in the population. Approximately a third will complete the early majority. In a symmetrical pattern, there are similar proportions of late adopters and laggards (one third and one sixth of the relevant population) that adopt the new practice very late or never.[2] Some innovations in local government are represented by a number of related practices that constitute an innovative approach. An example is the range of changes that constituted the 'reinventing government' (Osborne and Gaebler, 1992) or 'new public management' (NPM) approach. For these clusters of related innovations, diffusion is measured by the *number* of new practices that have been adopted.

Patterns of diffusion can be illustrated by examining the adoption of several clusters of innovation practices in the United States along with an example from Denmark. One pattern is illustrated by the results of surveys conducted by the International City/County Management Association (ICMA) in the past decade that determined whether local governments had adopted new practices in three different areas:

- Reinventing government (2003) – 1072 responses from cities with a population of over 10,000 / 33 percent response rate;
- Electronic Government (2004) – 1842 responses / 43 percent response rate;
- Strategic and participatory practices (State of the Profession survey, 2006) – 1273 responses / 37 percent response rate.

A total of 492 cities completed the three surveys, or 15 percent of the 3257 cities with a population of over 10,000.[3] For each area, ten measures were selected and the distribution of adoptions was calculated. The distribution of adoptions in all three surveys approximates a bell-shaped curve, although the emerging and fast-changing area of e-government was tilted somewhat toward the lower end of the adoption scale. In 2004, there were more low adopters and a substantial number of non-adopters of e-government practices compared with the other two areas of adoption.

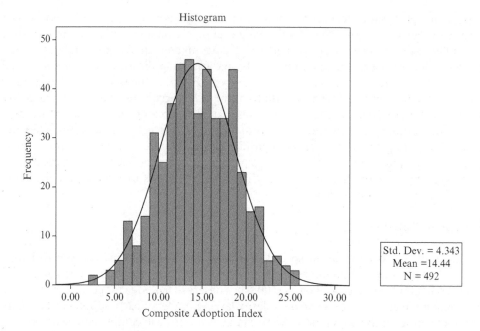

Source: Nelson and Svara (2012, Figure 1).

Figure 13.1   *Distribution of number of adoptions by city governments in the U.S.,*
2003–2006

The three separate adoption indices ranging from zero to ten points have been combined into a total adoption index that ranges from zero to thirty. Even though the cities that return surveys consistently may be different from those that respond selectively, the separate index scores are similar for the cities that returned all three surveys and the average score for all cities that returned each separate survey. The distribution of the adoption of a composite index that combines all three areas in innovation is presented in Figure 13.1. The results indicate a steep bell-shaped curve with 60 percent of the cities clustered within one standard deviation of the mean. Local government adoption from a range of options in three different types of innovation in the United States indicates a pattern familiar in the rates of individual adoption over time: a normal distribution with a small proportion of extensive adopters, the majority of moderately high and moderately low adopters, and a small proportion of limited adopters.

Other Patterns

A study conducted in Denmark in 2006 examined the extent to which practices associated with NPM had been adopted by municipal governments (Hansen and Svara 2007). Nine practices were listed and respondents were asked to state whether each had been adopted. The histogram measuring the responses is presented in Figure 13.2. The pattern is markedly different from the extent of adopting the similar reinventing government practices in the United States. The typical government was using all the practices and less than one

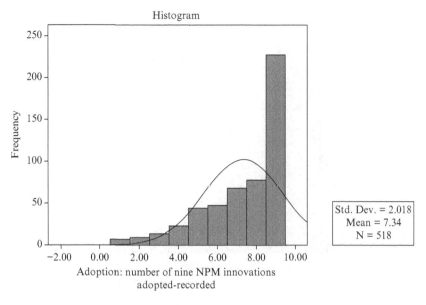

Source: Hansen and Svara (2007).

Figure 13.2 Distribution of number of NPM adoptions by city governments in Denmark, 2006

fifth of the municipalities were using five or fewer. The Danish case represents highly uniform diffusion and a high level of adoption. The factors that contribute to this uniformly high level of adoption may be the high level of professional networking among administrators in Denmark; the absence of very small municipalities after reorganization of local governments in the 1970s; greater uniformity in resources because of greater funding from the central government; and mandates from central government in selected areas, for example the requirement to offer alternative sources of certain social services.

A survey was conducted in 2010 in the United States by ICMA to determine the extent to which practices that are related to sustainability have been adopted. Specific indicators – policies, programs and activities that local governments can use to advance sustainability – were drawn from a number of sources,[4] and 109 actions were included in the survey, chosen to cover commonly used techniques as well as rarely used practices related to environmental protection, preservation of resources, economic development and social equity. As a consequence, the number of actions taken by the responding governments was likely to vary widely. The adoption rate for the responding cities and counties is displayed in Figure 13.3.

The striking feature in the adoption of sustainability practices is that most governments are bunched at the low end in the number of adoptions, and the innovators and early adopters are way out ahead of the rest. It appears that American local governments are still in the early stage of innovation, with most local governments closer to the lower end of the spectrum rather than in the middle or higher end. This relatively low adoption by most governments is puzzling in the sense that sustainability is not a new idea, but it may be understandable because of the relative newness of sustainability as a challenge

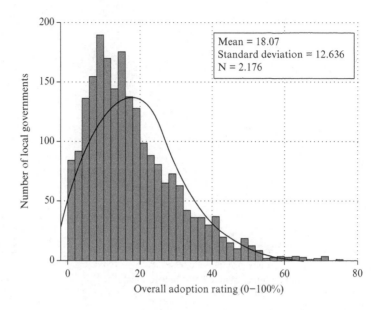

Source: Svara (2011).

Figure 13.3   Local governments arranged by the level of sustainability action

that *local* governments are taking on beyond the traditional activities like recycling and mandated activities like air quality control that they have been doing for some time.

Thus, the patterns of diffusion by local governments will typically approximate a normal distribution produced by variation in both the number and pace of adoptions. In the absence of mandates, a minority of governments start adopting sooner and adopt more of the practices in a cluster of related innovations. Larger numbers of governments adopt some or a few of the practices, and a minority lag behind. Some circumstances favor fairly uniform adoption, but, on the other hand, newly emerging areas of innovation like sustainability or rapidly changing areas, for example e-government may at least initially have pioneers and early adopters who move far faster and have relatively higher rates of adoption. Most local governments can be left behind. The question is whether a majority will move toward the middle of the curve by emulating the behavior of the leaders or whether the particular movement will fail to attract a majority of followers.

CORRELATES OF INNOVATION

A variety of factors affect the likelihood that local governments will adopt innovations from other organizations or will invent their own new approaches. The former approach to innovation has received much more attention in research.

The variables that have been found to be important in explaining higher rates of adoption in cross-sectional studies of local governments fall into two broad categories: external factors, such as community characteristics and pressures from the environment (e.g.

Table 13.1   Factors related to level of adoption of innovation

External characteristics	Internal characteristics
• Socio-economic factors (population, economic health level, per capita income);[1, 2, 9] size[3, 6, 8, 10] • Environmental (urbanization, community wealth, population growth, unemployment rate, complexity).[4] In the U.S., located in Sunbelt (southern and western states)[1] or west[3, 10] • Environmental factors (service need, diversity of need, changes in social, political and economic context facing the service)[5] • Institutional characteristics: in U.S. council-manager form[1, 2, 3, 8, 9, 10] • Vertical integration with central government policies[5] • State policies on sustainability[10] • Enterprise zone[8] • Community policy priorities[10] • Other external factors (public pressure, public competition, service provider competition, coercion from auditors and inspectors)[5]	• Managerial tenure[1, 2, 4] • Managerial background (age, gender, education)[4] • Manager's values (NPM values, traditional administrative values, political ideology);[1, 2] managerial values regarding innovations[4] • Importance of good relations with superiors/peers (negative)[6] • Effective strategic planning[7] • Managerial leadership;[5] importance of being a change agent and central to organizational change;[6] leadership commitment to innovation[7] • New manager from outside[5] • Operating department director versus city manager (negative)[6] • Unions (negative);[1, 2, 3] frequency of trade union contacts[6] • Application of IT[8] • Organizational size;[4, 5] economic health, unions, external communication[4] • Learning from associations and peers[5] • Involvement of private business[8] • Political leadership[5] • Goal formulating and visionary politicians[6]

Sources: 1. Kearney, Feldman and Scavo (2000); 2. Moon and deLeon (2001); 3. Kearney (2005); 4. Damanpour and Schneider (2006); 5. Walker (2006); 6. Hansen and Svara (2007); 7. Kim, Lee and Kim (2007); 8. Kwon, Berry and Feiock (2009); 9. Nelson and Svara (2012); 10. Svara (2011).

economic conditions and unemployment), on the one hand, and internal factors, such as leadership and organizational characteristics, on the other. The variables that have been found to be important in explaining higher rates of adoption in cross-sectional studies of local governments are presented in Table 13.1.

The variation in innovation associated with form of government has been an important topic in the United States, with its two major formal structures that local governments use. The record of elected executives in mayor-council cities as change agents after election to office is noteworthy (Wolman, Strate and Melchior 1996). They can be innovators who generate popular support and leverage limited political and governmental resources to carry out an agenda of change (see summary in Svara 1990, ch. 3). Despite this reputation, however, council-manager cities have appointed executives who are extensively involved in policy leadership (Mouritzen and Svara 2002) and a stronger record of innovation in the studies reported in Table 13.1. With a council that sets policy and oversees administrative performance and a city manager who advises the council and directs the administrative organization, it is more likely that the city government will set clear goals and develop long-term strategies to meet them. These cities are also more receptive to change in administrative and management practices. Council-manager cities are more active adopters of management change, new technology, economic development strategies, citizen participation and sustainability practices. Kwon, Berry and Feiock (2009), who compared adoption rates of economic development strategic planning tools based on surveys in 1999 and 2004, found that council-manager cities were more likely to be early adopters, overall adopters and abandoners who dropped the tools over the five year period – perhaps for new tools not covered by the survey – whereas mayor-council cities had a higher proportion of non-adopters and late adopters.

The research findings of Nelson and Svara (2012) add insights to the current debate over what is happening with forms of government in American cities. There is a widespread impression that form of government is less important than certain specific structural features. In this line of argument, all cities with chief administrative officers (CAOs) or elected mayors are more like each other than they are other cities with the same form that lack the specific feature (Frederickson, Johnson and Wood 2004, pp. 100–101). This analysis shows, however, that there are clear distinctions related to form but not necessarily distinctions related to variations within each form of government. The presence of an elected mayor in council-manager cities does not produce the same lower level of adoption found in mayor-council cities with a CAO. In fact, council-manager cities with and without a directly elected mayor have nearly the same rate of innovation, contrary to the adapted cities expectation. Council-manager cities generally perform better than mayor-council cities with regard to adopting innovations. The variations in the council-manager cities make little difference in adoption rate. The presence of a CAO in mayor-council cities, on the other hand, is linked to greater adoptions and this effect is enhanced when the mayor and council are both involved in the selection of the CAO. The evidence does not support the argument that the stronger the mayor, the higher is the level of innovation (Krebs and Pelissero 2009).

Variations by Type of Innovation

Two studies examine how determinants vary with different types of innovations. Walker (2006, p. 334) used 22 survey items to measure innovations in local government in England. Rather than referring to specific practices, survey respondents were asked to indicate the extent to which they agreed that the following characteristics were a 'major part of our approach' to innovation in the city government.

- Centralization (e.g. organizing services at our head office).
- Contracting out/outsourcing (e.g. the same/similar service delivered by another agency under contract).
- Working more closely with our users.
- Decentralization (e.g. organizing services on a neighborhood basis).
- Delayering.
- Developing local strategic partnerships (e.g. voluntary partnerships to coordinate funding, policy, implementation, etc).
- Developing statutory partnerships (e.g. crime and disorder partnerships).
- Developing new methods of raising income (e.g. charging for services).

- Providing existing services to new users.
- Significant changes in external communications (e.g. regular newsletters, citizens' forums).
- Externalization (e.g. passing/selling a service to another agency; e.g. disposal of residential homes for the elderly to another agency, council housing stock transfer).
- Enhancing coordination and joint working with other departments (integration).
- Significant changes in internal communications (e.g. intranets, roadshows).
- New approaches to improvement (e.g. EFQM (European Foundation for Quality Management), re-engineering, charter marks).
- New approaches to service planning/budgeting (e.g. redirecting resources to priority areas).
- The introduction of new information technology systems (e.g. computer hardware).
- The introduction of new management information systems (e.g. performance management systems).
- New management processes (e.g. new job descriptions, establishing new teams of staff).
- Providing new services to existing users.
- Providing new services to new users.
- Relayering.
- Restructuring the organization (e.g. creating new departments, moving services between departments).

Several of these elements could have been combined in a single innovation.

Major innovation types were identified from this list by factor analysis, and validity and reliability of the types were assessed with scale analysis. Five groups were identified. First, governments innovated by developing new products. Secondly, they innovated in three areas of process: new information and communication technology; market orientation such as service delivery through externalization and contracting and generating new ways of raising income; and changes in organizational structure and management practices. Finally, governments expanded boundary-spanning partnerships. These innovations included both internal changes such as integration of departments and also new external ties by the organization with outside groups.

Walker measured the drivers of innovation by examining three categories of variables. First, the external environment of local authorities was measured by data on need, diversity and political disposition, along with changes as perceived by the respondent in the social, political and economic context. Secondly, organizational determinants included perceptions of the importance of political leadership, managerial leadership and changes in management from the outside.[5] Thirdly, so-called 'diffusion determinants' included perceptions of the importance of public pressure from external sources, other external pressures such as the media, pressure from users and citizens, learning about good practices from professional associations/networks, competition with local authorities, competition from other service providers, pressure from central government policies, and reports from central government auditors and inspectors.

Walker found that the adoption of different types of innovation was influenced by different factors. 'In short,' he concludes, 'the pattern of innovation adoption and diffusion in English local government is contingent and complex' (2006, p. 325). New product innovations that entail providing a new kind of program, product or service to residents were not explained by environmental variables in this analysis but were associated with diffusion factors such as demands from users and citizens and organizational characteristics including political leadership. Coercion from auditors and organizational size were negatively correlated to new products; that is, external reviewers acted as a constraint on local officials and smaller organizations developed new products.[6]

In contrast, innovations in information and communications technology (ICT) were associated with organizational characteristics – size, change in management from outside, perhaps because new staff members were recruited to bring new technological expertise and experience – along with public pressure in the form of user and citizen demands and competition among service providers. Market orientation innovations are associated with changes in the environment along with competition from other service providers. These results suggest that authorities who focused on contracting and externalization-type actions were likely to be extremely aware of the external environment and the actors within it. Organizational innovations were influenced by changes in the social, political and economic context and political leadership. Finally, the expansion of partnerships was related to increasing diversity in the population and a higher proportion of the electorate voting Labour. Two other related factors were competition among service providers and user and citizen demands.

A number of variables stand out for their failure to affect innovation diffusion as predicted. These include the level of service need (measured with objective data) and the perceived importance of managerial leadership, pressure from the media, sharing of information through professional associations and networks, and central government policies despite the centralized nature of local government in England. The absence of significant relationships suggests that these factors that have commonly been thought to affect the likelihood of adoption of new approaches should be examined further in future research.

Variations have also been found in the U.S. in the factors related to innovations in the three surveys mentioned earlier that were conducted by ICMA between 2003 and 2006. Form of government is related to adoption of reinventing government practices, e-government technology, and strategic planning and citizen participation practices, but population is related to only the latter two. Adoption of e-government technology is related to education level of the population. Reinventing government is related to population, location in or closer to the center of metropolitan areas, and being in the sunbelt region (the southern and western states); but adoption of strategic practices varies only with population.

The varied practices themselves may be adopted at differing levels. There was only a weak correlation between reinventing government and e-government reforms, although there was more co-variation between reinventing government and strategic and participation practices and even stronger links between new technology and practices to plan and involve citizens.[7] The cities responding to all three surveys can be grouped into five clusters reflecting differing levels and combinations of adoptions. Five groups of cities of similar size are presented in Table 13.2. Almost one in five cities is generally reluctant to adopt new approaches of any kind, on the one hand, or is willing to accept most of the new approaches working their way through the local government system, on the other.

Table 13.2   Clusters based on average ratings on three indices

	Clusters				
	Adoption resisters	Reinventers	Strategists	Reinventing strategists	Adoption leaders
Reinventing government index	3.09	6.14	4.08	7.57	7.70
E-government index	2.28	2.82	4.94	2.31	5.68
Strategic practices	3.96	2.52	6.58	5.84	7.24
Number (490)	19.8% (97)	18.0% (88)	24.1% (118)	21.8% (107)	16.3% (80)

In between are groups of more specialized adopters that select relatively heavily from one or two kinds of innovation. The uses of new information technology were expanding but governments were generally slower in keeping up with this developing area than they were in adopting the other better known and more stable practices.

Thus, innovating governments vary in the extent to which they specialize in distinct areas of change or combine adoptions from more than one area. The adoption resisters uniformly reject change, whereas the adoption leaders are broadly receptive to new approaches. It is likely that acceptance of change in any particular area builds on changes that have already been adopted. The leaders may be transforming governments that are continuously remaking themselves.[8] In general, adoption of new practices in distinct areas does not occur at the same pace and may be driven by differing combinations of factors inside and outside government except those governments that have a broad commitment to innovation.

LEADERSHIP AND ORGANIZATIONAL FACTORS: INTENTIONS AND CAPACITY

The factors identified in the previous section provide some explanation for the differing patterns of diffusion and suggest the need for identifying additional factors. In addition to these characteristics, a variety of organizational factors affect organizational capacity (Lundquist 1987) to recognize new external information, assimilate it and apply it effectively to accomplish organizational ends (Cohen and Levinthal 1990, p. 128), including the capacity to absorb change. Organizations need to develop the behavioral and cultural capacity for innovation (Ahmed and Prajogo 2006). Organizations with leaders who have the characteristics of early adopters – that is, younger, more educated, better networked, less rigid and more innovation minded in general (Rogers 2003) – are more likely to be innovative. Leadership is important to initiating adoption (Moynihan and Ingraham 2004; Kim, Lee and Kim 2007) and successfully implementing it (Damanpour 1991; Fernandez and Rainey 2006; Hansen and Svara 2007). Research on business organizations indicates that key leadership styles required for high level, sustained innovation are the ability to resolve gaps between strategy and performance and to develop strategies and values that transform the organization, but these 'action logics' are found in only one in six private sector leaders (Rooke and Torbert 2005). The innovative organization does not rely entirely, however, on the leader to direct the innovation effort (Light 1998; Martin 2011). The literature on learning organizations strongly suggests that organizational structures and performance feedback routines can stimulate innovation (Greve 2003; Moynihan 2008; Berry, Jang and de Lancer Jules 2009).

Another kind of innovation is the invention of an approach that is both new to the organization that creates it and unique across organizations (Kimberly 1986). In the private sector, innovation-generating organizations develop new approaches to enter markets whereas adopting organizations are innovative in the assimilation of new approaches (Damanpour and Wischnevsky 2006). The factors that support innovation in organizations that are mainly 'adopters' may be different from those that are primarily innovation 'generators' (Damanpour and Schneider 2006, p. 231).

In addition to the factors already discussed with regard to adoption, studies of cities that invent new approaches have identified other characteristics that may also be related to high and especially early adoption. They may have specialized knowledge and an organizational culture that supports creativity and risk taking. Innovative organizations emphasize empowerment and participation of staff, push authority downward, encourage collaboration and communication across boundaries, and support staff when they fail (Light 1998; Denhardt and Denhardt 2001). Many award-winning ideas come from the mayor or other politicians (36 percent) or top administrators (36 percent) (Borins 2000, p. 500.) Still, it is beneficial for top administrators to encourage subordinates to take on new responsibilities and develop new approaches because Borins shows that many inventions come from middle-level (45 percent) and front-line (29 percent) staff. Organizations that more fully utilize the capabilities and skills of staff are more likely to be innovative (Al-Yahya and Vengroff 2004). The larger one's 'tool box' of knowledge and experience, the greater is one's capacity to create new combinations and to innovate (Arthur 2007).

External forces are as important to invention, as they are to adoption. Crisis was a factor in over one quarter of award-winning innovations, especially those initiated by politicians, whereas professional administrators were more likely to pursue new opportunities or proactively address problems before they became crises (Borins 2000, p. 503). The limited research on cutback management and budgetary retrenchment has demonstrated a distinction between organizations that creatively adapt and innovate, on the one hand, and those that respond reactively in ways that evade problems and ignore new conditions, on the other (Levine 1979; Miller and Svara 2009). Most governments take the latter approach. In the past, only a minority of governments used cutback conditions as the occasion for eliminating low priority programs and positions and looked for ways to improve processes or reorganize activities in ways that strengthened their performance when conditions improved (Kelman 2008). The proportion of local governments using proactive and strategic approaches to making cuts appears to be higher in the current fiscal crisis in the United States than in previous cutback periods (Miller 2010; Svara 2010), but the introduction of innovations as a long-term approach to enhancing performance at lower cost is still limited (Thoreson and Svara 2011).

The difference between innovative and non-innovative organizations is little studied but is recognized as an important issue. In their examination of Korean central government agencies and municipal organizations, Kim, Lee and Kim (2007) report that almost half the organizations reported no innovations during the year studied and a few organizations accounted for most of the adoptions. Walker, Avellaneda and Berry (2007), who divide cities into above and below average groups, find that higher innovation cities learn from professional associations and networks and take advantage of vertical influence from central government, whereas lower innovation cities are more likely to innovate in reaction to external pressure (similar to differences observed by Senge et al. 1994). Organizations with high and low innovation are likely to have leaders that follow different 'action logics' (Rooke and Torbert 2005).

In addition to identifying instances of initiating innovation, it is important to examine the process of incorporating innovations into organizational practice and the impact of innovation (Zaltman, Duncan and Holbek 1973; Klein and Sorra 1996). As noted in the survey of Danish municipal officials, there was relative uniformity in the adoption of NPM techniques. There was substantial variation, however, in the impact of implementing the new techniques on how the organization functions (Hansen and Svara 2007). Effective leadership and management are more strongly associated with the extent of implementation than adoption. While adoption can be a relatively superficial activity and can reflect simple conformity to prevailing management norms, extensive implementation tends to require a more dedicated and committed managerial effort and stronger political support (Damanpour 1991; Kim, Lee and Kim 2007).

There are obvious leadership qualities and organizational characteristics that can deter staff members from proposing changes (Kanter 1985), and organizational climate and 'innovation management capacity' affect the number of innovations in a city (Gabris et al. 2008). Networking and other 'discovery skills' are practiced by entrepreneurial leaders in business (Dyer, Gregersen and Christensen 2009). There is evidence to suggest that innovation leaders, whether individuals (Joy 2004) or organizations, seek to be different and advance a 'broader ideal' to which the organization is committed (De Miranda et al. 2009, p. 530). For example, the early leaders in adopting and developing sustainability practices in U.S. local governments have a strong commitment to addressing the issue of climate change and getting a communitywide commitment to action (Svara 2011). It is important to better understand the drivers in organizations that are 'out front' and cannot simply follow widely held values or accept practices with verified efficacy.

It seems likely that leaders will differ in their intentions regarding how innovative their organization should be. The bell-shaped curve identified in adopting practices from a number of related innovations is presumably influenced by a similar distribution of resources among local governments. It may to some extent also match variation in the attitudes of leaders about how they want the organization to approach innovation. Reflecting the stages in the process of diffusion, there are presumably corresponding levels of commitment or organization intention:

- Encouraging inventions and being the first to adopt new approaches (innovators).
- Supporting inventions and actively seeking out newly emerging ideas in other places that can be considered for adoption (early adopters).
- Monitoring new approaches developed in other local governments and adopting them when other local governments have tested them (early majority).
- Following other governments in adopting approaches that are proven to be worthwhile or effective (late majority).

- Maintaining current practices and considering change if the organization is clearly out of touch with prevailing practices or if local circumstances require a new approach (late and limited adopters).
- Preserving the status quo (laggards).

An indicator of intentions may be joining a network of governments committed to innovation. For example, based on my own research, among local governments that are members of the Alliance for Innovation in the United States, 84 percent had above average levels of adoption in the composite adoption index displayed in Figure 13.1, compared to 46 percent of non-members; three quarters were above average in adopting sustainability practices displayed in Figure 13.3, compared with one third of other governments. Presumably most of the governments that choose to join the network have intentions corresponding to the first three levels.

There may of course be discrepancies between more active intentions and actual capacity to identify and successfully incorporate new approaches, but private sector research indicates that leaders that do not stress change (Lohr 2010) and support it (Martin 2011) and are not willing to experiment with new approaches (Dyer, Gregersen and Christensen 2009) are unlikely to head innovative organizations regardless of advantageous internal and external factors. More research is needed to determine to what extent effective leaders can overcome obstacles and successfully innovate despite unfavorable circumstances.

CONCLUSION

Local governments need to innovate but they vary in their capacity to do so and they differ in the rate and scope of change that they accept. As is true in other areas of innovation, most local governments eventually incorporate many of the major new approaches that are introduced into the local government sector. It is possible, however, that the pace of change and effectiveness of implementation may not be sufficient to keep pace with new challenges. It is not enough, therefore, to expect that most will eventually catch up. More attention needs to be given to the leaders who develop new approaches or are willing to try out new ideas when they are still relatively unknown and untested. Isomorphism depends on pathbreakers and pace setters to identify options that other governments that are more cautious, less connected or lacking resources can consider. In addition, professional associations and organizations that specialize in public sector innovation need to continue to expand their capacity to disseminate information about good ideas and accelerate the diffusion process.

NOTES

1. An example in the United States is the Alliance for Innovation.
2. The cumulative number that adopts the innovation over time approximates an S-shaped curve.
3. Although response bias would seem to be a potential problem among these select high-response cities, the average index scores for all the cities that responded to each survey and the select cities are very similar. The average index scores for all cities and for the select respondents who returned all three surveys are as

follows: Reinventing Government: 5.6 / 5.6; E-Government: 3.4 / 3.6; Strategic practices: 5.0 / 5.3. The indicators used in each index are presented in Nelson and Svara (2011).

4. The sources included SustainLane (sustainlane.com/us-city-rankings/); Visible Strategies: Framework Adapted from U.S. Mayors (usmayors.visiblestrategies.com/); Portney (2003), p. 65; Go Green Virginia Green Community Challenge (gogreenva.org/?/challenge/participate/id/1); and an unpublished questionnaire provided by the ICMA Center for Performance Measurement.

5. Walker did not determine directly whether there was a new manager, but whether a new manager was important in driving improvement in the government's service.

6. Walker (2006, p. 326) speculates that this finding may reflect 'the recent reorganization of English local government, with the creation of around 40 unitary authorities, which are typically much smaller than the older county councils'.

7. The correlation between reinventing government and e-government was 0.05 (not significant) and with strategic and participation practices was 0.16 (significant at 0.000 level). The correlation between e-government and strategic and participation practices was 0.35 (significant at 0.000 level).

8. Among Alliance for Innovation members, only 1 percent had focused only on adopting reinventing government practices; 37 percent were adoption leaders compared with 13 percent among governments that were not members. On the other hand, 9 percent were resisters for whom membership in an innovation network appears to be more symbolic than real.

REFERENCES

Abrahamson, E. (1991). Managerial fads and fashions: the diffusion and rejections of innovations. *Academy of Management Review*, 16(3), 586–612.

Ahmed, P.K. and Prajogo, D.I. (2006). Relationships between innovation stimulus, innovation capacity, and innovation performance. *R&D Management*, 36(5), 499–515.

Al-Yahya, K. and Vengroff, R. (2004). Human capital utilization, empowerment, and organizational effectiveness: a comparative perspective. *Journal of Global Development Studies*, 3(3–4), 251–295.

Arthur, W.B. (2007). The structure of invention. *Research Policy*, 36, 274–287.

Berry, Frances Stokes and Berry, William D. (2007). Innovation and diffusion models in policy research. In Paul Sabatier (ed.), *Theories of the Policy Process*, 2nd edn. Boulder, CO: Westview.

Berry, F.S., Jang, H. and de Lancer Jules, P. (2009). *Assessing the Antecedents of Organizational Learning in American State, County and City Governments*. Paper prepared for the Public Management Research Association Conference, Columbus, Ohio, 1–3 October.

Borins, Sandford (2000). Loose cannons and rule breakers, or enterprising leaders? Some evidence about innovative public managers. *Public Administration Review*, 60, 498–507.

Cohen, Wesley M. and Levinthal, Daniel A. (1990). Absorptive capacity: a new perspective on learning and innovation. *Administrative Science Quarterly*, 15, 128–152.

Cyert, Richard M. and March, James G. (1963). *A Behavioral Theory of the Firm*. Englewood Cliffs, NJ: Prentice-Hall.

Damanpour, Fariborz (1991). Organizational innovation: a meta-analysis of effects of determinants and moderators. *Academy of Management Journal*, 34(3), 555–590.

Damanpour, F. and Evans, W.M. (1984). Organizational innovation and performance: the problem of 'organizational lag'. *Administrative Science Quarterly*, 29, 392–409.

Damanpour, Fariborz and Schneider, Marguerite (2006). Phases of the adoption of innovation in organizations: effects of environment, organization and top managers. *British Journal of Management*, 17, 215–236.

Damanpour, Fariborz and Wischnevsky, J. Daniel (2006). Research on innovation in organizations: distinguishing innovation-generating from innovation-adopting organizations. *Journal of Engineering and Technology Management*, 23(4), 269–291.

De Miranda, Paulo C., Aranha, José Alberto S. and Zardo, Julia (2009). Creativity: people, environment and culture, the key elements in its understanding and interpretation. *Science and Public Policy*, 36, 523–535.

Denhardt, Janet V. and Denhardt, Robert B. (2001). *Creating a Culture of Innovation: 10 Lessons from America's Best Run City*. Washington, DC: IBM Center for the Business of Government.

DiMaggio, Paul J. and Powell, Walter W. (1983). The iron cage revisited: institutional isomorphism and collective rationality. *American Sociological Review*, 48, 147–160.

Dyer, Jeffrey H., Gregersen, Hal B. and Christensen, Clayton M. (2009). The innovator's DNA. *Harvard Business Review*, (December), 61–67.

Fernandez, S. and Rainey, H.G. (2006). Managing successful organizational change in the public sector. *Public Administration Review*, 66, 168–176.

Frederickson, H.G., Johnson, G.A. and Wood, C.H. (2004). *The Adapted City: Institutional Dynamics and Structural Change*. Armonk, NY: M.E. Sharpe.

Gabris, Gerald, Koenig, Heidi, Nelson, Kimberly and Wood, Curtis (2008). *Exploring Innovation Management in Local Government: An Empirical Analysis of Northern Illinois Municipalities*. Paper presented at the 2008 Annual Conference of the American Society for Public Administration, Dallas, Texas, 7–11 March.

Greve, Henrich (2003). *Organizational Learning from Performance Feedback*. Cambridge: Cambridge University Press.

Hansen, Morten Balle and Svara, James H. (2007). *The Diffusion of Administrative Innovations*. Discussion Paper.

Joy, Stephen (2004). Innovation motivation: the need to be different. *Creativity Research Journal*, 16, 313–330.

Jun, Kyu-Nahm Jun and Weare, Christopher (2011). Institutional motivations in the adoption of innovations: the case of e-government. *Journal of Public Administration Research & Theory*, 21(3), 495–519.

Kanter, Rosabeth Moss (1985). *Change Masters*. New York: Free Press.

Kearney, Richard C. (2005). Reinventing government and battling budget crisis: manager and municipal government actions in 2003. *Municipal Yearbook 2005*. Washington, DC: International City/County Management Association, pp. 27–32.

Kearney, Richard C., Feldman, Barry M. and Scavo, Carmine, P.F. (2000). Reinventing government: city manager attitudes and actions. *Public Administration Review*, 60, 535–548.

Kelman, Steven (2008). The 'Kennedy School' of research on innovation in government. In Sandford Borins (ed.), *Innovations in Government: Research, Recognition, and Replication*. Washington, DC: Brookings, chapter 3.

Kim, Seok Eun, Lee, Jung Wook and Kim, Byong Seob (2007). *The Quality of Management and Government Innovation: An Empirical Study*. Paper delivered to the 7th Public Management Research Association Conference, University of Arizona, Tucson, 25–27 October.

Kimberly, J.R. (1986). The organization context of technological innovation. In D.D. Davis (ed.), *Managing Technological Innovation*. San Francisco, CA: Jossey-Bass, pp. 23–43.

Klein, K.J. and Sorra, J.S. (1996). The challenge of innovation implementation. *Academy of Management Review*, 21, 1055–1080.

Krebs, T.B. and Pelissero, J.P. (2010). Urban managers and public policy: do institutional arrangements influence decisions to initiate policy? *Urban Affairs Review*, 45(3), 393–411.

Kwon, M., Berry, F.S. and Feiock, R.C. (2009). Understanding the adoption and timing of economic development strategies in U.S. cities using innovation and institutional analysis. *Journal of Public Administration Research and Theory*, 19, 967–988.

Levine, Charles H. (1979). More on cut-back management: hard questions for hard times. *Public Administration Review*, 39, 179–183.

Light, Paul C. (1998). *Sustaining Innovation: Creating Nonprofit and Government Organizations that Innovate Naturally*. San Francisco, CA: Jossey-Bass Publishers.

Lohr, Steve (2010). Steve Jobs and the economics of elitism. *New York Times*, 30 January. Available at: http://www.nytimes.com/2010/01/31/weekinreview/31lohr.html (accessed 28 November 2011).

Lundquist, Lennart (1987). *Implementation Steering: An Actor-Structure Approach*. Lund: Studentlitteratur.

Martin, Roger L. (2011). The innovation catalysts. *Harvard Business Review*, 89 (June), 82–87.

Meier, K.J. and O'Toole, L.J. (2001). Managerial strategies and behavior in networks: a model with evidence from U.S. public education. *Journal of Public Administration, Research, and Theory*, 11(3), 271–294.

Miller, Gerald (2010). Weathering the local government fiscal crisis: short-term measures or permanent change? *The Municipal Year Book 2010*. Washington, DC: International City/County Management Association, pp. 33–36.

Miller, G.A. and Svara, J.H. (2009). *Navigating the Fiscal Crisis*. Washington, DC: ICMA/Alliance for Innovation.

Moon, M. Jae and deLeon, Peter (2001). Municipal reinvention: managerial values and diffusion among municipalities. *Journal of Public Administration Research and Theory*, 11, 327–351.

Mouritzen, Poul Erik and Svara, James H. (2002). *Leadership at the Apex: Politicians and Administrators in Western Local Governments*. Pittsburgh, PA: University of Pittsburgh Press.

Moynihan, Donald P. (2008). Learning under uncertainty: networks in crisis management. *Public Administration Review*, 68(2), 350–361.

Moynihan, Donald P. and Ingraham, Patricia W. (2004). Integrative leadership in the public sector: a model of performance-information use. *Administration and Society*, 36(4), 427–453.

Nelson, Kimberly and Svara, James H. (2012). Form of government still matters: fostering innovation in U.S. municipal governments. *American Review of Public Administration*, 42(May), 257–281.

Osborne, David and Gaebler, Ted (1992). *Reinventing Government: How the Entrepreneurial Spirit is Transforming the Public Sector*. Reading, MA: Addison-Wesley.

Portney, Kent E. (2003). *Taking Sustainable Cities Seriously*. Cambridge, MA: MIT Press.

Rogers, Everett M. (2003). *Diffusion of Innovations*, 5th edn. New York: The Free Press.

Rooke, David and Torbert, William R. (2005). Seven transformations of leadership. *Harvard Business Review*, 83(April), 67–76.

Senge, P.M., Kleiner, A., Roberts, C., Ross, R. and Smith, B. (1994). *The Fifth Discipline Fieldbook: Strategies and Tools for Building a Learning Organization*. New York: Crown Business.

Strang, David and Soule, Sarah A. (1998). Diffusion in organizations and social movements; from hybrid corn to poison pills. *Annual Review of Sociology*, 24, 265–290.

Svara, James H. (1990). *Official Leadership in the City: Patterns of Conflict and Cooperation*. New York: Oxford University Press.

Svara, James H. (2010). Local government leadership in the fiscal crisis in the United States of America. *International Journal of Policy Studies*, 1(1), 5–24.

Svara, James H. (2011). The early stage of local government action to promote sustainability. *The Municipal Year Book 2011*. Washington, DC: International City Management Association, pp. 43–60.

Thoreson, Karen and Svara, James (2011). How local governments are navigating the fiscal crisis: taking stock and looking forward. *The Municipal Year Book 2011*. Washington, DC: International City Management Association, pp. 37–42.

Walker, Richard M. (2006). Innovation type and diffusion: an empirical analysis of local government. *Public Administration*, 84, 311–335.

Walker, Richard M., Avellaneda, Claudia and Berry, Frances Stokes (2007). *Explaining the Diffusion of Innovation Types Amongst High and Low Innovative Localities: A Test of the Berry And Berry Model*. Paper delivered to the 7th Public Management Research Association Conference, University of Arizona, Tucson, 25–27 October.

Wolman, H., Strate, J. and Melchior, A. (1996). Does changing mayors matter? *Journal of Politics*, 58, 201–223.

Zaltman, G., Duncan, R. and Holbek, J. (1973). *Innovations and Organizations*. New York: Wiley.

14. Strategic management and change in the public services
Paul Joyce

INTRODUCTION

Change and innovation in the public services are often poorly managed. A survey of senior civil servants in the UK found that only a third of them judged their departments to be good at managing change (Capability Reviews Team 2007, p. 31). In this chapter we look at the case for using strategic management as a tool for change and innovation. Can strategic management produce successful change and innovation, and how does it do this?

Strategic management is often seen as having developed from strategic planning. Berry (2007, p. 332) has stated: 'Strategic Management involves taking the strategic planning process and extending it into an ongoing management paradigm of anticipating and managing organizational change and environmental uncertainty.' For practitioners strategic management is also linked to change and innovation in the public services. Box 14.1 shows some of the outcomes in the minds of senior civil servants and public services leaders when trying to develop and deliver strategic plans in government. In general these outcomes imply change and innovation.

It might seem self-evident that strategic management is a useful tool to manage change. Using strategic management, public services leaders articulate rationales for change and even strategic visions of the future that are potentially inspiring targets for change efforts. They use its analytical techniques to understand, among other things, situations and the needs and wishes of service users and other stakeholders. Strategic management underlines the need for rigorous attention to planning and managing the execution of strategic changes. In recent years, strategic management's emphasis on implementation and execution of change has been seen as requiring performance measurement and budgetary decisions to be integrated into the strategic decision-making process (Berry 2007). All of these points support the idea that strategic management offers advantages as an approach for managing change and innovation.

But formal strategic planning has long had critics who considered it an ill-advised approach to managing change and innovation. (It should be noted that we are referring here to strategic planning and not strategic management, and that critics tended to characterise strategic planning as top down decision making, concerned with planning prior to action, and little concerned with implementation and learning.) The doubts about formal strategic planning were raised first in respect of private sector businesses. It was labelled bureaucratic and criticised by some as dominated by headquarters staff and as failing to adequately recognise the virtues of informality, experimentation, strategic learning and emergent decision making (Peters and Waterman 1982; Mintzberg 1994).

Despite the attention that was paid to these types of criticisms in business schools,

BOX 14.1   DESIRED OUTCOMES FROM STRATEGIC
MANAGEMENT IN GOVERNMENT

(a) Government Performance

- To develop a culture of continuous improvement
- To transform government in terms of its performance and degree of client satisfaction
- To improve efficiency and effectiveness
- To improve accountability of government to the public
- To improve transparency
- To improve trust in government as an organisation

(b) Sound Decisions

- To improve the task of assessing strengths and weaknesses
- To convert weaknesses into strengths
- To eliminate threats
- To take account of risk in strategic planning and manage that risk

(c) Systems

- To improve long-term policy-making capacity
- To improve linkages between policy making, budgeting and strategic planning
- To improve accountability of managers to elected politicians

strategic planning and mission and vision statements flourished in the private sector during the 1990s and during the first few years of the 21st century (Rigby and Bilodeau 2010). Moreover, studies of managers in public services found that they evaluated their experiences of strategic planning as beneficial (Berry and Wechsler 1995; Flynn and Talbot 1996). For example, Flynn and Talbot (1996) presented survey evidence from UK local government managers suggesting that formal strategic planning was widespread and managers thought it helped them to achieve goals and objectives, define milestones for achievement and make better use of resources. A survey by Berry and Wechsler (1995) of state agencies in the United States indicated that setting programme and policy direction was the most important objective of the strategic planning process. It was reported that goal setting was widely used in strategic planning, and that setting management direction and clarifying agency priorities were the most important outcomes for many respondents.

In the current climate it seems likely that politicians and policy makers will assume that strategic management should be used to manage change and innovation. It is often assumed that public services reforms and modernisation should be realised through strategic planning and management (OECD 2000). Then, in addition, there are signs that the idea of the strategic state seems to be catching on (Prime Minister's Strategy Unit (PMSU) 2006; Parker et al. 2010). This new concept proposes that the government centre will set out strategic priorities and encourage innovation in government services that are run in a more decentralised way than in the past. There has certainly been the emergence of the idea that civil servants need to be strategic and to have skills in strategic thinking and strategic management (Boyle 1995a).

This whole topic has another layer of complexity as a result of the fact that the practice of strategic management may be differentiated into different types, and they appear to require different explanations of how they work (different 'mechanisms'). In the next section we will consider four different types of strategic management: formal strategic planning, strategic transformation, strategic issue management and a public value-based strategic management.

TYPES OF STRATEGIC MANAGEMENT

Change is often seen as something forced on the public services organisation by the external world. Nutt (2004), in fact, outlined a model which contained the proposition that a public organisation's internal capacity determines if it can respond to pressures for change. This same coupling of pressures for change and capacity was to be found in a model of public services reform in the UK offered by the Prime Minister's Strategy Unit (PMSU 2006).

There may be arguments about points of detail in how external pressure and internal capacity are conceptualised and how they are seen as interrelated in the management of change and innovation, but together they offer a perspective for thinking about strategic approaches to change and innovation in the public services. For example, strategic leadership may be defined as responsible for leveraging resources as adroitly as possible in response to external pressures; and strategic plans may be defined as important in developing and adjusting capacity to ensure successful results in terms of public value (Heymann 1987; Moore 1995).

Turning to the first type of strategic management, formal strategic planning, there is not one single meaning of this in practice. What is called 'strategic planning' varies in its components and even, in a sense, in its completeness from one organisation to another. Strategic planning is defined as a process used for whole organisations or major parts of organisations. It may produce a plan that is written down and therefore contains explicit strategic thinking. The plan provides statements about the 'targets' of actions and these are expressed in terms of the future of the organisation; this statement might include ideas and proposals about mission, strategic vision, and goals and objectives. Strategic planning involves some degree of environmental screening and assessment so that targeting and action planning can be considered in terms of suitability and feasibility. Strategic planning should involve planning of implementation and should identify and determine budgetary decisions and allocations necessary to implement actions. Delivery of the strategic planning should be monitored and reported using performance indicators and targets. Finally, we can note that strategic planning may be carried out on the basis of a single organisation, but may also be multi-organisational or community based (Joyce 1998; Berry 2007).

In practice, there are examples of public services strategic plans where there are missions and goals and even planned actions, but little or no attention has been given to an assessment of the environment. Then again, some strategic plans may be poor on planning for implementation and monitoring. They may have very weak linkages to budgetary decisions, and processes of performance measurement and reporting for purposes of monitoring implementation may be non-existent (Poister and Streib 2005). So, we could say that strategic planning is often poor in respect of its concern for implementation; indeed, from a contemporary point of view we might say that this is an incomplete type of strategic planning. Where it is complete, it is possible that strategic leaders may give the impression that change is 'programmable' through a strategic planning process. By this is meant, that change is planned with confidence that there is no need for learning and that change will be largely acceptable to various stakeholders.

A second type of strategic management is the strategic transformation approach. This label is intended to suggest its affinity to the thinking and writing done on transformational leadership (as distinct from transactional leadership). One of the interesting propositions in the leadership literature is the idea that leaders are important because they get others to think in new ways and to question the 'givens' of the situation. In one well-known theorisation of transformational leadership, it is suggested that leaders get the people who follow them to put aside their self-interest and to think up new solutions to problems (Bass and Avolio 1994). The role of leadership is, therefore, to bring about not just change, but change that transforms organisations and industries in which this type of leadership is exercised.

But how does a leader persuade followers to put aside their self-interest and challenge the givens of a public service system? The answer given is that it is by strategic communications from the leaders to the followers. In consequence, language is important and the abilities of leaders to present their ideas – orally and in writing – are critical.

Many familiar elements of strategic planning and management can be used to carry through this strategic transformation approach to change. The leader can carry out strategic analysis, including assessing the external environment and internal capabilities and resources, prior to developing a statement of strategic vision. Strategic choices can be made, leading to new services and programmes. The strategic actions chosen can be implemented through training and development programmes and through joint developments with other public services organisations. But the key point is that it is the strategic communications of the skilful transformational leader that open the organisation up to new possibilities and radical change, and inspire not only new thinking but also the willingness of people to abandon their sectional interests. This can sound naïve and over optimistic.

The third type of strategic management is known as 'strategic issue management'. The tendency in the 1980s was to describe a strategic issue management approach in the public services as requiring a creative approach to designing change (Eadie 1983). Whereas the strategic planning described above is target oriented, strategic issue management is focused on strategic issues, which can be defined as constraints on, or opportunities for, the realisation of strategic goals. The constraints could have their origins, for example, in the dependence of strategic leaders on support and co-operation by people and organisations in the external environment. Environmental assessment (internal as well as external environments) is an important part of the strategic thinking process in the case of strategic issue management. This can be a way of flushing out strategic issues, but might also be seen as an input into creative thinking to address the issues (Nutt and Backoff 1992). Because of this emphasis on creativity, it was also possible to link this type of strategic approach with change which represented an innovation. The strategic issue management approach tended to emphasise the use of strategic planning techniques that enabled creativity, such as the nominal group technique.

At least one variant of strategic issue management acknowledged the significance of conflicting interests in strategic management (Nutt and Backoff 1992). Change is then the result of the struggle between a coalition of interests that want to maintain the status quo and a coalition that favours change. Consequently, the need for creativity is only one reason for the difficulty of addressing strategic issues. Another reason is that conflicting interests can be hard to resolve and strategic leaders have to recognise that resistance will occur in defence of interests. The obvious point that follows is that creativity may be pointing to a change that can be seen by strategic leaders as an innovation, but not all stakeholders will welcome that change even though it is an innovation. Recognition of this point leads to the advocacy within this variant of strategic issue management of stakeholder analysis techniques and actions aimed at stakeholder management (Nutt and Backoff 1992).

Evidently, strategic issue management is not an easy approach to use in order to bring about change: it sets strategic leaders two challenges. These are the challenge of creativity (knowing what to do) and the challenge of controlling the situation (getting enough support and co-operation to make change feasible).

The final type of strategic approach discussed here emerged from studies of experiences in the public services in the US. It is labelled here as the 'public value theory' of strategic management. It has been clearly described by both Heymann (1987) and Moore (1995) and provides a very simple conceptual framework for strategic management in the public sector. Essentially, both Heymann and Moore argued that strategic planning in public services should align three things: desirable goals that meet social needs (strategic vision), organisational capacities and external support (see Figure 14.1). This conceptual framework was used by both to analyse a series of case studies and it worked well in appreciating both major innovations in public services systems and even turnaround situations.

We will briefly examine each of the three strategic factors in turn. First, Heymann had interesting things to say about the desirable goals, but it was Moore that linked this to the concept of public value. (We might note here that Michael Porter had earlier also highlighted the concept of value in his framework for looking at business strategy in the private sector, especially in relation to his idea of analysing and evaluating the 'value chain' to implement strategic choices; see Porter 2004.) Heymann took the view that desirable goals should be aligned to two things: the values of the public services organisation and important social needs (as perceived by politicians and others to whom the organisation was accountable). It is possible to deduce from Heymann's view that desirable goals would be seen as having value to people in the organisation (because the goals were in keeping with the values) and would be of value to politicians and others in an oversight role because they saw the goals linked to important social needs. Moore (1995, p. 71) argued that strategy (which could be defined as the desirable goals plus the planned action) had to be 'substantively valuable', which he defined as the public services organisation delivering 'things of value to overseers, clients and beneficiaries at low cost in

Sources: Heymann 1987; Moore 1995.

Figure 14.1   Strategic triangle

terms of money and authority'. For Moore, value was fundamentally a matter of the citizens' desires and perceptions. We can link this to the idea that goals are also desired goals; hence even the phrase 'desired goals' can be seen as flagging up the idea of public value, since the goals are desired ones and not just goals.

The second factor in this model of strategic management is organisational capacities, which as a first approximation can be linked to the skills and values of the people working for the public services organisation. These two dimensions provoke the thought that capacity is not only a function of what people can do but also a function of what they want to do (or not do) based on their values. (I have often heard managers say about their staff who they think are not doing their job properly: is it because they can't or because they won't?) The inclusion of organisational values as a dimension of capacity means we need to think about the possibility that strategic leaders will face conflicts and resistance to change because some staff may not want to change their values to bring about consistency between desirable goals, organisational capacities and external support. Of course, the inclusion of skills as an aspect of organisational capacities suggests that the Heymann and Moore approach to strategic management has an overlap with the resource-based theories of strategic management which became popular in the 1990s (Hamel and Prahalad 1994).

Both Heymann and Moore saw strategic planning and management in the public sector as different in some respects from that found in the private sector. Indeed, Moore described his account of strategic management as adapted for the public sector. One example of this differentiation from private sector strategic management could be seen in the third factor, external support. Heymann thought that public services strategic leaders had to share power with outsiders much more than did their counterparts in private companies. Heymann saw this fact of sharing power with outsiders as an expression of democracy. Strategic leaders in public services, therefore, need to pay attention to the views of outsiders (including the politicians to whom they are accountable) because they need their support. They need to do this when identifying and clarifying the goals. If these goals are developed and communicated with the outsiders in mind, then the strategic leaders may get the external support they need. This means being aware of, and understanding, the interests of external people and organisations. Heymann took the view that there were limits to how successful a leader could be in gathering external support: not all outside interests would be satisfied.

Heymann and Moore both contributed to a public sector model in which strategic planning identifies the necessary steps to develop organisational capacity and external support in order to meet new strategic goals, which they saw as goals aligned to social needs. When implemented, the strategic plan should, ideally, create public value (i.e. be valuable).

Clearly, changing public attitudes, new social problems, changing political priorities, and political trends and developments are all obvious sources of pressures for change if we adopt the public value theory of strategic management. Because of the environment of the public services organisation, therefore, strategic leaders who can adapt the organisation through strategic planning and management are essential. In Moore's (1995) view it is not enough for the public services organisation to focus on maintaining itself and only concern itself with increasing efficiency in its operations. Strategic leadership is necessary because public services organisations have got to revise their goals and be innovative and experimental.

In summing up this section, we should note that each of the approaches can be linked to different propositions about change. So, a formal strategic planning approach might be seen as likely to lead to an assumption that change is programmable. The strategic transformation approach assumes that change and innovation come about because a strategic leader uses strategic communications and because they have abilities as a communicator to foster the voluntary desire of followers to challenge the givens of the situation and to put aside their self-interest so that the organisation can pursue transformations in the general interest. In the case of strategic issue management the proposition is that strategic approaches encourage creativity and lead to innovations. In at least one variant of strategic issue management it is made evident that issues are difficult to address not only because the best course of strategic action is not always obvious but also because change occurs through the clash of interest groups. The public value theory of strategic management assumes that pressure for change is inevitable and organisations would be mistaken to rely only on actions that serve to maintain the status quo or focus only on efficiency in current operations. It recognises the limitations on the ability of leaders to please all stakeholders in change situations and also draws attention to the issue of organisational values in planning strategic changes.

Before we move on from this review of theory, we should note the fact that there are a range of change situations and this probably deserves more attention from researchers into strategic management in the public services. It is true that Moore (1995) has shown that the public value theory approach can address a range of change situations, from strategic change through to public sector turnarounds. But, still, more attention needs (for all the theories) to be focused on how strategic management works in different change situations. For example, public services reforms are change situations but we should not assume they are essentially the same as, say, a change situation in which a failing organisation is in a crisis and it is decided it needs to be turned around. Nor should we assume that reform situations are all the same. The UK reforms of the 1980s are arguably fundamentally different from the reforms of the early years of the 21st century. Specifically, recent reforms have involved reconstructing the relationship between public services and the public (e.g. patient choice in the public health services), whereas the 1980s reforms were more focused on achieving greater efficiency through provider competition and management changes. The implications of this theoretically are that change situations provide a context in which strategic approaches are applied and may affect the consequences. For example, each type of change situation may have its own specific change issues. Take the case of recent public services reforms:

> many reform programmes in different countries include the goal of putting the customer first. It follows, therefore, that leaders have to change their organizations to better suit the public, and this means disrupting those who work for the organization to put the public first. It is also likely that the public will be relatively silent beneficiaries (silent supporters) of reforms, whereas those who are disrupted or suffer loss will make clear to leaders they are unhappy with the changes. Leaders in such a situation may find that they will have to endure opposition by employees to changes meant to provide a service until the new service becomes established – as happened in the case of Jobcentre Plus in 2002. (Joyce 2012, p. 72)

Jobcentre Plus, a UK government agency, was formed by merging staffs from two separate government departments and was intended to improve the service to unemployed people by bringing together the work of job finding and the work of paying benefits into a single branch network. The new branches were piloted in 2001–02 and resistance to change began almost at once. A national strike by the Public and Commercial Services Union lasting six months was called in protest at the absence of screens to separate staff and clients. It was seen by the union as a safety issue. It was seen by the leadership of the new agency as an issue of customer service. In the event, the new service was established as a largely unscreened environment.

SOME RESEARCH EVIDENCE

The study by Poister and Streib (2005) of cities with strategic planning showed not only the absence of strategic planning in many cases but also what we might describe as the incompleteness of the process even when there was a strategic plan. As shown in Figure 14.2, many of the US municipal governments they surveyed had a strategic plan document but did not use performance measures to track strategic goals and objectives. This is important because there was evidence from this same study that tracking performance over time mattered in relation to the impact of strategic planning, and thus if performance measures are not used to track strategic goals and objectives then planned change (impact) is likely to be less. Likewise, the impact of strategic planning was associated with new money in the budget being used to advance strategic goals and objectives. It is a plausible inference from this that programmed change through strategic planning is more likely where strategic documents are delivered through budgetary decisions and performance management and reporting against strategic goals and objectives. That is to

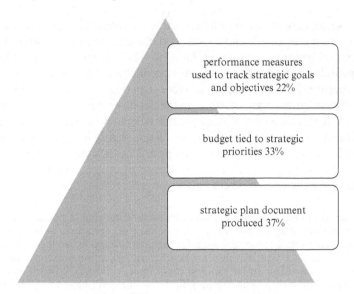

Figure 14.2   Poister and Streib (2005): survey of US municipal governments with populations over 25,000

say, that strategic planning processes should ensure the strategic plan guides the budgetary process and the plan should be monitored through performance measurement and reporting. In this sense, a strategic planning process that does not shape budgetary decisions and does not involve performance monitoring and reporting is incomplete.

There were also important findings about the need to tie in individual managers to the delivery of the strategic planning by setting their objectives on the basis of the strategic plan and using annual reviews to check their contribution to the delivery of the plan. So, again, there is much more to worthwhile strategic planning than the existence of a strategic plan document. The impact of strategic planning depends on securing the commitment of individual managers to its realisation, which it appears can be done through the performance management of the individual manager.

The findings above might be summarised as showing that a systems view of strategic management is justified, by which is meant the view that the strategic goals and strategy of an organisation need to provide the basis for an integration of budgeting, performance management, stakeholder management and management generally (Berry 2007, p. 341).

There is a qualitative study that offers evidence that a strategic transformation approach is relevant to the public services and that transformative change can result from it. The study was by Frost-Kumpf and colleagues (1993), who collected and analysed data on changes at the Ohio Department of Mental Health, a state agency in the United States. This was a transformation which involved fundamental change in the agency's system of public services. The state Department of Mental Health, as a result of the change, transformed its primary focus on a service delivery role into a commissioning role. This involved making use of community-based boards and local agencies. The changes began in 1983 and the researchers claimed that the Department's reputation for the quality of its health care had dramatically improved by 1990.

The researchers concluded that there were three 'streams' of strategic action: the leadership's use of language to set out a new strategic direction, the development of capabilities, and creating co-operative ventures with other government agencies. They also analysed nine patterns of strategic action which may have been linked to the streams identified. These were: taking symbolic actions; developing new programme thrusts; empowering key constituencies; developing alternative revenue sources; responding to opposition; building internal capacity; developing technical expertise; utilising training; and gaining external co-operation. There are some obvious points of similarity with the ideas of Heymann and Moore (e.g. building internal capacity and gaining external co-operation). The distinctive contribution of this research is to highlight the leadership dimension and the role of language and symbolic action.

As might be guessed, the leaders developed a new vision for the future of the Department, articulated the values of the new organisational model, and provided a critique of its failings. More importantly, the researchers report that it was leadership use of language that provided to others the important stimulus to the development of new ideas about this public service. The picture of the process that is conveyed by this is not leaders operating in a command and control manner but leaders who use symbolic action to empower others. Arguably, leaders emerge from this as chiefly stimulating change through providing a new language and new vocabulary. Presumably the leaders' strategic intent was idealistic, reflecting a new set of underlying values, and having to be conveyed in words because it was so different from the current reality of the organisation.

If we turn now to the public value theory approach to strategic change, we can usefully return to the Poister and Streib (2005) study one more time. Poister and Streib found evidence which can be read as showing that the impact of strategic planning may be increased by, first, adopting an inclusive approach to the development of strategic plans so that the public and other stakeholders are involved, and, secondly, by reporting on performance to the public regularly. This supports the public value theory of strategic management, with its assumption about the importance of external support. It will be recalled that Heymann considered it important that public services strategic leaders shared power with outsiders much more than did leaders in private companies. In democratic societies strategic plans for public services need to have popular support. In any case, involving the public and other stakeholders in preparing strategic plans is a very obvious way of strategic leaders in public services paying attention to the views of outsiders.

Moore's (1995) case studies of Boston Housing Authority and the Houston Police Department illustrate the public value theory assumption that political support for strategic plans is vital. The leaders in both cases sought external support from politicians, and this support produced resources and authorisation. These two case studies also highlighted the significance of top management effectiveness as an aspect of organisational capacity, although the leaders tackled improving top management effectiveness in very different ways – one leader bringing in new people and one leader making top managers more accountable. Both these cases might be described as organisational turnarounds and therefore we can suggest that strategic approaches are also applicable to turnarounds as well as other types of change.

STRATEGIC APPROACHES TO INNOVATION IN PUBLIC SECTOR HEALTH SYSTEMS

So far we have looked at strategic approaches and some empirical studies of strategic planning and management which allowed some marshalling of the evidence for the theories. Now we turn to a case study in the public sector in which the authors draw lessons on an inductive basis that provides further insights into strategic management and change. Fajans and his colleagues (2006) describe a strategic approach to innovations in reproductive health policies and programmes which was implemented in 25 countries. They report its first use in 1993 in Brazil and the last one in Moldova in 2005. They characterise this approach as follows (Fajans et al. 2006, p. 439): 'The Strategic Approach is an innovation for policy and program development that has produced beneficial results in a growing number of developing countries. It builds on principles of strategic planning and organization development.'

Fajans and his colleagues make a number of observations about these applications of the strategic approach which are worth considering here. First, they observed that the strategic approach had the advantage of enabling government officials to learn about the conditions of service delivery and public needs. They quoted an official from Mongolia (2006, p. 438), which implemented the strategic approach in 2003: 'We sit in our offices and think we are doing it right; then we do this strategic assessment and find that it is not right for doctors or the women.'

Secondly, they highlighted the importance of stability in the personnel who are in programme leadership roles and in professional roles at all levels. Without stability in the people occupying leadership roles, for example, strategic planning becomes more difficult in respect of long-term vision and planning. And it is people, they argue, that push implementation forward; they refer to policy champions. They report that Human Resources (HR) policies can undermine stability in personnel; a 1998 project in Myanmar, which was focused on health services at district level, took place in the context of an HR policy which moved senior team members to a new district every two years.

Thirdly, Fajans and his colleagues drew attention to a receptivity factor which they termed 'the opening of a policy window'. These windows are political in nature – comprising a period of political opportunity when policy and programmes can be changed. The problem is that these windows are relatively short time periods whereas the strategic approach requires a longer period. Arguably, a version of this issue has been recognised in relation to federal-level strategic planning in the United States, where the original legislation setting up strategic planning had specified a planning cycle that did not integrate with the political cycle of American politics. Recent legislative changes have sought to fix this problem in the US case so that the planning cycle is linked to the political cycle.

Fourthly, they identified the importance of the strategic approach being seen as relevant within the country concerned. For example, the Ministry of Health in Vietnam (1994) were receptive to the strategic approach because it offered them a way of broadening the contraceptive methods available and because they wanted to improve the quality of services. This point by Fajans et al. seems to be consistent with the experience of the UK government in the early years of the 21st century: the leading politicians wanted to change public services and took up strategic plans (in 2004) because they were seen as useful tools for delivering changes in public services systems.

All of these four observations from this case study could be seen as affirming existing theories of strategic management or extending and elaborating them. For example, the first observation about the advantages of the strategic approach for understanding conditions of service delivery and public needs affirms the idea that strategic management has to address the stakeholders of public services. The second observation about the stability of personnel extends our understanding of strategic leadership – leaders need to stick around and provide persistence to the pursuit of a strategic vision.

The last two observations (i.e. policy windows and the importance of the strategic approach being seen as relevant to the concerns or priorities of those in charge) offer developments of our understanding of the conditions in which political support is more likely to be forthcoming. This would elaborate the public value theory of strategic management, with its emphasis on the importance of strategic leaders getting political support for their strategic plans.

SUMMARY

This chapter has reviewed a number of theories of strategic management and has explored their implications for the management of change and innovation. It has also looked at research evidence and case study findings.

As a result it has been shown that influential commentators on strategic planning in the private sector who rejected strategic planning as bureaucratic and overly rational are not a reliable guide to the advantages and disadvantages of using strategic management in the public services for the delivery of change and innovation. Strategic planning has reportedly been one of the most widely used management tools over the last 20 years in large businesses, and surveys of the public services have revealed that managers found benefits from the use of strategic planning.

When strategic management – with its concern for implementation, monitoring, learning and general integration of management processes – is deployed, research has shown that it achieves results. Some of the key conclusions from research into public services include the importance of:

- Ensuring strategic plans are actually implemented through budgetary decisions and through the use of performance measurement and management.
- Getting individual managers to focus on strategic goals and getting them to make a personal contribution to implementing strategy.
- Ensuring strategic plans deliver the priorities of politicians and thereby address the need to secure the ownership of strategic plans by politicians, which, if not addressed, could deny strategic leaders in public services the support they need.
- Linking the planning cycle to the political cycle and being sensitive to the opportunities offered by policy windows.
- Increasing the level of understanding of public officials about the needs of the public and the conditions in which public services are delivered.
- Involving the public in preparing governmental/public service strategic plans and ensuring they are regularly informed of the performance of the public services against strategic goals.

- Developing strategic leadership capabilities in communicating strategic vision and future direction and in using language and vocabulary that encourage others to design new strategic actions.
- Adopting HR policies which favour the stability of personnel occupying key leadership and professional positions in the public services organisations.

Finally, it is critical that the application of strategic management in the public services is looked at realistically. It achieves varying degrees of success in practice (Poister and Streib 2005). This is in part because strategic management is a practice and requires the use of understanding, insights, foresight and skills. Strategic management in the public services is not without its challenges and can be expected to result in varying degrees of success depending on how well the challenges are met.

BIBLIOGRAPHY

Bass, B.M. and Avolio, B.J. (1994). *Improving Organizational Effectiveness Through Transformational Leadership*. Thousand Oaks, CA: Sage Publications.

Berry, F.S. (2007). Strategic planning as a tool for managing organizational change. *International Journal of Public Administration*, 30, 331–346.

Berry, F.S. and Wechsler, B. (1995). State agencies' experience with strategic planning: findings from a national survey. *Public Administration Review*, 55, 159–168.

Boyle, R. (1995a). *Developing Management Skills*. Dublin: Institute of Public Administration.

Boyle, R. (1995b). *Towards a New Public Service*. Dublin: Institute of Public Administration.

Capability Reviews Team (2007). *Capability Reviews Tranche 3: Findings and Common Themes. Civil Service – Strengths and Challenges*. London: Cabinet Office. Crown copyright (Ref: 279915/0307/D2.4).

Crozier, M. (1964). *The Bureaucratic Phenomenon*. London: Tavistock.

Eadie, D.C. (1983). Putting a powerful tool to practical use: the application of strategic planning in the public sector. *Public Administration Review*, 43, 447–452.

Fajans, P., Simmons, R. and Ghiron, L. (2006). Helping public sector health systems innovate: the strategic approach to strengthening reproductive health policies and programs. *American Journal of Public Health*, 96(3), 435–440.

Flynn, N. and Talbot, C. (1996). Strategy and strategists in UK local government. *Journal of Management Development*, 15, 24–37.

Frost-Kumpf, L., Wechsler, B., Ishiyama, H.J. and Backoff, R.W. (1993). Strategic action and transformational change: the Ohio Department of Mental Health. In B. Bozeman (ed.), *Public Management*. San Francisco, CA: Jossey-Bass.

Hamel, G. and Prahalad, C.K. (1994). *Competing for the Future*. Boston, MA: Harvard Business School Press.

Heifetz, R.A. (1994). *Leadership Without Easy Answers*. Cambridge, MA: The Belknap Press of Harvard University Press.

Heymann, P.B. (1987). *The Politics of Public Management*. London: Yale University Press.

Joyce, P. (1998). Management and innovation in the public services. *Strategic Change*, 7, 19–30.

Joyce, P. (2012). *Strategic Leadership in the Public Services*. Abingdon: Routledge.

Martin, J. (1999). Leadership in local government reform: strategic direction v administrative compliance. *Australian Journal of Public Administration*, 58(2), 24–37.

Miles, R.E. and Snow, C.C. (1978). *Organizational Strategy, Structure, and Process*. London: McGraw-Hill.

Mintzberg, H. (1994). The fall and rise of strategic planning. *Harvard Business Review*, 72(1), 107–114.

Moore, M. (1995). *Creating Public Value: Strategic Management in Government*. London: Harvard University Press.

Nutt, P.C. (2004). Prompting the transformation of public organizations. *Public Performance & Management Review*, 27(4), 9–33.

Nutt, P.C. and Backoff, R.W. (1992). *Strategic Management of Public and Third Sector Organizations*. San Francisco, CA: Jossey-Bass.

OECD (2000). *Government of the Future*. Paris: OECD.

Osborne, D. and Gaebler, T. (1992). *Reinventing Government: How the Entrepreneurial Spirit is Transforming the Public Sector*. Reading, MA: Addison Wesley.

Parker, S., Paun, A., McClory, J. and Blatchford, K. (2010). *Shaping Up: A Whitehall for the Future*. London: Institute for Government.

Peters, T. and Waterman, R. (1982). *In Search of Excellence*. New York: Harper Collins.

Pettigrew, A. and Whipp, R. (1993). *Managing Change for Competitive Success*. Oxford: Blackwell.

Pettigrew, A., Ferlie, E. and McKee, L. (1992). *Shaping Strategic Change*. London: Sage.

PMSU (2006). *The UK Government's Approach to Public Service Reform*. London: Strategy Unit, Cabinet Office.

Poister, T.H. and Streib, G. (2005). Elements of strategic planning and management in municipal government: status after two decades. *Public Administration Review*, 65(1), 45–56.

Porter, M. (2004). *Competitive Advantage: Creating and Sustaining Superior Performance*. New York: Free Press.

Rigby, D. and Bilodeau, B. (2010). *Management Tools for Turbulent Times*. Available at: http://www.bain.com/bainweb/Consulting Expertise/hot topics/detail.asp?id=56 (accessed 17 April 2010).

Wechsler, B. and Backoff, R.W. (1986). Policy making and administration in state agencies: strategic management approaches. *Public Administration Review*, 46, 321–327.

15. Public procurement of innovation[1]
Jakob Edler and Elvira Uyarra

INTRODUCTION

Recent years have witnessed a renewed interest, both in academia and in policy discussions, in the influence of public procurement on the development and introduction of new goods and services. Public procurement – understood as the acquisition of goods and services by government or public sector organisations – has also been an integral part of recent demand-side innovation policy initiatives. Edler (2010, p. 177) defines demand-side policies as 'a set of public measures to increase the demand for innovations, to improve the conditions for the uptake of innovations and/or to improve the articulation of demand in order to spur innovation and the diffusion of innovations'. Whilst debates about the influence of 'demand' on innovation are not new, the broad interest in the use of *public demand* as a driver of innovation is a significant development in innovation policy design.

For instance, procurement for innovation was an element of the European Commission's Action Plan to raise R&D expenditure to the 3 per cent Barcelona target. Subsequent programmatic European innovation policy papers (Kok et al. 2004; Aho et al. 2006) emphasised a need to promote policies driving demand for innovation, including public procurement. Consequently, the EU Commission set up the European Lead Market Initiative (EU COM 2007a; CSES and Oxford Research 2011), focused largely on sectors in which the state is an important purchaser, and considered public procurement to be one of the key instruments for the creation of 'lead markets' in Europe. More recently, the Europe 2020 strategy sees public procurement as one of the market-based instruments that should be used to achieve the objectives of smart, sustainable and inclusive growth (EU COM 2010a). The 2011 Commission Green Paper on 'the modernisation of procurement policy' (EU COM 2011) states that existing procurement tools and methods should be modernised in order to make them better suited to deal with the evolving political, social and economic context. This includes support of common societal goals such as protection of the environment, promoting innovation and social inclusion, and ensuring the best possible conditions for the provision of high quality public services.[2]

The promotion of demand-side innovation policies, including procurement, has also been supported by many OECD countries and the OECD itself. An OECD Project on Demand-Side Innovation Policies was launched in 2008 under the auspices of the Working Party on Innovation and Technology Policy and the Committee on Industry, Innovation and Entrepreneurship as an input to the OECD Innovation Strategy (see OECD 2011; also Myoken 2010). The overview in OECD (2011) indicates how very different countries seek to establish public procurement as one element in the enlarged instrument mix fostering the demand for innovation. This also includes very small countries (e.g. Georghiou et al. 2010), a few catching up central and east European countries (Edler 2011) and emerging economies such as China (Edler et al. 2008; Li 2011).

Against this background, this chapter reviews the main academic arguments and the state of the art in relation to public procurement and innovation. It first outlines how the interest in public procurement of innovation has developed over the last two decades. It then presents key theoretical arguments for the use of public procurement to spur innovation. The next section summarises the different types of public procurement of innovation referred to in the literature, followed by a discussion of the challenges, barriers and potential drawbacks associated with its use in practice. The final section concludes with some general considerations as regards the limited use of public procurement for innovation to modernise public services.

ACADEMIC DEBATE ON PUBLIC PROCUREMENT AND INNOVATION: RECENT EVOLUTION

In line with the evolution in academic thinking about innovation policy, the academic discussion about the role of procurement in innovation has shifted over time, from selected mission-oriented application of procurement (mainly in defence) and its implication for the development of technologies and markets to the role of general procurement to spur innovation and foster societal needs. The interest in procurement as a tool for innovation policy also coincides with a broadening of the discussion of innovation policy to incorporate a wider range of instruments and a realisation of a relative failure of traditional innovation policies to boost competitiveness (Flanagan et al. 2011). This failure has been attributed to a suboptimal use of the instrument mix portfolio and to a bias towards supply-side measures (Edler and Georghiou 2007). Finally, the academic and policy interest in procurement relates to an interest in the public sector as an innovative actor in its own right (Flanagan et al. 2011) although, as will be noted later, scholarly debates on public sector innovation have so far failed to engage sufficiently with discussions on the innovation effects of public procurement.

Early interest in public procurement was centred on the influence of US defence procurement on the emergence of high-technology sectors (Molas-Gallart 1997; James 2004). A number of studies showed how post-war national security-oriented procurement expenditure in the US influenced the emergence of industries such as semiconductors and commercial aircraft (Mowery 1997). For instance, Geroski (1990) reviewed key successful innovations that emerged as a result of (mainly defence related) public procurement, such as computer, civilian aircraft and semiconductor industries, and concluded that procurement was under-valued as a means to drive innovation. In the 1980s and 1990s the debate went beyond defence, and public procurement was advocated as a suitable tool for industrial policy (Rothwell 1984) and as one effective means of encouraging technological prowess and R&D spending more generally. Rothwell and Zegveld (1981) compared R&D subsidies and state procurement contracts and concluded that procurement was more effective in generating innovation than R&D subsidies. Other studies confirmed this innovation effect of public procurement (Dalpé et al. 1992; Dalpé 1994), with Geroski (1990, p. 183) claiming that procurement policy 'is a far more efficient instrument to use in stimulating innovation than any of a wide range of frequently used R&D subsidies'.

The interest in the use of procurement for innovation declined in the 1990s, only to increase again with added emphasis in the 2000s, focusing at first on the strategic use of technology and finally on innovation procurement. A first wave of interest centred around public *technology* procurement, focused on large-scale, national-level public sector infrastructure projects (Edquist et al. 2000; Rolfstam 2005; some examples also in Myoken 2010). For instance, these national and sectoral (mainly telecommunications) case studies of technology procurement reported in Palmberg (1997) and Edquist et al. (2000) corresponded to sectors characterised by a high concentration of public sector buying power, often linked to 'natural monopolies' and strong network externalities. More recently, academic interest has broadened into understanding, empirically, the processes and structures within public procurement that are favourable to the development and adoption of innovations more generally (Edler et al. 2006; CSES and Oxford Research 2011; Lember et al. 2011).[3] Such case study-based qualitative studies made no claim of the effects of public procurement on innovation across the board of public procurement, but focused instead on good practice and its preconditions. More quantitative analyses include the research of Aschhoff and Sofka (2009), comparing the effects of procurement vis-à-vis other instruments (regulation, R&D subsidies and university research) on the innovation activities of German enterprises. They found that both public procurement and the provision of knowledge infrastructure in universities had positive effects on innovation success, procurement being particularly effective for smaller firms in regional areas under economic stress and in distributive and technological services. Whilst providing some evidence of impact, Aschhoff and Sofka (2009) fall short of explaining how such effects take place, namely the procurement processes, modes, structures and rationales that are more conducive to innovation.

It must also be stressed that many of the positive effects identified in empirical studies on suppliers and on competitiveness of locations were found to be not so much the result of a coherent or explicit use of public procurement as innovation policy but rather a side effect of 'everyday' or general procurement activities (see Uyarra 2010; Lember et al. 2011).

HOW DOES (OR HOW COULD) PROCUREMENT INFLUENCE INNOVATION?

Procurement is a complex instrument consisting of multiple decisions and multiple forms of intervention, contributing to multiple and varied effects on innovation. One important implication of this is that, regardless of whether public procurement is explicitly oriented towards innovation, procurement decisions are likely to have innovation impacts via their influence on intermediate outcomes such as competition, industrial structure and network effects (Cabral et al. 2006; Uyarra and Flanagan 2010). As Dalpé (1994, p.66) argues, 'decisions concerning prices, quantities, and standards affect innovation, positively or negatively, in a group of industries involved in government procurement'. It is important to understand these effects, whether they are actively sought or not. A related implication is that innovation impacts go beyond the procurement of goods and services that 'do not exist'. The procurement of a new product or service, for instance a one-off product development, is not a sufficient, sometimes not even a necessary, condition for systemic innovation effects to emerge. Geroski (1990, p. 192) thus notes that 'using procurement policies to encourage firms to develop new capabilities does not imply that one ought to uncritically encourage them to generate something new'. Analysis should go beyond the act of purchasing a new good or service and include adoption and medium- or longer-term effects in the market, including dynamic effects on competition and the supply chain. However, knowledge about the nature of supply chains resulting from public procurement contracts, and the spatial and environmental 'footprint' of those supply chains, is limited (Uyarra and Flanagan 2010).

A key consideration is therefore not *whether* but *how* innovation is stimulated; in other words, which procurement designs best encourage potential suppliers to produce and sell innovative products and services. As Cabral et al. (2006, p. 485) note, 'the buyer must ensure that the suppliers have enough incentives to invest in the innovative knowledge that will eventually be incorporated in the goods it needs'.

Justifications to Use Public Procurement to Spur Innovation

The rationales commonly exercised for the use of public procurement as a demand-side innovation policy stem, first and foremost, from the potential of public procurement to alleviate a number of *market and systemic failures* hindering innovation. Such failures preventing the market introduction and diffusion of innovations can arise when, for instance, demand is insufficient to stimulate innovative products and services; when the number of users is too low to enable network effects; or when there are insufficient incentives or high switching costs associated with the shift to a new technology and therefore a strong demand pull is required to incentivise investment. Systemic failures can occur when users are unable to articulate and signal their needs to manufacturers or are unaware of potentially innovative goods and services the market can offer; or interaction between users and producers is required to define the innovative solution. The presence of these failures provides a potential for public policy intervention that can improve the overall level of welfare (Edler and Georghiou 2007). Additional justifications to use public procurement to spur innovation rest on the assumptions that innovation procurement can contribute to the achievement of particular economic and societal goals (e.g. actively shaping particular markets/technologies, promoting sustainable development and social inclusion) and considerably improve public service provision in the long run. These rationales are discussed in turn.

Procurement to overcome system and market failures

Buyer–supplier interaction has been identified as an important trigger for innovation (Lundvall 1992). However user–producer interaction and communication can sometimes be poor, especially if demand is not articulated sufficiently to make suppliers read the signals and translate them into innovations. Procurement can help alleviate such information problems. As Edler and Georghiou (2007, p. 950) state, "not only demand as such, but also the interaction between demand and supply has crucial implications for innovation dynamics'. Systems of innovation approaches emphasise the interactive nature of innovation and in particular the influence of users and user–producer interaction in the production of innovations. Rigid procurement procedures and practices have however been found to severely constrain buyer–supplier collaboration (Erridge and Greer 2002).

To overcome this, procedures such as 'competitive dialogue' were introduced by the 2004 EU procurement directive to allow pre-qualified tenderers to engage in a discussion to fine tune the solutions proposed (Arrowsmith and Treumer 2012; Treumer and Uyarra 2012).

Public procurement can have significant effects on innovation via its impact on the market and has even been used as a market transformation tool (most recently by the EU Lead Market Initiative). Cabral et al. (2006) identify three such kinds of (indirect) influence of public procurement: by enlarging the market for new goods; by facilitating the adoption of new standards; or by changing the market structure so as to make it more conducive to innovation. Similarly, Porter (1990) argued that public procurement can act as a positive force for upgrading national competitive advantage in several ways: by providing early demand for advanced new products and services (as indicated above, the lead market argument); by government acting as a demanding and sophisticated buyer; by reflecting international needs in the setting up of specifications; through facilitating innovation; and through encouraging competition. These conditions can be mutually reinforcing and each may have its greatest significance at different stages of an industry's evolution.

If of a significant scale, public sector demand can 'pull' innovation by guaranteeing a significant level of production and a reduction in uncertainty that allow firms to benefit from economies of scale and technological investment. The scale of demand is particularly important in those industries characterised by heavy R&D requirements, substantial economies of scale in production, large generational leaps in technology or high levels of uncertainty (Porter 1990). Sizeable public demand reduces market risks by guaranteeing a certain amount of sales, enabling innovative firms to generate early economies of scale and learning, increase productivity and lower costs.

Further, a number of scholars have highlighted the role of government as potential 'lead users' (von Hippel 1986) or 'first users' of innovation (Rothwell and Zegveld 1981; Dalpé et al. 1992), creating new niche or even lead markets for new products and services (Beise 2004; Meyer-Krahmer 2004). Dalpé has shown that in particular research-intensive fields, public administrations can be more demanding than industry or final consumers and therefore are more likely to act as 'lead users' for new innovations (Dalpé et al. 1992, p.258). A public sector body with the necessary technical competences can also act as an 'experimental user' (Malerba et al. 2007), pushing suppliers to innovate in order to keep up with user requirements or even engaging in co-invention.

The influence of public sector demand is relative to the total demand of a particular market, its influence being stronger when the public sector is the sole (monopsonistic) buyer or is amongst a few large buyers in the market (oligopsony) (Rothwell and Zegveld 1981; Edquist and Hommen 2000). This purchasing power is therefore particularly strong in sectors such as health, construction and defence. Greater purchasing power can also be achieved by centralising or aggregating demand, a practice which can however disincentivise small potential bidders from bidding, and effectively reduce innovation by reducing variety and narrowing technological paths.

Public demand can also have a strong influence in goods and services that exhibit network effects (whereby additional users increase the value associated with the use of that particular good or service or of complementary goods and services). Network effects can allow dynamic increasing returns but can also lead to market failures (e.g. excess inertia and lock-in). When purchasing innovative goods and services on a large scale, public administrations can influence the outcome of the technology adoption process by their decision to choose a new technology or a particular version or standard of a new technology (Cabral et al. 2006). Coordinated procurement decisions to adopt a particular standard or technology will increase its value by increasing the installed base of that technology, thus encouraging adoption and preventing lock-in and excess inertia. More generally, public sector demand can lead to softer reputational or brand effects through demonstrating new functionalities to potential users.

Finally, procurement can influence innovation via the impact it exerts on competition (OFT 2004; Cabral et al. 2006). The relation between competition and innovation is complex: some economists argue that innovation declines when there is greater competition as it reduces monopoly rents, as suggested by Schumpeter (1934), whilst others consider that there is a positive correlation between competition and innovation. A third position is that there is an inverted U-shaped relationship, whereby competition effects dominate for low initial competition levels, whilst Schumpeterian effects are stronger at higher levels of product market competition (Aghion et al. 2005). Linked to this debate is the importance of dynamic vis-à-vis static or short-term efficiency gains (based on the optimum utilisation or allocation of existing resources). For instance, Rothwell and Zegveld (1981, p.96) differentiate between 'short-term efficiency of procurement as buying the best that industry has to offer, and long-term efficiency as improving the offering that industry has to make'. Such static and dynamic effects may be mutually reinforcing or cancel each other out over time (Caldwell et al. 2005; Uyarra and Flanagan 2010). Rothwell and Zegveld (1981) consider a potentially virtuous effect where the short-term efficiency could (of itself) lead to long-term efficiency, in that highly informed procurement could stimulate suppliers that are technologically competent. However, the structure of public tendering (for instance privileging large bundled contracts, or selection criteria privileging size or experience) can be such that it reinforces incumbents' advantages and locks other suppliers out of the market (Cabral et al. 2006).

Procurement to satisfy societal needs

Additional rationales are suggested by the need to satisfy social needs that are unlikely to be met by the market (Edquist and Hommen 2000; Edler and Georghiou 2007). Indeed, there are instances where the public sector may be willing to pay a premium cost or bear some efficiency losses if it wants to encourage certain policy goals and tackle societal needs, such as innovation, sustainability, health and social inclusion (McCrudden 2004; Edler and Georghiou 2007; Morgan 2008). Cave and Frinking (2003) consider that innovation can be an explicit secondary objective in certain instances, for instance in order to ensure that vital government functions can be secured against a range of shocks and threats (mission-critical procurement). Indeed many areas associated with public procurement, from environmentally friendly products to energy technologies, space technology and defence, typically have objectives linked to perceived societal needs (Edler et al. 2006). Related to this, public procurement of innovation also can make the provision of existing public service and the achievement of societal goals more effective and efficient.

Different Ways to Influence – Different Ways to Procure

Public procurement of innovation has been associated with instances where public agencies act to purchase, or place an order for, a product-service, good or system that does not exist at the time but which could be developed within a reasonable period; that is, that requires innovative work to fulfil the demands of the buyer (Edquist and Hommen 2000; Edler et al. 2006). This is in contrast with regular procurement, where governments place orders for 'off-the-shelf' products.

However, this definition is not differentiated enough if we want to understand procurement effects as innovation policy tool. We can distinguish between *general* procurement that might or might not have effects on innovation behaviour of suppliers (unintended), on the one hand, and *strategic* innovation procurement that is *intended* to spur innovation (see, for example, Cave and Frinking 2003).

We can further distinguish between procurement of solutions that do not exist yet and thus need to be developed (triggering demand) and procurement to acquire and adopt a service that exists in the marketplace, but is new for the organisation (responsive demand). Edquist et al. (2000, p. 21) differentiate between 'developmental' and 'adaptive' public technology procurement. Developmental procurement occurs where completely new products, processes or systems are created, whilst adaptive procurement is the procurement of goods and services not new to the world but new to the country of procurement.

Innovation can be triggered through intelligent functional specifications – whereby the public buyer asks for a solution to a specific problem rather than specifying the concrete product or services to buy – and through market intelligence and interaction with the market (see below). One extreme form of triggering a new solution is first to purchase an R&D service up to a prototype, with a view to their possible purchase at a later stage through a normal public procurement procedure. This procedure is commonly labelled 'pre-commercial procurement', as it precedes the market purchase of the final good. Pre-commercial procurement has been introduced in various forms in different European countries (EU COM 2007b, 2010b), mainly by innovation promotion agencies in a number of member states, which have introduced their own scaled-down version of the first model of this scheme – the US Small Business Innovation Research (SBIR) programme –adapted to national innovation policy objectives.

If public procurement is *responsive* to innovations that are out there in the marketplace, the public purchase mainly accelerates diffusion (Miles et al. 2009). This potentially contributes to the quality of a market as being innovation friendly, which is important for the adoption and the speed of diffusion of innovation and thus for the attractiveness of markets (e.g. Tellis et al. 2003; Trott 2003; Veryzer 2003). Responsive demand requires the ability of organisations to adopt and adjust to the innovation, and to bear the learning and transaction cost of this adoption.

A further distinction relates to the degree to which public procurement intends to spur markets. Public procurement is in general done to fulfil a specific need from a particular public organisation; that is, the public buyer is also the end user. However, as a tool to trigger or transfer markets, public procurement has been used in conjunction with private procurement. In the Swedish Market Transformation Programmes private and public demand have often been bundled together (cooperative procurement) or else public buyers have deliberately procured in areas in which private demand was then expected to take over (catalytical procurement; Suvilehto and Överholm 1998).

Finally, and reflecting on the various ways in which public procurement can influence innovation, Uyarra and Flanagan (2010) suggest four stylised types of procurement. Their starting point is that procurement influences innovation through shaping the size, specificity, technical sophistication or standardisation of demand. It can do so through pooling requirements, aggregating contracts, opening or restricting competition through tendering procedures, setting standards, defining specifications, and through engaging with users and suppliers. This leads to the following four types of procurement: *experimental*, whereby procurement provides a testing-ground for innovative products; *technological*, creating demand 'pull' by guaranteeing a level of production and a reduction in uncertainty that enables R&D investment; *efficient*, setting up or encouraging particular standards for products and systems, thus allowing diffusion and market creation; and *adapted*, tailoring existing technologies to identified niches which satisfy unmet user needs.

CHALLENGES ASSOCIATED WITH THE USE OF PROCUREMENT TO STIMULATE INNOVATION

The intentional use of public procurement to promote innovation is challenging. Difficulties associated with taking this agenda forward include regulatory complexity, potential conflict between policy objectives, and capacity and resource constraints in contracting authorities. In monitoring terms difficulties also arise in defining what constitutes innovation in procurement terms, and in relation to measuring the extent and impact of such innovations.

First, fragmentation of public demand (often between different levels of government) can limit potential scale effects for innovative procurement. Indeed 'effective technology procurement depends on a high concentration of buying power and a comprehensive "articulation of demand"' (Edquist and Hommen 2000, p.72). Even when the public sector accounts for a significant share of the total demand in a particular market, buyer power cannot be made effective if different functions or departments are buying the same goods individually and in an un-coordinated fashion. Even seemingly 'unitary' parts of the public sector often do not act as a coherent whole in practice (Caldwell et al. 2005), for they comprise different decision-making and purchase points. Furthermore, many agencies with responsibilities for public procurement operate separately from line ministries or government agencies with a remit to foster innovation.

Another barrier hindering innovation may result from a lack of coherence in the way public sector needs are transmitted to the market. Geroski (1990) highlighted the importance of defining a clear set of needs towards which innovative efforts can be directed. Lack of consensus over priorities, inconsistent definition of needs or even frequent changes in policy would have the effect of increasing uncertainty and decreasing the likelihood of innovation (Rothwell and Zegveld 1981). A tendency to 'bolt on' many policy objectives to the public procurement function may be confusing to procurers and practitioners, who may struggle to adequately weight the different priorities and policy agendas, and send contradictory messages to the marketplace (Uyarra 2010). Adequate planning, definition and communication of needs and market engagement very early on in the procurement process is crucial to drive innovative solutions onto the market although, as HM Treasury (2010) notes, the pre-procurement phase is often the most neglected and poorly executed part of the procurement process.

A further set of challenges relates to the organisation of the procurement. This, first, relates to the very definition of needs. To define a future need and turn it into specifications for a concrete tender process, and then to channel this through the procurement process and back into adoption, require that the 'business owners' within the organisations – that is, the budget holders – are actively engaged both with the internal end user or those responsible to deliver the service, and the procurers. Secondly, institutional barriers such as decentralised or 'silo' budgets may also hinder the adoption of innovations. Rolfstam et al. (2011), in their description of the introduction of Bardex catheters into the UK NHS, noted how the benefits of the new catheter were not visible to the budget holder affected by the purchasing of a more expensive product, but to another department within the organisation, which slowed down the adoption of the new product within the organisation. Sound internal coordination and appropriate interfaces between the organisation and the market have been identified as major success factors for innovation procurement (as identified in the cases analysed in Edler et al. 2006).

Further, explicitly designating public procurement as an innovation policy tool leads to significant coordination challenges, as sectoral ministries or agencies (e.g. police force, department of health, etc.) need to engage with innovation policy agencies or departments in order to make the best use of existing supporting measures and adjust framework conditions as and if needed; whilst innovation policy makers need to engage and seek commitment from decision makers in those sectoral bodies.

An additional limitation relates to a potential lack of leadership, capacity and resources in the procurement function. As noted by the UK Treasury in their review on the use of competitive dialogue, 'the outcome of a procurement will be influenced as much by the capacity and capability of those party to the process as by the nature of the contract to be delivered' (HM Treasury 2010, p. 7). Rothwell and Zegveld (1981) early on highlighted a potential discrepancy between the capabilities held by procurers and the skills required for procuring innovative solutions. They argued that whereas relatively little in-house competence is needed when procuring off-the-shelf goods for the lowest possible price, greater competence is required to encourage suppliers to innovate. Particularly at lower levels of governance and in procurement systems that are decentralised, there may be a shortage of professional procurers and therefore the lack of skills for innovative purchasing becomes an important challenge (Uyarra 2010; OECD 2011). Finally, in terms of procurement procedures, additional barriers include a poor uptake of lifecycle costing practices vis-à-vis a traditional focus on lowest price and the use of overly narrow functional specifications. Specifications defined in terms of outcomes or performance allow the market to propose better solutions to problems.

Numerous studies have also suggested that the position and status of procurement professionals in the internal hierarchy of organisations tend to be lower than those of professionals in other functional areas, which can limit the influence of procurers over corporate-level strategic decisions and in managing relations with suppliers (Zheng et al. 2007). Leadership and senior management support and the presence of innovation champions have been identified as crucial in securing the success of certain innovations (Phillips et al. 2007; Yeow et al. 2011).

It has also been shown empirically that the risk-averse culture typically prevailing in public agencies 'can also act as a barrier to the adoption of appropriate, innovative, reactive and proactive supply strategies' (Cox et al. 2005, p. 1). This risk for the purchasing organisation is related to the often higher entry costs of an innovation and the uncertainty of whether the solution can be developed and subsequently adopted by the organisation. Inside organisations there can be a challenging mismatch between those who benefit if the innovation is successfully adopted and those who bear the consequences of failure (procurers, highest level decision makers). Reducing risk aversion and allowing risk sharing have thus been pinpointed as important factors for strengthening the role of public procurement as a means to stimulate innovation (Aho et al. 2006; Nyiri et al. 2007; Tsipouri et al. 2010).

A common pitfall when using public procurement as an innovation and economic policy instrument is to privilege national and/or regional suppliers. However, favouring local and regional contractors may not work in the best interest of service users and can even be counterproductive for suppliers. Evidently, it can exclude innovative solutions that may be available elsewhere, and which could represent better value for money and contribute to improved public services as well as to the technological upgrade of a location. Indirect effects via technology leakages and spillovers from such innovations may be more significant than local direct contracting, and could be secured through, for example, subcontracting practices, licensing, and purchasing of complementary products and services such as maintenance services (Uyarra 2010).

Finally, there is a whole range of strategic intelligence challenges; that is, challenges associated with the design (ex ante), implementation, ex post evaluation and re-design of procurement initiatives that seek to spur innovation. Whilst for supply-side innovation policies (grants, tax credits, etc.) ex ante and ex post evaluation are well established and implemented, until recently only very few evaluations of demand-side and procurement policies were made (Suvilehto and Överholm 1998; OECD 2011). With the renewed interest concepts are being developed and implemented (Edler et al. 2009; SEES and Oxford Research 2011). However, the challenges are manifold: relevant markets and market actors are hard to define and public statistics inadequate – as by definition what the relevant markets are might change because of the intervention – and the attribution of market and societal effects of purchasing decisions is hard to establish (Edler et al. 2009). Further, the actor landscape is complex and effects range from micro (changed behaviour of procurers) to meso (new networks of procurers, new innovation-oriented innovation between supply and demand) and macro (transformation of markets). Last but not least, there needs to be a strong formative element in the evaluation, as procurement of innovation involves learning within public organisations at all levels.

CONCLUSIONS

Scholarly evidence suggests that, under certain conditions, public procurement has significant potential to support the emergence and diffusion of innovation and to improve the attractiveness and competitiveness of locations as markets. At the same time it can improve public services and contribute to the solution of societal problems. However, policy developments during the financial crisis in many OECD countries are a demonstration that many decision makers perceive public procurement of innovation as a luxury to afford in good economic times, but too high a burden when budgets are cut. Further, in economic crises public budgets are seen as means to nourish domestic firms, even though they may be less likely to supply the most innovative solution. Above all, the lack of capabilities and internal coordination, the problematic mismatch of benefit and risks within organisations, and the failure to realise the *long-term* financial and service benefits of innovations purchased by public bodies appear to pile up to a mountain of obstacles for public procurement of innovation.

A decade-long experience in introducing new practices around public procurement has demonstrated that the mere intention, the action plans and guidelines, are not enough. A turn towards using public procurement more intelligently for innovation would involve the combination of three major developments. First, the capabilities and internal coordination within procuring organisations need to be radically improved. Once internal users, budget holders and procurers have integrated structures and are able to define and signal needs and interact with the market, innovation will be more likely to occur. Secondly, the purchase of innovative goods or services needs to be more closely linked to the debate of modernising public services, both in academia and in policy practice. The academic literature and the current debate on innovation in the public sector appear currently to be entirely de-linked from the procurement debate (e.g. Mulgan 2007; Hughes et al. 2011), whilst the debate on public procurement fails to sufficiently stress the long-term benefit for the effectiveness and efficiency (and thus long-term cost savings) of many innovative goods and services. Thirdly, the public purse could be used more intelligently in areas in which public demand represents a large share of overall demand and/or can act as an experimental user with a view to transfer markets in directions that are socially desirable.[4] As long as this triad is not internalised and is not linked across government, the hopes for public procurement to deliver major innovation dynamics will remain just that – hopes.

NOTES

1. This work was funded through the UK Economic and Social Research Council Grant R111539 with contributed support from the Department of Business Innovation and Skills, NESTA (National Endowment for Science, Technology and the Arts) and the Technology Strategy Board. The authors would like to acknowledge their generous support. Beyond normal peer review input they have no influence on the content of this chapter or the decision to publish.
2. The European directives on public procurement (Directive 2004/18/), published in 2004, already incorporated some adjustments so that contracting authorities encourage the market to propose innovative solutions. For instance, under the design contest procedures participants can propose ideas outside of the strict terms of reference and that may be used in a future procurement procedure. In the case of complex contracts the directive allows for the use of competitive dialogue which enables the contracting authority to open up 'a dialogue the aim of which shall be to identify and define the means best suited to satisfying their needs' (Article 29, § 3).
3. For an overview see a compilation of case studies produced within the context of an ESRC-funded project UNDERPIN: http://ec.europa.eu/environment/gpp/pdf/compilation%20case%20studies.pdf (accessed 11 July 2012). As Dimitri et al. (2006, p.4) note: 'there is not a one-size-fits-all measure for effective

procurement design: the variety and complexity of situations in which procurement decisions are made means that appropriate purchasing procedures must take into account many aspects, and be tailored to each single situation'.

4.   Edler et al. (2011), for example, argue to link the sustainability agenda much more closely to the innovation agenda and use public procurement as one means to achieve this.

REFERENCES

Aghion, P., Bloom, N., Blundell, R., Griffith, R. and Howitt, P. (2005). Competition and innovation: an inverted U relationship. *Quarterly Journal of Economics*, 120(2), 710–728.

Aho, E., Cornu, J., Georghiou, L. and Subira, A. (2006). *Creating an Innovative Europe*. Report of the Independent Expert Group on R&D and Innovation appointed following the Hampton Court Summit, 27 October 2005, Luke Georghiou, Rapporteur; Brussels.

Arrowsmith, S. and Treumer, S. (eds) (2012). *Competitive Dialogue in EU Procurement*. Cambridge: Cambridge University Press.

Aschhoff, B. and Sofka, W. (2009). Innovation on demand – can public procurement drive market success of innovations? *Research Policy*, 38(8), 1235–1247.

Beise, M. (2004). Lead markets: country-specific drivers of the global diffusion of innovations. *Research Policy*, 33(6–7), 997–1018.

Cabral, L., Cozzi, G., Denicolo, V., Spagnolo, G. and Zanza, M. (2006). Procuring innovations. In N. Dimitri, G. Piga and G. Spagnolo (eds), *Handbook of Procurement*. Cambridge, MA: Cambridge University Press, pp. 483–530.

Caldwell, N., Walker, H., Harland, C., Knight, L., Zheng, J. and Wakeley, T. (2005). Promoting competitive markets: the role of public procurement. *Journal of Purchasing and Supply Management*, 11(5–6), 242–251.

Cave, J. and Frinking, E. (2003). Public procurement for R&D. Available at http://www2.warwick.ac.uk/fac/soc/economics/staff/faculty/cave/publications/pp_for_rd.pdf (accessed 19 October 2009).

Cox, A., Chicksand, D. and Ireland, P. (2005). Overcoming demand management problems: the scope for improving reactive and proactive supply management in the UK health service. *Journal of Public Procurement*, 5(1), 1–22.

CSES (Centre for Strategy/Evaluation Services) and Oxford Research (2011). *Final Evaluation of the Lead Market Initiative*. Final Report, July. Available at: http://ec.europa.eu/enterprise/policies/innovation/policy/lead-market-initiative/files/final-eval-lmi_en.pdf (accessed 11 December 2011).

Dalpé, R. (1994). Effects of government procurement on industrial innovation. *Technology in Society*, 16(1), 65–83.

Dalpé, R., DeBresson, C. and Ciaoping, H. (1992). The public sector as first user of innovations. *Research Policy*, 21(3), 251–263.

Dimitri, N., Piga, G. and Spagnolo, G. (2006). Introduction. In N. Dimitri, G. Piga and G. Spagnolo (eds), *Handbook of Procurement*. Cambridge, MA: Cambridge University Press, pp. 3–13.

Edler, J. (2010). Demand oriented innovation policy. In R. Smits, S. Kuhlmann and P. Shapira (eds), *The Theory and Practice of Innovation Policy: An International Research Handbook*. Cheltenham and Northampton, MA: Edward Elgar, pp. 177–208.

Edler, J. (2011). Innovation in EU CEE: the role of demand-based policy. In S. Radosevic and A. Kaderabkova (eds), *Challenges for European Innovation Policy: Cohesion and Excellence from a Schumpeterian Perspective*. Cheltenham and Northhampton, MA: Edward Elgar, pp. 177–208.

Edler, J. and Georghiou, L. (2007). Public procurement and innovation – resurrecting the demand side. *Research Policy*, 36(7), 949–963.

Edler, J., Corvers, S. and Xielin, L. (2008). Public procurement and innovation: OECD experience and reflections on China. In OECD (ed.), *OECD Reviews of Innovation Policy*: China and Paris: OECD.

Edler, J., Georghiou, L., McMeekin, A. and Uyarra, E. (2011). *Closing the Procurement Gap: The Costly Failure to Mobilise Sustainable Procurement for Innovation*. A Provocation written as a background paper for the discussion forum at Business Innovation and Skills, London, 7 April, organised by the Sustainable Consumption Institute, The University of Manchester.

Edler, J., Blind, K., Georghiou, L., Uyarra, E., Cox, D., Rigby, J. and Nugroho, Y. (2009). *Monitoring and Evaluation Methodology for the EU Lead Market Initiative – A Concept Development* - Final Report. Brussels: EU Commission.

Edler, J., Edquist, C., Georghiou, L., Hommen, L., Hafner, S., Papadakou, M., Rigby, J., Rolfstam, M., Ruhland, S. and Tsipouri, L. (2006). *Innovation and Public Procurement: Review of Issues at Stake*. Final report, Brussels: EU Commission. [ftp://ftp.cordis.lu/pub/innovation-policy/studies/full_study.pdf].

Edquist, C. and Hommen, L. (2000). Public technology procurement and innovation theory. In C. Edquist, L. Hommen and L. Tsipouri (eds), *Public Technology Procurement and Innovation*. Norwell, MA: Kluwer Academic Publishers, pp. 5–70.

Edquist, C., Hommen, L. and Tsipouri, L. (2000). *Public Technology Procurement and Innovation*. Norwell, MA: Kluwer Academic Publishers.

Erridge, A. and Greer, J. (2002). Partnerships and public procurement: building social capital through supply relations. *Public Administration*, 80(3), 503–522.

EU COM (2007a). *A Lead Market Initiative for Europe*. COM (2007) 860 final, Brussels.

EU COM (2007b). Precommercial Procurement: Driving Innovation to Ensure Sustainable High Quality Public Services in Europe. COM(2007) 799, Brussels.

EU COM (2009a). *Lead Market Initiative for Europe Mid-term Progress Report*. Brussels: Commission Staff Working Document, Commission of the European Communities.

EU COM (2009b). *Exploring Public Procurement as a Strategic Innovation Policy Mix Instrument*. Final report of the EU funded OMC-PTP project. Available at: http://www.innovation.lv/ino2/publications/Publicprocur. pdf (accessed 15 July 2010).

EU COM (2010a). *Innovation Union*. SEC(2010) 1161, Brussels.

EU COM (2010b). EU SBRI – options paper and study of international best practice. Proposal for establishment of EU SBIR. 3rd Inno-Partnering Council meeting in Delft. Workshop A, 18th November.

EU COM (2011). *Green Paper on the Modernisation of Procurement Policy: Towards a More Efficient European Procurement Paper*. 27.1.2011 COM(2011) 15 final, Brussels.

Flanagan, K., Uyarra, E. and Laranja, M. (2011). Reconceptualising the 'policy mix' for innovation. *Research Policy*, 40(5), 702–713.

Georghiou, L., Li, Y., Uyarra, E. and Edler, J. (2010). *Public Procurement for Innovation in Small European Countries*. Report to the European Commission in the context of the ERAPRISM OPMC-Net project (Policies for Research and Innovation in Small Member States to Advance the European Research Area), Manchester / Brussels. Available at: http://www.eraprism.eu/documents/4.4%20and%204.5%20del%20 public%20procurement.pdf (accessed 21 August 2012).

Geroski, P.A. (1990). Procurement policy as a tool of industrial policy. *International Review of Applied Economics*, 4(2), 182–198.

HM Treasury (2010). *Review of Competitive Dialogue*. London: HM Treasury.

Hughes, A., Moore, K. and Kataria, N. (2011). Innovation in the Public Sector: A Pilot Survey for Measuring Innovation Across the Public Sector. NESTA report, March. Available at: http://www.nesta.org.uk/about_ us/assets/features/innovation_in_public_sector_organisations (accessed 15 July 2011).

James, A. (2004). *U.S. Defence R&D Spending: An Analysis of the Impacts*. Rapporteur's report for the EURAB Working Group ERA Scope and Vision. EURAB 04.011, Manchester. Available at: (http://europa.eu.int/ comm/research/eurab/pdf/recommendations10.pdf (accessed 14 July 2011).

Kok, W. et al. (2004). *Facing the Challenge: The Lisbon Strategy for Growth and Employment*. Report from the High Level Group. Brussels: European Commission.

Lember, V., Kalvet, T. and Kattel, R. (2011). Urban competitiveness and public procurement for innovation. *Urban Studies*, 48(7), 1373–1395.

Li, Y. (2011). *Public Procurement as a Demand-Side Innovation Policy Tool in China – a National Level Case Study*. Paper presented at the DRUID 2011 conference, Innovation, Strategy and Structure, Copenhagen Business School, Denmark, 15–17 June.

Lundvall, B.A. (1992). User–producer relationships, national systems of innovation and internationalization. In B.A. Lundvall (ed.), *National Systems of Innovation*. London: Pinter, pp. 47–70.

Malerba, F., Nelson, R., Orsenigo, L. and Winter, S. (2007). Demand, innovation, and the dynamics of market structure: the role of experimental users and diverse preferences. *Journal of Evolutionary Economics*, 17(4), 371–399.

McCrudden, C. (2004). Using public procurement to achieve societal outcomes. *Natural Resource Forum*, 28, 257–267.

Meyer-Krahmer, F. (2004). Vorreiter-Märkte und Innovation. Ein neuer Ansatz der Technologie und Innovationspolitik. In F.W. Steinmeier and M. Machnig (eds), *Made in Germany '21. Innovationen für eine gerechte Zuknft*. Hamburg: Hoffman und Campe, pp. 95–110.

Miles, N., Bleda, M., Clark, J., Edler, J. and Simmonds, P. (2009). *The Wider Conditions for Innovation in The UK. How the UK Compares to Leading Countries*. Report to NESTA. London: NESTA.

Molas-Gallart, J. (1997). Which way to go? Defence technology and the diversity of 'dual-use' technology transfer. *Research Policy*, 26(3), 367–385.

Morgan, K. (2008). Greening the realm: sustainable food chains and the public plate. *Regional Studies*, 42(9), 1237–1250.

Mowery, D. (1997). U.S. post-war technology policy and the creation of new industries. In OECD (ed.), *Creativity, Innovation, and Job Creation*. Paris: OECD.

Mulgan, G. (2007). *Ready or Not? Taking Innovation in the Public Sector Seriously*.NESTA Provocation, April, London. Available at: http://www.nesta.org.uk/library/documents/readyornot.pdf (accessed 14 July 2011).

Myoken, Y. (2010). Demand-orientated policy on leading-edge industry and technology: public procurement for innovation. *International Journal of Technology Management*, 49(1/2/3), 196–219.

Nyiri, L., Osimo, D., Özcivelek, R., Centeno, C. and Cabrera, M. (2007). *Public Procurement for the Promotion of R&D and Innovation in ICT*. Institute for Prospective Technological Studies, European Commission, EUR 22671 EN.

OECD (2011). Demand Side Innovation Policy. Paris: OECD. Available at: http://www.oecd-ilibrary.org/science-and-technology/demand-side-innovation-policies_9789264098886-en (accessed 14 July 2011).

OFT (2004). *Assessing Impact of Public Sector Procurement on Competition*. London: Office of Fair Trading.

Palmberg, C. (1997). *Public Technology Procurement as a Policy Instrument? Selected Cases from the Finnish Telecommunications Industry*. VTT Group for Technology Studies, Working Paper no. 28/97.

Phillips, W., Knight, L., Caldwell, N. and Warrington, J. (2007). Policy through procurement: the introduction of digital signal process (DSP) hearing aids into the English NHS. *Health Policy*, 80, 77–85.

Porter, M.E. (1990). The Competitive Advantage of Nations. New York: Simon and Schuster

Rolfstam, M. (2005). *Public Technology Procurement as a Demand-Side Innovation*. Policy Instrument – an Overview of Recent Literature and Events, Lund University.

Rolfstam, M., Phillips, W. and Bakker, E. (2011). Public procurement of innovations, diffusion and endogenous institutions. *International Journal of Public Sector Management*, 24(5), 452–468.

Rothwell, R. (1984). Creating a regional innovation-oriented infrastructure: the role of public procurement. *Annals of Public and Cooperative Economics*, 55(2), 159–172.

Rothwell, R. and Zegveld, W. (1981). Government regulations and innovation – industrial innovation and public policy. In R. Rothwell and W. Zegveld (eds), *Industrial Innovation and Public Policy*. Westport, CT: Greenwood Press, pp.116–147.

Schumpeter, J. (1934). *The Theory of Economic Development*. Cambridge, MA: Harvard University Press.

Suvilehto, H.-M. and Överholm, E. (1998). *Swedish Procurement and Market Activities – Different Design Solutions on Different Markets*. Presentation at the 1998 ACEEE Summer Study on energy efficiency in buildings, Pacific Grove, California.

Tellis, G.J., Stremersch, S. and Yin, E. (2003). The international takeoff of new products. *Marketing Science*, 22, S.188–208.

Treumer, S. and Uyarra, E. (2012). Competitive dialogue and contractual design fostering innovation and need analysis. In G. Piga and S. Treumer (eds), *The Applied Law and Economics of Public Procurement*. London: Routledge.

Trott, P. (2003). Innovation and market research. In L. Shavinina (ed.), *International Handbook on Innovation*. Amsterdam: Elsevier, pp.835–844.

Tsipouri, L., Edler, J., Rolfstam, M. and Uyarra, E. (2010). *Risk Management in the Procurement of Innovation: Concepts and Empirical Evidence*. Brussels: EU Commission.

Uyarra, E. (2010). *Opportunities for Innovation through Local Government Procurement: A Case Study of Greater Manchester*. NESTA research report, May. Available at: http://www.nesta.org.uk/library/documents/opportunities-for-innovation18May2010.pdf (accessed 11 July 2011).

Uyarra, E. and Flanagan, K. (2010). Understanding the innovation impacts of public procurement. *European Planning Studies*, 18(1), 123–143.

Veryzer, R.W. (2003). Marketing and the development of innovative new products. In L. Shavinina (ed.), *International Handbook on Innovation*. Boston: Elsevier Science, pp.845–855.

Von Hippel, E. (1986). Lead users: a source of novel product concepts. *Management Science*, 32(7), 791–805.

Yeow, J., Uyarra, E. and Gee, S. (2011). *Sustainable Innovation through Public Procurement: The Case of 'Closed Loop' Recycled Paper*. Manchester Institute of Innovation Research Working Paper. Manchester: Manchester Business School.

Zheng, J., Knight, L., Harland, C., Humby, S. and James, K. (2007). An analysis of research into the future of purchasing and supply: a critical review research. *Journal of Purchasing and Supply Management*, 13(1), 69–83.

16. Ethical innovation in the public services
Michael Macaulay and David Norris

Organizational ethics is a practical business. Those engaged in debating moral and ethical issues in the workplace should be able to provide insights into real-world problems. One area that may benefit from the gaze of organizational ethics is that of public service innovation, which has become increasingly well documented and applied to a broad spectrum of research into public service performance (Windrum and Koch 2008; Baxter et al. 2010). Recently there has been increasing interest in the ethics surrounding innovation, which has focussed predominantly on conceptual and philosophical issues, for example Glor (2003) who discusses some of the fallacies that can befall those who attempt to implement innovation. Others seek to promote a particular philosophical framework as a means by which the ethics of innovation can be better understood: Emison (2010), for example, highlights pragmatism as a suitable philosophy for professionals involved in innovation, whereas Fuglsang and Mattsson (2009) argue that innovation can best be viewed through the prism of care ethics. Perhaps most interestingly, commentators such as Jennings (2008) have cited innovation as a key factor in *unethical* organizational behaviour, although there can be little doubt that in an age of global austerity the quest for further innovation will continue apace.

Several commentators have suggested that the values of ethics and innovation are somehow opposed. Mehanna and Yazbeck (2008, p. 1) have portrayed ethics and innovation as 'two seemingly unrelated principles', although they subsequently suggest that there is a point of convergence centred on public prosperity. Interestingly, similar dichotomies are often found in the ethics literature and, as this chapter will show, are equally often found to be false.

This chapter therefore seeks to draw a broader framework of organizational ethics to innovation, using the compliance/integrity spectrum. It will argue that innovation may in one sense seem anathema to organizational ethics, whose promotion of accountability, integrity and transparency may act as a barrier to the flexibility and adaptability needed by innovate practices. The chapter will discuss some of the major fault lines and dilemmas in innovation (including innovation as means–ends dilemma, innovation and leadership cabals, innovation as a driver for performance manipulation) and how these can negatively impact on public service organizations, and then outline different responses by the main school of ethical thought. Finally, it will show how ethical innovation can be embraced by moving away from strictly compliance views of organizational ethics towards an integrity approach.

WHOSE ETHICS?

To begin, however, it may be useful to note the key schools of thought in ethics (consequentialism, deontology, virtue ethics) as well as more recently adapted schools (justice ethics, care ethics). All ask slightly different questions regarding public service innovation: thus any ethical dilemma that one may face will be framed and shaped by one's initial ethical orientation. More importantly, each of these perspectives asks very different ethical questions about innovation, which can be summarized as thus:

- *Consequentialism*: What are the outcomes of the innovation? Who do they benefit? Do these outweigh any costs?
- *Deontology*: Has the implementation of the innovation fulfilled policy and professional obligations?
- *Justice ethics*: Is the innovation fair? Is the innovation equitable to all stakeholders?
- *Virtue ethics*: Does the innovation promote good character?
- *Care ethics*: Does the innovation fully recognize individuals? Is the innovation empathetic to individuals?

These perspectives may seem to offer a series of either–or choices (consequentialism *or* deontology, justice *or* virtue); this does not necessarily need to be the case and instead leads to unhelpfully restrictive frameworks within which to deal with the very practical problems faced by administrators. Although organizational ethics touches upon each of these perspectives it does not necessarily endorse any one of them as either better or worse than the others. Each perspective therefore offers insights into various ethical issues that can arise in the innovation process.

The classic *consequentialist* position of utilitarianism (as outlined by writers such as Jeremy Bentham and James Mill) invokes a debate on the greatest good for the greatest number of people. Thus a consequentialist perspective would look at the outcomes and ask who benefits of any given innovation and whether or not these are outweighed by any costs. Utility is a key aspect of the creative aspects of the innovation process. As Sternberg (1999) suggests, for any innovation to be successful requires two distinct elements: that it is both original and useful. The question of how we determine the utilitarian value of an innovation is clearly not as straightforward as Mill or Bentham may have envisaged but it does require some essential foundations: perhaps most importantly, that there is a sufficient evidence base upon which to innovate in the first place. Is the innovation one that has an expressed public value or is it innovation for its own sake? How is the utility of the innovation understood, and how is this evaluated during implementation?

A *deontological* perspective (most famously, but not exclusively, outlined by Immanuel Kant) looks at ethics through the prism of obligations rather than consequences. Kant's (2002, p. 46) second formulation of the moral law tells us to treat each other as ends rather than means: 'act so that you use humanity, as much as in your own person as in the person of every other, always at the same time as end and merely as means'. Consistency in behaviour is key: Kant not only proposes a universalist view of humanity but also a requisite moral obligation to act consistently to each of our fellow persons. To donate to one charity while ignoring others can level accusations of moral inconsistency against us, and thus making our behaviour unethical. Such debates are extremely illuminating when considering the scope of public service innovations. Policy makers and public managers cannot realistically expect to treat all stakeholders in the same way, even if they have an obligation to promote the public good. This begs the question, to whom do obligations arise? In the private sector, for example, Friedman (1970) famously exhorted that the only obligation managers have is to create maximum profits for shareholders. The same is clearly not true for public managers, and there is a much broader spectrum of stakeholders who may have a legitimate expectation that they have rights that need to be fulfilled.

The most famous modern example of *justice ethics* is Rawls's justice as fairness, which was a direct response to classical utilitarianism and an attempt to establish Kantian-like universal principles, although Rawls subsequently revised this claim. Rawls sought to establish principles of justice through a hypothetical thought experiment, the 'veil of ignorance', which removes all concrete human experience (e.g. specific cultural, social, gender, knowledge, etc.) and leads to what was termed the 'original position'. Although Rawls accepted that the thought process of the veil of ignorance was designed purely to elicit the principles of justice that the author had already identified (Rawls 1972, p. 12), the theory nevertheless poses an interesting perspective on innovation. It accepts that universalism cannot be viewed in terms of equality, as other deontological perspectives may lead, and instead works on the principle of equitability: that where people cannot be treated the same they must be treated in a way that maximizes an equitable outcome for all; an interesting variant on the utility calculus expounded above. A veil of ignorance is, to some extent, what any innovation is forged in: even with the strongest evidence implementing something new will, inevitably, pose a risk of failure. Along with the risk, however, is the potential for unintended consequences and – a greater ethical challenge – perverse incentives. Innovation for its own sake (Jennings 2008) can become self-propelling in organizations that are desperate to be ahead of the game and can lead to risk taking that is either excessive or unchecked (Mainelli 2010; see also Mullen 2004 for perverse incentives and performance).

To take such risks, however, often requires a particular mindset, which leads on to the perspective of *virtue ethics*. Aristotle offered the original (Western) concept of public virtue, which inextricably linked morality to political life through the application of practical wisdom. 'Political wisdom and practical wisdom are the same state of mind, but their essence is not the same' (1947, 1141b, pp. 25–30). Machiavelli praised the *virtù* of political leaders, which was more closely related to the notion of the virtuoso rather than the virtuous (Wootton 1994), and thus denoted more general skills and excellences pertaining to leadership, including military prowess, diplomatic sensitivity, an understanding of one's subjects' characters, and so on. The most striking modern variant has been MacIntyre's *After Virtue*, which infamously depicted the character of the modern bureaucratic manager as distinctively lacking in virtue (1885). MacIntyre argues that whether operating in a private or public organization, the bureaucratic manager relies on a system of knowledge that promotes efficiency and effectiveness, which looks at controlling means rather than ends. There is little, if any, room for moral debate therefore. MacIntyre accordingly portrays managers not as omniscient and all-powerful but as impotent, affecting their organizations despite rather than because of the managerial expertise.

These are important perspectives for a number of reasons. First, commentators have started using virtue as a means by which to develop the notion of ethical competency (Bowman et al. 2004; Macaulay and Lawton 2006). Secondly, the concept of practical wisdom is closely aligned with that of pragmatism, which, as has been argued recently, is an ideal philosophy for dealing with the 'prescriptions and dynamic conditions' that are prevalent in public service innovations (Emison 2010, p. 3). Finally, and perhaps the most challenging aspect of all, is the problem of what Jennings (2006) labels the 'innovative personality', whose inherent strengths (dynamism, creativity, risk taking, action oriented) become potential ethical liabilities. Jennings demonstrates, for example, that the innovations at Enron were frequently justified on the grounds that those undertaking them were on the 'side of the angels', and suggests that the personality type exhibits consistent over-confidence and an exaggerated sense of being able to control external events.

These ideas reflect an older concern with the entrepreneurial personality (see, for example, Lessem 1996 for the conflation of the entrepreneurial and innovative personality types), which has been equated with social deviancy (Kets de Vries 1977, 1985, 1991; also Zaleznik and Kets de Vries 1975; McKenna 1996). The research in these areas does not suggest that innovators (or entrepreneurs) are bad or immoral people; rather, their character traits can lead towards a belief that the usual rules of engagement need not apply to them, and any form of regulation comes to be regarded as unnecessary restriction. The virtue ethics perspective thus asks innovators to look at the character traits that lie behind motivations for innovation.

Finally, *care ethics* has developed out of feminist theory (Gilligan 1982; Noddings 1984; Benhabib 1993) and argues that ethical decisions are founded in concrete relationships rather than abstract reasoning. To care is to be able to self-reflect and display empathy for the moral dilemmas that others face: it is therefore concerned directly with the context of a particular issue (the 'concrete-other') rather than a reliance on universal principles (the 'abstract-other'). In this way care ethics embraces the perspectives identified above but argues that without reference to concrete situations, each of them lacks explanatory power. Care inevitably moves into consequentialism, for example, but only insofar as it looks at very specific consequences: it cannot be used in the same way as Bentham's utility calculus but as a means of assessing costs/benefits in a specific situation. Similarly, care ethics opposes the notions of universal obligations posted by deontological reasoning, although it would still look at rights as one of the factors affecting moral decision making. Care ethics seeks fairness, but is against the abstraction of concrete humanity that Rawls's justice ethics requires. It has recently been argued that this approach is ideally suited to the ethical dilemmas of innovation (Fuglsang and Mattsson 2009) although it is acknowledged that it inevitably offers a partial ethical theory.

INNOVATION DILEMMAS AND FAULT LINES

The ability to innovate is increasingly viewed as the single most important factor in developing and sustaining competitive advantage (Tidd et al. 2001). It is no longer adequate to do things better; it is about 'doing new and better things' (Slater and Narver 1994). Due to the fast-paced, changing nature of the modern knowledge-based economy the question of 'newness' becomes pertinent. Varis and Littunen (2010) suggest that merely associating innovation with the term 'newness' asks a further question of 'new to whom or new in what way?'

Although it is fair to say that most innovation literature is still based on research into the private sector, studies of public sector innovation have become increasingly important. Osborne (2010) has recently argued that much new public management (NPM) research has effectively been misplaced, relying on manufacturing concepts instead of more suitable services management literature. This orientation has been particularly acute in the realm of public sector innovation, which focusses upon the innovation of processes rather than products or services themselves (Osborne 2010, p. 6). Nevertheless, important strides have been made into classifying and understanding the nature of public services innovation; for example, Osborne and Brown's (2005) classification of innovation in public services (regular innovation, niche-creation innovation, revolutionary innovation, architectural innovation). Savory (2009) looks at innovations in the NHS and argues that much public innovation is about process rather than product. He distinguishes between continuous and discontinuous innovation (Savory 2009, p. 152), and also suggests that public service innovation can still be imitative: what may be innovative in the NHS can be regarded as an established practice in other areas. Indeed, most innovations are adaptations from external sources rather than the creation of people within the health service.

Drucker (1986) argues that there are seven sources of innovation. Some innovation can come from a spark of genius; however, most innovation comes as a result of a conscious search for innovation opportunities and in any case can be categorized into internal sources and external sources of innovation. The four internal drivers for innovation can be: unexpected occurrences, incongruities, process needs, and industry and market changes. Three further opportunities for innovation can be highlighted and sourced as being external to the organization, namely demographic changes, changes in perception and acquisition of new knowledge.

The sources of innovation can be related directly to the three output categories of innovation: product, process and organizational. The ability to discover and systematically engage with a conscious search for innovation is essential. The ability to uncover sources of innovation can be directly related to an organization's capabilities and resources. In this way it can be argued that organizations need to be structured in a way that supports innovation. It is also suggested that culture plays a major role in an organization's ability to innovate or adopt innovation (El Sawy et al. 2001).

Innovation theory has historically converged around two core themes of process innovation and product innovation. Product innovation refers to the development and introduction of new or improved products and/or services that are successful in the market (Neely et al. 2001). This form of innovation is often the most obvious innovation for consumer groups as the tangible nature of the product innovation makes it simple to understand. The second typology of innovation, process innovation, refers to the adoption of improving methods that enhance the manufacturing, delivery and distribution levels of service. It is argued that the implementation of a process of innovation requires a supportive organizational structure (Humphreys et al. 2005). Tidd et al. (2001) suggest that the most innovative organizations are those that find a strategic fit between structure, operating contingencies and flexibility. This can be a challenging process, particularly in larger organizations, given the often complex organizational structures and policies.

These two areas offer a wide scope in which innovations can be of a large or micro scale and the effects of the innovation can be measured through increased customer satisfaction, profitability and sales.

Research is further developing, and it involves the concept of organizational innovation (Bates and Flynn 1995). Neely et al. (2001, p. 115) state that: 'Organisational innovation can result in the more effective use of human and physical resources.' Due to the current economic climate, innovation has been seen as a method to achieve sustained competitive advantage, and as such much emphasis has been placed on building innovative organizations and the management of the innovation process as essential elements of organizational survival. For organizations to achieve innovation, in any of its forms, they must first understand the potential sources of innovation, and secondly must be able to develop a process to enable innovation.

Endless innovation has recently been identified as one of the seven signs of ethical collapse in both public and private sector organizations (along with a larger-than-life CEO; a weak board; an organizational culture beset with fear and silence; unrelenting conflicts; mitigating unethical behaviour with some good actions; and the pressure on maintaining numbers (Jennings 2008)). In addition innovation can cause unease and fear among a workforce; for example, innovations in technology may be perceived as removing skills or even leading to the demise of entire organizations. Many of the potential ethical fault lines found in innovation, however, relate to process rather than product innovation. Although there are some classic dilemmas to consider (whether or not, for example, Einstein was ultimately responsible for the deaths at Hiroshima and Nagasaki), product innovation is, by and large, less ethically challenging in the public service context.

With its emphasis on accountability and transparency, organizational ethics is sometimes regarded as diametrically opposed to innovation. Where innovation needs room to be flexible, ethics encases in rules and regulations. Innovation requires speed, ethics requires reflection. Emison (2010) argues that the public service ethos is one that is cautious and risk averse, which puts it against the entrepreneurial tendencies of the innovator. Such risk aversion is frequently the default position of many organizations in regard to ethics. There is an emphasis on simply staying within the law and only implementing the minimal levels of ethical compliance: there is an emphasis on avoiding harm rather than doing good (Cameron 2006). Some theorists have recently posited that the distinctions between public and private sector values are becoming increasingly aligned (see, for example, Van der Wal et al, 2008; Malloy and Agarwal 2010), but the perceived difference between different sectors is crucially important to questions of organizational ethics because the supposed clash of culture (between public and private) forms perhaps the most significant fault line between ethics and innovation.

The appeal for organizations to innovate either processes, products or the organization as a whole drives many organizations forward and research has suggested that an organization's capacity to innovate has a positive influence on organizational performance (Low et al. 2007). However, there is also a range of issues that make innovation both difficult to develop and manage (Oster 2010). A review of the literature highlights a range of areas for innovation dilemmas, including managing the innovation process, leadership of innovation and developing innovative capabilities.

Most of the research focusses on barriers towards injecting innovation or developing innovation within an organization. Christensen and Raynor (2003) highlight another major dilemma caused by innovation, suggesting that most organizations are concerned with sustaining/incremental innovation in the beginning but that success often causes them to move from incremental innovation to disruptive innovation, normally in pursuit of competitive advantage, increased profits are a combination of the two. This often causes major issues as disruptive innovation can be seen as a mechanism that takes the organization away from a customer orientation. Many ethical and value-based issues lie at the centre of innovation theory and more importantly at the heart of a range of innovation dilemmas.

One of the organizations that managed to beat the innovation dilemma highlighted by Christensen was Apple, which did so by focusing on two core themes: staying true to the business mission and bending the 'traditional' rules of disruptive innovation. These two elements, although being distinctively unique, were at the core of Apple's widely reported recovery from near bankruptcy to becoming one of the most influential organizations in the world. Apple saw innovation not as a way to drive profits but as a way to develop great products/services and its own organization. It beat Christensen's innovation dilemma through believing in a focussed mission and vision and not through using innovation as merely a profit-generating strategic initiative.

The question now becomes, therefore, how best to bring together the different perspectives offered in the organizational ethics literature and the ideas prevalent in innovation studies.

ETHICAL INNOVATION

As previously mentioned, perhaps the most significant innovation dilemma and ethics is the perceived clash of cultural values between the bureaucratic needs of public management and the entrepreneurial requirement of innovation. Golembiewski and Vigoda (cited in Vigoda-Gadot et al. 2008) argue that the values of innovation and bureaucracy are fundamentally opposed, and that attempts to innovate within a bureaucratic structure are doomed to fail (see also Borins 2001; Vigoda-Gadot et al. 2008). The public services' reliance on hierarchy, accountability and control is regarded as anathema to the need for creativity and dynamism required by the innovator. Pärna and von Tunzelmann (2007, p. 109) share the same concerns: 'Many people believe that the very notion of an innovative government is paradoxical. Innovation is presumed to thrive in dynamic, flexible business enterprises and not in rigid, bureaucratic government organisations.' Marsh and Edwards (2009, p. 410), citing Australian federal government's experiences of policy innovations, identify three specific obstacles that affect the public sector exclusively: the political nature of such innovations; the complexity of dealing with a multi-agency approach; and 'the capacity of a sensationalist media to hobble innovative proposals'. Moore (2005) suggests that there is a greater risk of failed innovations being punished in the public sector, which develops a more risk-averse approach.

In a sense these concerns reflect the supposed cultural divisions identified in the earliest NPM literature over the compatibility of values of public and private sector organization (e.g. Dunleavy and Hood 1994). The difference in such values was thought to create new grey areas in which ethical dilemmas could emerge; for example, in public/private partnerships (Lawton and Doig 2006).

Recent research has begun to suggest, however, that such concerns can be successfully resolved. Pärna and von Tunzelmann (2007) have demonstrated that although there are differences between the *motivation* for public and private innovation adoption, the principal drivers remain the same: both require strong institutional support; rely on organizational learning from both external and internal sources; and the success of the innovation is often predicated on the strength of leadership behind it. Wu (2005) argues that the impact of ethics legislation such as the US *Foreign Corrupt Practices Act* has effectively forced private businesses to become innovative in the way they self-regulate. Similarly, Mehanna and Yazbeck (2008) have suggested that organizational ethics and innovation converge in relation to economic prosperity. In short, the goals of public and private innovations are not polarized even if the institutional arrangements behind them differ: the potential ethical fault line is, therefore, not as wide as may commonly be suspected.

Ethics and innovation have been linked by the very useful framework provided by Harting et al. (2006), who map organizations (defined as innovative or imitative) against stakeholders (defined as exploitative or supportive). In so doing they describe four different intersections: destructive innovation, garden variety corruption, ethical engagement and ethical innovation. Destructive innovation (innovative/stakeholder exploitative) charts innovative behaviour that succeeds in gaining competitive advantage but at a palpable cost to stakeholders involved; the most obvious example would be criminal business activity such as the illegal drug trade. Garden variety corruption (imitative/ stakeholder exploitative) occurs when the exploitation is known and understood, and a number of competing organizations imitate each other in following the practice. There is nothing new about any one organization's actions but rather there is a mutual cycle of unethical conduct. Ethical engagement (imitative/stakeholder supportive) explains the usual notion of following rules and regulations, without extending or developing new practices from within. Ethical innovation (innovative/stakeholder supportive) occurs when organizations create new avenues by which to improve ethically, most commonly in terms of environmental practices such as waste management, and which offers competitive advantage as a result (Harting et al. 2006).

This is a useful starting point for bringing ethics and innovation together but the focus on stakeholder exploitation/support is very much in the consequentialist mode, and looks at the external impacts that innovations may bring. What is missing is an understanding of the internal conditions of organizations under which ethical innovation can develop in the first place. To do so, we can use another perspective from the organizational ethics literature: the continuum of compliance and integrity continuum (e.g. Skelcher and Snape 2001; Lewis and Gilman 2005; Macaulay and Lawton 2006; Lawton and Macaulay 2009). A compliance approach focusses upon accountability mechanisms and regulation to promote an ethical culture (e.g. code of conduct, protocols, etc.): it is usually a legalistic outlook that is reactive and implements the minimum standard of whatever laws are proscribed. An integrity-based organization has a more proactive approach to ethical conduct, which relies on developing individuals rather than rules. It promotes ethics as an essential component of all major organizational activity (e.g. HR policy, marketing) and has clear alignment between organizational values and everyday practice.

We can map the innovative/imitative spectrum onto the compliance/integrity continuum as shown in Figure 16.1. This matrix suggests not only that innovation and ethics can be linked, but that the development of each can lead to mutual benefits. An organization that is characterized by *reactive regulation* (Compliance/Imitation) is one that will simply follow whatever external directives (legislation, codes of conduct, etc.) are enforced upon it. A *best practice* (Integrity/Imitation) organization will adapt the ethical practices of other organizations but will not necessarily think of its own approach. A *new*

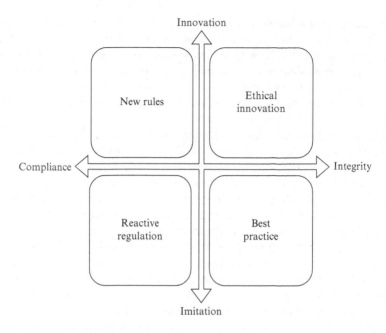

Figure 16.1   The innovation ethics matrix

rules (Compliance/Innovation) organization will innovate, but generally in regard to regulations and compliance mechanisms: for example adopting a voluntary code of conduct. An *ethical innovator* (Integrity/Innovation) will develop new ways of taking ethics forward. It is characterized by ethical leadership and organizational learning, so that the risk inherent in innovation can be mitigated against by learning from failure and building on success.

CONCLUSION: THE RANGE OF THE POSSIBLE?

Hofstede and Hofstede (2005) suggested that organizational culture looks to the range of the possible and we suggest that this can be extended into the arena of ethical innovation. We began this chapter with the oft-repeated assertion that ethics and innovation are somehow in opposition, or even a paradox. Hopefully we now see that they in effect act as counterweights to one another: the restrictions of each of the five ethical perspectives put forward show the limitations in the scope of nature of public service innovations. The dynamism and creativity inherent in innovation allow us to consistently adapt and develop our sense of ways in which we can define and expand on the nature of the public good and civic morality. We are not the first to make this connection. Vigoda-Gadot et al. (2008, p. 325), for example, have argued that the 'creation of an appropriate ethical and moral climate' is crucial to improving public sector innovation. Jennings (2008, p. 204) has suggested that 'innovation without the other tools of business, including ethics and those antidotes for this sign [of ethical collapse] and the others, is a common thread in companies that experience ethical collapse'.

Innovation can, therefore, be implemented in conjunction with proper control and accountability mechanisms, but these cannot be allowed to conflict: the straitjacket of traditional bureaucracy can be equally as destructive as unfettered innovation. The crucial aspect is to achieve a balance that allows creative solutions to flourish rather than mutate. We suggest that the tension between organizational ethics and innovation is better understood as a tension between compliance models of ethics and innovation. Indeed, adopting an integrity approach, rather than a compliance approach, allows an ethical approach to public service innovation to flourish. Far from being polar opposites, the relationship between ethics and innovation can be, therefore, mutually beneficial to public service organizations.

REFERENCES

Aristotle (1947). *Nicomachean Ethics,* translated by W.D. Ross. New York: Random House.

Baxter, D., Schoeman, M., Goffin, K. and Micheli, P. (2010). *The Role of Commercial Partnerships.* Cranfield: Cranfield School of Management.

Benhabib, S. (1993). *Situating the Self.* London: Routledge.

Borins, S. (2001). Encouraging innovation in the public sector. *Journal of Intellectual Capital,* 2(3), 310–319.

Bowman, J., West, J.P., Berman, E.M. and Van Wart, M. (2004). *The Professional Edge Competencies in Public Service.* New York: M.E. Sharpe.

Brenkert, G.G. (2009). Innovation, rule breaking and the ethics of entrepreneurship. *Journal of Business Venturing,* 24(3), 448–464.

Cameron, K. (2006). Good or not bad: standards and ethics in managing change. *Journal of Management Learning,* 5(3), 317–323.

Christensen, C. and Raynor, P. (2003). *The Innovator's Solution.* New York: Harvard Business Press.

Drucker, P.F. (1985). The discipline of innovation. *Harvard Business Review,* 63(3), 67–72.

Dunleavy, P. and Hood, C. (1994). From old public administration to new public management. *Public Money and Management,* 14(3), 9–16.

El Sawy, O., Eriksson, I., Raven, A. and Carlsson, S. (2001). Understanding shared knowledge creation spaces around business processes: precursors to process innovation implementation. *International Journal of Technology Management,* 22(1), 149–173.

Emison, G.A. (2010). Ethics of innovation for public service professionals. *The Innovation Journal: The Public Sector Innovation Journal,* 15(3). Available at: http://www.innovation.cc/volumes-issues/vol15-no3.htm (accessed 1 September 2012).

Friedman, M. (1970). The social responsibility of business is to increase profits. *New York Times Magazine,* 13 September.

Fuglsang, L. and Mattsson, J. (2009). An integrative model of care ethics in public innovation. *Services Industries Journal,* 29(1), 21–34.

Gilligan, C. (1982). *In a Different Voice.* Cambridge, MA: Harvard University Press.

Glor, E.G. (2003). Innovation traps: risks and challenges in thinking about innovation. *The Innovation Journal: The Public Sector Innovation Journal,* 8(3). Available at: http://www.innovation.cc/volumes-issues/vol8-iss3_ethics.htm (accessed 1 September 2012).

Greene, I. (2003). The ethics of innovation and the development of innovative projects. *The Innovation Journal: The Public Sector Innovation Journal,* 8(3), 1–13.

Harting, T.R., Harmeling, S.S. and Venkataraman, S. (2006). Innovative stakeholder relations: when 'ethics pays' (and when it doesn't). *Business Ethics Quarterly,* 16(1), 43–68.

Hofstede, G. and Hofstede, G.J. (2005). *Cultures and Organizations: Software of the Mind.* New York: McGraw Hill.

Hull, R. (2000). Ethics, innovation and innovation studies. *Technology Analysis and Strategic Management,* 12(3), 349–355.

Humphreys, P., McAdam, R. and Leckey, J. (2005). Longitudinal evaluation of innovation implementation in SMEs. *European Journal of Innovation Management,* 8(3), 283–304.

Jennings, M. (2006). *The Seven Signs of Ethical Collapse.* New York: St Martin's Press.

Kant, I. (2002). *Groundwork for the Metaphysics of Morals,* trans. A.W. Wood. New Haven, CT: Yale University Press.

Kets de Vries, M.F.R. (1977). The entrepreneurial personality: a person at the crossroads. *Journal of Management Studies*, 1, 34–57.

Kets de Vries, M.F.R. (1985). The dark side of entrepreneurship. *Harvard Business Review*, November–December, 160–167.

Kets de Vries, M.F.R. (1989). Leaders who self-destruct: the causes and cures. *Organizational Dynamics*, 17(4), 5–17.

Kets de Vries, M.F.R. (1991). Whatever happened to the philosopher king? The leader's addiction to power. *Journal of Management Studies*, 28(4), 339–351.

Lawton, A. and Doig, R.A. (2006). Researching ethics for public service organizations: the view from Europe. *Public Integrity*, 8(1), 11–33.

Lawton, A. and Macaulay, M. (2009). Ethics management and ethical management. In R. Cox III (ed.), *Ethics and Integrity in Public Administration: Cases and Concepts*. New York: M.E. Sharpe, pp. 107–120.

Lessem, R. (1996). *Intrapreneurship: How to be a Successful Individual in a Successful Business*. Aldershot: Wildwood House.

Lewis, C. and Gilman, S. (2005). *The Ethics Challenge in Public Service: A Problem Solving Guide*, 2nd edition. New York: Wiley.

Low, D.R., Chapman, R.L. and Sloan, T.R. (2007). Inter-relationships between innovation and market orientation in SMEs. *Management Research News*, 30(12), 878–891.

Macaulay, M. and Lawton, A. (2006). From virtue to competence – changing the principles of public service? *Public Administration Review*, 66(5), 1–9.

Machan, T.R. (1999). Entrepreneurship and ethics. *International Journal of Social Economics*, 26(5), 596–609.

MacIntyre, Alasdair (1985). *After Virtue*, 2nd edition. London: Duckworth.

Mainelli, M. (2010). Failure is not an option: perverse incentives. *Journal of Risk Finance*, 10(1), 91–94.

Malloy, D.C. and Agarwal, J. (2010). Ethical climate in government and nonprofit sectors: public policy implications for service delivery. *Journal of Business Ethics*, 94, 3–21.

Marsh, I. and Edwards, L. (2009). Dilemmas of policy innovation in the public sector: a case study of the National Innovation Summit. *Australian Journal of Public Administration*, 68(4), 399–413.

McKenna, S.D. (1996). The darker side of the entrepreneur. *Leadership and Organization Development Journal*, 17(6), 41–45.

Mehanna, R.A. and Yazbeck, Y. (2008). Business innovation, ethics and prosperity: the primacy of microeconomics. *Journal of Business Strategies*, 26(2), 1–17.

Miles, M.P., Munilla, L.S. and Covin, J.G. (2004). Innovation, ethics and entrepreneurship. *Journal of Business Ethics*, 54, 97–101.

Moore, M.H. (2005). Break-through innovations and continuous improvement: two different models of innovative processes in the public sector. *Public Money and Management*, 1, 43–50.

Mullen, P. (2004). Using performance indicators to improve performance. *Health Services Management Research*, 17(4), 217–228.

Neely, A., Filipini, R., Forza, C., Vinelli, A. and Hii, J. (2001). A framework for analysing business performance, firm innovation and related contextual factors: perceptions of managers and policy makers in two European regions. *Integrated Manufacturing Systems*, 12(2), 114–124.

Noddings, N. (1984). *Caring: A Feminine Approach to Ethics and Moral Education*. Berkeley, CA: University of California Press.

Osborne, S. (2010). Delivering public services: time for a new theory? *Public Management Review*, 12(1), 1–10.

Osborne, S. and Brown, K. (2005). *Managing Change and Innovation in Public Service Organisations*. London: Routledge.

Oster, G. (2010). Characteristics of emergent innovation. *Journal of Management Development*, 29(6), 565–574.

Pärna, O. and Von Tunzelmann, N. (2007). Innovation in the public sector: key features influencing the development and implementation of technologically innovative public sector services in the UK, Denmark, Finland and Estonia. *Information Polity*, 12, 109–125.

Rawls, J. (1972). *A Theory of Justice*. Oxford: Oxford University Press.

Savory, C. (2009). Building knowledge transition capability into public sector innovation processes. *Technology Analysis and Strategic Management*, 21(2), 149–171.

Skelcher, C. and Snape, S. (2001). *Political Executives and the New Ethical Framework*. Birmingham: INLOGOV.

Slater, S.F. and Narver, J.C. (1994). Market orientation and the learning organization. *Journal of Marketing*, 59(3), 63–74.

Sternberg, R. (ed.) (1999). *Handbook of Creativity*. Cambridge: Cambridge University Press.

Tidd, J., Bessant, J. and Pavitt, K. (2001). *Managing Innovation: Integrating Technological, Market and Organisational Change*. Bognor Regis: Wiley.

Van der Wal, Z., de Graaf, G. and Lasthuizen, K. (2008). What's valued most? Similarities and differences between the organizational values of the public and private sector. *Public Administration*, 86(2), 465–482.

Varis, M. and Littunen, H. (2010). Types of innovation, sources of information and performance in entrepre-neurial SME's. *European Journal of Innovation Management*, 13(2), 128–154.

Vigoda-Gadot, E., Shoham, A., Schwabsky, N. and Ruvio, A. (2008). Public sector innovation for Europe: a multinational eight-country exploration of citizens' perspectives. *Public Administration*, 86(2), 307–329.

Windrum, P. and Koch, P. (2008). *Innovation in Public Sector Services*. Cheltenham and Northampton, MA: Edward Elgar.

Wootton, D. (1994). 'Introduction'. In *Selected Political Writings*. Indianapolis: Hackett Publishing.

Wu, X. (2005). Corporate governance and corruption: a cross country analysis. *Governance*, 18, 151–170.

Zaleznik, A. and Kets de Vries, M.F.R. (1975). What makes entrepreneurs entrepreneurial? *Business and Society Review*, 17, 18–21.

PART IV

ICT, E-GOVERNMENT AND INNOVATION

17. E-government and innovation: the socio-political shaping of ICT as a source of innovation
Victor Bekkers

INTRODUCTION

'My Administration is committed to creating an unprecedented level of openness in Government. We will work together to ensure the public trust and establish a system of transparency, public participation, and collaboration. Openness will strengthen our democracy and promote efficiency and effectiveness in Government.' These were the opening lines of the statement of President Obama of the United States when he launched his Open Government Initiative on 21 January 2009. In his view information and communication technology (ICT) had to play an important role to innovate government in this way. ICT is considered as a major source of innovation.

In this chapter I analyse the innovation potential of e-government for the modernization of public administration and assess the kind of innovations that e-government has brought to the organization and functioning of public administration. E-government can be described as the use of ICT to design new or redesign existing information, communication and transaction relationships between governments and citizens, companies and non-governmental organizations as well as between different government organizations and layers in order to achieve specific goals. Relevant goals are the improvement of the access to government, the enhancement of the quality and efficiency of public service delivery processes, the improvement of internal and external efficiency, the support of public and political accountability, the support of the political participation of citizens and the strengthening of interorganizational cooperation (OECD 2003; Moon 2004). E-governance, a term often used in this context, can be seen as the governance of the conditions to achieve these goals (Dawes 2008).

In the next section I will explore the innovation potential of e-government. I will argue that the innovation potential of e-government is partly defined by a number of relevant characteristics that are embedded in the technologies to be used. However, these characteristics are not given. They are not neutral, because they are shaped by the interactions of stakeholders who are involved in the development and introduction of these technologies. I then address the major changes that e-government has brought to public administration by looking at a number of different innovations and discuss some barriers to be broken. However, electronic government is also changing the governance potential of government in two profound ways. These ways will be sketched in the fourth section. In the final section some conclusions will be drawn.

THE INNOVATION POTENTIAL OF E-GOVERNMENT

Innovation refers to a process of creative destruction in which new combinations arise that depend on the exploration and exploitation of new and existing resources; combinations that represent a discontinuity with the past, with existing practices (Schumpeter 1942; March 1999; Osborne and Brown 2005). One of these resources is technology. What is the innovation potential of ICT? One step is to look at a number of relevant technological developments.

Some Technological Developments

What are currently relevant technological developments that help understanding of the innovation potential of ICT, and thus will influence the shaping of e-government?

First, and also looking at the history of computing, we notice that the processing capacity of computers is still increasing (in terms of speed), which facilitates the handling of large quantities of data which become larger and larger. This also depends on the increased memory capacities of computers. This development is also known as Moore's law. Moreover, we also notice that computers and other related technologies have become *smaller* and *smaller*.

Secondly, technologies to be used and the content which they carry have become more *integrated*, due to two developments. The first development refers to the process of digitization. The data that not only books, documents, speeches, communications but also pictures, videos and films contain can be translated in digitized data, which have two major advantages (Castells 1996). These data can be transported much more easily and they can be manipulated much more easily, so that data (and their carriers) can be integrated much more easily into new information (and new carriers). Moreover, digitization facilitates the exchange of these data, all over the world. Also the development of so-called 'open standards' and 'open source software' helps to link and integrate data, infrastructures and applications much more easily. On the one hand, standards facilitate integration because software and hardware applications can 'talk' to each other, while on the other hand standards frustrate integration, if applications are based on different standards (which leads to all kinds of incompatibilities) and companies are not willing to share their computing source code (e.g. Microsoft versus Apple). Open standards and open source software are based on a development process that takes place in open and decentralized communities of peers in which ideas regarding and changes in the computing code are based on trial and error, a free flow of ideas and peer review. This code (as a source of knowledge) is open and thus accessible to everybody who wants to use it. An example is the Linux software (Bekkers 2003).

The second development refers to the fact that the essence of these new technologies is their capacity to link. Network technology like the internet makes it possible to connect people to other people, information and knowledge sources. Geographical, physical, functional and temporal boundaries are no longer hurdles which have to be overcome in order to have access to information, to share this information or to communicate with people (Castells 1996). Presence availability as a necessary condition for effective coordination can be organized online and in real time. An example is the use of social media, like Facebook and Twitter, in the organization of the protests that took place in many

Arabic countries, including Egypt, in the Spring of 2011. Moreover, people in Europe and America almost got a real-time account of the events that took place in the streets of Cairo and Tunis: boundaries did not play a significant role.

Thirdly, ICT has become more *open* and more *interactive*. As a result some people talk about 'the social internet' or 'Web 2.0'. The social and interactive nature of Web 2.0 is what distinguishes it from the older generation (Web 1.0), which is more static and supply oriented. Examples are social networks like Twitter, Facebook or Linked-In but blogs, wickis and mash-ups can also be mentioned. These applications emphasize the importance of user participation, openness and network effects (Boulos and Wheeler 2007; Stanyer 2009). Users are no longer the passive consumers of content; they have become co-creators. As a result, an organic and flexible process of open content production, collaboration and content sharing occurs (Benkler 2006). Relevant content to be shared can be information, knowledge, contacts, photos, video and experiences. Network effects emerge because the network's added value increases for its users with the number of users that make use of it; because new information, knowledge, contacts or experiences are added to the existing ones. This opens the door to new social practices that are closely interwoven with the open and interactive nature of these new technologies. An example is 'crowd sourcing'. Crowd sourcing tries to exploit the scattered knowledge and experience (especially people, information and data sources) – the intelligence – that is present on the internet by bringing it together, in relation to a specific goal or problem to be solved. The underlying idea is that a group of people know more than a single person, especially if people bring in different sources of knowledge and experiences, and thus different perspectives. The challenge is to confront and link these perspectives to each other so that new perspectives emerge. This idea is also known as 'the wisdom of crowds' (Surowiecki 2004). For instance, Brabham (2008) reports on how crowd sourcing has been used to support the participation of citizens and the generation of ideas in urban and transit planning.

Fourthly, ICT has become more *mobile*, due to its tendency to become smaller and more integrated. Instantaneity has become more important. People like to have instant access, at any time and in any place, to relevant information and people. As a result advanced mobile technologies create new services, which are called location or area-based services. These are services which are provided, if a citizen enters a specific area or stands in a specific location. For instance, he/she is able to acquire tourist information (monuments, hotels, restaurants) at the moment that he/she is in a specific spot. Hence, a new form of e-government may emerge, which is called mobile (m-) government.

Fifthly, technologies have become increasingly *visual*. First, due to the multimedia character of ICT, we see that ICT is not only used for word processing and data calculations; it is also used to make, manipulate and watch photos, films and videos. A typical example is the internet telephone, which cannot only be used to phone, but also to send small text messages, to search on the internet, to e-mail, to make use of Twitter or Facebook, to make pictures and videos, to listen to the radio, to listen to music which has been downloaded from the internet, and so on. As a result, our mobile phone has been upgraded to advanced multimedia application. Secondly, we see that gaming in which users actually create, participate in and manipulate visual events has become popular. For instance, in the Netherlands gaming technologies are provided to citizens to redesign their own neighbourhood. Thirdly, the access to geographical information and geo-graphical information systems (GIS) has also pushed the desire to visualize information that can also be used for simulation purposes. Moreover, GIS makes it easy to link data sets, if these data sets share a location-based information element. An example is Google Maps, which not only shows relevant restaurants in a neighbourhood, but also shows where road blocks can be found. Another example is the visualization of the crime rates and types of crime in neighbourhoods. Pictures have the advantage that they can combine all kinds of data regarding complex issues and visualize them, so that the information provided can be understood in an easy, integrated and transparent way. The last type of technology is the use of digital cameras that record and register the behaviour of people in streets, squares and buildings, like CCTV cameras. Also webcams can be mentioned. Due to webcams, nurses can provide the necessary (feedback) information to sick or elderly people (e.g. diabetics, people with heart disease) about their medical treatment without having to visit them.

Sixthly, ICT has become more *embedded*, due to the use of microchips. Hence, it is possible to add a specific form of intelligence to objects like goods, people, locations and movements without being visible, which can be monitored. The necessary information can be read from a distance. An example is Radio Frequency Identification (RFID) tags which, for instance, are used to follow the whereabouts of containers that are being shipped. These chips not only make it possible to identify people, goods and flows but they also give information about their location and movements. For instance, in the Netherlands the police use bikes that are fitted with RFID tags that they can follow in order to deal with the massive theft of bikes.

Seventhly, ICT is also increasingly being used for *identification* purposes, especially in relation to the use of biometrical data. In a global world – in which economic, social, cultural and political activities and corresponding interactions between people become flexible and fluid while at the same time there is an increased feeling of anxiety and fear (e.g. the war on terrorism) – governments find it very important to establish the identity of people (but also that of houses and companies). In order to answer the question 'who is who', not only is residential information important, but also person-specific, and thus unique, information is being used. Examples are DNA information, face recognition and iris scan-based information and fingerprint information.

Last but not least, there is the *semantic* web, also called Web 3.0. 'Semantic web' refers to the proactive and integrated presentation of information that is present on the World Wide Web and that might be of interest to you as a consumer or citizen. Advanced data mining and profiling techniques are used to create highly personalized services. The pres-entation of these data is done by intelligent robots and is based on the meanings in which these robots think you might be interested. What does this mean? If you look for 'e-government' in Google you will get a large list of links that contain relevant informa-tion. Semantic web will give you all the relevant information about e-government (without links) according to the meanings that you have in your mind, when referring to e-government, based on meanings you previously gave to e-government as they can be understood from your previous search behaviour and preferences.

However, these developments stress specific features which play an important role in the (re-) design of the relationships between government, citizens and companies. They are also an indication of the innovation potential of ICT.

Main Characteristics

If we look at the main characteristics which are embedded in the technology that is used for e-government purposes, a number of characteristics are relevant (Bekkers 1998).

First, we can look at the *calculation* and *transaction* potential of these technologies. ICT makes it possible to compute (literally, in terms of calculation) large amounts of data in more sophisticated ways. Very often these calculations are related to transactions that take place. A classical e-government example is the digital filing and assessment of taxes. Another example is the calculation program, often in combination with the electronic forms to be filled in, that gives you an indication of the amount of benefits you might receive when applying.

Secondly, *access* and *transparency* can be mentioned. ICT makes it possible to have access to relevant information, knowledge and persons. It is possible 24 hours per day and 7 days per week to download relevant information in order to apply for a social benefit or a building permit. Access to specific information or databases facilitates also the transparency of government, so that citizens can get a better understanding about, for instance, the results of primary schools. This better understanding can also be achieved when specific data are matched – within a database or between databases. Data mining and profiling are examples of this desire to achieve transparency, for instance in order to attack fraud or to develop more tailor-made services.

Thirdly, *transparency* often opens the door to discipline and control behaviour. ICT is used to control people, organizations or movements – not only because their behaviour can be watched or reconstructed (for instance through the matching of data), but also because the use of ICT presupposes standardization and formalization of communication and information exchange and processing processes and activities. This can also be seen as a way of disciplining behaviour. For instance, one goal of the electronic filing of taxes is that tax administration is able to control the quality of the information that is given by citizens and companies in a better and more efficient way: wrong or insufficient information can be detected in advance, which helps to reduce the chance that mistakes or miscalculations occur.

Fourthly, *communication* is another feature. E-mail and instant messaging programs in combination with the network character of ICT make it possible that government and citizens communicate with each other, in order to exchange and share questions, opinions, knowledge and views. For instance, citizens can be invited to participate in a digital platform or a discussion group which is set up by government to discuss the reconstruction plans for a neighbourhood, or they can be invited to express their opinions and thoughts about how to improve the quality of specific service-delivery processes.

The last relevant characteristic is *visualization* and *simulation*. ICT can be used to visualize specific events and developments – in combination with graphics, gaming technology and specific (geographical) data sets – in order to make them more transparent. For instance, ICT helps to show what the effects of specific government measures would be in order to provoke discussion and deliberation. Simulation technology in combination with geographical information systems can be used, for example, to show citizens and other relevant stakeholders what the effects of global warming will be for their region, especially if this region is below sea-level.

However, these characteristics are not given and neutral. For instance, transparency and control may have different meanings for the tax and customs administration than for (dis)obedient taxpaying citizens and companies. Therefore, it will be hardly any surprise that tax administrations try to influence the kind and degree of transparency and control in such a way that ICT serves their needs and interests. ICT is not only used as a set of tools but also as a powerful resource to politically shape e-government practices.

E-government as the Socio-political Shaping of Technology

The assumption behind many e-government policies is that technology is a neutral tool in the hands of policy makers who can determine what effects can be accomplished if they have clear goals in mind and are able to control and manage the environment in which these tools are being introduced and used (e.g. Heeks 1999; OECD 2003). However, this assumption can be questioned (Chadwick and May 2003; Bekkers and Homburg 2007). Research into the effects of ICT in public sector organizations, and e-government in particular, shows that the desired effects are not always general and intended. They are rather specific and context driven, and also all kinds of unforeseen side-effects occur (e.g. Snellen and Van de Donk 1998; Andersen and Danziger 2001; Dawes 2008). In order to explain these effects, it is important to question the role of technology and its proclaimed neutrality and instrumentality. Three insights are relevant.

First, some authors argue that the nature of e-government innovations can be understood from an *ecological* perspective (Davenport 1997; Nardi and O'Day 1999; Bekkers and Homburg 2005). Technology changes in public organizations blend with socio-economic changes in society, organizational changes in public administration, the embracing of specific management conceptions and political ideologies (like New Public Management or Open Government) and with changes in the information and communication behaviour in society, like the use of social media (Chadwick and May 2003; Dunleavy et al. 2005; Lips and Schuppan 2009). E-government innovations can be seen as the local, contingent outcome of the process of co-evolution between the changes that occur in different (socio-cultural, economic, technological and political) environments. An example is the way the Dutch Ministry of Agriculture has used crowd sourcing (as a new social communication practice in society) to engage the public in specific discussions about how to regenerate the socio-economic vitality of rural areas in the Netherlands.

Secondly, an ecological perspective, however, does not really discuss the role that actors, with different views and interests, fulfil in the linking of these changes. How, and under what circumstances, can these changes be linked to each other? And who benefits from a specific coupling? Hence, actors may have different views on the added value of technology to be developed or to be used in an e-government practice. The '*cui bono*' question helps us to understand e-government as the outcome of a *social* and *political* shaping process in which different stakeholders frame the blessings of e-government and the blessings of technology in a specific way. However, vital questions are: Which frame will survive as the most dominant frame (Orlikowski 1991, 2000)? Which frame is included in the technologies to be developed and used and which frames have been excluded? This is important, because actors (or specific coalitions of actors) use ICT and the kind of information gathered, processed and exchanged to define social reality in such a way that it favours their interests and views. In doing so, actors push forward specific frames in which their expectations regarding the strengths and weaknesses of the technology to be developed or used and the effects to be expected are expressed (Bijker et al. 1987; Orlikowski 1991, 2000; Fountain 2001). If we want to understand the nature of e-government, we have to understand the negotiations between the involved actors, frames and discourses which emerge from these negotiations as the most relevant and powerful ones. For instance, despite the rhetoric of many e-government programmes, many e-government services are still being framed from a top-down, government-centric perspective that is based on compliance with the rules and procedures that citizens have to take into account. In many cases the perspective of citizens and companies, for instance stressing the reduction of red tape, is not seriously being taken into account (Bekkers and Homburg 2007; Taylor and Lips 2008).

Thirdly, the introduction of ICT in an organization or in a policy sector can also be seen as an intervention in a policy network, which influences the position, interests, values and the (information) domains of the actors involved (Kling 1987; Knights and Murray 1992; Bellamy and Taylor 1998). Thus the introduction of ICT is not a neutral intervention but a political one. ICT is considered as a powerful resource. Choices with respect to ICT influence the (grown and established) access, use and distribution of information among actors and their communication. Furthermore, ICT also influences (new and existing) information and communication relations and patterns between these actors and the (inter)dependency between them. As a result 'game like' interactions between these actors occur (Dutton and Guthrie 1991). Therefore scholars point at the local and political shaping of ICT in and between organizations (Kraemer and King 1986; Kumar and Van Dissel 1996). From this perspective the nature of e-government and the changes that occur can be understood in terms of *resource politics*, in which the use of ICT is seen as a strategy to reduce dependency in the exchange of information (Pfeffer and Salancik 1978; Kraemer and King 1986). For instance, the Dutch Vehicle Licence Registration Agency systematically uses ICT to discipline the exchange of information with all kinds of other public (e.g. the police) and private (e.g. garages and insurance companies) organizations that execute tasks that use or produce information that is relevant for the agency, in order to create a position in which it views itself as a spider in a network of mutually linked supply chains.

The next question is, what is the outcome of this information politicking process? Research shows that in the public sector, ICT very often strengthens the existing frames of reference, power relations and positions of the already privileged actors within an organization or within a policy sector (Kraemer and King 1986, 2006; Andersen and Danziger 2001; Fountain 2001; Moon 2004; Margetts 2009). Up till now ICT has tended to reinforce the already vested positions, relationships, views and interests, which does not imply that no innovations have taken place. However, these results are primarily based on the study of pre-internet and Web 1.0 based-technologies. However, it is questionable if this conclusion is still valid when the effects of Web 2.0 (social media based) technologies are taken into account.

ICT AS A CARRIER FOR INNOVATION

Innovation and e-government often go hand in hand. In order to understand this blending, I will show how ICT acts as a carrier for change and innovation. The following types of innovation can be discerned, although they are not exclusive (Moore and Hartley 2008).

Product and service innovations. ICT can be used to create new products or services. For instance, due to the coupling of specific data (in order to create transparency) citizens can be warned in advance that they need to have a new passport or driving licence. ICT can also help to create a single digital entry point ('portal') for citizens and companies and to link relevant data that refer to different legal regimes and that are uploaded from different databases in order to present in a coherent way all the information needed, for example, to apply for a building permit.

Technological innovations that emerge through the use of new technologies. An example is the use of cell broadcasting to warn citizens in case of an emergency. Another example is the use of biometrical and face recognition data by the police and customs at airports for identification purposes so that citizens do not have to line up for passport control.

Process innovations, focused on the improvement of the quality and efficiency of internal and external business processes. An example is the redesign of service delivery processes in order to reduce administrative burdens by using and sharing data that are only collected at one point and at one moment but are used by several agencies. This prevents the same questions being asked in other or related information-processing processes by other agencies or organizations that fulfil different but adjacent roles and activities in one service delivery process.

Organizational and managerial innovations, focused on the creation of new organizational forms, and the introduction of new management techniques and new working methods. An example is the development of chain management concepts to improve public service delivery processes, which is necessary to create forms of 'joined up government'. These forms of government are very often organized in terms of 'virtual organizations' which coordinate the sharing of information by creating a common information and communication space in which different people or organizations participate (Bekkers 2003). For instance, harbour information systems create such a platform because they help all kinds of different organizations that are active in a harbour – like the customs and tax administration, coast guard and harbour authorities, but also the captains of ships, pilotage employees, shipping and transport companies, stevedores, and so on – to share relevant information when a ship is entering or leaving the harbour, so that a complex chain of logistic activities can be planned by sharing the same clock time – as well as information about the nature of the shipment.

Conceptual innovations. These innovations occur because the characteristics of ICT might offer a new paradigm, a new frame of reference or a new concept for looking at things. For instance, the linking capacities of ICT make it possible to develop ideas about 'one stop shops' or distributed networking. In doing so a qualitative new approach can be developed on how governments should organize themselves, how they should provide services or how they can use the knowledge that citizens have.

Governance innovations reflect new ways of how to use the self-organizing capacities of society in order to organize collective action by the fact that autonomous but interdependent actors make use of ICT to share information, knowledge, contacts and experiences. This offers all kinds of possibilities for cooperation and participation (Rhodes 1997). An interesting example is Fix My Street, in which UK citizens add new and almost real-time information on road problems to a state-owned website which gives citizens an up-to-date account of where they can expect traffic problems. In doing so citizens become a co-producer in creating public value (Meijer 2011).

Institutional innovations refer to fundamental transformations in the basic principles which lie behind the relationships and positions of public organizations, companies and citizens. E-petitions illustrate how ICT can be used to gather the amount of (digital) signatures that are necessary, for instance, to force government to organize a public vote. In doing so ICT is used to strengthen the position of citizens as voters in order to create a counterbalancing force.

In sum, the innovation potential of e-government addresses changes in:

- the relationships between a number of relevant stakeholders in the public and private domain, like the relationships between citizens, companies, societal organizations and the state, and the relationships between different government organizations and layers of government. In these relationships, for instance, new processes, new organizational forms and new governance concepts are being introduced;
- the information and communication flows between these stakeholders in terms of the sharing and exchange of information, knowledge, experiences and communications;
- the qualities of the technologies (calculation, transparency, control, communication, etc.) to be used, due to all kinds of technological developments.

E-government innovations imply change. However, in order to implement these changes, some hurdles have to be overcome. Most hurdles deal with the fact that e-government innovations cross internal and external boundaries, which question the existing and grown practices within and between organizations. One of the interesting things about e-government is that, due to the linking capacity of the technology that is being used, organizations or organizational units are forced to cooperate with each other. However, cross intra- and interorganizational cooperation implies the integration of information domains (Dawes 1996; Bellamy and Taylor 1998). An information domain is a unique sphere of influence, ownership and control over information – its specification, format, exploitation and interpretation. Domain integration evokes several interoperability problems that are described in Table 17.1 (Bekkers 2007).

The changes that e-government brings to the public sector not only refer to a more efficient, more client-friendly or more open government. In a more profound way, e-government also changes the governance potential of government.

E-GOVERNMENT AS GOVERNANCE CAPACITY

The use of ICT also refers to the capacity to influence specific societal outcomes and occurrences. This can be understood as an act of governance: who governs whom (Rhodes 1997)? Governance capacity deals with the problem-solving capacity of an actor, which depends on his or her ability to mobilize and combine relevant resources (like ICT) in a structured way in order to achieve specific goals or to handle societal

Table 17.1   E-government interoperability problems

Types of interoperability problem	Elaboration
Administrative interoperability	Conflicting, exclusive or overlapping jurisdictions and accountability regimes
Legal interoperability	Different legal regimes with conflicting rights and obligations, e.g. in relation to privacy and safety regulations
Operational interoperability	Different working processes and information processing processes, routines and procedures
Technical interoperability	Incompatibility of specific 'legacy' ICT infrastructure (hardware and software)
Semantic interoperability	The idiosyncrasy of information specifications and the lack of common data definitions
Cultural interoperability	Conflicting organizational norms and values, communication patterns, and grown practices and habits

problems (Scharpf 1997). As such e-government can be seen as a governance act in which governments try to deal with problems regarding, for instance, the quality of public services.

E-government and the Intelligent State

In the intelligent state, the interactions between government on the one hand, and citizens, companies and other government agencies on the other, are mainly database driven (e.g. Bellamy and Taylor 1998; Fountain 2001). Access to these databases, as well as to the combination of different data sets which stem from different databases located in different organizations, plays a vital role in the rendering of integrated, but often obligatory, services. These services occur as a result of the need to exchange and process information during the implementation and enforcement of specific programmes, rules and regulations. Database technology as an important resource is used to increase the transparency of citizens or companies when they apply for specific benefits (e.g. social benefits) or when they comply to specific rules (e.g. permits, tax assessments) in order to assess whether their claims or obligations meet the formulated requirements. Governments also use ICT as a governance source to discipline or control the information exchange processes with these companies and citizens as well as with other government agencies. Through the employ of all kinds of electronic formats, and digitized routines and procedures, governments try to enhance the quality of the communications, data transfers and transactions that take place. Hence, the emphasis lies on the design of transparent, formalized, standardized and thus controlled information-processing processes. These processes are organized around databases or the referral indexes which act as an information broker to enable agencies to share data that are located in different back offices. A Dutch example is the Vehicle Licence Chain, which resulted from the implementation of the Vehicle Licence Registration Act. In fact this chain consists of some different sub implementation chains, that share and are linked with each other by the New Vehicle Licence Registry (established in 1995). The registry is owned by the Vehicle Licence Agency on behalf of the Traffic Ministry. This registry was established to improve traffic safety by increasing the effectiveness in terms of liability of vehicle ownership (mostly used cars) through a better exchange of information. The registry is a central, common pool database in which information about the status of a vehicle and its owner is stored and can be used by other organizations, such as the Tax and Customs Administration (in order to assess road taxes), garages (when they periodically execute safety checks on cars, older than two years), insurance companies (to assess the legal status of a car in order to handle insurance requests) and post offices (when functioning as the front office of the Vehicle Licence Agency for citizens to provide information about the status of a car when they sell or buy a used car). On the one hand, the Vehicle Licence Agency is dependent on private garages, insurance companies and post offices to execute a number of tasks on its behalf. On the other hand, the Vehicle Licence Agency attempts to control the discretion of the organizations through the introduction of well-specified information-processing and exchange procedures and norms, which are based on the legal status of the Agency as owner of the registry.

The database becomes the vital core, the heart of the organization, to which most of the activities in the organization are directed. Around this database concentric circles of users – within the agency, but also outside the agency – can be discerned (Zuboff 1988; Beniger 1989; Fountain 2001; Bekkers 2003). The outer circle is companies or citizens who, through the use of the internet and web-based applications, have centrally controlled access to this database and are able to add new or change existing information. In doing so a process of inclusion occurs. However, the desire to develop integrated service delivery and enforcement programmes, which presupposes a more organic, joined-up working of government, stimulates the further elaboration of this concentric organizational model (Fountain 2001; Margetts 2009). Around a central database one may notice the emergence of dedicated service or enforcement (supply) chains – more or less sequential organized coalitions of public and private organizations – which all use the same data from the database, or which share different data owned by these organizations, through the use of a common information broker.

Castells (1997, p. 301) has described this development in terms of 'Little Sisters'. 'Rather than an oppressive "Big Brother" it is a myriad of well wishing "little sisters", relating to each of us on a personal basis because they know who we are, who have invaded all the realms of life.' Others, however, question the good intentions of these Little Sisters, and point to the informational power that is in the hands of a small number of organizations. They question, for instance, the way in which this power and possible misuse are controlled. Hence, they talk about the rise of a panoptical state in a surveillance society (Lyon 1992) or the e-Ubiquitous State (Taylor and Lips 2008) which is based on the values of transparency and control. These governance ambitions may therefore influence the way in which e-government is framed and shaped. In doing so e-government practices may constitute an intelligent state, which favours a rather government-centric top-down perspective on how to shape e-government. An important driver for the creation of these centrally controlled networks is the wish to increase the efficiency, effectiveness and coherence of service delivery and enforcement processes. In doing so e-government aspirations and New Public Management goals co-evolve (Dunleavy et al. 2005; Margetts 2009; Lips and Schuppan 2008).

E-government and the Intelligent Society

The governance capacities that ICT provide are not only restricted to government. Also citizens, companies and non-governmental organizations can use them, not only to communicate to government but also in terms of sharing – access and exchange – relevant information, knowledge, preferences and experiences. Hence, it is interesting to see how the collective – but dispersed – intelligence present in society can be used by governments in shaping e-government practices. Three ways can be discerned.

First, the intelligence of society can be inserted into e-government practices by monitoring and measuring the preferences of citizens and citizen groups – for instance through instant polling through internet-based, focus group-oriented surveys – in order to get a more transparent and integrated picture of citizens, which helps to develop target-based services. In this view citizens are primarily based as a source of information that can be 'tapped' to find the earlier mentioned top-down, government-centric perspective on e-government (Taylor and Lips 2008).

Secondly, the intelligence of society can also be inserted into e-government practices, when citizens are considered as relevant co-producers in service delivery processes. In doing so, e-government practices try to make use of the knowledge, experiences and views of citizens. By sending a text message to citizens on their mobile phones, citizens can be asked to assist in finding a missing child or looking for a burglar. In doing so the police mobilize the attention of many people in a neighbourhood or city, thereby asking them to assist the police, by inviting them to act as co-producers in achieving public safety. Also more personalized service delivery processes can be achieved, when citizens have the opportunity to participate in the design of their own service process (Leadbetter 2004). A Dutch example is the agency that is responsible for the rendering of unemployment benefits (UWV). This agency deliberately tries to insert the experiences of the applicants to improve and redesign the application processes (Meijer 2011). However, although in e-government personalization has become more important – for instance in terms of 'my. . .' – citizens have, in general, not been involved in the design of this type of personalization. Personalization is primarily defined in terms of the integration of data that are available towards an individual citizen, but from the perspective of government (Anthopoulos et al 2007; Taylor and Lips 2008).

Other examples of co-production are interactive forums – digital discussion platforms of digital town halls. Citizens are given the opportunity to discuss, for example, policy proposals, and to come up with alternative views and proposals. In order to facilitate this, governments create a virtual platform organization for debate and deliberation (Bekkers 2003). However, in many cases results are ambivalent. Four critical factors, among others, can be mentioned (Mayer et al. 2005; Coleman and Bumler 2009; Hindman 2010). First, it should be clear to citizens, if and how the outcomes of the discussions will be used in the policy formulation and decision-making process and how the participation of citizens will be balanced against the primacy of politics in the system of representative democracy. Many cases show that, in the end, not only politicians but also public managers are quite reluctant to use these outcomes, for they interfere with their own ideas and interests. It requires a shift towards another, more responsive conception of democracy, in which dialogue, and trial and error learning are embraced as an important value (Barber 1984). Hence, politicians and public managers try to influence the format as well as the operation of these online discussions (Wright and Street 2007). Secondly, there is the quality of the discussion. Opinions and statements are exchanged but a shared learning and deliberation process is not always present. Soundbites seem to prevail. In order to create this learning process, it is important to understand how technology can support social interaction. Interaction does not happen but has to be organized in such a way that it makes sense. Thirdly, questions are also raised regarding the number and types of people who participate in the discussion. People who have already decided to participate are often given an additional forum for participation. Digital discussion forums have difficulty in attracting new participants. Also a lack of access to the internet (in terms of capacities and capabilities) excludes some groups of citizens from participating in these online deliberations (the so-called digital divide; see Dijk and Hacker 2003). Fourthly, the participation of people is also closely related to the trust they have in government as well as their willingness to exploit the scarce resources they have (like time). Berman (1997) argues that citizens are quite sceptical about the effects of their participation efforts.

The third manifestation of the intelligence of society refers to citizens who operate in virtual but social networks in which, separated from government, information, knowledge, contacts and experiences are produced, shared and exchanged which might be relevant for governments (Benkler 2006). Through the (re-)combination of these, although scattered, information sources new information and intelligence can be created. An example is discussion about the claims that are put forward on the internet regarding the reliability of information that is produced by the UN Panel on Global Climate Change which was used in the discussion at the UN Meeting on this subject in Copenhagen in 2010. These discussions refer to knowledge and information that, according to the participants in these lists, are not being referred to in the official government documents and reports. The linked intelligence that is present on the net has been used to produce alternative knowledge which defies the government's information and knowledge monopoly and the framing of public policy problems and approaches which are based on it. However, the challenge is how to connect these social networks to the established and institutionalized world of politicians and policy makers (Coleman and Bumler 2009). Moreover, some people question the quality and representativeness of the knowledge that is produced in these networks, because they often require a specialized and professional training and education (Keen 2007).

CONCLUSION

Due to the fact that ICT is a major source of innovation, e-government and innovation blend. However, just like innovation, e-government suffers from the idea that it is a 'good thing', that it has a virtue of its own. In order to understand the power of ICT as a source of innovation, we have to open the black box which is called e-government and the role of ICT in it. In order to do so it is important to take a number of considerations into account that have been put forward in this chapter. First, I have discussed several technological developments and relevant features that give us a glimpse of the innovation potential of ICT. However, these developments and features are not a given. They are not neutral. I have questioned the instrumental perspective which dominates the e-government literature. The technology itself is not enough to explain the nature of e-government and its innovation potential. The technology used is the result of a specific, contextually determined, political and social shaping process, in which demands (for change) that stem from different environments co-evolve. In this shaping process different actors with different frames regarding the blessing of ICT try to influence the content and effects of e-government practices. Due to the fact that ICT is not only a major source for innovation but also a major power resource that strengthens or weakens the existing positions, views and relations, innovative e-government practices are often subjected to a process of politicking, in which specific frames survive and others are rejected. However, in general we see that ICT tends to reinforce existing biases, which does not imply that no innovations take place. Moreover, if we want to understand the innovative potential of e-government we do not only have to look at changes in terms of more efficiency, more openness or more personalization. E-government also changes the governance capacity of actors. And again, this governance capacity is based on the fact that ICT is an important source of innovation and power. How is the governance capacity used? I have argued that predominantly ICT is used in e-government practices to build an intelligent state. However, this potential can also be used to create an intelligent society, although I have put forward a number of critical remarks regarding the quality of this intelligent society. However, for the next generation of e-government programmes an important challenge is how to link the governance capacities that are present in the intelligent state with those of the intelligent society.

REFERENCES

Andersen, K. and Danziger, J. (2001). Impacts of IT on politics and the public sector. *International Journal of Public Administration*, 25(5), 129–159.

Anthopoulos, L., Siozos, P. and Tsoukalas, I. (2007). Applying participatory design and collaboration in digital public services for discovering and re-designing e-Government services. *Government Information Quarterly*, 24(4), 353–376.

Barber, B. (1984). *Strong Democracy*. Berkeley, CA: University of California Press.

Bekkers, V.J.J.M. (1998). New forms of steering and the ambivalency of transparency. In I.T.M. Snellen and W.B.J.H. van de Donk (eds), *Public Administration in an Information Age*. Amsterdam: IOS Press, pp. 341–358.

Bekkers, V. (2003). E-government and the emergence of virtual organizations in the public sector. *Information Polity*, 8(3/4), 89–102.

Bekkers, V. (2007). The governance of back office integration. *Public Management Review*, 9(3), 377–401.

Bekkers, V. and Homburg, V. (2005). E-government as an information ecology. In V. Bekkers and V. Homburg (eds), *The Information Ecology of E-Government*. Amsterdam: IOS Press, pp. 1–19.

Bekkers, V. and Homburg, V. (2007). The myths of e-government. *The Information Society*, 23(5), 373–382.

Bellamy, C. and Taylor, J. (1998). *Governing in the Information Age*. Buckingham: Open University Press.

Beniger, J. (1986). *The Control Revolution*. Cambridge: Cambridge University Press.

Beniger, J. (1989). Conceptualizing information technology as organization and vice versa. In J. Fulk and Ch. Steinfeld (eds), Organizations and Communication Technology. Sage: Newbury Park, pp. 29–45.

Benkler, Y. (2006). *The Wealth of Networks*. New Haven, CT: Yale University Press.

Berman, E. (1997). Dealing with cynical citizens. *Public Administration Review*, 57(2), 105–112.

Bijker, W., Hughes, T. and Pinch, T. (1987). *The Social Construction of Technological Systems*. Cambridge, MA: MIT Press.

Boulos, K. and Wheeler, S. (2007). The emerging Web 2.0 social software: an enabling suite of sociable technologies in health and healthcare education. *Health Information and Libraries Journal*, 24(1), 2–23.

Brabham, D. (2008). Crowdsourcing as a model for problem solving: an introduction and cases convergence. *International Journal of Research into New Media Technologies*, 14 (February), 75–90.

Brabham, D. (2009). Crowdsourcing the public participation process for planning projects. *Planning Theory*, 8(3), 242–262.

Castells, M. (1996). *The Rise of the Network Society*. Cambridge, MA: Blackwell.

Castells, M. (1997). *The Power of Identity*. Cambridge, MA: Blackwell.

Chadwick, A. and May, C. (2003). Interaction between states and citizens in the age of the internet: e-government in the United States, Britain and the European Union. *Governance*, 26(2), 271–300.

Coleman, S. and Bumler, J. (2009). *The Internet and Democratic Citizenship*. Cambridge: Cambridge University Press.

Davenport, T. (1997). *Information Ecology*. Oxford: Oxford University Press.

Dawes, S. (1996). Interagency information sharing: expected benefits, manageable risks. *Journal of Policy Analysis and Management*, 15(3), 121–147.

Dawes, S. (2008). The evolution and continuing challenges of e-governance. *Public Administration Review*, 68(8), 82–102.

Dijk, J. van and Hacker, K. (2003). The digital divide as a complex and dynamic phenomenon. *The Information Society*, 19(4), 315–326.

Donk, W. van de and Snellen, I. (eds) (1998). *Government in the Information Age*. Amsterdam: IOS Press.

Dunleavy, P., Margetts, H., Bastow, S. and Tinkler, J. (2005). New Public Management is dead – long live digital era governance. *Journal of Public Administration Research and Theory*, 16(3), 467–494.

Dutton, W. and Guthrie, K. (1991). An ecology of games: the political construction of Santa Monica's public electronic network. *Informatization and the Public Sector*, 1(1), 279–301.

Fountain, J. (2001). *Building the Virtual State*. Washington, DC: Brookings Institution Press.

Heeks, R. (ed.) (1999). *Reinventing Government in the Information Age*. London and New York: Routledge.

Hindman, M. (2010). *The Myth of Digital Democracy*. Princeton, NJ: Princeton University Press.

Keen, A. (2007). *The Cult of the Amateur*. New York: Doubleday.

Kling, R. (1987). Computerization as an ongoing social and political process. In G. Bjerkness, P. Ehn and M. Kyng (eds), *Computers and Democracy*. Aldershot: Ashgate, pp. 117–136.

Knights, D. and Murray, F. (1992). Politics and pain in managing information technology: a case study in insurance. *Organization Studies*, 13(2), 211–228.

Kraemer, K. and King, J. (1986). Computing and public organizations. *Public Administration Review*, 46, 488–496.

Kraemer, K. and King, J. (2006). Information technology and administrative reform: will e-government be different? *International Journal of E-government Research*, 2(1), 1–20.

Kumar, K. and van Dissel, H. (1996). Sustainable collaboration: managing conflict and collaboration in interorganizational information systems. *MIS Quarterly*, 20(3), 279–300.

Leadbetter, C. (2004). *Personalization through Participation*. London: Demos.

Lips, M. and Schuppan, T. (2009). Transforming e-government knowledge through public management research. *Public Management Review*, 11(9), 739–749.

Lyon, D. (1992). *The Electronic Eye*. Cambridge: Polity Press.

March, J. (1999). *The Pursuit of Organizational Intelligence*. Oxford: Blackwell.

Margetts, H. (2009). Public management change and e-government. In A. Chadwick and P.N. Howard (eds), *Oxford Handbook of Internet Politics*. Oxford: Oxford University Press, pp. 114–128.

Mayer, I., Edelenbos, J. and Monnikhof, R. (2005). Interactive policy development: undermining or sustaining democracy. *Public Administration*, 83(1), 179–199.

Meijer, A. (2011). Networked coproduction of public services in virtual communities. *Public Administration Review*, 71, 598–607.

Moon, M. (2004). The evolution of e-government among municipalities. *Public Administration Review*, 64(4), 424–433.

Moore, M. and Hartley, J. (2007). Innovations in governance. *Public Management Review*, 10(1), 3–20.

Nardi, B. and O'Day, V. (1999). *Information Ecologies*. Cambridge, MA: MIT Press.

OECD (2003). *The E-Government Imperative*. Paris: OECD.

Orlikowski, W. (1991). The duality of technology. *Organization Science*, 3(3), 398–427.

Orlikowski, W. (2000). Using technology and constituting structures. *Organizational Science*, 11(4), 404–428.

Osborne, S. and Brown, K. (2005). *Managing Change and Innovation in Public Service Organizations*. London and New York: Routledge.

Pfeffer, J. and Salancik, G. (1978). *The External Control of Organizations*. New York: Harper and Row.

Pinch, T. and Bijker, W. (1987). The social construction of facts and artefacts. In W. Bijker, T. Hughes and T. Pinch (eds), *The Social Construction of Technological Systems*. Cambridge, MA: MIT Press, pp. 17–50.

Rhodes, W. (1997). *Understanding Governance*. Buckingham: Open University Press.

Scharpf, F. (1997). Introduction: the problem solving capacity in multi-level governance. *Journal of European Public Policy*, 4(4), 520–538.

Schumpeter, J. (1942). *Capitalism, Socialism and Democracy*. New York: Harper.

Snellen, I. and Van de Donk, W. (1998). *Public Administration in the Information Age: A Handbook*. Amsterdam/Berlin/Oxford/Tokyo/Washington DC: IOS Press.

Stanyer, J. (2009). Web 2.0 and the transformation of news and journalism. In B. Chadwick and P. Howard (eds), *Handbook of Internet Politics*. Abington: Routledge, pp. 201–214.

Surowiecki, J. (2004). *The Wisdom of Crowds*. New York: Little, Brown.

Taylor, J. and Lips, A. (2008). The citizen in the information polity. *Information Polity*, 13(3/4), 139–152.

Wright, S. and Street, J. (2007). Democracy, deliberation and design: the case of online discussion forums. *New Media and Society*, 9(5), 849–869.

Zuboff, S. (1988). *In the Age of the Smart Machine*. Oxford: Heinemann.

18. Analyzing policies for government innovation in practice: electronic government policy in Italy, 1993–2003

Valentina Mele

INTRODUCTION

A main theme of public sector innovation is the use of Information and Communication Technologies (ICTs)[1] to strengthen state capacity. These reforms often involve efforts to improve state economic and social programs, its relationships with citizens and its internal operations by exploiting ICTs (Brown 2005). In public administration, 'the use of ICTs, and particularly the Internet, as a tool to achieve better government' has been defined as Electronic Government (OECD 2003, p. 1). This term was coined in the wake of the Internet-driven transformations in the modus operandi of entire business sectors, known as Electronic Commerce. After its debut in the early 1990s,[2] the concept of Electronic Government gained currency among policymakers. It has become, first, a significant component of the modernization and innovation agenda in developing and developed countries and, since 2000, the main target of numerous administrative reforms.

Paralleling its spread in the policy arena, Electronic Government has been progressively incorporated in the studies on public management and is currently used as an umbrella category under which separate research streams have coalesced. Despite the variety of these research streams, the process of Electronic Government policy-making, must be analyzed further. This chapter develops research arguments about the politics of Electronic Government, analyzed as an instance of innovation and change in a public services context.

In the frame of this section of the book – dedicated to the analysis of concrete experiences of innovation – this chapter reports and then analyzes a decade-long episode of Electronic Government in Italy. The efforts to launch and sustain Electronic Government policy in this country were initiated with the establishment of an Authority for IT in Public Administration in 1993 and continued throughout the decade, resulting in a high number of ad hoc laws, institutional rearrangements, initiatives and projects. The episode analyzed is used as an instrumental case to answer two empirically grounded questions: (a) How did the innovative content of E-Government evolve in the decade under analysis? (b) Why and how was the issue of Electronic Government introduced in the agenda in the three policy cycles?

Answering these questions, in turn, contributes to inform an analytically significant question on what explains the trajectory of the E-Government policy in Italy.

The chapter proceeds as follows. The next section features the theoretical underpinnings of the study and the methodology. A narrative of the policy episode follows. The narration is organized into three intervals of policy-making. The narrative provides the empirical basis for the analysis of the policy cycles thus providing insight into the *process* of innovation in the context of public services. In conclusion, the chapter offers some analytical insights and implications for policymakers.

CONCEPTS AND METHODS

As the literature on Electronic Government evolves, what remains communal is the accepted view that ICTs are a set of technical means, processes and skills enabling not only the creation of and access to information but also an unprecedented level of integrated communication systems. Besides this communality, three distinct thematic areas of the Electronic Government literature can be identified. The first strand aims at recognizing the role of ICTs in enabling revolutionary change in public administration. The central question is whether government would become dramatically different if the technological possibilities of ICTs were fully exploited. In fact, scholars have formulated a singular issue around which they have developed various scenarios. Several basic analytical devices have been employed to comment on the issues. These devices include holistic concepts such as paradigm shifts and very stylized notions of the processes operating within the output side of government (Moore 1995), such as public service delivery. For example, some argue that the advent of ICTs is shifting governments away from the traditional bureaucratic model (La Porte, Demchak and De Jong 2002; Thompson and Jones 2008), triggering a new form of governance and setting in motion an information polity (Taylor and Williams 1990). Others have investigated the dynamics between the paradigm of New Public Management (NPM) and the paradigm of government informatization (Bellamy and Taylor 1992, 1994). More recently, the ICTs-driven paradigm superseding NPM has been conceptualized as 'digital era governance' (Dunleavy and Margetts 2000), a constellation of ideas and reforms that grant a central role to ICTs in a wide-ranging series of alterations of how public services are organized and delivered to citizens (Dunleavy, Margetts, Bastow and Tinkler 2006).

A further stream of literature can be considered as a contingency version of the one described above. The work of the scholars writing in this strand challenges the optimistic claims of inevitability of the first approach. In particular, it shows that such universal expectations cannot possibly be accurate. The evidence, in fact, confirms that the relationship between an intention of E-Government and its outcome is highly conditional (Ho and Ni 2004; Gil-García and Pardo 2005; Kim 2005; Luna-Reyes, Gil-García and Cruz 2007; Rose and Grant 2010). Studies in this strand are focused on the identification of critical issues and success factors of E-Government policy design and implementation. These studies typically try to identify salient predictors of the decision and successful implementation of E-Government policy. For example, Carter and Weerakkody (2008) have investigated the country variation in citizens' E-Government adoption. By comparing data from the US and UK they conclude that determinant factors driving citizens' willingness to use E-Government services are the level of their perceived utility and the level of trust in the public agency offering such services. Similarly, Dimitrova and Chen (2006) have attempted to profile the adopters of E-Government services according to non-demographic characteristics such as perceived usefulness, perceived uncertainty and civic mindedness. Other scholars have investigated the supply side, offering that specific institutional arrangements and the availability of resources, such as IT budget allocation,

IT staff and IT training, are conducive to positive outcomes of E-Government initiatives. For example, Luna-Reyes, Gil-García and Cruz (2007) argue that institutional arrangements and organizational forms affect the way in which technology is understood, designed and used in a particular inter-organizational project.

The third stream of literature analyzes the output side of government. Instead of the holistic perspective on Electronic Government seen before, these studies adopt an empirical approach and ground their commentary on a clearly argued appraisal of a particular technical innovation within programs (Moore 1995). There is a lot of variety in the required performance characteristics of E-Government projects and their outcomes. Illustrative of this approach are some studies that appraise ICTs-based projects in relation to their effectiveness in cutting red tape (Peled 2001), others in increasing the direct interaction with citizens (Thomas and Streib 2003) or in channeling a democratic input into the policy-making process (Torres, Pina and Acerete 2006). It should also be noted that many of these design criteria, such as the level of public agencies' accountability (Pina, Torres and Royo 2007), are familiar to public administration studies, while some, such as system openness, appear to be novel and specific to this domain (Wong and Welch 2004).

These works seem to conclude that there is little variation in relation to the valued criteria to appraise the expected change. The results are even worse compared with the rhetoric that may have come with the creation of the capability. In particular, the rhetoric of a fully fledged integrated and transactional E-Government is compared with the reality of merely informational websites or of online services with an unsatisfactory take up (Moon 2002; Norris and Moon 2005; Scholl 2005; Nasi, Frosini and Cristofoli 2011). It should be noted that not only has this stream questioned whether the incorporation of new ICTs assets changes the performance characteristics of a public program (i.e. it is truly conducive to innovation in public services), but it has also attempted to diagnose failures in implementation. Such failures are mainly associated with the fact that Electronic Government often only exacerbates the existing nature and attributes of public bureaucracies (Wong and Welch 2004) and pre-existing practices, thus preventing innovative projects from unleashing their full transformative potential (Torres, Pina and Acerete 2006).

In synthesis, the literature on Electronic Government has recognized the importance of variation in the broad environment of public sector innovation and the associated effects on its performance. Yet, these studies do not acknowledge that policy-making is an important component of the broad Electronic Government enterprise. Some do not because they conceptualize E-Government holistically. Others study Electronic Government in its components but develop a narrow interest for the utilization of such innovative technical features of delivery systems, thus missing the stage where decisions on these features are taken.

A minority strand of research focused on single-country cases of Electronic Government (Hudson 2002; Acaud and Lakel 2003; Margetts 2006; Lofgren 2007; Liou 2008). Most of these studies are commentaries on the evolution of the Electronic Government policy in one country. Yet, they represent encouraging precedents in that they show how an interest in policy-making is not entirely idiosyncratic with the literature on Electronic Government.

This chapter posits that analyzing continuity and change in Electronic Government policy should be a substantive inquiry, and one that responds also to recent calls for a better understanding of the political dynamics among the actors that lead to the decision to launch Electronic Government initiatives. Moreover, the research should entail a greater use of out-of-office data-gathering. Some scholars have identified, as a limitation of this literature, the narrow range of research methods being used, with little empirical work or website development as the main indicator (Norris and Moon 2005). While this does not per se invalidate the findings of the research, the fact that 'most e-government researchers appear to do little more than sit at their PCs' tends to exclude events and opinions from the analysis and triangulation of large tranches of data (Heeks and Bailur 2007, p. 257). This methodological choice might, in turn, be mutually reinforced with the lack of interest for the policy-making processes behind E-Government developments (Yildiz 2007).

Therefore, this chapter analyzes the instrumental case of Electronic Government in Italy (Ragin 1987; Yin 1994; Abell 2004) in the frame of a research approach on public management policy change (Barzelay 2003; Barzelay and Gallego 2006, 2010). This program seeks to develop a middle-range, historically based, causal theory of public management policy-making. Public management policies are government-wide institutional rules and routines that carry out administrative functions, such as expenditure planning and financial management, civil service and labor relations, procurement, organization and methods, and audit and evaluation (Barzelay 2001). The synthesis scheme is built around Kingdon's theorization of the policy-making process, composed of the three phases of agenda-setting, alternative specification and decision-making (Kingdon 1984). The middle-range theory is structured around the dynamics of each component phase and their interfaces (Barzelay and Gallego 2006).

The standard unit of analysis for investigating this process is the policy cycle and, considering that the E-Government policy in Italy during the decade under analysis included three waves, this chapter analyzes a multi-cycle case. Details of the study design, sources examined and interviewees are in Appendix A.

NARRATING E-GOVERNMENT POLICY IN ITALY

Activities for promoting IT were formally started in 1993 with the establishment of the Authority, designed to be a key player over the following decade for this policy domain. Since the beginning, the mandate of the Authority has been two-fold: the spread of IT usage in public administration and to exert control over IT procurement processes. Its main achievements include the issuing of organic plans for IT application in the public sector and a project to create a system network of local Italian public administration. The political context during this decade was a turbulent one, resulting in the continuous turnover of Executives. Thus the responsibility for strategic planning relating to IT in the public sector fluctuated between the Authority and the Ministry for Public Administration. Moreover, the policy arena for IT in the public sector saw the rise and fall of several Commissions, Units and Centers. Despite this institutional turmoil, there has been substantial continuity and evolution of IT as a policy issue and practice.

The following sections present a narration of a decade-long policy cycle organized around three turning points, namely the establishment of the Authority in 1993, the launch of the Action Plan for E-Government in 2000 and the Call for an E-Government project in 2002. These three decisions represent the outcome of intentional efforts aimed at changing practices and principles embedded in the public administration. The narrative is focused on the phase preceding each decision, structured around the above-mentioned meta-categories of agenda-setting, alternative specification or program development, and finalizing and launching the program. The synthesis of the events selected and narrated is presented in Appendix B.

Previous Events

The beginning of the policy cycle on E-Government in Italy is conventionally associated with the establishment of an ad hoc Authority in 1993. The nature and mission of the Authority, however, represented a controversial matter for its entire mandate, which ended a decade later. Analyzing the phase that preceded the Authority's launch helps to account for the ambiguities that marked the interplay between context and actors during this decade-long episode.

In 1993, ICTs in public administration were not a new issue in the debate on administrative modernization. From the late 1970s, one of the Commissions charged with assessing the status quo of the Italian bureaucracy and its modernization needs focused on ICTs. The Commission denounced the scarce level of technological penetration in public offices, while it recognized the tremendous potential of automated procedures for public office modernization. Simultaneously, studies on e-administration flourished, though their main interest was limited to the legal validity of documents managed and archived through prototype PCs.

Throughout the 1980s, cultural and technological developments provided the foundations for the modern conception of E-Government in the country. Several scholars and intellectuals became advocates of the democratic potential of ICTs, influenced also by the French experience with Minitel. In the words of one of our informants: 'Not only did we believe that new technologies were improving the internal efficiency of public agencies, the most remarkable progress brought by the advent of technology regarded communication between citizens, between public administrations, and, above all, between citizens and administrations.'

At the same time the distribution of basic technological equipment per public sector office increased conspicuously, though 'in 1990 Italy was still lagging behind the other industrialized countries' (interview with a top bureaucrat of the Public Administration Department). The issue was given some attention also from the Executive throughout the second half of the 1980s. In 1984 the Public Administration Ministry established a Commission for IT in Public Administration. Five years later the Commission delivered a decree on the coordination and planning of IT in central agencies, which 'can be considered a turning point in the conception of the bureaucratic machine as an entity in charge of delivering services to citizens also through new technologies' (interview with the former Minister for Public Administration). However, the advisory nature of the Commission and the relatively low status of this issue on the Executive agenda prevented this decree from producing actual change in the procedures of central agencies.

Efforts aimed at rationalizing IT developments continued throughout the period in office of the following Executive, when the Public Administration Ministry issued an ad hoc memorandum and guidelines for IT standardization in government. Nevertheless, despite the increase in investment, the process of IT diffusion in the local and central public organizations was developing in a fragmented fashion, with scattered projects and applications.

Direct effects of such a fragmented approach were that 'the systems being implemented were hardly ever compatible' (Finocchiaro 1991, p. 49), the potential economies of scale were hindered and the bargaining power of public administrations with vendors was limited. In 1992, the figures on ICT penetration showed an uneven distribution, with the coexistence of some public organizations, both at the central and at the local level, that were technologically advanced while the majority of public organizations were still relying on backward ICT systems. In fact, the President for the Commission on IT coordination in public administration affirmed, 'We lacked a comprehensive development model. Several of our initiatives were praiseworthy. Yet, they turned out to be like the *tesserae* of a mosaic whose shape and content had not been defined in advance.'

Therefore, despite the establishment of an ad hoc Commission, investments in ICT in public administration proceeded with scant coordination. Moreover, ICT investments – as well as any significant public procurement decision – had to be authorized by the State Account and Controller General. However, the role of this Controller was limited to checking the legal validity of the procurement procedures. Strategic planning, coordination and standardization were far beyond its mandate (Cammarata 1994–2004). Let us now turn to the first phase of this decade-long episode.

The Authority for IT in Public Administration (1993)

Setting the agenda

In 1992 the issue of ICT in government moved from the specialized agenda of the Public Administration Minister to the congested agenda of the Executive, after a phase of political and economic turbulence. In 1992 the 'clean-hands' scandal had reached its peak, and the media had exposed civil society to the evidence collected over years of investigations on political corruption and bribery. At the same time, the currency crisis of 1992, which mirrored the global financial crisis, together with the struggle to meet the EU standards, prompted the Executive to introduce emergency measures.

The issue of ICT in government found a receptive audience in the two Executives that ruled the country during, and in the immediate aftermath of, the scandal. The two technical governments have been considered as a continuum, as, for the first time, they were not composed of career politicians and parliamentary members. The first of these two Executives was headed by Giuliano Amato and, under his short mandate, 'the coordination of ICT strategies and expenditure in public administration, a process which had matured slowly, abruptly exploded' (interview with the former Prime Minister). The mandate of Amato focused almost entirely on the drafting and approval of a 'package' through which he intended to delegate the economic rationalization of the public system to the Executive. The package interested domains and jurisdictions as diverse as healthcare, social security, civil service, financial accounting and expenditure. He was also familiar with the specific challenges of reforming the Italian bureaucracy, as he had participated in the attempts to reform it since the early 1970s, thus he developed a maturing awareness of the role of ICTs as an enabler of streamlining and administrative simplification.

Alternative specification/developing the Authority

The Prime Minister's familiarity with the main problems of Italian public administration, including the lack of a coordinated policy for ICTs in government, led to the inclusion of IT in the agenda. The last mile for the inclusion, however, was gained as a serendipitous result of the intense negotiations with the unions that preceded the approval of the Amato package. The labor unions' leadership, in fact, was concerned that the austerity measures were excessively penalizing for civil servants, who had been forced to give up some of their established benefits. Thereby, the Prime Minister was asked to introduce parallel measures clearly attending to the need for austerity but 'signaling that civil servants were not the only scapegoat' (interview with the former Prime Minister). The result was two oddly disparate alternative measures to be included in the austerity package: an additional tax for luxury motorcycles and the establishment of an entity aimed at coordinating, and thus controlling, the public expenditure on ICTs. The inclination of the Prime Minister and the current debate on the need to increase the efficiency of public administration determined the inclusion of the latter issue in the Amato package, approved right before the Executive resigned amid corruption allegations in 1992.

The President of the National Statistics Institute was appointed *ad interim* as Special Commissary for IT in Public Administration. He drafted the regulations for the new entity, conceiving it as a qualified structure with high technical expertise. It was beyond his mandate, however, to determine the legal status of the new organization; to exercise the choice between establishing an Agency or an Authority. While the former was considered as semi-autonomous from the Executive (Fedele et al. 2007), the latter had the status of a completely independent organization.

Finalizing and launching the Authority

The following Executive discarded the alternative of an Agency and opted for an Authority. By creating an Authority completely independent of the political parties, the Executive signaled its commitment (Gilardi 2002; Elgie and McMenamin 2005) to fight the corruption of elected officials. Hence, in 1993 the Authority was officially launched with a vast and ambiguous mandate.

The Authority was expected to support the process of ICTs diffusion in the public sector, rationalize the adoption of ICTs and review the regulations for technology procurement: 'the Authority was created to stimulate and coordinate technological developments in public organizations as well as to regulate their procurement procedures in the aftermath of the dirty-hands scandal. These two distinct needs determined a bi-cephalous entity' (interview with a former top bureaucrat of the Authority for IT in Public Administration). A further ambiguity marked the establishment of the Authority. Notwithstanding the intention of its President to create an Authority completely independent of the Executive, the Public Administration Minister considered it an Agency, subject to the priorities of the Executive and, more specifically, to those of his own department. In the words of one of our informants: 'Basically the Executive launched an Authority, but regarded it as an Agency.'

The Authority operated with three-year plans that were to be updated annually and with a main focus on ICTs in central administration. Ministries were requested to submit their ICTs procurement contracts to the Authority, in charge of assessing the contracts' conformity to the annual plan. The appropriateness of the contracts was assessed not only on the basis of formal compliance with the procurement standards, but also on their substantial coherence with the Authority ICTs plan.

The E-Government Action Plan (2000)

The second cycle of this decade-long episode is associated with the launch of the E-Government Action Plan. While efforts to draft the Plan had been rapid and intense, it had taken a few years for the issue to be widely recognized in the political and administrative arena, both at national and at European levels, and for the community of interest to coalesce around the Public Administration Department.

Setting the agenda

In the period from 1994 to 1996 the Authority performed two main tasks. First, it assessed a considerable number of central ICTs procurement contracts – an activity considered as the primary tool for steering the ICTs policy. Secondly, it worked on the ambitious project of an Internet-like information system, which should have connected all the Italian public administrations through a network based on the Internet Protocol. In 1996, in fact, Italy and the Scandinavian countries were the only European countries to have an Internet Protocol.

While the Authority mandate was focused on central administrations, local administrations such as the Municipalities of Bologna, Milan and Modena started to experiment with electronic community networking. Such developments were aligned with European Union guidelines on the Information Society, which prepared the ground for the inclusion of Internet development as a priority in the EU agenda for development and social cohesion.

The new Executive elected in 1996 soon recognized the importance of ICTs in the public sector. First, it established the Information Society Forum, composed of key representatives from different Ministries, assigning it the mission of promoting the Information Society and supporting the creation of a favorable regulatory framework. Secondly, it included the development of a Unitarian Telematic Network in the comprehensive reform of the public sector launched by the Public Administration Minister. The Minister also established a Technical Center, in charge of managing the Unitarian Network.

The prominent status gained by the issue of the Information Society in the agenda was strengthened further over the following months. Early in 1999 the Executive established a new organizational structure for promoting the Information Society, composed of three boards reporting directly to the Prime Minister. The three boards, in charge of drafting a new 'Action Plan for the Development of the Information Society', were supported by a permanent Task-force within the Prime Minister's Council. Regional and local authorities were involved in the activities of the Information Society Forum, and an ad hoc Coordination Center for E-Government in Local Administrations was set up in Turin.

In the two-year timeframe between 1997 and 1999, the work of both the newly established bodies and the Authority led to the approval of a significant number of laws and decrees, which promoted and ruled the use of new technologies in the public sector. Documents produced by civil servants through digital devices were granted legal status, while digital signature, optical archives and digital documents were introduced. The practice of tele-working for civil servants was pioneered in Italy while the online management of the revenue service and the land registry was introduced and became a best practice at the EU level.

Developing the Action Plan

During the same period, between 1997 and 1999, the European Commission was developing a draft strategy for the Information Society. The eEurope Action Plan, endorsed by European heads of government at their summit in June 2000, was aimed at fostering the Information Society, considered a crucial component of European competitiveness. The eEurope Action Plan also marked a shift in the conception of ICTs usage by public administrations. The Plan legitimized Electronic Government as a key asset of the European strategy for development and, more importantly, it signaled its policy salience as an autonomous cross-country issue.

In parallel, after a reshuffle of the Italian Executive in late 1999, Electronic Government was confirmed as a policy priority. In particular the Executive established the institutional role of an Under-Secretary at the Prime Minister's Office for Technological Innovation. Another significant indication of the issue's rise in status on the policy agenda was the inclusion of a chapter on Electronic Government in the Action Plan for an Information Society drafted by the Committee of Ministers for the Information Society. The chapter was drafted by the Public Administration Minister with the support of an E-Government Working Group, a think-tank mainly composed of experts from academia. A few days after the Information Society Action Plan had been approved, the chapter was extracted from the general strategy and was launched as the 'E-Government Action Plan 2000–2002'. The document promoted Electronic Government as a main instrument for modernizing the public sector, and it was packaged as instrumental to the structural reforms initiated by the coalition in 1996. In particular, the main pillars of the public administration reform were strengthening the managerial tools available for public officials, such as performance evaluation systems; simplifying the administrative procedures, thus reducing red tape; and devolving new functions and service delivery to local governments. Unsurprisingly, the Action Plan for Electronic Government mirrored these priorities and was organized around the building-blocks of ICTs-based decision support systems for public managers, streamlining bureaucratic procedures and delivering online services. This chapter was also the result of the intense cooperation with a group of a few local administrations which had experimented with cutting-edge ICTs applications, typically for streamlining internal procedures or for activating online communication channels with groups of citizens. The exchange and collaboration of the E-Government Working Group with these local administrations led to the immediate endorsement of the Electronic Government Action Plan by the Joint Conference of Central, State and Local Administration, a step that ensured higher visibility and consensus to the Action Plan.

Launching the Action Plan for E-Government and reorganizing the policy domain
In 2000, Giuliano Amato, the Prime Minister who had led the Transition Executive in 1993, once again received the mandate to lead a Transition Executive before the political elections of 2001. As a consequence, the same Premier who had launched the Authority for IT in 1993 was responsible for approving the E-Government Action Plan in June 2000.

The Plan laid out the details of specific E-Government initiatives, such as the establishment of an Internet connection among all public agencies, the development of an electronic ID card and the use of electronic signature to certify online procedures. These goals required high-level technological expertise. The institutional venue with the highest concentration of expert staff whose skills ranged from computing engineering to legal aspects of information systems was a Unit within the Authority – the Technical Center. The Unit had been established in 1997 to tackle the complex issues associated with the development of the Unitarian Network for public administration, the most ambitious project of the Authority. This project had never been fully deployed. In fact, the lengthy process of authorizing and setting up the Network lagged behind the pace of technological innovation so that, by the time the Authority defined the technical and legal standards of the Unitarian Network project, alternative fully fledged Internet solutions had been made available 'off the shelf', making this complex architecture technologically obsolete. Over time, the substantial failure of this and other minor projects, announced and never delivered by the Authority, undermined its reputation. The reservations held by an increasing number of experts and civil servants on the effectiveness of the Authority in building capacity and in coordinating large ICTs projects were exacerbated by an ill-timed mismatch between the scope of its mandate and the emerging needs of Electronic Government projects (interviews with two top bureaucrats at the Public Administration Department and with one academic consultant of the Authority). On the one hand, the target of the projects launched by the Authority had been limited since its inception to central administrations. On the other hand, local administrations had become the key enablers of Electronic Government developments, and especially of what was progressively considered to be at the heart of the national strategy for E-Government, namely online service delivery. Therefore, the exclusive focus of the Authority on Ministries and large central agencies was no longer compatible with the dominant conception of Electronic Government and with the current shift towards the devolution of public functions to local entities.

These factors prompted Bassanini, the Public Administration Minister, to move the Technical Center from the Authority to the Prime Minister's Council. This shift also marked the end of a period during which the Authority had been in charge of strategic planning on ICTs. Bassanini created a new Permanent Unit for implementing the E-Government Action Plan within the Public Administration Department. The Unit included representatives of local administrations, well-known academics, experts and top officials. At the same time, the reorganization of the Public Administration Department offered the opportunity to include an Office for ICT and Public Digital Networks in the new organizational chart. In 2000 the Public Administration Department completed the process of appropriating jurisdiction over Electronic Government matters by incorporating the Technical Center, which previously had been part of the Authority.

The prominence gained by the issue of Electronic Government by early 2001 ensured the allocation of a significant amount of funds to implement the Action Plan.[3] This was the last act of the Electronic Government policy under the four Executives of the left-wing coalition that had ruled the country during a five-year legislature.

Call for E-Government Projects (2002)

Setting the agenda

The issue of E-Government remained a priority for the right-wing coalition chaired by Silvio Berlusconi, who won the elections in May 2001. During the electoral campaign and in the following years, modernization of the bureaucracy was addressed as a matter of so-called 'digital state' and E-Government became the one-size-fits-all solution to cut red tape, to improve country competitiveness and to strengthen business–government and business–citizen relations. The 'digital revolution' was expected to spill over from the public administrations to schools, universities, businesses and citizens.

Consistent with the priority given to innovation and ICTs in the electoral campaign, the Premier established a new office in his Cabinet, namely the Ministry for Innovation and Information Technologies and appointed Lucio Stanca as Minister. Mr Stanca had over 30 years of professional experience at IBM and had served as CEO of IBM Italy. The initial mandate of the Ministry for Innovation and IT swept across different policy domains. The Ministry was in charge of steering any policy on the Information Society, science, technology and innovation, including basic research. However, despite such a broad mandate Electronic Government immediately became the focal point of the Ministry's activities, thanks to the availability of ad hoc funds, allocated by the previous Executive to the implementation of the E-Government Action Plan.

Developing the call for projects

While the available funds and the institutional mandate created a favorable context for the Minister to launch incisive actions and to implement the Action Plan for E-Government, Mr Stanca struggled to assemble a team under his leadership. When he took office in 2001, the policy domain of E-Government was difficult to coordinate. The Authority was still in place and claiming its autonomy from the Executive. As for the Technical Center, its shift from the Authority to the Executive had brought it closer to the leadership of the Minister. Yet, its Director had been appointed during the previous Legislature. In his view, the next steps to implement the E-Government Action Plan entailed investing in the infrastructure and the back offices of public administrations, while the new Minister was keen on immediately strengthening front-office services highly visible to citizens and corporations.

The distribution of the institutional mandate for Electronic Government was complicated by the presence of the Permanent Unit for managing the E-Government Action Plan and of the Office for ICTs and for Public Administration Networks. Both entities, whose institutional locus was the Department of Public Administration, were composed of members designated by the previous Executive. Such a fragmented policy sub-system was not compatible with the existence of a newly established Ministry for Innovation and IT that had been granted both the clear mandate and the resources to steer Electronic Government initiatives. Consequently, between 2001 and 2002 the Electronic Government domain was restructured. First, responsibility for policy-making shifted definitively from the Authority of IT in Public Administration to the Ministry for Innovation and Technologies. Secondly, within the new Ministry an Office of E-Government for Local Administrations was created. The drivers to do so were partly political and partly instrumental to the goal of implementing the Action Plan. At the political level a debate initiated in the early 1990s, over the need to devolve functions downward and to empower local administrations, had intensified. This pressure was fueled by the inclusion of the Northern League in the ruling coalition; a Political Party very attentive to the needs and requests of local administrations. The decision to actively involve local administrations was not only driven by the perception of political opportunity, but also by the awareness of the Minister and his staff that local administrations represented the 'administrative backbone of the country. Without the support of local administrations, delivery of services to citizens and businesses would have remained wishful thinking' (interview with a top bureaucrat at the Ministry for Innovation and IT). The Minister appointed as Director General of the Office of E-Government for Local Administrations an experienced top official who had been working at the Authority for IT in Public Administration, and then headed the Office for IT and digital networks at the Public Administration Department. His work and profile were well known among central and local agencies. Therefore, his appointment facilitated the liaison between the Ministry and local administrations. The following months were characterized by intense negotiations between local administrations and the Ministry over a crucial decision: the modalities and criteria to allocate the funds already appropriated by the previous Executive for Electronic Government. The alternatives being evaluated could be roughly synthesized into two approaches. The top-down approach required that the new Ministry select a few priorities for the development of Electronic Government and then invest the funds in building capacity at the local and central level by ensuring that technological infrastructure, system integration and *ex officio* removal of the administrative barriers were in place. In the bottom-up approach, central and local administrations were expected to define their own strategies to enact Electronic Government projects and the Ministry had to provide the adequate resources.

Launching the call for projects and restructuring the policy domain

The latter approach prevailed, mainly due to the complexity of a centralized, top-down approach in terms of institutional capacity needed to orchestrate the initiative as well as in terms of resistance by local administrations to give up some of their prerogatives. In 2002, the Minister launched the first call for E-Government projects, open to any administration delivering services to citizens and businesses. The previous initiatives had given priority to less visible aspects such as back-office re-engineering and systems interoperability (i.e. making different applications and technological architecture compatible with each other). Instead, the most important criterion for selecting projects was identified in the visibility of the outcomes for citizens and businesses.

The Minister completed the restructuring of the policy domain in June 2003, when the Executive replaced both the Authority and the Technical Center with the National Center for IT in Public Administrations (CNIPA). The new entity was responsible for the implementation of the E-Government plans devised by the Minister for Innovation and Technologies, and became the operating unit of the Ministry.

ANALYZING PROGRAMS FOR CHANGE

This section attempts to provide a basic understanding of E-Government policy-making in Italy between 1993 and 2003. The idea pursued in this chapter is that E-Government can be analyzed as an innovative public management policy, related specifically to the role of central coordinating agencies (Barzelay 2007, p. 21). The episode presented here includes three policy cycles, each resulting in the launch of an entity or a project for E-Government.

The first question concerns the evolution in the innovative content of Electronic Government policy.

The analysis of this episode shows a significant evolution in formulating and implementing a policy aimed at fostering an innovation, namely IT in the public sector. When the Authority was established in 1993, it was considered innovative in terms of potential impact on the IT procurement procedures and on the harmonization of the IT procurement policies. The system put in place to monitor the public expenditure for IT consisted of mandatory approval by the Authority of each IT public procurement contract. It is also important to highlight that the Authority's mandate was only exerted over central administrations.

When the Action Plan for E-Government was launched in 2000, the concept of IT-related innovation had evolved tremendously. First of all, ICTs were regarded as instrumental to the general reform of the public sector, and particularly to the project initiated by the Minister himself, that is, launching the E-Government Action Plan. Secondly, the emphasis was not on changing IT procurement procedures, but rather on upgrading the system-wide country competitiveness through the new available technologies. Thirdly, while in 1993 the Authority was established to control and possibly reduce IT expenditure, the 2000 Action Plan came along with an allocation of ad hoc resources. The last substantial difference is that, consistently with the general public sector reform, the Action Plan addressed both central and local administrations.

The third phase was the call for E-Government projects in 2002. The alternation from left-wing to right-wing in the ruling majority introduced by the political elections in 2001 did not significantly change the trajectory of E-Government policy. Yet, the notion of IT-related change was redefined and increasingly associated with the impact on the end users' experience. The initiatives were formulated accordingly, and the funds available were distributed to the central and local administrations whose projects were employing ICTs to improve the service delivery, thus increasing end users' satisfaction.

The second question is focused on why and how the issue of Electronic Government became introduced in the policy agenda in the three policy cycles.

The inclusion in the agenda which led to the establishment of the Authority for IT in Public Administration in 1993 can be explained by the interplay between the context factors and the quality of participation of the policy entrepreneurs. The concept of IT in public administration, in fact, was not a novelty when it was added to the agenda in 1993. Ever since the late 1970s experts in the policy community had brought the IT issue to the attention of a specialized audience and included it among the critical factors for bureaucratic modernization. Encouraging signs also came from the political stream, where parliamentary members managed to create ad hoc Commissions to discuss and analyze the implications connected to the introduction of IT in public administration. Yet, this subject could have remained a low priority issue on the Cabinet agenda, had it not been for the quality of participation of the policy entrepreneurs and for the malleability of the issue image of IT in public administration. On the one hand, the political turmoil of the early 1990s determined an abrupt turnover of the whole establishment and the majority of the members of the transitional Executives were co-opted from academia. These experts, who had participated in the Commissions for the reform of Public Administration in the late 1970s, had been given crucial positions in the so-called 'technical' government. For example, the quality of participation of the Prime Minister in the IT policy domain in 1992 was influenced by his previous experience as a member of the working groups in charge of assessing the problems of the Italian bureaucracy 15 years previously. On the other hand, the issue definition process played a crucial role in 1992, as IT in the public sector was introduced on to the agenda under the guise of an action aimed at fostering control and transparency in public procurement.

Turning to the following policy cycle, the period started with the election of a new Coalition in 1996 and culminated with the launch of the E-Government Action Plan in 2000. The issue of IT in the public sector had not scored particularly high in the electoral program. However, it found a secondary entrance as the pressure to improve the country's competitiveness and the struggle to meet the EU standards called for reform in the public sector. The issue of IT in this context was defined as instrumental to bureaucratic modernization. The institutional *locus* around which the community of experts and civil servants coalesced was the Public Administration Ministry, and this reinforced the overlap between public sector reform and IT in the public sector policy domains. Also, the Minister in charge of the government-wide reform of public administration became the champion of IT (E-Government). Changing the label of these initiatives from ICTs to Electronic Government was a consequence of his participation in the EU ministerial meetings for the eEurope Action Plan. However, being part of such international polity also had a domestic outcome in terms of issue and actor certification.

Last, in the third policy cycle, the recognition received by the issue at the national and international levels, together with the availability of funds appropriated for E-Government, persuaded the incoming Executive to build on the issue and to reinforce its status. This was due to the fact that during the electoral campaign Digital Government had become the substitute for the discourse on bureaucratic modernization. The issue, however, had to be repackaged in terms of devolution, which was consistent with the political milieu of the Executive. A newly established Ministry for Innovation and IT was the natural candidate to aggregate the policy community and to channel the different initiatives. Thus, despite some internal resistance and the slow pace, the competencies for E-Government were ultimately shifted from the Public Administration Ministry and from the Authority to the Ministry for Innovation and IT.

CONCLUSIONS

This chapter has combined the previously distinct streams of literature on Electronic Government and public management policy change, thus responding to calls for a better understanding of the policy dynamics that lead to the initiation of E-Government initiatives. In particular, these calls have suggested the importance for the literature on

Electronic Government to extrapolate its theoretical underpinnings from established public policy frameworks (Hudson 1999) and to tie the subject of E-Government to mainstream public administration research.

The longitudinal perspective taken allows for a comparison of the three cycles, thus distilling analytical insights on what explains the overall trajectory of the E-Government policy in Italy. On the one hand, the resilience of the E-Government policy, more surprising considering the unstable Italian political context over the decade under study, can be partially explained by the features of the issue image, and particularly by its malleability. The subject of IT in the public sector was packaged in the first cycle and repackaged in the following two cycles around the leading themes of the political or electoral agenda. Transparency and austerity, country competitiveness and bureaucratic reform, devolution and visibility for the end users have, in sequence, shaped the issue image of E-Government in this decade-long episode. Such flexibility of the issue did not activate interference effects from the champions of competing policy domains. A further reason for the extended career of E-Government (as a mainstay of public administration policies) in Italy was the fact that it echoed policy developments at the European Union level, thus triggering the certification of the issue and of the policy entrepreneurs.

On the other hand, despite its early start and the significant resources allocated to the E-Government policies, several experts and scholars question whether these actually resulted in a more efficient, responsive and transparent administration at the central and local level. Among the factors that may have hindered a systemic development of ICTs in public administrations, this chapter has identified the features of the policy sub-system, considered as a sticky institutional context to be understood in its evolutionary nature (Baumgartner and Jones 1993) and characterized by a certain degree of contention over its jurisdiction. In fact, the period under analysis witnessed a continuous reconfiguration of the E-Government policy sub-system, with ad hoc working groups, inter-ministerial and central–local coordination units coexisting with the dedicated Authority and, in the final phase, a new Ministry taking over the issue of E-Government. Two interrelated determinants explain the turnover in the policy sub-system, namely the instability characterizing the political and institutional context over the decade combined with the ambiguity in the mandate that has marked the functions and activities of the Authority since its inception.

The present study is not without limitations. In particular the research design does not lend itself easily to the assessment of the policy outcomes. Therefore, it would be meaningful to investigate the results further in the conceptual frame of a policy process analysis.

To conclude, previous studies warned public managers that designing and implementing E-Government initiatives require careful consideration of the technological and organizational conditions that enable the innovation. The evidence presented in this chapter supports the notion that also the dynamics of policy-making are not to be overlooked.

NOTES

1. In this chapter the acronyms IT (Information Technology) and ICT (Information and Communication Technologies) are used interchangeably. For a complete account of the shift from IT to ICT see Castells

(1996). IT policy and E-Government policy are also used without distinction, although E-Government as a label was coined much later when the first IT policies were launched.
2.   The term first appeared in the 1993 US National Performance Review.
3.   The funds totaled approximately 410 million Euros, coming from the auctioning of licenses for UMTS (Universal Mobile Telecommunications System) to telephone companies.

REFERENCES

Abell, P. (2004). Narrative explanation: an alternative to variable-centered explanation? *Annual Review of Sociology*, 30, 287–310.
Acaud, D. and Lakel, A. (2003). Electronic government and the French state: a negotiated and gradual reform. *Information Polity*, 8, 117–131.
Barzelay, M. (2001). *The New Public Management: Improving Research and Policy Dialogue.* Berkeley, CA: University of California Press.
Barzelay, M. (2003). Introduction: the process dynamics of public management policy making. *International Public Management Journal*, 6(3), 251–282.
Barzelay, M. (2007). Learning from second-hand experience: methodology for extrapolation-oriented case research. *Governance*, 20(3), 521–543.
Barzelay, M. and Gallego, R. (2006). From 'New Institutionalism' to 'Institutional Processualism': advancing knowledge about public management policy change. *Governance*, 19, 531–558.
Barzelay, M. and Gallego, R. (2010). The comparative historical analysis of public management policy cycles in France, Italy, and Spain: symposium introduction. *Governance: An International Journal of Policy, Administration, and Institutions*, 23(2), 209–223.
Bassanini, F. (2003). *Good Government Strategies: A Prospect for Integration. Reflection from the Italian Experience.* Fifth Global Forum on Reinventing Government, 3–7 November, Mexico City.
Bauer, M.W. and Gaskell, G. (2000). *Qualitative Researching with Text, Image and Sound.* London: Sage.
Baumgartner, F.R. and Jones, B.C. (1993). *Agendas and Instability in American Politics.* Chicago, IL: University of Chicago Press.
Bellamy, C. and Taylor, J. (1992). Informatisation and new public management: an alternative agenda for public administration. *Public Policy and Administration*, 7(29).
Bellamy, C. and Taylor, J.A. (1994). Reinventing government in the information age. *Public Money & Management*, 14, 59–62.
Brown, D. (2005). Electronic government and public administration. *International Review of Administrative Sciences*, 71, 241–254.
Cammarata, M. (1994–2004). Dieci anni di società dell'informazione, InterLex. Available at: http://www.inter-lex.it/attualit/1994-2004.htm (accessed January 2012).
Carter, L. and Weerakkody, V. (2008). E-government adoption: a cultural comparison. *Information Systems Frontiers*, 10, 473–482.
Castells, M. (1996). *The Rise of the Network Society.* Oxford: Blackwell.
Creswell, J.W. (1994). *Research Design: Qualitative and Quantitative Approaches.* London: Sage.
Dimitrova, D.V. and Chen, Y.C. (2006). Profiling the adopters of e-government information and services: the influence of psychological characteristics, civic mindedness, and information channels. *Social Science Computer Review*, 24, 172–188.
Dunleavy, P. and Margetts, H. (2000). The advent of digital government: public bureaucracies and the state in the internet age. Paper presented at the Annual Conference of the American Political Science Association, Omni Shoreham Hotel, Washington DC, 4 September.
Dunleavy, P., Margetts, H., Bastow, S. and Tinkler, J. (2006). New Public Management is dead – long live digital-era governance. *Journal of Public Administration Research and Theory*, 16, 467–494.
Elgie, R. and McMenamin, I. (2005). Credible commitment, political uncertainty or policy complexity? Explaining variations in the independence of non-majoritarian institutions in France. *British Journal of Political Science*, 35(3), 531–548.
Fedele, P. et al. (2007). Disaggregation, autonomy and re-regulation, contractualism: public agencies in Italy (1992–2005). *Public Management Review*, 9(4), 557–585.
Finocchiaro, G. (1991). *Informatica e pubblica amministrazione.* Bologna: Clueb.
Gilardi, F. (2002). Policy credibility and delegation to independent regulatory agencies: a comparative empirical analysis. *Journal of European Public Policy*, 9(6), 873–893.
Gil-García, J. Ramón and Pardo, Theresa A. (2005). E-government success factors: mapping practical tools to theoretical foundations. *Government Information Quarterly*, 22, 187–216.

Heeks, R. and Bailur, S. (2007). Analyzing e-government research: perspectives, philosophies, theories, methods, and practice. *Government Information Quarterly*, 24(2), 243–265.

Ho, A.T.K. and Ni, A.Y. (2004). Explaining the adoption of e-government features: a case study of Iowa County treasurers' offices. *American Review of Public Administration*, 34, 164–180.

Hudson, J. (1999). Informatization and public administration: a political science perspective. *Information, Communication & Society*, 2, 318–339.

Hudson, J. (2002). Digitising the structures of government: the UK's information age government agenda. *Policy and Politics*, 30, 515–531.

Kim, S. (2005). Individual-level factors and organizational performance in government organizations. *Journal of Public Administration Research and Theory*, 15, 245–261.

Kingdon, J. (1984). *Agendas, Alternatives, and Public Policies*. Boston, MA: Little, Brown.

La Porte, T.M., Demchak, C.C. and De Jong, M. (2002). Democracy and bureaucracy in the age of the web: empirical findings and theoretical speculations. *Administration & Society*, 34, 411–432.

Liou, K.T. (2008). E-government development and China's administrative reform. *International Journal of Public Administration*, 31, 76–95.

Lofgren, K. (2007). The governance of e-government: a governance perspective on the Swedish e-government strategy. *Public Policy and Administration*, 22, 335–352.

Luna-Reyes, L.F., Gil-Garcia, J.R. and Cruz, C.B. (2007). Collaborative digital government in Mexico: some lessons from federal Web-based interorganizational information integration initiatives. *Government Information Quarterly*, 24, 808–826.

Margetts, H. (2006). E-government in Britain – a decade on. *Parliamentary Affairs*, 59, 250–265.

Marshall, C. and Rossman, B.B. (1995). *Designing Qualitative Research*. Thousand Oaks, CA: Sage.

Moon, M.J. (2002). The evolution of e-government among municipalities: rhetoric or reality? *Public Administration Review*, 62, 424–433.

Moore, M.H. (1995). *Creating Public Value: Strategic Management in Government*. Cambridge, MA: Harvard University Press.

Moore, M.H. (2005). Break-through innovations and continuous improvements: two different models of innovative processes in the public sector. *Public Money and Management*, 25(1), 43–50.

Nasi, G., Frosini, F. and Cristofoli, D. (2011). Online service provision: are municipalities really innovative? The case of larger municipalities in Italy. *Public Administration*, 89(3), 821–839.

Norris, D.F. and Moon, M.J. (2005). Advancing e-government at the grassroots: tortoise or hare? *Public Administration Review*, 65, 64–75.

OECD (2003). *The e-Government Imperative*. OECD e-Government Studies, Paris: France.

Peled, A. (2001). Do computers cut red tape? *American Review of Public Administration*, 31, 414–435.

Pina, V., Torres, L. and Royo, S. (2007). Are ICTs improving transparency and accountability in the EU regional and local governments? An empirical study. *Public Administration*, 85, 449–472.

Ragin, C. (1987). *The Comparative Method*. Berkeley, CA: University of California Press.

Rose, W.R. and Grant, G.G. (2010). Critical issues pertaining to the planning and implementation of e-government initiatives. *Government Information Quarterly*, 27, 26–33.

Scholl, H.J. (2005). Organizational Transformation Through E-Government: Myth or Reality? *Lecture Notes in Computer Science*, 3591, 1–11.

Taylor, J. and Williams, H. (1990). Themes and issues in an information polity. *Journal of Information Technology*, 5, 151–160.

Thomas, J.C. and Streib, G. (2003). The new face of government: citizen-initiated contacts in the era of e-government. *Journal of Public Administration Research and Theory*, 13, 83–102.

Thompson, F. and Jones, L.R. (2008). Reaping the advantages of information and modern technology: moving from bureaucracy to hyperarchy and netcentricity. *International Public Management Review*, 9, 142–186.

Torres, L., Pina, V. and Acerete, B. (2006). E-governance developments in European Union cities: reshaping government's relationship with citizens. *Governance*, 19, 277–302.

Wengraf, T. (2001). *Qualitative Research Interviewing: Biographic Narrative and Semi-Structured Methods*. London: Sage.

Wong, W. and Welch, E. (2004). Does e-government promote accountability? A comparative analysis of website openness and government accountability. *Governance: An International Journal of Policy, Administration, and Institutions*, 17, 275–297.

Yildiz, M. (2007). E-government research: reviewing the literature, limitations, and ways forward. *Government Information Quarterly*, 24(3), 646–665.

Yin, R.K. (1993). *Applications of Case Study Research*. Beverly Hills, CA: Sage.

Yin, R.K. (1994). Discovering the future of the case study method in evaluation research. *Evaluation Practice*, 15(3), 283–290.

APPENDIX A

The 'corpus construction' (Bauer and Gaskell 2000, p. 23) has been built considering the criteria of relevance, triangulation (Creswell 1994; Yin 1994; Marshall and Rossman 1995) and saturation, through the analysis of the documents collected and the interviews conducted during the field research (2003–2005). Two main sets of documents were used for the study. One set included official documents such as Cabinet submissions, internal reports and project evaluation reports from the Italian Archive of the Prime Minister Council, from the Department for Public Administration and from the Ministry for Innovation and Technology. Another set of documents included research papers and feasibility studies conducted by academics and consultants of the Prime Minister Council. The list of the 20 relevant actors that were interviewed is: (1) a former Prime Minister; (2) a former Minister for Public Administration; (3) the former Director of the National Center for IT in Public Administration; (4) the former President of the Authority for IT in Public Administration; (5) the former Director of the Area 'Innovation, Regions and Local Administration' at the Department for Innovation and IT; (6) the Director General of the Public Administration Department; (7) the former Senior Official at the Public Administration Department in charge of E-Government; (8) a Senior Official at the Public Administration Department; (9) a Senior Official at the Department for Innovation and IT; (10, 11) two former consultants for the Public Administration Department and for the Department for Innovation and IT in charge of innovative projects; (12, 13, 14) three academics who worked as consultants for the E-Government projects during the episode; (15, 16, 17) three top managers of large IT vendors (IBM Italia, Oracle Italia and Microsoft Italia) in charge of analyzing and interacting with the public sector during the episode; and (18, 19, 20) three top bureaucrats of local administrations (Modena, Siena and Reggio Emilia) which received funding from the Public Administration Department for their Electronic Government pilot projects. These bureaucrats also participated in the preliminary stages of the Electronic Government Action Plan.

The semi-structured interviews took place mostly in the interviewees' offices. The duration ranged from 90 minutes to three hours. Four interviewees were consulted twice. Interviews were conducted taking into consideration the peculiarities of 'elite interviewing' (Bauell and Gaskell 2000) for the rapport-building and the interview schedules. Consistent with Wengraf's recommendations (2001), the research questions (i.e. main research questions and research sub-questions) have been distinguished from interview questions/prompts. Access both to internal documents and to the interviewees was facilitated by the author's work as consultant for the Public Administration Department at the Prime Minister Council (1999 and 2000). Atlas was used for coding, retrieving and recording the documents and interview text.

APPENDIX B

Establishing the Authority for IT in Public Administration AIPA (1992–1993)	Launching the E-Government Action Plan (1996–2000)	Launching the E-Government Funding Projects (2000–2002)
Setting the agenda – Packaging of IT coordination in terms of austerity and market competition *Developing the proposal for an Authority for IT in Public Administration (AIPA)* – Consulting with the unions and considering alternatives – Appointing an Extraordinary Commissioner for IT in Public Administration (1992) – Formulating the mission of the Authority – Projecting the Authority resources and personnel needs *Finalizing and launching Authority for IT in the Public Administration (AIPA)*	*Setting the agenda* – Establishing the Information Society Forum within the Prime Minister Council (1996) – Including the issue of IT in the wider public sector reform issue (1997) – Establishing a Technical Center for the Government Digital Network (1997) – Establishing a new Unit for the Information Society, reporting directly to the Prime Minister (1999) *Developing the Action Plan* – Gathering ideas and working with the EU DG on the Information Society (1998, 1999) – Collaborating with the new structure for the Information Society and the permanent task-force in the Office of the Prime Minister (1999) – Negotiating with the local authorities (establishment of a Coordination Center for Territorial Authorities (1999)) – Gathering ideas from academics and consultants – Negotiating the resources with the Executive *Finalizing and launching the Action Plan*	*Setting the agenda* – Creating an ad hoc Unit for E-Government within the Ministry for Public Administration (2000) – Creating an ad hoc Ministry for Innovation and ICTs (2001) – Certifying part of the previous team – Repackaging the issue in terms of federalism *Developing the initiative* – Appropriating 410 million Euros from the UMTS licenses sale to fund the E-Government Action Plan (2001) – Negotiating with local administrations and establishing the Regional Competence Network on E-Government (2002) – Gathering ideas from academics and consultants *Finalizing and launching the call for projects*

19. Innovation and information in public/third sector partnerships for older people's services: case studies from England and Italy

Rob Wilson, Sue Baines and Mike Martin

INTRODUCTION

The last decade has seen numerous initiatives to transform care and health services through electronic government (e-government) initiatives at central, regional and local levels. E-government (also known variously as digital era and transformational government) has been defined as using Information and Communications Technologies (ICTs) to support modernised public services (Silcock 2001). More recently, as public management has become increasingly inter-organisational, the emphasis has been on multi-agency and partnership-oriented developments involving statutory agencies, the voluntary and charitable sector, and commercial suppliers (Pestoff and Brandsen 2010). Importance attached to Third Sector Organisations (TSOs) in public services is an international phenomenon (Milligan and Conradson 2006). Many governments have been looking for new ways to involve them; however, there are national variations in rationales for doing so as well as in the established roles and responsibilities of different sectors (Lyon and Glucksmann 2008; Pestoff and Brandsden 2010).

Arguments for enrolling charities, social enterprises and community-based organisations in public services rest on claims that include: they are embedded within communities (of place and identity); they are responsive to the needs of service users; and, perhaps most of all, they can innovate. Together these have been described as important resources for service transformation (Lewis 2005). This chapter concerns innovations intended to develop and deploy ICTs to improve services in health and social care for older people. Its focus is on such innovations when they involve forms of partnership across the public and third sectors. We consider the varied and challenging nature of interactions between third sector service providers and state agencies on the frontline, drawing upon the influential concept of 'co-production' that emphasises the 'shared character of the production process' in services (Brandsen and Pestoff 2006, p.496). Such a vision of modernised, co-produced public services, we note, is often essentially about the sharing of information (Wilson, Cornford, Baines and Mawson 2011).

There is a substantial and growing literature around the independence and distinctiveness of TSOs, and how these can become compromised by taking on public services (Curtis 2008; Milbourne 2009; Macmillan 2010). It has been argued that when they choose (or are constrained) to deliver to state agenda, TSOs adopt characteristics of statutory agencies, and even work towards 'a bureaucratic mandate laid down by the state' (Hodgson 2004, p.140). Something that has been much less well rehearsed is the explosion of information that is moving between TSOs and public agencies. As TSOs

– especially larger charities and social enterprises – have become increasingly central to the delivery of state-sponsored social care, they have been required to professionalise their administration and, as a side effect, become more adept at managing information both internally and externally (Wilson, Martin, Walsh and Richter 2011). While many large TSOs have sophisticated ICTs and data-handling, others are at the opposite end of the informationalisation spectrum. For some, all this points to a need for the sector to embrace the information economy. Others are sceptical about the advantages of the collection and use of information, seeing it variously as a bureaucratic overhead, a trend promoting reductions in diversity within the sector, and a threat to client consent and confidentiality. It must be emphasised, of course, that the TSO is large and diverse. There are arguments about where its boundaries lie and, indeed, if it can reasonably be called a 'sector' (Halfpenny and Reid 2002). It is 'complex in the sense that there are a great many types of organisations of different sizes and structures, doing many different things in many different ways' (Chapman et al. 2009, p. 14). The recent momentum gained by 'social enterprise' has increased interest in organisations that use business tools and techniques to achieve social aims (Di Domenico, Tracey and Haugh 2009; Dey 2010). A useful working definition is that the TSO consists of organisations that are formal or institutionalised; separate from government; self-governing and non-profit-distributing. Moreover, they typically involve some degree of voluntary participation (Billis and Glennerster 1998).

We turn next to consider innovation across the public and third sectors, and introduce a typology of TSO goals to reflect on the contested nexus of innovation, partnerships and information. Then we illustrate these themes with examples from our engagement as academic partners in projects that attempted to implement ICTs-based improvements to older people's services within complex partnership contexts where a variety of innovation dynamics were in play. We reflect on how these projects confronted challenges in the areas of governance, trust, and the distribution of tasks and responsibilities for care.

PUBLIC SERVICE INNOVATION ACROSS SECTORS

Much innovation theory has been limited to products and processes in the private sector and derived from studies of science and technology. One useful broad definition of innovation that can be applied to the public sector is:

> Doing something new i.e. introducing a new practice or process, creating a new product (good or service), or adopting a new pattern of intra- or inter-organisational relationships (including the delivery of goods and services). (Green, Howells and Miles (2001), quoted in Cunningham (2005))

This definition can encompass development of new services and the application of technologies to service improvement as well as new market relations and change in the welfare mix. Importantly, it can accommodate social innovation, defined as 'new ideas that meet unmet needs' (Mulgan 2006, p. 4) and 'innovations in governance', which refers to innovations that 'burst the boundary of an organization's hold on a given (and complex) problem' (Moore and Hartley 2008, p. 15). Caring services for older adults are perceived as ever more demanding on public resources, one of the difficult social problems (sometimes called 'wicked' problems) that demand innovation and better use of technology (Department of Health 2006). Across Europe ICTs developments are increasingly prominent in attempts to transform the cost-effective delivery of health and care (Commission of the European Union 2009).

In the UK, enhancing the role of the 'third sector' in public services became a key strand of the drive to improve public service delivery under the new Labour government, especially in its second and third terms, when it put in place mechanisms to harness the contributions of a much more diverse range of partner organisations to tackle social and health inequalities (HM Treasury 2007). After the 2010 election the new coalition government declared its intention to 'support the creation and expansion of mutuals, cooperatives, charities and social enterprises, and support these groups to have much greater involvement in the running of public services' (Cabinet Office 2010, p. 2). The 'Big Society' agenda and the debates around it have intensified interest in TSOs (including social enterprises) and raised expectations for their capacity to deliver better services across the UK in an era of public spending cuts. There is, however, some evidence of increased divergence between England and the UK's devolved administrations (Alcock 2010; Danson and Whitham 2011).

Much of the positive case for engaging the TSO in public services is around claims that it is close to service users and incorporates their needs into the shaping of services better than the statutory sector (Paxton, Pearce, Unwin and Molyneux 2005; Blackmore 2006). This form of closeness is captured in the notion of 'stakeholder ambiguity' (Billis and Glennerster 1998). Stakeholder ambiguity refers to the lack of clear-cut differentiation between the various roles of employer, employee, provider, recipient and volunteer. This implies a flexible, changing and informal structure capable of responding more sensitively than the state or the market to the disadvantages of service users. In this process, the distinctions embodied in the concepts of value-adding, value-extracting and evaluation are also blurred. The other strong assumption that underpins the case for enhanced involvement of TSOs in public services is innovation, in contrast to a public sector where innovation can be seen as 'an optional extra or an added burden' (Mulgan and Albury 2003). TSO capacity for innovation is often taken for granted; indeed, innovation in the sector has been described as the 'very crux of [its] distinctiveness' (Public Administration Select Committee 2008, p. 29). These positive arguments for the shift in responsibility to deliver care must be balanced by the more negative issues of cost-saving, transfer of risk and the shrinking of the traditional public sector, a contrast which underlines the political and social complexity of the contexts and developments we are discussing.

In many Western states voluntary groups initially pioneered the services that became part of statutory welfare in the twentieth century and continued to be innovative as pathfinders and experimenters after the establishment of welfare states (Billis and Glennerster 1998; Osborne, Chew and McLaughlin 2008). There have been some outstanding examples of new thinking and new ways of responding to unrecognised and unmet need. Children's hospices, for example, were an innovation that grew from a third sector response to the closure of long-stay hospitals in the UK in the latter part of the twentieth century (Jackson and Robinson 2003). In the context of services for older people, TSOs typically offer so-called 'low level' services that can be innovative in responding creatively to the importance older people attach to support to care for themselves, rather than being recipients of care (Clark et al., 1998). There is evidence of enormous creativity and resourcefulness in the sector in finding ways to do things differently (Amin 2009).

Research by surveys conducted in Britain in 1994 demonstrated that claims for innovative capacity in the third sector could be well founded although innovation was a response to imperatives from central and local government rather than an innate sectoral characteristic (Osborne 1998). A follow-up study in 2006 found that innovative activity of TSOs had shrunk in that 12-year period (Osborne, Chew and McLaughlin 2008). The authors argued that this apparently counterintuitive finding was explained largely by changes in government notions of innovation, rather than changes within the sector. New Labour government pronouncements invoked innovation but it was identified with continuous improvement rather than discontinuity, as under the New Public Management framework favoured by its Conservative predecessor. Osborne, Chew and McLaughlin (2008) also argued that commissioning processes dominated by local authority approaches to risk management privilege the tried and tested over the innovative. In other words innovation is not always possible when working to risk-averse public policy frameworks (Osborne, Chew and McLaughlin 2008).

As a heuristic device for talking about the various dimensions of innovations and TSOs we borrow a typology of generic third sector outcomes (Harris, Mainelli and O'Callaghan 2002). Harris, Mainelli and O'Callaghan propose four outcomes across the sector: service delivery (i.e. meeting identified and accepted needs); communitarian (i.e. addressing needs through communal activity such as volunteering); expanding frontiers (i.e. moving into new areas to mitigate needs); and changing systems. This last category invokes 'conceptual innovations – in the sense of introducing new missions, new worldviews, objectives, strategies and rationales' (Halvorsen, Hauknes, Miles and Røste 2005, p. 2). These are not types of organisation but orientations towards outcomes that can co-exist within the same organisation and change and develop over time.

The distinction in this typology between delivery of existing services and notions of pursuing new areas and new ideas is consistent with Blackmore's (2006) analysis that in order to contribute to the improvement of public services TSOs not only deliver but identify gaps in service provision and help to discover and design new solutions. The Harris et al (2002) four fold typology (see Figure 19.1) is very close to Osborne and Flynn's (1997) four types of innovation: totally new; expansionary (i.e. existing service to new group): evolutionary (i.e. new service to existing groups); and developing existing services. We prefer the Harris et al. typology because it explicitly includes the communitarian which can recognise new democratic spaces and ideas of reciprocity and re-distribution. It helps us to think clearly about links and tensions between third sector and public sector goals, and kinds of information they need to exchange.

METHODS OF ENQUIRY – 'BIG AND RICH' PICTURES

We turn now to a series of cross-sector partnerships that have worked towards innovation in services for older people. The first is an electronic single assessment process (SAP) which was intended to help transform services for older people by making their personal information available across organisations and agencies. The second is about innovations in care for older people in the context of a telecare system developed as part of a European

Typology of Third sector
outcomes

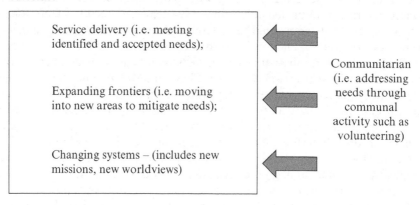

Source: Adapted from Harris et al. (2002).

Figure 19.1   Typology of partnership innovation

Framework project and trialled in Italy. In the final example we return to England and consider a much more TSO-driven example of innovation which includes public sector partners.

The authors were involved in each of these projects in roles that included summative and formative evaluation and, particularly in the first two examples, working with participants towards practical outcomes and new understanding. The team has a longstanding commitment to action research grounded in real-life problems to produce change. Our methodological approach uses multiple methods including exploratory case studies and facilitated workshops, often using multi-media-based visualisation and simulation.

Innovation in Partnership: Example from the Field

The single assessment process was intended to ensure joined-up care for older people by supporting inter-organisational and inter-professional information-sharing. SAP systems were introduced across England following the recommendations of the third national Service Framework for Older People (2001). One of the major arguments in favour of moving to a SAP was clinical research evidence for the success of structured assessment approaches to deliver strong long-term management and effective support for survival and function in older persons. SAPs were an innovation in practice designed to provide a common approach to sharing information across different agencies concerned with care for an older person. They involved new inter-organisational relationships, improving co-ordination, referral and discharge between the different parts of the statutory care network. SAPs were developed and deployed as paper-based or computer-based forms that structured the practitioner assessment processes. They used formal structured assessment process tools including combinations of tick boxes, validated assessment scores and some free text. In this section we are concerned with the implementation of an electronic SAP in the north west of England. This was part of one of the national e-government projects known as Framework for Information Environments (FAME) (see www.fame-uk.org). FAME puts information systems in place at a local level in pilot sites to support information-sharing in various services (e.g. to vulnerable older people). The FAME SAP in the north west of England involved seven partners who were from local authorities and the health service, plus a charity that is part of a national federation dedicated to the well-being of older people. The Project Initiation Document recognised that it required joint working across a wide range of partners 'where perhaps this has not been done to such an extent before'.

The difficulty of working across the health/social care divide in England is well documented, and the challenges in this respect were foreseen in FAME and, for the most part, successfully mitigated by project planning and hard work (Gannon-Leary, Baines and Wilson 2006). There were, however, unforeseen tensions that raised more difficult questions about the nature and limits of ICTs-enabled integration in older people's services (for details see Wilson and Baines 2009). One of these tensions was about the inclusion of a service provider from the third sector. There was already a local information-sharing protocol (ISP), which the project hoped to adopt as a convenient short cut to devising one specifically for this partnership. It transpired after most of the partners thought the ISP was in place that it did not take account of the working practices of the third sector partner, in particular its use of volunteers as well as employees in advice and support roles. The ISP had to be hastily revised at some cost to meeting timescales in progressing the project. Referrals to the central duty team (social services) were usually from third parties – such as neighbours or family – who cannot give consent to sharing personal information about individuals with others. The difficulty was overcome with a workaround by referring the case within the local authority to the social services or occupational therapy service, which would later need to seek consent from the user to share information with other agencies. These problems are important because they illustrate how boundaries around agencies can be defined and managed in complex multi-agency environments and how the contributions of volunteer-using charities, families and informal carers in the community can be recognised. A key lesson from this SAP was the limitation of local formal solutions that failed to accommodate the roles of non-statutory participants (third sector organisations and also neighbours, carers and friends of service users). Taking the typology in Figure 19.1 as a frame or analysis, it was a public service-driven change project mainly situated in the 'service delivery' level. It could not accommodate the diverse values and assumptions about client relationships – and client information – of a TSO partner. The communitarian practices and values of the partner, in this case its involvement with volunteers, formed a barrier that was awkward to overcome in partnership with statutory agencies.

We turn now to a project known as Older People's Services at Home (OLDES) that was a collaboration between 11 European partners, including local government, system developers, service providers and a multi-disciplinary university research team of which the authors were part. In order to meet the priorities under Ambient Assisted Living for the Ageing Society, the OLDES project partners undertook to develop low-cost, easy-to-use telecare technologies offering entertainment services as well as health care monitoring for older people in their homes. There were two aspects: a feature called 'tele-accompany' involving a 'digital companion' delivered through the activities of specialist call centre operators and members of voluntary organisations to combat the isolation of older people living alone, and health monitoring consisting of sensors for vital functions and movement detection. Both these technologies were trialled in the Municipality of Bologna in the Italian region of Emila-Romagna.

The role of the third sector in health and social care is weaker in Italy than in many other European countries (Lyon and Glucksmann 2008). In Bologna, however, OLDES became associated from the inception with a local political vision of increased participation by the city's voluntary associations in the care of its older people. Two social institutions, the Catholic Church and the Communist Party, run voluntary associations in Bologna. These associations provide facilities such as bars and recreation centres, reading and TV rooms, exercise classes, leisure activities and social events (Wilson et al., in press). They receive some funding from the state but are autonomous and largely run by volunteers, who are often older people. The voluntary associations were not formally partners in OLDES and had no funding from the project. The associations nevertheless became energetic champions of OLDES because it seemed to them to offer future strategies to bring older people together and fight their isolation. The pilot system failed to work when initially installed in older people's homes and had to be removed for further technical development. Dealing with this event was mediated on behalf of the project by the parishes and social centres. Their intervention with older people at this stage was vital to ensure that the project recovered from such a serious setback. The Municipality of Bologna aims at offering the whole system to all people over 75 in the city (about 30,000 persons could be involved in the medium term). In terms of the typology, this project is about expanding frontiers; that is, being able to do more, both for the municipality and the associations. Its success depended on introducing its technical innovations in ways that respond to social, cultural and ethical constraints and conditions of older people, their families and carers. The communitarian nature of the organisations in this context was a significant strength when it became aligned with the Municipality and the Framework project. Information was a resource for strategic and tactical decision-making.

The final example is part of an innovation programme in the north east region of England that was initiated in 2010 to support innovative and collaborative projects that would deliver service efficiencies to local authorities and care providers, and improve outcomes for people who use services. Unlike the other projects discussed, this is ongoing at the time of writing. The project we highlight is led by a social care charity that develops services to empower people with dementia and their carers within the life of their local community. The charity, which has an annual turnover of four million pounds and 210 employees, originated in a pilot project funded from 1993 to 1994 as a joint initiative between health and social services to test the feasibility of supporting people with dementia in their own homes. When the initial short-term funding ended, the project manager set up the charity with carers and former carers as advisors. Its aim from the outset was to provide alternative ways to deliver care and it has been dedicated to developing new approaches with people living with dementia to ensure they are at the centre of any decision-making process. It has gained a very high profile. For example, it became one of the Department of Health social enterprise pathfinders and the chief executive won a social entrepreneurship award. The aim of the project is to put people with dementia and their carers in the lead by developing, implementing and reviewing a value-based 'Enriched Support and Development Plan' in collaboration with the Department of

Health and three local authorities. It is also training carers as volunteer 'peer navigators' whose roles include collecting life histories with multi-media including photos and music. Another strand is about piloting assistive technology in the home to minimise risks and promote independence of people with dementia and their carers. The emphasis in all this is on innovation and changing systems by challenging established ways of doing dementia care with new ideas. Innovation in this case, unlike the two examples discussed above, is driven by the TSO partner. The charity is deeply embedded in communitarian values and dedicated to ensuring that the voices of people with dementia are constantly listened to and influence thinking and practice, in the spirit of co-production. The information this requires is specific, localised, 'entangled' (Carlson and Anderson 2007) information capable of producing what has been called 'knowledge-in-action based on practical experience' (Ledwith 2007). Such local knowledge or contextual information may be limited, however, by lack of scalability (Zahra, Gedajlovic, Neubaum and Shulman 2009).

DISCUSSION AND CONCLUSIONS

The transformation of public services is increasingly understood to require the sharing of data from multiple agencies in order to construct a rounded or 'whole systems' view of issues and problems (Varney 2006). The decline of the state as a direct provider of welfare is associated with marketisation and with a push for charities, community groups, user-led organisations and social enterprises to become more active and innovative service providers (Bull 2008; Amin 2009). In this chapter we have drawn upon examples of our longstanding engagement with public services in diverse contexts to consider some innovations involving partnerships with TSOs. We have tentatively mapped these onto a typology of TSO outcomes to start to think about the intersection of information, innovation and cross-sector partnership.

Information and innovation are important because they encompass activities that cut across boundaries of services, innovation and governance. There are many reasons to pay closer attention to cross-sector innovation and information, including information management, information security, safeguarding of personal client information, personal and organisational identity, and roles and responsibilities with regard to information about services. The typology draws in the goals of the third sector as a means of understanding what information and innovation might mean and how they may interact in different service contexts. Further, it raises questions about the communitarian ideals of individual organisations and the ways in which innovation is valued in a range of partnership contexts.

As in other multi-agency environments, managers and professionals from the public and third sector domains often struggle to find ways of bridging their respective 'social worlds'. Participants in our research sometimes express a desire to improve understanding between the sectors. The metaphor of speaking and learning a 'common language' was often invoked to explain these tensions. How can we as academic researchers meet such theoretical, conceptual, political and practical challenges? We suggest that it is by bringing organisations together in addressing the 'multi-ness' of the challenges in a way that supports the development of 'big and rich' pictures as a means of shaping the agenda for further action and the shaping of an environment to support innovation, rather than by prescribing individual service-level innovations. In order to cultivate a richer set of discourse(s) we need to ask who is sharing what information, what is being interpreted, for whom, for what purpose and in what context (Wilson, Cornford, Baines and Mawson 2011).

REFERENCES

Alcock, P. (2010). Big society or civil society? A new policy environment for the third sector. Available at: http://www.tsrc.ac.uk/LinkClick.aspx?fileticket=PwhvBXnPGAU%3D&tabid=716 (accessed January 2012).

Amin, A. (2009). Extraordinarily ordinary: working in the social economy. *Social Enterprise Journal*, 5(1), 30–49.

Billis, D. and Glennerster, H. (1998). Human services and the voluntary sector: towards a theory of comparative advantage. *Journal of Social Policy*, 27(1), 79–98.

Blackmore, A. (2006). *How Voluntary and Community Organisations can Help Transform Public Services.* London: NCVO.

Brandsen, T. and Pestoff, V. (2006). Co-production, the Third Sector and the delivery of public services: an introduction. *Public Management Review*, 8(4), 493–501.

Bull, M. (2008). Challenging tensions: critical, theoretical and empirical perspectives on social enterprise. *International Journal of Entrepreneurial Behaviour and Research*, 14(5), 268–275.

Cabinet Office (2010). *Building the Big Society*. London: Cabinet Office.

Carlson, S. and Anderson, B. (2007). What are data? The many kinds of data and their implications for data re-use. *Journal of Computer-Mediated Communication*, 12(2), article 15.

Chapman, T., Robinson, F., Brown, J., Shaw, S., Ford, C., Bailey, E. and Crow, R. (2009). Mosaic, jigsaw or abstract? Getting a big picture perspective on the Third Sector in North East England and Cumbria. Northern Rock Foundation Third Sector Trends Study. Available at: www.nr-foundation.org.uk/thirdsec tortrends (accessed November 2010).

Clark, H., Dyer, S. and Horwood, J. (1998). *'That Bit of Help': The High Value of Low Level Preventative Services for Older People*. Bristol: The Policy Press.

Commission of the European Union (2009). Overview of the European strategy in ICT for ageing well. Available at: http://ec.europa.eu/information_society/activities/einclusion/docs/ageing/overview.pdf (accessed January 2012).

Cunningham, P. (2005). Innovation in the health sector: case study analysis. Publin Report D19. Available at: http://www.step.no/publin/reports/d19-casestudies-health.pdf (accessed January 2012).

Curtis, T. (2008). Finding the grit that makes a pearl. *International Journal of Entrepreneurial Behaviour & Research*, 14(5), 276–290.

Danson, M. and Whittam, G. (2011). Scotland's civic society v England's Big Society? Diverging roles of the VCS in public service delivery. *Social Policy and Society*, 10(3), 353–363.

Department of Health (2006). *Our Health, Our Care, Our Say: A New Direction for Community Services*. Available at: http://www.dh.gov.uk/en/Publicationsandstatistics/Publications/PublicationsPolicyAnd Guidance/DH_4127453 (accessed January 2012).

Dey, P. (2010). The politics of narrating social entrepreneurship. *Journal of Enterprising Communities: People and Places in the Global Economy*, 4(1), 85–108.

Di Domenico, M., Tracey, P. and Haugh, H. (2009). Social economy involvement in public service delivery: community engagement and accountability. *Regional Studies*, 43(7), 981–992.

Gannon-Leary, P., Baines, S. and Wilson, R. (2006). Collaboration and partnership: a review and reflections on a national project to join up local services in England. *Journal of Interprofessional Care 2006*, 20(6), 665–674.

Green, L., Howells, J. and Miles, I. (2001). Services and innovation: dynamics of service innovation in the European Union. Available at: http://europa.eu.int/comm/economy_finance/epc/documents/annexg_en.pdf (accessed January 2012).

Halfpenny, P. and Reid, M. (2002). Research on the voluntary sector: an overview. *Policy and Politics*, 30(4), 533–550.

Halvorsen, T., Hauknes, J., Miles, I. and Røste, R. (2005). On the differences between public and private sector innovation. Publin Report No. D9, Oslo.

Harris, I., Mainelli, M. and O'Callaghan, M. (2002). Evidence of worth in not-for-profit sector organizations. *Strategic Change*, 11, 399–410.

Haugh, H. and Kitson, M. (2007). The Third Way and the third sector: New Labour's economic policy and the social economy. *Cambridge Journal of Economics*, 31(6), 973–994.

HM Treasury (2007). *Building the Evidence Base: Third Sector Values in the Delivery of Public Services*. Available at: http://www.hm-treasury.gov.uk/media/2/8/thirdsectorreview_buildingtheevidence.pdf (accessed January 2012).

Hodgson, L. (2004). Manufactured civil society: counting the cost. *Critical Social Policy*, 24(2), 139–164.

Jackson, P. and Robinson, C. (2003). Children's hospices: where do they fit? *Critical Social Policy*, 23(1), 103–112.

Ledwith, M. (2007). Reclaiming the radical agenda: a critical approach to community development. *Concept* 17(2), 8–12. Available at: http://www.infed.org/community/critical_community_development.htm (accessed January 2012).

Lewis, J. (2005). New Labour's approach to the voluntary sector. *Social Policy and Society*, 4(2), 121–131.

Lyon, D. and Glucksmann, M.G. (2008). Comparative configurations of care work across Europe. *Sociology*, 42(1), 101–118.

Macmillan, R. (2010). The third sector delivering public services: an evidence review, Birmingham, TSRC. Available at: http://www.tsrc.ac.uk/LinkClick.aspx?fileticket=l9qruXn%2fBN8%3d&tabid=712 (accessed 10 October 2010).

Milbourne, L. (2009). Remodelling the third sector: advancing collaboration or competition in community based initiatives? *Journal of Social Policy*, 38(2), 1–21.

Milligan, C. and Conradson, D. (2006). *Geographies of Voluntarism: New Spaces of Health, Welfare and Governance*. Bristol: The Policy Press.

Moore, M. and Hartley, J. (2008). Innovations in governance. *Public Management Review*, 10(1), 3–20.

Mulgan, G. (2006). Social innovation: what is it, why it matters, how it can be accelerated. Young Foundation. Available at: www. youngfoundation.org.uk (accessed January 2012).

Mulgan, G. and Albury, D. (2003). *Innovation in the Public Sector*. London: Strategy Unit, Cabinet Office.

Osborne, S.P. (1998). *Voluntary Organizations and Innovation in Public Services*. London: Routledge.

Osborne, S. and Flynn, N. (1997). Managing the innovative capacity of voluntary and non-profit organizations in the provision of public services. *Public Money and Management*, 17(4), 31–39.

Osborne, S.P., Chew, C. and McLaughlin, K. (2008). The once and future pioneers? The innovative capacity of voluntary organisations and the provision of public services: a longitudinal approach. *Public Management Review*, 10(1), 51–70.

Paxton, W., Pearce, N., Unwin, J. and Molyneux, P. (2005). *The Voluntary Sector Delivering Public Services: Transfer or Transformation?* York: Joseph Rowntree Foundation.

Pestoff, V. and Brandsen, T. (2010). Public governance and the Third Sector: opportunities for co-production and innovation. In S. Osborne (ed.), *The New Public Governance? Emerging Perspectives on the Theory and Practice of Public Governance*. London: Routledge, pp. 223–236.

Public Administration Select Committee (2008). *Public Services and the Third Sector: Rhetoric and Reality – Eleventh Report of Session 2007–08*. London: HMSO.

Silcock, R. (2001). What is e-government? *Parliamentary Affairs*, 54(1), 88–102.

Varney, D. (2006). *Service Transformation: A Better Service for Citizens and Businesses, a Better Deal for the Taxpayer*. London: HM Treasury.

Wilson, R. and Baines, S. (2009). Are there limits to the integration of care for older people? In B.D. Loader, M. Hardey and L. Keeble (eds), *Third Age Welfare: Health and Social Care Informatics for Older People*. London: Routledge, pp. 17–27.

Wilson, R., Cornford, J., Baines, S. and Mawson, J. (2011). Information for localism? Policy sensemaking for local governance. *Public Money and Management*, 31(4), 295–300.

Wilson, R., Maniatopoulos, G., Martin, M. and McLoughlin, I. (in press). *Innovating Relationships: Taking a Co-productive Approach to the Shaping of Telecare Services for Older People*. Information, Communication and Society.

Wilson, R., Martin, M., Walsh, S. and Richter, P. (2011). Re-mixing digital economies in the voluntary community sector? Governing identity information and information sharing in the mixed economy of care for children and young people. *Social Policy & Society*, 10(3).

Zahra, S., Gedajlovic, E., Neubaum, D. and Shulman, J. (2009). A typology of social entrepreneurs. *Journal of Business Venturing*, 24(5), 519–532.

PART V

COLLABORATION, NETWORKS, CO-PRODUCTION AND THE ROLE OF THE THIRD SECTOR IN INNOVATION IN PUBLIC SERVICES

20. Collaborative innovation in the public sector
Jacob Torfing

INTRODUCTION

The public sector is far more dynamic and innovative than its reputation. Take, for instance, the spectacular changes in health care, employment policy and environmental protection that we have been witnessing over the last 30–40 years. The organization and the mode of governance in the public sector have also undergone dramatic transformations, and so has the relation between citizens and public authorities as a result of the arrival of new digital means of communication. However, public innovations in policy, organization and services are often one-off episodes driven by more or less accidental events such as public scandals, the recruitment of new managers, public spending cuts or technological inventions (Borins 2001, p. 313). Moreover, the efforts to produce innovative solutions are typically confined to public organizations that are facing considerable pressures and have an experimental culture or a proactive leadership. Hence, the attempt to improve public services and break policy deadlocks requires the development of a new innovation agenda that aims to turn innovation into a permanent and systematic activity that pervades the entire public sector from local institutions and municipalities, over ministries and government agencies, to international and supranational governance structures.

Today, there is a growing demand for innovation in the public sector. It is impossible to meet the rising expectations of citizens and private firms in a situation with limited, or even shrinking, public budgets without generating new and smarter services. The mounting ambitions of professionals, public managers and elected politicians are unattainable in our increasingly complex and fragmented societies if we do not learn to think and act more creatively in relation to crosscutting problems. Finally, the solution of the increasing numbers of 'wicked problems', which cannot be solved by standard solutions or by spending more money, calls for innovative solutions.

Public innovation is sometimes a result of heroic efforts of individual entrepreneurs. Competitive markets and bureaucracies with stable procedures for adaption might also spur public innovation. However, this chapter explores another source of public innovation as it highlights the role of *multi-actor collaboration* in spurring innovation relating to public policies, organizations and services. In recent decades there has been an astonishing proliferation of networks, partnerships and other forms of interactive governance. Governance networks are arenas for collaborative interaction that facilitate creative learning, the cross-fertilization of ideas, coordinated implementation and the creation of joint ownership to innovative solutions. However, as we shall see, many things can go wrong in the contingent processes of networking, collaboration and innovation and the precarious links between them. As such, some kind of innovation management is required in order to remove barriers, enhance drivers and keep the processes of collaborative innovation on track.

In the attempt to elucidate the role of collaborative innovation for reinvigorating the public sector, this chapter proceeds as follows. The first section explores the ambivalence of New Public Management in relation to public innovation and suggests that the development of the emerging forms of New Public Governance will help to unleash the innovative potential of collaboration. The second section defines innovation and collaboration. It also explains how collaboration can enhance public innovation and discusses the advantage of collaborative innovation vis-à-vis other innovation strategies. The third section presents some empirical examples of collaborative innovation while the fourth section assesses the risk of failure and the need for managing collaborative innovation. The final section provides an overview of how different strands of governance network theory can help us in studying collaborative innovation in the public sector.

FROM NEW PUBLIC MANAGEMENT TO NEW PUBLIC GOVERNANCE

Driven by the neoliberalist criticisms of the public sector for being too big, too inefficient and too expensive, a wave of New Public Management reforms has swept through the public sector in most Western countries (Pollitt and Bouckaert 2004). The key ambition of New Public Management is partly to increase the use of market-driven governance mechanisms based on competition and free consumer choice in order to create a more dynamic and flexible public sector; and partly to develop new and more effective forms of public management based on clear objectives, performance measurement and economic incentives that aim to enhance the motivation and entrepreneurial spirit of public managers and their employees (Hood 1991).

Some of the protagonists of New Public Management have seen themselves as leaders of a reform movement aiming to enhance public innovation. According to Osborne and Gaebler (1992), New Public Management aims to foster an entrepreneurial spirit that will reinvigorate the public sector. One of the key ideas is that competition between public and private contractors will stimulate service innovation. Another idea is that public managers should take responsibility for developing the public sector through a stronger focus on results, a flexible use of rules and resources, and an increasing emphasis on user satisfaction. Finally, New Public Management has recommended the formation of public–private partnerships as a means to enhance innovation through the mobilization of private resources and the sharing of risks (Hodge and Greve 2005).

Although the partnership strategy paves the way for a collaborative approach to public innovation, there are several barriers to collaborative innovation inherent to New Public Management. First of all, the emphatic concern for greater cost efficiency tends to marginalize discussions of the content and quality of public services that are often the primary interest of public employees and private stakeholders and the key to getting these actors involved in collaborative innovation. Secondly, the privileged role of public managers tends to exclude the important contribution of public employees, users and elected politicians to public innovation. Thirdly, the competitive spirit that pervades the governance arrangement associated with New Public Management tends to preclude the development of mutual trust that is the *sine qua non* for collaborative innovation. Public and private actors that are competing for public money and contracts find it difficult to share knowledge and collaborate on the development of new methods and services. Finally, the strong demand for standardized services, documentation of activities and measurement of past performance is not only costly in terms of time and resources, but also tends to inhibit innovation since the innovative public agency may have stopped delivering the services that are being measured and thus the innovative practices are not properly documented. As a result, an innovative public agency might risk being penalized for innovating.

Fortunately, we are currently seeing a gradual shift from New Public Management to New Public Governance (Osborne 2006, 2010). Whereas New Public Management tends to view public monopolies as the key problem and enhanced competition as the preferred solution, New Public Governance tends to see complexity and fragmentation as the key challenge and the formation of interactive forms of collaborative governance that cuts across organizational and institutional boundaries as the way forward (Torfing et al., 2012). New Public Governance replaces the intraorganizational view and the input and output focus of New Public Management with an interorganizational approach to governance and a focus on processes and outcomes (Osborne 2006). As such, it offers a new paradigm for studying how a plurality of interdependent public and private actors, who are operating in a complex and fragmented world, engage in collaborative processes and produce innovative solutions that lead to desired outcomes. Such a paradigm will help to unleash the innovative potential of collaborative interaction, as its more or less explicit focus on the institutional conditions for collaboration (Peters and Pierre 2000) and its recognition of the need to govern self-regulating systems of interaction (Kooiman 2003) enable us to identify and remove barriers to collaborative innovation through a combination of institutional design and administrative and political leadership.

COLLABORATIVE INNOVATION IN THE PUBLIC SECTOR

Innovation is often defined in short and catchy phrases such as 'new ideas that work' (Mulgan and Albury 2003) or 'new stuff that is made useful' (McKeown 2008). Although such brief definitions might well capture the gist of the concept, we shall here offer a more elaborate definition of innovation as an intended, but inherently contingent, process that involves the development, adoption and spread of new and creative ideas that challenge conventional wisdom and bring about a qualitative change in the established practices within a specific context (Sørensen and Torfing 2011). In the public sector, innovation can take the form of service innovation, process innovation, organizational innovation, policy innovation and system innovation (Hartley 2005).

Innovation is a complex, non-linear and iterative process. However, as shown in Figure 20.1, we can identify four constitutive phases in the innovation cycle (Eggers and Singh 2009). The *generation of ideas* involves the development, presentation and enrichment of ideas, but it presupposes the identification of problems and opportunities, the clarification of relevant goals and values, and the questioning of long-held assumptions. *Selection of ideas* involves decisions about which ideas are worth pursuing. Ideally, ideas should be big, bold and transformative, and, at the same time, feasible, flexible and broadly accepted among the key stakeholders. From this it follows that negotiation, conflict resolution and compromise formation are key features of the idea selection.

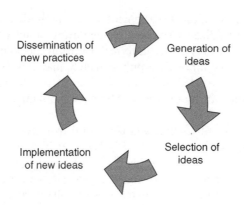

Figure 20.1   The innovation cycle

Implementation of new ideas involves conversion of ideas into new strategies, procedures and practices. Changing existing patterns of behaviour is a difficult task that requires the exercise of leadership, the construction of ownership and the creation of positive incentives. *Dissemination of new practices* involves the diffusion of innovation throughout an organization or from one organization to another. Spreading innovative practices requires highlighting the gains obtained by first movers, establishing contacts to potential followers, and overcoming standard objections such as 'we do not need any changes' and 'this is not invented here'. It also involves adapting innovative solutions to new and different circumstances.

The four phases seldom follow neatly after each other, but are often jumped, rearranged, combined, integrated and repeated in and through various feedback loops (Van de Ven et al. 2007). Nevertheless, the four phases are key components in the open-ended and often relatively messy processes of innovation.

New information technologies and scientific breakthroughs have prompted numerous innovations in the public sector, especially in health care, civic engagement and customer services. However, we should not forget that innovation is always driven by social and political actors who face specific problems and choose to exploit new opportunities by combining them with existing practices in order to craft novel and creative solutions. Based on this recognition, there has been a growing interest in the entrepreneurial role of different kinds of 'innovation champions' who are seen as the vehicle of public innovation (Mulgan 2007). In his now classic study, Polsby (1984) focuses on the entrepreneurial role of political executives who need to advance new ideas as a part of constitutional routines and when competing for votes. The protagonists of New Public Management emphasize the role of public managers and private contractors who are responding to competitive pressures (Hood 1991). Human Resource Managers and some European labour-market organizations emphasize the importance of tapping into the ideas and resources of the employees (Kesting and Ulhøi 2010). Finally, inspired by Hippel (1988), there has also been a growing interest in user-driven innovation, especially in the health care sector, where public managers and employees aim to learn from or about different user groups in order to reshape public policies, services and organizations in response to new or previously undiscovered needs (Røtnes and Staalesen 2009).

Despite the important and unique contributions of these different innovation champions, public innovation is seldom the result of the individual efforts of singular actors (Csikszentmihalyi 1996). In most cases public sector innovation requires *collaboration* between a host of public and private actors, including politicians, civil servants, experts, private firms, user groups, interest organizations and community-based associations (Borins 2001, p. 312). Collaboration can in this context be defined as the process through which a plurality of actors aim to arrive at a common definition of problems and challenges, manage conflicts in a constructive way, and find joint solutions based on provisional agreements that may coexist with disagreement and dissent (Gray 1989). The focus on collaborative innovation opens up the innovation process to the active participation of a broad range of actors since 'the locus of innovation is determined by the availability of innovation assets and not by the formal boundaries of a bureaucratic organization' (Bommert 2010, p. 16).

Multi-actor collaboration seems to have a large potential for spurring public innovation. The argument in support of this claim is that each of the constitutive phases in the innovation cycle can be strengthened through collaboration between relevant and affected actors (Bommert 2010, pp. 22–23). The argument rests on four propositions. The first proposition is that the generation of ideas is spurred when different experiences and ideas are circulated, challenged, transformed and expanded through multi-actor collaboration that facilitates mutual learning. The second proposition is that the selection of ideas is improved when actors with different perspectives and forms of knowledge participate in a joint assessment of the content and the potential gains and risks of competing ideas. In addition, collaborative interaction will facilitate the formation of compromise and agreement, so that stalemates are prevented and the role of veto players is mitigated. The third proposition is that the implementation of the selected ideas is enhanced when collaboration creates joint ownership to new and bold initiatives, so that implementation resistance is reduced. Collaboration in the implementation phase also helps to mobilize resources, ensure flexible adjustments and compensate eventual losers. The final proposition is that the dissemination of innovative practices in the public sector is propelled by the formation of social and professional networks. Networks with 'strong ties' have a short reach but provide a strong basis for communication and mutual support, whereas networks with 'weak ties' have a limited bandwidth but a longer reach that enables dissemination of novel ideas (Granovetter 1973).

The innovative potential of collaborative processes raises the question of how collaboration is facilitated. The new research on interactive governance answers this pertinent question by showing that governance networks provide crucial arenas for multi-actor collaboration (Kickert, Klijn and Koppenjan 1997; Rhodes, 1997; Sørensen and Torfing 2007). Governance networks can contribute to the exchange of information and resources and help to coordinate intra- or interorganizational policymaking, but they may also facilitate collaboration. Some actors will tend to join a governance network in order to prevent or obstruct collective action because they fear the outcomes. However, as Gray (1989) argues, the majority of the network participants will tend to engage in a constructive management of differences in order to find a common ground for solving multi-party problems. Governance networks are formed because the social and political actors realize that they cannot solve the problems they are facing alone as they do not possess the relevant knowledge, skills and resources. The stronger network actors might try to realize their own solutions to a joint problem through imposition, but such a strategy will encounter constraints imposed by the other parties and create externalities for the other network actors. Hence, the inevitable result is the development of conflicts. The actors may choose to fight them, but an adversarial approach to conflict resolution will often be extremely costly and will generate unsatisfactory outcomes and a long-lasting mistrust. By contrast, a collaborative approach will pave the way for the crafting of win–win solutions and promote trust and positive relationships (Gray 1989, p. 50). As such, the social and political actors will be better off choosing a multilateral and collaborative approach to societal problem solving in governance networks formed on the basis of interdependency.

Governance networks are by no means the only source of public innovation. Public bureaucracies and the new kind of quasi-markets that are introduced by New Public Management may also spur innovation. Public bureaucracies have a lot of resources, competence and expertise. They might also have stable routines for adapting to new developments through exploration and exploitation and their large size makes it possible for them to absorb the costs of innovation failures. Likewise, the competition between private contractors in publicly initiated quasi-markets may spur public service innovation and so will the increasing orientation towards the needs of the users in those quasi-markets that are competing for customers. However, risk-averse politicians, administrative rules and lack of economic incentives tend to hamper innovation within public bureaucracies, and the combination of hierarchical command systems, bureaucratic silos and strong professional identities tends to prevent them from reaping the fruits of collaboration. Moreover, competitive quasi-markets are difficult to create and sustain, and cut-throat competition in the less than lucrative quasi-markets tends to prevent trust-based collaboration about the development of new methods and services. What is important in this connection is, of course, that the formation of collaborative forms of network governance can help to overcome the problems and limitations associated with public bureaucracies and quasi-markets by bringing a plurality of public and private actors together in problem-driven processes aiming to find new and creative solutions. As such, governance networks provide a valuable and somewhat underexplored supplement to hierarchies and markets in the field of public innovation.

STUDIES OF COLLABORATIVE INNOVATION

The positive impact of collaboration on innovation is not only confirmed in studies of innovation in strategic alliances of private firms (Teece 1992; Powell and Grodal 2004), but also in empirical analyses of public sector innovation. A meta-analysis of studies of organizational innovation shows that diversity among the participating actors, the dispersion of power in organizational settings, and the presence of internal and external communication have a positive impact on innovation in both public and private organizations (Damanpour 1991). Apparently, a variety of specialists broadens the common knowledge base and facilitates the cross-fertilization of ideas. The dispersion of power in participatory arenas enhances the involvement and commitment of key actors, and the presence of internal and external communication facilitates the exchange of ideas and the dissemination of innovative solutions.

Another quantitative study underscoring the relevance of the concept of collaborative innovation is Borins' (1998, 2001) analysis of the semi-finalists in the US-based Ford-KSG Innovation Award Program between 1990 and 1994. The analysis shows that 29 per cent of the innovation projects claim that they coordinated several organizations to deal with the problem at hand and that in 28 per cent of the projects a formalized public–private partnership was observed (Borins 1998, pp. 19–29).

Numerous qualitative studies confirm the positive impact of stakeholder collaboration on the ability to find new and innovative solutions in the public sector. A single case study from the US conducted by Roberts and Bradley (1991) shows that collaboration has a positive impact on policy innovation. Having failed to pass a new law about open enrolment in public schools, the governor convened a group consisting of the representatives of 24 stakeholders and asked them to produce a visionary statement for state education. The sustained collaboration, which lasted more than a year, resulted in an innovative policy proposal. The policy innovation was less radical than the governor had hoped for because the stakeholders had been constrained by the various constituencies.

Another case study from the US confirms the role of collaboration in spurring innovation (Steelman 2010, pp. 70–100). Population growth in the state of Colorado has put an increasing pressure on open land, farm land and wildlife habitat. However, in a setting with strong political concerns about maintaining private property rights, preserving the ability to find local solutions and preventing 'overregulation' of land use, the scope for effective land protection was limited. In this situation an innovative policy solution was fostered by a collaborative Citizens' Committee that brought together business, conservationists and political leaders from across Colorado. The Citizens' Committee proposed, lobbied for and got the voters' approval of the establishment of a Trust that was financed by a dedicated funding mechanism and enabled local governments and non-profit land protection organizations to purchase, enhance and protect land.

A comparative case study of urban development in large northern Italian cities finds that urban planning has been much more innovative in Turin than in Milan (Dente, Bobbio and Spada 2005). The difference in innovative capacities of the two cities is explained by the higher diversity and density of the urban governance network in Turin. Hence, the richness of urban policy ideas was larger in Turin because there were more different actors involved in the urban governance network. At the same time, the ability of the urban governance network in Turin to develop innovative solutions through mutual learning and compromise formation was bigger because the public and private actors were better and more intensely connected over a longer period of time.

A comparative case study from Britain concludes that local authorities with weak inter-agency and stakeholder networks tend to have less extensive patterns of innovation (Newman, Raine and Skelcher 2001). The empirical analysis shows that governance networks and partnerships are on the rise and that collaboration enhances public innovation. However, the significance of networks and partnerships as drivers of innovation tends to be mediated by the pre-established political culture in terms of the embeddedness of networks in different organizations, the receptivity of public agencies to new ideas and their stance towards partnership agencies. As such, empirical analysis supports the idea that multi-actor collaboration provides an important source of public innovation. The studies suggest that contextual factors, institutional design and public management play a crucial role in determining the success of collaborative innovation in the public sector.

THE RISK OF FAILURE AND THE NEED FOR COLLABORATIVE INNOVATION MANAGEMENT

Despite the great potential of collaborative interaction for enhancing innovation in the public sector, deliberate attempts to facilitate collaboration and spur innovation in inter-active arenas might fail. Actors may interact because they need to exchange or pool ideas and resources in order to solve urgent policy problems, but collaboration may be pre-vented by large power asymmetries, the prevalence of mistrust and opportunistic behav-iour, strategic and substantial uncertainty, conflicting cognitive and discursive frameworks, and the lack of leadership and facilitation (Gray 1989; Straus 2002; Koppenjan and Klijn 2004; Ansell and Gash 2008).

Even when the actors engage in enduring collaborative efforts, these may not foster innovation. As such, repeated collaboration in closed and stable networks consisting of the 'usual suspects' who over time have developed more or less the same world views will tend to stifle creativity and prevent generation of new and bold ideas (Skilton and Dooley 2010). Moreover, if the actors have different interests, they may settle for solutions based on the least common denominator in order to avoid the conflicts associated with the attempt to develop more ambitious and innovative solutions (Scharpf 1994). In addition, we should not forget that the heightened level of strategic uncertainty and the incomplete institutionalization of collaborative arenas may prevent an effective implementation of innovation ideas (O'Toole 1997). Finally, the diffusion of innovative solutions within and across public agencies is sometimes prevented by the presence of 'structural holes' that emerge when actors who could benefit from communication are not connected (Burt 1992).

The truth is that the link between interaction, collaboration and innovation is contin-gent and there is a persistent risk that we will not be able to reap the fruits of collaborative innovation. At least, good intentions to collaborate and to explore and exploit new bold ideas are not enough to ensure collaborative innovation in the public sector. In order to drive the process from interaction, via collaboration, to public innovation, the social and political actors will need to exercise some kind of collaborative leadership and innovation management. Management of processes of collaborative innovation can be provided either by trained facilitators or by organic leaders who are connected to and familiar with the stakeholders in the interactive arena. Centrality, legitimacy, access to resources and organizational back-up are the fundamental institutional conditions for collaborative innovation managers, who must also possess an array of personal competencies such as reflexivity, flexibility, open-mindedness, and boundary spanning and communicative skills.

In the process of managing collaborative innovation the managers will have to perform different functions relating to different challenges. In order to create well-functioning interactive arenas with active and committed actors, the managers must act as *stewards*. The steward convenes the actors, sets the initial agenda, frames the collaborative efforts and represents the collaborative process as a whole both in relation to the participants and in relation to the external environment and the sponsors (Ansell and Gash 2008; Page 2010; Scott 2011). In order to facilitate and drive collaboration between the stakeholders, the managers must act as *mediators*. The mediator aims to clarify interdependencies, manage the process, build trust and resolve disputes by aligning interests, constructing

Table 20.1 Comparison of different forms of public management

	Bureaucratic management	New public management	Collaborative innovation management
Focus	Programme management	Inputs and outputs	Creative problem solving
Objective	Stable service provision	Cost-efficient service provision	Break policy deadlocks and improve public services
Instrument	Rule-based regulation	Management by objectives and performance measurement	Regulation of more or less self-regulated collaboration
Public employees	Hold on to stable, reliable and professional employees	Enhance the productivity of the specialized employees	Nurture and recruit creative talents who are well connected
Interorganizational relations	Create clear organizational and professional boundaries and resolve boundary wars	Enhance competition between public and private organizations	Encourage interdisciplinary boundary spanning and create borderless organizations
Citizens and private stakeholders	Perceived as subjects and clients	Perceived as users and customers	Perceived as potential co-creators
Governmental rationality	Enhance coordination and control	Enhance 'auditability' as a means to create legitimacy	Enhance transformative learning and capacities
Handling of slack	Establish an organizational buffer by sustaining slack	Enhance efficiency by eliminating slack	Create innovation by mobilizing slack
Role of managers in relation to change	Must ensure transparency and stability and make marginal adjustments	Must assume responsibility for strategic organizational development	Must facilitate and lead collaboration as a means to spur innovation

common frameworks and removing barriers to collaboration (Straus 2002; Crosby and Bryson 2010). Finally, in order to spur innovation, the managers must act as *catalysts*. The catalyst exercises an entrepreneurial leadership that encourages re-framing of problems, explores existing and emerging constraints and opportunities, and encourages transformative learning and 'out of the box' thinking (Crosby and Bryson 2010; Morse 2010).

In order to better understand what collaborative innovation management really involves in terms of content, we can compare this new kind of innovation management with the traditional forms of bureaucratic management and the recent emphasis on New Public Management. Table 20.1 provides such a comparison in relation to key aspects of public organizations. As we can see, collaborative innovation management radically changes the role, orientation and practices of public managers. However, the message derived from the comparison of the three kinds of public management is not that public managers should stop exercising bureaucratic management or New Public Management and focus exclusively on the exercise of collaborative innovation management. Rather, the point is that public managers should combine all three types of management in a flexible and reflexive manner. Public managers must learn to juggle the different managerial roles in order to wear the right hat in the right circumstances. That being said, it is clear that if the demand for public innovation continues to grow stronger and stronger, collaborative innovation management will move to the fore.

STUDYING COLLABORATIVE INNOVATION

The main analytical vantage point for studying collaborative innovation in the public sector is provided by the theories of network governance (Sørensen and Torfing 2007). Although the primary focus of governance network theory is the production of public value rather than the creation of public innovation, it persistently emphasizes the need to involve a plurality of public and private actors in the formulation, implementation and revision of public policy (Bommert 2010, pp. 17–18). Therefore, the study of collaborative public innovation will benefit greatly from a critical engagement with different strands of governance network theory: rational choice institutionalism, normative institutionalism, interpretative governance theory, network management theory and governmentality theory. A brief *tour de horizon* will reveal the comparative advantages of the different theories of network governance.

Rational choice institutionalism (Ostrom 1990; Scharpf 1994, 1998) perceives public policy and governance as a result of the interaction of social and political actors who are pursuing their interests on the basis of a bounded rationality that permits them to make satisfactory rather than optimal choices. This actor-centred view of public policy and governance is combined with an institutionalist view of how institutions, defined as systems of rules, provide opportunity and incentive structures that help rational actors to overcome collective action problems, reduce the level of conflict and facilitate non-hierarchical coordination (Ostrom 1990). The interaction between the social and political actors takes place in governance networks that are defined as informal institutional structures, which shape the games played by the actors (Scharpf 1994). Rational choice institutionalism helps us to understand the role of institutions for the building of trust, the reduction of different kinds of transaction costs, and the provision of incentives for collaboration and innovation. It also highlights the strategic uncertainty in the implementation of innovative solutions in network settings and draws our attention to the importance of risk assessment and risk management for the willingness of the network actors to produce innovative solutions (O'Toole 1997; Vangen and Huxham 2010). However, despite the importance of these arguments, rational choice institutionalism can be criticized for reducing actors to calculating agents and for reducing institutions to incentive structures (March and Olsen 1995). Although actors are sometimes placed in circumstances where they are expected to act on the basis of a more or less incomplete calculation of costs and benefits that are shaped by institutional incentives, this only captures a fragment of what actors are and institutions are doing.

Normative institutionalism (March and Olsen 1989, 1995) solves both of the problems inherent in rational choice institutionalism. It claims that social and political actors are not acting according to a 'logic of consequentiality' that bids them to calculate and compare the consequences of different actions in relation to pre-given preferences and objectives. Actors are essentially rule-followers as they act in accordance with institutionally embedded rules, norms and scripts. Social and political actors are placed in institutional contexts that are dominated by a particular 'logic of appropriateness' that prescribes what actors with a certain socially constructed identity are supposed to do in a particular situation. The institutionalized logic of appropriate action is defined in terms of an ensemble of rules, norms, values, cognitive scripts, cultural codes and rituals (March and Olsen 1989). Governance networks are in this context defined as institutional arenas of interaction that bring together relevant and affected actors who become normatively integrated through the institutionalization of common rules, norms, values and forms of knowledge (Powell and DiMaggio 1983; March and Olsen 1995). Normative institutionalism urges us to appreciate the role of identity and the impact of institutional rules and cultural norms when studying processes of collaborative innovation. Social identities and institutional traditions and cultures may hamper or encourage collaboration and innovation. For example, some public administrators may see themselves as guardians of well-established norms and rules, while others may perceive themselves as policy entrepreneurs. Such differences in role perceptions are often shaped and sustained by the institutional context of the public administrators. Normative institutionalism also draws our attention to the existence of stable procedures for adaptation and change and offers a non-rationalistic theory of learning. Learning in collaborative arenas of public governance seldom takes the form of scientific investigations that provide hard evidence of what is the best solution. Rather, it involves pragmatic experimentation through which new ideas are developed, tested and evaluated on the basis of normative criteria and institutional norms. Despite these advantages, normative institutionalism is hampered by its weak account of the active role of agency in changing institutional structures and reforming public policy and governance. Normative institutionalism insists that actors play an active role in matching rules and norms to the particular situations in which they are going to be applied and in interpreting the content of the often ambiguous rules and norms they are facing (March and Olsen 1995). However, the normative and integrative force of institutions seems to outweigh the transformative capacities of autonomous agents. As such, the space for an effective agency is limited. At least, the active role of individual capacity to create new interpretations of the world is downplayed and there is no account of power and power struggles as a way of transforming public governance.

Interpretative governance theory (Bevir and Rhodes 2006; Bevir and Richards 2009; Bevir 2010) offers a decentred approach to public governance that focuses on 'the social construction of a practice through the ability of individuals to create and act on meaning' (Bevir and Richards 2009, p. 3). Compared with normative institutionalism, the focus is on the individual actors and the meanings that they are constructing and acting upon, rather than on what Bevir (2010) terms 'reified institutions'. Interpretative governance theory shares its focus on individual actors as does rational choice institutionalism, but the individual actors are not calculative but act on the basis of interpretations. The actors interpret their beliefs, desires and actions against the background of different more or less sedimented traditions and often in response to particular dilemmas or problems. Dilemmas may arise from the clash between different traditions and discourses, and problems are constructed when public governance produces failures that conflict with people's beliefs. People confront the different dilemmas and problems differently because they draw on different traditions and discourses, and this results in political conflicts over the nature of the puzzles and problems and how to solve them (Bevir and Richards 2009, p. 7). The political conflicts are fought out and partly resolved through networked interaction. As such, governance networks are defined as emerging patterns of interaction between actors who are constructing and acting upon particular narratives. Interpretative governance theory enables us to understand how public innovation is conditioned by the interweaving of narratives that construct problems as urgent and manageable and solutions as feasible and desirable. Narratives are powerful tools for motivating actors to act on specific problems and collaborate to find a joint solution. Interpretative governance theory also provides a bottom-up account of the formation of governance networks and portrays these as arenas of public contestation and problem solving, which – despite the presence of formal and informal rules of conduct – can create innovative solutions as a result of contingent combinations of dissimilar experiences, ideas and opinions advanced by the social and political actors. On the down-side, interpretative governance theory seems to be so busy trying to avoid reifying conceptions of aggregate social phenomena that it fails to provide a proper account of the institutional and organizational conditions for social and political action.

Network management theory is associated with the Dutch 'governance club' at Erasmus University in Rotterdam (Kooiman 1993; Kickert, Klijn and Koppenjan 1997; Koppenjan and Klijn 2004). In sharp contrast to Bevir's interpretative governance theory, it emphasizes the institutional conditions for the complex policy interactions that bring together interdependent actors who act strategically on the basis of uncertain perceptions of substantive issues, political interests and the strategic importance of different policy arenas (Koppenjan and Klijn 2004). Governance networks are defined as interorganizational arenas for interest mediation between self-interested actors who interact because of the presence of a mutual resource dependency. The absence of a joint utility function means that their interaction and the emerging policy outcomes are marked by conflicts, but the actors are kept together by their interdependency and the development of shared norms, perceptions and ideologies. The policy performance of governance networks depends on cooperation, and public network managers play a crucial role in generating improved interactions between the existing members and in making changes to the existing networks in terms of the membership and institutional framework (Kickert, Klijn and Koppenjan 1997). Network management theory helps us to understand both the centrifugal and the centripetal forces of governance networks, which is crucial in order to enhance the prospect for collaboration. It also pays attention to the need to manage uncertainty in complex networks and to the limits of collaborative innovation, which is frequently hampered by the regulative and normative framework for networked interaction that tends to be a result of old and long-forgotten compromises. Policy making is path dependent and often ends up preserving the status quo. The critique of network management theory is that it tends to treat governance networks as tools for pragmatic problem solving. Governance networks are institutional mechanisms that are formed and manipulated with the purpose of getting things done. As such, there are almost no reflections on the constitutive role of power in shaping identities, interactions and the institutional frameworks of network governance.

Governmentality theory is a poststructuralist approach to the analysis of the state, governance modes and concrete acts of government (Foucault 1991; Dean 1999; Rose 1999). It focuses on the collective and institutionalized ideas, perceptions, rationalities and technologies that are articulated in a historically contingent governmentality, which shapes the way that people are governing and are being governed (Foucault 1991). Concrete acts of government are conditioned and formed by hegemonic discourses that construct the subjects and objects of regulation as well as the modes and telos of public regulation (Dean 1999). Governmentality theory does not make any references to 'governance networks', but power is not seen as emanating from a sovereign state, but rather conceived in terms of decentred networks of social and political forces that are acting on each other. Moreover, the way that Western societies are governed has shifted and, today, the dominant governmentality tends to favour the use of power technologies that facilitate some kind of 'regulated self-regulation'. According to the prevailing governmentality, advanced liberal societies should neither be regulated from above through the exercise of sovereign power and the deployment of disciplinary institutions and normalizing discourses, nor from below through a neoliberal reliance on the allegedly self-regulating market forces. Rather, societal regulation should involve the creation and regulation of self-regulatory assemblages of actors who are capable of crafting responsible and legitimate solutions through a more or less institutionalized interaction (Dean 1999). With its emphasis on the role of 'regulated self-regulation', governmentality theory reveals how freedom and power are really two sides of the same coin. On the one hand, advanced liberal societies deploy 'technologies of agency' in order to mobilize the competencies, resources and energies of free and responsible actors through the construction of networks, partnerships and other forms of interactive governance. On the other hand, they use 'technologies of performance' in order to ensure that actors engaged in governance practices use their free and empowered actions in a way that conforms to the overall goals of the political and administrative system. Governmentality theory does not focus on public innovation, but it can help us to see public innovation and the construction of collaborative arenas as a part of a particular governmentality, which is shaped by discursive power strategies. It also encourages us to understand the negotiated interactions between different actors in terms of decentred power struggles that are not merely driven by resource asymmetries, but also involve attempts to shape the institutional conditions of individual and collective action. Hence, collaborative innovation is not an innocent attempt to improve public policy, services and organizations by developing new ideas and doing the right thing, but a power-ridden practice which is shaped by discursive power strategies that operate at both the macro level through campaigns and institutional technologies, and at the micro level where social and political actors struggle to define the agenda, the rules of the game and the meaning of the past, the present and the future. The problem with governmentality theory, however, is that it does not say much about why and how actors are interacting within relational assemblages and does not analyse the conditions for these actors to produce policies and regulations that are both continuous and discontinuous with the past. Despite its focus on concrete governmental technologies, governmentality theory remains at a fairly general and abstract level of analysis.

In sum, it seems clear that each of the five theoretical perspectives has something important to offer to the analysis of processes of collaborative innovation. Rational choice institutionalism highlights the institutional conditions for strategic action in the context of risk and uncertainty. Normative institutionalism emphasizes the role of identity, cultural norms and pragmatic experimentation for the adaptation of public institutions to new conditions. Interpretative governance theory draws our attention to the role of narratives and bottom-up processes of networked collaboration. Network management theory insists that governance networks must be designed and managed in order to function properly and claims that policy renewal is path dependent. Last but not least, governmentality theory highlights the role of discursive power strategies for shaping new forms of governance and the actions of social and political actors engaged in public governance. As shown above, the different governance network theories also engage in different kinds of problems, but together, and in different combinations, they offer a strong foundation for developing a theoretical framework for analysing collaborative innovation in the public sector.

CONCLUSION

The emerging shift from New Public Management to New Public Governance makes it possible to envisage a new strategy for public innovation that highlights the role of multi-actor collaboration. This chapter has defined innovation and collaboration and aimed to show why collaboration may help us to spur public innovation that can help us to break policy deadlocks and improve the quality of public services. It has also provided empirical evidence in support of a collaborative approach to innovation and discussed the risks of failure and the need to manage the collaborative efforts and ensure that they foster innovation.

Collaborative innovation in the public sector is a new research area, but existing strands of governance network theory can help us to further explore the key questions about the conditions for collaborative public innovation and the role of institutional design and public management. It goes without saying that governance network theory cannot stand alone. Insights from economic innovation theory, collaborative planning, learning theory, design thinking and theories of collaborative leadership must be added in order to develop a fuller picture of the potential for reinvigorating the public sector through collaborative innovation.

REFERENCES

Ansell, C. and Gash, A. (2008). Collaborative governance in theory and practice. *Journal of Public Administration Research and Theory*, 18(4), 543–571.
Bevir, M. (2010). *Democratic Governance*. Princeton, NJ: Princeton University Press.
Bevir, M. and Rhodes, R.A.W. (2006). *Governance Stories*. London: Routledge.
Bevir, M. and Richards, D. (2009). Decentring policy networks: a theoretical agenda. *Public Administration*, 87(1), 3–14.
Bommert, B. (2010). Collaborative innovation in the public sector. *International Public Management Review*, 11(1), 15–33.
Borins, S. (1998). *Innovating with Integrity*. Washington, DC: Georgetown University Press.

Borins, S. (2001). Encouraging innovation in the public sector. *Journal of Intellectual Capital*, 2(3), 310–319.

Burt, R.S. (1992). *Structural Holes*. Cambridge, MA: Harvard University Press.

Crosby, B.C. and Bryson, J. (2010). Integrative leadership and the creation and maintenance of cross-sector collaboration. *The Leadership Quarterly*, 21(2), 211–230.

Csikszentmihalyi, M. (1996). *Creativity: Flow and the Psychology of Discovery and Invention*. New York, NY: Harper Collins.

Damanpour, F. (1991). Organizational innovation: a meta-analysis of effects of determinants and moderators. *Academy of Management Journal*, 34(3), 555–590.

Dean, M. (1999). *Governmentality: Power and Rule in Modern Society*. London: Sage.

Dente, B., Bobbio, L. and Spada, A. (2005). Government or governance of urban innovation? *DIPS*, 162, 1–22.

Eggers, B. and Singh, S. (2009). *The Public Innovator's Playbook*. Washington, DC: Harvard Kennedy School of Government.

Foucault, M. (1991). Governmentality. In G. Burchell, C. Gordon and P. Miller (eds), *The Foucault Effect*. Hertfordshire: Harvester Wheatsheaf, pp. 87–104.

Granovetter, M. (1973). The strength of weak ties. *American Journal of Sociology*, 78(6), 1360–1380.

Gray, B. (1989). *Collaborating: Finding Common Ground for Multiparty Problems*. San Francisco, CA: Jossey-Bass.

Hartley, J. (2005). Innovation in governance and public service: past and present. *Public Money and Management*, 25(1), 27–34.

Hippel, E.V. (1988). *The Sources of Innovation*. Oxford: Oxford University Press.

Hodge, G. and Greve, C. (eds) (2005). *The Challenge of Public–Private Partnerships*. Cheltenham and Northampton, MA: Edward Elgar.

Hood, C. (1991). A public administration for all seasons? *Public Administration*, 69(1), 1–19.

Kesting, P. and Ulhøi, J. (2010). Employee-driven innovation: extending the license to foster innovation. *Management Decision*, 48(1), 65–84.

Kickert, W.J.M., Klijn, E.-H. and Koppenjan, J.F.M. (eds) (1997). *Managing Complex Networks*. London: Sage.

Kooiman, J. (ed.) (1993). *Modern Governance*. London: Sage.

Kooiman, J. (2003). *Governing as Governance*. London: Sage.

Koppenjan, J. and Klijn, E.-H. (2004). *Managing Uncertainties in Networks*. London: Routledge.

March, J.G. and Olsen, J.P. (1989). *Rediscovering Institutions*. New York: The Free Press.

March, J.G. and Olsen, J.P. (1995). *Democratic Governance*. New York, NY: The Free Press.

McKeown, M. (2008). *The Truth about Innovation*. London: Prentice Hall.

Morse, R. (2010). Integrative public leadership: catalyzing collaboration to create public value. *The Leadership Quarterly*, 21(2), 231–245.

Mulgan, G. (2007). *Ready or Not? Taking Innovation in the Public Sector Seriously*. London: NESTA.

Mulgan, G. and Albury, D. (2003). Innovation in the public sector. Working Paper, Version 1.9, October, The Strategy Unit, The UK Cabinet Office.

Newman, J., Raine, J. and Skelcher, C. (2001). Transforming local government: innovation and modernization. *Public Money and Management*, 21(2), 61–68.

Osborne, D. and Gaebler, T. (1992). *Reinventing Government: How the Entrepreneurial Spirit is Transforming the Public Sector*. Reading, MA: Addison-Wesley.

Osborne, S.P. (2006). The new public governance? *Public Management Review*, 8(3), 377–387.

Osborne, S.P. (ed.) (2010). *The New Public Governance*. London: Routledge.

Ostrom, E. (1990). *Governing the Commons*. Cambridge: Cambridge University Press.

O'Toole, L.J. (1997). Implementing public innovations in network settings. *Administration and Society*, 29(2), 115–138.

Page, S. (2010). Integrative leadership for collaborative governance: civic engagement in Seattle. *The Leadership Quarterly*, 21(2), 246–263.

Peters, B.G. and Pierre, J. (2000). *Governance, Politics and the State*. Basingstoke: Macmillan.

Pollitt, C. and Bouckaert, G. (2004). *Public Management Reforms*. Oxford: Oxford University Press.

Polsby, N.W. (1984). *Political Innovation in America: The Politics of Policy Initiation*. New Haven, CT: Yale University Press.

Powell, W.W. and DiMaggio, J. (1983). The iron cage revisited: institutional isomorphism and collective rationality in organisational fields. *American Sociological Review*, 48(2), 147–160.

Powell, W.W. and DiMaggio, J. (1991). *The New Institutionalism in Organizational Analysis*. Chicago, IL: University of Chicago Press.

Powell, W.W. and Grodal, S. (2004). Networks of innovators. In J. Fagerberg, D.C. Mowery and R.R. Nelson (eds). *The Oxford Handbook of Innovation*. Oxford: Oxford University Press, pp. 56–85.

Rhodes, R.A.W. (1997). *Understanding Governance*. Buckingham: Open University Press.

Roberts, N.C. and Bradley, R.T. (1991). Stakeholder collaboration and innovation. *Journal of Applied Behavioural Science*, 27(2), 209–227.

Rose, N. (1999). *Powers of Freedom*. Cambridge: Cambridge University Press.

Røtnes, R. and Staalesen, P.D. (2009). *New Methods in User-Driven Innovation in the Health Care Sector*. Oslo: Nordic Innovation Center.

Scharpf, F.W. (1994). Games real actors could play: positive and negative coordination in embedded negotiations. *Journal of Theoretical Politics*, 6(1), 27–53.

Scharpf, F.W. (1998). *Games Real Actors Play: Actor Centred Institutionalism in Policy Research*. Boulder, CO: Westview Press.

Scott, C. (2011). A case study of collaborative governance: health care law reform in Georgia. *Conflict Resolution Quarterly*, 28(4), 441–462.

Skilton, P.F. and Dooley, K. (2010). The effects of repeat collaboration on creative abrasion. *Academy of Management Review*, 35(1), 118–134.

Sørensen, E. and Torfing, J. (eds) (2007). *Theories of Democratic Network Governance*. Basingstoke: Palgrave-Macmillan.

Sørensen, E. and Torfing, J. (2011). Enhancing innovation in the public sector. *Administration and Society*, 43(8), 842–868.

Steelman, T.A. (2010). *Implementing Innovation*. Washington, DC: Georgetown University Press.

Straus, D. (2002). *How to Make Collaboration Work*. San Francisco, CA: Berrett Koehler Publishers.

Teece, D.J. (1992). Competition, cooperation, and innovation. *Journal of Economic Behaviour and Organization*, 18(1), 1–25.

Torfing, J., Peter, B.G., Pierre, J. and Sørensen, E. (2012). *Interactive Governance: Advancing the Paradigm*. Oxford: Oxford University Press.

Van de Ven, A., Polley, D., Garud, R. and Venkataraman, S. (2007). *The Innovation Journey*. Oxford: Oxford University Press.

Vangen, S. and Huxham, C. (2010). Introducing the theory of collaborative advantage. In S.P. Osborne (ed.), *The New Public Governance*. London: Routledge, pp. 163–184.

21. Innovation in an inter-organisational context
Tony Kinder

This chapter argues that whole system models of public service design and delivery are emerging in response to changing service user values, creating a new inter-organisational environment in which new forms of learning and innovation are flourishing. It suggests a new framework for conceptualising public service innovation.

The next section sets out a new framework for inter-organisational innovation. It discusses values and purposes and then unpacks key aspects of the innovation system: operations, professionals, information processing, resources and co-producers, culture and learning. These aspects are brought together in a brief discussion of how innovation processes affect accountability, efficiency and sustainability, fairness and, finally, quality. In the third section I suggest some key 'lessons' from this approach for innovative public service managers. I then give a brief illustrative example of the framework operating in Scottish care services and, in conclusion, suggest that though models of public service design and delivery vary enormously across and within countries, the whole systems innovation framework may have general usability.

Since some 80 per cent of GDP value and jobs in Europe and the US are in services, innovation in services, especially knowledge-intensive services, is significant. Sadly, much of the management literature continues to envision innovation related to physical products. For example, Porter's (1985) metaphoric value chain has services as an add-on at the end of the chain. This chapter contributes a conceptual framework for innovation by networks of local public service providers. My perspective, like Osborne (2010b), is that new inter-organisational governances will grow in importance as local service providers move beyond intra-organisational managerialism towards a whole system approach to addressing service user needs, offering more personalised solutions. It further presumes, as Lapsley (2009) argues, an environment in which (unlike new public management ideology) the complexity of local services such as education, health and care is acknowledged. This perspective interconnects with the research agenda posed by Andrews and Boyne (2010): change, organisation, performance and their inter-relationships. Working increasingly in network contexts is likely to shift public sector managers' thinking towards more closely connecting the micro with the macro (a holistic view), driven, I will argue, by more closely interrogating the values and needs of both service users and other stakeholders.

My argument is that service user values are changing to demand whole system solutions to user needs; these drivers of innovation are symbiotically interacting with supply-side models of service delivery focusing around the inter-organisational which are transforming the landscape of public services.

Normann's (2002) perspective on service management argues that services are personally experienced by users, co-produced between users and providers, and involve interactivity between users and providers. This suggests some degree of close *psychic distance* between providers and users. I borrow the idea of psychic distance from comparative social capital studies (Shenkar 2001) and international trade (Kogut and Singh 1988) to mean degrees of empathetic understanding and desire to meet user needs as characterising the relationship between service providers and users. Psychic distance stands in contradistinction to supply-led models of public service design and delivery. Low psychic distance suggests trust and interdependency (Brouthers and Brouthers 2001) within the non-market setting of local public services (LPSs): openness to vulnerability and managed (not eradicated) risk and experimentation of the sort Freidson (1988) suggests characterises relations between professionals and their clients. These values are (re)-emerging in advanced public service settings and challenge traditional silo'd, functionally separated modes of organising service design and delivery.

Rising public service user expectations cannot be delivered by functionally structured organisations; user needs are multifaceted and interconnected. For example, the person moving house (Kinder 2003) may need a new school for children, new care arrangements, new registrations. Typically, user needs cross intra-organisational functional boundaries and inter-organisational boundaries. Innovations such as one-stop-shops, interoperability and joined-up government reflect the need for a whole system approach to meeting user needs. My argument is that the emerging transformed model of public service design and delivery is both a cause and a result of meeting changing service user values for whole system solutions to their needs. This transformative model organises the design and delivery of public services as a whole system, transgressing previous functional-unit and organisational boundaries.

This emerging environment for modern public services is not simply a new organisational setting or (another) restructuring; it suggests new ways of working to co-produce public services and new ways of innovating. As Hudson (2002, p. 6) points out, 'mere structural integration evidently does not guarantee well-coordinated practice on the ground'. This is because, as Bateson (1973, p. 303) argued, 'the rate of learning must equal or exceed the rate of change'. A whole system approach poses new issues for learning and innovation. Kooiman and Jentoft (2009) make the profound point that meta-governances are created in strategic and practice community conversations addressing values, norms and principles arguing the importance of embedding learning in structures: processing information into knowledge and innovation. Innovative new organisations are *clumsy* (Thompson 1997) and the diversity of public service design and delivery seems set to expand. Emerging whole system service design and delivery models whilst creating the need for training and reflective practitioner learning; and also deutero-learning (new ways of learning) characterises the completely new environment of whole systems. Structures are important, but from a social learning perspective (Wertsch 1998), learning is sense-making involving cognition (individual and distributed) formed by mediating artefacts with heritage learning and thinking. Learning processes, Engeström (1987) argues, feature learners (implicitly or explicitly) in interpreting artefacts: reinforcing or challenging interpretations and their embeddedness into social structures, including rules, operating procedures and mores.

LITERATURE

This section presents a conceptual framework for innovation in a networked public services setting and then seeks to support and justify the framework by referencing general theory and, in a later section, an illustrative case.

Types of Inter-organisational LPS Systems

For Weick (1995) framing issues is the process of creating a thought-corridor (including terms and value parameters); a paradigm in which to solve puzzles. Discourse around issues is a social process; frameworks only become valid (useful) when they are shared as meaningful. Discourse around innovation and public services, as Rawls (2005) argues, gains most legitimacy when conducted in (shared) *public reason*. The framework I present aspires to be recognisable as relevant by those designing, delivering and using public services, whilst also suggesting new connections and processes that *inspire* innovation.

A network is a set of nodes connected by channels; in the case of business and social networks, the channels, governances and goals characterising the network can gain agility from loose ties (Granovetter 1973), positive externalities and (where there is requisite variety; Grabher 1993) the 'wisdom of crowds'. The problem with all systems thinking (Child 1984) is that purpose and goals are contested; governances unclear; boundaries ill defined; and causal relationships between actors misunderstood. Where ownership, governances (including leadership), purpose and goals and causal relationships are explicit, shared and stable, then a loose network can become a system (Stinchcombe 1990) acknowledged by participants and stakeholders.

The framework proposed here does not presume organisational integration as a response to service fragmentation (Scott 1995), nor am I suggesting, as the UK Government-sponsored Care Services Integration Programme (CSIP 2005) and Thistlethwaite (2004) do, that there is a linear progression from autonomy to coordination and then integration. Rather, in the tradition of Ostrom (1973) and Bardach (1998), I am arguing that situationally relevant *whole systems* for designing and delivering public services are emerging, driven by the desire to provide integrated services; the ownership, goals, governances and causal relationships of which reflect the diverse heritages and statutory settings, often resulting in clumsy organisational forms. Precisely because my framework is about service processes and not organisational form it has the disadvantage of appearing abstract, with the advantage of potentially recontextualising across a wide range of contexts. If Castells' (1997) point is correct, that markets and networks increasingly resemble the other, then emergent whole systems for local public service design and delivery appear clumsy. One consequence of Klijn and Koppenjan's (2006) argument that structural design is the result of learning processes is that since learning is socially situated, a diversity of delivery models will arise. The framework below presumes some degree of shared destiny amongst users and their providers guided by eroding functional and organisational barriers.

Framework and Analytical Tools

Figure 21.1 is not a stage or linear framework: innovation processes iterate and parallel track. It begins with a negotiated (compromise) shared notion of what value outputs the system aims to produce, migrating values into clear purpose and goals creating strategic and performance metrics. The whole system and its governances (including leadership) are the service design and delivery supported by six key elements of innovation, chosen from Bardach (1998) as significant in inter-organisational innovation. An example of

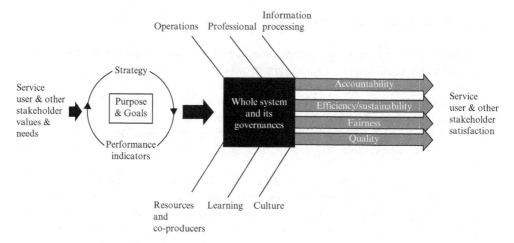

Figure 21.1   Innovation processes in the networked service

such a system could be integrated care for the elderly or person-centred care for people with learning difficulties. Four outputs from the whole system are chosen, again from Bardach (1998), to represent successful innovation leading to user and stakeholder satisfaction.

Values and Needs

Values and needs in public services are likely to be always contested (Van der Wal et al. 2011). The point about low psychic distance is that empathy and discourse between service providers, users (including informal users such as family) and wider stakeholders (such as funders and suppliers) present a better opportunity for innovations suiting user values and needs than supply-driven services: value implies non-value; that is, supplied services that are redundant as not meeting user values. As Gronroos (1983, p. 24) argues: 'value for customers is created throughout the relationship by the customer, partly in interactions between the customer and the supplier or service provider'. Value is discernible (e.g. using value stream mapping) and measurable (e.g. using Parasuraman (1985) gap analysis). Without a clear and shared view of values, service systems cannot be sure that innovations take them closer to users.

Contexts, resources, standards and heritage systems differ. The purpose and goals of any service system will therefore relate to context. For local service providers and innovators performance metrics and strategy symbiotically inter-relate, mutually shaping the other (Neely 2001), the link being the capabilities to meet user values: here represented by the whole system box. Effective strategies are rooted in the delivery context: as Hope (2007) argues, there can be no all-purpose set of performance indicators. Simple performance metrics, such as Sink and Tuttle (1989) and Stern's (2000) economic value added, fail to address complexities in public service delivery in user values and areas such as social accountability (Kinder 2010b), echoing Power's (2003) critique of centralised target setting. An important implication of transparent strategies and performance metrics linking user values and competences is staff motivation resulting from processes creating shared destiny; linking to low psychic distance. Organising continuous innovation and improvement relies heavily on staff motivation (Williams 2002) and ideally produces commitment-based human relations (Brown 2007).

Whole System and Innovation

Operations, professionals and craft and information processing

Stability, dependency and quality standards are essential in any worthwhile public service. Innovative service providers may use programmed continuous improvement projects (such as lean) within a service paradigm for process improvement, whilst periodically reviewing the design and delivery of the whole system. This cycle of freeze–unfreeze–refreeze (Lewin 1947) is especially important where a whole system (such as care for the elderly) remains a project drawing upon staff and resources from autonomous bodies (such as hospitals, social workers and police) that continue to run their own operations systems.

Local services offer professional problem solving: the exercise of judgement based upon specialist education and cumulated wisdom (Svensson 1990). Rivalry and a pecking order amongst professions can create antagonism to inter-organisational working (Bardach 1998). As Sennett (2008) argues, professionals are characterised by doing the best job possible, *for the sake of it*. Modernising local service providers are increasingly innovating multidisciplinary teams, for example of doctors, community care, social workers and housing, in care of the elderly.

Whilst many local service professionals work closely informally (Hollander and Pallan 1995), multidisciplinary team working can widen the scope of accountability, broadening professionals' knowledge and competence domains. Some professionals thrive whilst others are challenged by hybridity (Friedson 1994) or the evolution of their profession (Torstendahl 1990). A particular issue for professionals in inter-organisational working is the possibility of being line managed or accountable to middle managers from outside the profession or from another profession in 'interlocking chains of accountability' (Bezzina et al. 2001, p. vi). As Wilson et al. (2004) argue, the aspirations of the citizenry as a whole may conflict with issues of professional integrity and budgeting accountability. Teams need the time to negotiate a joint language and meanings, for example in shared user assessments; this is especially so for online forms and databases (Perri et al. 2004). Time together helps erode any distrust (Glen 2003) and adherence to earlier governance systems (Causer et al. 1999), and may allow professionals to redesign service systems around users with the ability to up-skill support staff, relieving (costly) professionals of non-professional duties. Innovative inter-organisational and multidisciplinary working relies for success not on combining technologies and systems, but on bringing people together.

Beer's (1979) information-processing theory argues that the performance of any organisation is constrained by its ability to process information, and in environments characterised by uncertainty, complexity and ambiguity the dangers are either over-centralisation (slow) or functionally self-contained service units (duplicative and costly). Since, as Stinchcombe (1990) argues, in complex organisations coherent decision taking requires real-time relevant information, multi-organisational working is IT-hungry and is best structured to ease information flows rather than by silo'd functions (Haux 2006). Shared, effective and real-time information flows are referred to by Siehl et al. (1991) as a 'rite of integration'. There are tensions between process cost reduction and adding richness into service products, and the pace of service integration and the ability of information systems to support it and to restructure accordingly (Tushman and Nadler 1978). Further, devolving decision taking to multidisciplinary teams may disrupt previous decision-taking patterns and therefore power and prestige distribution.

Taking a whole system view of information flows is likely to require new protocols and database synthesis, not easy where organisations are not co-terminus or part of national systems. Inter-organisational working using functional rather than information processing-led structures is costly. One way forward is to parallel track, building a whole system vertical information system, but a bottom-up dashboard of real-time information to support service decisions in teams.

Resources and co-producers, culture and problem solving, learning and innovation

A danger of conflating inter-organisational working with organisational integration is the defensive protection of budgets. Bardach (1998) characterises inter-agency working as *shared strategies* (project by project), coordinating processes without necessarily pooling resources or new organisational forms. Joint working is thus best led by service needs, creating a whole system from the viewpoint of the user, who is often agnostic about back-office ownership and controls. Huxham's (1993a, 1993b) work in Glasgow illustrated the advantages of collaboration in a wide social innovation setting, developing the idea of meta-strategies: managing relationships with other organisations in the public sector (1993a, p. 26).

All services are co-produced and increasingly whole system services involve a mixture of statutory bodies, the voluntary sector and the user (perhaps also family as informal users) in delivering services. Effective co-production is not simply at the point of service use; rather (drawing on the idea of psychic distance) services are altered incrementally as a result of user feedback and are designed jointly with users. Examples of using tele-democracy to continually improve public services are widespread (Kinder 2002). In the private sector, Cusumano (1998) details how Microsoft involves users at every stage of new product design (see also von Hippel 1988). The point of user engagement in co-producing (re)designs of services is to capture their tacit knowledge of using services. As Chesbrough (2011) points out, this is a version of the open innovation framework: opening up design to intra- and inter-organisational knowledge flows, including environmental scanning and benchmarking.

Public services solve problems (medical diagnoses, social care packages) when users may not have the knowledge or resources themselves. In doing so service professionals cumulate tacit knowledge (Polanyi 1958) which becomes embedded in organisational rules, morés and ways of working. Ironically, this accumulation can give an organisation *as a whole* a bureaucratic mindset that becomes self-referencing. The idea of organisational learning is a lazy metaphor, often substituting mere information accumulation (on intranets) for the active reflection of practitioners: organisations do not think; only people think. There is merit in the idea of distributed cognition: organisations or communities of practice sharing ideas and using the wisdom of crowds to propose new solutions. Modernising inter-organisational working seeks root cause problem solving and is unafraid of structural change (Argyris' (1977) double-loop learning). In short, effective inter-organisational working has a culture of problem solving.

Engeström's (1987) third-generation activity theory of cycles of expansive learning is a good model for a culture of problem solving: continually asking why and what if, posing deeper and wider questions. For Engeström and Kerouac (2007), context is everything; learners recombine heritage and new conceptualisations by ever-deeper understanding of what changes are necessary to innovate *in context* (see also Nardi 1996). Since innovators must take staff and service users with them on this journey, enacting plausible and coherent narratives (Weick 1995) is an important aspect of reducing ambiguity and legitimising performance-seeking innovation processes (Brown 2005). In a logic of appropriateness (March and Olsen 1989) or organisational logic (MacDuffie 1997) or thought-corridor (Douglas 1986) narratives can become *social facts*. These are processes of shared understandings envisaged by Wenger (1998) in communities of practice and Czarniawska's (1997) ever-producing narratives.

The centrality of learning and its operationalisation are central to inter-organisational working, since this is at the heart of service innovation. As Gallouj (2002) points out, what differentiates innovation in services results from their intangible and co-produced character: innovations are less supply driven (e.g. new technologies) and more the result of gathering and acting upon tacit knowledge. In effect, the whole system, involving users and providers from separate organisations, becomes a new platform from which to innovate (see Cusumano's (1998) idea of platforms from which to innovate, in the case of holistic service systems). For example, banks use their service platform from which to extend the range of services to customers; in similar fashion local education and payment services in inter-organisational contexts are expanding their service ranges. Innovative whole system local services are likely, then, to be characterised by continual rounds of experimentation, cycles of expansive learning and pilot projects testing new ways of working.

Such a learning environment is far removed from the world of centralised targets and transfer of tools and techniques from other sectors: new public management (Osborne 2010a). Local public services are often essential to the quality of life of vulnerable people (children, the elderly, the disabled, the excluded). Ethical considerations are therefore paramount as local public services share data, share assessment, join up services and work in multidisciplinary teams. Only close psychic distance ensures that ethics are not lost in a more dynamic environment. Paul Ricoeur (1995) argues for *human time*, time to negotiate meanings, between actors in arenas of rapid social change. New ways of organising multidisciplinary and holistic services require human time between users and providers and amongst sets of providers. Learning and change are likely to alter the identity of users and providers, especially professionals (Torstendahl 1998), in a world of relational ethics (Gilligan 1982; Held 2006) populated by relational persons (Friedman 1993; Mackenzie and Stoljar 2000).

Whole System and its Outputs

Having explored some of the theory and empirical work relating to whole system inter-organisational working, this section examines the outcomes from whole systems working, again referencing criteria used by Bardach (1998) in their classic study of inter-agency working.

Quality and effectiveness – transformed models

Introducing the user's experience into service evaluation introduces subjectivity. When evaluating independent living in smart housing, Kinder (2002) employed the criteria of use, usefulness, usability and usage as measures of quality and effectiveness; a study concluding that the innovativeness was in reconfigured networks – a new business model. Many service innovations (especially for people at risk) deploy mature rather than technically risky technology and techniques (Miles 2005). (Business model here means value proposition: the transformation of inputs into outputs satisfying users.) More conventionally, quality is measured using Parasuraman et al.'s (1985) service quality determinants based upon gap theory, later developed by Zhu et al. (2002) into SERVQUAL, which itself has been criticised for underplaying performance (Hemmasi and Strong 1994). Recently, whole system inter-organisational bodies have developed performance measurement approaches synthesising into a particular context with appropriate metrics; an example is in Kinder (2011).

Accountability

Accountability measures, records, reports, justifies and responds to performance metrics presuming the acceptance of responsibility by agents as the *cause of effects* (Kennett 2001), whilst in reality outcomes may be the result of moral luck (Nagel 1993). Increasingly, accountability systems use *indeterminate* forms of accountability (Rhodes 1997), for example 360-degree appraisal and evaluation. For Behn (2001, p.52) the accountability dilemma is 'trading-off between accountability for finances and fairness and accountability for performance'. Modernising inter-organisational local service providers avoid such trade-offs: with staff engagement and continuous improvement it is possible to create equity *and* efficiency, volume *and* variety, quality *and* quantity: in short, more from less by being more effective and efficient. Since inter-organisational working is novel, it is likely to measure its own social accountability (equality, environmental impact) and be subject to social accountability measurement by others. Where the private sector attempts to dis-intermediate the competition to capture market share, the public sector seeks integration to cut process costs.

Efficiency, sustainability and fairness

Do parts of the public sector suffer Baumol's disease, whereby efficient sectors of the economy shrink in size whilst inefficient ones expand? This is the view of those who argue that the public sector is always less productive than the private (e.g. Osbourne and Gaebler 1993). Yet if Baumol's theorem has value does it not apply to public *and* private services? Does it apply to Japanese retailing and agriculture compared with its manufacturing? Staying with services, all services innovate (and perform) differently from manufacturing, according to Tether (2005), because they are personalised (variety rather than flow) and co-produced (craft rather than mass production). Taking Prahalad and Bettis' (1986) idea of a dominant logic in sectors, Vargo and Lusch (2004) argue that discourse on innovation and performance remains product centred: accounting systems, valuation of intellectual property, measurement of work in progress are all rooted in physical product systems, whereas the utility of services is not embedded in a physical product but *experienced* by the user. A growing body of theory supports the idea of sectoral systems of innovation: sector institutional arrangements support different innovation processes

(Geels 2004). Important tools measuring what matters in service innovation include activity-based costing, benchmarking and the contextualisation of all performance metrics.

The normative moral purpose of providing public services includes social cohesion and fairness, funded by taxpayers (Andrews and Boyne 2010); here fairness is not only simply public goods which everybody can access (policing, roads, water); it is fairness in the sense of wealth redistribution, ensuring that people with particular needs, whatever their income, have a social minimum standard of wellbeing (health care, disability access, special educational needs). Fair access to public services by the *citizenry as whole* (Ostrom 1973; Behn 2001) is a challenge for inter-organisational whole systems for several reasons. Whole systems can only be sure that diverse users (clients, patients, pupils, tenants, defendants) gain fair access and outcomes from local public services by measuring (e.g. epidemiological studies cross-correlating demographics and service use for medical services), ensuring that close psychic distance with one set of users does not disadvantage others. In Scotland each local Council and Health Trust must produce an annual *joint* community care plan and set outcome targets for crime prevention jointly with the local police. There is a tension between stakeholders (including users) demanding fairness from public service providers, and innovative leaders, who necessarily take actions privileging a particular set of services and their users. There is no price mechanism drawing access to public services towards equilibrium; allocative fairness can only be ensured by measuring and justifying service use.

Satisfaction

Figure 21.1 begins with values and ends with the user and stakeholder satisfaction question. Buckmaster (1999) poses some of the difficulties: qualitative and quantitative performance measures, weighting between sets of stakeholders, individual or community levels of satisfaction, measures of stable quality versus measures of innovation and change. Context is everything for both values and satisfaction measurement: are they explicit, are expectations suitably managed, is performance accurately and appropriately measured and does the system have feedback loops driving continuous improvement? These questions all need contextually situated answers. In that sense, Andrews and Boyne (2010) are justified in asserting that public services require public discourse. For holistic systems to support meaningful discourse around satisfaction, real-time and effective information flows are essential. Bringing services together in inter-organisational arrangements also poses identity questions: who are we, what do we want to become? These are questions posed for all of the participants, much more sharply posed (because of the choices faced) than in an environment of fragmented services in which social problems may have (more) individual solutions.

Holistic Thinking

Modernising inter-organisational LPSs seek knowledge flows from users, partners and stakeholders; they are characterised by clear value flows, low inventory, teamworking, active problem solving and commitment-based human relations: what Csikszentmihaly (1991) calls *flow*. As Goldratt and Cox (1993) point out, improving flow means continually seeking and eliminating bottlenecks. Typically, bottlenecks stifle throughput and increase both inventory and operating costs: an hour lost at a bottleneck is an hour lost to the system. Inter-organisational working challenges the procedures, standards and outcomes to change intra-organisationally for each participating organisation. Inter-organisational services challenge innovators' comfort zones to adopt the new ways of learning (deutero-learning). In short, inter-organisational provision of local public services challenges everyone involved to adopt a new way of thinking about their community, its identity and their own identity.

IMPLICATIONS FOR THE MANAGEMENT OF INNOVATION IN PUBLIC SERVICES

Let me suggest three lessons for the management of innovation in local public services, in each case posing the lesson not in terms of exhortations, 'great leaders' or the latest management fad, instead each lesson is a contrived balance, a mindset inviting the reconciliation of seemingly competing pathways.

First, the inter-organisational innovation framework suggests that managers should, *at the same time*, press for continuous improvement within their organisation by (for example) benchmarking and eliminating bottlenecks, whilst *at the same time* thinking more widely about the networks they operate in and the opportunities for innovative joining up of services to deliver better solutions for users. This is what Ogle (2007) calls *ideas space*: perpetually seeking a new big idea by learning from one's networks. Joining up capacity and resources can often mean more from less – better service solutions with less resource input.

Secondly, key service users are a significant source of innovative ideas for public service managers. Provided values are mutual and destinies shared, listening to complaints and ideas from service users can paint an invaluable picture of what services might look like: a new vision. Indeed, one of the differentiating factors between service and physical product innovation is that service innovations are experienced (subjective feelings), so that successful change *always involves users*.

A third lesson for managers is not to be afraid of asymmetric organisation. Innovation often breeds clumsy organisational forms and emergent governances. As Christensen et al. (2008, p. 203) point out, isolating a project to create an innovation is often necessary to allow experimentation and enable new ways of working to emerge – this is what agile organisations do! Stability and prescribed processes are essential to deliver public services, *at the same time*; so too are innovative projects with clumsy organisational forms and governances.

ILLUSTRATIVE CASE EXAMPLE

To illustrate the value of the inter-organisational innovation framework, this section presents a truncated illustrative case study of health and social care in West Lothian (WL), Scotland. It has been cited in numerous papers and is the result of 20 years' observer-participation and formal research by the author. The WL Community Health and Care Partnership (WL CHCP) builds upon close and co-terminus working arrangements to deliver £120 million of primary health and care services previously delivered by WL Council and the local NHS hospital trust.

Values and Needs

WL's 160,000 population mainly lives in small communities and Livingston, a bustling new town. It is a working class area. Most of the middle class professionals work in the public sector and use local services: there is a close psychic distance between service users and providers. Its mining heritage supports a high voluntary sector participation rate and pride in local public services: in 2006 the local Council won the UK Best Council award.

Whole System and Innovation

From 1998 onwards, the Council embarked on a strategy of independent living for the elderly and disabled, previously accommodated in residential care: a small number of new-build homes in hub-and-spoke formation and 8,000 home conversions. Smart housing consists of alert, alarm and assistive technologies supported by an integrated service network, bringing together different agencies (health, social care, housing, police) often in co-located services, with the entire service network accessible via one-stop-shops, home Internet-enabled televisions and call centres. The smartness was in the network of formal and informal carers. As part of this popular move, the WL CHCP built upon a heritage of joint working (e.g. aids and adaptations), pooling social care and primary health care budgets.

WL CHCP immediately established its own IT, finance and Human Resources arrangements. Staff began working in multidisciplinary teams, soon using a shared online joint assessment of clients designed by doctors, social workers, community health, housing and police. An intensive training programme ICT-enabled community health and social care staff. Professional staff embarked on joint groups redesigning service processes; these groups and overall strategy groups included local voluntary organisations. Service quality and innovation groups mushroomed, levels of learning and change were high, and professionals from other areas began applying for jobs as service quality rose and the service model transformed.

Whole System and its Outputs

Using the synthetic WL Assessment Model to set high standards of service and innovation targets, quality and effectiveness of services transformed over a five year period. Although clumsy in organisational form, with accountability to its two parent bodies (the Council and NHS), internal and external accountability systems matured. Costs fell and service quality rose. Service users supported the new services, which gave access to previously under-represented groups.

Holistic Thinking

WL became the first Council area in the UK to achieve international quality standards and outcome agreement status. Holistic person-centred service design and delivery continue to drive innovation; for example, piloting touch-screen televisions for service communications and community education.

PROSPECTS AND CONCLUSIONS

Though highly condensed, the WL CHCP case illustrates that the analytical framework in Figure 21.1 readily structures the narrative of inter-organisational innovation and change in West Lothian.

My purpose has been to set out a framework through which local public service providers can envision inter-organisational service provision and the innovation opportunities it offers over the next ten years. It should be noted that in West Lothian the transformation of services from average to excellent took less than ten years.

Linear transplantation of so-called best practice rarely works: both the source and the target context require careful interrogation, including the service heritage, its governances, the leadership and the engagement of service providers and users. Reducing inter-organisational innovation to shared IT or back-office caps its potential to transform services; the more ambitious challenge requires investing time to allow service providers and users to think themselves into the new world, to negotiate new meanings and feel comfortable with new identities. Time to the first innovation implementation by inter-organisational groups is likely to be longer than with command and control hierarchies and, as Bardach (1998) points out, may cost more before savings begin to be crystallised.

Whole system, person-centred public services offer service users the opportunity to pass a public service version of Alan Turing's famous computer test (Kinder 2003, p. 156): 'The usefulness to users of interoperable public service systems increases in proportion to the extent to which systems are moulded so that users cannot detect where one organisation's system begins and another ends'. The challenge for local public services over the next ten years is to pass this test whilst innovating to meet rising service user and stakeholder expectations.

BIBLIOGRAPHY

Andrews, R. and Boyne, G. (2010). The Moral Purpose of Public Management Research. *Public Management Review*, 12(3), 307–321.
Argyris C, (1977). Double loop learning in organisations. *Harvard Business Review*, September–October.
Argyris, C. and Schön, D. (1978). *Organisational Learning: Theory of Action Perspective*. Boston, MA: Addison Wesley.
Bardach. E. (1998). *Getting Agencies to Work Together*. Washington, DC: Brookings Institution.
Bateson, G. (1973). *The Logical Categories of Learning and Communication: Steps to Ecology of Mind*. Chicago, IL: University of Chicago Press.
Beer, S. (1979). *The Heart of Enterprise*. Chichester: Wiley.
Behn, R.D. (2001), *Rethinking Democratic Accountability*. Washington, DC: Brookings Institution.
Bezzina, M.B., Fischer, L.B., Harden, L., Perkin, K. and Walker, D. (2001). Leadership in uncharted territory: developing the role of professional practice leader. *International Journal of Health Care Quality Assurance*, June, vi–xi.
Brouthers, K.D. and Brouthers, L.E. (2001). Explaining the national cultural distance paradox. *Journal of International Business Studies*, 32(1), 177–189.
Brown, A.D. (2005). Making sense of the collapse of Barings Bank. *Human Relations*, 58(12), 1579–1604.
Brown, A. (2007). Measuring the performance of England's primary school teachers: purposes, theories,

problems and tensions. In A. Neely (ed.), *Business Performance Management*. Cambridge: Cambridge University Press, chapter 16.

Buckmaster, N. (1999). Association between outcome measurement, accountability and learning for non-profit organisations. *International Journal for Public Sector Management*, 12(2), 186–197.

Castells, M. (1997). *The Information Age: The Rise of the Network Society, Vol. One*. Oxford: Blackwell.

Causer, G. and Exworthy, M. (1999). Professionals as managers across the public sector. In M. Exworthy and S. Halford (eds), *Professionals and the New Managerialism in the Public Sector*. Buckingham: Open University Press.

Chesbrough, H. (2011). *Open Services Innovation*. San Francisco, CA: Wiley.

Child, J. (1984). *Organisation: A Guide to Problems and Practice*. London: Harper and Row.

Christensen, C.M., Horn, M.B. and Johnson, C.W. (2008). *Disrupting Class – How Disruptive Innovation Will Change the Way the World Learns*. London: McGraw-Hill.

Csikszentmihaly, M. (1991). *Flow: The Psychology of Optimal Experience*. New York: Harper Collins.

CSIP (2005). *Integration and Partnership Working*. Integrated Care Network. Available at: http://www.integratedcarenetwork.gov.uk (accessed August 2006).

Cusumano, M.A. and Nobeoka, K. (1998). *Thinking Beyond Lean*. New York: Free Press.

Cusumano, M.A. and Selby, R.W. (1995). *Microsoft Secrets*. London: HarperCollins.

Czarniawska, B. (1997). *Narrating the Organization: Dramas of Institutional Identity*. Chicago, IL: University of Chicago Press.

Douglas, M. (1986). *How Institutions Think*. New York: Syracuse University Press.

Engeström, Y. (1987). *Learning by Expanding: An Activity-Theoretical Approach to Development Research*. Helsinki: Orienta-Konsultit.

Engeström, Y. and Kerouac, H. (2007). From workplace learning to inter-organisational learning and back: the contribution of activity theory. *Journal of Workplace Learning*, 19(6), 336–342.

Freidson, E. (1988). *Profession of Medicine: A Study of the Sociology of Applied Knowledge*. Chicago, IL: University of Chicago Press.

Friedman, M. (1993). *What are Friends For? Feminist Perspectives on Personal Relationships and Moral Theory*. New York: Cornell University Press.

Gallouj, F. (2002). *Innovation in the Service Economy: The New Wealth of Nations*. Cheltenham, UK and Northampton, MA: Edward Elgar Publishing.

Geels, F.W. (2004). From sectoral systems of innovation to socio-technical systems. *Research Policy*, 33, 897–920.

Gilligan, C. (1982). *In a Different Voice: Psychological Theory and Women's Development*. Cambridge, MA: Harvard University Press.

Glen, S. and Reeves, S. (2003). Developing interprofessional education in the pre-registration curricula: mission impossible? *Nurse Education in Practice*, 4, 45–52.

Goldratt, E.M. and Cox, J. (1993). *The Goal*. Aldershot: Gower.

Grabher, G. (1993). *The Embedded Firm*. London: Routledge.

Granovetter, M. (1973). The strength of weak ties. *American Journal of Sociology*, 78(6), 1360–1380.

Gronroos, C. (1983). *Strategic Management and Marketing in the Service Sector*. Bromley and Lund: Studentlitteratur.

Haux, R. (2006). Health information systems – past, present, future. *International Journal of Medical Informatics*, 75(3–4), 268–281.

Hemmasi, M. and Strong, K.C. (1994). Measuring service quality for strategic planning and analysis in service firms. *Journal of Applied Business Research*, 10(4), 24–34.

Hollander, M.J. and Pallan, P. (1995). The British Columbia Continuing Care System. *Aging*, 7, 94–109.

Hope, A. (2007). Risk taking, boundary performance and intentional school Internet misuse. *Discourse*, 28(1), 87– 99.

Hudson, B. (2002). *Whole Systems Working, Care Services Improvement Partnership*. Available at: http://www.integratedcarenetwork.gov.uk (accessed August 2006).

Huxham, C. (1993a). Pursuing collaborative advantage. *Journal of Operational Research Society*, 44(6), 599–611.

Huxham, C. (1993b). Collaborative capability: an intra-organisational perspective on collaborative advantage. *Public Money & Management*, July–September, 21–28.

Kennett, J. (2001). *Agency and Responsibility*. Oxford: Clarendon Press.

Kinder, T. (2000). A sociotechnical approach to the innovation of a network technology in the public sector: the introduction of smart homes in West Lothian. *European Journal of Innovation Management*, 3(2), 72–90.

Kinder, T. (2002). Vote early, vote often? Tele-democracy in European cities. *Public Administration*, 80(3), 557–582.

Kinder, T. (2003). Mrs Miller moves house: interoperability of local public services in Europe. *Journal of European Social Policy*, 13(2), 141–157.

Kinder, T. (2010a). Social innovation in services: technologically assisted new care models for people with dementia and their usability. *International Journal of Technology Management*, 51(1), 106–120.

Kinder, T. (2010b). Evolving accountabilities and outcome agreements: experience and prospects from Scottish public services. In A. Ball and S. Osborne (eds), *Social Accounting and Accountability*. London: Routledge, chapter 6.

Kinder, T. (2012). Learning, innovating and performance of locally delivered public services. *Public Management Review*, forthcoming.

Kinder, T. and Burgoyne, T. (2012). Lean and learning in healthcare services. *Financial Accountability & Management*, forthcoming.

Kinder, T., Klaes, M. and Molina, A. (1999). Sociotechnical alignment in the build-up of a telemedicine constituency in Scotland. *Science and Public Policy*, 26(6), 415–435.

Klijn, E-H. and Koopenjan, J. (2000). Public management and policy networks. *Public Management*, 2(2), 135–158.

Klijn, E-H. and Koopenjan, J. (2006). Institutional design: changing institutional features of networks. *Public Management Review*, 141–160.

Kogut, B. and Singh, H. (1988). The effect of national culture on the choice of entry mode. *Journal of International Business Studies*, 19(3), 411–432.

Kooiman, J. and Jentoft, S. (2009). Meta-governance: values, norms and principles, and the making of hard choices. *Public Administration*, 87(4), 818–836.

Lapsley, I. (2009). New Public Management: the cruellest invention of the human spirit? *ABACUS*, 45(1), 1–21.

Leutz, W. (2005). Reflections on integrating medical and social care: five laws revisited. *Journal of Integrated Care*, 13(5), 3–12.

Lewin, K. (1943). Defining the field at a given time. *Psychological Review*, 50, 292–310.

Lewis, A.G. (2001). *Streamlining Health Care Operations*, San Francisco: Jossey-Bass.

MacDuffie, J.P. (1997). The road to 'root cause:' shop-floor problem-solving at three auto assembly plants. *Management Science*, 43(4), 479–502.

Mackenzie, C. and Stoljar, N. (eds) (2000). *Relational Autonomy: Feminist Perspectives on Autonomy, Agency and the Social Self*. Oxford: Oxford University Press.

March, J.G. and Olsen, J.P. (1989). *Rediscovering Institutions: The Organizational Basis of Politics*. New York: Free Press.

Miles, I. (2005). Innovation in services. In J. Fagerberg, D.C. Mowery and R.R. Nelson (eds), *The Oxford Handbook of Innovation*. Oxford: Oxford University Press.

Nagel, R. (1993). *Experimental Results on Interactive, Competitive Guessing*. University of Bonn Working Paper.

Nardi, B.A. (1996). Studying context: a comparison of activity theory, situated action models and distributed cognition. In B.A. Nardi (ed.), *Context and Consciousness*. Boston, MA: MIT, chapter 4.

Neely, A. (2001). The performance measurement revolution: why now and what next? *International Journal of Operations & Production Management*, 19(2), 205–228.

Normann, R. (2002). *Services Management: Strategy and Management in Service Business*. Chichester: Wiley.

Ogle, R. (2007). *Smart World: Breakthrough Creativity and the New Science of Ideas*. Boston, MA: Harvard Business School Press.

Osborne, D. and Gaebler, T. (1993). *Reinventing Government*. London: Penguin.

Osborne, S.P. (2010a). Public governance and public service delivery: a research agenda for the future. In S.P. Osborne (ed.), *The New Public Governance?* London: Routledge, chapter 23.

Osborne, S.P. (2010b). The (New) Public Governance: a suitable case for treatment. In S.P. Osborne (ed.), *The New Public Governance?* London: Routledge, chapter 1.

Ostrom, V. (1973). *The Intellectual Crisis in American Public Administration*. Tuscaloosa, AL: Alabama University Press.

Parasuraman, A., Zeithaml, V.A. and Berry, L.L. (1985). A conceptual model of service quality and its implications for future research. *Journal of Marketing*, 49, 41–50.

Perri 6, Leat, D., Seltzer, K. and Stoker, G. (2002). *Towards Holistic Governance*. London: Palgrave.

Polanyi, M. (1958). *Personal Knowledge*. London: Routledge & Kegan Paul.

Porter, M. (1985). *Competitive Advantage*. New York: The Free Press.

Power, M. (2003). *The Audit Society: Rituals of Verification*. Oxford: Oxford University Press.

Prahalad, C.K. and Bettis, R. (1986). The dominant logic: a new linkage between diversity and performance. *Strategic Management Journal*, 7, 485–501.

Rawls, J. (2005). *Political Liberalism*. New York: Columbia University Press.

Rhodes, R.A.W. (1997). *Understanding Governance: Policy Networks, Governance, Reflexivity and Accountability*. Buckingham: Open University Press.

Ricoeur, P. (1995). *Oneself as Another*. Chicago, IL: University of Chicago Press.

Schön, D.A. (1983). *The Reflective Practitioner*. New York: Basic Books.

Scott, W.R. (1995). *Institutions and Organisations*. London: Sage.

Sennett, R. (2008). *The Craftsman*. London: Allen Lane.

Shenkar, O. (2001). Cultural distance revisited: towards a more rigorous conceptualization and measurement of cultural differences. *Journal of International Business Studies*, 32(3), 519–535.

Siehl, C., Bowen, D.E. and Pearson, C.M. (1991). The role of rites of integration in service delivery. *International Journal of Service Industry Management*, 2(1), 15–34.

Sink, D.S. and Tuttle, T.C. (1989). *Planning and Measurement in Your Organisation of the Future*. Norcross, GA: Industrial Engineering and Management Press, chapter 5.

Stern, E. (2000). *The Value Mindset*. New York: Wiley.

Stinchcombe, A.L. (1990). *Information and Organisations*. Los Angeles, CA: University of California Press.

Svensson, L.G. (1990). Knowledge as a professional resource: case studies of architects and psychologies at work. In R. Torstendahl and M. Burrage (eds), *The Formation of Professions: Knowledge, State and Strategy*. London: Sage, chapter 7.

Tether, B. (2005). Do services innovate (differently)? Insights from the European Innobarometer Survey *Industry and Innovation*, 12(2), 153–184.

Thistlethwaite, P. (2004). *Integrated Working: A Guide (Bringing the NHS and Local Government Together)*. Integrated Care Network. Available at: http://www.integratedcarenetwork.gov.uk (accessed August 2006).

Thompson, M. (1997). Cultural theory and integrated assessment. *Environmental Modeling and Assessment*, 2, 139–150.

Torstendahl, R. (1990). Essential properties, strategic aims and historical development: three approaches to theories of professionalism. In M. Burrage and R. Torstendahl (eds), *The Formation of Professions: Knowledge, State and Strategy*. London: Sage, chapter 1.

Tushman, M.L. and Nadler, D.A. (1978). Information processing as an integrating concept in organisational design. *Academy of Management Review*, 3(3), 613–624.

Van der Wal, Z., de Graff, G. and Lawton, A. (2011). Competing value in Public Management: introduction to the symposium issue, 13(3), 331–341.

Vargo, S. and Lusch, R. (2004). Evolving to a new dominant logic for marketing. *Journal of Marketing*, 68 (January), 1–17.

Von Hippel, E. (1988). *The Sources of Innovation*. Oxford: Oxford University Press.

Weick, K.E. (1995). *Sensemaking in Organizations*. San Fracisco, CA: Sage.

Wenger, E. (1998). *Communities of Practice*. Cambridge: Cambridge University Press.

Wertsch, J.V. (1998). *Mind as Action*, Oxford: Oxford University Press.

Williams, R.S. (2002). *Managing Employee Performance: Design and Implementation in Organisations*. London: Thomson.

Wilson, S., Butler, M., James, K., Partington, D., Singh, V. and Vinnicombe, S. (2004). The fallacy of integration. *Women in Management Review*, 19(4), 186–195.

Zhu, F.X., Wymer, W. and Chen, I. (2002). IT-based services and service quality in consumer banking. *International Journal of Service Industry Management*, 131, 69–90.

22. Innovation in complex public service systems
Mary Lee Rhodes

INTRODUCTION

Understanding the nature of innovation in public services as *complex systems* requires some upfront definitional work – which may give pause to the reader with limited time to spare. To provide some incentive for the wary (and weary), the following arguments are put forward in this chapter. To start with, the argument from Osborne[1] (2010, p. 415) that 'a *systemic* approach is required' to study contemporary public services sets the stage. While Osborne suggests an open natural systems perspective for this approach, we will argue that complex adaptive systems (CAS) models – specifically those proposed by Siggelkow and Levinthal (2003) and their collaborators – are shown to be consistent with empirical studies of innovation in the public and community and voluntary sectors. This allows us to compare the findings from the empirical studies with those from the CAS model-based research to highlight those features of innovation in public services that are likely to prove most fruitful for developing robust theory that can be tested empirically, as well as via model-based simulations. Furthermore, there is reason to believe that ongoing research into the 'rules' that enable complex organizational systems to operate at the 'edge of chaos' (Kauffman 1995; Brown and Eisenhardt 1998; Miller and Page 2007) could shed light on how public service managers and the systems they influence could be better positioned to adapt to changing circumstances and achieve improved outcomes through innovation. Institutional rules and their relevance to public management and policy systems are familiar ground (Scott 1995; Koppenjan and Klijn 2004) and the CAS perspective can easily incorporate elements from this literature. These features and the potential for policy and management insights are summarized in the conclusion to this chapter.

WHAT ARE COMPLEX PUBLIC SERVICE SYSTEMS?

We start out by defining the concept(s) of *complex public service systems* by bringing together recent work in systems theory and service management and relating this to the current reality of public service delivery. Beginning with public service delivery, we observe that in the post-New Public Management world, public services are unlikely to be delivered uniquely or even largely by the public sector. While it was never the case that health, education, transport, housing, communications, and so on were provided by the public sector on its own, the reforms of the last 30 years have resulted in increasing reliance on private, non-profit and community sector organizations to deliver public services. They are delivered by a plethora of actors with heterogeneous motives and capacities interacting to greater or lesser extent with highly variable results and with limited ability to hold any one organization accountable.

Compounding the organizational impact of reforms on the delivery of services, the development of theory on the nature of services has highlighted the significant management challenges arising from intangibility, perishability, co-creation and perception. Osborne (2010) highlights the mismatch of manufacturing-based operations theory to issues of public service delivery that underpins much of the recent adaptation of private sector practices to the public sector. The private sector has long since moved on from many of the 'modern' reforms introduced into the public sector. Service-Dominant Logic is an approach to understanding and delivering services that has been developed by R.F. Lusch and S.L. Vargo (2006) and provides many of the underlying concepts for the proposed new 'discipline' of Service Science being promoted by IBM and assorted academics.[2] At its core, Service-Dominant Logic requires that service firms (and, by implication, public sector service organizations) fundamentally change how they view what they do.

Service-Dominant Logic has yet to become a mainstream element of management theory and it has its critics in the marketing discipline in which it was born (Achrol and Kotler 2006). However, the basic differences between the manufacturing of products and the creation of services are well established in private sector management theory and practice. Theory and practice concur that service takes place at the interaction between customer and provider, and that attention to all aspects of that interaction is an imperative for service firms. Reforms such as the 'Quality Customer Service' initiative in the Irish public sector pay some heed to this imperative, but in the end it fails to really engage with the implication for fundamental change in the way services are designed and delivered. In healthcare, the research and practice reforms aimed at improving the 'patient journey' are moving in the direction of Service-Dominant Logic, but the medical professional model and the manufacturing paradigm still provide the underlying assumptions on how best to deliver healthcare. A basic discussion of the implications of Service-Dominant Logic for innovation may be found in Hazdra (2010), and Osborne (2010) suggests that the adoption of a service management perspective in the public sector is long overdue.

Understanding of services as experienced interactions and public services as complex networks of heterogeneous service providers are two of the three definitional tasks required to complete the definition of complex public service systems. The third is the definition of a system. We start with the identification of three fundamental types of systems: closed, open and complex. Closed systems are those that exist without any significant interaction with their environment, largely confined to mechanical systems such as waste, water and electrical systems in a public service context. Open systems are those that interact with their environment, via the exchange of information and/or the transformation of inputs (from the environment) into outputs. All living systems are considered open systems. Complex systems have the same basic characteristics as open systems, but display unpredictable behaviour due to interactions among elements, adaptation of system components and emergence of new properties over time. These types of systems have only been explored in any detail over the last 25 years or so and their application to human organizational systems has emerged only over the last 15 years (Anderson 1999). Complex systems theory has been identified by public administration scholars as having the potential to address the increasingly messy business of public service provision, and several books and special issues of journals have been devoted to exploring this potential.[3]

Systems theorists have identified several types of complex systems. *Dissipative systems* are those that draw energy from the environment in a continual process of self-organization and – at least for a period – appear to defy the Second Law of Thermodynamics. These systems exist in a kind of semi-equilibrium state, importing energy to maintain their shape for a while but then suddenly collapsing into disorder before reaching a 'bifurcation point', after which a new form is adopted and becomes the new equilibrium state of the system. Models of dissipative systems are based on the work of the physicist/chemist and Nobel prize-winner, Ilya Prigogine, and are most often applied in the natural sciences, although the concept of 'punctuated equilibrium' in organizations (Romanelli and Tushman 1994) is similar to the ideas of Prigogine.

Chaotic systems are another archetype of complex systems, theories of which are derived from the work of the meteorologist, Edward Lorenz. Chaotic systems follow precise 'laws' of behaviour, but nevertheless exhibit unpredictable outcomes due to interactions between the various laws and/or small differences in initial conditions. Applications of chaos theory are concerned with discovering the laws and conditions that govern the behaviour of a particular system and mapping out the potential set of patterns that the system can display. Chaos-based models tend to be heavily mathematical and are used extensively in financial and economic analyses.

A third type of complex systems is *complex adaptive systems*. Like all complex systems, CAS are self-organizing in that there is no controlling entity within or outside of the system. However, patterns of actions/interactions that emerge over time may create conditions that constrain the behaviour of agents in future periods. Furthermore, agents can 'learn' from their previous actions and outcomes and adapt their behaviour to suit their individual purpose(s). There are many proponents of complex adaptive systems theory; among the most well known and cited are the biologist, Stuart Kauffman and the computer scientist/psychologist, John H. Holland. In contrast to models based on chaos theory, CAS models tend to be implemented in the form of computer simulations and 'fuzzy logic' formulations, which are more easily applicable to the social sciences. Daniel Levinthal and Nicolaj Siggelkow[4] and their collaborators have explored a number of organizational models based on Kauffman's 'NK' model[5] of complex adaptive systems, and Sidney Winter (2005) has suggested that NK models have significant potential for the development of management theory. We return to Levinthal and Siggelkow's work later in this chapter.

In our research into public sector systems in Ireland over the last 10 years,[6] we have proposed that CAS models have the greatest potential for exploring the nature and dynamics of public and non-profit service delivery. A detailed mapping of a selection of public service systems to CAS elements may be found in Rhodes et al. (2011). Furthermore, the shift to multi-agent public service delivery over the past 20 years and the re-conceptualization of services described above lend further weight to the argument that CAS have empirical as well as theoretical relevance to the public services today.

We may summarize the above by stating that complex public service systems are most closely aligned to CAS, and that the key elements of these systems are the agents that interact in a particular environment to produce outcomes. Agents can learn from their interactions and the resulting behaviour and can adapt over time to improve (from their perspective) outcomes. Furthermore, agent interactions over time may create 'rules' that will constrain future behaviour, and there may also be rules and outcomes extant in the environment arising from previous systems that influence agent behaviour.

CAS AND INNOVATION

Having made a case for complex public service systems as CAS, the next step is to discuss what *innovation* means in CAS. In so doing, we will also define some of the basic dynamics in CAS and how these have been identified in several relevant studies of public management innovation.

There is no lack of definitions of innovation. For the purposes of this chapter, we use one from Walker (2008, p. 592): 'a process through which new ideas, objects, and practices are created, developed or reinvented, and which are new for the unit of adoption'. The author goes on in the same article (p. 592) to state: 'in public organizations, one-off or stand-alone innovations are not the norm. Innovation is evolutionary rather than radical', a view echoed by Osborne et al. (2008) as well as Piening (2011). In this definition of innovation as an evolutionary process of change, we can already discern the basic dynamic of *adaptation* in CAS. Adaptation is defined as the changes made by agents in response to the actions of other participants, environmental conditions or emergent systems characteristics and is generally conceived of as a feature of goal-seeking behaviour of agents in a CAS (Kauffman 1993; Holland 1998). There are several different mechanisms by which agents can adapt, one of the most popular of which is based in evolutionary theory and typified by Beinhocker's (2007) phrase: 'differentiate, select, amplify'. The search process on the performance landscapes in Levinthal and Siggelkow's work is an example of this kind of adaptive mechanism. In their models, 'agents' can change one or more strategic choices in a given time period and the combination of choices will result in a (randomly assigned) performance outcome. Agents will move towards higher performance 'peaks' by searching neighbouring[7] combinations of choices to determine if performance will improve as a consequence of the adaptation. Examples of adaptation by public sector organizations abound, and Osborne et al. (2008) provide a plethora of evidence for the adaptive behaviour of voluntary and community organizations to changes in the UK policy environment between 1994 and 2006.

Innovation as discontinuous change is also accommodated in complex systems theory, but is more often seen in models based on dissipative structures theory (Prigogine and Stengers 1984; Prigogine 1997). In these models, *bifurcation* is the process of change that can come about abruptly as a result of the system reaching a critical 'bifurcation' or 'tipping' point. While there is evidence that bifurcation occurs in public service systems (see Rhodes et al. 2011), this is not a feature of the empirical studies on innovation examined here. However, the concept of discontinuous change as a dynamic of innovation is certainly contained in the literature.

A CAS dynamic that is found in innovation studies and is strongly associated with both CAS and dissipative systems theory is path-dependency. *Path-dependency* refers to the tendency for systems to lock into a particular set of behaviours and/or characteristics early on in the lifecycle due to initial conditions in the environment and/or the nature of the agents and their early interactions. An oft-cited example of the dynamic of path-dependency is the evolution of the QWERTY keyboard design for computers, which developed out of the original design for typewriters in 1870. The QWERTY layout of keys for the typewriter was designed to prevent the jamming of the type bars while typing at speed and in 140 years the design of the keyboard has not changed, in spite of successive waves of innovation in computing and information processing. Often linked to path-dependency – but conceptually distinct – is the notion that complex systems are characterized by their sensitivity to *initial conditions* (Prigogine 1997), which are the specific characteristics of the environment and/or the agents at the time of the system's start-up. The state of technology at the time of the invention of the early typewriter is an example of 'initial conditions'. Path-dependency and initial conditions generally appear as contingencies in innovation theory and reference to path-dependency in healthcare management may be found in the recent study by Piening (2011).

Two dynamics of complex adaptive systems that do not feature in any obvious way in the innovation literature are 'self-organization' and 'emergence'. *Self-organization* is a defining feature of CAS and refers to the ability of systems to emerge spontaneously from the interaction of agents following their own 'local' rules and responding to feedback from other agents and their environment (Kauffman 1993, 1995; Anderson 1999). The interaction of these agents over time results in patterns and regularity (rule-based behaviour) without the intervention of a central controller. The existence of 'standard practices' in professions, sectors and industries is a practical example of self-organization by interacting agents, as is the creation of markets or the geography of urban streets and neighbourhoods. *Emergence* at its simplest is the creation of new properties (Emmeche et al. 1997), that is, properties that could not be predicted based on the antecedent actions or component elements of the phenomena that led to or comprise the resulting (emergent) phenomena. Emergence also implies properties that are at a higher level of abstraction than the antecedent actions and/or elements (de Wolf and Holvoet 2005); for example the emergent properties (market price, range and roles of firms and agencies, standard building practices, etc.) of housing markets arising from the building, buying and selling of houses over time. Holland (1998) suggests that the dynamic of emergence results in recurring, although not necessarily predictable, patterns across multiple instances of the system examined and 'involve patterns of interaction that persist despite a continual turnover of the constituents' (Holland 1998, p. 7).

REINTERPRETING RECENT STUDIES IN PUBLIC MANAGEMENT INNOVATION USING CAS

In the previous sections we made the case that CAS theory – both its basic elements and dynamics – is relevant to innovation in complex public service systems. In this section we reinterpret some recent studies of innovation in public services to demonstrate how CAS theory would describe/explain how innovation 'works'. The innovation studies we examine are found in Piening (2011), Walker et al. (2011), Osborne et al. (2008) and Walker (2008).

In each of the four studies, (public and non-profit) organizations represent 'agents' in the system that operate in an environment characterized by: 1) other agents, and 2) environmental factors that are selected for their potential relevance for innovation processes and outcomes. Environmental factors – such as service need, political turbulence, rules and levels of competition, and so on – and organizational characteristics – such as structure, size, resources, capabilities, and so on – are hypothesized as being important for predicting whether the organizations will innovate. Furthermore, in the Walker studies, there is implicit recognition of interdependencies among factors as the regressions are set up to introduce groups of factors in stages, and their regression coefficients vary significantly with the introduction of new factors. Finally, in three out of four studies (Osborne 2008; Walker 2008; Walker et al. 2011), different types of innovation are identified – with the attendant hypotheses that organizational/environmental features will have different relevance for different types of innovation.

Heterogeneous agents (organizations) operating in an environment made up of multiple dimensions that affect outcomes interdependently is exactly what the CAS performance landscape models of Levinthal and Siggelkow explore. The difference between the CAS models and the analytical framework used in the innovation studies is that the dependent variable in the CAS models is 'performance' while the dependent variable in the innovation studies is 'innovation'. It is not a significant leap of logic, though, to argue that organizations innovate in search of better performance. In fact, in Walker (2008), the existence of a performance management system in an organization is a statistically significant indicator of the likelihood to innovate across all innovation types. The only other independent variable in this study (and in the later Walker et al. 2011 study) that is positively correlated with all types of innovation is service need/demand. Osborne et al. (2008) also suggest that innovation (or the lack of it) by voluntary and community organizations (VCOs) is driven by their need to meet expectations from government funding agencies – another example of performance-driven innovation.

If user demand and measures of performance together provide the basic impetus for innovation, and innovation is 'a process through which new ideas, objects, and practices are created, developed or reinvented' (Walker 2008, p. 592), we have the basics of a performance landscape model. The process of innovation reinterpreted is the search process that agents undertake as they vary one or more dimensions of their own 'DNA' (i.e. their strategies and/or organizational processes) and also seek to alter features of their environment to meet user need and increase performance. The landscape includes relevant features of the environment, and the range of choices that organizations make in relation to strategy, structure and process. Furthermore, the landscape is made up of performance peaks and valleys that represent how different combinations of environmental features and organizational choices interact and impact on performance.

Figure 22.1 represents a performance landscape that arises from the performance characteristics of two dimensions (X, Y) and the interaction between them. Agents occupying a particular location (X, Y coordinate) will exhibit a specific level of performance in the environment, as shown by the circles A, B, C, and D. Multidimensional landscapes incorporating any number of dimensions (N) may be modelled mathematically.[8]

What is striking about the comparison between the performance landscape models and the innovation studies is the convergence of the key drivers and dynamics of innovation and performance. We have already discussed the fact that performance and need are identified as fundamental drivers of innovation in both literatures. In addition, both the innovation studies and the performance landscape models find that organizational structure, the type of innovation/search and features of the environment have significant impact on outcomes. We discuss each of these in turn below.

In the performance landscape models, the main organizational variable in the landscape models is 'structure' – in particular the choice between 'centralized' or 'decentralized' decision making. For example, in Rivkin and Siggelkow (2003), the authors demonstrate when, how and why an 'active vertical organization' (i.e. a centralized

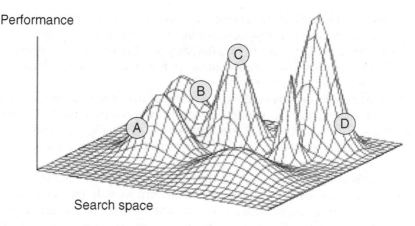

Figure 22.1   Performance landscape

structure) will achieve better performance on a landscape made up of six dimensions (N) with varying levels of interdependency (K) among the dimensions. One of their findings is that under conditions of environmental complexity,[9] centralization is less effective (results in lower average performance) than decentralization, although there are other organizational design decisions that can mitigate this effect. In Siggelkow and Levinthal (2003), the authors find that under conditions of environmental complexity *and* change, organizations that temporarily operate in a decentralized fashion and then shift into a more centralized structure perform better on average. In both cases the problem with the centralized structure is that organizations lock into performance 'traps' too early and fail to explore possibilities that could result in higher performance. A performance trap in these models is represented by a peak in the performance landscape that is not the highest peak achievable overall. In Figure 22.1, the location at point C represents a performance trap as organizations occupying this location would be unlikely to make an incremental change since all of the neighbouring locations result in lower performance. However, in the system overall there is a higher performance peak that could be achieved.

In Walker (2008), organizational structure also plays a central role in the determination of whether a firm will innovate or not. Interestingly – and consistent with the performance landscape models – the effects of organizational structure are amplified by the incorporation of environmental dimensions into the regression models. 'Specialization' is positively related to levels of innovation while 'devolved management' has a negative impact – and both are particularly apparent in relation to 'marketization' innovation, although the relationship of specialization to organizational and ancillary innovations is also statistically significant, if not quite as strong.

At first, the innovation findings appear to contradict the performance landscape models. 'Devolved management' in the Walker study is the same concept as 'decentralization' in the Siggelkow models, and in the latter the decentralized structure increases the search capability of the organization on the landscape. However, *this is only valuable in a complex environment.* When there are no interdependencies or changes in performance characteristics of the various environmental dimensions, a centralized structure does very well. Innovation (search) stops once the ideal performance peak is reached – which happens quite quickly. One might suggest that the findings in Walker (2008) are representative of a relatively low complexity environment with a plethora of mature organizations. Given that the study is based on local authorities in the UK, this would not be a huge stretch of the imagination. Furthermore, in the most complex regression reported by Walker (2008), the regression coefficient for devolved management becomes statistically significant in a *positive* direction for service innovation – which is consistent with the Siggelkow models.

Similarly, the regression coefficients for specialization, when combined with those for centralization in the Walker study, are consistent with Siggelkow et al. models. In Walker's study, centralization is found to be weakly inversely related to innovation – particularly with respect to organizational innovation – while specialization is positively related to innovation. This is consistent with the performance landscape model findings that decomposability and subordinate knowledge (features of specialization) improve the performance of organizations through improved search capability. On the other hand, Osborne et al. (2008) suggest that the shift towards specialization by VCOs in the UK in the mid-2000s is associated with a decrease in innovation by these organizations. A careful reading of this article, however, suggests that the specialization referred to by managers of these organizations is not what Siggelkow and Levinthal are describing, but rather a refocus of the VCOs' activities to align with the needs of the commissioning bodies – that is, the local authorities. In this case, specialization does improve performance under the new rules, but it is not via an increased capacity to innovate.

It is interesting to note that the significance of centralization and specialization, not to mention devolved management, in the Walker study only holds as long as previous and current innovation variables are not included in the regression. What this suggests – and what is explicitly proposed in Piening (2011) – is that organizational path-dependency has an important role to play in any model of organizational innovation. Path-dependency is one of the defining features of complex systems as described above. What Walker (2008) and Piening (2011) find is that path-dependency is a feature of organizational innovation as well – namely, that organizations with a history of innovation are more likely than those without such a history to engage in future innovation. In summary, organization structure matters and there are observable patterns in how it affects innovation that can be simulated in a performance landscape model.

This brings us to the next major area of overlap – namely the innovation/search process itself. In the performance landscape models innovation is represented as a search process in which agents innovate based on the potential return arising from changing the value of one or more environmental/organizational dimensions – or movement around the landscape. The 'rules' governing search are crucial to the outcomes of the performance landscape models and there are two main types of rules that apply. The first is how far away from its current position an agent can move – represented by how many different dimensions can be changed in one period. The second is how many different combinations of dimensions can be evaluated in one period. For example, in a six-dimension landscape, the search rules might be that agents can vary up to two dimensions, but can only evaluate one option beyond their current position. This means that in any one period there are up to four different combinations that are possible, but the agent can only decide between two of these. This would be a fairly restrictive innovation/search process, while an increase in either the number of changes that are possible or that can be considered represents more far-reaching innovation/search capacity.

To reinterpret the innovation studies using the CAS search framework, we first need to consider the typology of innovation that is present in the empirical studies. All of the studies recognize the basic typology proposed by Osborne (1998) that service innovation consists of changing one or both of the dimensions of type of services or type of customers. These are generally perceived as the outward-/market-facing types of innovation and the studies show that service need (user demand) and performance management are positively correlated with this type of innovation. With one stroke we have defined two dimensions of the strategic choices that organizations have on the landscape. Osborne defines changing both customers and services as 'total' service innovation, while changing the customers to whom similar services are delivered is 'expansion' and changing the services delivered to the same customers is 'evolution'. 'Total' service innovation is considered to be more difficult to undertake – which is consistent with the performance landscape model of movement across more dimensions as a greater 'leap'.

The second category of innovation includes process (or developmental) innovations – which are those innovations that relate to the internal activities of the organization. In Osborne et al. (2008), these are explicitly characterized as 'incremental' innovations as opposed to the more ambitious and risky innovations in the service category. Walker et al. (2011) further decompose these types of innovations (which Walker calls 'process' innovations) into three types: organizational, marketization and technological. While the basic point is that these innovations would align with more restrictive movement on the performance landscape, what is interesting about the Walker findings is that environmental/organizational characteristics appear to correlate differently with different sub-types of process/developmental innovation. We return to this point later on.

The third and final category of innovation in the Walker studies is called 'ancillary' innovation and has to do with network building, partnerships and inter/intra-organizational communication. We can (re)interpret this type of innovation as an expansion of the number of different changes that an agent may be aware of – although not necessarily evaluate – in a given period. One very intriguing finding in the Walker studies is that ancillary innovations are strongly positively correlated with service innovations, both in the period in which they occur and lagged one period before – suggesting that ancillary innovation (or expanded search capability) increases the likelihood of the outward facing (or more ambitious) service innovations.

To summarize, the typologies in the innovation studies are consistent with the types of searches in performance landscape models. The service/ancillary innovation type is consistent with an 'exploration' search in which agents can jump significant distances on a performance landscape, but a jump may or may not bring them to a higher performance level. Process/developmental innovations are consistent with 'exploitation' searches in that they focus on moving short distances on the performance landscape with more assurance of an increase in performance – that is, moving steadily up a performance peak. In the CAS literature, a hierarchical (centralized) organizational structure is often linked with exploitation searches, while a more organic (decentralized) structure is linked with exploration search processes.

The last main area of convergence between the innovation studies and performance landscape models is the specification of the features of the environment and the link between the environment and the organization (agent). We have already highlighted how the dimensions of the environment as described in the innovation studies are similar to those described in the performance landscapes of Siggelkow and Levinthal and their collaborators. This is also the case for the dynamics of the interaction between environment and organization. For example, level of service need is positively correlated with all innovation types in the Walker studies – which is consistent with the dynamics of agents on a performance landscape seeking to improve their performance by offering better service.

What is interesting in this comparison of innovation and CAS is the consistency between the findings in Walker in regards to diversity of need and the performance landscape models – that is, that diversity of need decreases innovation, particularly with respect to ancillary innovations. Diversity of need may be understood as a dimension that increases the complexity of the environment in which an organization operates. Environmental complexity in a performance landscape is largely captured by the interaction among different dimensions (as in diverse but interdependent user needs). As complexity increases, agents on a highly complex landscape often find themselves in performance traps, stuck on low-lying performance hills from which they cannot perceive or move to the higher performance peaks. A further elaboration of the performance model (for the public sector) is suggested by the Walker innovation regressions; that is, that competition among agents is positively correlated with marketization but not so much with other types of innovation. This suggests that while competition will facilitate exploitation-type movement on the landscape it will not affect/encourage exploration. This dynamic is different from what is typically incorporated into private sector-oriented performance landscape models as the assumption in these models is that competition motivates both kinds of innovation/search processes.

Osborne et al. (2008) propose that changes in the external environment are key drivers of the type of innovation that non-profit organizations undertake. The authors studied the innovation behaviour of UK VCOs over a 12-year period and found that a significant shift had occurred. In the mid-1990s, a significant proportion (38 per cent) of VCOs had engaged in 'innovative' behaviour and 14 per cent had engaged in 'developmental' change.[10] By the mid-2000s the proportions had nearly reversed – with 19 per cent undertaking innovative projects and 36 per cent reporting developmental projects. The authors make a convincing argument that 'innovation was seen as a core element of the provision of social services by VCOs in the early 1990s' (Osborne et al. 2008, p. 60), and that this was driven by government policy rhetoric as well as funding streams. By the mid-2000s, policy (and funding) in regards to innovation in the UK was 'profoundly different', emphasizing continuous improvement rather than organizational transformation to deliver specialist services and improve efficiency. Essentially, while innovation in some form was still encouraged, the focus was now on making incremental changes to improve existing service provision.

Osborne et al.'s (2008) categories of 'innovative' and 'developmental' behaviour align well with the concepts of 'explorative' and 'exploitative' search on the performance landscape. The idea that changes in the environment can change the search processes is also well documented in such models. Osborne et al. also show that organizational characteristics are statistically correlated with likelihood of innovative behaviour, with age (younger organizations) and the presence of paid staff both having positive relationships to innovation. This finding, too, aligns with the performance landscape model, in that organizational characteristics are regularly assumed to influence search behaviour as well as performance. Osborne et al. (2008) are strongly aligned with the idea that environment drives organizational behaviour, as evidenced in their conclusion that 'the prime driver for this shifting pattern of organizational activity has been a significant change in the public policy context of VCOs' (p. 66).

We may conclude that the relevant features of the environment are described similarly in the empirical and performance landscape literature and they affect innovation in similar ways. The typologies for innovation and for searching the landscape were also shown to be similar. Overall, in this section we have presented a reinterpretation of empirical findings in innovation in the public sector that indicates a remarkable consistency between these findings and the CAS organizational performance landscape modelling literature, supporting the case for CAS as a valid and potentially useful perspective for exploring the nature and dynamics of innovation. But, so what?

THE (POTENTIAL) CONTRIBUTION OF COMPLEX SYSTEMS THEORY TO INNOVATION THEORY AND PRACTICE IN PUBLIC MANAGEMENT

This chapter has provided a detailed comparison of recent empirical studies in innovation in the public and voluntary/community sectors with a particular type of complex adaptive systems model, namely performance landscapes. We have argued that the empirical studies generate similar findings to simulations of organizational behaviour on CAS performance landscapes and this provides a significant opportunity to deepen our understanding of the dynamics of innovation, as well as to more accurately specify performance landscape models to facilitate the study of complex organizational behaviour. We believe that there are the following potential benefits to the theory and practice of innovation from further research in this direction:

● *Clarification/further specification of innovation concepts and causal relationships* – for example, path-dependency, innovation (search) types, relevant organizational and environmental features, and so on. The rigour required to specify a computer simulation forces a clarity of thought that can extend our understanding of exactly what is meant by these terms and how different dimensions of a model of innovation may exhibit different states. For example, the different types of 'service' innovation are relatively easily understood as a particular combination of choices on the performance landscape, but the meaning of a 'marketization' or 'ancillary' innovation needs to be more carefully defined if it is to be modelled as a specific (set of) choice(s) on the landscape. Marketization appears to be a type of 'exploitation' search which changes the internal processes of the organization for efficiency gains – and CAS theory suggests that organizations go through periods of exploitation and exploration, but rarely do both at the same time. Additional efforts at clearly specifying concepts from innovation theory into a performance landscape model are likely to generate a range of testable hypotheses to advance theory.
● *Insights into dynamics of innovation in public services and contribution to CAS organizational theory.* In the review of the innovation studies for this chapter, the

application of the CAS framework suggested a number of patterns that begin to tell a modelling story about the statistical correlations found in the empirical data. One such story is as follows: service need/demand in the environment appears to be a fundamental driver for innovation, although there are several organizational features that work against the innovation pull of demand, such as devolved management, high levels of trust, high proportions of paid staff (in VCOs) and slack resources – which limit marketization innovations in particular. However, high levels of trust will increase the probability of ancillary innovation. Furthermore, the greater the diversity of service need, the less likely organizations are to innovate. Nevertheless, if the organization can somehow engage in ancillary innovation (exploratory search), it can kick-start service innovation (which has a significant positive correlation with ancillary innovation in period $t - 1$ as well as in period t in the Walker 2008 study, and is also proposed in Piening 2011). This will then set off a flurry of downstream innovations, until such time as the organization gets to a performance peak at which only incremental efficiency changes are possible. Does this story make sense – is it an accurate picture of reality? More research is required. But the good news is that with the performance landscape models in our research toolkit, we can construct any number of 'experiments' without having to undertake costly and time-consuming empirical data collection and narrow down our search. Furthermore, CAS models can be enhanced by empirical 'docking' in the rich quantitative and qualitative data already gathered.

• *Contribution to public sector practice.* This is one of the most difficult challenges for CAS-based researchers, as the nature of complex systems is that they are not amenable to developing predictable, causal relationships. Managers want 'if/then' sorts of guidance from theory – even though they know in practice that those 'if/then' relationships may not play out as anticipated. Nevertheless, in terms of how a manager's practice might be affected, we believe that CAS and the performance landscape perspective challenge the professional to engage in prior and real-time analysis that is not generally part of the traditional process methods and assumptions of either the classical bureaucratic model or the rational–analytic, rational choice models that underpin much of the New Public Management tradition. The importance of path-dependency, initial conditions and environmental and organizational adaptation means that managers must make the appropriate analysis of history as well as real-time assesments of their own organization and environment, else they seem doomed to mis-specifying the purpose and the path of innovation and implementation.

Where to next? The conceptualization of the process of innovation as searching for higher performance on a landscape consisting of a myriad of interrelated organizational choices and environmental factors may seem a bit daunting – and perhaps even unnecessarily complicated. However, when one considers that both the empirical data and the simulation models of organizational innovation are identifying regular patterns of structure, strategy, environmental configurations and path-dependencies that affect innovation processes, there is potential here to imbue our policy and practice choices with a bit more knoweldge and a bit more certainty – even in a fundamentally uncertain world. The development of models of complex public service systems, involving multiple heterogeneous agents operating on a landscape of shifting policy and relevant environmental factors, could provide a 'petri dish' for observing the (theoretical) innovation behaviour of organizations in any one of a number of policy domains. Resulting patterns in outcomes or organizational dynamics could then be researched empirically, and findings used to inform policy instruments and/or management practices that would prove more robust in a rapidly changing public sector environment. This is just one of the ways to adopt a more 'systemic' approach to the study of contemporary public services, but one that has significant potential, and builds on a solid foundation of theoretical and empirical work done to date.

NOTES

1. Systems theory in public management has a long (and somewhat chequered) history. Hoos (1972) and Stacey and Griffin (2006) present convincing critiques; however, there are numerous voices calling for the re-introduction of systems thinking in public management – see Boston (2000), Chapman (2002) and Weber (2005).
2. See the 'wiki' on Service Science at: https://www.ibm.com/developerworks/mydeveloperworks/wikis/ home/wiki/We2324b49e6c0_406d_8107_5b36d9b7cc47/page/Learn%20about%20Service%20Science?lan g=en.
3. *Emergence: Complexity and Organization* (2005), 7(1); *Public Administration Quarterly* (2005), 29(3/4); Stacey and Griffin (2006); *Public Administration Quarterly* (2008), 32(3); *Public Management Review* (2008),10(3); *The Leadership Quarterly* (2007), 18(4); Dennard et al. (2005).
4. Levinthal (1997); Levinthal and Warglein (1999); Siggelkow and Levinthal (2003); Siggelkow and Rivkin (2005).
5. NK models refer to work originally described in Kauffman (1995) which looked at biological evolution as a search function on an environmental landscape made up of 'N' options (gene expressions), with 'K' interdependencies (the average number of options that together contributed to the likelihood of survival). Kaufman called these 'fitness landscapes'.
6. Rhodes (2008a/b, 1999, 2012); Rhodes et al. (2011); Rhodes and Mullins (2009); Rhodes and Donnelly-Cox (2008); Rhodes and Murray (2007); Rhodes and MacKechnie (2003).
7. A 'neighbouring' location in this context refers to a combination of choices that is different from the existing set of choices by some small number of variations (usually no more than two).
8. For example, Siggelkow and Levinthal (2003) set N equal to 6 in their models.
9. Complexity in this model is defined as 'non-decomposability' – meaning that there is a medium to high level of interdependency among dimensions (K > 3) and that it is not possible to fully decompose the set of decisions into groups that only influence each other.
10. 'Innovative' change was defined as the three service/market-related categories used in earlier studies by Osborne as well as by Walker, while 'developmental' change was defined as incremental improvements to the same services delivered to the same clients.

REFERENCES

Achrol, Ravi S. and Kotler, Philip (2006). The service-dominant logic for marketing: a critique. In R.F. Lusch and S.L. Vargo (eds), *The Service-Dominant Logic of Marketing: Dialog, Debate, and Directions*. Armonk, NY: M.E. Sharpe, pp. 320–333.
Anderson, P.W. (1999). Complexity theory and organizational science. *Organization Science*, 10(3), 216–232.
Beinhocker, E.D. (2007). *Origin of Wealth: Evolution, Complexity, and the Radical Remaking of Economics*. Boston, MA: Harvard Business School Press.
Boston, Jonathan (2000). *The Challenge of Evaluating Systemic Change: The Case of Public Management Reform*. Paper presented at the IPMN Conference, 'Learning from Experience with New Public Management', Macquarie Graduate School of Management, Sydney, 4–6 March.

Brown, Shona and Eisenhardt, Kathleen M. (1998). *Competing on the Edge: Strategy as Structured Chaos*. Boston, MA: Harvard Business School Press.

Chapman, Jake (2002). *System Failure: Why Governments Must Learn to Think Differently*. London: Demos.

de Wolf, T. and Holvoet, T. (2005). Emergence versus self-organization: different concepts but promising when combined. In S. Brueckner, G. Di Marzo Serugendo, A. Karageorgos and R. Nagpal (eds), *Engineering Self-Organizing Systems: Methodologies and Applications*. Berlin: Springer Verlag, pp. 1–15.

Dennard, L., Richardson, K. and Morcol, G. (eds) (2005). Special issue on complexity and policy analysis. *Emergence: Complexity and Organization*, vol 7(1).

Emmeche, Claus, Koppe, Simo and Stjernfelt, Frederik (1997). Explaining emergence: towards an ontology of levels. *Journal for General Philosophy of Science*, 28, 83–119.

Hazdra, Adam (2010). *Service-Dominant Logic: Why, Where and What it Means for Innovation*. Available at: adamhazdra.com/Hazdra_Service-dominant_Logic_(2010).pdf (accessed 4 May 2011).

Holland, J.H. (1998). *Emergence: From Chaos to Order*. Cambridge, MA: Perseus Books.

Hoos, Ida R. (1972). *Systems Analysis in Public Policy: A Critique*. Berkeley, CA: University of California Press.

Kauffman, S.A. (1993). *The Origins of Order: Self-Organization and Selection in Evolution*. New York, NY: Oxford University Press.

Kauffman, S.A. (1995). *At Home in the Universe: The Search for Laws of Self-Organization and Complexity*. New York, NY: Oxford University Press.

Koppenjan, Joop and Klijn, Erik-Hans (2004). *Managing Uncertainties in Networks*. London: Routledge.

Levinthal, Daniel (1997). Adaptation on rugged landscapes. *Management Science*, 43(7), 934–950.

Levinthal, D. and Warglein, M. (1999). Landscape design: designing for local action in complex worlds. *Organization Science*, 10(3), 342–357.

Lusch, R.F. and Vargo, S.L. (2006). *The Service Dominant Logic of Marketing: Dialog, Debate and Directions*. Armonk, NY: M.E. Sharpe.

Marion, R. and Uhl-Bein, M. (eds) (2008). Special issue on leadership and complexity. *The Leadership Quarterly*, 18(4).

Miller, John H. and Page, Scott E. (2007). *Complex Adaptive Systems: An introduction to Computational Models of Social Life*. Princeton, NJ: Princeton University Press.

Morcol, G. (ed.) (2008). Special issue on complexity of public policy and administration. *Public Administration Quarterly*, 32(3).

Osborne, Stephen (1998). *Voluntary Organizations and Innovation in Public Services*. London: Routledge.

Osborne, Stephen (2010). *The New Public Governance? Emerging Perspectives on the Theory and Practice of Public Governance*. London: Routledge.

Osborne, Stephen, Chew, Celine and McLaughlin, Kate (2008). The once and future pioneers? The innovative capacity of voluntary organizations and the provision of public services: a longitudinal approach. *Public Management Review*, 10(1), 51–70.

Piening, Erk P. (2011). Insights into the process dynamics of innovation implementation: the case of public hospitals in Germany. *Public Management Review*, 13(1), 127–157.

Prigogine, I. (1997). *The End of Certainty: Time, Chaos and the New Laws of Nature*. New York: The Free Press.

Prigogine, I. and Stengers, I. (1984). *Order out of Chaos: Man's New Dialogue with Nature*. New York: Bantam Books.

Rhodes, M.L. (1999). *A Strategy for Systems Thinking in Urban Services*. Presented at the 3rd International Research Symposium on Public Management, Birmingham, UK, March.

Rhodes, M.L. (2008a). Complexity and emergence in public management: the case of urban regeneration in Ireland. *Public Management Review*, 10(3), 361–379.

Rhodes, M.L. (2008b). Agent-based modeling for public services: a new framework for policy development, In Linda Dennard, K. Richardson and Goktug Morcol (eds), *Complexity and Policy Analysis: Tools and Concepts for Designing Robust Policies in a Complex World*. Goodyear, AZ: ISCE Publishing, chapter 20.

Rhodes, M.L. (2012). Systems theory in housing. In Susan J. Smith, Marja Elsinga, Lorna Fox O'Mahony, Ong Seow Eng and Susan Wachte, (eds), *International Encyclopedia of Housing and Home*, vol. 7, Oxford: Elsevier, pp. 134–137.

Rhodes, M.L. and Donnelly-Cox, G. (2008). Social entrepreneurship as a performance landscape: the case of 'front line'. *E:CO*, 10(3), 35–50.

Rhodes, M.L. and MacKechnie, G. (2003). Understanding public service systems: is there a role for complex adaptive systems theory? *Emergence*, 5(4), 58–85.

Rhodes, M.L. and Mullins, D. (2009). Market concepts, coordination mechanisms and new actors in social housing. *International Journal of Housing Policy* 9(2), 107–119.

Rhodes, M.L. and Murray, J. (2007). Collaborative decision-making in urban regeneration: a complex adaptive systems perspective. *International Public Management Journal*, 10(1), 79–101.

Rhodes, M.L., Muir, J., Murphy, J. and Murray, J. (2011). *Public Management and Complexity Theory: Richer Decision-Making in Public Services*. London: Routledge.

Rivkin, Jan W. and Siggelkow, N. (2003). Balancing search and stability: interdependencies among elements of organizational design. *Management Science*, 49(3), 290–311.

Romanelli, E. and Tushman, M.L. (1994). Organizational transformation as punctuated equilibrium: an empirical test. *Academy of Management Journal*, 37(5), 1141–1166.

Scott, W.R. (1995). *Institutions and Organizations.* Thousand Oaks, CA: Sage Publications.

Siggelkow, N. and Levinthal, D. (2003). Temporarily divide to conquer: centralized, decentralized, and reintegrated organizational approaches to exploration and adaptation. *Organizational Science*, 14(6), 650–669.

Siggelkow, N. and Rivkin, J. (2005). Speed and search: designing organizations for turbulence and complexity. *Organization Science*, 16(2), 101–122.

Stacey, R.D. and Griffin, D. (eds) (2006). *Complexity and the Experience of Managing in the Public Sector.* London: Routledge.

Teisman, G. and Klijn, H.-J. (eds) (2008). Special issue on complexity theory and public management. *Public Management Review*, 10(3).

Walker, Richard (2008). An empirical evaluation of innovation types and organizational and environmental characteristics: towards a configuration framework. *Journal of Public Administration Theory (JPART)*, 18(4), 591–615.

Walker, R.M., Avellaneda, C.N. and Berry, F.S. (2011). Exploring the diffusion of innovation among high and low innovative localities: a test of the Berry and Berry model. *Public Management Review*, 13(1), 95–125.

Weber, J. (ed.) (2005a). Special issue on complexity and public administration. *Public Administration Quarterly*, 29(3/4).

Weber, J. (2005b). Introduction to chaos, complexity, uncertainty and public administration: a symposium. *Public Administration Quarterly*, 29(3), 262–267.

Winter, Sidney (2005). Developing evolutionary theory for economics and management. In Ken G. Smith and Michael A. Hitt (eds), *Great Minds in Management: The Process of Theory Development*, Oxford: Oxford University Press, pp. 509–546.

23. Innovation, networks and leadership
Myrna P. Mandell and Robyn Keast

INTRODUCTION

There has been a growing realization among policy makers, managers and practitioners that the public sector must work differently if it is to respond adequately to a rapidly changing operating environment, characterized by decreasing funds and increasingly higher service demands and expectations. As a consequence, government and community services are displaying a stronger interest in innovation to refine strategies, processes and service delivery models for more effective, efficient, and therefore sustainable, solutions to new and emerging problems as well as those that are more entrenched and intractable (Walker 2006; Tinkler 2008; Martin et al. 2009).

The process of innovation is lengthy, requires considerable resources and the coming together of diverse talents and skills. These factors have combined to limit the vision and scope of innovative practice and programme development within the public sector. The refocusing of a single body of effort into a cohesive endeavour via networks has allowed those in the public service a vehicle by which innovations can more easily be attempted. Thus, networks have become an innovation in and of themselves as well as a mechanism to create innovation. Unfortunately, although a number of studies (Ferlie et al. 1984; Osborne 1998; Osborne and Brown 2005) have been undertaken to better understand and enhance innovation within the public arena, they have largely overlooked the detailed functioning of networks as innovation drivers and creators. The recent work by Considine et al. (2009), which examined the norms, practices and structures of innovation networks within the Australian public sector, represents a comparatively rare effort to interrogate this phenomenon and expand our conceptualization of what constitutes innovations through networks.

Accomplishing innovations in networks, however, is not an easy thing to do. Establishing the correct culture for innovation and building the necessary relationships within and across complex government departments and other sectors require new leadership skills and capacity. Unfortunately, only a few studies (Mandell and Keast 2004; Martin et al. 2009; McGuire and Silva 2009) have been undertaken to indicate how this leadership is accomplished in networks, especially innovation networks.

The purpose of this chapter is to analyse and explain how networks create/impact on the process of innovation in the public sector and the different leadership styles required. First, it outlines the different types of innovations available to the public sector. This is followed by an examination of the different types of networks and their innovation potential. We then analyse different types of leadership styles and relate these to the different types of networks. Three case studies are used to illustrate how leadership can make a difference in networks. The chapter concludes with the implications of developing innovations through networks.

PUBLIC SECTOR INNOVATION

In general, innovation refers to the creation and implementation of new processes, services or new ways of delivering services (Rogers 1983). Unlike the business arena, where the motivation is profit, for the public sector these new ideas, strategies, concepts and organizational forms are directed at creating public value (Currie et al. 2008). That is, innovation must not only be new and novel, it must also add value.

A distinction is also made in the literature between five types of innovation (IDeA Knowledge 2005, p. 6) as follows:

- *Strategy/policy*: new missions, objectives, strategies and rationales.
- *Service/product*: changes in features and design of services/products.
- *Delivery*: new or altered ways of delivering services or otherwise interacting with clients.
- *Process*: new internal procedures, policies and organizational forms.
- *System interaction*: new or improved ways of interacting with other actors and knowledge bases; changes in governance.

Finally, Mulgan and Albury (2003) proposed that innovation is not a single state but rather is represented by a continuum from incremental to radical to transformative innovation.

Incremental innovations are minor improvements or simple adjustments in current offerings. These are critical to sustaining and enhancing relationships in current markets, with a focus on improving existing products and services, and are synonymous with innovation that is 'evolutionary' (Osborne 1998, p. 23). By contrast, it is argued that radical innovations lead to or equate with breakthrough initiatives. Radical innovations 'either involve the development of new services or the introduction of fundamentally new ways of doing things, in terms of organisational processes or service delivery' (IDeA Knowledge 2005, p. 7). Transformative innovations are the rarest type of innovation. They involve the transformation of 'entire sectors, and dramatically change relationships between organisations' (IDeA Knowledge 2005, p. 7).

In the context of service delivery systems, however, it is argued that there can be few genuinely new models, and that innovation generally consists of the adoption of existing approaches or the mixing of elements. Such an evolutionary/incremental approach is sometimes referred to as 'bricolage', or making do with what you have at hand, including networks (Innes and Booher 2010). This suggests in the majority of cases an incremental approach to innovation within the public service delivery system, which draws on ideas and practices from other sectors or services, rather than the development and implementation of radical or transformative changes.

This does not mean that there are no radical or transformative innovations in the public sector. Instead, it points to the difficulties of getting the entrenched organizations and agencies in the public sector to embrace any kind of major changes to their systems. To overcome this, networks and their associated new forms of leadership have come to the fore as both the mechanism for and the products of innovation in the public sector across many developed countries (Agranoff 2006; Keast et al. 2004). In order to fully understand how networks have impacted the ability to innovate in the public sector, however, we must first understand the different types of networks.

DIFFERENT TYPES OF NETWORKS AND THEIR INNOVATION FOCI

Increasingly it has been recognized that networks provide a powerful source for new information and knowledge and that this can be reconfigured to produce new products, processes and services. The horizontal nature of networks, with their emphasis on exchanges, shared experiences, trust and reciprocity, provides a social space in which new knowledge and practices can result. Networks are based on horizontal relationships in which top-down authority is not considered the guiding factor. Although the reality is that not all participants are equal in terms of their positions of power, networks are nevertheless seen as arenas where decisions are made, not unilaterally, but through a more consensus-building mode (Innes and Booher 2010).

Although much has been written on networks, the literature has generally treated networks as undifferentiated (Brown and Keast 2003). That is, the term 'network' is used to broadly denote the various ways in which organizations might work together, from arrangements that are merely loose, temporary forms to those that are much more complex and enduring (Agranoff and McGuire 2003; Kamensky and Burlin 2004; Koppenjan and Klijn 2004). More recent literature focuses on important differences among types of networks (Mandell and Steelman 2003; Agranoff 2006; Keast et al. 2004, 2007). Most notable is the emphasis on the different purposes of networks and the related variation in required relationship strength, with three main types of horizontal integration relationships highlighted: cooperation, coordination and collaboration. Brown and Keast (2003) and Keast et al. (2007) have defined these as the '3 C's'.

Cooperative networks involve the exchange of information and/or expertise among relatively independent organizations with few risks involved. Members are generally involved in the sharing of routine information, making referrals and the building of initial relationships. A typical example of this type of network is professional social workers who routinely exchange information about best practices for dealing with their clients. The looser, more sporadic exchanges between members in cooperative networks and the lower level of information sharing and trust mean that their innovation production is limited to minor changes in the way services are delivered (service/product innovations) and these changes are incremental in nature. Innovation, in this context, often remains with the participating network members and is directed towards doing their work differently and better.

In a *coordinative network*, organizations, groups and/or individuals go one step beyond merely exchanging information and explicit knowledge. They interact with each other to better align their individual efforts. Most of the literature on networks is based on these types of interactions, with the work of Provan and Milward (1995, 2001) in the mental health field particularly notable. In this type of network coalitions are formed whereby interdependent and strategic actions are taken but the purpose(s) are narrow in scope and all actions occur within the participant organizations themselves or involve the sequential or simultaneous activity of the participant organizations. Adjustments to policies and/or practices may occur, but they are limited to dealing with a specific action at a specific time.

Coordinated networks involve changes to the way organizations interact with each other, but there are no major changes in the way they do business. They can involve service/product or delivery innovations. These are radical innovations in that they involve new ways of doing business with other organizations; however, the organizations involved do not make any major changes in how they do business overall.

Collaborative networks occur when the nature of the problem is so complex and critical that cooperating or coordinating efforts are not enough. Instead, there is an understanding among all participants that in a collaborative network the participants are *reciprocally interdependent*. This means members know they are dependent on each other in such a way that for the actions of one to be effective they must rely on the actions of another. There is an understanding that 'they cannot meet their interests working alone and that they share with others a common problem' (Innes and Booher 2000, p. 7). This goes beyond just resource dependence, data needs, common clients or geographical issues, although these may be involved. It involves a need to make a collective commitment to change the way in which they are operating (systems changes) (Mandell 1994; Keast et al. 2004).

In collaborative networks the participants recognize their interdependence and no longer see themselves only as independent participants in the network. Rather, they are committed to building a new whole, involving systems changes and building new relationships. For innovations to occur in these networks, participants must change the way they think and recognize that they can only engage each other based on reciprocity of actions.

Collaborative networks involve major systems changes and require new types of behaviour among participants. The innovations that can occur include strategy/policy, process and system interactions. These can be defined as transformative, as participants and the organizations they represent must be willing to take major risks and change the way they do business. They cannot make only minor changes or changes at the margins of their organizations.

The issue of how these different types of innovations occur relates not only to the differences in the different types of network, but to the differences in the leadership needed in each type of network.

LEADERSHIP

The current literature on leadership (Vangen and Huxham 2003; Moynihan and Ingraham 2004; Crosby and Bryson 2005; Mandell and Keast 2009; Martin et al. 2009) is on the influence of the leader's behaviour. Different leadership theories have focused on this critical element.

Models of leadership in the private sector have focused on the transformational leader. The idea of a transformational leader is that the leader is 'a single, heroic figure at the apex of the organization' (Martin et al. 2009, p. 772) who infuses his/her followers with a vision that leads them to higher expectations. As Martin et al. (2009) indicate, however, the context of networks does not lend itself to a single 'heroic' type of leader. Rather, more recent studies have tended to focus on the notion of leadership as a distributed process. These new models emphasize the importance of follower participation, democratic involvement and decision making, and make a claim for a less formalized, hierarchical model of leadership. That is, leadership is perceived as an evolving property of a group or network of interacting individuals rather than a phenomenon that arises from the personality or attributes of the individual. Further, because leadership within this perspective is centred on performing acts that assist the network/group to meet goals and maintain itself, varieties of expertise are distributed across many actors rather than a few.

Thus, over time there has been a shift in the theorizing and practise of leadership such that it no longer emphasizes the properties of individuals or organizations but recognizes the growing interaction and interdependence between people and the various contributions that can be made by diverse members. Many of the new leadership aspects, with their emphasis on facilitation rather than direction, their focus on interactions not individuals and their distributed orientation, now have strong resonances with networks and network leadership characteristics.

For cooperative and coordinative networks a distributive approach to leadership (Chrislip and Larson 1994; Korac-Kakabadse and Korac-Kakabadse 1997; Murrell 1997), where the leadership functions and tasks are shared across the membership according to expertise or the assignment of a leadership 'turn', is appropriate. That is, network leadership is about creating the space and processes to enable members to learn about and from and appreciate each other, push the boundaries and look for areas of commonality and joint effort. Although more informal in these types of networks, the leadership role needs to focus on maintaining good relationships and open lines of communication.

In collaborative networks, however, a unique feature is the synergy that can be created by the diverse membership that will allow participants to manage systems changes (Lasker et al. 2001). But synergy will not occur without the type of leadership that is able to build relationships, and identify and capitalize on the opportunities that arise from the pooling of resources and the merging of human capital. Leaders need to leverage the particular mix of properties inherent in collaborative networks that allow the synergies to be created. As Goleman (2007) notes, this requires more than leaders who influence and direct; rather, it is about leadership that is 'fully present [in the process] and being in synch' (p. 106). At the same time, there needs to be a level of stability maintained within the network.

Since collaborative networks are characterized by a more complex, dynamic process the leadership function shifts to a focus on the interactions and processes that are required to build strong and ongoing relationships capable of breaking through existing mechanisms and creating new systems and innovative responses. The term 'process catalyst' (Mandell and Keast 2009) has been used to describe this new type of leadership, highlighting the ability to identify, create and facilitate strategic synergies among participants that will eventually lead to innovative solutions and outcomes. Leadership in this context, 'produces rather than a solution to a known problem, a new way of framing the situation and developing unanticipated combinations of actions that are qualitatively different from the options on the table at the outset' (Innes and Booher 1999, p. 12).

In order for problems to be solved in any type of network, therefore, different patterns of leadership and action are needed. This would include being able to address the interconnections between problems, stakeholders and orchestrate intra/inter-organizational complexities.

These roles and styles are needed before, as well as during, the workings of the network. For Vangen and Huxham (2003, p. S62) leadership involves 'the mechanisms that *make things happen* in a collaborative'. This involves an emphasis, not so much on an individual leader, per se, but rather on the structures, processes and participants on which leaders need to focus in order for networks to be effective. The emphasis, therefore, in all networks is on how to build and maintain relationships critical to the operation of any network.

But as has been pointed out, 'shared leadership ultimately requires both a willingness to cede leadership on the part of organizational heads and the capacity of other actors to take it on' (Martin et al. 2009, p. 772). This emphasizes the relationship between those in power and reliance on stakeholders in how effective leadership can be. Martin et al. (2009) point out that although leadership may be distributed among all participants in a network, the network's operation can be stymied by external stakeholders, such as policy makers who may constrain the actions of those within the network. What is needed is 'an enactment of leadership that seeks to manage a multiplicity of stakeholders, facilitating and consolidating change by concentrating on process and outcomes' (Martin et al. 2009, p. 775). This is referred to (p. 787) as 'dispersed leadership'. This leadership type is relevant in coordinative as well as collaborative networks. In collaborative networks, where the complexity of the issues and diversity of participants make leadership especially difficult, it is particularly important to have the strong support, not only of the parent organizations, but also of relevant external stakeholders (Vangen and Huxham 2003; Mandell and Keast 2009).

Table 23.1 summarizes the characteristics of each of the three networks, including the innovation foci and the different leadership capacities/roles. The table provides a conceptual framework/outline against which the following three case studies may be analysed.

CASE STUDIES

The case studies selected represent the three different types of networks. They are: The International Budget Project (IBP) (cooperative network); Life Services Systems (LSS) (coordinative network); and Services Integration Project (SIP) (collaborative network). These cases represent a cross-national approach as well as being drawn from multiple levels.

IBP: A Cooperative Network

IBP was formed in 1997 within the Centre on Budget and Policy Priorities to enhance civil society's capacity to analyse and influence government budget processes, institutions and outcomes. The overall aim of the project is to make budget systems more responsive to the needs of society and to make these systems transparent to the public. The network focuses on organizations working with the poor and low-income people in developing countries or new democracies. Members are primarily from Latin American countries, but also include groups from India and several countries in Africa. The relationships between member organizations are loose and flexible and more or less on an informal basis.

Table 23.1   Summary of characteristics, leadership and innovation in different types of networks

Type of network	Cooperative	Coordinative	Collaborative
Characteristics	– low risk – loose links/low intensity level – independent organizations – purpose: sharing information/expertise	– medium risk – medium links/some level of stability – independent/ minimum degree of interdependence – purpose: integrate services for efficiency; minor changes at the margins	– high risk – tight links/highly interdependent: reciprocal relations – purpose: building new relations/ways of working; systems change; building a new whole
Leadership style	– distributed; informal	– distributed/ dispersed; more formal	– process catalyst informal and formal
Type of innovation	– service/product – small changes in service to clients	– service/product – some changes in service to clients – delivery: changes in how services are delivered	– strategy/policy – building a new whole – process – changes in organizations' procedures, policies and forms – system interaction – new relationships, changes in governance
Level of innovation	– incremental	– radical	– transformative

To build the social and political capital of the participating organizations, members have participated in IBP's training programmes and attend IBP's conferences where they are able to exchange information with members from other countries. Over the period of its operation IBP has convened several conferences, collected information and brokered IBP to other groups, as well as fostering and facilitating training, technical assistance and research. As a relatively loose network IBP is well regarded, with members valuing the learning experiences and the ability to share information with each other. Most importantly, the primary benefits of IBP are directed to member organizations in terms of providing support and assisting in their individual programmes. The primary benefit of this network has been to build the capacity of its individual members to deal with problems in their own country.

The effectiveness of this network is argued to be due to the flexibility of IBP and its leadership. Although there is a director, member organizations are involved in the decision-making process and the uptake of informal leadership roles is encouraged across the network according to areas of expertise or the identification of projects/activities that will benefit individual organizations. The distributed leadership that this represents has enabled members to contribute to the shaping of IBP and its actions, and in so doing has helped to increase the relevance of the network to the members and increased the flow of information and expertise available. With its core business centred on sharing information and expertise among its members and its relatively loose exchange/relational arrangements, IBP meets the definition of a cooperative network. In terms of innovation it falls within the service/product type of innovation and involves incremental innovation. There are some areas, however, in which members believe IBP could be improved, including the establishment of increased international relations between all the organizations in the participating countries to find out what they are doing and to share their knowledge and to learn new methods. Extending its network connections might lead to a different purpose and different innovation outcomes; it will also call for an expanded leadership role.

LSS: A Coordinative Network

This programme was initiated through a grant from the Michigan State Developmental Disabilities Program in 1980. Its purpose was to provide integrated services to developmentally disabled adults. It was engaged in a number of programmes, ranging from integrating health, education and employment services to the provision of educational programmes in hospitals and schools about the need for early intervention services for this target group.

Seven state agencies and their counterparts in four counties, plus a number of private human service agencies were involved in the network. The agency forming the network took the lead in directing participants to coordinate their efforts to realize the goal of making sure that disabled adults would not get 'lost' in the social services system. All agencies were able to follow their existing case management rules and regulations but had to work in a coordinated effort in this programme. In order to remain in the programme each agency had to agree to work within a case management framework set up by the lead agency. The network was effective to the extent that the case management framework allowed for better access for clients and cut back on the redundancy in the total system. It was also able to identify areas where the system was failing and to correct these gaps.

It is clear that LSS meets the definition of a coordinated network in that its purpose was to integrate the efforts of the members of the network. In terms of innovation it falls into two categories: service/product and delivery. This is seen in the perceptions of the participants of this network who understood LSS as having two functions. One is a system-wide function in which LSS coordinates the efforts of all the agencies and private groups who service the developmentally disabled (delivery innovation). The other function is to provide more meaningful services to clients based on a holistic view of the client (service/product innovation). They did this by reaching out to other key stakeholders in order to make the programme more meaningful to their clients. It is considered a radical innovation.

Although there was a lead agency, all members were encouraged to mould the programme to meet their needs and to take on a leadership role in terms of making decisions that would have an impact on how their individual organizations would interact with the others involved in the network. In addition, by including stakeholders outside the network they were able to expand the impact of the programme. This follows the model of distributed and dispersed leadership.

The effectiveness of the network, however, was limited. The network remained in its competitive mode and used the grant to solidify existing arrangements and to strengthen the existing case management strategies, restricting the type of innovation that could be accomplished.

SIP: A Collaborative Network

SIP was established in response to a critical incident in the community of Goodna, Australia when an elderly man was murdered by a group of teenagers. The state government supported the community demands that the agencies responsible for addressing the social and economic problems culminating in this incident should do something different in order to prevent this from happening again. The result was a network of cross-sectional representation from federal, state and local government, community-based agencies and community members. It was recognized by the participants from the beginning that a fundamental change in the service delivery system was required and, further, that such a change in the delivery system could only be accomplished by establishing much better relationships between concerned agencies and the community than had been the experience in the past (Keast et al. 2004). A deliberate programme of collaboration via a human services network was commenced, using a range of relationship-building vehicles such as shared training programmes, workshops and an agreed programme of work. As a result of the enhanced relationships between members, the project effected a dramatic shift in orientation from single agencies to a collective approach. The project was able to secure many layers of direct and indirect organizational and community benefit such as locality-specific services and programmes and a new governance regime, training initiatives to aid service and community capacity building, and improved infrastructure and facilities (Boorman and Woolcock 2002; Keast et al. 2004).

SIP meets the definition of a collaborative network. The problem was of such a critical nature that the participants recognized immediately that they could no longer continue working in their usual way. They recognized that they were not just independent organizations working together, but rather that they were inextricably related (*reciprocal interdependence*) in such a way that unless each of them agreed to work in new ways, the problem would only reoccur. The critical innovations created by this network were process and system interaction innovations, as they completely changed the way that members interacted with and behaved towards each other and changed the way their organizations worked. This is considered a transformative innovation.

The innovations allowed participants to build a sustained commitment not only to solving the crisis, but to work more effectively with each other on future issues (Boorman and Woolcock 2002; Keast et al. 2004). These innovations, which have been embedded into the local region and continue to operate, were due in large part to the different leadership approach adopted by members. The focus from the outset was the need to build new relationships for further efforts. Rather than distributed leadership, where the focus is on all members being involved in making decisions, the members of SIP focused on how to change the process in which they had been working (process catalyst leadership). By attending the Graduate Certificate Program, all participants were able to better understand each other and, rather than competing with each other (as occurred in LSS), they were able to build on the synergy they discovered within the total membership. In essence, rather than just focusing on how to better deliver services (although that was involved), they were able to focus on the process of finding a pool of shared meaning leading to 'a new collective whole' (Innes and Booher 1999, p. 13).

Each of these cases was effective in developing different types and levels of innovation. In so doing, they drew upon different network types with associated leadership styles. A number of implications can be derived from these cases.

IMPLICATIONS

Each of these cases confirms the ability to develop innovations through networks. The difficulty is that many officials who set up networks expect results that they are often not able to generate. They do not understand the differences among networks and what needs to be done in order for them to be effective. Not all networks are equal, nor do they produce similar innovation outcomes. By understanding that there are different types of networks, each requiring a different type of leadership, involving a different degree of risk and resulting in different outcomes, the expectations of these officials might be better met.

The attitudes of these officials, as well as other relevant stakeholders, will have an impact on whether or not the change(s) required for innovations to be achieved will be accepted. It will therefore be necessary for leaders to focus, not only on what is happening within the network, but on the impact of those outside the network (Martin et al. 2009). This means that not only the participants in the network need to be on board but also the parent organizations represented in the network, as well as any relevant stakeholders.

A further implication is the need to strategically design the network structure to achieve the type of innovation desired. An ongoing debate in the network literature has centred on whether innovation requires sparse and weak (Granovetter 1973) or dense and strong (Coleman 1988) ties. Sparse and weak ties are argued to be limited to the transfer of simple information, thus facilitating only incremental innovation. Regardless of this, sparse ties are argued to be important sources of new and novel information. That is, much of the information circulating around a network is considered to be redundant, with most of the members already aware of it. By shedding redundant ties to focus effort on the specific set of ties that bridge 'structural holes' (Burt 1992) networks can be made more efficient and targeted in their innovation approach. Time and energy are then able to be redirected towards sourcing and activating new contacts that are able to bring in new knowledge and resources. It is also viewed that intense and long-lasting ties can lead to reduced variety in input, less opportunity for learning and therefore group-think, which limits innovation.

Strong ties are argued to be better conduits for the transfer of complex knowledge (Uzzi 1997), as well as to provide a foundation for the higher level of cohesion which is necessary for trust to develop and synergies leveraged to produce radical and break-through innovation. By understanding the different types of networks, it becomes clear that both sparse and tight ties can be appropriate. The key is that different types of networks require different strengths of relationships. To achieve radical innovation requires dense ties. For incremental innovation the cost of redundant (tight ties) could be a concern and therefore loose ties will be more appropriate. For transformative innovations, however, strong ties are needed to provide the cohesion and strength to create something new.

The above also has implications for the governance of these networks. Weak ties (cooperative networks) allow for a contract-type governance where they are steered from a distance. Strong ties (coordinative and collaborative networks) where relationships, norms, and so on are the key in governance are more appropriately governed by network governance modes. In both instances, government is faced with a push/pull type of problem. On the one hand it only governs at an arm's length or at best equally with network participants (rather than being the key player). On the other hand the political and social ethics of government means that it is held to a higher level of responsibility and accountability and therefore should have a more central role. The challenge is to deal with these dichotomies while keeping the network/collaboration flexible enough to produce innovations.

Networks are like any other structural arrangement. They have to be designed (structure and ties) and monitored and leveraged for maximum advantage. The implication for leaders is that a contingency approach is called for, in which the leader(s) should be constantly monitoring the network and its ties.

CONCLUSION

Networks have become one of the primary means by which to achieve innovation in the public sector. There are many different ways to develop innovations through networks, and without a full understanding of the different types of networks and their innovation potential this will be difficult to accomplish. In effect, not all networks are equal nor do they produce the same types of innovation outcomes. Some will have a greater impact than others, but they will also require a greater commitment to work differently and accept a higher degree of risk in the process. In addition, the different types of innovations and the level of innovation that can be achieved through networks need to be fully understood. Finally, in order for networks to be effective, the type of leadership needed within them must be recognized.

There is no guarantee that investing in a network will produce meaningful innovations, but at least by recognizing and understanding the complex relationships between these different elements, networks will be better designed and have sufficient leadership strength to live up to the expectations placed upon them.

REFERENCES

Agranoff, R. (2006). Inside collaborative networks: ten lessons for public managers. *Public Administration Review, Special Issue, Supplement to Issue*, 66(6), 56–65.

Agranoff, R. and McGuire, M. (2003). *Collaborative Public Management*. Washington, DC: Georgetown University Press.

Boorman, C. and Woolcock, G. (2002). The Goodna Service Integration Project: government and community working together for community well-being in Goodna. In T. Reddel (ed.), *Governing Local Communities:*

Building State and Community. Occasional Paper Series No. 4. Brisbane. Brisbane, Australia: School of Social Work and Social Policy, pp. 57–81.

Brown, K. and Keast, R. (2003). Community–government engagement: community connections through networked arrangements. *Asian Journal of Public Administration*, 25(1), 107–132.

Burt, R. (1992). Structural holes: the social structure of competition. In N. Nohria and R. Eccles (eds), *Networks and Organization: Structure, Form and Action*. Boston, MA: Harvard Business School Press, pp. 57–91.

Chrislip, D. and Larson, C. (1994). *Collaborative Leadership: How Citizens and Civic Leaders Make a Difference*. San Francisco, CA: Jossey-Bass.

Coleman, J.S. (1988). Social capital in the creation of human capital. *American Journal of Sociology*, 94, 95–120.

Considine, M., Lewis, J. and Alexander, D. (2009). *Networks, Innovation and Public Policy: Politicians, Bureaucrats and the Pathways to Change Inside Government*. Basingstoke: Palgrave Macmillan.

Crosby, B.C. and Bryson, J.M. (2005). *Leadership for the Common Good: Tackling Public Problems in a Shared-Power World*. San Francisco, CA: Jossey-Bass.

Currie, G., Humphreys, M., Ucbasaran, D. and McManus, S. (2008). Entrepreneurial leadership in the English public sector: paradox or possibility? *Public Administration*, 86(4), 987–1008.

Ferlie, E., Challis, D. and Davies, B. (1984). Models of innovation in the social care of the elderly. *Local Government Studies*, 10(6), 67–82.

Goleman, D. (2007). *Social Intelligence: The New Science of Human Relationships*. New York: Arrow Books.

Granovetter, M. (1973). The strength of weak ties. *American Journal of Sociology*, 78, 1360–1380.

IDeA Knowledge (2005). *Innovation in Public Services – Literature Review*. Available at: http://www.idea.gov. uk/adk/aio/118552 (accessed 25 January 2010).

Innes, J.E. and Booher, D.E. (1999). Consensus building as role playing and bricolage: toward a theory of collaborative planning. *Journal of the American Planning Association*, 65(1), 9–24.

Innes, J.E. and Booher, D.E. (2000). Collaborative dialogue as a policy making strategy. *Institute of Urban and Regional Development, Working Paper 2000-05*. Berkeley, CA: University of California Press.

Innes, J.E. and Booher, D.E. (2010). *Planning With Complexity*. London and New York: Routledge.

Kamensky, J.M. and Burlin, T.J. (eds) (2004). *Collaboration: Using Networks and Partnerships*. Oxford: Rowman and Littlefield Publishers, Inc.

Keast, R., Brown, K. and Mandell, M. (2007). Getting the right mix: unpacking integration meanings and strategies. *International Journal of Public Management*, 10(1), 9–16.

Keast, R., Mandell, M., Brown, K. and Woolcock, G. (2004). Network structures: working differently and changing expectations. *Public Administration Review*, 64(3), 363–371.

Koppenjan, J. and Klijn, E.-H. (2004). *Managing Uncertainties in Networks*. London and New York: Routledge, Taylor and Francis.

Korac-Kakabadse, A. and Korac-Kakabadse, N. (1997). Best practice in the Australian public service (APS): an examination of discretionary leadership. *Journal of Managerial Psychology*, 12(7), 1–37.

Lasker, R.D., Weiss, E.S. and Millier, R. (2001). Partnership synergy: a practical framework for studying and strengthening the collaborative advantage. *The Milbank Quarterly*, 79(2), 179–205.

McGuire, M. and Silva, C. (2009). Does leadership in networks matter? Examining the effect of leadership behavior on managers' perceptions of network efficiency. *Public Performance and Management Review*, 33(1), 34–62.

Mandell, M.P. (1994). Managing interdependencies through program structures: a revised paradigm. *American Review of Public Administration*, 24(1), 99–122.

Mandell, M.P. and Keast, R. (2009). A new look at leadership in collaborative networks: process catalyst. In J.A. Raffel, P. Leisink and A.A. Middlebrooks (eds), *Public Sector Leadership*. Cheltenham and Northampton, MA: Edward Elgar Publishing, pp. 163–178.

Mandell, M. and Steelman, T. (2003). Understanding what can be accomplished through interorganizational innovations: the importance of typologies, context and management. *Public Management Review*, 5(2), 197–224.

Martin, G.P., Currie, G. and Finn, R. (2009). Leadership, service reform and public-service networks: the case of cancer-genetics in the English NHS. *Journal of Public Administration Research and Theory*, 19(4), 769–794.

Moynihan, D.P. and Ingraham, P.W. (2004). Integrative leadership in the public sector: a model of performance information use. *Administration and Society*, 36, 427–453.

Mulgan, G. and Albury, D. (2003). *Innovation in the Public Sector*. London: Strategy Unit, Cabinet Office.

Murrell, K. (1997). Relational models of leadership for the next century not-for-profit organization manager. *Organization Development Journal*, 15(3), 35–42.

Osborne, S.P. (1998). *Voluntary Organisations and Innovations in Public Services*. London: Routledge.

Osborne, S. and Brown, K. (2005). *Managing Change and Innovation in Public Sector Organizations*. Abingdon: Routledge.

Provan, K.G. and Milward, H.B. (1995). Theory of interorganizational effectiveness: a comparative study of four community mental health systems. *Administrative Science Quarterly*, 40, 1–13.

Provan, K.G. and Milward, H.B. (2001). Do networks really work? *Public Administration Review*, 61(4), 414–423.

Rogers, E.M. (1983). *Diffusion of Innovations* (3rd edn). New York: Free Press.

Tinkler, J. (2008). *Innovation in Government Organizations, Public Service Agencies and Public Service NGOs: Draft Working Paper*. NESTA (National Endowment to Science, Technology and the Arts). Published as part of the Innovation Index Project in the UK. London: London School of Economics and Political Science.

Uzzi, B. (1997). Social structure and competition in interfirm networks: the paradox of embeddedness. *Administrative Sciences Quarterly*, 42, 35–67.

Vangen, S. and Huxham, C. (2003). Enacting leadership for collaborative advantage: dilemmas of ideology and pragmatism in the activities of partnership managers. *British Journal of Management*, 14, S61–S76.

Walker, R. (2006). Innovation type and diffusion: an empirical analysis of local government. *Public Administration*, 84, 311–335.

24. Policy networks and innovation
Jenny M. Lewis, Damon Alexander and Mark Considine

INTRODUCTION

Innovation has come to be seen as a defining value of both economic and political development in the global era. It is not difficult to see why this should be the case in a context where revolutionary new technologies and novel organisational methods are the subject of competition among the world's leading corporations. At a somewhat less visible level, innovation has also helped frame issues and priorities within the public sectors of many developed countries over the last decade. Pressure for governments at all levels to do more with less in response to shrinking budgets and expanding community service obligations has led to a much greater focus upon how the public sector manages change and innovation (Bartlett and Dibben 2002). Such pressures are likely to increase exponentially in light of the impact of the Global Financial Crisis on government expenditure (Osborne and Brown 2011). A heightened focus on innovation in the public sector has created a pressing need to understand the innovative capacity of public organisations. This has not been matched by empirical work on the topic, with a few notable exceptions (e.g. Osborne, Chew and McLaughlin 2008a, 2008b).

This chapter examines the normative outlooks and networking behaviours of recognised policy and programme innovators within the public sector, using an Australian study of municipal governments (Considine, Lewis and Alexander 2009). As such, it is situated within an approach that recognises the importance of networks as a distinct organisational form – from Powell (1990), through to recent elaborations of the 'new public governance' (Osborne 2010). The analysis provides little support for the common claim that innovative policy makers are 'frame-breakers' with fundamentally different normative orientations. However, it does provide solid evidence that the networking patterns of recognised innovators are indeed different from those of people who are not recognised as such.

NETWORKS AND INNOVATION

The new public governance (see Osborne 2010) provides a conceptual starting point for this examination of innovation and networks, with its emphasis on network theory, relationships and open systems, and the recognition of the various pressures and competing values that enable and constrain public policy. Osborne describes five strands of public governance, two of which are pertinent here: public policy governance and network governance. The first relates to how policy networks shape the policy process and the second to how inter-organisational networks function in implementing policy and delivering services.

Policy networks have been discussed at length in the public policy and public administration literature, particularly since the Marsh and Rhodes (1992) book. Policy networks are important 'soft' structures, built on the relationships between actors, which establish how interests within a given sector are interlinked. These networks have important effects on the policy-making process. Interest in network governance followed this interest in policy networks, with a greater emphasis on the implementation and management of networks (e.g. Rhodes 1997; Koopenjan and Klijn 2004). More recently, new public governance has been described as an alternative to traditional public administration and the new public management (Osborne 2010). As a conceptual tool based on network (rather than hierarchy or market) ideas, it is a useful frame for the central concerns of this chapter – the relationships between individuals and the link between (policy and governance) networks and innovation capacity.

At its core, innovation is essentially a socially constructed concept (Newman, Raine and Skelcher 2001). Osborne, Chew and McLaughlin (2008a) demonstrated that the innovative capacity of voluntary organisations is contingent on the policy frameworks they are situated within. A supportive environment that privileges innovation enhances this capacity, while a downplaying of it will reduce this capacity. It seems that government funding drives innovation – encouraging these organisations both to be more innovative and to portray themselves as such. Conversely, if innovation is an optional extra, neither something to regard as a core activity nor something that organisations should be seen to be doing, it will (perhaps not surprisingly) become a lower priority (Osborne, Chew and McLaughlin 2008a, 2008b).

Our first departure point is to explore the normative frames that people use to define innovation, to locate their own role and the role of government in the innovation process, and to evaluate the main governmental institutions, procedures and processes that might be used to create innovations within their environment. In this context, we were interested in how actors defined innovation. Did they see innovation as being about major structural disjuncture or gradual incremental change? Could they see a role for governments as innovative forces or did they regard them as having a limited or non-existent role in innovation? Did they find the legislative system conducive to innovation? Was the planning and budget process helpful to innovation or a source of blockage? Such norms, we suspected, provide actors with a type of mental map to navigate their work. This map would be crucial in shaping how individuals and organisations approach the task of innovation.

The second main departure point is networks. The importance of networks in facilitating innovation and shaping innovation pathways at the organisational, sectoral and national level has long been recognised within the private sector innovation literature (see for example: Lundvall 1992; Nelson 1993; Conway 1995; Jones, Conway and Steward 1998; Jones and Beckinsale 1999; Love 1999). Relationships have also been acknowledged as important in the public sector literature, particularly in the context of the diffusion of innovative ideas and practices, with networks a prime means to facilitate information exchange within organisations and governments. Being linked to other organisations provides opportunities to learn new ways of doing things (Borins 2000; Martin 2000; Hartley 2008; Staronova and Malikova 2008), and, in this context, the innovative capacity of local governments has been linked to the presence of strong internal and external networks (Newman, Raine and Skelcher 2001). Hence, networks are expected to play a key role in shaping the approach of governments and individual actors towards innovation.

The empirical approach taken was as follows. We called for volunteers from the municipalities in the state of Victoria in Australia, through an umbrella local governance organisation. In response to this call, 11 municipalities expressed interest in participating, and all of them were included. The top four levels of bureaucrats (the CEO, directors, managers and team leaders/coordinators) and all of the politicians in each of these governments were surveyed using a self-completed questionnaire. Overall, 765 of the possible 947 respondents (81 per cent response rate) completed the survey. The questionnaire collected information on how these people frame innovation as a concept; on their views regarding the impact of a range of political, institutional and procedural factors on the innovation process; and data on who they communicate with (their interpersonal networks) in order to get advice and strategic information. Four of these governments were then chosen as sites for more in-depth examination, and in each of these, respondents were asked to identify the key innovators in their municipality. In these four, interviews were conducted with some 250 politicians, senior and middle-ranking bureaucrats and community leaders (see Considine, Lewis and Alexander 2009 for full details, and Lewis, Considine and Alexander 2011 for a summary).

In many respects, our findings for all 11 municipalities confirmed that both normative frames and networks were important to innovation. Different governments showed evidence of place-specific 'cultures of innovation' characterised by unique normative frames and perceptions of the role played by different institutions, processes and procedures in helping or hindering innovation. These frames varied in relation to where an individual sat within the hierarchy and whether they were on the political or bureaucratic side of the fence (Considine and Lewis 2005). However, they were only weakly correlated with innovator status, with innovators slightly more positive about the role of institutional factors and managerial procedures. We found clear evidence of distinct networking cultures across governments, with some more hierarchical in their networking patterns than others, and some more externally focused (Considine, Lewis and Alexander 2009). Perhaps most significantly, our research confirmed a clear link between innovator status and network placement: actors widely recognised as innovators were significantly more central in networks, and network centrality was the strongest predictor of innovator status (Considine and Lewis 2007).

This chapter draws out in finer detail how the normative outlooks and networking behaviour adopted by those recognised by their peers as innovators differ from those of their colleagues. We examine whether or not the key innovators have outlooks which run counter to the dominant frames within their organisations – a situation which would sit comfortably with suggestions that innovators tend to be 'frame-breakers' (Jones 2002), or at least prone to bend or break rules and to feel less constrained by norms or consensus (Isaksen, Lauer and Wilson 2003). In relation to networks, we analyse whether innovators structure their patterns of contact in substantially different ways from their colleagues.

CASE STUDY: THE CITY OF KILBOURNE

One of the four municipalities involved in the second, more in-depth component of this study – Kilbourne (pseudonyms were used to prevent governments being identified) – is used as a case study here. We narrowed the focus to a single case largely for the sake of parsimony, and chose Kilbourne because it had the highest response rate among the four municipalities in the second stage of the research. While, as previously flagged, our findings suggest that the normative framing and networking behaviour of actors do differ significantly across governments, the relative placement of 'key innovators' on these measures compared with their colleagues – which is our current focus – shows no uniform or meaningful variation across the four cases. To put it another way, the same general similarities and differences between what recognised innovators and others think and how they network that we found at Kilbourne, are also evident at the other three municipalities. Using a single representative case in this context allows us to explore important issues with greater clarity without any substantial loss of the overall picture.

Kilbourne is located approximately 20 kilometres southeast of Melbourne's Central Business District in the shadows of the Dandenong Ranges. Home to over 140,000 residents, the city is one of the most rapidly growing urban centres in Victoria, and has been for two decades. Much of this growth and local economic development has been propelled by historically low land prices. Most of the suburbs within Kilbourne could be characterised as true 'mortgage belt' suburbs, peopled by large numbers of young middle-class families enjoying a comfortable but not wealthy living standard.

Kilbourne follows the council-manager model characteristic of all Australian local governments. The municipality is governed by a nine-member popularly elected council and members serve four year terms. It is headed by a Mayor, who is elected by other members of the council for a one year term. These politicians are paid a relatively small annual allowance – $18,000 (approximately £11,000) at the time of the study, with the Mayor receiving $57,000 (£34,000). As is typical in Australian local governments, only a minority of Kilbourne's elected members held overt party affiliations. The municipal organisation itself is one of the larger local governments in Victoria, with well over 900 staff.

A council-appointed CEO is responsible for implementing and administering municipal policy. At the time of the study, the municipal organisation was split into five divisional silos covering Finance, Organisational Development, Infrastructure, Environment and Planning, and Community Services. Each division was headed by a Director who reports to the CEO. The CEO at Kilbourne had been in place for just under a year, with the remainder of the management team also quite new, averaging just 2.5 years in position. In comparison, the seven elected members who participated in the study had served an average of 6.25 years.

Identifying the 'Key Innovators'

For the purposes of this chapter we focus our attention on the top five key innovators in Kilbourne, comparing their normative views of innovation and their networking behaviour with those of their colleagues. These top five innovators have been identified on the basis of data collected from structured interviews with a cross-section of 26 politicians, senior bureaucrats and middle-managers at Kilbourne. During these interviews, respondents were asked to name those people they regarded as the 'key innovators' in Kilbourne. An open approach to the notion of who is an innovator was taken. Nominations could include politicians, bureaucrats or members of the community, and there were no

Table 24.1   Top five key innovators at Kilbourne

	Evan (middle manager)	Kate (middle manager)	Andy (middle manager)	Joe (senior bureaucrat)	Ian (senior bureaucrat)	Mean
Key innovator nominations	18	13	11	11	7	1.37

limitations placed on the number of people listed. The assumption here is that innovation is a visible property to proximate actors in a governmental system, even when it sometimes involves confidential processes and partial information. That is, it is possible for people to recognise the innovators in their municipalities, even when the full details of the innovations these people have introduced might not be known to them. We acknowledge that reputational approaches such as this arguably run the risk of bias in favour of high profile and more senior actors. However, the material collected via qualitative interviews, combined with the strong correlation between key innovator nomination patterns and involvement in actual case studies of innovation conducted ($p = 0.68$), gives us confidence that the innovators have been successfully identified.

Table 24.1 shows the five highest-placed individuals at Kilbourne (pseudonyms have been used) based on the number of nominations they received along with the mean number of nominations per capita for respondents to the survey in Kilbourne. As the table shows, the top-placed 'key innovator' at Kilbourne was a middle-manager (Evan), who received 18 nominations out of a possible 26. This compares to an overall mean of 1.37 nominations per person. Two other managers, Kate and Andy, also received a high number of nominations, with 13 and 11 respectively. Indeed, middle-managers dominate the list, filling out three of the top five positions. In this respect, Kilbourne was different from the other municipalities. Joe and Ian are senior bureaucrats (hold either CEO or Director level positions). The absence of politicians from the list is another factor setting Kilbourne apart, with none of the nine politicians in office at the time of the original survey receiving more than a single nomination from the 26 respondents interviewed.

Innovation Norms and Procedures

To locate their own normative orientations to innovation, politicians and bureaucrats in the 11 local governments were asked to respond to a series of 16 statements concerning the concept's nature and meaning. These statements included items relating to three themes: defining innovation, innovation and government, and innovation structures and people (see Appendix A). Each respondent was asked to indicate their level of agreement with these statements on a five point Likert scale, ranging from strongly disagree to strongly agree. The 16 items were then factor analysed using principal components analysis, in order to determine underlying or latent structures in the ways innovation was understood.[1] The five factors that emerged from the factor analysis we have called institutional, structural, sceptical, incremental and adaptive accounts of innovation. The *institutional* factor describes innovation as the work of internal structures and certain standard organisational factors. The *structural* type refers to innovation as radical, externally focused and sometimes based on conflict. The *sceptical* outlook defines innovation as being of limited applicability to the public sector, while the *incremental* factor refers to the role of small and planned efforts. The notion that innovation is largely about *adaptation* refers to sourcing ideas from elsewhere, while also seeing governmental innovation as quite different from other types.

Figure 24.1 plots the mean factor scores for each individual, as well as the scores for each of the top five innovators at Kilbourne, across the five normative outlooks on innovation. The results indicate that four of the five innovators at Kilbourne are more likely than average to view innovation as being about internal structures and organisational factors, the exception being one of the senior bureaucrats (Ian). The five are more evenly split on the structural norm, with two middle-managers and a senior bureaucrat slightly under the mean (i.e. less likely than average to view innovation as involving major change) and one of each above the mean. All five innovators are fairly tightly clustered around the means for the sceptical and incremental dimensions. They display more dispersed views on the adaptive norm, and Ian and Joe (the two senior bureaucrats) are more positively inclined to this view than the three middle-managers.

Using the same approach, respondents were also asked to assess, using a five point Likert scale, the extent to which 13 key procedures and instruments used in local government helped or hindered innovation. These items included such things as statutory meetings, the budget, corporate plans, election campaigns and their organisation's pay and promotion system (see Appendix A). Three coherent positions expressing different views of the procedures most likely to help and hinder innovation emerged from the analysis. The position that we have called *political* covers assessments of all the formal legislative procedures of local government such as municipal meetings and committees. The annual budget process and the corporate plan load on both this factor and the *managerial* factor, reflecting the fact that these items are seen as part of both political and internal management procedures. *Managerial* also includes the internal management procedures associated with the organisational machinery of each municipality and its staff (e.g. pay and performance, quality procedures), but not politicians. The items making up the *electoral* factor centre on the role played by elections, state government regulation and the culture, values and other characteristics of local politicians, so far as innovation is concerned.

Figure 24.2 plots the mean factor scores for these three procedural normative dimensions for each survey respondent at Kilbourne along with the scores for each of the key innovators.[2] As Figure 24.2 shows, at Kilbourne the key innovators registered factor scores well away from the mean on the political procedures measure, although in divergent directions – three rating the latter as being helpful for innovation and one (Ian) quite negative about their impact. All four converged quite closely on the managerial procedures factor, registering scores slightly above the mean, while three of the four were below the average in their rating of the impact of electoral procedures on the innovation process.

Two key findings emerge from the results, both somewhat at odds with what we might expect from the literature on innovation. First, there is very little evidence of convergence in terms of how the key innovators frame innovation either on the five innovation norms or the three procedural dimensions. The positions adopted by the innovators are dispersed relatively widely across most of the factors, with the exception of the managerial procedures measure, where all four innovators were very closely placed. There is also no discernible pattern in terms of any particular individual diverging regularly from the other innovators.

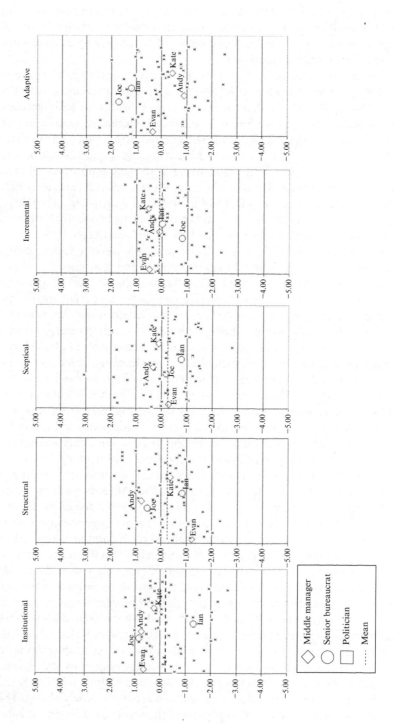

Figure 24.1   Kilbourne: distribution of 'norms' factor scores

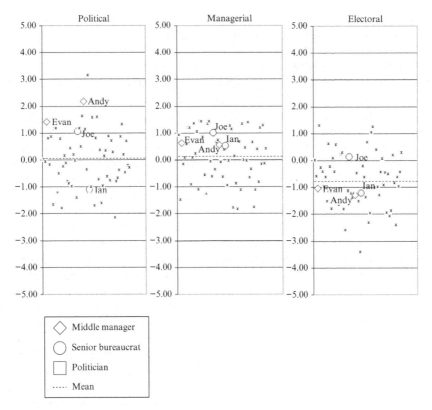

Figure 24.2   Kilbourne: distribution of 'procedures' factor scores

Secondly, there is very little evidence to indicate that the innovators are in any sense 'frame-breakers' or 'rule-benders'. While the top five innovators do sometimes adopt positions away from the mean on the norms and procedures measures, the extent of their divergence is for the most part relatively minor, with major departures rare. Mean scores are provided in Appendix B.[3] Indeed, for the norms measures, the key innovators only stray further than one standard deviation from the mean on 16 per cent of occasions (4/25), with the drift slightly higher on the procedures measures at 25 per cent (3/12). Overall, then, and somewhat contrary to our expectations, there is little evidence to suggest that innovators differ significantly in terms of their normative framing of innovation or in terms of how they view the contribution that various institutions, procedures and processes make towards the innovation process. Instead of struggling against the normative current, the top innovators generally appear to swim with the prevailing tide.

Networks

As noted at the outset of this chapter, one of our underlying contentions was that the networking behaviour of highly recognised innovators was likely to be quite different from that of their colleagues, and that this would be reflected in the structure and content of the different kinds of networks they form. To test these assumptions we used a name generator to collect information on the strategic information networks of politicians and bureaucrats across 11 municipalities.[4] Name generators invite actors to name the people with whom they interact in regard to some critical issue such as the getting or giving of advice or information, or the solving of a problem (Burt 1984; Straits 2000). Respondents were asked to list up to five people from inside their organisation that they had gone to over the previous six months to get strategic information about something in their government/organisation.[5]

Strategic information – knowing in which direction the organisation is headed and having a strong sense of the institutional and political obstacles that policy will need to overcome – was selected because it is a crucial resource for policy innovators. Key innovators should be well placed within this type of policy network, so that they are able to easily link to crucial actors, if they are not occupying the most important strategic positions themselves. Social network analysis was used to explore the positions of policy actors. *In-degree centrality* provides an indication of the popularity of an individual actor, and is based on the number of ties directed towards an individual (Wasserman and Faust 1994).[6] *Eigenvector centrality* moves beyond simply measuring popularity by taking into account the strategic positioning of an individual actor within a network (Hanneman and Riddle 2005).[7] Comparing means of these measures for the key innovators and their political and bureaucratic colleagues enabled us to explore differences in their network characteristics.

Innovation implies a capacity to reach out of normal work routines and communicate with potential policy actors, stakeholders or decision makers elsewhere in the system. So, how different is the boundary-spanning behaviour of our innovators compared with that of their colleagues? Do they tend to reach out more extensively than others across divisional boundaries in search of new ideas and support for their innovations? Do they more readily bridge functional barriers between, for example, politicians and bureaucrats? To capture these networking patterns we calculated the number of strategic information ties each key innovator receives from and directs to people outside of their immediate domain. For bureaucrats we counted ties directed to and received from other divisions across the organisation and those to and from politicians; for politicians, we counted ties directed to or received from across the political–bureaucratic divide to and from bureaucrats.

Finally, examining the placement of innovators within global network structures is one way of building a picture of how actors make use of the embedded resources within networks in order to get things done. Examining the structure and make-up of the ego-networks of our key innovators is another. These ego-networks are each individual's unique set of connections, incorporating all direct ties to and from the person being examined (ego) and all ties between those with direct connections to ego. Measuring the size of each actor's ego network, or more specialised social network measures such as *normalised brokerage* and *two-step reach*,[8] helps to characterise the nature of these networks. Our expectations concerning the uniqueness of our key innovators' networks can then be tested.

Table 24.2 provides scores on each of these measures for the top five innovators at Kilbourne as well as the mean score for Kilbourne. As Table 24.2 shows, in terms of the global network measures we can see that the key innovators at Kilbourne tend to reside in much more central positions in the strategic information network than average. The

Table 24.2   Kilbourne strategic information network measures

	Evan (MM)	Kate (MM)	Andy (MM)	Joe (SB)	Ian (SB)	Mean
Normalised in degree	17.11	22.37	11.84	18.42	25.00	4.33
Eigenvector centrality	31.36	26.67	23.45	29.34	41.85	12.91
Ties out to external directorate	5.00	2.00	3.00	3.00	4.00	1.69
Ties in from external directorate	11.00	6.00	5.00	3.00	11.00	1.49
Ego network size	15.00	18.00	11.00	17.00	21.00	5.92
Two-step reach	84.21	65.79	68.42	78.95	82.89	46.78
Normalised brokerage	0.46	0.47	0.43	0.46	0.46	0.38

highest normalised in-degree centrality score (25.00 for Ian) is a remarkable six times larger than the average score returned across all survey respondents at Kilbourne. Even the least central of Kilbourne's key innovators (11.84 for Andy) was almost three times as central as his colleagues. The eigenvector centrality measure tells a similar story, with scores across the key innovators ranging from two to three times the mean. The global measures indicate that the key innovators were much more cross-organisational in their networking behaviour both in terms of seeking strategic information and especially in terms of disseminating the latter. This was particularly the case for Evan, whose five out ties were all directed externally, and who along with Ian received 11 ties from actors outside of his directorate.

The measures contained in Table 24.2 also indicate that the structure and composition of our key innovator's ego networks are quite different from the norm. First and most obviously, they are uniformly larger than average, again ranging from between two and three times the mean. They also tend to have far greater reach across their organisation, either directly or through a single intermediary, as measured by two-step reach. Finally, it appears that our innovators are also more likely than others to serve as brokers linking pairs of actors who would not otherwise be connected. This is likely to place them in a position of significant strategic advantage by providing them a degree of control over the flow of information across the organisation (Burt 2005).

With such small numbers it is obviously impossible to make any conclusive judgements on whether or not the networking behaviour of key innovators is fundamentally different from others working in local government.[9] The results suggest that this might be the case, and this pattern is repeated in each of the other three municipalities in this study. It is clear that the innovators tend to occupy central, strategic positions within strategic information networks; that their networks are larger; and that they tend to have greater reach across their organisations. They also tend to be more cross-organisational in their networking behaviour, and to hold network positions which give them greater control over the flow of information to their colleagues.[10] These are important findings which support the contention that innovators sit at important strategic junctures within organisational networks. The structure of their relationships with other actors means they are well placed to be able to initiate policy, to persuade others of the importance of their ideas, and to carry them through the necessary internal processes.

CONCLUSIONS

Returning to our two launching points – the social construction of innovation and the importance of networks – we can now draw some conclusions. First, it is clear that, contrary to expectations, key innovators in public sector settings might be those who swim with rather than against the tide, in regard to their normative orientations. This interesting finding links to that of Osborne, Chew and McLaughlin's (2008a) point about the importance of the policy context to innovation: if there is high level policy support for innovation it is more likely to happen, and to be reported as such. If there is no policy support, it is unlikely to happen and also to be claimed. Being someone who stands out from the crowd in an environment where this is at best unimportant, and at worst risky to your career, is unrewarding. Even if you do (surreptitiously) innovate, you are unlikely to want others to see you as an innovator if that term lacks positive connotations. The safer option is to fit within the prevailing culture.

Secondly, it is clear that networks are a key part of the innovation story. Actors with high recognition as innovators were far more likely to be central in communication networks than their colleagues, and had larger networks and superior cross-organisational reach. This confirms earlier research on the importance of networks to innovators as a source of inter-organisational learning, knowledge sharing and innovation diffusion in the public sector (Teske and Schneider 1994; Martin 2000; Borins 2001; Walker and Enticott 2004; Walker 2007). Such networks are crucial to innovation because the interpersonal connections they are based upon generate embedded resources.

Networks provide a shadow structure of policy influence which can be used to wield informal power within a policy sector, to significantly shape the policy agenda, and to structure policy choices (Laumann and Knoke 1987; Lewis 2005). While traditional institutional pathways and structures are important in shaping innovation's trajectory, it is often these patterns of informal communication which underpin the process by allowing policy entrepreneurs to reach out beyond organisational boundaries, move more easily across divisional or departmental borders, and bridge the role divide between politicians, bureaucrats and non government actors engaged in the policy-making process. These networks are an important part of the innovation culture which shapes individuals' normative orientations, through their connections to others. While others have shown the importance of networks, few have been able to demonstrate their relative importance. This is an important conclusion: networks are more important to innovation than the other factors considered in this study (Considine, Lewis and Alexander 2009).

In this chapter, we have established that both the particular innovation outlooks of individuals, and the policy and governance networks they sit within, drive the innovation process. In doing so, this research constitutes one of the few attempts to integrate an analysis of social networks with an examination of cognitive processes at the individual level. Highly innovative policy actors are not rule-breakers – they have very similar innovation orientations to their colleagues. It seems more important to sit comfortably within the prevailing policy context. But the importance of networks to innovation inside government is crystal clear. Policy networks have previously been shown to be crucial at numerous points in the policy process and in a variety of contexts. This study confirms the old truism that it's not just what you know, but who you know. Who you are connected to and how you are connected underpin innovation.

NOTES

1. Full details of the principal components analysis are available in Considine, Lewis and Alexander (2009).
2. Unfortunately, no factor scores could be computed for Kate as she failed to complete this bank of questions.
3. Independent sample T-Tests confirmed that there were no statistically significant differences in the means recorded by 'key innovators' and their colleagues across the five 'norms' and three 'procedures'.
4. Data on advice networks were also collected but are not discussed here, as strategic information networks were the better of the two in predicting innovator status.
5. While name generators could effectively be unlimited in the number of nominations, we limited the scope to five names each on the assumption that this would be a manageable number for the actors to recall and describe with a reasonable degree of validity. Longer lists, while giving more information, might also open the door to various kinds of self-congratulation or desirability bias.
6. Given that this measure is dependent upon network size, a normalised figure which makes results comparable across networks (governments) of different sizes was used (Scott 2000).
7. Calculating individual eigenvector centrality gives more weight to ties to actors who themselves have high in-degree centrality scores because ties to actors with multiple connections potentially provide access to more of the network and, hence, more extensive resources.
8. Normalised brokerage measures the extent to which ego serves as a broker linking pairs of actors in his/her ego network not otherwise directly connected. This is calculated by dividing the number of pairs in the ego network not directly connected by the actual number of pairs. Two-step reach measures the percentage of actors in the whole network who ego is able to reach either directly or through a 'friend of a friend' (Hanneman and Riddle 2005).
9. Given that no politicians were identified among the key innovators in Kilbourne, our findings relate only to government officers.
10. Independent sample T-Tests confirmed statistically significant differences ($p<0.05$) in the means recorded by the five 'key innovators' and their colleagues across all network measures except for normalised brokerage.

BIBLIOGRAPHY

Bartlett, D. and Dibben, P. (2002). Public sector innovation and entrepreneurship: case studies from local government. *Local Government Studies*, 28(4), 107–121.
Borins, S. (2000). Loose cannons and rule breakers, or enterprising leaders? Some evidence about innovative public managers. *Public Administration Review*, 60(6), 498–507.
Borins, S. (2001). The challenge of innovating Government. The Pricewaterhouse Coopers Endowment for The Business of Government. Innovation in Management Series. February.
Burt, R.S. (1984). Network items and the General Social Survey. *Social Networks*, 6, 293–339.
Burt, R.S. (2005). *Brokerage and Closure: An Introduction to Social Capital*. New York: Oxford University Press.
Considine, M. and Lewis, J.M. (2005). Mapping the normative underpinnings of local governance. In P. Smyth, T. Reddel and A. Jones (eds), *Community and Local Governance in Australia*. Sydney: UNSW Press, pp. 205–225.
Considine, M. and Lewis, J.M. (2007). Innovation and innovators inside government: from institutions to networks. *Governance*, 20(4), 581–607.
Considine, M., Lewis, J.M. and Alexander, D. (2009). *Networks, Innovation and Public Policy: Politicians, Bureaucrats and the Pathways to Change Inside Government*. Houndmills: Palgrave Macmillan.
Conway, S. (1995). Informal boundary-spanning communication in the innovation process. *Technology Analysis and Strategic Management*, 7(3), 327–342.
Hanneman, R.A. and Riddle, M. (2005). *Introduction to Social Network Methods*. Riverside, CA: University of California, Riverside. Published in digital form at http://faculty.ucr.edu/~hanneman/ (accessed 19 July 2012).
Hartley, J. (2008). Does innovation lead to improvement in public services? Lessons from the Beacon Scheme in the United Kingdom. In S. Borins (ed.), *Innovations in Government: Research, Recognition and Replication*. Washington, DC: Brookings Institution Press, pp. 159–187.
Isaksen, S.G., Lauer, K.J. and Wilson, G.V. (2003). An examination of the relationship between personality type and cognitive style. *Creativity Research Journal*, 15(4), 343–354.
Jones, O. and Beckinsale, M. (1999). *Analysing the Innovation Process: Networks, Micropolitics and Structural*

Change. Research Paper 9919. Aston Business School, Aston University, Birmingham. Available at: http://www.abs.aston.ac/UK/ (accessed 19 July 2012).

Jones, O., Conway, S. and Steward, F. (1998). Introduction: social interaction and innovation networks. *International Journal of Innovation Management* (Special Issue), 2(2), 123–136.

Jones, R. (2002). Leading change in local government: the tension between evolutionary and frame-breaking reform in NSW. *Australian Journal of Public Administration*, 61(3), 38–53.

Koopenjan, J. and Klijn, E.-H. (2004). *Managing Uncertainties in Networks*. London: Routledge.

Laumann, E. and Knoke, D. (1987). *The Organisational State: Social Choice, National Policy Domains*. Madison, WI: University of Wisconsin Press.

Lewis, J.M. (2005). *Health Policy and Politics: Networks, Ideas and Power*. Melbourne: IP Communications.

Lewis, J.M., Considine, M. and Alexander, D. (2011). Innovation inside government: the importance of networks. In V. Bekkers, J. Edelenbos and B. Steijn (eds), *Innovation in the Public Sector: Linking Capacity and Leadership*. Basingstoke: Palgrave Macmillan, pp. 107–132.

Love, J. (1999). Patterns of networking in the innovation process: a comparative study of the UK, Germany and Ireland. Research Paper 9913. Aston Business School, Aston University, Birmingham. Available at: http://www.abs.aston.ac/UK/ (accessed 19 July 2012).

Lundvall, B. (1992). *National Systems of Innovation: Towards a Theory of Innovation and Interactive Learning*. London: Pinter Press.

Marsh, D. and Rhodes, R.A.W. (eds) (1992). *Policy Networks in British Government*. Oxford: Oxford University Press.

Martin, J. (2000). *Innovation Strategies in Australian Local Government: Occasional Paper 4*. Melbourne, Australian Housing and Urban Research Institute. Available at: http://www.ahuri.edu.au/downloads/publications/Occasional_Paper_4.pdf (accessed 19 July 2012).

Nelson, R. (1993). *National Systems of Innovation*. Oxford: Blackwell.

Newman, J., Raine, J. and Skelcher, C. (2001). Transforming local government: innovation and modernization. *Public Money and Management*, 21(2), 61–68.

Osborne, S.P. (ed.) (2010). *The New Public Governance*. London: Routledge.

Osborne, S.P. and Brown, L. (2011). Innovation in public services: engaging with risk. *Public Money and Management*, 31(1), 4–6.

Osborne, S.P., Chew, C. and McLaughlin, K. (2008a). The once and future pioneers? The innovative capacity of voluntary organisations and the provision of public services: a longitudinal approach. *Public Management Review*, 10(1), 51–70.

Osborne, S.P., Chew, C. and McLaughlin, K. (2008b). The innovative capacity of voluntary and community organisations: exploring the organisational and environmental contingencies. In S. Osborne (ed.), *The Third Sector in Europe: Prospects and Challenges*. London: Routledge, pp. 134–156.

Powell, W. (1990). 'Neither market nor hierarchy: network forms of organisation. *Research in Organisational Behavior*, 12, 295–336.

Rhodes, R.A.W. (1997). *Understanding Governance*. Buckingham: Open University Press.

Scott, J. (2000). *Social Network Analysis: A Handbook* (2nd edn). Thousand Oaks, CA: Sage.

Staronova, K. and Malikova, L. (2008). Learning to innovate in a transition country: developing quality standards for elderly residential care in Slovakia. In P. Windrum and P. Koch (eds), *Innovation in Public Sector Services: Entrepreneurship, Creativity and Management*. Cheltenham and Northampton, MA: Edward Elgar Publishing, pp. 208–227.

Straits, B. (2000). Ego's important discussants or significant people: an experiment in varying the wording of personal network name generators. *Social Networks*, 22, 123–140.

Teske, P. and Schneider, M. (1994). The bureaucratic entrepreneur: the case of city managers. *Public Administration Review*, 54(4), 331–340.

Walker, R.M. (2007). An empirical evaluation of innovation types and organisational and environmental characteristics: towards a configuration framework. *Journal of Public Administration Research and Theory*. [Advanced access copy published October 25, 2007.]

Walker, R.M. and Enticott, G. (2004). Using multiple-informants in public administration: revisiting the managerial values and actions debate. *Journal of Public Administration Research and Theory*, 14(3), 417–434.

Wasserman, S. and Faust, K. (1994). *Social Network Analysis: Methods and Applications*. New York: Cambridge University Press.

APPENDIX A: INNOVATION NORMS AND PROCEDURES ITEMS

Table 24A.1   Innovation norms' items

Defining innovation	1. Innovation means making small, continuous improvements
	2. Innovation is when you develop or adapt a new technology or product that is better than the one you had before
	3. Innovation means making major changes
	4. Innovation is any planned effort to improve a process, service or programme
Innovation and government	5. To be innovative in local government you have to work closely with the community
	6. I have never thought of innovation as something that governments do
	7. In local government, innovation means resolving conflicting priorities
	8. Accountability requirements mean that innovation in local government is very limited
Innovation – structures and people	9. To be innovative you need to be able to move outside regular channels
	10. I do *not* see much difference in the roles played by experts, politicians and managers when it comes to innovation
	11. I see myself as an innovator
	12. Our structures encourage us to bring forward ideas for innovation
	13. Councillors are elected to identify needs, officials are there to then create the innovations to meet those needs
	14. I believe our organisation values individuals who strive to be innovators
	15. My strength is that I can adapt innovations produced by someone else to my situation
	16. I find it difficult to be innovative in our organisation

List of 'Innovation Procedures' Items

1. The annual budget process
2. Council corporate plan
3. Council statutory committee meetings
4. Council advisory committee meetings
5. Council meetings
6. Pay and promotion system
7. Values and culture of Executive management
8. Divisional structure of Council
9. Quality of proposals coming from officers
10. Council election campaigns
11. State government regulation of local government
12. Values and culture of elected Councillors
13. Quality of policy proposals coming from Councillors

APPENDIX B

Table 24A.2   Factor scores for key innovators at Kilbourne

		Evan (MM)	Kate (MM)	Andy (MM)	Joe (SB)	Ian (SB)	Kilbourne (Mean)[a]
Norms	Institutional	0.64	0.24	0.73	0.83	−1.31	−0.16
	Structural	−1.19	−0.34	0.77	0.53	−0.83	−0.15
	Sceptical	−0.29	0.10	0.32	−0.19	−0.79	−0.10
	Incremental	0.49	0.50	0.09	−0.81	−0.02	−0.01
	Adaptive	0.34	−0.42	−0.90	1.70	1.19	0.05
Procedures	Political	1.42	–	2.17	1.05	−1.11	0.07
	Managerial	0.63	–	0.56	1.00	0.52	0.16
	Electoral	−1.03	–	−1.29	0.13	−1.22	−0.76

Note: [a] Factor scores were calculated across respondents from all 11 municipalities. As a result mean factor scores from Kilbourne do not sum to zero.

25. Co-production and innovation in public services: can co-production drive innovation?

Kirsty Strokosch

INTRODUCTION

This chapter uses an integrated typology of co-production to consider co-production and the innovation of public services. The chapter is divided into two parts. The first discusses co-production through the integration of two theoretical standpoints: services management (Normann 1991; Venetis and Ghauri 2004; Gronroos 2007; Johnston and Clark 2008; Vargo et al. 2008) and public administration (Whitaker 1980; Parks et al. 1981; Brudney and England 1983; Bovaird 2005, 2007; Pestoff 2006). This integration has led to the development of a typology of co-production which can be used to differentiate co-production at the individual and organizational levels. Referring to these types of co-production, the discussion will turn to innovation. The vast literature on innovation will not be covered here. Rather, the focus will be upon the role of co-production in innovating public services.

Using the data collected during a study of co-production in the case of asylum seekers in Glasgow, the second part of the chapter will consider whether co-production is a mechanism that can be used to drive innovation in public services.

UNDERSTANDING CO-PRODUCTION: INTEGRATING THE THEORIES

Traditionally, public services management has been firmly situated within the public administration debate, with limited insight being taken from the services management literature. Although the conception of consumerism has been abstracted, the supporting elements of the services logic have not been applied thoroughly (Jung 2010). It will be argued here that this is imperative to understanding how public services are produced, noting particularly the importance of the service interaction and the potential for innovation through different forms of co-production. Thus, the approach taken in the first part of this chapter is to integrate the public administration and services management literatures to develop a more comprehensive understanding of co-production, laying the foundations for understanding whether co-production can drive innovation.

Co-production, from the public administration perspective, originated from the work of Ostrom (1972), who examined the relationship between the community and public service organizations, showing that a police force relied as much upon the community as the community did on the police force. This body of literature was further developed predominantly in the United States, Europe and Australia (Whitaker 1980; Parks et al. 1981; Brudney and England 1983; Levine and Fisher 1984; Rosentraub and

375

Warren 1987; Alford 1998, 2002; Brandsen and Pestoff 2006; Pestoff, 2006; Bovaird 2007).

Using this literature, co-production can be differentiated from the 'traditional' model of public service production where 'public officials are exclusively charged with responsibility for designing and providing services to citizens, who in turn only demand, consume and evaluate them' (Pestoff 2006, p. 506). Indeed, Moore and Hartley (2008) describe service user participation as one type of governance innovation that can provide space and opportunity for individuals to contribute where government had previously exercised full control.

Public administration has strong tendencies towards manufacturing production logic, where production and consumption are discrete processes (Vargo et al. 2008). Services are conceptualized as goods, produced by service providers/professionals and consumed (relatively) passively by service users. This has implications for how co-production is both initiated and managed. It becomes a normative, voluntary good that will add value to the public service production process, rather than being intrinsic to it. Perceived in this way, co-production also becomes dependent upon service professionals' willingness and ability to provide opportunities to co-produce. Furthermore, the extent of co-production will rest on service organizations' resources, their predisposition to 'share' power and also whether service users have an appetite to co-produce (Whitaker 1980; Brudney and England 1983; Pestoff 2006).

The services management literature offers unique insights to the understanding of public services management (Osborne 2010) and specifically the integral role played by service users during service production. The theory is rooted within three concepts of inseparability, intangibility and co-production (Gronroos 2007). Understanding these concepts allows us to place public services more firmly within the services logic. *Inseparability* differentiates services from manufactured goods, explaining that they are produced and consumed simultaneously in time and location (Gronroos 2007; Johnston and Clark 2008). Services are also distinguished from goods as *intangible* processes. Finally, services are *co-produced*. This means that the service user's contribution is integral to service production and the interaction they have with the service provider is intrinsic and fundamental to the service encounter (Gronroos 2007). Indeed, central to the services management literature is the service encounter or 'the moment of truth' (Normann 1991), where the interaction between service user and provider takes place. The service encounter is the point at which service quality is gauged by the service user: 'Service encounters are critical moments of truth in which customers often develop indelible impressions of a firm . . . From the customer's point of view, these encounters are the service' (Bitner et al. 1997, pp. 139–140).

Developing a Typology: Individual and Organizational Co-Production

Integrating these two theories creates a more comprehensive understanding of the co-production of public services. Indeed, three distinct types of co-production can be differentiated for the individual service user: consumer, participative and enhanced. Each type can be achieved through various mechanisms and entails different levels of input from the service provider and service user.

Consumer co-production stems from a services management literature, where the consumer plays a tripartite role: consuming the service, contributing to the production process and evaluating the quality of the service. Thus, the act of service consumption is the cornerstone of co-production, as it is this action that results in service users' contribution to service production at the most basic level. As a result of the interrelated nature of production and consumption, co-production is an inherent component of service production and, as such, is involuntary and unavoidable on the part of both the service user and provider.

The public administration literature sets the stage for *participative co-production*. It extends beyond the consumption logic of a single service alone and into the overall public policy process (including planning, delivery and evaluation). Here, service providers facilitate various mechanisms of engagement to allow service users to engage in the service production process. Arnstein's (1969) typology of citizen participation illustrates eight levels of participation in a ladder, and is a helpful reference point in understanding what forms participative co-production might take (e.g. information, consultation, partnership) (although this model is not without criticism; for example, Tritter and McCallum 2006).

Enhanced co-production combines the two previous types and is rooted within the integration of the literature discussed above. Consumer-based mechanisms in the service encounter can be used to enhance participative co-production. For example, choice and complaints procedures, as well as the co-design of service innovation, can be employed to enhance the achievement of public policy objectives. Enhanced co-production can also be achieved through the use of participative mechanisms during the service interaction, using the service encounter or Normann's (1991) 'moment of truth' to achieve deeper engagement.

The discussion so far has focused upon co-production at the individual level, but developing a comprehensive understanding of how co-production might drive the innovation of public services also requires an integration of the organizational level. Indeed, the existence of individual forms of co-production is unlikely to supersede inter-organizational working; both types are likely to co-exist, particularly given the political drive for partnership and collaborative working. Scotland, for example, has a history of collaborative working in the delivery of public services which has become embedded latterly by the establishment of the 2007 Concordat and the subsequent development of Single Outcome Agreements between the Scottish government and local-level Community Planning Partnerships (Osborne et al. 2011).

Working across organizational boundaries, specifically with the third sector, has strong theoretical lineage in the public administration literature. In their seminal book, *To Empower People*, Berger and Neuhaus (1978) discuss third sector organizations as mediating structures with the capacity to solve dilemmas around extending the welfare state without expanding the boundaries of overly bureaucratic government structures. The argument for mediating structures starts with the presumption that people are the best experts in their own lives; the mediating structure taps into this expertise and is said to represent people's needs to policy makers and public service organizations. Furthermore, third sector organizations are typically regarded as being closer to service users and therefore well placed to understand and articulate local need (Haugh and Kitson 2007). Third sector involvement might also lead to the inclusion of groups that might not have the necessary resources or organizational capacity to be otherwise involved (Kearns 1995),

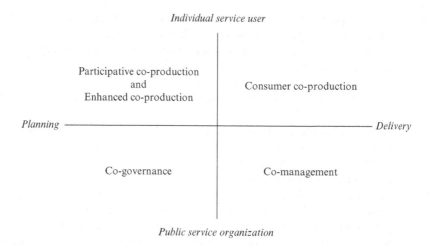

Figure 25.1   Typology of co-production at the individual and organizational levels

which is applicable in the case of asylum seekers discussed in the second part of this chapter.

Brandsen and Pestoff (2006) differentiate two types of inter-organizational co-production. They use the term *co-management* to describe instances where third sector organizations collaborate with the state to produce services, and *co-governance* to describe where third sector organizations contribute to both the planning and delivery of a service. However, there is some disagreement over the extent to which such relationships are positive and there is an ongoing debate about whether they genuinely enhance co-production – through the strength of collective action – or actually diminish it – by placing a mediating organization between the individual service users and their services (Brenton 1985; Hartley and Benington 2006; Pestoff et al. 2006).

The insights from the individual and organizational forms of co-production can be combined in a conceptual typology. Figure 25.1 depicts a matrix to illustrate the different ways in which public services can be co-produced. The vertical axis illustrates that either individual service users or other public service providers can co-produce public services with public service organizations, while the horizontal axis shows that either party can co-produce during service delivery or planning/decision making about the services.

The two upper quadrants of the typology comprise individualized co-production. They both differentiate between involvement in service delivery alone and involvement in service planning as well, and between more active and passive forms of co-production. Thus, *consumer co-production* refers to co-production by service users as part of the service experience, while *participative* and *enhanced co-production* refer to co-production that is explicitly sought by service managers in order to achieve some third objective, whether in relation to that service (such as innovation) or broader public policy objectives.

The two lower quadrants of the matrix illustrate organizationally based co-production, involving inter-organizational relationships between, for example, public service organizations and third sector organizations. In these organizational modes, an organization can collaborate with a public service organization /government agency (*co-management*) to produce services or it can be responsible for service planning and delivery (*co-governance*).

Co-production and Innovation

Innovations are not always initiated at the top of an organization by decision makers or strategists. Service managers, professionals and service users can be a source of the ideas needed for innovative practice (Albury 2005). Furthermore, innovation is not always manufactured internally, but also results from the process of 'learning from others' outwith the organization. Co-production, in its various modes – particularly participative, enhanced, co-management and co-governance – arguably allows a public service organization to harness the knowledge and capabilities of various others for the benefit of the service.

Theorists from the public administration debate have typically teamed co-production with innovation, with participative co-production being associated conventionally with efforts to improve democracy by placing service users at the heart of decision-making processes (Bovaird 2007). Indeed, Pestoff and Brandsen (2009) suggest that directly participating in service delivery through co-production contributes to the process of democratization by empowering service users and reducing the gap between service professionals and their clientele. Furthermore, co-production has been described as an innovative method of engaging and communicating with the public who can directly influence policy and service delivery (Bovaird and Downe 2009). Analysing policy documentation, Bovaird and Downe argue that mechanisms of participative co-production have been adopted to achieve service improvement. They also discuss the innovative approaches used to consult hard-to-reach groups such as young people.

The services management literature makes a further contribution, broadening our understanding of the innovation of public services. At its most basic level, consumer co-production exists as an integral element of the service interaction which involves an exchange between service provider and user (Prahalad and Ramaswamy 2004). It can improve customer satisfaction, through understanding the nature of services and particularly the inseparability of consumption and production in the service encounter. However, co-production can also be enhanced to achieve various forms of innovation.

Essentially, enhanced co-production involves the use of consumer mechanisms to enhance the achievement of public policy objectives. By establishing mechanisms of choice, for example, public service organizations can promote independent advocacy, which can shift responsibility and control away from the service provider and towards service users (Jack 1995), transforming them to active contributors to service production (Gronroos 2007).

The services management literature further suggests that service users are typically better placed to make functional innovations because they have a greater understanding of their own needs than service providers and thus have specialized competencies that cannot otherwise be replicated (Magnusson 2003; Prahalad and Ramaswamy 2004; Zwick et al. 2008; Oliveira and von Hippel 2011). Thus, through enhanced co-production, innovation can arguably be promoted by changing the relationship between the service user and provider, placing greater responsibility in the hands of service users. Zwick et al. (2008) reinforce this point, arguing that service innovations can no longer be achieved through a two-prong approach which scrutinizes and then satisfies the customer. Instead, they recommend that service organizations position themselves as a 'facilitator and partner of consumer ingenuity and agency' (p. 173). Such an approach, they contend, is dependent on communication and co-operation.

The services management literature also contends that services users can benefit indirectly from the innovations made by others (von Hippel 2007); the rewards of innovations are not exclusive to those who contributed to their making. However, von Hippel (2007) argues that those who contribute directly to the process of innovation are likely to receive a higher economic and personal benefit.

Kristensson et al. (2008) differentiate between two types of relationships that can exist between customers and service organizations for the purposes of service innovation: customization and co-creation. *Customization* places the responsibility for designing the service with the service provider, who draws up the design specification according to service users' needs (Prahalad and Ramaswamy 2000). The customer's role is therefore at the end of the reform process, where they suggest changes to a near finalized prototype.

The term *co-creation* was coined by Prahalad and Ramaswamy (2000), who discuss the changing role of customers within the service relationship. The traditional role of the relatively passive buyer with whom the service provider interacts via market research and customer service programmes has been extended. Customers can be co-creators of value, who co-develop personalized service experiences through an active and equal dialogue with service providers through the service encounter. Describing personalization, Prahalad and Ramaswamy (2000, p. 84) argue that the customer becomes 'a cocreator of the content of their experiences', enhancing consumer co-production by offering less restrictive choices and offering opportunities for the customer to share ideas with experts and other customers. Co-creation thus extends beyond the service interaction, which is the basis of consumer co-production, offering a deeper opportunity for customers to shape the service experience. The service organization proactively seeks to discover, understand and satisfy 'latent needs', rather than simply reacting to expressed needs (Kristensson et al. 2008). The mechanisms through which customers co-create in service design include brainstorming, interviews, mock service delivery and team meetings (Alam 2006). The task for service managers is establishing and maintaining co-operation with co-creators, which Prahalad and Ramaswamy (2000) argue can be achieved by shaping their expectations through two-way communication and education.

Services management also places conditions upon the extent to which these forms of enhanced co-production can be captured by service organizations. Oliveira and von Hippel (2011), for example, argue that innovation through service users will take place only if there is an expectation that service users will benefit from using that service. How much time and resources they have to invest in such activities also bears weight over the extent of their involvement. Furthermore, capitalizing upon the recognized competencies of the consumer co-creators is a challenge for service managers, who have to engage in an active and continuous dialogue with an often diverse group of customers (Prahalad and Ramaswamy 2000). Furthermore, Alam (2006) argues that over-customization in service innovation can result in service fragmentation and inefficiency.

Challenges around enhanced co-production have also emerged from the public administration literature. First, public service organizations are typically highly professionalized and may be resistant to accepting the actual premise of enhanced co-production and the associated sharing of power, or its challenges to their own professionalism (Osborne 1994; Bovaird and Loffler 2003). Secondly, over-empowering service users in service production may lead to inefficiencies in public spending (Peters and Pierre 2000). Finally, introducing consumer mechanisms to enhance co-production is only effective where the results of such activity are implemented to reform the services. Indeed, the use of consumer mechanisms to enhance co-production does not guarantee this level of co-production because service providers can take a passive or even tokenistic approach to responding to these mechanisms (Sinclair 2004).

At the organizational level, innovation has the potential to occur through co-management and co-governance, benefiting from the perceived 'closeness' of third sector organizations to service users. Pestoff and Brandsen (2009) suggest that innovation can be a collective process, involving a network of, in this case, third sector organizations rather than one organization acting alone. As a result, they describe the process of innovation as an interaction between organizations. Inter-organizational working to drive innovation has also been discussed from the services management perspective. Prahalad and Ramaswamy (2000), for example, discuss how organizations and their suppliers collaborate to develop products and share information to ensure need is met.

CAN CO-PRODUCTION DRIVE INNOVATION? THE CASE OF ASYLUM SEEKERS

The second part of this chapter considers the case of asylum seekers and the provision of social welfare services in Glasgow in order to better understand what bearing co-production has on the innovation of these services.

The case of asylum seekers offers a fertile ground through which to explore co-production. Their marginal position in society may affect their capacity to co-produce. Asylum seekers sit in a contentious position, having exercised their legal right under the Geneva Convention (1951) to apply for asylum but remaining a non-citizen while they await the outcome of their case. Their lives are regulated and constrained by strict immigration laws, which are rooted within and built upon 'policies of deterrence' (Williams 2006). The legislation has built a very much stratified system of social rights which limits asylum seekers' access to services and singles them out as a visibly in-need group distinct from mainstream society (Sales 2002). This is compounded by negative media attention and political rhetoric (see, for example, Crawley 2003; Hickley 2009).

Although immigration is a reserved issue, the devolved government in Scotland is responsible for the provision of public services to asylum seekers. Statutory agencies in Scotland are responsible for various support functions, including housing, a reception visit from a case-worker, access to GPs, education for children and social care needs (Wren 2004). Furthermore, the third sector has historically played a leading role in supporting asylum seekers in the UK, responding on an ad hoc basis in reaction to individual crises and establishing support programmes (Wren 2007). Research conducted by Lewis (2006) also suggested greater tolerance for asylum seekers in Scotland than England. Indeed, the Scottish media has latterly tended to be less suspicious of asylum seekers compared with English counterparts (see, for example, Johnston 2003; Anon 2001, 2005).

Despite the more favourable conditions for asylum seekers in Scotland in terms of the rhetoric espoused from the Scottish Government and public perception, they remain a group of non-citizens and this ultimately has implications for the type and extent of their involvement. The identity of non-citizen has a negative impact on their capacity to engage politically. They cannot vote or have a say over the way in which their host country is governed.

The study took a mixed methods approach and comprised three stages. First, using a purposive sample, seven policy interviews were conducted with key national and city-wide organizations, including the Scottish Government and UK Borders Agency. These interviews were used to establish a policy framework for co-production and the trajectory for service user involvement. The second stage was a Glasgow-wide postal survey of service managers in those public service organizations providing social welfare services to asylum seekers and third sector organizations working on behalf of asylum seekers. The survey sampled the whole population of organizations providing social welfare services to asylum seekers in Glasgow; in total 107 questionnaires were sent out and a 40 per cent response rate was achieved. The survey data were used to map the extent of co-production in services for asylum seekers in Glasgow and the institutional forms that this takes.

The final element of the empirical research was a cross-sectional case study of Glasgow. This comprised 24 interviews with service managers and front-line staff and 10 interviews with asylum seekers using the services. In addition, eight direct observations were conducted and key policy and organizational documents were also gathered and analysed. The case study was used to explore the nature of co-production within welfare services for asylum seekers in Glasgow.

Can Co-production Drive Innovation?

The study found confirmatory evidence of each type of co-production. However, the focus here will be on participative, enhanced and organizational types of co-production, as these were described as the most likely drivers of innovation in the preceding discussion.

Innovation through participative co-production

There was some agreement among service providers that participative co-production results in more personalized services which better meet the needs of asylum seekers as service users. Giving asylum seekers a 'voice' was key for most service providers who wanted to give them the space and opportunity to contribute to services. The two most commonly identified mechanisms used to achieve participative co-production were consultation and volunteering.

Various consultation exercises with asylum seekers were observed and discussed by respondents. These typically focused on gathering views around the nature of the service environment and the changes that could be made to improve and tailor services to need. However, respondents also discussed the challenges associated with consulting asylum seekers. Language barriers were significant, particularly when multiple interpreters were present, which made consultation exercises long and convoluted. Also, a challenge lay in getting asylum seekers to contribute to the consultation process, as their focus is invariably upon their own individual needs rather than those of the wider service or, indeed, broader social objectives. A lack of willingness of asylum seekers to engage due to fears of this negatively impacting upon their claim for asylum was also considered a strong barrier to engagement. Despite this, the asylum seekers who participated in the study were largely keen to speak up about the services they receive: 'Nothing would stop me voicing my opinion.'

Volunteering was considered to lead to a host of benefits for asylum seekers, including improving their English, fostering cultural exchange and giving them a sense of self-worth through engaging with the community. Furthermore, asylum seeker volunteers were seen, in some instances, to improve service provision, given their experience and cultural knowledge. One large third sector organization, for example, provided volunteering opportunities for asylum seekers and refugees to support new arrivals to the city. These volunteers were considered well placed to provide support as they had experienced the hardships of the asylum process; the service also benefited from their skill set, cultural knowledge and language skills. Thus, the service was arguably benefiting from what Oliveira and von Hippel (2011) termed 'functional innovations', honing in on the specialized competencies exhibited by past service users (Zwick et al. 2008; Oliveira and von Hippel 2011).

However, participative co-production with asylum seekers was challenging for service providers, who suggested that some participative mechanisms were better suited to the indigenous population. At the local government level, a formal consultation process that facilitates input to decision making does not exist for asylum seekers, and the extent to which structures through which the indigenous population participates are accessible to asylum seekers is dubious. One respondent reflected upon the general challenge of getting service users, and particularly hard-to-reach groups, to engage:

> There's issues about public engagement with services generally; how do we get our service users more involved in the planning and delivery of services? . . . whether it's local homeless people, people with addiction issues, people with learning disabilities, people with mental health problems . . . (Strategic Manager)

Interestingly, however, a respondent from the third sector spoke of the Resident's Association that had been established for asylum seekers to give them a voice in running the accommodation – the first of its kind in the UK.

Although respondents from across the public and third sectors spoke of attempting to involve asylum seekers as partners, akin to those in Arnstein's ladder (1969), in network planning sessions or board meetings, logistical difficulties (e.g. language barriers) and an unwillingness among organizations to have asylum seekers contribute were seen as barriers to deeper forms of participative co-production.

Innovation through enhanced co-production

Developing trusting service relationships with asylum seekers was fundamental. Respondents often referred to the vulnerability of asylum seekers as a group of service users who often needed dedicated support from one individual with whom they could establish and maintain a strong communicative relationship. Not only do these relationships reflect Normann's conception of the 'moment of truth' in service relationships and the importance of individual interactions at the point of service delivery (which is the base point for consumer co-production), they also point to enhanced co-production and innovation at the service level.

There was, for example, a public sector organization that went beyond its original (bureaucratically defined) function of providing accommodation, to ensure new arrivals were aware of other services and were in receipt of the appropriate asylum support. Such a diversification may constitute an innovation at the level of service provision, but it is unclear whether it would transpire into an innovation at the structural level of service provision given that accommodation is also provided by the third and for-profit sectors. The for-profit service provider, in particular, was not deemed to establish the same level of interaction with or care for asylum seeker respondents.

Various consumer mechanisms were also implemented to customize services through enhanced co-production. Service evaluation, for example, was common. The completion of structured 'happy sheets' and broader feedback about how the service made a difference to an individual's life were used to make service improvements and to drive forward innovation in public services. Informal opportunities during service delivery to raise concerns were used as a vehicle to listen to the views of asylum seekers and to improve services in an ad hoc manner. Service providers played an invaluable part, not only providing asylum seekers with choice, but also helping them to make choices about services available through the provision of information and advice.

Examples of innovation through co-creation and customization (Kristensson et al. 2008; Prahalad and Ramaswamy 2000) were also found. One example highlighted that service users can co-create innovations through the design of services to meet needs, rather than through higher-level policy making or strategic planning. A service manager working with young asylum seekers explained that her organization supported asylum seekers to develop a 'Welcome Pack' containing the information that they thought was important: 'And it was young people who came up with the ideas and design.'

Another interesting example pointing to the importance of fostering trust through the service relationship was the orientation service provided by the Scottish arm of a UK-wide third sector organization. The service was described as 'client led', with the service being planned and executed on an individual level:

> We call it . . . non-directional advocacy, so you can advocate on behalf of somebody . . . it's assisting someone who can't quite make their point, not going . . . into a meeting and saying 'She needs this, she needs that.' . . . It is about that person saying 'I would like this service. . .'.

Through the service relationship, trust was built over time, allowing the provider to improve service provision by developing knowledge of what services are required by the individual service user. This example has strong connotations with the co-creation of personalized experiences described by Prahalad and Ramaswamy (2000, 2004).

In terms of customization, a large third sector organization used group-based brainstorming events through sticky note exercises in order to gather views on reviewing its organizational strategy. Such an exercise is closely related to consultations conducted under participative co-production but the difference was the timing of the session, which took place during the service encounter, thereby capitalizing both on the inseparability of service production and consumption and on the relaxed atmosphere in which service providers had established trust with the asylum seekers.

Framework for Dialogue groups operating throughout the city played a dual role as 'information provision networks' and 'consultation mechanisms'. They offered a means through which to achieve service innovations by gathering the views of groups of asylum seekers. The idea underpinning the groups was to provide 'a refugee/asylum seeker voice in the assessment of need process, the development of service bids and in the leadership of the networks themselves' (Service Manager). Indeed, the structure provided a means through which asylum seekers could raise any issues with services with those sitting in more strategic positions. They were linked at an operational level to Integration Networks working in the local areas, upon which various service providers sit to plan services together. The two structures were described as having 'conterminous boundaries', with each sharing the function of 'building bonds'. The direct link with Integration Networks provided asylum seekers participating in Framework for Dialogue groups with a voice in the process of service planning. Furthermore, asylum seekers spoke of the structure as offering a volunteering opportunity, which they associated with a host of benefits which improved the quality of their lives in Scotland.

Innovation through co-management and co-governance

The study also identified various inter-organizational relationships that had become established as a means of improving public service provision. Underpinning these relationships, respondents emphasized a Scottish mindset of partnership working which was facilitated by geography, government support and perceived benefit at an organizational level. Furthermore 'personal' relationships existed across organizational boundaries, both at a strategic and operational level, making it easier to collaborate to improve service provision.

In terms of co-management, the Scottish Government funded both large voluntary organizations and smaller community groups to plan and deliver services for asylum seekers, ranging from support around integration to the provision of drop-in centres or arts and crafts activities. Furthermore, the Scottish Government benefited from the knowledge and trust granted to large charitable organizations, which consulted asylum seekers on its behalf and also had strong links to smaller community organizations. The UK Borders Agency also contracted organizations from the public, for-profit and third sectors to house asylum seekers in Glasgow. However, respondents from the public sector accommodation provider described a tension with the government Agency. Furthermore, the contractual relationship did not promote collaboration on a strategic level, with Scotland tending to be 'tagged on, rather than an integral part to that [policy] cycle' (Strategic Manager). On a policy level, the devolved government was described as easier to work with than Westminster, due to the shared mindset towards integration.

Co-governance was demonstrated at various levels. On the ground, examples were found of organizations working together to deliver shared services such as crèches to allow asylum seekers to use other services and also sports services which were used to promote the integration of asylum seekers. Referring back to Berger and Neuhaus' (1978) conception of mediating structures, respondents from public sector organizations often described third sector organizations as key players, operating between asylum seekers and public sector bodies. Indeed, one manager suggested that rather than implementing participative mechanisms like tenant surveys or participative groups, a 'trusting dialogue' should be facilitated and maintained with 'critical friends' who will take up issues for asylum seekers.

Beyond these relationships, structures operated within the city which facilitated collaborative service planning and delivery. Three models were apparent. First, bodies such as Glasgow City Council, the Scottish Government, the UK Borders Agency and the Scottish Refugee Council sat together on a Strategic Partnership Group that discussed policy at this level.

Secondly, various third sector organizations and public sector agencies (such as the police and Community Healthcare Partnerships) collaborated on Integration Networks to share information and work together to plan services on an operational level (public funds were distributed to Integration Networks via Community Planning Partnerships). The networks were established initially to support asylum seekers and refugees (during the time of this research, the remit had recently been extended to include migrant workers and the settled Black Minority Ethnic communities) and aid their integration into the Scottish community. The networks planned, delivered and evaluated services and also fed back any valid information to funders. This integrated approach was considered to improve service effectiveness and efficiency:

> we want to see the network having a primacy in planning and delivering and monitoring what's happening locally. And it's not that helpful when you've got people operating in a maverick way and wasting money or duplicating services or whatever ... So an integrated approach is something that we would favour. (Service Manager)

Indeed, having relevant organizations and agencies sitting round the table, sharing information and communicating with one another was said to improve service provision, making it easier for the appropriate organizations to be involved at appropriate times.

For service managers networking at the operational level was also important for building relationships, exchanging information and promoting interest in and extending services to other clients. However, being party to such a structure was limited by resources as the extra work it brought could have a detrimental effect on the service providers' day jobs: 'It's easy to get sucked into what the network as a whole is organizing' (Service Manager).

Thirdly, at the neighbourhood level, eight Framework for Dialogue groups were in operation across Glasgow. As mentioned previously, these acted both as an information provision network for asylum seekers and as a consultation mechanism for public service providers. They were depicted as important mechanisms through which operational considerations could be filtered up through Integration Networks to strategic decision-making level. Co-governance thus arguably requires operational collaboration as an essential component of any strategic-level action.

Respondents further emphasized that co-governance may not always be about positive relationships – it may also involve adversarial ones. Indeed, some service providers, particularly from the third sector, played a dual role, managing services and working on an adversarial basis to represent asylum seekers and campaign on their behalf around issues of immigration and for improved services. The perception around this adversarial role differed among respondents. One public official, for example, described the role as: 'Not helpful, not productive because this is an ideal opportunity for them, literally, to get up on their soapbox . . .' (Policy Respondent). Other respondents referred to the strong foundations that had been put in place to facilitate fruitful discussions with other service providers and with government. Respondents recognized that there was a need to communicate up to higher echelons, but recognized the need to communicate as one voice – whether that be for Scotland as a whole or the third sector – and provide evidence in support of any arguments made.

SUMMARY

This chapter has examined the different forms that co-production can take within the provision of public services at both the individual and organizational levels: consumer co-production; participative co-production; enhanced co-production; co-management; and co-governance.

The discussion began by pointing to a new starting point for theorizing about service production, referring to the integral nature of consumer co-production in the production process (Normann 1991; Gronroos 1997; Johnston and Clark 2008). This set the scene for discussion of how innovation in public services can be driven by co-production. While consumer co-production was identified as a means of improving customer satisfaction at the base level, the achievement of broader societal goals, such as integration in the case of asylum seekers, was striven for both through participative and enhanced co-production at the individual level and through co-management and co-governance at the organizational level.

The case study framed participative co-production as an important mechanism which offers asylum seekers a voice in service production. However, this was clouded by logistical challenges such as time, language barriers and hurdles placed by professionals who do not see a place for service users. Enhanced co-production was presented as a more appropriate and fruitful route for innovation in the case of asylum seekers. Building trusting relationships through service interactions was an underpinning feature of the services provided to asylum seekers. The aim, for service providers, was to better understand and therefore meet service users' needs, and, in some cases, to achieve personalized services to cater for individuals' needs.

Inter-organization working through co-management and co-governance has also been described as an important driver of innovation. In the case of asylum seekers, the role of the third sector has been vital. The integrated approach to operational planning which feeds off established service user groups has been developed to improve service effectiveness and efficiency. Furthermore, a similarly integrative (and evidence based) approach has been developed to communicate with government, with the intention of impacting policy.

REFERENCES

Alam, I. (2006). Removing the fuzziness from the fuzzy front-end of service innovations through consumer interactions. *Industrial Marketing Management*, 35, 468–480.
Albury, D. (2005). Fostering innovation in public services. *Public Money and Management*, 25, January, 51–56.

Alford, J. (1998). A public management road less travelled: clients as co-producers of public services. *Australian Journal of Public Administration*, 57(4), 128–137.

Alford, J. (2002). Why do public-sector clients coproduce? *Administration and Society*, 34(1), 32–56.

Anon. (2001). Let Scotland sort out the asylum mess. *The Glasgow Herald*, 14 August.

Anon. (2005). Deal means asylum seeker raids continue. *The Scotsman*, 25 November.

Arnstein, S.A. (1969). A ladder of citizen participation? *Journal of the American Institute of Planners*, 35(2), 216–224.

Berger, P.L. and Neuhaus, R.J. (1978). *To Empower People: The Role of Mediating Structures In Public Policy*. Washington, DC: American Enterprise for Public Policy Research.

Bitner, M.J., Faranda, W.T., Hubbert, A.R. and Zeithaml, V.A. (1997). Customer contributions and roles in service delivery. *International Journal of Service Industry Management*, 8(3), 193–205.

Bovaird, T. (2005). Public governance: balancing stakeholder power in a network society. *International Review of Administrative Sciences*, 71(2), 217–228.

Bovaird, T. (2007). Beyond engagement and participation – user and community co-production of public services. *Public Administration Review*, 67, 846–860.

Bovaird, T. and Downe, J. (2009). *Innovation in Public Engagement and Co-production of Services*. Policy Paper for the Department of Communities and Local Government. Cardiff: Cardiff Business School.

Bovaird, T. and Loffler, E. (2003). Understanding public management and governance. In T. Bovaird and E. Loffler (eds), *Public Management and Governance*. London: Routledge, pp. 3–12.

Brandsen, T. and Pestoff, V. (2006). Co-production, the third sector and the delivery of public services. *Public Management Review*, 8(4), 493–501.

Brenton, M. (1985). *The Voluntary Sector in British Social Services*. London: Longman.

Brudney, J.L. and England, R.E. (1983). Toward a definition of the co-production concept. *Public Administration Review*, January/February, 59–65.

Crawley, H. (2003). Presumed guilty: asylum seekers are now portrayed not only as welfare scroungers, but as would-be terrorists too. *The Guardian*, 22 January.

Gronroos, C. (2007). *Service Management and Marketing: Customer Management in Service Competition*, 3rd edn. Chichester: John Wiley and Sons.

Hartley, J.F. and Benington, J. (2006). Copy and paste, or graft and transplant? Knowledge sharing through inter-organizational networks. *Public Money and Management*, 26, 101–108.

Haugh, H. and Kitson, M. (2007). The third way and the third sector: New Labour's economic policy and the social economy. *Cambridge Journal of Economics*, 31, 973–994.

Hickley, M. (2009). 90% of failed asylum seekers remain in the UK – and the backlog of undecided cases doubles in a year. *Daily Mail*, 23 January.

Jack, R. (1995). Empowerment in community care. In R. Jack (ed.), *Empowerment in Community Care*. London: Chapman and Hall, pp. 11–42.

Johnston, I. (2003). Work ban on asylum seekers condemned. *Scotland on Sunday*, 25 May.

Johnston, R. and Clark, G. (2008). *Service Operations Management: Improving Service Delivery*. Harlow: Prentice Hall.

Jung, T. (2010). Citizens, co-producers, customers, clients, captives? A critical review of consumerism and public services. *Public Management Review*, 12(3), 439–446.

Kearns, A. (1995). Active citizenship and local governance: political and geographical dimensions. *Political Geography*, 14(2), 155–175.

Kristensson, P., Matthing, J. and Johansson, N. (2008). Key strategies for the successful involvement of customers in the co-creation of new technology-based services. *International Journal of Service Industry Management*, 19(4), 474–491.

Levine, C. and Fisher, G. (1984). Citizenship and service delivery: the promise of co-production. *Public Administration Review*, 44, 178–189.

Lewis, M. (2006). *Warm Welcome? Understanding Public Attitudes to Asylum Seekers in Scotland*. London: Institute for Public Policy Research.

Magnusson, P.R. (2003). Benefits of involving users in service innovation. *European Journal of Innovation Management*, 6(4), 228–238.

Moore, M. and Hartley, J. (2008). Innovations in governance. *Public Management Review*, 10(1), 3–20.

Normann, R. (1991). *Service Management: Strategy and Leadership in Service Business*, 2nd edn. Chichester: John Wiley and Sons.

Oliveira, P. and von Hippel, E. (2011). Users as service innovators: the case of banking services. *Research Policy*, 40, 806–818.

Osborne, S. (1994). The language of empowerment. *International Journal of Public Sector Management*, 7(3), 56–62.

Osborne, S. (2010). Delivering public services: time for a new theory? *Public Management Review*, 12(1), 1–10.

Osborne, S., Bond, S., McQuaid, R. and Honore, E. (2011). *The Opportunities and Challenges of the Changing*

Public Services Landscape for the Third Sector in Scotland: A Longitudinal Study Year One Report: Baseline Findings. Edinburgh: Scottish Government.

Ostrom, E. (1972). Metropolitan reform: propositions derived from two traditions. *Social Science Quarterly*, 53, 474–493.

Parks, R.B., Baker, P.C., Kiser, L., Oakerson, R., Ostrom, E., Ostrom, V., Percy, S.L., Vandivort, M.B., Whitaker, G.P. and Wilson, R. (1981). Consumers as co-producers of public services: some economic and institutional considerations. *Policy Studies Journal*, 9(7), 1001–1011.

Pestoff, V. (2006). Citizens and co-production of welfare services. *Public Management Review*, 8(4), 503–519.

Pestoff, V. and Brandsen, T. (2009). *The Governance of Co-production*. Paper presented at the 13th Annual Conference of the International Research Society for Public Management, 6–8 April, Copenhagen.

Pestoff, V., Osborne, S.P. and Brandsen, T. (2006). Patterns of co-production in public services. *Public Management Review*, 8(4), 591–595.

Peters, B.G. and Pierre, J. (2000). Citizens versus the new public manager: the problem of mutual empowerment. *Administration and Society*, 32(1), 9–28.

Prahalad, C.K. and Ramaswamy, V. (2000). Co-opting customer competence. *Harvard Business Review*, January/February, 79–87.

Prahalad, C.K. and Ramaswamy, V. (2004). Co-creation experiences: the next practice in value creation. *Journal of Interactive Marketing*, 18(3), 5–14.

Rosentraub, M. and Warren, R. (1987). Citizen participation in the production of urban services. *Public Productivity Review*, 10(3), 75–89.

Sales, R. (2002). The deserving and undeserving? Refugees, asylum seekers and welfare in Britain. *Critical Social Policy*, 22, 456–478.

Sinclair, R. (2004). Participation in practice: making it meaningful, effective and sustainable. *Children and Society*, 18, 106–118.

Tritter, J.Q. and McCallum, A. (2006). The snakes and ladders of user involvement: moving beyond Arnstein. *Health Policy*, 76, 156–168.

Vargo, S.L., Maglio, P.P. and Archpru Akaka, M. (2008). On value and value co-creation: a service systems and service logic perspective. *European Journal of Management*, 26, 145–152.

Venetis, K. and Ghauri, P. (2004). Service quality and customer retention. *European Journal of Marketing*, 38(11/12), 1577–1598.

von Hippel, E. (2007). Horizontal innovation networks – by and for users. *Industrial and Corporate Change*, 16(2), 293–315.

Whitaker, G.P. (1980). Coproduction: citizen participation in service delivery. *Public Administration Review*, May/June, 240–246.

Williams, L. (2006). Social networks of refugees in the United Kingdom: tradition, tactics and new community spaces. *Journal of Ethnic and Migration Studies*, 32(5), 865–879.

Wren, K. (2004). *Building Bridges: Local Responses to the Resettlement of Asylum Seekers in Glasgow*. Glasgow: Scottish Centre for Research on Social Justice.

Wren, K. (2007). Supporting asylum seekers and refugees in Glasgow: the role of multi-agency networks. *Journal of Refugee Studies*, 20(3), 391–413.

Zwick, D., Bonsu, S.K. and Darmody, A. (2008). Putting consumers to work: co-creation and new marketing govern-mentality. *Journal of Consumer Culture*, 8(2), 163–196.

26. The once and future pioneers? The innovative capacity of voluntary organizations and the provision of public services: a longitudinal approach[1, 2]

Stephen P. Osborne, Celine Chew and Kate McLaughlin

THEORETICAL AND EMPIRICAL BACKGROUND

The innovative capacity of voluntary and community organizations (VCOs) as public service providers has long been a key assertion of the public policy debate in the UK, stretching back for almost one hundred years. This ascribed capacity has its basis in historical fact, as VCOs were the prime innovators of social welfare, and other, public services in the nineteenth century (Webb and Webb 1911). Subsequently this perception became embedded as the official view of this capacity (e.g. Beveridge 1948; Ministry of Health 1959; Home Office 1990; Labour Party 1990). Yet, despite such reification of this innovative capacity, little research has taken place to evaluate this claim. The only study of any substance is the American study of Kramer (1981) – now limited both by its American context and considerable age. Reviewing the literature in 1998, Osborne (1998a) concluded that such studies as there were, were limited by: (i) their reliance on normative argument rather than empirical data; (ii) their lack of attention to the mainstream innovation studies literature (e.g. Rogers and Shoemaker 1971; Rothwell 1975; Abernathy et al. 1983; Van de Ven et al. 1989; Herbig 1991) and the potential that this literature has for offering theoretical and empirical insights into the public service context; and (iii) the possibility of situating this capacity within a contingent framework that recognized the impact of the public policy environment upon innovativeness.

In the broader public services arena, there have also been a limited number of studies of innovation in public services (see Osborne and Brown 2005 for a more extensive literature review). Most notably in this literature, Borins (2001) has explored the public policy–public services delivery interface and its impact on innovation in public services. Despite its importance, this work is hampered in its applicability to the UK by its national specificity within the US public policy system. In a European context, Koch and his colleagues in the EU *Publin* programme (e.g. Koch and Hauknes 2005; Malikova and Staranova 2005; Koch et al. 2006) have explored the public policy context of innovation within public service organizations in the European Union. However, whilst this is useful work at the industry level, the issue of the innovative capacity of VCOs is wholly absent from their work.

Finally, much of this work has not been grounded in the 'innovation studies' literature, above, that might give a more robust theoretical, as opposed to normative or empirical, basis to the debate (Osborne and Brown 2005). Consequently the previous work of the lead author of this chapter (Osborne 1998a), in the 1990s, was the first research study in the UK that:

- mapped this innovative capacity of VCOs and developed a contingent model of it, within the field of social welfare in the UK; and
- drew upon the organization theory and innovation studies literature to inform our understanding of the innovative capacity of VCOs.

Crucially it developed a typology of innovation (Osborne 1998c) in the social sector that differentiated between:

- *the traditional activity of VCOs* in providing specialist services but without any significant element of change or innovation (situated within the 'traditional organizations' in this chapter);
- *the developmental activity of VCOs* involved in the incremental change of their services (situated within the 'developmental organizations' in this chapter); and
- *the innovative activity of VCOs* that changed the paradigm of their services and/or their skills base (situated within the 'innovative organizations' in this chapter) – and also separated this innovative activity into three distinct modes, as discussed further below.

It is important to note that this differentiation does not suggest any normative difference between these modes of work – they can all have a positive or negative impact upon an organization or its services (see, for example, Rosner 1967; Kimberly 1981; Mole and Elliot 1987). Over time, for example, a series of smaller service innovations may produce a much more profound effect upon a service than a single innovation (e.g. Van de Ven 1998). However, as the innovation studies literature makes clear, innovation does pose distinctive organizational and managerial challenges, compared with either traditional or developmental activity.

Osborne (1998c) argued further that the innovative capacity of VCOs was not a function of their organizational characteristics, such as their structure or culture (as much of the policy literature invariably suggested), but rather it arose out of the interaction of these organizations with their institutional and policy environments. *That is, it was the action and policy context created by central and local government that encouraged innovative activity by VCOs rather than it being an inherent consequence of their organizational structure or culture.* Subsequent work by other researchers has confirmed and developed this model in other fields beyond social care – such as the work of Walker et al. (2001) in the field of housing.

PURPOSE OF THIS CHAPTER

The original study by Osborne (1998a) provided a significant empirical study of the organizational and environmental factors that mediated the innovative capacity of VCOs in the provision of social care services. The present chapter reports on the longitudinal development of this original study and considers its implications both for public management theory and for the policy context and management of public services. Such longitudinal studies are an essential part of the social science process and allow both original hypotheses to be re-tested and a test of the impact of changing contingencies upon emergent models – though they have been frequently lacking in the field of public management.

METHODOLOGY

This chapter utilizes survey and case study data from two studies carried out in 1994 and 2006 in three localities in England – an urban, suburban and rural locality. The purpose is to map the extent of the innovative, developmental and traditional activity of VCOs, to examine any key differences between them across the two studies, and to explore the potential contingencies that might explain the innovative capacity of VCOs.

The initial plan had been for an exact replication in 2006 of the 1994 study. However, at a late juncture the key stakeholder for one of the original research sites (the suburban locus) withdrew involvement because of its own financial crisis and subsequently a replacement locality was identified. Whilst this diminishes the exact replication of the original research, it nonetheless provides a robust longitudinal test of the sustainability of the innovative capacity of VCOs. Three loci were thus surveyed in each study – an urban (Midwell), suburban (Bellebury in 1994 and Siliton in 2006) and rural (Southshire) locus.[3]

The survey element of each study was based upon cluster sampling, which excluded pre-stratification of the sample population and used rather a census of all identifiable VCOs in each locality (de Vaus 1986). Such an approach might not provide a precise sampling frame for the VCO sector in each locality. However, given the poor quality of most local databases about the sector (see Osborne and Hems 1995 for a discussion of this issue), such an approach provided a convincing sampling frame for this study.

In the survey, respondents were invited to say whether they had been involved in developing a new service over the past three years, and to describe it. Where respondents identified a new service, this was classified using a typology of innovation developed by the author (Osborne 1998b). This classified the new work of VCOs along two dimensions – its *mode of production* (whether it was a modification of an existing service of the organization or the growth of a new one) and its *market* (whether it was serving an existing client group/need of the organization or a new one). This produced a classification of four types of new services – three innovative forms (that differentiated further the work of the innovative VCOs identified above) and one of incremental development (that refers to the work of the developmental VCOs above).[4] These are:

- *total innovation* (involving working with a new client group and providing new services);
- *expansionary innovation* (involving working with a new client group, but using the existing services/methods of work of the organization);
- *evolutionary innovation* (involving working with the same client group, but providing new services); and

- *incremental development* (involving working with the same client group and providing the same services, but incrementally improving them).[5]

In addition to these four modes of organizational change, *traditional* service delivery was identified, where VCOs continued to provide their existing services to their existing client group, without any change or development (the traditional VCOs, above).

Inevitably such a classificatory process involves the exercise of judgement by the lead researcher. In these studies both the reliability and validity of these judgements were tested. Their reliability was tested by a test–retest process whereby a random sample of 10 per cent of the questionnaires was reclassified by this researcher after a three month interval, with 93 per cent agreement in both studies. Their validity was approached in two ways. First, methodological triangulation was used (Denzin 1970) to cross-validate the findings of the study through the use of two approaches to data analysis – Chi-Square tests and Discriminant Analysis. Secondly, the judgement of the lead researcher in allocating each questionnaire response to one of the five classificatory domains above was validated by asking another member of the research team to similarly classify a random 10 per cent sample of the questionnaires. This produced an 80 per cent level of agreement in the 1994 study and a 90 per cent level in 2006, suggesting a robust level of validity in the judgements exercised.

Subsequent to this survey, three cross-sectional case studies of the innovative capacity of VCOs were carried out – one in each of the research sites. These involved ten mini-case studies of VCOs in each locality, covering the range of innovative, developmental and traditional VCOs. They utilized semi-structured interviews with a range of organizational staff together with interviews with key national and local stakeholders. They explored whether the innovative capacity of VCOs was structured by one of four contingencies – the structural characteristics of VCOs, their internal culture, their external environment and their relationship with it, and their institutional and public policy context. The findings presented here combine data from both these approaches.

SURVEY FINDINGS[6]

Table 26A.1[7] lays out the profile of the innovative activity of VCOs in both the 1994 and 2006 surveys. The original study found that innovation was a significant but not all-embracing activity for VCOs – 37.9 per cent of organizations were engaged in innovative activity. Almost 13.9 per cent of VCOs were also engaged in developmental activity, whilst just over 48.2 per cent continued their traditional work, without modification.

The contrast in 2006 is stark. In this survey, the innovative activity of VCOs has shrunk to 19.1 per cent whilst their developmental work has increased to 35.7 per cent. The traditional activity has stayed almost constant at 45.2 per cent. *Therefore, far from being a constant element of the organizational activity of VCOs, innovation appears as a contingent variable.* This contrast is shown diagrammatically in Figure 26A.1.

An important conclusion of the 1994 study was that governmental policy, at a central and local level, was the key contingency in the priming of the innovative capacity of VCOs, rather than any inherent organizational characteristics. A question raised by this replication study was therefore: *have the policy imperatives of governmental policy changed to lessen the innovative imperative upon VCOs?* This is returned to later in this chapter.

Further light is thrown upon this pattern of innovative, developmental and traditional activity, as defined above, when the organizational characteristics of the three types of VCOs were compared through the use of Chi-Square tests. In 1994, little was found to differentiate the innovative and developmental VCOs. The developmental VCOs did tend to be older (i.e. founded at least six years previously) than their innovative counterparts and the innovative organizations were less likely to be purely volunteer based – though neither of these relationships was statistically significant. Developmental organizations were significantly more likely to have larger staff groups than innovative organizations and the innovative VCOs accounted for almost 95 per cent of the smaller organizations with less than five paid staff. Little continuity exists between 1994 and 2006 in this pattern. In 2006, and in contrast with 1994, innovative VCOs were significantly more likely to be younger organizations than their developmental counterparts and significantly larger.

In terms of the distinction between the innovative and traditional VCOs, a stable pattern of certain characteristics emerged across 1994 and 2006. The innovative VCOs were significantly more likely than the traditional VCOs

- to be younger organizations (i.e. founded in the last five years);
- to have some paid staff (i.e. at least a half-time member of paid staff), rather than being volunteer based alone;
- to be other- rather than self-oriented (i.e. to be concerned with the needs of members of the wider community rather than of their own members only); and
- to have substantial governmental funding (from either service contracts or grants) rather than voluntary income or fees.

With regard to funding patterns, in 1994, the innovative organizations had accounted for 73.8 per cent of those VCOs citing governmental funding as their most significant source of income (whilst the traditional organizations accounted for 64.2 per cent of those citing voluntary income and fees as their major income source). By 2006 this had shifted appreciably. Traditional VCOs still accounted for the baulk of those organizations with voluntary income and fees as their major funding source (76.6 per cent). However, they now also accounted for 59.3 per cent of those VCOs with substantial governmental funding. In contrast to 1994, the innovative VCOs were split equally between the two funding sources – though with a non-significant orientation towards governmental funding.

It should be emphasized that these statistics do not provide any *predictors* of the innovative activity of VCOs. They simply describe different groups of organizations rather than imbue any causality into the classification. The appropriate formulation is thus the descriptive 'innovative VCOs tend to have at least one member of paid staff' rather than the causal 'because a VCO has at least one member of paid staff it is likely to be an innovator'. To explore the potential predictors of innovative activity, it was necessary to employ the more predicative statistical approach of Discriminant Analysis (Eisenbis and Avery 1972; Klecka 1980).

The Discriminant Analysis

In this stage of the analysis, the relationship between the dependent variable (innovation status) and seven independent variables (age, location, client group, the presence (and number) of volunteers, the presence (and size) of a paid staff group, organizational orientation and major funding source) was explored. Using SPSS (the Statistical Package for the Social Sciences), the analysis proceeded in a stepwise manner, removing a variable as its contribution to the analysis was identified.

In the 1994 study, two discriminating functions were identified. The first function included three variables: government funding, VCOs aged under six years old and the absence of paid staff (this latter variable as a negative one). The second function also included three variables: charging fees for services, employment of six or more paid staff and the absence of paid staff. The first variable was found to be by far the strongest one, accounting for 83.48 per cent of the variance in the analysis and with an eigenvalue[8] of 0.5407. This function differentiated between the innovative and traditional organizations. Taking the canonical coefficients into account, this function was found to correlate positively with the innovative organizations and negatively with the traditional ones. The second function was much weaker, accounting for only 16.52 per cent of the variance in the analysis and with a comparatively low eigenvalue of 0.1070. It correlated positively with the developmental organizations but with a very weak predicative power – indeed random choice was more successful than this function in predicting the developmental organizations (Osborne 1998a, pp. 98–105).

This analysis thus confirmed that it was possible to differentiate between innovative and traditional VCOs in 1994 on the basis of the organizational characteristics identified above. Whilst a second function was allied to the developmental organizations, its discriminating ability was extremely weak.

In the 2006 study, two discriminating functions were uncovered sharing three significant variables: VCOs being aged under six years, the absence of paid staff, and five and under paid staff employed. In function one, all three variables are significant coefficients, though in function two only the variable of five or more paid staff is significant (as measured by the standardized canonical coefficients of the Discriminant Function). Function one is also revealed to be the most powerful, accounting for 79 per cent of the variance in the analysis. However, the eigenvalues for both functions are low, suggesting that they are not as robust as the functions identified in 1994. This is emphasized further by the high values of Wilks Lambda in the functions in 2006 (0.727 and 0.921 respectively) compared with 1994. This coefficient has a maximum value of 1.0 and varies in inverse proportion to the discriminating power of the functions, again suggesting that this power is much weaker in 2006 than in 1994.

Finally, Figure 26A.2 displays diagrammatically the relationship between these two functions and the VCO population in 2006. Again, function one is discriminating most strongly between the innovative and traditional VCOs whilst function two discriminates (weakly) the developmental organizations from both the other groups.

Discussion of the Survey Data

These longitudinal data have revealed two significant trends. On the one hand, the innovative capacity of VCOs appears to have shrunken appreciably over this period – from
37.9 per cent to 19.1 per cent (Table 26A.1). On the other hand, whilst the work of the
traditional and non-innovative, organizations has remained roughly static (48.2 per cent
and 45.2 per cent respectively), there has been a dramatic and inverse growth in the
amount of developmental work carried out by VCOs – from 13.9 per cent to 35.7 per cent.
As identified above, this is work carried out by VCOs involving some incremental service
improvement but not characterized by the discontinuity that is a core characteristic of
innovative change.

   One could explain this shift between the innovative and developmental work of VCOs
in three ways. First, that it is a product of unreliability and a lack of validity in the data
analysis process employed – and particularly of the judgement exercised by the research
team in denoting the activity of a VCO as innovative, developmental or traditional.
However, the earlier reliability and validity checks carried out precisely on this judgement
(in both 1994 and 2006) would seem to discount this as an explanation.

   Secondly, it may be that the amount of innovative work of VCOs has indeed simply
shrunken and the developmental work has increased.

   Finally, the explanation may lie with those VCOs engaged in developmental work. The
1994 study found that many 'developmental' VCOs actually portrayed their work as
innovative – because this was essential if they were to receive funding under the dominant
government schemes at that time. Therefore, it is possible that underlying this shift of
emphasis between the innovative and developmental work of VCOs is in fact a change to
the institutional framework, established by government, for VCO public service provision
– that is, innovation is no longer a core policy driver and expectation of VCOs and so
there is no longer any need for VCOs to portray their work as innovative, irrespective of
its true merit. In this context it is interesting to note that, in the 2006 survey, governmental funding has disappeared from the Discriminant function, which has remained fairly
constant otherwise. This raises the question as to whether it was precisely this governmental funding that was driving the innovative capacity of VCOs (both in terms of
encouraging genuine innovation and in terms of encouraging VCOs to portray their
developmental work as innovative) in 1994 but which has now begun to drive developmental work instead. The cross- sectional case studies therefore explored this specific
question in more detail.[9]

THE POLICY FRAMEWORK FOR INNOVATION IN PUBLIC SERVICES AND VCOs

The Policy Framework in 1994

It is unquestionably true that innovation was seen as a core element of the provision of
social care services by VCOs in the early 1990s. At the broadest policy level, the introduction of non-statutory, and especially VCO, service providers was argued to stimulate the
development of services that 'met individual needs in a more flexible and innovative way'

(Department of Health 1989, para. 3.4.3), and the influential Griffiths Report had also argued for the use of VCOs to provide social care services in order 'to widen consumer choice, stimulate innovation and encourage efficiency' (Griffiths 1988, para. 1.3.4). One influential commentator at the time argued that this shift was itself a paradigmatic shift from the community development roots of social care (as epitomized by Abrams et al. 1989) and towards one of 'market development and market management' (Wistow et al. 1994, p. 22; see also Le Grand 1991).

This policy focus on innovation as a normative good was also mirrored in the key professional social care organizations at the time. The Kings Fund Institute (1987) had early argued for the centrality of innovation in the impending 'Griffiths Report' community care reforms. In a similar vein, Smale and Tuson (1990) at the National Institute of Social Work argued for innovation to become 'almost synonymous with social work' (p. 158).

A key policy driver in 1994 was undoubtedly the influential 'New Right' think-tank, the Adam Smith Institute, epitomized by the work of its Director, Madsen Pirie (1988) and which embraced the model of competitive advantage (Porter 1985). This placed innovation at the heart of the effective workings of the market. Its tenets are well summarized by Nelson (1993): 'For-profit business firms in rivalous competition with each other are the featured actors [in innovation]. Firms innovate in order to gain competitive advantage over their rivals . . . A firm that successfully innovates can profit handsomely' (p. 364).

It has been argued convincingly elsewhere that it was this model of competitive advantage that influenced the public policy models of the Conservative government of the early 1990s, predicated upon assumptions that the introduction of market disciplines to public services would lead to both greater economy and efficiency in service delivery (see Wistow et al. 1996 for a full discussion of this issue).

As innovation thus became more ingrained in public policy in the early 1990s, so too did the ascribed role of VCOs in bringing this capacity to the provision of public services. This was embodied both by the then efficiency scrutiny of VCOs by the government (Home Office 1990), that lauded their ability to be 'in the forefront of developing new [public] service approaches', and the pronouncements of both the Labour and Conservative Parties in the run-up to the 1992 general election (Labour Party 1990; National Council for Voluntary Organisations 1991). Finally, the VCO sector was itself not slow in heralding its innovative capacity, in its efforts to establish itself as a mainstream public service provider alongside, or instead of, local government (e.g. Burridge 1990).

This macro-level public policy context influenced profoundly the structure of government funding of VCOs in the early 1990s. Thus, the then Department of Health placed innovation firmly at the heart of its funding rules for VCOs. An example of this was Section 64 of the *Health Services and Public Health Act 1968*. In the early 1990s, the first page of the application form for these grants emphasized that, for a VCO project to be considered for a grant, it 'must be innovatory'. Similar conditions were also found in the 'Inner City Partnership Scheme' of the Department of the Environment. Finally, the Department of Health also adopted the 'outcome funding' model of the Rensselaerville Institute (Williams and Webb 1992) as a means through which to stimulate innovation in relation to the Department's 'Drugs and Specific Alcohol Grants 1994–1995' – and engaged the self-styled 'Innovation Group' to administer this scheme.

The 1994 study found this national public policy emphasis upon innovation as key funding parameter of VCOs active at the local level also. All three local authorities in the case study sites had strategic plans on their relationship with the VCO sector and all emphasized the importance of their innovative capacity. The Bellebury document asserted that VCOs had a 'capacity to innovate, experiment and test new ideas' and explicitly related funding them to their ability to innovate in public services delivery, whilst the Midwell document identified innovation as one of four key funding priorities in relation to VCOs (Osborne 1998a, p. 150).

Importantly, as well as being a policy imperative, innovation was also seen as a useful tool through which to allocate scarce resources. One central government policy officer in 1994 explained that they did not use a strict definition of innovation but rather used a loose one that 'allowed [us] to support and help [VCOs] to do things that we would like them to do' – a position echoed at the time by the Research Director of one of the large charitable Foundations that funded VCO activity. This approach to innovation as an allocative mechanism invariably drew an angry response from VCO workers:

> Things have to be innovative for the [funding body], whether they are needed or not. It's just dressing things up as innovative to get money. What we want is an appropriate response to an appropriate problem ... but we have to dress it up as innovative for them. The process is tortuous. (Quoted in Osborne 1998a, p. 151)

Finally, as at the national level, VCOs were not slow to ascribe to themselves this innovative capacity, if they thought that it could assist in gaining governmental funding. For example, a leading VCO intermediary body in Southshire in 1994 prefaced its contribution to the Community Plan of the local authority by emphasizing the 'adaptive and innovative' character of VCOs in that area.

The early 1990s thus presented a set of interlocking factors that all privileged the ascribed innovative capacity of VCOs as a core expectation when they sought governmental funding:

- a government influenced by the market approach to the provision of public services and the centrality of competition and of innovation to this;
- subsequently, government public policy that required innovation as a precondition of governmental funding of VCOs;
- practice at a local level that both reflected these national priorities and that used innovation as a useful tool by which to allocate scarce public resources; and
- both local and national VCOs actively encouraging the perception of themselves as innovative in order to attract governmental funding and to assert their hegemony over local government as the 'provider of first choice' for public services.

The net result of these factors, it is argued, was both to encourage VCOs to engage in innovative activity rather than to provide and/or develop their traditional 'specialist' services *and* to portray their services as innovative, irrespective of their true nature, in order to gain governmental funding within the prevailing rules of the game at the time.

The Policy Framework in 2006

Analysis of the core policy documents from the contemporary period and the stakeholder interviews from the three cross-sectional case study sites reveals three significant changes in the place of innovation in public policy and the role that VCOs can play in it. These are:

- a reformulation of innovation not as discontinuity but as 'continual improvement';
- a re-evaluation of the role of the VCO sector in innovation in public services; and
- a changing orientation towards innovation at the local level, in terms of the operation of funding regimes for public services.

The reformulation of innovation

At the outset it is vital to emphasize that innovation has not disappeared from the public policy environment. This is far from the truth. Innovation has been at the core of the 'modernizing government' agenda of the current Labour government since the publication of the *Modernising Government* White Paper in 1999 (Cabinet Office 1999). At that time, the Public Audit Forum emphasized that this White Paper 'encourages public bodies to adopt innovative and flexible approaches to [public] service delivery' (Public Audit Forum 1999). Subsequently, national government initiatives such as the Invest to Save Budget have been predicated upon the need 'to promote successful innovation and to deliver better public services' (House of Commons Select Committee of Public Accounts 2003, p. 2), whilst the National Endowment for Science, Technology and the Arts (NESTA) has emphasized the links between innovation in public services, public procurement policy and the efficient and effective provision of public services (NESTA 2007).

What has occurred, however, has been a reformulation of the nature of innovation. As noted, in 1994 that understanding of innovation was rooted in Porter's model of competitive advantage and it emphasized the view of innovation as 'creative destruction' by which existing service paradigms were transformed by discontinuous organizational change. This approach is at the heart of the innovation studies literature and is encapsulated in the definition and classification of innovation used in this study and presented above.

Significantly, the view of innovation employed within the current policy framework is profoundly different – and indeed somewhat at odds with the academic advisors to the government who have continued to emphasize the transformational nature of innovation (e.g. Hartley 2006). The *Modernising Government* White Paper (Cabinet Office 1999) portrays innovation as central to creating a culture of organizational learning by public service organizations – and the creation of 'learning organizations' (Argyris and Schon 1978; Senge 1990). It situates innovation not as a process of organizational discontinuity and transformation but rather as one of the '*continuous improvement* in central government policy making and service delivery' (para. 4.9, our emphasis).

Such an approach has been central to a range of policy documents since the publication of the 1999 White Paper (such as National Audit Office 2005; Prime Minister's Strategy Unit 2006; Museums Libraries Archives Partnership 2007), as well as to the Best Value performance regime for local authorities (e.g. Office of the Deputy Prime Minister 2003).

The reformulation is best captured, though, in the text of a speech by the British Prime Minister, Tony Blair, in 2004. This criticized the 'failed neo-conservative experiment' that relied upon markets and competition to drive forward public services and offered an alternative vision:

> Public services have a crucial role to play in our society . . . [I]t is only by truly transferring power to the public through choice, through personalising services, through enhanced account-ability, that we can create the drivers for *continuous improvement* in all our services . . . [O]ur strategy for *continuous improvement* [in public services] through giving power to people involves greater choice, greater voice and more personalised services. (Blair 2004, our emphases)

Re-evaluating the role of VCOs in innovation in public services

The early part of this chapter noted the reification of the innovative capacity of VCOs in public policy from the turn of the twentieth century up to the mid 1990s. Current govern-ment policy, whilst not dismissing this, is rather more circumspect. The influential *Cross Cutting Review* of the role of the sector in delivering public services (H.M. Treasury 2002) noted that, whilst 'at best' VCOs could be 'flexible and innovative', the extent of this was 'difficult to test and . . . the empirical evidence was inconsistent'.

In subsequent policy documents, both the VCO and public sectors are posed as equally innovative, though with problems of sustainability (Office of the Third Sector 2006, para. 93). Crucially, the innovative capacity of VCOs is argued not as something intrinsic to the sector but rather as a capacity that can only be activated in partnership with govern-ment:

> The third sector's potential to improve public services and help deliver better value for money can only be fully realised if there is joint working with local authorities . . . to help the sector build its capacity to play a more effective role. (H.M. Treasury/Cabinet Office 2006)

From being the pre-eminent source of innovation in public services, the VCO sector has thus become a conditional one – and then only under the hegemony of the govern-ment.

The changing orientation towards funding VCOs at the local level

An important starting point for understanding the institutional framework for the inno-vative work of VCOs at the local level is the observed gap between the policy level and actually existing management practice in the delivery of public services. Mulgan and Aubury (2003), drawing attention to this gap, have concluded that in reality innovation is invariably 'an optional extra or an added burden' for public sector organizations, rather than a core activity.

This observation is verified when the commissioning guidance for these organizations in relation to VCOs is examined. A key document here is the guidance issued by the Office of the Third Sector (2006). This fifty-seven page document does indeed contain two pages exhorting the importance of innovation by VCOs. Its recommendations, however, are precisely the sort of 'add ons' noted by Mulgan and Aubrey – an 'Innovation Exchange' and an 'Innovation Team' within the Office of the Third Sector, for example, rather than mainstream service requirements. Moreover, in its detailed guidance on commissioning and procurement, covering thirteen pages, there is no mention of how to optimize the innovative activity of VCOs by these processes.

If the reality of government practice in relation to the innovative capacity of VCOs does not seem to match up to the public policy framework, this becomes even more problematic at the local level. Here, the spending targets and assessments of local government dominate – and nowhere is innovative activity recognized in these. This was made quite explicit by both the local authority and the VCO staff in the cross-sectional case studies:

> Everything is funding-led of course. It is impossible to make a strategic decision to take a certain direction, like to be innovative and then look for money. You have to follow the money. It's all targets. And innovation is not one of them. (CVS[10] organizer in Southshire)

> The role [of VCOs] has changed. I'd have given you a different answer in the nineties. Now the ability of the statutory bodies in the Partnership to fund innovation is reduced dramatically. This is because of changes in government policy and funding streams. We no longer fund the sector to innovate. And we are very unhappy mainstreaming innovations as well. We just don't have the capacity to do this. So we say 'why bother funding a pilot scheme if we can't afford to mainstream it?' The capacity has gone. (Local authority representative in Southshire Local Strategic Partnership)

> Local Area Agreements? A good idea gone wrong. They are too top down and lacked reality at the sharp end. It's all set by above to targets from above. Innovation doesn't figure. (District Authority Service Manager in Southshire)

> We do need the voluntary sector to innovate. Local government doesn't have the capacity. We are driven by statutory duties. But now so is the voluntary sector through our commissioning. We need to re-create freedom to fail. We've lost it. Risk management and minimization dominates our commissioning – and this destroys the freedom to fail and the capacity to innovate. (Local Authority member of Siliton Local Strategic Partnership)

> When I first came into the [voluntary] sector it was all innovation. You couldn't get money for anything else. Now the irony is it's all changed. Local government doesn't want innovation anymore. You can develop a service, yes. Especially if it helps you to meet a target. But innovation? Not a chance – too risky and it doesn't feature on the targets radar. Maybe it will come around again – who knows? (Manager of VCO in Siliton)

> The strength of voluntary organizations is that they do things differently. They innovate. But our contract specifications don't encourage or reward this. It's lost. It is funding driven. We can only buy services now that fit our specifications and targets – and innovation is not one of these. (Midwell Social Services Department Service Manager)

> Innovation is not a burning issue any more. The key issue for [local government] is the transfer of public services – getting them off their books and onto ours. It's transfer not transformation the government wants! (Manager of local VCO in Midwell)

CONCLUSIONS

Using longitudinal data from two research studies in 1994 and 2006, this chapter has demonstrated a reduction in the innovative activity of VCOs and a concomitant increase in their developmental activity over this period. Far from being a 'constant' in terms of their role in delivering public services, innovation has been revealed as a variable. It has been argued that the prime driver for this shifting pattern of organizational activity has been a significant change in the public policy context of VCOs. In 1994 this context privileged innovative activity above other types of activity. This led VCOs both to focus more of their activity on innovative work and to portray their other work as innovative, irrespective of its true nature, in order to gain governmental funding.

In 2006, this context has shifted to favour the development and provision of specialist services that enable local authorities to meet their own performance targets from central government. Underlying this shift in context and activity have been three elements: a reconceptualization of innovation in public services as 'continuous improvement' rather than transformation; a change in perception of the innovative capacity of VCOs to emphasize the importance of the leadership of, and partnership with, government in producing innovations in public services; and a re-orientation of government performance targets for local public services to emphasize specialization rather than innovation. Ironically, it may well be the case now that innovative VCOs are being driven to portray their work as developmental in order to secure important governmental funding of their activities. Innovation as 'continuous improvement' rather than 'service transformation' has become the watchword.

In conclusion, at the theoretical level, this chapter emphasizes the need to understand the innovative capacity of VCOs as a variable organizational capacity, with its key contingencies in the institutional and policy environment rather than an inherent element of these organizations. This is a significant shift in our understanding of the contribution of VCOs to public services provision.

At a service level, this has implications for policy makers and VCO managers alike – in the UK and elsewhere. First, public policy makers and managers need to understand and take seriously the impact that their policy decisions have upon the structure and activity of VCOs. These organizations are not in a 'steady state', with inherent capabilities to bring to public services provision. Public policy makes as much difference to the activities of these organizations as it does to public sector ones.

Secondly, for VCO managers, it is important to emphasize that *appropriate innovation* is an important activity for VCOs to undertake. *Funding-driven innovation*,[11] though, risks skewing the vital role that they can play in the provision of public services – and undermines the, at least, equally important contributions that they can make both by providing specialist services and by the incremental improvement of such services. VCO managers thus have to achieve a difficult balance. On the one hand, they need to be sensitive to the aspirations and requirements of public policy and assess what, if any, contribution they can make to this (and its impact upon them if they are so dependent upon such funding for survival). On the other hand, they need to be clear about their distinctive contribution to public services, if they have one, and whether this involves innovative, developmental or specialist services.

Finally, this chapter serves also as a warning to VCO managers and staff not to attach too great a significance to the sectoral rhetoric of innovative capacity. In the past it was too easy a rhetoric to adopt in order to establish hegemony over public sector organizations. Yet such rhetoric both is prone to obsolescence and is liable to undermine other equally important capacities that VCOs may possess – such as specialist expertise. The research upon which this chapter is based serves as a warning against such easy sophistry.

NOTES

1. Previously published in a special symposium in *Public Management Review*, 10(1) on 'Innovation in Public Services' (January 2008).
2. The research upon which this chapter is based was funded by ESRC Research Grant RES-153-25-0051-A. Responsibility for its content and the views expressed therein remains, as always, with the authors.
3. The names 'Midwell', 'Bellebury', 'Siliton' and 'Southshire' are pseudonyms to ensure the anonymity of the organizations and agencies involved in this study.
4. The key differentiator between the innovative and developmental work identified here was the element of *discontinuity* with the prior work of the organization, as discussed above.
5. Again, no normative distinction is being made here between the value of incremental development and innovative activity. In the long term a series of apparently minor incremental developments might actually lead to a more fundamental change in the nature of organizational activity. However, the distinction is important in terms of the managerial and front-line activity of VCOs – innovation and incremental change involve different tasks, because of the element of discontinuity and organizational destruction that innovation involves compared with incremental development (Abernathy and Clark 1988).
6. A summary of these survey findings is presented in this chapter. The full statistical analyses are available in the web-based ESRC Public Services Programme Discussion Paper from this project (DP0701): S. Osborne, C. Chew and K. McLaughlin (2007), *The Innovative Capacity of Voluntary Organizations: Survey Evidence from a Replication Study* (http://www.publicservices.ac.uk/Publications/Discussion_Papers/DP0701_VCO_Innovation.pdf).
7. All figures and tables are contained in Appendix 1 to this chapter.
8. This is a measure of the discriminating power of the variable and for a value of 0.4 or more considered to be 'excellent' (Hedderson and Fisher 1993, p. 148).
9. The evidence from the cross-sectional case studies is explored more fully in Osborne et al. (2007).
10. Council for Voluntary Service.
11. And, for that matter, 'funding-driven continuous improvement' – whatever that means.

REFERENCES

Abernathy, W. and Clark, K. (1988). Innovation: mapping the winds of creative destruction. In M. Tushman and W. Moore (eds), *Readings in the Management of Innovation*. Cambridge, MA: Ballinger, pp. 55–78.

Abernathy, W., Clark, K. and Utterbach, J. (1983). *Industrial Renaissance*. New York: Basic Books.

Abrams, P., Abrams, S., Humphreys, R. and Snaith, K. (1989). *Neighbourhood Care and Social Policy*. London: HMSO.

Argyris, C. and Schon, D. (1978). *Organizational Learning: A Theory of Action Perspective*. Boston, MA: Addison Wesley.

Beveridge, W. (1948). *Voluntary Action*. London: Allen Unwin.

Blair, T. (2004). Speech at the Guardian's Public Services Summit. *Guardian Unlimited*. Available at: http://society.guardian.co.uk/futureforpublicservices/comment/0,,1134531,00.html

Borins, S. (2001). *The Challenge of Innovating in Government*. Washington, DC: IBM Center for the Business of Government.

Burridge, D. (1990). *What Local Groups Need*. London: NCVO.

Cabinet Office (1999). *Modernising Government*. London: HMSO.

de Vaus, D. (1986). *Surveys in Social Research*. London: George Allen and Unwin.

Denzin, N. (1970). *The Research Act in Sociology*. London: Butterworth.

Department of Health (1989). *Caring for People*. London: HMSO.

Eisenbis, R. and Avery, R. (1972). *Discriminant Analysis and Classification Procedures*. Lexington, MA: Lexington Books.

Griffiths, R. (1988). *Community Care*. London: HMSO.

Hartley, J. (2006). *Innovation and Its Contribution to Improvement*. London: Department for Communities and Local Government.

Hedderson, J. and Fisher, M. (1993). *SPSS Made Easy*. Belmont, CA: Wadsworth.

Herbig, P. (1991). A cusp catastrophe model of the adoption of industrial innovation. *Journal of Product Innovation Management*, 8(2), 127–137.

H.M. Treasury (2002). *The Role of the Voluntary and Community Sector in Service Delivery: A Cross Cutting Review*. London: H.M. Treasury.

H.M. Treasury/Cabinet Office (2006). *Local Area Pathfinders – Building Public Service Partnerships*. London: H.M. Treasury/Cabinet Office.

Home Office (1990). *Efficiency Scrutiny of Government Funding of the Voluntary Sector*. London: HMSO.

House of Commons Select Committee of Public Accounts (2003). *Improving Public Services Through Innovation: The Invest to Save Budget. Sixteenth Report of Session 2002–03*. London: House of Commons.

Kimberly, J. (1981). Managerial innovation. In P. Nystrom and W. Starbuck (eds), *Handbook of Organizational Design*. Oxford: Oxford University Press, pp. 84–104.

Kings Fund Institute (1987). *Promoting Innovation in Community Care*. London: Kings Fund Institute.

Klecka, W. (1980). *Discriminant Analysis*. Beverley Hill, CA: Sage.

Koch, P. and Hauknes, J. (2005). *On Innovation in the Public Sector*. Oslo: NIFU STEP.

Koch, P., Cunningham, P., Schwabsky, N. and Hauknes, J. (2006). *Innovation in the Public Sector: Summary and Policy Recommendations*. Oslo: NIFU STEP.

Kramer, R. (1981). *Voluntary Agencies in the Welfare State*. Berkeley, CA: University of California Press.

Labour Party (1990). *Labour and the Voluntary Sector*. London: Labour Party.

Le Grand, J. (1991). Quasi markets and social policy. *Economic Journal*, 101, 1256–1267.

Malikova, L. and Staroòová, K. (2005). *Innovation in the Social Sector – Case Study Analysis*. Oslo: NIFU STEP.

Ministry of Health (1959). *Report of the Working Party on Social Workers in the Local Authority Health and Welfare Services*. London: HMSO.

Mole, V. and Elliot, D. (1987). *Enterprising Innovation*. London: Frances Pinter.

Mulgan, G. and Albury, D. (2003). *Innovation in the Public Sector*. London: Cabinet Office.

Museums Libraries Archives Partnership (2007). *A Blueprint for Excellence. Public Libraries 2008–2011*. London: Museums Libraries Archives Partnership.

National Audit Office (2005). *Improving Public Services through Better Construction*. London: HMSO.

National Council for Voluntary Organisations (NCVO) (1991). Political supplement. *NCVO News*, June.

Nelson, R. (1993). Technological innovation: the role of non-profit organizations. In D. Hammock and D. Young (eds), *Nonprofit Organizations in a Mixed Economy*. Ann Arbor, MI: University of Michigan Press, pp. 363–377.

NESTA (2007). *Driving Innovation through Public Procurement*. London: NESTA.

Office of the Deputy Prime Minister (ODPM) (2003). *Local Government Act 1999: Part I. Best Value and Performance Improvement*. ODPM Circular 03/2002. London: ODPM.

Office of the Third Sector (2006). *Partnership in Public Services: An Action Plan for Third Sector Involvement*. London: Cabinet Office.

Osborne, S. (1998a). *Voluntary Organizations and Innovation in Public Services*. London: Routledge.

Osborne, S. (1998b). The innovative capacity of voluntary organizations: implications for local government. *Local Government Studies*, 24(1), 19–40.

Osborne, S. (1998c). Naming the beast: defining and classifying service innovations in social policy. *Human Relations*, 51(9), 1133–1154.

Osborne, S. (1998d). Organizational structure and innovation in voluntary associations: applying the Aston Measures. *Voluntas*, 9(4), 345–362.

Osborne, S. (2000). Reformulating Wolfenden? The roles and impact of local development agencies in supporting voluntary and community action in the UK. *Local Government Studies*, 26(4), 23–48.

Osborne, S. and Brown, K. (2005). *Managing Change and Innovation in Public Service Organizations*. London: Routledge.

Osborne, S. and Hems, L. (1995). The economic structure of the charitable sector in the UK. *Nonprofit and Voluntary Sector Quarterly*, 24(4), 321–326.

Osborne, S., Chew, C. and McLaughlin, K. (2007). The innovative capacity of voluntary and community organizations: exploring the organizational and environmental contingencies. In S. Osborne (ed.), *The Third Sector in Europe: Trends and Prospects*. London: Routledge.

Pirie, M. (1988). *Privatization: Practice and Choice*. Aldershot: Wildwood House.

Porter, M. (1985). *Competitive Advantage*. New York: Free Press.

Prime Minister's Strategy Unit (2006). *The UK Government's Approach to Public Service Reform*. London: Prime Minister's Strategy Unit.

Public Audit Forum (1999). *The Implications of Audit for the Modernising Government Agenda*. London: PAF.

Rogers, E. and Shoemaker, F. (1971). *Communication of Innovation*. New York: Free Press.

Rosner, M. (1967). Economic determinants of organizational innovation. *Administrative Science Quarterly*, 12, 614–625.

Rothwell, R. (1975). *Project SAPPHO – Some Hypotheses Tested*. Stockholm: Paper to the Innovation Symposium, Royal Swedish Academy of Engineering Science.

Senge, P. (1990). *The Fifth Discipline: The Art and Practice of the Learning Organization*. London: Random House.

Smale, G. and Tuson, G. (1990). Community social work: foundations for the 1990s and beyond. In G. Darvill and G. Smale (eds), *Partners in Empowerment: Networks of Innovation in Social Work*. London: NISW.

Van de Ven, A. (1998). Central problems in the management of innovation. In M. Tushman and W. Moore (eds), *Readings in the Management of Innovation*. Cambridge, MA: Ballinger, pp. 103–122.

Van de Ven, A., Angle, H. and Doole, M. (1989). *Research on the Management of Innovation*. New York: Harper and Row.

Walker, R., Jeanes, E. and Rowlands, R. (2001). *Managing Public Services Innovation: The Experience of English Housing Associations*. Bristol: The Policy Press.

Webb, S. and Webb, B. (1911). *Prevention of Destitution*. London: Longman.

Williams, H. and Webb, A. (1992). *Outcome Funding*. New York: Rensselaerville Institute.

Wistow, G., Knapp, M., Hardy, B. and Allen, C. (1994). *Social Care in a Mixed Economy*. Buckingham: Open University Press.

Wistow, G., Knapp, M., Hardy, B., Forder, J., Kendall, J. and Manning, R. (1996). *Social Care Markets*. Buckingham: Open University Press.

Wolfenden Committee (1978). *The Future of Voluntary Organisations*. London: Bedford Square Press.

APPENDIX 1:   SURVEY ANALYSIS TABLE AND FIGURES

Table 26A.1   The innovative activity of VCOs

Type of activity	Locality				
	Bellebury	Siliton	Midwell	Southshire	Overall
Innovative 1994	43.1	N/A	35.0	36.5	37.9
Innovative 2006	N/A	18.8	24.2	18.8	19.1
Developmental 1994	13.8	N/A	19.0	9.5	13.9
Developmental 2006	N/A	33.3	30.3	44.1	35.7
Traditional 1994	43.1	N/A	46.0	54.0	48.2
Traditional 2006	N/A	47.9	45.5	41.2	45.2
TOTAL	100	100	100	100	100

Notes:
1994. 376 organizations surveyed with 196 organizations responding – a response rate of 52.1 per cent (potentially rising to 67.6 per cent allowing for organizational morbidity).
2006. 356 organizations surveyed with 115 responding – a response rate of 32.0 per cent (potentially rising to 42.0 per cent allowing for organizational morbidity).

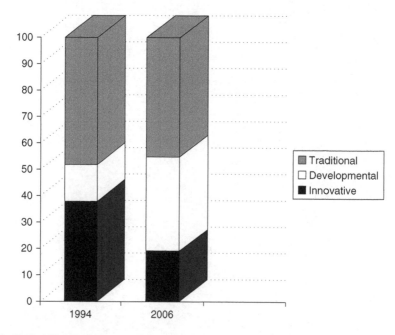

Note: [a]See Table 26A.1 for the exact percentages.

Figure 26A.1   The activity of VCOs in 1994 and 2006 (%)[a]

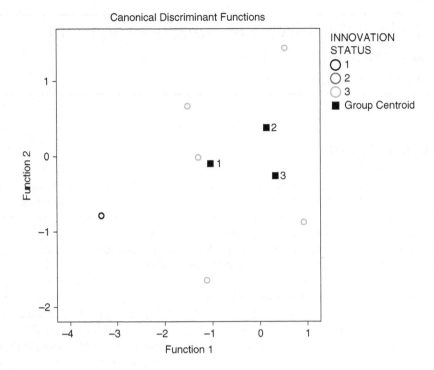

Innovation status key
1: Innovative VCOs
2: Developmental VCOs
3: Traditional VCOs

Figure 26A.2   Territorial map of functions and variables

27. Role of third sector organizations in health innovation networks
Paul Windrum

INTRODUCTION

This chapter addresses the role played by third sector organizations in forming and managing health innovation networks, and their contribution to the co-production of new health services. The third sector has grown significantly, both in terms of the number of third sector organizations which exist and the range of sectors in which they operate. Research on the third sector is nascent but intensifying as national governments and the EU consider its social and economic role (Osborne 2009).

Third sector organizations are found in a variety of sectors in Europe, and take a variety of organizational forms. Kendal and Knapp (1995) describe the third sector as a 'loose and baggy monster'. Hasenfeld and Gidron (2005) highlight the complex organizational forms that are developing in not-for-profit organizations and link this to specialization and differentiation. Brandsen et al. (2005) and Evers (2005) propose that the traditional ideal-type characterization of voluntary organizations no longer applies because these hybrid organizational forms mix core values, cultures and organizational forms which were previously thought to be discrete and particular to the public and the private sector.

Scholars have highlighted the role of government policy in promoting social enterprises in the co-production of public service provision (see Defourny 2001; Aiken 2006). Co-production involves a constellation where governments and social actors share 'conjoint responsibility in producing public services' (Marschall 2004, p. 232). This differs from conventional definitions of political participation, in which participants take the initiative to engage in activities that seek to influence public decision making. Here, participants demand something from the government and use participation as a way to communicate their preferences, with the expectation that government will 'deliver' (Marschall 2004). Lelieveldt et al. (2009) observe that, with co-production, citizens and organizations are invited by governments to take part in policy making, and are much more actively engaged in one or more phases of the policy process. Depending on the issue at hand, they may be informed, consulted, asked to think about policy options, entitled to allocate budgets and/or entrusted with implementing such policies.

Osborne (2009) has drawn attention to the lack of research on the role played by third sector organizations in innovation networks which contain multiple private and public sector organizations. The paucity of research in this area, together with a lack of quantitative data sets, hampers discussions regarding the role of third sector organizations in Europe, their contribution to efficient and effective delivery of public and private services, to questions of co-production and co-governance and, more widely, to social policy and economic development (Cunningham and James 2010).

Table 27.1   Description of cases by country, innovation category, third sector membership and central role of third sector organization

Innovation	Country	Category	Third sector	Central role
Diabetes education	UK	Intangible service	Yes	Yes
Capacity planning	UK	Organizational/process	No	
Health school for illness prevention	Denmark	Intangible service	No	
Public–private network for elderly care innovations	Denmark	Network	Yes	Yes
IT risk-adjustment software tool	Spain	Technology mediated service	No	
Social network site for health professionals	Spain	Network	Yes	Yes
Handheld defibrillators	Austria	Network and technology mediated service	Yes	Yes
Virtual reality rehabilitation therapies	France	Technology mediated service	No	
Supersonic imaging	France	Technology mediated service	No	
Public–private partnership for research	France	Organizational/process	No	

This aim of this chapter is to identify a set of critical factors which affect the successful organization and management of health innovation networks, the specific network contributions that are made by third sector organizations and their role in the co-production of innovations, and the external factors which affect the successful roll-out and diffusion of those innovations. The empirical research presented in this chapter is based on a cross-cutting meta analysis of ten case studies that were developed in the EU-funded Public–Private Services Innovation (ServPPIN) project.[1] The findings provide insights for third sector managers engaging in the setting up and management of health networks, and a set of testable hypotheses and stylized facts in three areas: the drivers and barriers of health innovation networks; the role played by key organizations in the structuring and managing of the networks; and the co-production of new services.

META ANALYSIS

Description

Table 27.1 provides information, for each case study, of the country in which the innovation network is located, the category of innovation produced by the network, whether the network contains one or more third sector organizations, and whether a third sector organization played a central role in the formation and management of the network.

Four of the ten cases include one or more third sector members. What is more, in each case it is a third sector organization which plays a central role in the formation and management of the network. In the UK case study of the development of a patient-centred diabetes education programme for Type 2 diabetics, it was a third sector education establishment which set up the development of the programme, co-produced its content with the diabetes education unit of a local primary care trust (PCT), and trained the PCT's staff in the delivery of patient-centred education. It also organized the clinical trial procedure and conducted the data analysis. Funding for development was found by the third sector organization while the costs of running the trials of the new programme were met by the PCT.

A Danish case study examines the activities of a third sector organization that organizes and brokers collaborative public–private innovation networks. This particular study examined its role in the establishment of innovation networks to develop elderly care innovations, and to trial these innovations in five nursing home centres in the local municipality. Once established, the third sector organization removes itself from the picture. Its contribution is development of an idea, the establishment of the network and organizing the opportunities to pilot service innovations. It does not provide technological inputs or involve itself in the specification or development of new services.

A third sector network organizer is also at the heart of the Austrian handheld defibrillator case study. The key actor in this case is the Austrian Red Cross. It constructed a supply and demand network to ensure the development and successful adoption of handheld defibrillators. First, it engaged in a high profile media campaign, notably enrolling the ORF Austrian Broadcasting Corporation to raise public awareness of the prevalence of cardiac arrests and the benefits of defibrillators. The Austrian Red Cross gained funding for this media campaign from a range of private and public sector organizations At the same time it enrolled the General Hospital of Vienna (a public sector hospital) into the network to provide its scientific expertise, scientific inputs and supervision.

Having raised public awareness, the Austrian Red Cross worked with policy makers to pass legislation making it compulsory for all workplaces to have handheld defibrillators and to have staff trained in their use. To support this, the Red Cross organized the training of citizens. On the supply side, it worked with local manufacturers. At the outset there were no producers of handheld defibrillators in Austria. The Red Cross persuaded companies about the commercial opportunities of production (having created demand through the media campaign and the new workplace law) and facilitated collaboration with the General Hospital of Vienna to develop easy-to-use, affordable defibrillators.

The fourth network involving a third sector organization is located in Spain. A social network website was set up by a not-for-profit medical organization in Madrid. The aim is to improve the quality of health treatment by establishing good communications between different health professionals and institutions in Spain. The network is also open to medical practitioners in South America, and it has been very successful in attracting users from that region.

Six of the case studies do not contain a third sector member. The UK study of capacity planning concerns the implementation and embedding of a capacity planning process within a primary care trust. The trust brought in expertise from a private sector business and together they co-produced an IT-based planning system. This provides the information needed to cost services, which is essential for higher level managers in their negotiations with NHS groups that purchase services. The information is also useful for line managers to more effectively structure their resources and services. The Danish case study of a health school for illness prevention involves collaboration between a private sector healthcare organization and a local municipality. The health school is dedicated to the prevention of illnesses through the development of patient-centred health. The French public–private partnership for research is an organizational innovation between a private sector pharmaceutical company, CNRS (National Centre for Scientific Research) and a public sector research laboratory. It addresses the complex rules that demarcate public and private sector funding and research activities in France, in order to develop research programmes that are of mutual interest and benefit to the partners.

The remaining three case studies involve information and communication technologies. A Spanish IT risk-adjustment software tool is designed to manage budgets for pharmaceutical expenditure. This promises to better support regional health authorities to allocate budget resources for pharmaceutical expenditure. The French case study of rehabilitation therapies involves the development and application of new therapies using interactive 3D technology (Virtual Reality). The key to their clinical success is the service innovation – the way to approach the therapy for the patient – rather than the software and peripherals that are used. Finally, the supersonic imaging case study involves the application of waves and acoustic technology to the development of new, non-destructive testing and medical imaging. This has great potential benefits in areas such as cancer treatment.

A range of different categories of innovation outputs is being developed by these health networks. These fall into one of four generic categories:

- knowledge services which are intangible (e.g. health education programmes);
- technology mediated services (e.g. strongly connected with new medical devices, or new ICT hardware/software products);
- organizational/process innovations which seek to improve the efficiency or effectiveness of patient-facing service delivery and/or administrative back-office activities; and
- the construction of innovation networks themselves.

As can be seen in Table 27.1, there is an even spread of case studies over the four categories. Two involve the invention and development of intangible knowledge service products, four involve the development of new artefacts and physically mediated services, two involve the development of new organizational processes, and three of the cases have as their goal the construction of innovation networks.

Of the four case studies which contain third sector members, three involve the construction of innovation networks. This suggests that network building is itself a highly important aspect of innovation in public health services, and that third sector organizations can play a major role in this activity. The Austrian defibrillator case study provides a particularly good illustration of this. While the focus of innovation activity is ostensibly the development and diffusion of a physical artefact (the defibrillator), its success depended on the construction of a supply side and demand side network to create, support and develop the artefact. The Austrian Red Cross had sufficient prestige, connections and competences needed to build this network of political, public sector, private business and citizen interests.

Features of Innovation Networks

Cowan and Jonard (2008, 2009) propose that innovation networks differ from social networks. Innovation networks are formed purely on the basis of competence fit between the partners. A common feature of the empirical evidence is an inverted-U curve in cognitive distance (see, for example, Gulati 1995; Gilsing et al. 2008). Partners which are too similar have nothing to learn from or contribute to one another, so a degree of competence differentiation is important. However, if the cognitive distance is too great then there is no absorptive capacity and partners cannot work with, or learn from, each other. This results in sparse, clustered networks containing few partners, with highly skewed link distributions (i.e. small world networks with large structural holes). A third feature is the tendency for repeated interactions between partners. Innovation is risky, and information on the quality of potential partners is expensive to collect – often it involves learning-by-doing. Hence, there is a tendency for networks to be formed that include at least some partners with which there have been good experiences in prior innovation projects.

These features are found across the ten case studies. These European health innovation networks are collaborative alliances among public, private and third sector organizations. They are alliances which bring together and develop complementarities and synergies between the specialist knowledge, competences, services and financial resources of each partner. Each partner has a specific role and makes a specific contribution to the co-production of the service innovation.

With regards to competences, two important aspects are identified in the case studies. The interviewees highlighted the importance of complementary competences (including skills and knowledge) among network partners. Just as important, the interviewees stressed, was non-rivalrous commensurability among partners. Where there is more than one private sector organization present within a network, or more than one third sector organization, it was important that these organizations were not direct rivals, or even from the same field.

It is notable that the case studies contain relatively few partners. The one notable exception is the Austrian defibrillator case, which has eight network organizations. In the other case studies, there were typically just three or four partners. Hence, they are less like social networks and more akin to the types of strategic alliances and research consortia formed among private sector firms, and university–industry consortia found in the USA and in Europe.

In line with Gulati's (1995) research, there are previous ties between partners. In eight of the ten case studies, one or more members had some form of prior connection. Sometimes this is through previous collaborative projects; sometimes the connections were between individuals who had previously worked together within an organization. Only in one of the French case studies was there a deliberate attempt to seek out expertise from individuals and/or organizations which were unknown. In this particular case it was to recruit medical expertise from the USA.

In terms of network composition, the case studies tend to comprise a public and a private sector partner (four out of ten case studies), or else a third sector, public sector and private sector partner (also four out of ten case studies). Perhaps the most striking feature is the absence of end-users – that is, patients – in these health networks. Despite the rhetoric of health policies in many European countries concerning greater direct patient participation, and a growing academic literature and policy literature on user engagement in innovation, there is no evidence here of active end-user participation in the co-production of innovation. In these ten studies, at least, patient participation does not appear to be a factor, either in formation and management of innovation networks, or defining and developing new services. This is not to say that medical practitioners and other groups do not have knowledge of patients' medical needs. Clearly they do, built up over many years of interactions with patients and of experience in developing and trialling service innovations. However, the success of certain types of service requires active patient participation – notably the patient-centred health programmes in diabetes and the preventative medicine case studies. It is therefore surprising that patients were not directly involved in the networks.

The lack of direct patient involvement could be a factor explaining the powerful advocacy role played by charities and other third sector organizations in many European public health systems. As noted previously, a wide range of third sector organizations is to be found in public health, from unincorporated and voluntary associations to trusts, charities and foundations, not-for-profit business enterprises and social enterprises. These bring a variety of specialist knowledge about patients as well as distinct medical and non-medical competences. The strong presence of medical charities and other third sector organizations may also be due to the restricted access of private sector businesses in European public health systems.

Third sector advocacy groups are seen as 'honest brokers' whose primary interests are to improve the quality of healthcare. In four of the ten case studies, third sector organizations were the initiators and the lead network partner – that is, in all cases in which a third sector partner was present. In the other six case studies, leadership was jointly shared by a public and a private organization in three cases, a private business took the lead in two cases, and a public sector organization was the lead partner in one case study. As noted, this was an unanticipated finding of the research. It was not expected that third sector organizations would play such a prominent role in the formation, organization and management of health innovation networks.

Critical Success Factors

Two sets of critical success factors are identified in the case studies. The first set comprises 'network factors' which influence the composition and strength of the network. The findings are presented in Figure 27.1. The importance of finance is highlighted in all of the case studies. Of the three innovation networks which ended in failure, two failed due to a lack of finance. The case studies highlight that access to finance can be the key attribute which a partner brings to a network.

We have discussed the importance of compatibility in the knowledge and competence of partners and the role of previous contacts in reducing risk. Compatibility was identified as a significant factor in nine of the studies, and previous contact in seven studies.

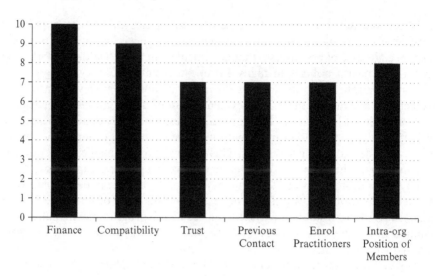

Figure 27.1   Network factors by case study

Trust between members is highlighted as a key factor in seven cases. This is in line with empirical research on strategic alliances between private sector organizations and university–industry collaboration. More surprising, perhaps, is that formal contracts were drawn up in just five of the ten case studies. This indicates a particularly high degree of trust among network partners. This appears to be related to the existence of previous contact experience among the partners – either in terms of organizations having previously worked with one another or of having good personal contacts. The other contributing factor here is commensurability and non-rivalry between partners. Third sector and public sector bodies have very different, non-competing interests in the development of effective health innovations, as do private sector organizations. For public providers, the core interest is the development of improved service quality and greater efficiency in delivery and service organization. The core interest of health charities and other third sector interest groups is improvement in the welfare of the members which they represent. The interest of private sector businesses is the development of more effective services which return profits. Within this constellation of interests there is scope for mutually beneficial interaction.

The two remaining critical factors concern the quality and strength of links between the innovation network and its external environment. First, the ability to enrol medical practitioners is stressed – that is, doctors and nurses in hospitals and/or family doctors and practice nurses. Networks benefit significantly if they contain a prestigious medical practitioner or representative group, and face severe difficulties if they do not gain this support. For example, the Danish health school for illness prevention failed to engage local practitioners even though it was strategically set up within a local hospital. This resulting lack of referrals by hospital doctors and family practitioners killed the project. The second type of link that is highlighted is the intra-organizational position of network members; that is, the positions which individuals hold within their own organizations. Not only must they be champions/gatekeepers of the network within their organizations,

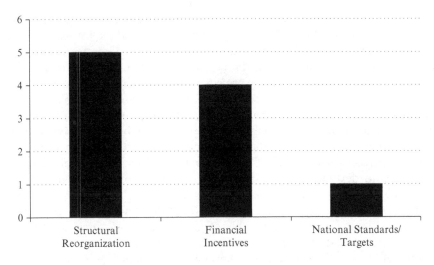

Figure 27.2   External factors by case study

they must have the power and authority within their organizations that are needed to ensure ongoing commitment to, and ongoing resources for, the network. This was dramatically emphasized by two of the cases in which the network failed. When key individuals left their organizations this led either to the ending of the network or else a radical reconstruction the network's aims and objectives.

'External factors' are a second set of critical factors which affect the success or failure of the network. As can be seen in Figure 27.2, three such factors are identified in the case studies: structural reorganization, financial incentives and national standards.

Structural reorganization is the reorganization of responsibility for local services and/ or the reorganization of organizations. This was a key factor in half of the case studies. For example, the capacity planning project was stimulated by a change in national policy which separated the purchasing arm of PCTs in the UK from local (public) service providers. This opened the way for purchasing from outside the local primary care trust. It has forced all local service providers to cost the range of services which their departments provide, and to engage in capacity planning. The capacity planning project is an example of the innovation that has been stimulated by this policy change.

The second external factor identified is financial incentives. It is perhaps surprising, given the attention placed on policy initiatives in the third sector literature and the importance of finance reported in these case studies, that policy funding incentives are only mentioned in four of the case studies. Certainly, policy funding was an important factor in both of the Danish case studies. Tax breaks for research were mentioned as a minor factor in two of the French case studies. This may indicate that funding incentives for innovation are not being fully exploited across the countries included in this sample of case studies. The third factor of national standards and targets was highlighted in one case study. Perhaps not surprisingly this was a UK study. Compared with the other countries in the sample, the UK has the most developed set of standards governing clinical care and medical practice.

It is useful to consider factors that are identified in case studies of failed innovation networks. Of the ten case study networks in this sample, three have ended (at the time of writing). The networks in the UK capacity planning study and the Danish health school study ended at the development/trial phase, and the UK diabetes education network ended at the diffusion phase.[2] The health school innovation ended due to an inability to obtain the funds needed to continue the project, and the inability to enrol local practitioners so that sufficient patients would be referred to make the service viable. The capacity planning network ended because it was successful. It started as a public–private initiative to develop a capacity planning process, and led to the collaborative development of an IT supported management tool for the public sector partner. Once the project ended, the public sector partner took control of the development of the capacity planning process and continues to develop the resources and operational procedures needed to fully support and exploit this organizational innovation.

The diabetes education network was successful in developing a new patient-centred education programme with demonstrable clinical benefits but failed at the diffusion stage. The clinical trial data of the education programme compare very favourably with the clinical data reported for the Desmond programme and the Xpert programme, which have become the two dominant standards for Type 2 diabetes education in the UK. However, the two partners in this case study – a public sector education unit within a local PCT and a third sector education group – were not interested in rolling out their programme nationally. The PCT education unit did not have the resources for a national roll-out. More importantly, these public health practitioners see their job as providing high quality local services to diabetics. They are not interested in becoming educators of practitioners. The members of the third sector education group were also not interested in becoming full time educators of diabetes practitioners. As a consequence, this innovation did not diffuse.

DISCUSSION

The empirical findings challenge a number of initial preconceptions and move us towards a set of hypotheses and stylized facts which can be tested by future research in other areas of health and in countries beyond those considered here. The innovation networks that make up our set have a set of identifiable features. They are organizational networks – not social networks – between public, private and third sector organizations. They typically contain a small number of partner organizations, at least in the invention and trial phase. These are goal-oriented networks. They typically come together to develop a particular research project and thereafter disband. Only in a small number of cases is the construction of a network an end goal in itself.

These are professional networks. The absence of patients (end-users) in these networks is striking. This is all the more remarkable given current discussions among academics and in policy circles regarding open innovation and the alleged importance of user-led innovation (Chesbrough 2003; Baldwin et al. 2006). The lack of direct patient involvement in the specification and development of new service innovations does not appear to be a critical factor affecting the success of this set of innovations. An issue which needs to be addressed in future research is the extent to which health practitioners' knowledge of patients' clinical needs, long-standing experience dealing with patients and the advocacy role played by third sector partners are sufficient to offset direct patient involvement in the innovation process.

Where there is a third sector partner in the network, that partner plays a key role in the construction, management and leadership of the health innovation network. They shape the nature, direction and timing of innovations, and play a key role in the co-production of the new service. The meta analysis results indicate that third sector organizations, such as charities, have a particular role within networks as advocates for patients while others are seen as 'honest brokers' whose primary interests are to improve the quality of health-care rather than commercial gain. This is important in public health systems in Europe which place strong restrictions on the access of private sector businesses.

Personal ties, and prior knowledge and experience of partners are highlighted across the case studies, as are complementarities between the competences of partner organizations. These are in line with prior research on alliances between private sector organizations and university–industry partnerships. Furthermore, commensurability and non-rivalry are found to be a key factor where more than one partner is from the private sector or third sector.

The meta study highlights the importance of key individuals who are leading members of the network. These actors must hold positions within their own organizations which are sufficiently senior to ensure the long-term commitment of resources to the network and access to the support needed to develop the health service innovation. The impor-tance of continuity among these core members, particularly in the invention and trial phase, is highlighted by the meta analysis results. The loss of key individual members from a network in this phase threatens the survival of the network. Where networks do survive, they are altered in either scope or objectives.

An issue which requires further investigation is the ability of these key actors to under-stand the different contexts and backgrounds of their partners. The literature on third sector organizations has identified the hybridization of values, cultures and organiza-tional forms which were previously thought to divide public and private sectors. Research is required to examine the ability of network actors to understand and successfully work with partners' values, cultures and organizational forms. Of particular interest would be a study of individuals who have worked in multiple private, public and third sector organizations, and who bring this experience to bear within innovation networks. This would complement research by Jain et al. (2009) on academic researchers who engage in the commercialization of their ideas. They found that, while commercialization leads academics to develop new professional identities, their academic identity remains their primary reference point. Our study identifies as a key success factor the ability of third sector, public sector and private sector actors to (a) communicate with one another, and (b) understand the drives and motivations of their partners.

Trust is another distinguishing feature of the health networks studied in this chapter. Formal contracts were only drawn up in half of the case studies. The data suggest this is partly explained by good understandings among partners and previous connections among key network members. Also important is the non-rivalrous composition of the networks. Where this is the case, each partner has different interests and goals in forming the network.

Finally, the research findings identify policy and practitioner enrolment as external factors that can be critical to the successful roll-out and diffusion of a service innovation.

As the diabetes education case study highlights, policy changes can stimulate or impede local innovation and service provision. The ability to enrol medical practitioners – that is, doctors and nurses in hospitals and/or family doctors and practice nurses – is another key factor determining the take-up and diffusion of health service innovations. Networks benefit strongly from having a prestigious medical practitioner or representative group within their membership.

As discussed, these insights and stylized facts, gleaned from the experiences of the case study networks, are a first step in filling the gap in the literature on third sector involvement in health networks. They provide guidance to managers in the planning, organization and implementation of collaborative innovation projects, while setting out a research agenda for further research in this field.

NOTES

1. ServPPIN was funded under the Seventh Framework of the Socio-economic Sciences and Humanities Programme. The individual case studies on which this meta analysis draws are Damm Scheuer (2009), Fuglsang and Damm Scheuer (2009), García-Goñi (2009a, b), Green and Windrum (2009), Merlin-Brogniart and Moursli-Provost (2009a, b, c) and Schartinger (2009).
2. Here we follow the Schumpeterian definition of innovation as a two-part process. The first phase is invention, followed by a second phase of diffusion. Innovation occurs in both phases. Radical changes tend to occur in the invention phase while more ongoing, incremental innovation occurs in the diffusion phase.

REFERENCES

Aiken, M. (2006). Towards market or state: tensions and opportunities in the evolutionary path of three UK social enterprises. In M. Nyssens (ed.), *Social Enterprise*. London: Routledge, pp. 259–271.

Baldwin, C., Hienerth, C. and von Hippel, E. (2006). How user innovations become commercial products: a theoretical investigation and case study. *Research Policy*, 35(9), 1291–1313.

Brandsen, T., Van de Donk, W. and Putters, K. (2005). Griffins or chameleons? Hybridity as a permanent and inevitable characteristic of the third sector. *International Journal of Public Administration*, 28(9/10), 749–765.

Chesbrough, H. (2003). *Open Innovation: The New Imperative for Creating and Profiting from Technology*. Boston, MA: Harvard Business School Press.

Cowan, R. and Jonard, N. (2008). If the alliance fits . . . : innovation and network dynamics. In J.A.C. Baum and T.J. Rowley (eds), *Network Strategy: Advances in Strategic Management*, 25. Oxford: JAI/Elsevier, pp. 427–455.

Cowan, R. and Jonard, N. (2009). Knowledge portfolios and the organization of innovation networks. *Academy of Management Review*, 34(2), 320–342.

Cunningham, I. and James, P. (eds) (2010). *Voluntary Organizations and Public Service Delivery*. Oxford and New York: Routledge.

Damm Scheuer, J. (2009). Private Hospital Valdemar. *WP 4 Report for ServPPIN Project*, August. Roskilde: Roskilde University.

Defourny, J. (2001). Introduction: from third sector to social enterprise. In C. Borzaga and J. Defourny (eds), *The Emergence of Social Enterprise*. London: Routledge.

Evers, A. (2005). Mixed welfare systems and hybrid organizations: changes in the governance and provision of social service. *International Journal of Public Administration*, 28, 737–748.

Fuglsang, L. and Damm Scheuer, J. (2009). Næstved Health School. *WP 4 Report for ServPPIN Project*, August. Roskilde: Roskilde University.

García-Goñi, M. (2009a). Adapting information technology for health care provision and the allocation of resources. *WP 4 Report for ServPPIN Project*, August. Madrid: Universidad Complutense de Madrid.

García-Goñi, M. (2009b). NETS: the creation of a social network for health service innovation and information. *WP 4 Report for ServPPIN Project*, August. Madrid: Universidad Complutense de Madrid.

Gilsing, V., Nooteboom, B., Vanhaverbeke, W., Duysters, G. and van der Oord, A. (2008). Network embeddedness and the exploration of novel technologies: technological distance, betweenness centrality and density. *Research Policy*, 37(10), 1717–1731.

Green, L. and Windrum, P. (2009). Implementation and embedding of capacity planning processes. *WP 4 Report for ServPPIN Project*, August. Manchester and Nottingham: MMUBS and NUBS.

Greve, C. (2003). Public sector reform in Denmark: organizational transformation and evaluation. *Public Organization Review*, 3(3), 269–280.

Gulati, R. (1995). Social structure and alliance formation patterns: a longitudinal analysis. *Administrative Science Quarterly*, 40(4), 619–652.

Hasenfeld, Y. and Gidron, B. (2005). Understanding multi-purpose hybrid voluntary organizations: the contributions of theories on civil society, social movements and non-profit organizations. *Journal of Civil Society*, 1(2), 97–112.

Henriksen, L.S., Zimmer, A. and Smith, S.R. (2009). At the eve of convergence? Social service provision in Denmark, Germany and the United States. Presented at the 38th Annual ARNOVA (Association for Research on Nonprofit and Voluntary Action) Conference, Cleveland, USA, 19–21 November.

Jain, S., George, G. and Maltarich, M. (2009). Academics or entrepreneurs? Investigating role identity modification of university scientists involved in commercial identity. *Research Policy*, 38(6), 922–935.

Kendal, J. and Knapp, M. (1995). A loose and baggy monster: boundaries, definitions and typologies. In J. Davis Smith, C. Rochester and R. Hedley (eds), *An Introduction to the Voluntary Sector*. London: Routledge, pp. 66–95.

Lelieveldt, H., Dekker, K., Völker, B. and Torenvlied, R. (2009). Civic organizations as political actors: mapping and predicting the involvement of civic organizations in neighborhood problem-solving and coproduction. *Urban Affairs Review*, 45(1), 3–24.

Marschall, M. (2004). Citizen participation and the neighborhood context: a new look at the coproduction of local public goods. *Political Research Quarterly*, 57(2), 231–244.

Merlin-Brogniart, C. and Moursli-Provost, A.-C. (2009a). Virtual rehabilitation: the ANR TecSan Reactive project. *WP 4 Report for ServPPIN Project*, August. Lille: Clersé and Iéseg, School of Management.

Merlin-Brogniart, C. and Moursli-Provost, A.-C. (2009b). SuperSonic imagine. *WP 4 Report for ServPPIN Project*, August. Lille: Clersé and Iéseg, School of Management.

Merlin-Brogniart, C. and Moursli-Provost, A.-C. (2009c). ISTMT (Institute for Drug Sciences and Technologies, Toulouse). *WP 4 Report for ServPPIN Project*, August. Lille: Clersé and Iéseg, School of Management.

Osborne, S. (2009). Key issues for the third sector in Europe. In S. Osborne (ed.), *The Third Sector in Europe: Prospects and Challenges*. Oxford and New York: Routledge, pp. 3–6.

Schartinger, D. (2009). The introduction of public access defibrillation in Austria. *WP 4 Report for ServPPIN Project*, August. Vienna: Austrian Institute of Technology.

28. Social enterprise and innovation in third sector organizations
Celine Chew and Fergus Lyon

INTRODUCTION

While the space between the public and private sectors has been explored extensively in the academic literature, policy makers are increasingly interested in the potential of organizations with social values, not-for-personal-profit aims and raising income through trading and contracts, to become involved in the delivery of public services. We refer to these entities as 'social enterprises'. Governments are particularly keen to embrace the concept of social enterprise as an alternative modus operandi for third sector organizations (TSOs) in their attempts at modernizing public service provision (Chew 2009a,b).

Using social services provision as an example, Evers (2005) argues that voluntary and community social enterprises have emerged from the New Public Management era due to a process of hybridization between third sector and public sector organizations, as various types of public services, governance mechanisms, networks and markets overlap and intertwine. This development has been particularly evident in the UK since the early 2000s where central and local governments have been urging TSOs to adopt the social enterprise model to effect social change, to deliver services to the local community more effectively and as an alternative means to sustain their operations (Department of Trade and Industry (DTI) 2002; Cabinet Office 2006).

Policy makers are particularly interested in TSOs undertaking social enterprise activities; that is, 'trading with the public body: undertaking specific activities in return for payment' (HM Treasury 2005, p. 19). At the same time, TSOs in the UK are perceived by institutional and government funders to be inherently innovative and better able to provide services to local communities where the state or the market cannot. Yet recent research (see, for example, Osborne 1998; Osborne, Chew and McLaughlin 2008) into the innovative capacity of third sector organizations in the UK suggests that the innovative capacity of TSOs is influenced by government policies and institutional factors, and is not an intrinsic consequence of their organizational structure or culture, as suggested in the previous literature.

Brandsen, Van de Donk and Putters (2005) suggest that the traditional ideal-typical characterization of TSOs is no longer applicable because these entities have developed hybrid organizational characteristics (e.g. adopting multiple goals – social, economic, environmental, resource mix and governance systems) as a response to external environmental pressures from the market and the state. Moreover, the typical meaning of organizational innovation (newness and discontinuity) is often garnered from private sector literature that is aimed predominately at manufacturing product innovation (Osborne and Brown 2005). This 'radical' form of innovation is arguably less prevalent in public service innovation, which could involve incremental organizational change and developmental activities (Osborne 1998, p. 65).

Westall (2007, p. 4) defines innovation in social enterprises as comprising a broad range of possible organizational changes such as developments in products, services and processes in order to adapt to new conditions and/or to meet needs in different ways in varying degrees. Innovation (the process and outcomes) can thus be better understood when it is viewed as part of organizational change (Normann 1971). In this regard, different types of organizational innovation (e.g. total, expansionary, evolutionary and developmental) could affect the actual services that a TSO offers and the target users/audiences that it is serving (Osborne 1998; Osborne and Brown 2005, p. 152). Moreover, Bessant and Tidd (2007) identify different sources from which innovation can emerge: products, processes, shifting market positions or evolving paradigms. Innovativeness is therefore a constructed and contingent criterion, rather than an inherent one that determines the extent of social enterprise activity in TSOs. However, there is scant empirical research that identifies these variables more explicitly in TSOs that have embraced the social enterprise model as a way to respond to external environmental changes. There is therefore a need to understand these relationships more fully in terms of the nature of offerings from TSOs and the impact this has on the relationship between the various actors (e.g. managers/staff in TSOs, end-users, funders) in the process of innovation, and in the innovation outcome.

This chapter is based on our research in social enterprise in the UK third sector and elsewhere, and on our earlier publications in various journals, in particular *Public Management Review, Public Money & Management* and the *Third Sector Research Centre Working Paper Series*. In this chapter, we examine the social enterprise practice of TSOs (within the wider third sector in the UK) and their innovative potential when they adopt the social enterprise approach to public service delivery. Drawing upon the contemporary literature in social enterprise in the third sector, we identify the drivers that have influenced the growing interest in the social enterprise model and the idea of a quasi-market in the third sector. Using three case studies, we illustrate the efforts of TSOs that have embarked on social enterprise activities in the provision of public services, either in line with their core social mission or in partnership with public/private sector bodies. We identify the innovative aspects of their activities and highlight the challenges that they face in the process of adopting the social enterprise approach to public service provision. While this chapter is based on the experiences of TSOs in the UK, it is equally applicable to third sector organizations elsewhere that are operating in increasingly competitive market/quasi-market environments.

SOCIAL ENTERPRISE IN THE UK THIRD SECTOR

Some forms of social enterprise have been operating in the UK third sector since the mid-1800s, e.g. cooperatives and community enterprises that used their trading surpluses to improve the economic situations of their members or disadvantaged neighbourhood groups (Social Enterprise Coalition 2003). However, there remains no single agreed definition of social enterprise in the UK, despite its historical roots. The UK DTI defines social enterprise as a business trading for a social purpose whose surpluses are principally reinvested for that purpose, or established in the community rather than maximizing profits for shareholders and owners (DTI 2002). There have been attempts to identify defined groupings within the commonly accepted definition of social enterprise in the UK. For instance, Lloyd (2003) identified distinct groupings of social enterprises. These groupings comprise a diverse range of organizational forms such as employee-owned businesses, credit unions, cooperatives, development trusts, social firms, intermediate labour market organizations, community businesses and charities trading arms – each having particular environmental and organizational distinctiveness. The diversity of social enterprise can also be seen as a continuum from the more philanthropic organizations with trading elements to the commercially oriented businesses that still have core social aims (Dees, Emerson and Economy 2001). Despite the considerable debate and attention to finding a definition of social enterprise, there remains much contestation as to what is meant by 'social' or 'trading'. Social enterprise can therefore be seen as a social construct that can be viewed from varying perspectives and dimensions (Lyon and Sepulveda 2009).

Social enterprise activities have been increasingly driving the UK voluntary sector economy since the early 2000s (National Council for Voluntary Organizations (NCVO) 2006). For instance, earned income from trading and non-voluntary sources of UK charities reached £17.4 billion in 2008, a 76 per cent increase from a decade ago (NCVO 2010, p. 46). Several drivers have been cited as causes for the emergence of social enterprise activities among charitable organizations in the UK in the past decade. A major impetus for the growth of social enterprise as an organized activity in the UK has arguably been the former Labour government's efforts to shape the role of charities and the wider third sector in a mixed economy of public service provision (Cabinet Office 1999; DTI 2002). In the UK, a nationwide governmental Social Enterprise Strategy was launched in 2002. It identified a range of policy initiatives aiming to increase the entrepreneurial potential of TSOs in the delivery of public services. They included the creation of a new legal form (the Community Interest Company) in 2005, improving access to social finance and procurement opportunities for social enterprises, and provision of advisory support. Developing social enterprise among TSOs under government policy initiatives has intensified under the new Conservative–Liberal coalition government since May 2010 (Cabinet Office 2010). The 'Big Society'[1] agenda sees a greater role for social enterprises in delivering public services and a growing interest in encouraging social enterprise and employee mutual spin-outs from the public sector.

At the same time, greater economic uncertainty and increasing competition for voluntary donations and statutory grants/contracts have contributed to a challenging funding environment for TSOs in the third millennium (NCVO 2004; Wymer, Knowles and Gomes 2006). The number of UK registered charities has grown appreciably from 120,000 in 1994 to 190,000 presently (Charity Commission 2010; Charity Commission for Northern Ireland 2010; Office of Scottish Charity Register 2010). The changing shape and size of the voluntary and charitable sector in the UK is partly attributed to the creation of new charities through the contracting out of public services by central and local governments. Consequently, these external factors have driven TSOs to increase their earned income and trading activities to generate additional revenue to sustain their core charitable work, and have blurred the distinction between what is considered non-profit and charitable, and what is not (Bruce and Chew 2011). Although undertaking trading activities for profit is legally permitted under current charity law in the UK, TSOs have to ensure that the financial and business risks associated with 'non-primary purpose trading'[2] for profits do not adversely affect their public benefit worth. The blurring of boundaries between organizations in the public, private and voluntary sectors is likely to continue and will further increase competition for financial, human and physical resources. These developments have put greater pressures on TSOs and have created new challenges for those entities with social enterprise operations in resource attraction, resource allocation and in managing new patterns of relationships with public and private sector organizations (Deakin 2000). Tension is thus emerging between the need for TSOs to maintain a strong strategic position anchored in their social mission and charitable purpose, preserving their core values and traditions, and being able to respond effectively and innovatively to the transient demands of their external environment.

INNOVATION PRACTICES IN TSOs INVOLVED IN PUBLIC SERVICES

We now illustrate the efforts of three TSOs that have embarked on social enterprise activities in the provision of public services in the UK in their respective ways, and highlight the innovative aspects of these activities. We employed a combination of data gathered from each case study; that is, organizational documents, published annual reports, media reports and interviews with key decision makers (where appropriate). The actual names of case organizations that are illustrated in this chapter have been replaced by pseudonyms to ensure their anonymity. Each case depicts a particular aspect of innovation from the TSO's perspective; namely, as an overarching organizational-wide philosophy to direct the entity's social enterprise activities (Case A); as new offerings (products/services) aimed at new/existing target audiences to maintain the organization's financial sustainability (Case B); and as an alternative financial model to encourage social inclusion and sustainability (Case C).

Case A: Innovation Based on a User-Driven Model for Social Enterprise Activities

Case A is a registered charity set up in 2001 in England that aims to help disabled people with physical and learning difficulties to live independent lives. From its inception, this charity has adopted a 'user-driven' model of organizational development, which served as a mantra to direct all its social enterprise activities. This model is based on a key assumption that the 'lived and shared experiences' (i.e. the needs, fears and aspirations) of disabled people, as users of public services, can and should play a leading role in the co-creation and co-production of the organization's offerings to its key target audience; that is, disabled people (Fenner and Martin 2010). The concept of co-production is not a new one in the context of public service delivery, and various perspectives (e.g. economic, social and organizational) can be found in the literature. However, a common characteristic among these definitions is the importance of collaborative long-term relations between citizens (as service users and co-producers), voluntary and cooperative forms of organizations (e.g. social enterprises) and the state to achieve public service improvements (Manfredi and Maffei 2008, p. 189). From an organizational perspective, the user-driven model employed by this case organization has been instrumental in guiding its social enterprise endeavours. It is an approach which affirms and supports an active and productive role for people who use public services, and the value of collaborative relationships in delivering the outcomes negotiated with the person using the service (Boyle and Harris 2009).

> The user-driven model is our innovative approach to achieve our mission – our way of working throughout the organization – to incentivize disabled people to be key drivers of their own destiny in life . . . it is unique to our context due to the lived experiences of our users. (Manager, Case A)

Being socially enterprising provides a means for the charity to achieve its social purpose in a financially sustainable way. While the user-driven model of working is not exclusive to this organization, it has nevertheless been effective in achieving its core mission of helping disabled people become independent by creating an innovative culture throughout the organization. For instance, a major social enterprise initiative was set up in 2006 to help young disabled people aged from 16 to 25 years to 'overcome barriers to work'. It was operated by and for young disabled people themselves. It strived to achieve this objective by running different educational and training activities for disabled youths who had been referred by various external parties (e.g. voluntary sector partners, government agencies, individuals and families) and it in turn helped them to find employment in the local area through securing apprenticeships with local private sector businesses. In 2009, the three 'original' apprentices were given full time employment contracts. They then employed three more young disabled people as apprentices to run the social enterprise project, and provided work opportunities for a further 21 young disabled people. The use of apprenticeships as a vehicle for young disabled people to access employment attracted attention nationally, resulting in a visit to the organization by the UK Minister for Apprenticeships in October 2009 to explore the possibility of applying this social enterprise initiative to other TSOs. In addition to using apprenticeships and work experience to enable disabled people to engage with the reality of work, the social enterprise also organized a Summer Job Forum in 2009 (funded partly by a local voluntary grant) where work and employment were explored through the use of a variety of media such as theatre, newspapers, and arts and crafts, as well as visits by well-known national/local celebrities.

A major challenge experienced by this organization was to become financially sustainable in the longer term and to reduce the dependency on public funding. It had been successful to a degree by reaching out to the private sector for alternative funding in place of government grants (e.g. lottery funding) and to avail work placements for young disabled people through its various social enterprise activities such as the one highlighted above. While this organization continues to try to change the perceptions of employers, it has ongoing concerns that employers are fearful of and ignorant in dealing with people with disability and have a lack of understanding regarding disability.

Case B: Innovation as Developing New Services for a Diverse Target Audience

Case B is an environmental conservation non-profit organization in Wales. It was set up in 1987 in direct response to the catastrophic decline in wildlife habitat and biodiversity in the farmed countryside in England and Wales. The organization's aim was to help reverse the process of degradation in farmlands in the local area without major interventions or capital expense and to monitor the speed and extent of the return of wildlife. Reinstating more traditional grazing regimes, encouraging haymaking, reversing drainage, stopping most fertilizer inputs and fencing off overgrazed hedgerows, streams and ditches were all used to help 'kickstart' natural processes. By 2010 it boasted of an environmentally rich and diverse meadow in the local region containing over 100 plant species and 46 bird species breeding, totalling over 200 pairs on 40 acres of land. The lake, pond and field scrapes now support 14 species of breeding dragonfly and damselfly – a notable diversity in west Wales. Large populations of small mammals, butterflies and ground invertebrates have returned to the meadows and pastures. This transformation has been recognized by the Countryside Council for Wales, which awarded the organization as a 'notable nature reserve' in the UK.

A major driving force behind the organization's ability to achieve its social and environmental objectives has been its focus on creating innovative education and training programmes for a diverse number of target audiences (e.g. conservation professionals, landowners and farmers, local authority land use managers and advisers, students and college groups) with an interest in the environment, the countryside and its wildlife. Hence, it was paramount that the organization's training courses were delivered by highly experienced tutors, ecologists and conservation professionals. These programmes included one-day practical workshops designed specifically for people who wanted to manage some or all of their land in a more wildlife-friendly way. There are also bespoke courses tailored to particular groups from a variety of conservation and land management agencies. Research-led projects that aim to identify, survey and record wildlife species in the local area have been created:

> Our courses are extensive and their prices are extremely competitive, making the social enterprise one of the most cost-effective and best-value training providers in the UK. We need to be more enterprising in order to deliver the services that they aim to deliver to their target users and in support of their social and environmental missions. (Manager, Case B)

Two key challenges faced by managers of this fledgling social enterprise were the organization's remote location in west Wales and its heavy reliance on grant aid from local and regional government agencies, and European Union and lottery funding for two thirds of its annual operating income. A key strategy of the organization's social enterprise activities (in particular its earned income efforts) was to focus on the area of biodiversity and eco-tourism using the nature reserve in order to generate more earned income from paying users.

However, a major dilemma faced by the management of this social enterprise was to balance adopting commercial principles/approaches in its operations and preserving its social mission in society. In 2010, the organization decided to initiate a collaborative network among other TSOs with different social missions in the regional community.

With the help of the Institute of Fundraising Wales, it was able to develop a more targeted marketing approach to promoting its services to new audiences in the community. This collaborative approach to marketing and fund raising endeavours has helped the organization and other TSOs in the network to increase their income from fee-for-service activities while maintaining their roots in the community:

> Our marketing and management operations need to be comparable with those of a business entity; we need to be innovative and increase our professionalism in the delivery of our services, but at the same time we need to be much more rooted into the community. If social enterprise activities are undertaken in a too capitalistic way, we will alienate ourselves from the very community that we strive to serve in the first place. (Manager, Case B)

Case C: Innovation as an Alternative Model for Funding its Services

This charitable organization defines itself as a social enterprise with the core purpose to build a better future for children, families and local communities through a commitment to excellence in early years education, training and research. It operates 20 nurseries in economically disadvantaged areas of London run by 300 staff serving 1500 children. The organization started at the turn of the twentieth century as an attempt to reduce infant mortality by helping mothers to learn about better childcare. In 1932, the organization started a one year nursery training scheme for day students not wanting to enter a residential institution. From the onset, it was able to make a financial surplus, which was used to support other activities such as a clinic to help mothers with breast feeding, an innovative 'roof garden sun room' and diphtheria testing. The innovative activity drew attention from a number of international health educators from 17 countries across four continents. The UK National Health Service, established in 1948, took responsibility for many public health services. However, the organization decided to retain its charitable status in order to continue to experiment and pioneer activities related to children's services and nurseries.

There are several core elements that differentiate the organization from other early years educational providers. First, its social aims go beyond simply caring for children – it has an equitable fee structure, with a range of fees payable to clients, depending on their financial ability to pay. Secondly, there is a focus on quality of service provision, such as good training for staff who deliver the teaching of early years education, quality food in its nurseries, and working with parents and the local community in new service development. Importantly, the organization emphasizes being enterprising in order to be less reliant on grants and donations. In this respect, it tends to operate very much like a 'business' that ensures its financial sustainability and attractiveness to institutional funders and investors. It strives to diversify its income sources in order to reduce the risk of income fluctuations due to unexpected external environmental shocks. All its enterprise activities have to cover their operating costs; surplus generation is encouraged, which is reinvested in the organization to further its social mission for wider community development.

The organization also prides itself on being innovative and able to adapt to different funding opportunities and challenges. For instance, from the early 1990s it began to enhance its public service delivery role by winning contracts from two civil service departments in 1991 and 1993, enabling it to run nurseries in the local community. In each of these successful contracts, much time and effort was invested in bid writing, developing the governance and management of the nurseries, and enhancing the quality of service delivery. Income from public service contracts continued to grow when it won tenders in 2005 from Westminster City Council and neighbouring communities to manage their nurseries, and children centres in other parts of London. Since adopting a more 'enterprising' approach to generating income, the organization has developed a portfolio of income sources. These comprise a mixture of nurseries and childcare centres that are fully funded by government contract fees, those that are purely funded by paid clients or by employers (located in more affluent areas), other nurseries that are funded by a tiered fee structure, and fees-for-training from students in early years education.

> Our organization is run as a business, but with the right ethos – the staff understand what social enterprise is and they buy into it. We operate on a mixed income model so as to be socially inclusive and financially sustainable. Also, we are a charity so we can raise funds where a business cannot. (Finance Director, Case C)

A key challenge that this organization faced was planning and managing the scaling up of its capacity/capability in service delivery as it responded to a competitive resource attraction environment. This included new ways to innovate while keeping a common framework of quality and standards. Scaling up its operations was also viewed in terms of increasing its social impact on new programmes working on intergenerational equity and recognizing the importance of tackling children's poverty through working with parents. Great attention was given to ethical procurement with sustainability factors, which were considered in the organization's resource and food purchasing for the nurseries. Finally, this case demonstrates that innovation comes about through a combination of various services that cuts across boundaries commonly found in the public sector, such as the health, education, training and employment agendas.

DISCUSSION

The case studies in this chapter illustrate the different ways in which innovation can be construed by third sector organizations in practice. They suggest that innovation is a complex process that could be triggered by both internal motives and external environmental opportunities, and that innovation can occur dramatically and on an incremental scale (Bessant and Tidd 2007). For instance, while there is radical innovation occurring in some of the case organizations (e.g. Case A), this is only part of the picture. The less dramatic changes related to changes within an organization or the innovations from creating hybrid services through combinations of existing activities (e.g. in Case B and Case C) should also be considered (Osborne and Brown 2005).

In terms of new product/service innovation, each of the case studies shows how it has developed something that is novel for its sector or its situation and was not there before. For example, in Case A, ways of improving the employability of disabled people were developed with Summer Job Forums and apprenticeship programmes. In Case B, new courses aimed at a wide range of different audiences were developed, delivered by highly experienced ecology researchers. Case C also had innovative products through bringing the various services for childcare that are often delivered by different government agencies under one roof. Evidence of process innovation is particularly evident in Case A. Through adopting a user-driven model for co-production and co-creation of services, the user, as key beneficiary of the organization, plays a leading role in strategy development and management of the social enterprise.

Positioning innovation is a form of incremental organizational change. It enables the TSO to alter the perception of the target audience about the benefits of existing products/services without significant changes in the actual service. This can be seen in Case B, where new markets for its existing training courses were created among target audiences who had not used these courses before, allowing it to build on opportunities arising from political developments, such as funding for land-owners to set up conservation projects. Similarly, Case C was able to develop positioning innovation to deliver its socially inclusive nursery services, and therefore benefit a wider range of families (particularly from ethnic groups) who were less willing to use early years' educational facilities and preschools.

Our case studies have also highlighted the challenges that social enterprises could face in the process of developing their innovative capacity and potential. This could come from a lack of investment available to start new projects, little willingness to take risks by senior management teams and trustees, or over-reliance on the government for funding. This situation is reflected in the UK where, since the 1990s, successive governments have attempted to increase the innovative capacity of social enterprises by providing more funding via public service contracts and other infrastructural mechanisms. However, such prescriptive funding can result in what DiMaggio and Powell (1983) refer to as 'institutional isomorphism' – where the greater the dependence of an organization for resources and legitimacy on another entity, the greater the risk that the dependent organization will change to become more similar to the resource-rich one. This is particularly prevalent where commissioners are more risk averse and tend to be overly prescriptive in the process and outputs requirements in public service delivery. At the same time, a heightened expectation by dominant stakeholders (such as government funders) of social enterprises to operate in a businesslike and innovative manner to address social problems and/or to sustain public policy objectives could potentially raise unrealistic performance standards too early in their organizational development (Chew 2008). There is also a need to develop a business-oriented operating culture among managers and staff who are responsible for the social enterprise activities in TSOs. However, the case studies underscore the high expectations imposed on social enterprises to demonstrate their social/community value, and the potential erosion of social values in charities that are pressured to develop a businesslike approach in their resource attraction in an increasingly competitive fundraising environment.

Finally, we argue that social enterprises in TSOs distinguish themselves from private sector enterprises by combining the social and enterprise goals in the process of responding to environmental opportunities, which was evident in the three case studies in this chapter. The process of social enterprise activity itself is an example of a paradigmatic shift in which voluntary and charitable organizations become more enterprising as an essential means for funding their activities, while preserving their social missions. This can be seen in Case C with the development of a socially inclusive fee structure where wealthier parents are charged more for childcare in order to enable poorer families to have access to high quality care. Similarly, Case B has developed eco-tourism as a new way of conserving wildlife habitats and complementing its existing training in environmental sustainability.

CONCLUSION

In the search for innovation in public service delivery, social enterprises have the potential to offer alternative models and solutions. The number of organizations in the third sector that consider themselves social enterprises is growing, although the extent to which this increase has been the result of specific governmental policies, the wider social changes or availability of market opportunities, is less clear (Lyon 2012). This lack of clarity is exacerbated by the confusion over what is meant by social enterprise, and the contested nature of this concept.

Despite the lack of a clear evidence base, there has been a continued and accelerating level of interest from consecutive governments in the UK to encourage social enterprise activities in TSOs in public service delivery. To those on the left of the political spectrum, social enterprises are seen as a means of prioritizing social equity goals using enterprise/ business mechanisms, while to those on the right of this spectrum, social enterprises are considered as ways of strengthening market mechanisms but with the benefits of maximizing social value. Within the 'Big Society' agenda of the current UK coalition government, there are a number of policies that are aimed at encouraging an innovative culture among social enterprises in delivering public services. These include policies that provide the right to challenge government policies and public sector agencies about the delivery aspects of a particular public service, encouraging entrepreneur spin-offs from the public sector, and developing new social investment vehicles such as the 'Big Society Bank' to help finance new social enterprise start-ups. However, due to the lack of rigorous research in this area, this policy trajectory is based on a presumed expectation of the economic and social benefits that social enterprises can provide, rather than on concrete empirical evidence (Lyon, Teasdale and Baldock 2010). Moreover, questions remain over the extent to which the claims of greater innovativeness in third sector social enterprises compared with organizations in the public and private sectors are substantiated (Osborne 1998). There are anecdotal cases of innovative organizations that can deliver new services, often cutting across traditional boundaries, whether they be sectoral, disciplinary or government departments (Mulgan, Tucker and Ali 2007). The three case organizations in this chapter attempt to illustrate the different ways in which an 'enterprising' culture can emerge in TSOs. They also highlight that care should be taken to avoid presenting too rosy a picture of innovation in TSOs as it can result in both benefits to, and challenges for, these organizations. More empirical research is needed to build a stronger evidence base in this area.

A further question persists about what should be done to create and support innovation in public service delivery in a way that recognizes the traditional 'social' roles of voluntary, charitable and other TSO organizations (e.g. advocacy and campaigning for the disadvantaged segments of civil society). On the one hand there is a need for a conducive environment that provides procurement and funding opportunities for social enterprises to grow. This is evident in the recent UK public service reforms that have availed more services that were originally delivered by public sector bodies to other providers in the third and private sectors. However, on the other hand, the case studies in this chapter have revealed that the innovative activities in TSOs often emerge as multi-faceted strategic responses by them to changes in the wider social and economic environment. We call for more comprehensive empirical research to understand these dynamics in greater breadth and depth.

NOTES

1. The 'Big Society' is an umbrella concept coined by David Cameron, the current British Prime Minister (since May 2010) and leader of the Conservative Party to mean empowering citizens, communities and local governments to work together to solve community and societal problems they face and to build the nation they desire. The concept has attracted both supporters and critics (see *The Numbers Behind the Big Society* at http://www.ncvo-vol.org.uk/networking-discussions/blogs/116/10/05/20/numbers-behind-big-society for an initial discussion).
2. UK charity law categorizes charities' trading activities as 'primary purpose trading' and 'non-primary purpose trading'. The former category is allowed if the activities contribute directly to the charity's purpose/objects, while the latter activities are carried out in order to raise additional funds for the charity rather than directly furthering the charity's purpose. Profits earned from non-primary purpose trading of charities are liable for corporate tax (or income tax for charitable trusts) (Charity Commission 2007).

REFERENCES

Bessant, J. and Tidd, J. (2007). *Innovation and Entrepreneurship*. Chichester: John Wiley.

Boyle, D. and Harris, M. (2009). *The Challenge of Co-production: How Equal Partnerships Between Professionals and the Public are Crucial to Improving Public Services*. London: NESTA. Available at: http://www.neweco nomics.org/sites/neweconomics.org/ files/The_Challenge_of_Co-production.pdf (accessed April 2011).

Brandsen, T., Van de Donk, W. and Putters, K. (2005). Griffins or chameleons? Hybridity as a permanent and inevitable characteristic of the third sector. *International Journal of Public Administration*, 28(9/10), 749–765.

Bruce, I. and Chew, C. (2011). Debate: the marketization of the voluntary sector. *Public Money and Management*, 31(3), 155–157.

Cabinet Office (1999). *Modernizing Government White Paper*. Government Cabinet Office. Available at: http:// archive.cabinet-office.gov.uk/moderngov/ (accessed February 2006).

Cabinet Office (2006). *Social Enterprise Action Plan – Scaling New Heights*. Available at: http://www.cabinet. office.gov.uk/third_sector/documents/ social_enterprise/se_action_plan_2006 (accessed July 2007).

Cabinet Office (2010). *Modern Commissioning: Increasing the Role of Charities, Social Enterprises, Mutuals and Co-operatives in Public Service Delivery*. London: Cabinet Office.

Charity Commission UK (2007). *Trustees, Trading and Tax: How Charities May Lawfully Trade*. Available at: http://www.charity-commission.gov.uk/publications/cc35.asp (accessed July 2008).

Charity Commission (2010). *How Many Charities?* Available at: http://www.charity-commission.gov.uk/ showcharity/registerofcharities/ registerhomepage.aspx?&=& (accessed October 2010).

Charity Commission for Northern Ireland (2010). *Register of Charities*. Available at: http://www.dsdni.gov.uk/ charity-commission-timeline-april-july.htm (accessed October 2010).

Chew, C. (2008). *Social Enterprise in Charities: Towards Hybrid Organizational Forms of Voluntary and Charitable Organizations in the UK*. Research Working Paper No. 49, ESRC Centre for Business Relationships, Accountability, Sustainability and Society (BRASS). Cardiff: Cardiff University.

Chew, C. (2009a). *The Extent and Impact of Formalized Social Enterprise Activities in Voluntary and Charitable Organizations involved in Public Service Provision in Wales*. Research Working Paper No. 53, ESRC Centre for Business Relationships, Accountability, Sustainability and Society (BRASS). Cardiff: Cardiff University.

Chew, C. (2009b). *Strategic Positioning in Voluntary and Charitable Organizations*. London: Routledge.

Deakin, K. (2000). *Putting Narrow-Mindedness Out of Countenance*. Civil Society Working Paper Series 4. Centre for Civil Society, London School of Economics and Political Science, London.

Dees, J.G., Emerson, J. and Economy, P. (2001). *Enterprising Nonprofits – A Toolkit for Social Entrepreneurs*. New York: John Wiley and Sons.

DiMaggio, P.J. and Powell, W. (1983). The iron cage revisited: institutional isomorphism and collective rationality in organizational fields. *American Sociological Review*, 48(2), 147–160.

DTI (2002). *Social Enterprise: A Strategy for Success*. UK Department of Trade and Industry. Available at: http:// www.dti.gov.uk/social enterprise (accessed April 2009).

Evers, A. (2005). Mixed welfare systems and hybrid organizations: changes in the governance and provision of social service. *International Journal of Public Administration*, 28(1), 737–748.

Fenner, N.P. and Martin, M. (2010). *User-Driven Social Enterprise: What Does it Mean in Practice?* Available at: http://www.hertspass.com/wp-content/uploads/2010/08/User-Driven-Social-Enterprise-Paper.pdf (accessed November 2010).

HM Treasury (1999). *Enterprise and Social Exclusion*. London: HM Treasury.

HM Treasury (2005). *Exploring the Third Sector in Public Service Delivery and Reform: A Discussion Document*. London: HM Treasury.

Lloyd, P. (2003). *Social Enterprise in the English RDAs and in Wales, Scotland and Northern Ireland*. London: Social Enterprise Coalition.

Lundvall, B. (ed.) (1992). *National System of Innovation: Towards a Theory of Innovation and Interactive Learning*. London: Pinter Press.

Lyon, F. (2012). 'Social innovation, co-operation, and competition: inter-organisational relations for social enterprises in the delivery of public services. In A. Nichols and A. Murdock (eds), *Social Innovation: Blurring Boundaries to Reconfigure Markets*. London: Palgrave, pp. 139–161.

Lyon, F. and Sepulveda, L. (2009). Mapping social enterprises: past approaches, challenges and future directions. *Social Enterprise Journal*, 5(1), 83–94.

Lyon, F., Teasdale, S. and Baldock, R. (2010). *Approaches to Measuring the Scale of the Social Enterprise Sector in the UK*. TSRC Working Paper 43, Third Sector Research Centre, Birmingham, UK.

Manfredi, F. and Maffei, M. (2008). Co-governance and co-production – from the social enterprise towards the public–private co-enterprise. In S.P. Osborne (ed.), *The Third Sector in Europe: Prospects and Challenges*. London: Routledge, pp. 183–208.

Mulgan, G., Tucker, S. and Ali, R. (2007). *Social Innovation: What It Is, Why It Matters and How Can It Be Accelerated*, Skoll Centre for Social Entrepreneurship Working paper. Available at: http://www.youngfoundation.org/files/images/03_07_What_it_is__SAID_.pdf (accessed August 2012).

NCVO (2004). *The UK Voluntary Sector Almanac 2004*. London: NCVO Publications.

NCVO (2006). *The UK Voluntary Sector Almanac 2006*. London: NCVO Publications.

NCVO (2009). *The State and the Voluntary Sector: Recent Trends in Government Funding and Public Service Delivery*. London: NCVO Publications.

NCVO (2010). *The UK Civil Society Almanac 2010*. London: NCVO Publications.

Normann, R. (1971). Organizational innovativeness. *Administrative Science Quarterly*, 16(2), 203–215.

Office of Scottish Charity Register (2010). *About the Scottish Charity Register*. Available at: http://www.oscr.org.uk/AbouttheScottishCharityRegister.stm (accessed October 2010).

Osborne, S.P. (1998). *Voluntary Organizations and Innovation in Public Services*. London: Routledge.

Osborne, S.P. and Brown, K. (2005). *Managing Change and Innovation in Public Service Organizations*. London: Routledge, pp. 115–168.

Osborne, S.P., Chew, C. and McLaughlin, K. (2008). The once and future pioneers? The innovative capacity of voluntary organizations and the provision of public services: a longitudinal approach. *Public Management Review*, 10(1), 51–70.

Social Enterprise Coalition (SEC) (2003). *There's More to Business than You Think: A Guide to Social Enterprise*. London: SEC.

Westall, A. (2007). *How can Innovation in Social Enterprise be Understood, Encouraged and Enabled?* London: Cabinet Office of the Third Sector.

Wymer, W., Knowles, P. and Gomes, R. (2006). *Nonprofit Marketing: Marketing Management for Charitable and Nongovernmental Organizations*. London: Sage Publications.

29. User involvement in public services innovation
Birgit Jæger

Innovation in public services is currently a government priority in many countries. In Denmark it rose to the top of the political agenda following the so-called Quality Reform (Regeringen 2007) launched by the government in 2007. The reform aims both to increase the quality of public services and to improve staff job satisfaction, and innovation is described as an important means to fulfil both aims. Given that the public sector has traditionally enjoyed a close relationship with public service users, User Driven Innovation (UDI) is expected to become a key driver of innovation in the public sector. But how are users involved in public services innovation in practice? This chapter seeks to shed light on this question by exploring the Danish case, which is particularly interesting to look at since Denmark has a long tradition of involving users in public service management and development.

This chapter begins with a brief overview of existing research on UDI. I then look more closely at public service users: who are they, and how can they participate in public sector innovation? These theoretical reflections will be followed by a discussion of user involvement in practice. I present two examples of how users are involved in innovation in different parts of the public sector in Denmark, and I analyse Danish policy papers to see how the user's role is defined. Finally, I reflect on some dilemmas which occur in user involvement in public service innovation processes.

USER DRIVEN INNOVATION

UDI is a further refinement of the concept of innovation. Classic innovation theory may be traced back to Schumpeter (1934), who used the concept to describe economic development in connection with private enterprises (Heertje 2006). Schumpeter defined innovation as *new combinations* of existing resources and he considered it a comprehensive concept since new combinations 'comprise a new product, a new method of production, the opening-up of a new market, the utilization of new raw materials and the reorganization of sectors of the economy' (Heertje 2006, p. 5). Ultimately, innovation should result in economic growth.

Schumpeter introduced the concept of entrepreneurship to capture the driving force of innovation. He initially described the entrepreneur as a person who thinks in untraditional ways, comes up with creative ideas, and combines existing knowledge and processes in new ways. While this may have been an adequate description during early capitalism, as production and the market became more complex, the institutional setting for innovation also became increasingly important (Fagerberg 2005, p. 10). By the mid 20th century, innovation processes were mainly institutionalized in laboratories and research and development (R&D) departments in big companies and universities. These changes led Schumpeter to modify the concept of entrepreneurship later in his career, when he redefined entrepreneurs as large companies which have the resources to do R&D. The entrepreneur was thus no longer regarded as a lone individual but as part of a team of researchers and designers who collaborated and became a 'collective entrepreneur' (Edquist and Hommen 1999, p. 74).

Schumpeter makes a sharp distinction between invention (a new idea, new technology or the discovery of new knowledge) and innovation (the application of inventions) (Heertje 2006, p. 6). This distinction has given rise to a widespread understanding of innovation as a linear process, and as an essentially applied science (Fagerberg 2005, pp. 8–9). In its simplest form, the linear model consists of three phases: 1) *invention*, where the scientist or engineer discovers new knowledge or has a creative idea; 2) *innovation*, where the entrepreneur(s) applies the new knowledge or idea, combines it with existing resources and transforms it into a new product or technology; and 3) *diffusion*, where the product/technology is diffused to society through the market (Hall 2005, p. 478). According to this understanding, innovation is generated by manufacturers and the user's role is that of a customer (von Hippel 2007) whose only involvement is deciding whether or not to buy the product.

However, this way of thinking has been widely criticized (Fagerberg 2005). Within the field of STS (Science, Technology and Society) both the linear model of innovation and the notion of distinct innovation phases have been questioned (Pinch and Bijker 1987; Williams et al. 2005). Several historical case studies of technological development show that this picture of innovation cannot be empirically documented. Due to this critique, the linear model has been rejected as a means of explaining innovation, but elements of the model are still understood as integral parts of the innovation process (Hall 2005, p. 479). Every innovation consists of a new idea/combination of existing resources which has to be applied somewhere and diffused to make a difference that can be called an 'innovation'.

Historical case studies of existing technology have also revealed that the users of technology sometimes play a much more active role than merely that of customers (Oudshoorn and Pinch 2003). In some cases, users play an active role in modifying a technology to fit their needs (Cronberg 1991), effectively becoming co-designers of the technology (Bijker 2010). In other cases, the user's needs may even turn out to be radically different from what the manufacturer had expected. This is clearly documented in a case study which describes how, a century ago, American farmers bought the first Ford T model, drove it to their farms, took off the wheels, and used the engine to run several other machines (Kline and Pinch 1996). Historical case studies have thus clearly shown that users must be understood as a relevant social group (Pinch and Bijke 1987) in the process of developing a technology.

Another strand of innovation studies similarly recognizes the active role of users. Here, innovation is understood as a learning process where new knowledge is created in the interaction between user and producer (Lundvall 1988). The core of the learning process is the user's experience with the product in question and the ideas that result about how to improve it in accordance with his/her needs. When these ideas are diffused back to the producer and taken seriously they can be used to generate new ideas for innovation. This was what happened in the American farmers' case. Some of the farmers left the wheels on their cars, but instead of driving them on the roads they used them in the fields to replace the plough horses. Initially, Ford was happy about this, but a couple of years later the company introduced the first tractor and started trying to persuade farmers to use tractors in their fields instead of the Ford T (Kline and Pinch 1996).

These findings are in line with von Hippel's (1988, 2007) studies of sources of innovation. Based on a series of empirical case studies carried out in different fields, von Hippel concludes that, 'empirical studies of the sources of innovation in both industrial and consumer goods' fields have shown that in many but not all of the fields studied, users rather than manufacturers are typically the initial developers of what later become commercially significant new products and processes' (von Hippel 2007, p. 7). Von Hippel's case studies reveal that users of, for instance, sports equipment come up with new ideas for the equipment or ideas for new ways to use the equipment, which they share with other sports enthusiasts. This pattern is also found in the development of open source software, where users continue to develop the software. Von Hippel defines this as User Innovation, and refers to the active users as Lead Users (von Hippel 2007, p. 9). Sometimes the innovation is shared within a network of users, or alternatively innovative ideas may be picked up by manufacturers and used for production.

Users' contribution to the innovation process is what von Hippel (1994) terms 'sticky information'. Based on Polanyi's concept of 'tacit knowledge' and Rosenberg's concept of 'learning by using', von Hippel describes how users develop knowledge about how to use a given technology. This knowledge is rooted in their needs and embedded in the local context. In technical problem solving, access to this information is crucial in order to generate further innovation. Sometimes this information is easy to access, but when it is 'costly to acquire, transfer, and use' it is termed 'sticky' (von Hippel 1994, p. 429).

Altogether, these case studies show that classical innovation theory, which overlooks users, is flawed. Users are the first to know how a specific product or service works and they are often able to come up with new ideas about how to improve it and/or optimize its use. According to this view, the users' role shifts from passive to active inasmuch as they either have specific ideas/requirements for a product or service, or can think of ways to improve it so that it fits their own needs.

In von Hippel's cases, it is the users who drive innovation. They experience a need, they come up with a solution, and they make it work in practice. In some of the Danish literature on UDI, the concept is defined rather more broadly. For example, Bason (2007) defines UDI as identifying users' real needs and then using this knowledge for innovation. Bason therefore prefers to talk about user *centred* innovation rather than user *driven* innovation. This raises the question of how involved users have to be for something to qualify as UDI. Do they actually have to drive the innovation, or is it enough if their needs and ideas for improvement are reflected in the innovation? There is no clear cut theoretical definition and, as we shall see in the following, both variants of the concept of UDI are used in practice.

PUBLIC SERVICE USERS AND THEIR INVOLVEMENT IN INNOVATION

Innovation theory is derived from studies of private sector innovation. If we want to apply these theories to the public sector we must ask: Who are public service users? And how can they be involved in public services innovation?

Even though the first question sounds very simple, there is no easy answer. To illustrate its complexity, consider the example of a state school pupil. The primary user is the child/student, and the pupil's relatives are indirect, or secondary (Bason 2007) users of the teaching service. But these are not the only two groups of users. Society as a whole can be regarded as a tertiary user group due to its dependence on the quality of the school service when former pupils are enrolled at university or employed in private or public organizations.

Seen from this perspective, we are all public service users because we are all affected by the quality of public services. Furthermore, private enterprises, non-governmental organizations and other civil society actors are not only tertiary users of public services. They are also primary users of a wide range of public services on which they depend in order to be able to run their businesses and carry out other activities. Yet despite this, public service users are still commonly defined as primary users or user representatives.

To answer the second question of how to involve users in innovation processes, we need to take a closer look at the roles that users can adopt when they engage with the public authorities (Jørgensen and Melander 1992). In the following, I briefly outline key user roles and explain how users can be involved in public service innovation processes.

In representative democracies, the individual's role is akin to that of a classic *citizen*, who elects politicians to represent him/her in the national parliament or local government. This role essentially defines the citizen as a user of society's democratic institutions. The best way to become involved in innovation is therefore to participate in the formulation of new policies, for instance by joining a political party or expressing one's political opinion in the public sphere.

With the emergence of policy networks in public sector governance (Sørensen and Torfing 2007) yet another role opens up for public service users – that of *participants* in a policy network. This role offers the user a variety of means to participate and become involved in innovation processes. According to Torfing (2008, p. 145), at least four participation channels are available to users: 1) public hearings; 2) user boards; 3) geographically limited democratic councils; and 4) local policy networks within different policy areas.

The fourth channel covers a range of different activities. Some of them are labelled 'social experiments', 'developmental projects' or 'design experiments'. Such experiments have flourished in the Danish public sector since the 1980s (Jæger 1993; Bogason 2001). Some take the form of large governmental development programmes while others are one-off local projects, but all are examples of projects that experiment with new ways to solve social problems through public service delivery. There is considerable variation in the scale, involved actors, methods and results of these projects, but altogether the Danish case offers a rich source of knowledge both about how to innovate in public services, and about how to include users and civil society actors in such experiments.

In welfare states, citizens also have a *client* role. Clients are users of a range of social services. Some clients are incapable of managing their own affairs and it is thus often difficult to involve them in public service innovation processes. In such cases, a secondary user can stand in as spokesperson for the client. Weak clients are often very dependent on public services, and often a very intimate relationship is formed between client and social workers. Social workers therefore typically possess detailed knowledge about the client's needs and wishes, which can be included in an innovation process on behalf of the client.

With the introduction of economic incentives in the public sector following various New Public Management reforms (Greve 2008), users have also acquired a new role as *customers*. This role is close to that described in classic innovation theory, as outlined above, as are the ways in which user involvement in innovation is envisaged. Here, users can choose among different services from either a public or private service provider, and if none of these meet their needs they can either attempt to modify the service themselves or ask the service provider to do so.

To sum up, there are a number of different ways in which users can be involved in innovation processes, depending on the type of relationship between governmental authorities and public service users. In some cases, users are involved in policy innovation, while in others they participate in service innovation. Importantly, a wide range of channels already exists for user involvement in Denmark. This tradition of involving citizens in policy processes and service delivery is a strong point of departure for introducing UDI in public services.

USER INVOLVEMENT IN PRACTICE

In this section, I turn to how user involvement in innovation processes plays out in practice in the Danish public sector. I present two examples from different parts of the public sector to illustrate how users are involved in public service innovation. I then analyse how UDI is depicted in policy papers written in connection with the Quality Reform.

UDI in Placement in Network Families

In Denmark, children whose parents are unable to assume their parental responsibilities are placed in a foster family. 'Network family' is the term used to describe a foster family which belongs to a child's existing network, such as a relative (e.g. grandparents), friends, neighbours or a teacher. In many cases, these network families would not normally be designated as foster families because they may not always possess the skills or resources to take care of a child in crisis. But they are selected because they have affective ties to the child and wish to give him/her a good childhood.

In 2008, one Danish municipal council noticed that 10 out of 15 network families failed to work out, with the result that the foster children had to find placements in new foster families. The council therefore launched an innovation project with a view to identifying new ways for family counsellors to support network families and prevent future breakdowns (Breiting 2010).[1]

The innovation process comprised four phases: 1) a start-up phase, 2) staff driven innovation, 3) user participation, and 4) user involvement. In the start-up phase, the project's idea and purpose were formulated, a project team was set up, and the manager of the department where the counsellors concerned worked offered his full support for the project.

In phase 2, the project team attempted to map the reasons why the network families had failed. Other professionals were also involved in this mapping, but not the users. The project plan stipulated that the mapping process should result in a proposal for a new praxis. During this process, however, the project team realized that the users' perspective was missing. The project leader therefore returned to the department manager and asked for a project extension and permission to involve the users.

In phase 3, the project team conducted 11 interviews with network families. As they analysed the interviews, the project team realized that they had underestimated the network families. They had not expected them to come up with ideas for improvements and new ways to solve problems, but the interviews yielded a great deal of insight into the 'sticky' information about the network families' everyday lives, and several ideas for improvement came up. Because of this, the project team decided to involve the network families directly in the innovation process, so they returned to the department manager with yet another petition to extend the project.

In phase 4, the network families were invited to a workshop together with the project team, the family counsellors and local politicians. Even though the network families were a little intimidated by this, most participated in the workshop and contributed with several new ideas for improving the counselling. The next step is to implement the new ideas, but it remains to be seen how this will work out in practice.

Breiting (2010, p. 68) concludes that so far the project has been a success, thanks to the ideas it generated about how to improve counselling for network families. She also concludes that such innovation processes are difficult to manage because they develop in unexpected directions due to the new knowledge generated during the process, and therefore they can take longer than estimated. Therefore, the support of the department manager is very important for the process.

The project learning process is also crucial. In the above case, the network families were not included from the outset. This was not due to bad intentions but to the social workers' routine work practices. They were simply not accustomed to regarding the network families as capable of making a useful contribution to such a project. Hence, it took some time before the staff realized that their input could be an asset to the innovation process. The families experienced a similar learning process. Through the interviews, they learned that the social workers were interested in their ideas, which gave them the self-confidence to participate in the workshop.

This case shows that even though we are dealing with public service users who are normally regarded as weak, it is possible to involve them in innovation processes that affect the services on which they depend. They may not be able to take the initiative themselves, but they can make a valuable contribution to a project set up by social work staff. Hence, staff play a key role in creating an enabling environment in which users can participate. This requires special training, which social workers currently do not receive. Consequently, the trade union 'Confederation of Professionals in Denmark' (in Danish 'FTF') recently pointed out that social work staff require further training if they are to fulfil the requirements stipulated in the Quality Report concerning UDI as a vehicle for public services innovation (Sørensen 2010).

Mindspot: UDI in a Library

From 2007–09, the main library in a large Danish city conducted a UDI project for young people between the ages of 14 and 20 under the slogan: 'Mindspot – Make it Your

Library' (Mindspot 2009). The idea was to find new ways to make the library relevant for youngsters, based on dialogue with them. The project received financial support from both Denmark and the EU, and to begin with 10 young people – the so-called 'Mindspotters' – were employed by the project for seven hours a week. They cooperated very closely with the librarians who worked on the project – the so-called 'Mindkeepers' – and they functioned as a link to other young people in the town.

From the outset, the idea was that Mindspot should be a physical place. However, it turned out to be impossible to find the right location and in the meantime the project developed in other directions. From its initial conception as a physical place, Mindspot developed into a universe which young people could meet at school, on the internet, in town or at the library. The project developed a range of new activities for young people. Mindspot staff visited schools to teach the pupils about information seeking, launched a blog, wrote a handbook for youngsters who wanted to start a new project, and arranged many different events. They even bought a caravan, which they christened the 'Spotmobil', in which they drove around the city and introduced the library's facilities in places where young people met up with each other (e.g. the beach in the summer, the art museum). They also initiated partnerships with two music festival organizations. The library itself served as a venue for hip hop music concerts, while the Spotmobil spread the word at other concerts around the country (Overgaard 2010).

In this project, UDI was enabled through dialogue. This was at its liveliest with the Mindspotter group, but also involved a group of voluntary youngsters who actively helped in arranging events and driving the Spotmobil, and who became important for the innovation process. During the project, the Mindkeepers realized that it wasn't a good idea to ask the young people their opinion about the future of the library because

> as soon as the word 'library' was mentioned the youngsters had a clear picture of what it was, hence it became very difficult to engage in a dialogue about what the library could become. Instead of using the Spotmobil conversations to get the youngsters to relate to the library of the future the Mindkeepers used them to gain insight into the needs of the users. (Mindspot 2009, p. 17)

The project was regarded as a success and most of the activities developed have since been continued.

One of the most difficult decisions that had to be taken during the project process was how to choose the Mindspotters. Many young people responded to the job advertisement, leaving the project managers with the tricky task of choosing the right people. Should they, for instance, select young people who 'loved the library' and described themselves as 'bookworms'? Ultimately, they decided to select a group of youngsters who recognized that the library was an important public service but at the same time thought it was old-fashioned and needed improvement. Besides this, they decided to go for a mixed group comprising Mindspotters of different ages, interests, competences and dreams for the future. This diversity was singled out in the final report (Mindspot 2009) as an important precondition for innovation.

This UDI project is quite different from the network families project. Here we are dealing with a group of staff who deliberately involved the targeted user group. They were also acutely aware that dialogue with the users was the core of the innovation process and, together with the Mindspotters, they facilitated this from the beginning. But, as in the case of the network families, Mindspot also had to modify the initial project idea. They had to drop the idea of creating a physical space for Mindspot, and come up with an alternative. It is no easy matter to change the initial idea for an innovation project, especially in a case like this when it is funded by external sources, but it turned out to be necessary.

UDI in Policy Papers

I now turn to a different example of user involvement: namely, how UDI is presented in policy papers written in connection with the Quality Reform. The analysis is based on policy papers drawn from three different sources (see Appendix 1). First, I examine the government's Quality Reform report which first introduced the reforms outlined earlier in the chapter. Secondly, I look at three policy papers published by the Council for Technology and Innovation (CTI), which was commissioned by the government to work on public sector innovation following the Quality Reform. At that time, the CTI had worked with innovation in the private sector for several years, but the public sector was a new area for it. Thirdly, I analyse two policy papers produced by the Danish Agency for Science, Technology and Innovation (DASTI), which was planning to run a new established research programme for UDI. I structure my analysis of the documents around four questions. The results are summarized in Table 29.1.

The definitions of UDI given in the table are quite similar, and mostly concur about what needs to be innovated. The Quality Reform's definition is the narrowest in that it refers to products and services, while the other two also include organizations and processes. However, it is remarkable that none of the three sources mentions policies as a target for innovation, and consequently they fail to reflect on the possibility of involving users in policy innovation processes. Conversely, all three sources agree that UDI should build on the users' needs, wishes and praxis, but differ as to whether or not future or unacknowledged needs should be included.

There is also some divergence in the way the users are defined. Whereas the Quality Reform defines users as customers or clients, the other two sources define users much more broadly, suggesting that the user might also be able to participate in policy networks.

Indeed, the greatest difference between the three sources is the way they address the users' role. The Quality Reform emphasizes that staff experience and knowledge about users' needs are useful in the innovation process. It also suggests that researchers, for instance sociologists or anthropologists, should map the users' needs and wishes. Seen from this perspective, the users' role is limited to answering questions in user satisfaction surveys and interviews, or being observed by researchers. The user may well come up with creative ideas, but the role of designing the new service is the preserve of researchers and staff. Hence, while the Quality Reform regards users as a passive source of knowledge, the CTI extends this definition and acknowledges that users can play an active role, and DASTI defines the user role as active co-designers of the innovation process.

These different views on how to integrate users mirror the different mandates of the agencies behind the respective policy documents. So these differences cannot only be

Table 29.1   User Driven Innovation in Public Services

	How is UDI defined?	How are the users defined?	What is the role of users?	What means are used to fulfil the objectives?
The Quality Report by the government	Development of new products or services based on identifying the user's needs and wishes	Users are patients in the health care system, elderly people dependent on daycare services, parents of kindergarten children	Passive – users are a necessary source of knowledge for innovation	Managers and staff work systematically with new ideas about how to improve quality
Council for Technology and Innovation	A systematic approach to the development of new services, processes, organizations and products based on research into the user's life, identity, praxis or needs, including unacknowledged needs	Users are clients, patients, staff, customers, firms and other partners	Users should be included either directly through dialogue, or indirectly by gathering knowledge about their lives	Programmes for innovation in the private sector should be adjusted accordingly and implemented in the public sector. Open innovation is recommended
Danish Agency for Science, Technology and Innovation	An approach for the development of new products, services and organizations, building on dialogue-based exploration of user's future praxis and needs	Users are consumers, customers, firms, citizens: everybody who applies what is developed and produced by people other than themselves	Active participation as co-designers	An interdisciplinary research programme based on 'Mode Two' methodology

attributed to the agencies' own interpretations. Notably also, despite their differences all the documents concur that it is the professionals who play the active role. None of the documents identifies public service users as agents. This shows that even if users are formally assigned an active role in the innovation process, its nature and extent are still defined by experts who also control the process.

As the above analysis shows, there is no clear cut definition of UDI in the policy papers, any more than there is in the academic literature. Everybody agrees that UDI has to take its point of departure in the needs of public service users, but it remains unclear who will identify the users' needs, what role they should have, and who should take charge of steering the process and meeting the project goals. The policy papers define user roles in a wide range of ways, from the completely passive user who is just a source of knowledge which staff, researchers and other experts can draw on in designing new public services, to the active user who functions as co-designer of new services. The only user role missing from the papers is one where the users themselves drive the innovation process, define their own problems and needs, steer the process and design the new services, as in the user innovation described by von Hippel.

Another notable feature of the policy papers is that they largely tend to describe UDI as something completely new. There is no mention of past experiments with user participation in policy networks, or social experiments and the like, which are a rich source of knowledge on how to involve users in innovation in public services.

CONCLUSION

In this concluding section, I reflect on four key dilemmas which arise in user involvement in practice. I link my discussion to the theoretical work on UDI outlined at the beginning of this chapter and to the examples outlined above of user involvement in practice drawn from both innovation projects and policy papers.

The first dilemma has to do with the question of who the users are. In the case of very specific public services (like network family counselling) the answer to this question is quite straightforward, but in other cases things become more complicated. Even when the users are defined as a special target group, as in the Mindspot initiative, the project team had to carefully reflect on how to select the young people to employ as Mindspotters. In projects where the users are not defined at the outset, project managers will always have to think carefully about this issue. Sometimes, lead users may be the best choice, while in other situations a representative group of users may be preferable. The choice depends on which kind of sticky information the project needs to gain access to in the innovation process.

The second dilemma is the degree of user involvement. As described above there are no clear parameters for this in the theoretical literature or in the examples presented. The network family case shows that social workers' perceptions about the user group, coupled with their own professional norms and routines, can be a barrier to UDI. However, after a learning process the staff realized that they had underestimated the users and it became possible to involve them in the process to a far larger extent than first anticipated. The case thus shows that user involvement depends partly on the ability and willingness of staff to learn and to modify their own norms and routines. It can therefore be misleading to talk about User Driven Innovation. If the innovation process is based on interaction between users and professionals, the term 'user involvement' is more accurate. This insight recently led an ongoing research project (Collaborative Innovation in the Public Sector – CLIPS) to shift its focus away from UDI, acknowledging instead that most public service innovation will take place through collaboration among users, professionals, politicians and sometimes civil society actors or the private sector (CLIPS 2008). This idea is akin to the concept of the 'collective entrepreneur', the difference being that the innovation process takes place in the social world and not in R&D departments in companies.

The third dilemma concerns how to manage innovation projects in practice. Especially in situations where a project has external funding, it is important to describe the idea and make a plan for activities from the outset. As we saw in the two cases described above, the project managers had to change both the plans and the basic project idea, and in the case of network families they even had to ask the manager to prolong the project twice. Mindspot describes this dilemma:

> How were we supposed to operate with fixed success criteria and at the same time try to ensure user involvement? We couldn't exactly tell the users that they were only allowed to think things that fit our predefined success criteria. So we were unsure what to prioritize – the initial success criteria or the ensuing experiences? (Mindspot 2009, p. 11).

The fourth dilemma concerns whether or not to use existing user involvement channels to create innovation. It may sometimes appear more efficient to go through some of these channels rather than launching a new project. However, such channels will typically have been created for other purposes so the question arises as to whether or not they can enable innovation. The trick is to find a balance between drawing on experience garnered from existing user involvement channels while simultaneously establishing new innovation areas through user involvement.

NOTE

1. The project is described in Tine Breiting's (2010) Master's thesis. She also worked as a part of the project team.

REFERENCES

Bason, C. (2007). *Velfærdsinnovation. Ledelse af nytænkning i den offentlige sektor.* Copenhagen: Børsens Forlag.
Bijker, W.E. (2010). How is technology made? That is the question! *Cambridge Journal of Economics*, 34, 63–76.
Bogason, P. (2001). *Fragmenteret forvaltning. Demokrati og netværksstyring i decentraliseret lokalstyre.* Århus: Systime.
Breiting, T. (2010). *Brugerne på banen. Brugerinddragelse og brugercentreret innovation.* Master's thesis from Department of Society and Globalization, Roskilde University.
CLIPS (2008). Collaborative Innovation in the Public Sector. Application for funding.
Cronberg, T. (1991). Experiments into the future. In T. Cronberg, P. Duelund, O.M. Jensen and L. Qvortrup (eds), *Danish Experiments – Social Constructions of Technology.* Copenhagen: New Social Science Monographs, pp. 9–23.
Edquist, C. and Hommen, L. (1999). Systems of innovation: theory and policy for the demand side. *Technology and Society*, 21, 63–79.
Fagerberg, J. (2005). Innovation: a guide to the literature. In J. Fagerberg, D.C. Mowery and R.R. Nelson (eds), *The Oxford Handbook of Innovation.* Oxford: Oxford University Press, pp. 1–26.
Greve, C. (2008). Konkurrencereformen og ledelsesstrategier. In J. Torfing (ed), *Ledelse efter kommunalreformen – sådan tackles de nye udfordringer.* Copenhagen: DJØF Publishing, pp. 121–140.
Hall, B.H. (2005). Innovation and diffusion. In J. Fagerberg, D.C. Mowery and R.R. Nelson (eds), *The Oxford Handbook of Innovation.* Oxford: Oxford University Press, pp. 459–485.
Heertje, A. (2006). *Schumpeter on the Economics of Innovation and the Development of Capitalism.* Cheltenham and Northampton, MA: Edward Elgar.
Jæger, B. (ed.) (1993). *Developmental Programmes as a Strategy to Innovate Social Policy.* Copenhagen: AKF Forlaget.
Jørgensen, T.B. and Melander, P. (eds) (1992). *Livet i offentlige organisationer.* Copenhagen: DJØF Publishing.

Kline, R. and Pinch, T.J. (1996). Users as agents of technological change: the social construction of the automobile in the rural United States. *Technology and Culture*, 37(4), 763–795.

Lundvall, B.-Å. (1988). Innovation as an interactive process: from user–producer interaction to the national system of innovation. In G. Dosi, C. Freeman, R. Nelson, G. Silverberg and L. Soete (eds), *Technical Change and Economic Theory*. London: Pinter Publishers, pp. 349–369.

Mindspot (2009). *Mindspot – Make it Your Library*. Århus: The Main Library.

Oudshoorn, N. and Pinch, T.J. (eds) (2003). *How Users Matter: The Co-construction of Users and Technologies*. Cambridge, MA: The MIT Press.

Overgaard, L. (2010). Mindspot partners up. *Scandinavian Public Library Quarterly*, no. 3, 11–13.

Pinch, T.J. and Bijker, W.E. (1987). The social construction of facts and artifacts: or how the sociology of science and the sociology of technology might benefit each other. In W.E. Bijker, T.P. Hughes and T.J. Pinch (eds), *The Social Construction of Technological Systems: New Directions in the Sociology and History of Technology*. Cambridge, MA: The MIT Press, pp. 17–50.

Schumpeter, J. (1934). *The Theory of Economic Development*. Oxford: Oxford University Press.

Sørensen, E. and Torfing, J. (eds) (2007). *Theories of Democratic Network Governance*. London: Palgrave-Macmillan.

Sørensen, M.B. (2010). *Styrkelse af fagligheden gennem brugerinvolvering*. FTF Documentation, no. 1. Copenhagen: FTF – Confederation of Professionals in Denmark.

Torfing, J. (2008). Strategisk styring af styringsnetværk i kommunerne. In J. Torfing (ed.), *Ledelse efter kommunalreformen – sådan tackles de nye udfordringer*. Copenhagen: DJØF Publishing, pp. 141–162.

von Hippel, E. (1988). *The Sources of Innovation*. New York: Oxford University Press.

von Hippel, E. (1994). 'Sticky information' and the locus of problem solving: implications for innovation. *Management Science*, 40(4), 429–439.

von Hippel, E. (2007). Horizontal innovation networks – by and for users. *Industrial and Corporate Change*, 16(2), pp. 293–315.

Williams, R., Stewart, J. and Slack, R. (2005). *Social Learning in Technological Innovation: Experimenting with Information and Communication Technologies*. Cheltenham and Northampton, MA: Edward Elgar Publishing.

APPENDIX 1:   LIST OF POLICY PAPERS

The Quality Report by the Government

Regeringen (2007). *Bedre velfærd og større arbejdsglæde – regeringens strategi for høj kvalitet i den offentlige service.* Available at: www.kvalitetsreform.dk (accessed 10 November 2011).

Council for Technology and Innovation (CTI)

Rådet for Teknologi og Innovation (2008a). *Innovation Danmark 2008. Handlingsplan fra Rådet for Teknologi og Innovation.* Forsknings- og Innovationsstyrelsen. Available at: www.fi.dk (accessed 10 November 2011).
Rådet for Teknologi og Innovation (2008b). *Øget videnspredning og innovation i den offentlige sektor. På vej mod en strategi.* Forsknings- og Innovationsstyrelsen. Available at: www.fi.dk (accessed 10 November 2011).
Rådet for Teknologi og Innovation (2008c). *Strategi for styrket innovation i den offentlige sektor.* Forsknings- og Innovationsstyrelsen. Available at: www.fi.dk (accessed 10 November 2011).

Danish Agency for Science, Technology and Innovation (DASTI)

Forsknings- og Innovationsstyrelsen (2006). *Brugerdreven innovation. Baggrundsrapport til et strategisk forskningsprogram.* Available at: www.fi.dk (accessed 10 November 2011).
Forsknings- og Innovationsstyrelsen (2008). *Fra inspiration til innovation – casesamling fra offentlige og private organisationer.* Available at: www.fi.dk (accessed 10 November 2011).

30. Citizens and the co-creation of public service innovations

Michelle Farr

INTRODUCTION

This chapter explores the question of how citizen involvement may facilitate innovations in public services, considering how changes can be instigated from the perspectives and initiatives of people who use public services. User involvement has been seen as a key source of innovation within the public sector (Department for Innovation, Universities and Skills 2008), and the role of citizens in creating innovation within public services can be analysed both through independent social welfare user movements and user-centred innovation practices (e.g. Von Hippel 2005). This chapter explores these different approaches and considers them within wider power relations and political contexts.

The chapter begins by exploring some of the definitions and typologies of innovation. It reflects on the differences between private sector and public service innovation, considering the issues associated with importing private sector innovation practices and theory into the political and policy context of public services. The chapter then explores both user-centred innovation literature and literature based on citizen and user participation within public services. These two different theoretical lenses are then used to analyse a local government case that developed an innovation programme based on user-centred innovation practices such as co-creation and co-production.

INNOVATION WITHIN PUBLIC SERVICES

There are significant differences between innovation in the context of public services in comparison to private sector goods and services. As Hartley (2008) notes:

> there has perhaps been 'over-adoption' of concepts, models and theories which derive from private sector manufacturing, with insufficient consideration of how the context, goals, processes and stakeholders of public service organisations and services can be different in ways which are significant for the application of innovation theory. (Hartley 2008, p. 198)

There are several different comparative aspects between private and public sector innovation that are considered to be important to the analysis within this chapter. First, whilst private sector innovation often focuses at the level of the firm or particular products or services, public sector innovation often concerns working across organisations to tackle complex social problems (Hartley 2011). Secondly, the drivers of innovation within public services can be different from those in the private sphere. Whilst economic competition is a key influence within the private sector, a catalyst for innovation within the public sphere can also concern changing aspects of society (Hartley 2011). Thirdly, the outcomes of innovation may be assessed differently within the private and public spheres, where private sector innovation is valued according to profit or market position whilst public service innovation may be valued according to different stakeholders' perceptions of public value, which could include effectiveness and efficiency (Hartley 2008) or social justice and equality. Fourthly, different dimensions of innovation within the public sector have been proposed (Hartley 2005). Whilst concepts of product, service, process, position (new context or users) and strategic innovations can overlap with private sector innovation literature, rhetorical innovation (new discourses, language and concepts) and governance innovation (new forms of decision-making and democratic institutions) have been less considered within the private sector literature (Hartley 2008, p. 201). Walker (2006), in his work on local government innovation, develops a different typology from Hartley (2005), differentiating between product, process and ancillary innovations. Product innovations are defined as new products or services, and incorporate 'total innovations' (new services or products to new users), 'expansionary innovations' (similar services to new groups of users) and 'evolutionary innovations' (providing a new service to existing users) (Walker 2006, p. 313). Process innovations alter relationships between organisational staff and might change rules, roles, procedures and structures, impacting the management of an organisation. Ancillary innovations involve working across organisational boundaries with other service providers or users where the successful implementation of the innovation 'is reliant upon others' (Walker 2006, p. 314). However, this typology does not cover rhetorical (discursive) or governance innovations, which may be important in innovations in the public sphere.

Public policy in its focus on public service innovation often conflates the two terms of 'improvement' and 'innovation'. However, there are important distinctions between facilitating innovation and improvement. Central to these is the idea that innovation involves 'discontinuous change' whereas improvement implies 'incremental development' (Osborne and Brown 2010). The processes of managing discontinuous change may demand distinctly different approaches to current institutional practices, involving changes in roles and relationships between service users and professionals (Hartley 2005), whereas improvements tend to build on existing organisational practices and processes. Lynn goes further in the description of innovation and is here worth quoting at length:

> Innovation must not be simply another name for change, or for improvement, or even doing something new lest almost anything qualify as innovation. Innovation is properly defined as an original, disruptive, and fundamental transformation of an organization's core tasks. Innovation changes deep structures and changes them permanently. Innovation necessarily involves all of the difficulties associated with arranging cooperative, collective action: conflict, defection, asymmetric information, and assessment and assignment of risks. A change unaccompanied by conflict and controversy is a change that is likely to have left the status quo untransformed and those in power more powerful still, and therefore is not an innovation. (Lynn 1997, p. 96)

This definition highlights how power dynamics and relationships may change and that 'conflict and controversy' might play a part in the process of innovation. Such conflict and controversy may occur to a greater extent within public policy innovations because of the essentially contested nature of public service provision. All innovation within public services takes place within a particular policy and political context and these policies and their goals and outcomes can be disputed. The governance of the public sphere takes place within a pluralist context, characterised by the proliferation of 'differences of culture, faith, lifestyle and values, differences which place public organisations at the intersection of conflicting needs and alternative definitions of the common good' (Hoggett 2006, p. 176). Politicians, policy makers and citizens may all have a particular interest in the development of particular innovations (Hartley 2008); however, these different groups and agents have unequal access to resources and processes to advocate and campaign for the representation of their diverse interests. Because of this it is important to consider the underlying power relations that operate within processes of innovation within public services. Understanding and analysing the dynamics of differential and possibly conflicting concerns in processes of innovation within a political context are particularly important within the arena of public policy. This chapter now considers two different theoretical approaches to understanding how the involvement of citizens within public services may create innovative developments. Initially user-centred innovation literature is considered, before exploring citizen participation theories and the role of independent welfare service user movements in promoting innovations within public services.

USER-CENTRED INNOVATION

'User-centred innovation' (Von Hippel 2005), 'distributed innovation' (Sawhney and Prandelli 2000) and 'co-creation' (Prahalad and Ramaswamy 2004) are terms that have developed within private sector innovation literature to explore how innovation can be created through dynamic interaction between companies and external customers, technologies and knowledge. Communication and shared learning between consumers and organisational employees enable knowledge to be created through 'a synergistic interplay between individual contributions and social interactions' (Sawhney and Prandelli, 2000, p.28). Transparency and risk sharing are seen as key, facilitating collaborative dialogue and trust (Prahalad and Ramaswamy, 2004). This process is governed by the organisation who defines the 'ground rules for participation' (Sawhney and Prandelli 2000, p. 25). Such innovation models have been increasingly applied within public services (e.g. Cottam and Leadbeater 2004; Bowden 2005; Bate and Robert 2007; Bessant and Maher 2009; Bason 2010) to describe examples of where consumers/service users collaborate with staff within organisations. Co-creation is used to denote a collaborative model where users develop partnerships with professionals, going beyond consultation to 'a more creative and interactive process which challenges the views of all parties and seeks to combine professional and local expertise in new ways' (Cottam and Leadbeater 2004, p. 22). As Bason (2010) notes, practices of co-creation often depend upon processes similar to deliberative democracy to make decisions. However, public service co-creation literature seems to have rarely critically analysed the role of power relations within these decision-making processes. The position of users within co-creation processes does not seemingly challenge policy directions, Bason (2010, p. 153) stating that citizen involvement in innovation is: 'Not about increasing democratic participation or legitimacy through the act of involvement in itself. It is about finding better solutions to achieve *politically defined visions of the future*' (emphasis added).

Because user innovation literature has been developed within the private sector and then applied to the public sector, it can overlook the political and democratic nature of citizen and service user participation. However, this chapter suggests that understanding the political and democratic nature of participation is essential to analyse the role of public service users and citizens in processes of the co-creation of innovations. This proposition is developed further by examining some of the theory and history of citizen participation within public services.

CITIZEN PARTICIPATION AND WELFARE SERVICE USER MOVEMENTS

Beresford (2002) notes how the analysis of participation in public services can often focus on technical aspects, abstracted from politics and ideology. He identifies two different approaches to service user participation within welfare services: the managerialist and the democratic models. Beresford (2002, 2009) sees that the last three decades of neo-liberalism have promoted managerialist models of participation, focusing on state concerns of efficiency and effectiveness. Here participation is often defined through state agendas, which can be limited in scope and substance, maintaining existing power relations. Informed by neo-liberal ideologies, participation is framed in market terms and is seen as a means to encourage innovation, individual choice and consumerism; however, the power of decision-making stays within institutions. In contrast to this, the democratic model of participation is built on the collective action of citizens and welfare service user movements and focuses on the redistribution and transformation of power relations. It is liberational and political and focuses on social change, with agency, autonomy and independence being prioritised through a rights agenda (Beresford 2002). Welfare service user movements have highlighted ingrained structural inequalities and illustrated how the state has tried to define the disadvantages that people have suffered as a result of individual conditions rather than exclusionary social structures. These groups focus on emancipatory changes, explicitly highlighting power relations and how some dominant social groups may, through their practices, harm the freedom and independence of less powerful social groups (Williamson 2010). Beresford and Croft (2004) assert that whilst managerialist and consumerist participation approaches have led to little transfer of power within decision-making, service user movements have been associated with major improvements and innovation in legislation, policy, culture, theory and provision of services, including the development of new discourses, an emphasis on human and civil rights, the social model of disability, direct payments which put users in control of their support and a campaigning force which works for the inclusion of users in all areas of the social world.

Some examples of innovations that have developed through welfare service user movements are now explored to highlight some of the important differences between user-centred innovation practices that have been developed within the private sector and the emancipatory focus of welfare service user movements. The disability movement has successfully campaigned to bring about significant changes in public service policy and practice to support disabled people's rights. Two particular achievements are the development of the social model of disability and direct payments. Both of these can be seen as examples of new and innovative ideas that have promoted discontinuous change within mainstream public service provision, developing new discourses and practices within the public sphere that have promoted disabled people's rights. Both have attempted to catalyse a transformation in the power relationships between disabled people, public service provision and wider society. For example, the redefinition of disability as a political and social issue was instigated by groups of disabled people, the Union of the Physically Impaired Against Segregation (UPIAS) redefining disability as socially created: 'Disability is something imposed on top of our impairments by the way we are unnecessarily isolated and excluded from full participation in society' (UPIAS 1975, p. 4).

This social model of disability proved highly influential and has increasingly been adopted within policy, research and wider social discourse. The social model of disability fits within Hartley's innovation dimensions as a rhetorical innovation that created a fundamentally different concept of disability. However, the social model of disability can be seen as much more than just a new concept; it essentially challenged the conception of disability as an individual issue and transformed understandings of disability as a social concept, highlighting the structural disadvantages and inequalities that disabled people faced in participating fully in society. In this sense the social model of disability can be seen as instigating a major paradigm shift and a radical innovation that promoted equality and social justice.

Turning to the field of mental health, the Hearing Voices Network (HVN) was inspired by the work of Marius Romme, a psychiatrist, and Sandra Escher, who pioneered new approaches to working with people who hear voices. HVN is run by voice-hearers themselves (Smith 2007) and the approach supports people to understand their voices in the context of their life history and experience, exploring the content of the voices with respect to a person's concerns (Garety 2001). The practices promoted by HVN are antithetical to traditional psychiatric treatment and challenged the dominance of medical conventions. Romme and Escher (1993) edited a book published by MIND entitled *Accepting Voices*, describing their approach, which provoked some critical response: 'If, as it says, this book is intended to be used by people who are beginning to hear voices then I believe it to be not just ill advised but potentially dangerous' (Cochrane 1994, p. 1649).

The extent to which such models have influenced mainstream thinking is mixed with some professionals exploring the potential of such models, developing therapeutic rather than medical approaches (e.g. Garety, 2001). The Hearing Voices movement is another example of a radical innovation and paradigm shift that promotes a fundamentally different understanding and treatment of the phenomenon of hearing voices. It promotes innovative changes in social relations between service users and providers, and can be classified as a bottom-up, ancillary innovation. Using Hartley's (2005) dimensions of innovation it can be seen as both a rhetorical innovation that promotes new concepts and understandings of a phenomenon, and an innovation in governance, whereby people who hear voices establish their own meanings to these voices rather than psychiatrists having the power of ascertaining and advocating medical meanings and treatments.

These different examples of innovation that have been promoted through welfare service user movements can be analysed with respect to some of the differences identified earlier between private sector and public service innovations. The examples operate at a macro, societal level, attempting to influence wider debate and instigate emancipatory changes within broader public spheres and social relations. The drivers for innovation can be seen to originate from personal experiences of the failure of traditional public services to meet the needs and rights of citizens who have had to use them, these service users having less power and control than service providers. Movements are often instigated and run by users and activists who may give their time freely, some of whom may have become radicalised as a result of adverse experiences of services (Williamson 2010). They can be seen to have developed in contestation to particular public policies and services, user groups disputing the labelling or treatment of particular phenomena as individualised experience and creating a politicised, collective agenda that highlights the political and social aspects of experience. They have challenged dominant paradigms of service provision and created alternative meanings and modes of support (Barnes and Cotterell 2011). In this way they do not find 'better solutions to achieve politically defined visions of the future' (Bason 2010, p. 153) but contest and challenge defined visions, highlighting power inequalities. They have challenged the locus of control and decision-making, arguing for what Moore and Hartley (2010, p. 52) define as governance innovations that 'redistribute the right to define and judge value'. The outcomes of innovation intend to transform wider structural power relations, and establish greater equality, social justice and the control of appropriate support.

Welfare service user groups have often operated outside institutions within independent spaces and civil society, rather than working inside organisations. In this way they follow Fraser's (1997, p. 81) concept of 'subaltern counterpublics' where 'parallel discursive arenas' can provide independent space for people to create and propagate 'counter-discourses' that account for people's own identified interests and needs. Both the disability movement and HVN can be seen as subaltern counterpublics, creating oppositional, counter-discourses within independent spaces, HVN having the support of radical professionals. In contrast to this, open innovation and co-creation models situate innovation processes within institutions, where organisations sponsor, endorse and host collaborative innovation. This chapter now considers examples of how co-creation processes have been applied within a specific local government case and reflects upon both the process and outcomes of this approach, in the light of both innovation and citizen participation literature.

CASE STUDY AND METHODS

The research described here was part of a wider study that explored the processes and outcomes of co-production, co-design and co-creation projects within different public services. Initially a realist synthesis (Pawson 2006) was conducted of co-production, co-design and co-creation literature, alongside eight expert interviews with facilitators and consultants who had been involved in a number of different projects based on these principles (labelled as 'expert interviews' within this chapter). Two longitudinal case studies were then researched, this chapter using data from an innovation programme within a local government organisation. My own role within this case was as an independent evaluator and researcher, observing the programme through meetings and events and interviewing different people about their involvement in the projects. The methodology and analysis were informed by both a morphogenetic approach (Archer 1995) and realistic evaluation (Pawson and Tilley 1997).

The local government case focused on a small-scale innovation programme, based on co-production and co-creation principles, that involved both staff and local citizens in developing person-centred public services and strategic policy-making. It engaged staff and service users in collaborative projects and worked in policy and service areas such as housing, public health and social services, working with local communities, families on low income and people who had been in prison. I followed the pathway of the project from its beginning (which had started before I began my research), tracking the various projects and their outcomes through documents and reports. I then interviewed 17 different staff and conducted 2 focus groups, one with 3 community participants and 2 members of staff, and another focus group with 3 members of staff (who were also interviewed separately). Staff included a range of senior managers, policy managers, service managers, front line staff and project co-ordinators, all of whom had worked with the programme in some way. Community participants had been involved in and worked on specific projects facilitated by the programme. Quotes are labelled as staff interviews or community participants, without job types to preserve anonymity. In addition to this, other data analysed included a wide range of documents and reports that detailed both the development of the programme and its projects.

CASE STUDY FINDINGS

The Projects

This chapter focuses on aspects of two different projects that the local government innovation programme facilitated. The Fathers' project developed within a centre for families and their young children where staff were concerned that their services weren't reaching fathers. They held several events to connect with fathers to find out how they could develop their centre to reach out to and support the needs of fathers in the local area. As a direct consequence of this work they employed a Fathers' worker. This project resulted in a 'total innovation' where new services were provided to a new group of people. The second project that is focused upon is a Community Shop that was an original idea of a group of local residents who then developed the project themselves with the support of the local government innovation programme, creating a new community resource in an area of deprivation that had been the subject of numerous regeneration initiatives. The Community Shop can also be seen as an example of a 'total innovation' where a new service was provided to new people. It also exhibits characteristics of a process or governance innovation whereby the community residents took on the decision-making, management and organisation of the Community Shop. It is also an ancillary innovation, as its success was dependent upon local residents' activities.

Processes of Involvement

The innovation programme usually began its processes of involvement by understanding the experiences, perspectives and aspirations of local citizens and service users within specific community areas or services. This work involved collecting narratives, stories and observations to provide rich, in-depth insights into everyday practices and experiences. Citizen and service user perspectives were then shared, which often had an important impact on staff, who commented on the power of these stories and the ways in which the stories made them think differently. Ideas were generated to tackle the issues that arose through these discussions and both staff and citizens then worked collaboratively to turn these ideas into action, generating different projects and services as a result. Creating the space for different people to come together and share their perspectives and experiences was facilitated in a number of different ways. The programme adapted its ways of working to ensure that different people felt comfortable in participating in the projects on their own terms. This meant a deliberative forum could take the shape of a curry evening or a morning get-together in a local café. For example, within the Father's project, an evening was organised for fathers to become involved in cooking a curry for everyone, where everybody collectively worked together. Working alongside people in informal activities could support conversations and engagement. The process could literally be walked into from off the street; for example, one participant saw the evening advertised as he was walking past, getting involved with the enticement of a free meal and a drink. Similarly, the Community Shop held all its meetings within a local café. Here a staff participant describes a typical meeting:

> The meetings aren't minuted, there is no agenda, people are having cups of tea and toast, children are pulling chairs and climbing and falling off things. People come, people go. Somebody is sent off to do something on the computer, comes back with this, and if they shout loud enough they can get heard. And then there are little conversations going on and it is one corner of the café, it is just a chaotic melee of things and that is how it works. And if you want to go for a cigarette and make a contact then that is fine, I like things better that way and it seems to work for them. People can turn up when they're ready, they don't have to be there at 9 o'clock. It's not formalised, they don't do all the proper things you would do but they somehow do know where they are up to and they do know what they want to do next and people go away with tasks that will help the next time and they do them and it works. (Local government interview)

The importance of basing participative processes within the context of people's own lives rather than institutions was also spoken of within an expert interview:

> Professionals have to become more creative, also more brave and basically go where the people are and there's still the thinking that users should come to where they are. If you want to have a discussion and involvement of users, you cannot make elderly people come to you, but you have to go to the bingo hall. You have to go to the pub on a Friday night, that's where most of the citizens are, at least in this country. (Expert interview)

Focusing upon the analysis of the content of participative discussions, within the Fathers' project, conversations derived from participants' own interests and concerns:

> It was an absolutely open discussion with dads about what they wanted. What [the area] was good for. What they wanted to do with their kids. (Local government staff interview)

Particularly within the Community Shop, community members saw that the content and outcomes of participation benefited themselves both socially and materially. Whilst the processes of involvement were not 'subaltern counterpublics', as described by Fraser

(1997), the innovation programme in effect attempted to host loose and engaging processes that fitted with local people's own interests, perspectives and needs. The role of staff within the innovation programme became to act as facilitators and hosts of these open spaces. Here part of the project's work became to facilitate a 'safe space' for the local residents to create and develop work as they wanted in consultation with the wider community.

> We have to be the buffers or the bodyguards and say, 'actually, no they need that space to go and do what they want to do' . . . just to allow them to have the free space to do what they want to do. (Local government staff)

Some ideas of the Community Shop group were in contradistinction with some organisational policies, yet it was seen as important to give community participants decision-making power and control over the process:

> it is their[s], not ours, it's theirs. That's what we keep saying, 'you may have given us the funding to do this project but actually it's not our project'. (Local government interview)

The organisational structure of the project was developed with local residents being appointed within key organisational roles. Community members got training in computer skills, the group developed the business plan, and logos and artwork were designed. There were collaborations between the shop and other local agencies that joined resources to develop the project further. New resources and services were developed and the project was seen as a success in practical, material and personal terms.

KEY LESSONS

Three different practices that supported these user-centred innovation processes can be identified from the research carried out.

Modes of Engagement

The local government case used different activities, alongside informal meetings in cafés, to involve different people and had considerable success in engaging with people that might be deemed 'hard to reach'. Its informal approach enabled easy access, and it has been highlighted in other studies on participation that more formalised professionally styled meetings may put some service users off becoming involved (Beresford et al. 2011, p. 322). Ensuring an easy and accessible format where people do not feel intimidated or nervous about becoming involved is important to ensure greater access to participative projects. Understanding people's motivation and interest in taking part was essential to keep people involved and engaged over a longer period of time. Developing the Community Shop meant that local community members would be able to buy particular goods at cheaper prices. Their motivation to become involved was facilitated by a process where they developed their own ideas, made the decisions and had control of the project's direction, getting feedback from the local community through local events and discussions. Where local people could see that their engagement and participation were making a significant difference, this created a virtuous circle which maintained their long-term involvement. Within the development of the Community Shop staff had ceded all decision-making power they could to the community members. This was commented upon by another member of staff as quite unusual practice:

> [They] have stepped back, which I wouldn't have done . . . My natural inclination would be to hold their hand all the way through and not direct them but lead them in the way we wanted it to go . . . I just would have panicked if it was my project, to hand it over. (Local government staff)

This illustrates how, when participative programmes are hosted by organisations, the power dynamics between those institutions and their service users can permeate the participative processes. Staff institutional roles meant they had some power and resource to facilitate the extent to which service users were influential within the collaborative processes.

An Open Systems Approach

The innovation programme brought together a number of different people from diverse areas, developing bridges to enable people who would not normally work together to share perspectives and experiences, supporting more collective approaches:

> It's all about building consensus, and a participatory approach to working across agencies and disciplines and only by setting it up like that will you then get those findings that are not only interesting, but mean something to all of those people that are on board and something will happen with them as well. Because all those people are on board and they are going to make something happen with them. (Co-ordinator)

These conversations enabled people to understand the different institutional contexts within which people worked and how wider systemic issues could impact people's working relationships:

> Within our own directorate people were saying to me, 'it was really interesting to have that conversation with somebody from that service because I never get to meet them' and when you create the conditions in which people have those conversations things take off don't they? (Local government staff)

Thus the processes enabled new links and networks across hierarchies, departmental silos and local communities.

Spaces and Political Mandate

Osborne and Brown (2010) illustrate how individual agency may be a necessary, yet not sufficient, condition for innovation, a theory borne out through this research. Organisational mandate and sponsorship of these innovation processes was essential to the success of the innovation programme. Whilst wide senior management support and sponsorship was not necessary for specific projects, endorsement and support from key senior figures of the innovation programme was important to its survival and success.

> The dynamics of the organisation, the politics and all of that was so important ... because it is threatening, it does challenge the way that things get done. (Local government interview)

Whilst community participants and staff's enthusiasm often drove these projects, resources and broader, structured organisational support were also needed to establish and embed the innovation programme within the wider institution.

DISCUSSION

These examples of co-creation and innovation are now analysed with respect to the earlier literature review on innovation and citizen participation. It was illustrated how service user movements were often built upon contestation of particular public services, with the drivers for user movements often being based on the failure of traditional services. This failure can be seen as a catalyst for radical change. In some contrast to this, the local government innovation projects focused on co-creation and shared interests, building a collaborative approach across diverse stakeholders where there was consensus and agreement for change. Processes were directed and co-ordinated by community members themselves rather than institutions. However, the projects operated at a micro level within specific areas, working within institutional and policy trajectories. The Community Shop became an illustration of the 'Big Society' in action. There was less space for the development of counter-narratives or the creation of groups of subaltern counterpublics that disputed aspects of these policies. In contrast to welfare service user movements, wider political contestation did not arise.

Whilst the projects that were developed were not radical paradigm shifts, they did build towards empowerment of participants. The outcomes generated by the projects tended to be small scale and localised, with some changes in the locus of decision-making within particular community contexts. The innovation projects successfully brought new groups of service users together who might not have joined welfare service user groups nor would they have set foot in professionally dominated participative arenas. 'Micro-emancipation' (Alvesson and Willmott 1992) tended to occur where localised reform brought welcome gains. For example, the confidence, self-esteem and skills of the participants involved in the Community Shop grew considerably, and the project had a positive impact on their material and social well-being and built greater social networks and bonds through the community.

The degree of power that service users had within these processes was partially dependent upon staff's approaches. It was within staff's 'gift' to facilitate changes in power relations and it was through their positions and roles that this was achieved. This was particularly apparent within the local government project's Community Shop, where staff had ceded all decision-making power they could to the community members:

> You can come up with an idea and they just turn round and say, 'yep, if you think that works'. (Community participant)

However, within the research there was no case where the actual public sector institutional power structures were changed – decisions about who could make the decisions remained with professionals:

> The power distribution in a normal hierarchy would still be there . . . the most powerful need to give permission for others to have power. (Local government and education expert interview)

The innovation programme supported changes in power relations and altered the locus of decision-making where it had the capacity and legitimacy to do so, as sponsored by the wider local government institution. In this way its empowering approach led to community members having greater power and responsibility dependent on the courtesy of institutional sponsorship. This again stands in contrast to welfare service user movements that contest and challenge institutional power structures.

CONCLUSION

The research examples within this chapter illustrate how the involvement processes of an innovation programme were based in the context of citizens' own lives, rather than focusing on institutional practices and concerns. More innovatory developments that were discontinuous with organisational trajectories tended to operate outside professionally based zones where projects worked in line with everyday practices and community contexts of local citizens, such as the Community Shop. This could on occasion produce dilemmas where citizens' pursuits and interests were not aligned with institutional structures. Within the local government case facilitators became the buffers between citizen-led projects and organisational requirements. They ensured that organisational logics and needs were fulfilled, yet at the same time facilitated an open space for community participants to develop their own projects. However, these free spaces that were created by the innovation programme did not exhibit the same qualities of welfare service user movements that may contend policy directions. Following Bason (2010, p. 153) the programme operated within 'politically defined visions of the future' rather than contesting wider structural power relations and political and policy trajectories.

Because user-centred innovation practices are initiated and hosted by institutions, this structural context can limit the agenda and framing of citizen participation. However, staff acting as 'tempered radicals' (Meyerson 2001) may contest and change some institutional practices. Inviting user movements and activists into these spaces may also initiate consideration of challenging issues and areas that institutions have not reflected upon (Williamson 2010). By bringing together innovation and participation theory and practice, this might enable both theorists and practitioners to reflect on and consider wider power relations within innovation in a political context.

REFERENCES

Alvesson, M. and Willmott, W. (1992). On the idea of emancipation in management and organization studies. *Academy of Management Review*, 17(3), 432–464.

Archer, M. (1995). *Realist Social Theory: The Morphogenetic Approach*. Cambridge: Cambridge University Press.

Barnes, M. and Cotterell, P. (eds) (2011). *Critical Perspectives on User Involvement*. Bristol: Policy Press.

Bason, C. (2010). *Leading Public Sector Innovation: Co-creating for a Better Society*. Bristol: Policy Press.

Bate, P. and Robert, G. (2007). *Bringing User Experience to Healthcare Improvement: The Concepts, Methods and Practices of Experience-Based Design*. Oxford: Radcliffe Publishing.

Beresford, P. (2002). Participation and social policy: transformation, liberation or regulation? In R. Sykes, C. Bochel and N. Ellison (eds), *Social Policy Review 14: Developments and Debates 2001–2002*. Bristol: Policy Press, pp. 265–290.

Beresford, P. (2009). Differentiated consumers? A differentiated view from a service user perspective. In R. Simmons, M. Powell and I. Greener (eds), *The Consumer in Public Services: Choice, Values and Difference*. Bristol: Policy Press, pp. 197–218.

Beresford, P. and Croft, S. (2004). Service users and practitioners reunited: the key component for social work reform. *British Journal of Social Work*, 34(1), 53–68.

Beresford, P., Fleming, J., Glynn, M., Bewley, C., Croft, S., Branfield, F. and Postle, K. (2011). *Supporting People: Towards a Person-Centred Approach*. Bristol: The Policy Press.

Bessant, J. and Maher, L. (2009). Developing radical innovations in health care: the role of design methods. *International Journal of Innovation Management*, 13(4), 555–568.

Bowden, A. (2005). Knowledge for free? Distributed innovation as a source of learning. *Public Policy and Administration*, 20(3), 56–68.

Cochrane, R. (1994). Views and reviews: accepting voices. *British Medical Journal*, 308, 1649.

Cottam, H. and Leadbeater, C. (2004). *Red Paper 01. Health: Co-creating Services*. London: Design Council.

Department for Innovation, Universities and Skills (2008). *Innovation Nation*. Norwich: Crown Publications.

Fraser, N. (1997). *Justice Interruptus: Critical Reflections on the 'Postsocialist' Condition*. London: Routledge.

Garety, P. (2001). Making sense of voices: by M. Romme and S. Escher. *Psychiatric Bulletin*, 25(10), 406–407.

Hartley, J. (2005). Innovation in governance and public services: past and present. *Public Money and Management*, 25(1), 27–34.

Hartley, J. (2008). The innovation landscape for public service organisations. In J. Hartley, C. Donaldson, C. Skelcher and M. Wallace (eds), *Managing to Improve Public Services*. Cambridge: Cambridge University Press, pp. 197–216.

Hartley, J. (2011). *A Comparison of Innovation in the Private and Public Sectors*. Paper presented at the ESRC Seminar Series on Innovation in Public Services, University of Bath, 11 February.

Hoggett, P. (2006). Conflict, ambivalence, and the contested purpose of public organisations. *Human Relations*, 59(2), 175–194.

Lynn, L.E. (1997). Innovation and the public interest: insights from the private sector. In A. Atchuler and R. Behn (eds), *Innovation in American Government: Challenges, Opportunities, and Dilemmas*. Washington, DC: Brookings Institution, pp. 83–103.

Meyerson, D.E. (2001). *Tempered Radicals: How People use Difference to Inspire Change at Work*. Boston, MA: Harvard Business School Press.

Moore, M. and Hartley, J. (2010). Innovations in governance. In S. Osborne (ed.), *The New Public Governance?* London: Routledge, pp. 52–71.

Osborne, S.P. and Brown, L. (2010). *Innovation, Public Policy and Public Services Delivery in the UK: The Word That Would Be King?* Paper presented at the European Group for Public Administration Conference, Toulouse, 8–10 September.

Pawson, R. (2006). *Evidence-based Policy: A Realist Perspective*. London: Sage Publications.

Pawson, R. and Tilley, N. (1997). *Realistic Evaluation*. London: Sage Publications.

Prahalad, C.K. and Ramaswamy, V. (2004). *The Future of Competition: Co-creating Unique Value with Customers*. Boston, MA: Harvard Business School Press.

Romme, M. and Escher, S. (1993). *Accepting Voices*. London: MIND Publications.

Sawhney, M. and Prandelli, E. (2000). Communities of creation: managing distributed innovation in turbulent markets. *California Management Review*, 42(4), 24–54.

Smith, D.B. (2007). Can you live with the voices in your head? *New York Times*, 25th March.

UPIAS (1975). *Union of the Physically Impaired Against Segregation: Comments on the Discussion between the Union and the Disability Alliance on 22nd November, 1975*. Available at: www.leeds.ac.uk/disability-studies/archiveuk/finkelstein/UPIAS%20Principles%202.pdf (accessed 20 August 2012).

Von Hippel, E. (2005). *Democratizing Innovation*. Cambridge, MA: MIT Press.
Walker, R.M. (2006). Innovation type and diffusion: an empirical analysis of local government. *Public Administration*, 84(2), 311–335.
Williamson, C. (2010). *Towards the Emancipation of Patients: Patients' Experiences and the Patient Movement*. Bristol: Policy Press.

PART VI

INNOVATION IN PUBLIC SERVICES IN PRACTICE

31. Evidence-based innovation in practice: experiences from health care and implications for the future
Gill Harvey

INTRODUCTION

Evidence-based policy and practice is a concept that has become the focus of growing attention and interest in public sector organisations. Since the initial emergence of the evidence-based medicine movement in the 1990s (Sackett et al. 1996), the basic idea that decisions should be more systematically based on sound evidence of effectiveness has spread to other disciplines in health care, other areas of the public sector and to other levels of decision-making, such as management and policy-making. There are close parallels between the literature on evidence-based health care and that on the diffusion of innovations, perhaps not surprising given the rapid advances in technological innovation in health care and the fact that many 'evidence based' initiatives result from technological developments in the field. Consequently, there is a large and growing body of literature, exploring the nature and process of technological innovation in health care (see, for example, Robert et al. 2010). This often links to the literature on evidence-based decision-making, and a number of authors (e.g. Fitzgerald et al. 2002; Ferlie et al. 2005) explicitly discuss and analyse the two concepts of health care innovation and evidence-based practice alongside each other.

One feature of both bodies of literature is that the nature of the innovation itself and the presence of strong research evidence are rarely sufficient to guarantee its uptake in practice. Whether focusing on the implementation and spread of innovation or the process of translating research evidence into policy and practice, the common experience seems to be that it is slow, resource-intensive and challenging. The reasons for this are often multiple and complex and relate to factors such as the nature of the adoption process, the role of scientific evidence in adoption decisions and the influence of context.

This chapter will explore the realities of evidence-based innovation at the level of service delivery, with a particular focus on health care. This will include examining to what extent evidence-based practice is a reality or a vision, what factors impede and facilitate the uptake of evidence into practice, and what the developing field of implementation science has to offer in terms of informing future strategies to translate innovation into practice.

EVIDENCE-BASED HEALTH CARE: THE BACKGROUND

Initial developments in evidence-based health care emerged at a clinical level, in response to widely recognised gaps between known evidence of best practice and what was actually happening in terms of the delivery of clinical care (Antman et al. 1992). Some studies (Schuster et al. 1998; Grol 2001) have suggested that 30 to 40 per cent of patients do not receive care complying with current scientific evidence. Others have highlighted the limited role that research evidence plays in managerial and policy decisions (Walshe and Rundall 2001), to the extent that decisions sometimes appear to fly in the face of available evidence (Pfeffer and Sutton 2006).

Responding to concerns such as these, early developments focused on making evidence more readily available and accessible and providing practitioners with the skills required to find and appraise evidence. For example, the international Cochrane Collaboration was established and made significant progress in terms of synthesising the large quantity of existing clinical research evidence in the form of systematic reviews. In some countries, such as England, Scotland, Canada and the United States of America, initiatives at a national level have also been established to collate, synthesise and publish evidence, typically in the form of clinical guidelines and technology appraisals. At the same time as producing evidence 'packages', attention also focused on developing knowledge and skills at the practitioner level to access and interpret evidence, typically through the development of critical appraisal skills (Ibbotsen et al. 1998).

However, despite the considerable investment in making evidence more readily available and accessible at both policy and practice levels, translating research into health care decision-making and practice continues to present a considerable challenge. The Institute of Medicine in the US established a Clinical Research Roundtable to address the issues facing the national research enterprise and concluded that failure to translate new knowledge into clinical practice and health care decision-making was one of the two major barriers preventing human benefit from the advances in biomedical sciences (Sung et al. 2003). Similarly in the UK, the Cooksey Report on UK health research funding (Cooksey 2006) identified the failure to implement new technologies and approaches into health care practice as the 'second translation gap'. For example, in England and Wales, the National Institute for Health and Clinical Excellence (NICE) was established in 1999 to undertake technology appraisals and produce clinical guidelines for the National Health Service (NHS), the aim being to generate more nationally recognised standards of health care and reduce the so-called 'postcode lottery' of NHS provision. Since this time, NICE has produced over 120 clinical guidelines and around 230 technology appraisals, alongside guidance for public health and cancer services. However, evaluations of the extent and pattern of implementation of guidance issued by NICE demonstrate highly variable levels of uptake, ranging from no change to significant changes in practice in line with the guidance (Sheldon et al. 2004). One specific example that illustrates the evidence–practice gap is the case of insulin pump therapy.

THE CASE OF INSULIN PUMP THERAPY

Type 1 diabetes affects around 250,000 people in the UK and rates have been increasing over time, with the greatest increase in children younger than 5 years. People with type 1 diabetes are unable to produce the natural hormone insulin, which is needed to control and use glucose. Most people with type 1 diabetes control their condition through multiple daily injections of insulin.

Insulin pumps are a technology that was developed as an alternative way of administering insulin. The pump provides a continuous subcutaneous insulin infusion, thus replacing the need for multiple daily injections of insulin, and typically produces better control of blood glucose levels. NICE issued technology appraisal guidance on insulin pump therapy in 2003, which was further updated in 2008, and recommended it as a clinically and cost effective treatment option for people with type 1 diabetes, whether adult or child, for whom multiple daily injections have failed, and for children under 12 if multiple daily injections are not deemed practical or appropriate (NICE 2008). Alongside the technology appraisal, NICE produced a Commissioning Guide to help health service commissioners plan and deliver services in line with the guidance. This suggests that the standard benchmark rate for the uptake of insulin pump therapy should be 12 per cent of people with type 1 diabetes, and 33 per cent for children younger than 12 years old.

A national working group on insulin pump services (Department of Health 2007) used a variety of sources, including national registers, manufacturer's records and published reports of pump practice in various countries, to estimate the uptake of insulin pump therapy at an international level. These data suggested that some countries (USA, Israel, Germany) were using pumps with about 15–20 per cent of people with type 1 diabetes. A typical figure for Europe (e.g. France, Sweden and the Netherlands) was around 10 per cent of people with type 1 diabetes using insulin pumps for routine management. In contrast, overall UK pump usage was estimated at around 1 per cent of people with type 1 diabetes.

A subsequent review of insulin pump therapy in England was undertaken by the Medical Technology Group in 2010. They carried out a survey of all primary care trusts (152) in England to ascertain levels of insulin pump provision. 87.5 per cent of primary care trusts responded to the survey and the data indicated that the average rate of pump use was 3.7 per cent, with rates across the country ranging from 0.25 to 13 per cent (Medical Technology Group 2010). Thus, whilst the rates are higher than those estimated by the Department of Health Working Group in 2007, they are still some way from the NICE-recommended benchmark of 12 per cent and considerably lower than in most other countries of comparable economic standing and level of health care provision. The central question of interest is why, despite evidence to support its use in practice, is the innovation (in this case, insulin pump therapy) not achieving higher levels of implementation in UK health care?

Whilst the example above has focused on one particular innovation, the experience is not atypical, as other evaluations of the uptake of evidence-based guidance have illustrated (see, for example, Ferlie et al. 1999; Dopson and Fitzgerald 2005). This suggests that there are more general challenges in translating research evidence into routine service delivery, reinforcing the so-called 'second translation gap' that has been recognised by policy makers (Cooksey 2006). In turn, this raises a whole series of issues that need to be explored further in relation to the implementation of evidence-based innovation in practice. For example, why do some innovations in health care get implemented whilst others do not? What factors influence the adoption and implementation process? Are some organisations better at implementing innovations than others? What can policy makers, managers, practitioners, patients and the public do to maximise the likelihood of successful implementation?

These are just some of the questions that have driven a growing interest and focus on understanding the processes of implementation: what actually happens in the process of moving from evidence to implementation (or not)? This has led to the growth of a new field of research in health care over the last 10 to 20 years, variously described by terms such as implementation science and knowledge translation, utilisation and mobilisation. This sits alongside, and has been informed by, a similar interest in understanding the processes of innovation in service delivery (see, for example, Greenhalgh et al. 2004). The following section discusses some of the key lessons to emerge to date from research into the processes of innovation and implementation.

UNDERSTANDING THE PROCESSES OF IMPLEMENTATION

A number of significant messages emerge from studies that have been undertaken to examine the implementation of evidence-based innovation in health care. These can be summarised as follows:

- Linear, rational models of the innovation and implementation process are over-simplistic and do not reflect the reality of implementation.
- Evidence is wider than research; it is typically contested, negotiated and socially constructed.
- Evidence can be used in different ways, both direct and indirect.
- Evidence use is mediated by a range of contextual factors at local, organisational and policy levels.

Each of these is discussed and illustrated in more detail below.

Linear, Rational Models of the Implementation Process are Over-simplified

Early models of evidence-based practice suggested a fairly straightforward, linear process of translating research into practice (Haines and Jones 1994), where once evidence was reviewed and collated (e.g. in the form of systematic reviews or clinical guidelines), then processes of dissemination, continuing professional development and clinical audit could be used to promote the uptake of the research in practice. Linear models of research use typically view research and practice as two separate communities and emphasise the flow of knowledge from researchers to the practice community (Nutley et al. 2007). Another way of viewing these more linear models is as 'producer push' approaches (Landry et al. 2001), with practitioners as the (passive) recipients of research. Linear conceptualisations of the evidence-based decision-making process can be seen to relate to the more deterministic models of the diffusion of innovations (Slappendel 1996; Robert et al. 2010), such as that proposed by Rogers (1995).

However, experiences in practice and studies to evaluate the implementation of research and innovation into practice have repeatedly highlighted the complexity of the process, linked to factors such as the multi-faceted nature of evidence, the influence of contextual factors and the mediating role of professional groups (Dopson and Fitzgerald 2005; Ferlie et al. 2005; Rycroft-Malone et al. 2002). As a result, there has been an increasing move away from viewing implementation as a rational, linear process. New models of implementation have been developed, which highlight the multi-faceted and dynamic processes involved in moving from evidence to action (Rycroft-Malone and Bucknall 2010). These include the Knowledge-to-Action cycle (Graham et al. 2006) and the Promoting Action on Research Implementation in Health Services (PARIHS) framework (Kitson et al. 1998, 2008). A recent review of models that have been developed to guide the knowledge transfer process (Ward et al. 2010) concluded that it is these interactive, multi-directional models of implementation that most accurately represent the knowledge transfer process in action. Again, this parallels much of the literature on the diffusion of innovations, with a shift from the more deterministic models to processual approaches, which acknowledge the more complex, contingent and fluid processes involved in adopting and assimilating new technologies into practice (e.g. Van de Ven et al. 1999).

Evidence is Wider than Research

Evidence derived from research is a central focus in most attempts to introduce evidence-based or evidence-informed policy and practice, where there is a conscious effort to close the gap between known best practice and what is currently happening. However, empirical studies repeatedly demonstrate the complex, multi-faceted and contested nature of evidence in the health care setting (Dopson et al. 2002; Ferlie et al. 2000), regardless of how scientifically a new technology has been developed and tested. Whilst rigorous techniques have been developed to increase the objectivity of research evidence (e.g. systematic review, technology appraisal and clinical guideline development), studies suggest that in practice health care professionals draw on and integrate a variety of different sources of evidence, encompassing both propositional and non-propositional knowledge. Sources of evidence that sit alongside research typically include knowledge derived from clinical experience, from credible colleagues, patients, clients and carers, and from the local context or environment (Thompson et al. 2001; Rycroft-Malone et al. 2004).

This experiential evidence presents a challenge to the traditional hierarchy of evidence within biomedical research, whereby 'gold standard' evidence is that derived from multiple, high quality randomised controlled trials or systematic reviews. In practice, evidence relating to the effectiveness of interventions is considered alongside a range of other criteria, including, for example, acceptability, accessibility, appropriateness and fit with local priorities. Thus, designing an implementation strategy to promote the uptake of a new technology that relies on a narrow definition of evidence as research (and ranking the strength of that research according to the research design) is likely to result in an approach that fails to acknowledge the complexity of decision-making at the level of clinical and service delivery.

Consequently, implementation strategies and approaches need to accept and encourage the adaptation of evidence to achieve an optimal level of 'fit' at a local level – a process described as 'tinkering' within the field of educational studies (Hargreaves 1998), where explicit knowledge from research blends with tacit, practice knowledge. This local melding of evidence sources is likely to enhance the acceptability and utility of research-based evidence. However, questions can be raised about the acceptable limits to which 'tinkering' with research evidence can go, for, as Nutley and Davies (2000) highlight, it can raise the possibility that untested innovations become widely disseminated, adapted and adopted. Rycroft-Malone et al. (2002) suggest that 'strong' evidence that is most likely to be implemented in practice comprises robust research evidence that closely matches practice-based experience and information and patient experience (in the case of health care).

Evidence Can be Used in Different Ways, Both Direct and Indirect

The multi-faceted nature of evidence has implications for the way in which research is implemented (or not) in practice. Whilst some strategies for getting research into practice, such as evidence-based clinical guidelines, assume a direct or instrumental process of research utilisation (Nutley et al. 2007), the reality in practice has been shown to be significantly more complex (Kitson et al. 1998). Dopson and Fitzgerald (2005) draw on comparative data from a total of 48 primary case studies of the careers of evidence-based innovations and highlight the importance of sense-making and the enactment of evidence in practice, in order to translate research evidence from information to new knowledge that can influence practice change. Other researchers have similarly highlighted that research evidence, although crucial to improving patient care, may not on its own inform practitioners' decision-making (Thompson et al. 2001; Bucknall 2003), because of the need to translate and particularise evidence in order to make sense of it in the context of caring for individual patients.

This links to the issues highlighted in the previous point, suggesting that evidence is perceived more broadly than research in the practice setting, and that to make sense of evidence a degree of 'tinkering' with the evidence takes place. It seems reasonable to assume, therefore, that the use of evidence in practice involves more than the direct, instrumental application of research findings. Indeed, typologies of research use that have been developed often make a key distinction between instrumental and so-called conceptual uses of evidence (see Nutley et al. 2007). Unlike instrumental use of evidence, which refers to the direct influence of research on a practice or policy decision, conceptual use is concerned with the more subtle and indirect influence of research. This may include the ways in which exposure to research evidence changes people's ways of thinking and understanding, sometimes referred to as 'enlightenment' (Weiss 1979).

Evidence Use is Mediated by a Range of Contextual Factors

Context can be defined as 'the environment or setting in which the proposed change is to be implemented' (Kitson et al. 1998) and is shaped by a range of different factors at the macro, meso and micro levels of health service delivery. Ferlie and colleagues (2009) identify context as a crucial determinant of the career of an evidence-based innovation, highlighting the influence of factors at the micro level in determining the receptiveness of an organisation to change – in particular, the engagement of clinical opinion leaders, the quality of relationships, change and project management capacity, senior management support, organisational complexity and a climate of organisational learning. McCormack and colleagues (2002) similarly note a range of contextual influences at the micro and meso organisational level that influence the uptake of research, including the existence of clearly defined boundaries; clarity about decision-making processes; clarity about patterns of power and authority; resources, information and feedback systems; active management of competing 'force fields'; and systems in place that enable dynamic processes of change and continuous development.

Alongside these micro and meso level contextual influences, wider macro level factors can also influence the uptake of evidence, for example linked to policy drivers, and economic, societal and political factors. In order to understand and manage the multiple contextual influences, implementation approaches need to have a clear strategy for assessing the organisational context in which implementation is to take place and have sufficient flexibility to tailor implementation to fit the specific needs of the context.

RETURNING TO THE CASE OF INSULIN PUMP THERAPY

Reflecting on these factors that are known to influence the translation and uptake of research evidence into practice, it is useful to return to the previously described example of insulin pump therapy and, in particular, to review whether this helps to shed light on why the adoption of pump therapy is relatively low in the UK. As previously described, the current rate of pump therapy in England is around 3.7 per cent, significantly lower than the NICE-recommended target of 12 per cent (Medical Technology Group 2010).

The NHS National Technology Adoption Centre (NTAC) set up a project to accelerate the rate of adoption of insulin pump therapy. Working with a number of implementation sites (supported by mentor sites that were already providing pump therapy services), NTAC supported project teams to identify and overcome the barriers to pump therapy provision at a local level. This resulted in the production of a web-based resource, known as a 'How to, why to guide', intended to be used by other NHS organisations wishing to improve the provision of insulin pump therapy to type 1 diabetics. Within the 'How to, why to guide', NTAC summarises the main benefits of adopting pump therapy at different levels of the service, alongside the barriers it has observed in practice (see Table 31.1).

As Table 31.1 illustrates, there are multiple factors that potentially influence the uptake of evidence around insulin pump therapy into both local policy and practice, again emphasising the complex and multi-faceted nature of implementation. Thus, whilst a NICE technology appraisal on insulin pump therapy summarises the available evidence and concludes that it is a clinically and cost effective intervention for people with type 1 diabetes, the process of applying this evidence in practice is far from being straightforward or rational. Making the evidence available in a synthesised form and disseminating this information to the health service, on its own, appears to have made limited impact. Key factors to emerge from the NTAC summary that contribute to the lack of uptake of the evidence include issues around knowledge, understanding and interpretation of the evidence by patients and clinical staff, linked to factors such as the availability of information and prevailing attitudes and behaviours. Perhaps most significantly, the insulin pump case highlights the complex web of contextual factors that need to be addressed to maximise the likelihood of translating evidence into day to day service provision. Such contextual factors exist at the service level (e.g. provision of time and funding for training provision), at the interface between different stakeholder groups such as providers and commissioners of the service, and at the wider policy level (e.g. in terms of how the innovation fits with existing payment systems in the NHS).

To address a diverse range of challenges such as these, implementation strategies need

Table 31.1   Perceived benefits and barriers to the adoption of insulin pump therapy in the National Health Service

Stakeholder group	Potential benefits of implementing the technology	Reasons for resistance to the technology
1. Patients	• Greater diabetes control and accuracy • Fewer blood glucose swings and reduced insulin dose • Lower risk of complications (e.g. possible reduction in heart disease, stroke, blindness, kidney disease, nerve damage and amputations leading to disability and premature mortality) • Greater freedom in eating and less disruption to sleep patterns • Improved quality of life for patients and their family • Better general health and improved treatment satisfaction • Reduced anxiety and depression • Reduced potential hospital admission as a result of Diabetic Ketoacidosis and hypoglycaemia	• Lack of information • Lack of understanding of insulin pump therapy • Lack of understanding of how to use an insulin pump effectively • Practicalities of living with pump therapy and impact on daily life • Trust in new technology
2. Clinical staff	• Improved patient outcomes • Enable the provision of an outreach and further developed outpatient service • Ensuring patient choice • Continued professional development • Informed patients and emphasis on self-management • Ability to reach Quality Outcomes Framework (QOF) Targets • Ability to respond to changes in health care requirements	• Agreeing a phased implementation can be time-consuming and difficult • Lack of time • Lack of funding • Lack of training of health care professionals • Unfamiliarity with technology • Embracing the new technology may require a change in attitude • Overcoming organisational barriers to adoption
3. Managers	• Opportunity to offer service to other providers • Reduce acute emergency admissions and overall length of stay • Opportunities to create a robust agreement with commissioners to secure the funding to enable service delivery • Opportunity to develop a new, integrated service	• Framing the arguments/articulating the downstream savings • Procuring the technology • Implementation can be time- consuming and difficult • Selection of cases (revision) and capacity-planning • Availability of professional resources to deliver the

Table 31.1   (continued)

Stakeholder group	Potential benefits of implementing the technology	Reasons for resistance to the technology
	• Change the way in which care is delivered and received in the community • Ability to respond to changes in health care requirements • Collaboration with Diabetes Network(s)	additional patient education and pump starts may not be in place • Coping with the backfill for health care professional training may have an impact on service delivery • Availability of sufficient funding within a primary care trust (PCT) or set of PCTs to purchase the pumps may be complex to agree
4. Commissioners	• Meet the NICE guidance for insulin pump therapy and objectives laid out in the Diabetes National Service Framework • Collaborative working partnership with provider trusts • Effective and enhanced management of diabetes within the health economy • Opportunity to improve buying power • Potential benefits to the Diabetes Network(s) with the introduction of specialised diabetes units within a given health economy	• Funding the technology/service change is complex as it sits outside the NHS Payment by Results regime • The risk of change is seen as greater than the risk of standing still • Technology implementation plan may be complex to initiate, monitor and evaluate • Availability of professional resources to deliver the additional patient education and pump starts may not be in place

Source: Adapted from National Technology Adoption Centre (2012).

to be broad in their focus, contextually sensitive and flexible enough to meet changing conditions or requirements. The final section of the chapter draws on the lessons learned to date in implementing evidence-based innovations in health care and outlines the implications for the future.

MOVING FORWARDS WITH IMPLEMENTATION: FUTURE IMPLICATIONS

Thinking around evidence-based practice in health care has developed from a position that was heavily influenced by a biomedical view of research, with its focus on questions of effectiveness, randomised controlled trials as a primary source of evidence and rational models of implementation, typically focused on change at the level of individual practitioners. As experiences with implementation have progressed over the last

20 years or so, accompanied by an increasing empirical base, the complexity of the implementation process has become apparent. This includes recognition of the multiple levels and stakeholders involved in making implementation successful and the need to pay attention to a wide range of issues at the individual, team, organisational and policy levels.

Reflecting on the lessons learned to date, a number of key implications can be identified – implications that need to be debated, considered and acted upon as the agenda around innovation and evidence-based or evidence-informed health care moves forward in the future. These implications are summarised as follows:

- The need for approaches that acknowledge the multi-dimensional, active nature of implementation.
- Acceptance of the contingent nature of evidence and the process of transformation to fit with local knowledge.
- The important influence of context at multiple levels of the system and a requirement for flexible and responsive approaches to implementation.
- Making use of available theories and empirical evidence to inform implementation.

The Need for Approaches that Acknowledge the Multi-Dimensional, Active Nature of Implementation

As case studies of adopting innovative technologies, such as the insulin pump therapy example, clearly illustrate, implementation does not typically take place in a linear, rational way. Rather it is a process that involves negotiation, contestation and multifaceted strategies to address the range of potential barriers that need to be overcome to achieve successful implementation of evidence into practice. Indeed, empirical evidence from the Cochrane Collaboration review group on Effective Practice and Organisation of Care has for some time confirmed the benefits of multi-faceted strategies that typically encompass a number of pre-disposing, enabling and reinforcing factors to promote and sustain the uptake of evidence into practice (Bero et al. 1998; Davies et al. 2010) (see Table 31.2).

A number of different models and conceptual frameworks have been developed which attempt to reflect the more dynamic and multi-dimensional nature of implementation (for overviews of these, see Nutley et al. 2007 and Rycroft-Malone and Bucknall 2010). An example of one of these frameworks is PARIHS, which proposes that the successful implementation of research evidence into practice is dependent on the complex interplay of the evidence to be implemented (how robust it is and how it fits with clinical, patient and local experience), the local context in which implementation is to take place (the prevailing culture, leadership and commitment to evaluation and learning), and the way in which the process is facilitated (how and by whom) (Kitson et al. 1998; Rycroft-Malone et al. 2002).

Each of the key concepts of evidence, context and facilitation is recognised to be multi-factorial and can be represented along a continuum from low to high, with uptake of the innovation likely to be greatest when all of the three elements are located at the high end of the continuum. Concept analysis of the *evidence* construct proposed

Table 31.2   *Evidence of effectiveness of interventions to promote evidence-based change among health professionals*

Consistently effective	Variable effectiveness	Little or no effect
Educational outreach visits • Reminders • Multi-faceted interventions (a combination that includes two or more of the following: audit and feedback, reminders, local consensus processes or marketing) • Interactive educational meetings (participation of health care providers in workshops that include discussion of practice)	• Audit and feedback (or any summary of clinical performance) • The use of local opinion leaders (practitioners identified by their colleagues as influential) • Local consensus processes (inclusion of participating practitioners in discussions to ensure that they agree that the chosen clinical problem is important and the approach to managing the problem is appropriate) • Patient-mediated interventions (any intervention aimed at changing the performance of health care providers for which specific information was sought from or given to patients)	• Educational materials (distribution of recommendations for clinical care, including clinical practice guidelines, audiovisual materials and electronic publications) • Didactic educational meetings (such as lectures)

Source: Bero et al. (1998).

that evidence comprised four key sub-elements, namely research, clinical experience, patient experience and local information (Rycroft-Malone et al. 2004). Where research evidence is 'high' (i.e. is rigorous/robust), but is not matched by a similarly high level of clinical consensus or does not meet with patients' needs and expectations, or perceived priorities at a local level, the process of translating an innovation into practice will be more difficult. A similar concept analysis of the *context* construct (McCormack et al. 2002) suggested that context comprised key elements of culture, leadership and evaluation. In a situation where evidence is 'high' (as measured in terms of the strength of the research, clinical and patient experience and local information), implementation will be more challenging where the culture is not conducive to change, the leadership is weak and there is not a prevailing evaluative culture within the unit or organisation.

Facilitation addresses the broader organisational dimensions of implementation and helps to create the optimal conditions for promoting the uptake of an evidence-based innovation into practice in the given context. Concept analysis of the facilitation dimension (Harvey et al. 2002) has shown that individuals appointed as facilitators (e.g. project leaders or educational outreach workers) can take on a number of approaches to facilitation, ranging from a largely task-focused, project manager role to a more holistic, enabling model where the facilitator works at the level of individuals, teams and organisations to create and sustain a supportive context for evidence-based care (e.g. by analysing, reflecting and changing attitudes, behaviours and ways of working). The key to successful implementation is seen to involve matching the role and skills of the facilitator to the specific needs of the situation.

Acceptance of the Contingent Nature of Evidence and the Process of Transformation to Fit with Local Knowledge

As highlighted earlier, and illustrated in the description of the PARIHS framework, at the point of implementation, evidence is interpreted more widely than research. Thus, straightforward replication of evidence from an original research study (e.g. to develop a technological innovation) to clinical, managerial or organisational level decision-making is highly unlikely. Rather a process of blending research evidence with more tacit forms of practice-based knowledge and experience is likely to take place – a process earlier referred to as 'tinkering' with the evidence (Hargreaves 1998).

This notion of adapting and transforming research evidence to make it 'fit' with local circumstances raises a number of interesting questions and potential dilemmas. First, it poses a fundamental challenge to the traditional hierarchy of evidence that underpins much of the thinking in medicine and health care. Whereas 'gold standard' evidence is that derived from multiple randomised controlled trials and systematic reviews of trials, clinical experience is rated a significantly 'lower' form of evidence and one that should only be drawn on when other more rigorous, robust forms of research evidence are not available. However, the reality of using evidence in practice calls into question the applicability of such a hierarchy (Upshur 2002) and suggests a need to view all sources of evidence as having a valuable contribution to make (Glasby et al. 2007). The issue is then not so much which is the 'best' evidence to use, but how can different sources of evidence be combined and integrated in the most meaningful way (Nutley et al. 2007). Building on the above points, it is also increasingly recognised that involving potential users of the research evidence in the actual conduct of the research itself is likely to enhance the relevance and transferability of evidence to practice – often referred to as a model of co-production (Nowotny et al. 1997; Bowen and Martens 2005).

The Important Influence of Context at Multiple Levels of the System and a Requirement for Flexible and Responsive Approaches to Implementation

Awareness and acceptance of contextual influences on the process of translating evidence into practice has been one of the areas of most significant growth and understanding over recent years. As empirical studies have repeatedly highlighted, context matters at all levels of the system when it comes to implementing evidence-based change and innovation (French et al. 2009). This suggests that implementation strategies need to adopt a proactive approach to assessing contextual factors that are likely to impinge on implementation and develop appropriate interventions to manage the different contextual hurdles or barriers. Such barriers may present themselves as part of both the inner and outer practice context, as the insulin pump therapy example illustrates. At an inner context level, barriers identified may include staff time and availability, skills and knowledge deficits, attitudes and behaviours, resistance to change, and so on. At the wider or outer context level, a different set of challenges may present, including existing policies and priorities, and fit of the evidence or innovation with prevailing structures and systems, for example in relation to payment or procurement of services.

In thinking about how to identify, plan for and address the numerous contextual factors that may be present, implementation strategies also need to consider what roles, relationships and communication processes are needed to support implementation. Typically this involves paying attention to both boundary-spanning roles and processes (Denis and Lehoux 2009). Within the field of evidence-based health care, various roles have been identified to support and lead boundary-spanning activities, including, for example, educational outreach workers, academic detailers, knowledge brokers, opinion leaders and facilitators (Soumerai and Avorn 1990; Harvey et al. 2002; Stetler et al. 2006; Dobbins et al. 2009). These roles vary in terms of the position of individuals in relation to the organisation (internal or external), their role and source of influence (e.g. professional versus non-professional), and the range of methods and techniques they might use to promote and support implementation (social marketing, influencing, education, leadership, facilitation).

Making Use of Available Theories and Empirical Evidence to Inform Implementation

A fourth and final implication to consider is how to make use of existing theories and evidence to inform more effective implementation. This is an area of growing interest in the field of health care, informed by a greater awareness of the broad range of factors that have the potential to enhance or hinder the translation of research and innovation in practice. As knowledge and understanding have accumulated, and the complexity of the implementation process has unfolded, so too attention has turned to a broader range of social science, psychological and organisational studies and learning theories that could help to inform implementation. Such theories are seen to provide a useful way of contextualising, planning and evaluating implementation strategies that typically comprise multiple interventions targeted at different groups and different levels within an organisation (see, for example, Eccles et al. 2005; Grol et al. 2007; Davies et al. 2010).

CONCLUSION

This chapter has traced the developments around evidence-based innovation and change in health care, with a particular focus on the implementation of evidence at the level of service delivery and practice. From its initial roots in the evidence-based medicine movement, the focus was predominantly on the rational and instrumental use of research evidence by individual practitioners to achieve more evidence-based practice. However, experience and empirical studies have clearly demonstrated that the process of achieving evidence-based innovation and change is more complex and context-dependent than originally envisaged. This has included the recognition of evidence as something that is wider than research, which can be used in both direct and indirect ways. Equally, the focus has shifted from decision-making by individual practitioners to understanding and addressing a broader set of organisational factors that influence the process of evidence-based innovation. This includes identifying specific roles and processes that can be employed to facilitate the exchange and implementation of evidence at multiple levels of the system, drawing on a range of individual and organisational level behaviour change theories.

REFERENCES

Antman, E.M., Lau, J., Kupelnick, B., Mosteller, F. and Chalmets, T.C. (1992). A comparison of results of meta-analyses of randomized control trials and recommendations of clinical experts: treatments for myocardial infarction. *Journal of the American Medical Association*, 268(2), 240–248.

Bero, L.A., Grilli, R., Grimshaw, J.M., Harvey, E., Oxman, A.D. and Thomson, M.A. (1998). Closing the gap between research and practice: an overview of systematic reviews of interventions to promote the implementation of research findings. *British Medical Journal*, 317, 465–468.

Bowen, S. and Martens, P. (2005). The need to know team: demystifying knowledge translation: learning from the community. *Journal of Health Services Research and Policy*, 10(4), 203–211.

Bucknall, T. (2003). The clinical landscape of critical care: nurses' decision making. *Journal of Advanced Nursing*, 43(3), 310–319.

Cooksey, D. (2006). *A Review of UK Health Research Funding: Sir David Cooksey*. London: The Stationery Office.

Davies, P., Walker, A.E. and Grimshaw, J.M. (2010). A systematic review of the use of theory in the design of guideline dissemination and implementation strategies and interpretation of the results of rigorous evaluations. *Implementation Science*, 5, 14.

Denis, J.-L. and Lehoux, P. (2009). Organizational theory. In S. Strauss, J. Tetroe and I.D. Graham (eds), *Knowledge Translation in Health Care*. London: Wiley-Blackwell and BMJ Books, pp. 215–225.

Department of Health (2007). *Insulin Pump Services: Report of the Insulin Pumps Working Group*. London: Department of Health.

Dobbins, M., Hanna, S.E., Ciliska, D., Manske, S., Cameron, R., Mercer, S.L., O'Mara, L., DeCorby, K. and Robeson, P. (2009). A randomized controlled trial evaluating the impact of knowledge translation and exchange strategies. *Implementation Science*, 4, 61.

Dopson, S. and Fitzgerald, L. (eds) (2005). *Knowledge to Action? Evidence-Based Health Care in Context*. Oxford: Oxford University Press.

Dopson, S., FitzGerald, L., Ferlie, E. and Gabbay, J. (2002). No magic targets! Changing clinical practice to become more evidence-based. *Health Care Management Review*, 27(3), 35–47.

Eccles, M., Grimshaw, J., Walker, A., Johnston, M. and Pitts, N. (2005). Changing the behaviour of healthcare professionals: the use of theory in promoting the uptake of research findings. *Journal of Clinical Epidemiology*, 58, 107–112.

Ferlie, E., Fitzgerald, L. and Wood, M. (2000). Getting evidence into clinical practice: an organizational behavior perspective. *Journal of Health Services Research and Policy*, 5(1), 1–7.

Ferlie, E., Wood, M. and Fitzgerald, L. (1999). Some limits to evidence-based medicine: a case study from elective orthopaedics. *Quality in Health Care*, 8, 99–107.

Ferlie, E., Fitzgerald, L., Wood, M. and Hawkins, C. (2005). The (non) diffusion of innovations: the mediating role of professional groups. *Academy of Management Journal*, 48(1), 117–134.

Ferlie, E., Dopson, S., Fitzgerald, L. and Locock, L. (2009). Renewing policy to support evidence-based health care. *Public Administration*, 87(4), 837–852.

Fitzgerald, L., Ferlie, E., Wood, M. and Hawkins, C. (2002). Interlocking interactions: the diffusion of innovations in healthcare. *Human Relations*, 55, 1429–1449.

French, B., Thomas, L.H., Baker, P., Burton, C.R., Pennington, L. and Roddam, H. (2009). What can management theories offer evidence-based practice? A comparative analysis of measurement tools for organisational context. *Implementation Science*, 4, 28.

Glasby, J., Walshe, K. and Harvey, G. (2007). What counts as 'evidence' in evidence-based practice. *Evidence and Policy*, 3(3), 325–327.

Graham, I.D., Logan, J., Harrison, M.B., Straus, S.E., Tetroe, J., Caswell, W. and Robinson, N. (2006). Lost in knowledge translation: time for a map? *Journal of Continuing Education in the Health Professions*, 26, 13–24.

Greenhalgh, T., Robert, G., Macfarlane, F., Bate, P. and Kyriakidou, O. (2004). Diffusion of innovations in service organizations: systematic review and recommendations. *The Milbank Quarterly*, 82(4), 581–629.

Grol, R. (2001). Successes and failures in the implementation of evidence-based guidelines for clinical practice. *Medical Care*, 39(8 Supp. 2), 1146–1154.

Grol, R., Bosch, M., Hulscher, M., Eccles, M. and Wensing, M. (2007). Planning and studying improvement in patient care: the use of theoretical perspectives. *The Milbank Quarterly*, 85(1), 93–138.

Haines, A. and Jones, R. (1994). Implementing findings of research. *British Medical Journal*, 308, 1488–1492.

Hargreaves, D.H. (1998). *Creative Professionalism: The Role of Teachers in the Knowledge Society*. London: Demos.

Harvey, G., Loftus-Hills, A., Rycroft-Malone, J., Titchen, A., Kitson, A., McCormack, B. and Seers, K. (2002).

Getting evidence into practice: the role and function of facilitation. *Journal of Advanced Nursing*, 37(6), 577–588.

Ibbotsen, T., Grimshaw, J. and Grant, A. (1998). Evaluation of a programme of workshops for the teaching of critical appraisal skills. *Medical Education*, 32(5), 486–491.

Kitson, A., Harvey, G. and McCormack, B. (1998). Enabling the implementation of evidence based practice: a conceptual framework. *Quality in Health Care*, 7(3), 149–159.

Kitson, A., Rycroft-Malone, J., Harvey, G., McCormack, B., Seers, K. and Titchen, A. (2008). Evaluating the successful implementation of evidence into practice using the PARIHS framework: theoretical and practical challenges. *Implementation Science*, 3,1.

Landry, R., Amara, N. and Lamari, M. (2001). Utilization of social science research knowledge in Canada. *Research Policy*, 30, 333–349.

McCormack, B., Kitson, A., Harvey, G., Rycroft-Malone, J., Titchen, A. and Seers, K. (2002). Getting evidence into practice: the meaning of context. *Journal of Advanced Nursing*, 38(1), 94–104.

Medical Technology Group (2010). *Pump Action: A Review of Insulin Pump Uptake and NICE Guidance in English PCTs, 27 August* Available at: http://www.mtg.org.uk/index.php/policy-initiatives/mtg-campaigns/32-pump-action (accessed 15 August 2012).

National Technology Adoption Centre (2012). *How To Why To Guide: Continuous Subcutaneous Insulin Infusion*. Available at: http://www.ntac.nhs.uk/HowToWhyToGuides/ContinuousSubcutaneousInsulin Infusion/Insulin-Infusion-Executive-Summary.aspx (accessed 15 August 2012).

NICE (2008). *Continuous Subcutaneous Insulin Infusion for the Treatment of Diabetes Mellitus. Review of Technology Appraisal Guidance 57*. London: NICE.

Nowotny, H., Scott, P. and Gibbons, M. (1997). *Re-thinking Science: Knowledge and the Public in an Age of Uncertainty*. Cambridge: Polity Press.

Nutley, S.M. and Davies, H.T.O. (2000). Making a reality of evidence-based practice: some lessons from the diffusion of innovations. *Public Money and Management*, 20(4), 35–43.

Nutley, S.M., Walter, I. and Davies, H.T.O. (2007). *Using Evidence: How Research can Inform Public Services*. Bristol: Policy Press.

Pfeffer, J. and Sutton, R.I. (2006). *Hard Facts, Dangerous Half-Truths and Total Nonsense: Profiting From Evidence-Based Management*. Boston, MA: Harvard Business School Press.

Robert, G., Greenhalgh, T., MacFarlane, F. and Peacock, R. (2010). Adopting and assimilating new non-pharmaceutical technologies into health care: a systematic review. *Journal of Health Services Research and Policy*, 15(4), 243–250.

Rogers, E.M. (1995). *Diffusion of Innovations*, 4th edn. New York: Free Press.

Rycroft-Malone, J. and Bucknall, T. (eds) (2010). *Models and Framework for Implementing Evidence-Based Practice: Linking Evidence to Action*. Oxford: Wiley-Blackwell.

Rycroft-Malone, J., Kitson, A., Harvey, G., McCormack, B., Seers, K., Titchen, A. and Estabrooks, C. (2002). Ingredients for change: revisiting a conceptual model. *Quality and Safety in Health Care*, 11, 174–180.

Rycroft-Malone, J., Seers, K., Titchen, A., Harvey, G., Kitson, A. and McCormack, B. (2004). What counts as evidence in evidence-based practice? *Journal of Advanced Nursing*, 47(1), 81–90.

Sackett, D.L., Rosenberg, W.M.C., Gray, J.A.M., Haynes, R.B. and Richardson, W.S. (1996). Evidence based medicine: what it is and what it isn't. *British Medical Journal*, 312, 71–72.

Schuster, M., McGlynn, E. and Brook, R.H. (1998). How good is the quality of health care in the United States? *The Milbank Quarterly*, 76, 517–563.

Sheldon, T.A., Cullum, N., Dawson, D., Lankshear, A., Lowson, K. and Watt, I. et al. (2004). What's the evidence that NICE guidance has been implemented? Results from a national evaluation using time series analysis, audit of patients' notes, and interviews. *British Medical Journal*, 329, 999–1003.

Slappendel, C. (1996). Perspectives on innovation in organizations. *Organization Studies*, 17, 107–129.

Soumerai, S.B. and Avorn, J. (1990). Principles of educational outreach ('academic detailing') to improve clinical decision making. *Journal of the American Medical Association*, 263(4), 549–556.

Stetler, C.B., Legro, M.W., Rycroft-Malone, J., Bowman, C., Curran, G., Guihan, M., Hagedorn, H., Pineros, S. and Wallace, C.M. (2006). Role of 'external facilitation' in implementation of research findings: a qualitative evaluation of facilitation experiences in the Veterans Health Administration. *Implementation Science*, 1, 23.

Sung, N.S., Crowley, W.F., Genel, M., Salber, P., Sandy, L., Sherwood, L.M. et al. (2003). Central challenges facing the national clinical research enterprise. *Journal of the American Medical Association*, 289, 1278–1287.

Thompson, C., McCaughan, D., Cullum, N., Sheldon, T.A., Mulhall, A. and Thompson, D.R. (2001). Research information in nurses' clinical decision making: what is useful? *Journal of Advanced Nursing*, 36(3), 376–388.

Upshur, R.E. (2002). If not evidence, then what? Or does medicine really need a base? *Journal of Evaluation in Clinical Practice*, 8(2), 113–120.

Van de Ven, A., Polley, D., Garud, R. and Venkataraman, S. (1999). *The Innovation Journey*. Oxford: Oxford University Press.
Walshe, K. and Rundall, T.G. (2001). Evidence-based management: from theory to practice in health care. *The Milbank Quarterly*, 79(3), 429–457.
Ward, V., Smith, S., Carruthers, S., Hamer, S. and House, A. (2010). *Knowledge Brokering: Exploring the Process of Transferring Knowledge into Action*. Leeds: University of Leeds, Leeds Institute of Health Sciences.
Weiss, C.H. (1979). The many meanings of research utilization. *Public Administration Review*, 39(5), 426–431.

32. NHS Direct: a UK health sector innovation study
Paul Cunningham

INTRODUCTION

This chapter provides an empirical case study of innovation in the public health sector, namely the introduction of NHS Direct in the United Kingdom. Although almost 15 years have passed since its introduction, it offers a number of common themes by which the process of public sector innovation may be contextualised. However, the chapter does not set out to evaluate the effectiveness or impact of the scheme. It concludes with a number of generic lessons which may have broader application to the management of innovation in the public sector.

The material for this chapter was collected in the context of the European Commission-funded PUBLIN study (2005–06),[1] which examined the commonalities between public and private sector innovation.[2] Analysis of the case studies (in the health and social sectors) carried out under PUBLIN necessitated the development of a set of drivers, barriers and facilitators (or shaping factors) as a broad analytical framework. Thus the approach, while not exactly 'grounded theory', was equally not a further development of an established approach. This is not to say that alternative frameworks – such as Sabatier's advocacy coalition framework (Sabatier and Jenkins-Smith, 1993, 1999) or the work of Geels (2004) on sociotechnical systems – are not relevant to public sector innovation: innovation processes are multifaceted as well as diverse, and research studies are confronted with choices as to what to focus on. Likewise, the conclusions of the PUBLIN study resonate strongly with some of the factors identified by Greenhalgh et al. (2004, 2005) in their review of the diffusion of innovations in health service delivery and organisation. The approach used in this study reflected a case study approach structured around the 'storyline' of the development of the innovation.

As in many public sector arenas, innovation in the NHS (the UK's National Health Service) is a controversial topic, pursued in order to 'modernise' and 'increase efficiency', but sometimes regarded with suspicion as a cover for reductions in services and jobs. NHS Direct provided a novel mechanism through which the public could access both critical and less urgent healthcare information (and subsequently base their decisions for further action), establishing an alternative to the existing sources of such information.

A BRIEF HISTORY

NHS Direct is a nurse-led, 24-hour telephone advice service which offers distance-based information to the public and allows them to make better informed decisions on their appropriate subsequent avenue to healthcare. Rather than the form of *triage* which is applied to patients on entry to a hospital Accident & Emergency (A&E) Department, NHS Direct allows patients and their immediate advisors to undertake their own assessment. It does this by combining an old technology (the telephone) and a new technology (Clinical Assessment Software, or CAS) in order to deliver healthcare and health service advice to the public. It thereby provides more extensive and cheaper access to healthcare, while at the same time alleviating pressure on healthcare services. In this sense, the innovation aspects concern the ability of CAS to reach appropriate decisions under a wide range of demands, together with issues of public trust, social reflexivity and social empowerment.

While forming a major part of the then government's policy for modernising the NHS, it also aimed to improve customer satisfaction and patient safety – empowering patients to make better informed choices about their own healthcare – and was thus in line with the general objectives of making public services more 'customer driven'. The need for the service originated from chronic concerns over the level of unnecessary attendances at hospitals, long queues and waiting times, and severe demands on emergency services in the winter time. Healthcare practitioners, including GPs (General Practitioners, or 'family doctors'), complained of the pressure induced by the presentation of non-urgent cases and it was evident that existing call-handling systems could not alleviate the delays suffered by needy patients. On the political side, the introduction of NHS Direct was high on the health priorities of the newly elected Labour government.

The origins of NHS Direct stemmed from a series of workshops[3] convened by the UK Chief Medical Officer, Sir Kenneth Calman, in response to the government's concerns over the perceived crisis in the provision of emergency care services. The earliest indication of the new service itself arose from a recommendation made in Calman's September 1997 report, *Developing Emergency Services in the Community*, which identified the potential benefits to over-stretched ambulance and A&E services from the provision of an alternative access to a high-quality 24-hour telephone advice system (National Audit Office (NAO) 2002).

The first official announcement of its establishment came with the publication of *The New NHS: Modern, Dependable* (Department of Health 1997b), although this contained only a short paragraph regarding the government's intention. A primary rationale for its launch was that ambulance services in the UK were struggling to cope with a huge rise in the number of emergency service calls, around an estimated two-thirds of which did not necessitate an emergency response, many being the result of 'nuisance' calls for trivial issues. Thus, the introduction of a system of immediate care advice lines was seen as a way both to improve the accessibility of appropriate information to patients in the event of a perceived emergency and, through the appropriate deployment of resources, to alleviate pressure on other NHS emergency and out-of-hours services.

The use of telephone help-lines was far from an original concept: the Health Information Service, a forerunner to NHS Direct, already provided information to callers, and a number of GP practices used CAS and computer-based triaging systems. Nevertheless, NHS Direct represented an important concept, and built on 'work pioneered by colleagues in primary care during the past five to ten years, in many parts of the UK' (Department of Health 1998).

The next developmental stage coincided with a change at ministerial level. The incoming ministerial team moved the project on, but transformed it into something far less sophisticated than Calman's original vision, and one which was, in addition, nurse-led.

In late 1997, a high-level political decision was taken to establish the service and to roll it out at three test sites. The idea to pilot was prompted partly by concerns that the service might stimulate an unmet demand for non-emergency healthcare services. In March 1998 three pilot schemes were set up, catering to approximately 1.3 million people, operated by the relevant regional ambulance services.

Due to its potential to involve and impact a large number of stakeholders, two consultative groups were set up: the National Advisory Group (which included voluntary organisations representing particular groups of users) and the Primary Care Implementation Group (involving the main GP representative organisations). Later developments further extended these consultative functions.

Between January and April 1999, a second wave of sites brought the service to a total of 20 million people, followed by a third wave between November and December 1999, adding a further 10 million people. The service was introduced into Wales in June and October 2000, with a set of fourth wave sites in England in place by November. Thus, within three years the service had been extended to cover the whole of England and Wales and was available to some 53 million people. NHS 24, a scheme to cover Scotland, was in place by the end of 2001, covering a further five million people (Munro et al. 2001).

During the early development phases, at the request of the Department of Health, a number of evaluations were undertaken (in 1998 and 2000, with a final report in 2001) by the Medical Care Research Unit, an independent health policy research group at the University of Sheffield. Overall, the evaluation was positive although some reservations were expressed and the conclusions were also cautious (Munro et al. 2001). Further close monitoring and a diverse programme of evaluation were among the recommendations.

Nonetheless, political reaction to the initial impact of the first wave pilots was extremely favourable and led to strong top-down pressure to accelerate the introduction of the service. The timescale for roll-out was very tight, from August 1998 to April 1999, during which time an entire infrastructure and staff had to be put in place. As noted by the 2002 report on NHS Direct by the government's expenditure 'watchdog', the NAO, this limited the time available to identify the 'champions' who could drive the new ideas forward at local level. Further plans and milestones were announced for the service in the NHS Plan (July 2000), mainly relating to a range of additional services, such as: calls from NHS Direct nurses to help patients manage their medicines and to check on older people living alone; advice provision; the launch of NHS Direct online, Digital TV and NHS Direct information points in key public places; and the availability of a translation and interpretation service through NHS Direct.

By mid-2000, the service had become much more than the simple 24-hour telephone help-line heralded in the 1997 White Paper and was presented as a more integrated, and accessible, component of the public healthcare system.

The process of change and acceptance was very rapid. The 2001/02 NAO review of NHS Direct in England noted that, in addition to responding to strong political demands and pressures in just five years, it had established an impressive track record for customer satisfaction and patient safety, empowering patients to make better informed choices about their own healthcare. The review also clearly identified the potential of the service to contribute to wider developments in the NHS.

A major factor in deciding the success, or otherwise, of NHS Direct was its impact on the public and its ability to generate a high degree of customer satisfaction while at the same time delivering a safe and effective service. Overall, the NAO review found that customer satisfaction was high and that NHS Direct performance measures were generally achieving their targets, with action being taken to address those which required improvement. Two causes of failure to meet performance targets were learning curve problems associated with the introduction of the national CAS system and staff recruitment shortfalls. However, solutions were foreseen in the networking of all sites by April 2002, which allowed the spread of workload from areas of high demand to those with lower demand, and the procurement of an automated staff rostering tool (NAO 2002). On the issue of patient safety, an independent analysis of caller records at the NHS Direct Hampshire site found that the service was operating safely (NAO 2002).

One interesting feature of NHS Direct was the way in which it integrated with complementary initiatives from other healthcare providers at the local level: a number of examples were cited by the 2002 NAO review. Such linkages were demonstrated to have made a number of useful contributions and further scope for broader application was evident, without any constraints to the capacity of existing NHS Direct functions.

In December 1999, the system was extended to include an internet-based delivery mode with the introduction of NHS Direct Online. This offered a simple questionnaire which aimed to assist people in knowing what they should do: either treat themselves, phone the NHS Direct service or call 999 (emergency services). Digital TV pilots were introduced the following year.

By 2002, four years after its initial introduction, the service had dealt with over 10 million calls providing healthcare advice and information; between October 2000 and October 2001, an average of 100,000 people called the service each week. In a follow-up to the NHS Plan (2000), the government announced the aim of extending capacity, handling all out-of-hours calls to GPs and taking up to 1 million low-priority ambulance calls (Secretary of State for Health 2002). Numbers of callers to NHS Direct increased steadily to over half a million a month by the end of 2003, and an equal number logged on to NHS Direct Online, which was expanded in November 2001 to offer a new health encyclopaedia. Further expansions and updates included the addition of the NHS Direct self-help guide, and in 2006 further features were added such as the Mind and Body magazine, current health news and features, and interactive health tools and quizzes, while accessibility was improved.

In April 2004 NHS Direct was established as a Special Health Authority with responsibility for all staff. By this time steady growth in use of NHS Direct was reported, with the number of calls reaching 6.4 million per year (up from 1.7 million in 2000), although well short of a projected target of 30 million. In addition, according to the NHS Improvement Plan, the NHS Direct website (http://www.nhsdirect.co.uk) recorded 6.5 million hits in 2003 (Department of Health 2003). By 2009, the number of hits had risen to approximately 18 million. Currently, the NHS Direct website receives over 1.5 million visits every month.[4]

The service has continued to integrate further innovations, including the introduction of mobile phone apps linked to the NHS Direct telephone service.

THE SERVICE CONTEXT

NHS Direct provides four categories of information relating to:

- advice on which action should be taken in response to specific symptoms of illness;
- particular health conditions;
- local healthcare services, such as doctors, dentists or late night opening pharmacies;
- self-help and support organisations.

The NHS Direct Online system offers further services both to the public and to other parts of the NHS.

Essentially, NHS Direct provides telephone callers with a nurse who uses computer-generated protocols to take a brief history and responds to on-screen prompts to give sound advice on the best management of the patient. Initially, the caller is dealt with by a call-handler, who takes baseline details and passes them on to a nurse if appropriate (i.e. for non-critical general information). The objective is for the consultation to finish with the patient being given either self-care advice or a referral for further care, which might include a 999 call, referral to an A&E department, referral to their own GP, or referral to an out-of-hours service. A follow-up call to the patient might also be scheduled, in the immediate or longer-term future. Nurses may have access to patient records and the system allows the development of a patient database which may be used to track previous contacts. The history-taking involves following a series of prompts, classified along a specific set of features (e.g. onset, location, description of symptoms, precipitating factors, etc.) (Royal College of General Practitioners 1999).

Following entry of the history, the nurse is able to access a list of over 1,000 protocols and follow the suggested advice with the patient or their representative. The final advice cannot be downgraded by the nurse but may be upgraded – thus the system errs on the side of caution. Local customisation of the systems is also possible, within a set of national guidelines. Voice recordings of calls are also made and these may be reviewed by supervisors/senior nurses at the request of nurses who are concerned about some element of the advice they have given. They may also be used to clarify any discrepancies that arise with the advice or the outcome of the patient's response to the advice.

NHS DIRECT AS A HEALTH SERVICE INNOVATION

NHS Direct represents an integration of three types of innovation: process, organisational and technical. The primary challenge faced by the innovation was to shift from the traditional face-to-face form of healthcare delivery via hospital A&E departments and GPs, to one that was expected to deliver extremely reliable assessments and diagnoses while overcoming public reluctance to adopt a completely new approach. Moreover, it had to integrate with and meet the needs of existing primary care delivery systems.

One major facet of the system's innovativeness is that its introduction represented a response to the development of a new form of patient – one who is proactive and confident and wishes to exert more control over their healthcare. Indeed, it has been argued that NHS Direct is also shaping its users to act more proactively and to share a greater proportion of their decision-making burden (Hanlon et al. 2003).

Generic NHS/Public Sector Issues

Innovation: definitions, interpretation and perception
Drawing on the definition of Green, Howells and Miles (2001), for the purposes of this study innovation was defined as 'deliberate change of behaviour at the level of institutions that includes a new or improved service, process, technology, or administrative tool'. The project recognised that at a broad level the process of innovation in the public sector could diverge from that which operates in the private sector. This notion of innovation appears to be recognised by employees within the UK public sector although it may be applied in the context of many activities. First, when used by 'front-line' employees at the 'ground' or operational level a number of findings emerged:

- The term 'innovation' is often not employed and is frequently subsumed in the more general context of 'modernisation' or 'change'.
- The process of innovation itself may not be recognised or is only seen in relation to the development or invention of 'new technology' or, less frequently, in the context of problem-solving. Thus, innovation may be categorised simply as an example of 'good practice'.
- Innovation is rarely encountered as a step change in practice or processes and it is often an incremental phenomenon.
- Innovation is often viewed as a process of adopting top-down guidelines, or of meeting targets.
- The diffusion or roll-out of new innovations forms a major management issue in the public sector, irrespective of whether they are top-down or bottom-up generated. Thus, employees in public sector management spend considerable effort on identifying, codifying and spreading good practice.

Whatever its form, innovation is far from a neutral process and, in addition to its impacts on its immediate environment (e.g. better levels of patient care, more effective treatments, reduction of waiting times), it frequently forms the driver for further organisational or process change and innovation.

Shaping factors for innovation
The UK public sector appears to offer a surprisingly large number of shaping factors (which here is used rather than the more loaded term 'barriers') for innovation. Eleven major types of factor were identified in relation to the NHS:

1. *Size and complexity*: The UK public health sector is an extremely complex organisation, composed of multiple-tiered interlinked systems with huge staff numbers (over 1.4 million in the NHS in 2010[5]); a large range of occupations, encompassing GPs, doctors, nurses, health visitors, dentists, opticians, pharmacists, therapists, technical staff, allied health professionals, ambulance staff, managers, support staff,

administrators and infrastructure support; and with many organisational arrangements and many service processes. Further rigidity is added to the system by the lack of 'patient information connectivity' between the various actors in the system.

2. *Heritage and legacy*: Public sector organisations are prone to entrenched practice and procedures. However, at the broader system level or in different institutional settings, it may be evident that established practice and procedures may not be working as effectively as desired. This problem is compounded by the difficulties of demonstrating the potential beneficial impacts of innovation and change (see point 6 below). Similarly, there may also be an unwillingness to accept novel ideas from outside the immediate organisational peer group.

3. *'Professionalised' resistance*: Several factors tend to operate within the UK health system, which comprises a number of distinct and well-established professional groups with their own communities of practice, rationales, perspectives and policy agendas to which they prefer to adhere. Thus, groups such as clinicians and the ambulance service, for example, form what has been described as a 'disconnected hierarchy'. Similarly, parts of the health system may operate according to varying command and control structures. The shift towards a customer/consumer-focused orientation may also engender a certain degree of reticence to embrace change and innovation, particularly on the part of those who are more committed to a professionally driven delivery system. Finally, another professionalised factor concerns the non-ownership of ideas and resistance to disseminating 'good ideas' that may be appropriated by others. At the technical level, this translates to problems over the ownership of intellectual property.

4. *Risk aversion*: Allied to professionalised resistance is the (fully understandable) inherent resistance of the medical professions to undertake changes which may result in an increased probability of risk to the patients in their care. The emphasis placed on the development of evidence-based medical and clinical practice is one consequence of the desire to minimise the unforeseen consequences of new health interventions. Paradoxically, this is counter-balanced by a reported tendency for the clinical professions to embrace innovation in the search for improved medical procedures and treatments. At a more general level – that is, including management practice in the equation – there is also a reported resistance to 'out of the box' thinking, partly explained by the factors described above. It should be noted that our definition of innovation implies novelty with its attendant lack of pre-knowledge on the possible outcomes. Moreover, innovations are rarely isolated phenomena and often depend upon, or engender, further changes and innovation, leading to a ripple effect across the entire system in which they are applied.

5. *High public/political profile and accountability*: In the health sector public service managers and politicians are wary of enacting changes that may result in negative outcomes, particularly if these engage the popular media. Against this is the argument that large-scale, radical (and, therefore, high-risk) policy changes are more attractive to politicians who are anxious to leave a legacy of their political careers rather than introducing a series of incremental but low-profile policy changes. Within the sector itself, there seems to be a tendency towards a blame culture, with its associated high levels of accountability. Added to this is the risk of litigation in

the event of adverse impacts, although it is also noted that in the US, with its strongly litigious culture, innovation and change are more widely embraced.

6.   *Need for consultation and likelihood of unclear outcomes*: As in all bureaucratic systems, but particularly in the health system where there is a huge range of stakeholder involvement, there is a strong requirement to consult and review any planned changes and modifications and to attempt to identify their potential consequences. The complexity of the system also militates against the ability to gain a clear picture of all the eventual effects of these actions – thus innovations may require piloting and careful evaluation prior to any large-scale roll-out. A related problem concerns the systemic nature of innovation, that is, the possibility that the introduction of one innovation may shift the underlying problem to another part of the system or may have unforeseen and adverse consequences. Thus, the introduction of any innovation requires close *ex ante* assessment, coupled with careful review and evaluation.

7.   *Pace and scale of change*: The NHS has been (and continues to be) subject to a large number of often radical changes, many of which have been at a very large scale. The pace of change has also been dramatic and has led to an environment of shifting targets and the absence of opportunities for reflection and assessment of the consequences of many of the innovations introduced. The introduction of new political ideologies, new 'world views' and so on, may also accelerate the pace at which policy makers (at all levels) wish to see change implemented. Thus, while 'political will' may be viewed as a driver for innovation and change, the systems to which it is applied may become 'innovation-fatigued' and resistant to further change. Given the requirements for consultation and appraisal of the effects outlined above, this has led to the creation of a vicious circle of uncertainty.

8.   *Absence of resources for innovation*: Although there has been a clear political imperative driving change and innovation, a lack of dedicated budgets specifically allocated to innovation at the Trust level hindered the realisation of innovative projects at the ground level. Naturally, the overall picture is somewhat patchy, and certain areas, such as surgery, will attract greater levels of investment than lower-profile areas, such as mental health.

9.   *Absence of capacity for organisational learning*: Despite the efforts of the (former) Modernisation Agency at disseminating good practice there was a recognised absence of structures and mechanisms within the UK public health system for the enhancement of organisational learning. A number of initiatives aimed at promulgating the diffusion of good practice were available but many were viewed as short-lived. In addition, the frequent reorganisations undergone by the NHS promote a lack of corporate memory.

10.   *Technical barriers*: The development of a new technology or technological application may serve as a strong driver or facilitator of process or organisational change. However, the absence of a technology which exhibits certain specifications may also hinder the development of a sought-for innovation. Thus, the application of new uses to existing equipment, for example, may push the technology to the limits of its capabilities and act as a driver for further technical innovation.

11.   *Public resistance to change*: Last but not least is a (postulated) general resistance of the public to reorganisation and changes in the way healthcare is delivered, although

this is possibly an over-generalisation; many innovations appear to be accepted very readily. While some sectors of the public may resist changes to their accepted ways of interfacing with the healthcare system, others are much more likely to embrace new ways of operating. Several factors may operate here, such as age, educational level, ethnic background, personal wealth, and so on.

Drivers and facilitators for innovation

A number of counters to the shaping factors noted above may also be discerned. These can be categorised as drivers for (i.e. pressures) and facilitators of (i.e. factors which aid uptake and dissemination) innovation in the public health system.

1. *Problem-oriented drivers*: Many innovations in the public health sector are introduced in response to one or more specific problems. Typical underlying causes include demographic factors, ageing population, fragmentation of families, and lifestyle, health and social problems. Thus, an innovation may be required to deal with new specific problems (i.e. the rapid increase in child obesity), or with generic problems (such as the need to reduce in-patient resident times as a means to free up hospital beds), or to speed up the processing of healthcare administrative tasks.

2. *Non-problem-oriented improvement*: Innovations may also be introduced because they represent an improvement on the prevailing situation, rather than addressing a specific problem. For example, doing things faster or more efficiently is generally a broad goal and not necessarily the answer to the specific problem in itself. Similarly, a new medical technique may confer improved quality of life for patients but may not offer any further advantages.

3. *Political push*: Clearly, the raft of changes introduced to the UK public health sector over recent years has been strongly driven by political ideologies, albeit ones that have shifted when faced with operational and financial realities. Three major trends may be identified: a drive towards the improvement of standards (greater patient choice and better delivery of services); a focus upon target-setting, which has engendered mixed levels of support; and 'disruptive policy-making', that is, the belief that an ongoing process of change and restructuring will stimulate the creation of new ideas, operating practices or approaches to problem-solving. Alongside the first two of these trends is the concomitant need for improved systems of review, evaluation and impact assessment (see above). At the delivery level, political goals may be reflected through the imposition of performance targets (which may facilitate innovation although with the danger that they can distort the behaviour of actors within the system in unanticipated and possibly undesirable ways) – see point 8 below.

4. *Growth of a culture of review*: A range of assessment practices have developed over the years in the public health sector, ranging from evidence-based guidance, health technology assessment and clinical audit through to broader-scale review activities (see above). The development of these techniques could, at least in theory, alleviate the problems associated with assessing the potential impacts of innovations and with promoting a culture of organisational learning.

5. *Input of major resources*: There has been a political recognition that change requires the allocation of substantial resources. Likewise, the management of change has also demanded increased resources but has been accompanied by claims that the NHS has

become top-heavy with administrators at the expense of those staff who actually deliver its services.

6. *Support mechanisms for innovation*: Allied to the allocation of resources is the provision of actual structures designed to promote, stimulate or disseminate innovation. Two major actors (or groups of actors) may be identified in this regard. First, the Innovation Hubs set up as 'innovation push' organisations. However, these are perceived as having a highly technology-based (intellectual property-oriented) focus with regard to innovations. In addition, technical innovation in the health sector is often driven by the suppliers of equipment and services rather than originating from within the public sector itself. The second 'innovation champion' was the Modernisation Agency. Tasked with promoting and assisting the process change at all levels, and with the dissemination of good practice and innovation, the Agency was able to offer support and advice but few resources. In addition, it looked at external sources, such as US models, for what it termed 'directed creativity' and examples of organisational innovation.[6]

7. *Capacity for innovation*: Many staff in the public health system were characterised by having a high level of expertise and exhibiting a high level of creativity and problem-solving, thus providing an environment in which innovation should both be generated and accepted. This can also be coupled to a very strong motivation for service towards the public, careers in many branches of the health service being highly vocational.

8. *Competitive drivers*: This set of drivers is rather questionable as it is based on the belief that a shift towards a competitive framework for healthcare delivery will provide incentives to staff (and management) and improve patient choice and drive resources (since money follows patients). The use of performance targets to derive 'league tables' (e.g. of hospitals, schools and universities) can encourage the use of innovative approaches in order to force up performance ratings. However, the use of such targets, indicators and league tables often distorts operational behaviours, sometimes with unintended and deleterious consequences (such as the refusal of GPs to operate accessible appointments systems in order to drive down waiting lists). Therefore, this is one example of a driver which may force innovation to operate in non-optimal ways.

9. *Technological factors*: Technological innovation can be a strong determinant or driver for subsequent innovation. The introduction or availability of new technology may provide an opportunity for another form of innovation (process, organisational, delivery, system interaction, etc.) to take place or to be implemented – a process sometimes termed 'innofusion' (see Fleck 1993).

Several of the shaping factors and drivers/facilitators described work in different directions when it comes to shaping innovations. The case study therefore provides a useful context for examining in more detail how these tensions work out in particular instances. We can begin to consider why it should be that particular resolutions are achieved.

NHS Direct as Part of the Innovation Framework

This section examines NHS Direct as an innovation event within the context of the generic sets of shaping factors and drivers. This approach enables us to draw a number of lessons on how potential barriers may be overcome and how the effects of drivers may be promoted or capitalised upon.

Shaping factors
The *size and complexity* of the UK public health system were to some extent surmounted (intentionally or unintentionally) through the gradual, phased introduction of NHS Direct through successive waves of pilot sites, expanding over three years to cover the entire country with a network of regional sites. The regional and local nature of the service was also significant as it allowed development to proceed according to the prevailing local conditions and introduced a degree of flexibility to what could have been a monolithic structure.

Heritage and legacy issues were to some extent overcome by the strong political pressure which drove the introduction of the service. Government and health ministers were very supportive and keen for NHS Direct to succeed, partly driven by existing pressures on A&E services and the need to be seen to be doing something in response. This strong top-down pressure was translated at the regional level by the use of local 'champions' – proactive and forward-thinking managers and executives with strong visions of what the service could deliver. Nevertheless, much groundwork was undertaken in order to prepare local stakeholders for the introduction of the service and to ensure their support. As the regional NHS Direct sites were brand new organisations, each was able to completely define its own culture (within broad NHS frameworks). Thus, in the absence of pre-existing policies, procedures or boundaries, Chief Executives were able to set new parameters, thereby offering organisational freedom which provided the opportunity to be exploratory, and hence facilitated further innovation and development. It also made the organisation and staff more receptive to new ideas; some sites explored a number of new areas, such as the opportunities for chronic disease management, telemetry, and so on, while other services explored the boundaries of the system and developed new areas and new innovations. However, this does not imply that the service lacked a clear set of objectives: the goals of NHS Direct were fully understood by all those involved.

Allied to the preceding factor is the issue of *professional resistance*: many groups and individuals in the NHS were quick to point out the potential obstacles and drawbacks of the new service, which generated much scepticism. Particular issues included concerns over patients' safety, the ability to carry out triage at a distance with no visual reference, and a belief that A&E presentations would increase through its use as a default response. There was also the major issue of recruitment and the belief that NHS Direct would 'cream off' the most skilled A&E nurses. Again, these concerns were overcome or deflected through the proselytising activities of local managers and executives to all stakeholders, combined with the integration of the system with ongoing local and regional services.

Professional resistance was exacerbated by the fact that the NHS reportedly suffers from a strong ethos of compartmentalisation and internal competitiveness. Again, the engagement and involvement of stakeholders were seen as key to overcoming this problem. For example, if nurses were being displaced through local Hospital Trust mergers, the regional NHS Direct offered to take them on. However, local NHS Direct managers had to guard against the perception that the service could provide a convenient place to which under-performing staff could be transferred.

A further way to overcome professional resistance was to demonstrate that the service was indeed having an impact on the demands for GP and emergency services. However, in the early phases, in the absence of any evaluations, there was no evidence, other than anecdotal, for success or failure and there was no clear message with regard to what worked and what did not. To complicate matters further, each of the pilots operated under different conditions and procedures and there was a lack of dissemination of their results. Such behavioural heterogeneity continued through into the second wave of sites and beyond. As more information emerged, many of the early concerns were removed, although the reaction from GPs with regard to NHS Direct remained inconsistent, both highly positive or equally negative. For example, the NAO study (NAO 2002) found that NHS Direct could reduce demands on health services provided outside normal working hours, and that the service was off-setting around half of its running costs by encouraging more appropriate use of NHS services. It was also apparently adding value by reassuring callers and saving them unnecessary anxiety.

Nevertheless, barriers of this nature were still present. For example, some NHS staff were convinced that the pool of potential cases had been broadened by the introduction of NHS Direct as it provides more opportunities for people to present to A&E and other primary care services, partially as a consequence of the removal of the 'gatekeeper' role of GPs. Moreover, the system is open to abuse – with patients claiming that they had received NHS Direct advice to go to A&E (in the absence of any such advice), while the service also attracted 'serial' callers, although some of these would have been displaced from making calls to other NHS services.

Finally, it may be argued that by adhering to the notion of patient empowerment, NHS Direct reduced the traditional professional barriers promoted by a small number of GPs and the concern felt by some patients that they did not want to present to A&E departments with what, in their view, may have been trivial conditions. Indeed, improving patient access to healthcare formed one of the key goals for the introduction of the service.

The NHS can be particularly rigid in terms of its career structures and paths. Hence, employees tend to be *risk-averse* and protective of their professional boundaries, and it may be difficult for employees to recognise or to seize opportunities. One interviewee noted that her colleagues had questioned her motives for joining NHS Direct and regarded her choice with some suspicion. Paradoxically, NHS Direct was also seen as a potential competitor to A&E nurse recruitment. Concerning the more specific issue of risk to patients, at the local level safeguards assumed major importance. For example, the clinical assessment software had a tendency to err on the side of caution in the advice provided and nurse advisors would also tend to opt for the more cautious recommendation offered. Software algorithms also underwent several iterations and were adjusted to respond to local conditions. Regularised collection of patient information was also implemented, both to gauge data on participants' reactions and for safety checking (as noted, all calls are logged and recorded). Overall performance of the system was monitored using 'mystery shoppers' who make controlled calls and test the system. Around 1 in 20 patients would also be audited, although regional practices varied.

The problem of clinical risk and the perception that uncertainty can be equated with professional failure was addressed through a cultural shift by encouraging nurse advisors who were concerned about a call or that they might have made a mistake or error of judgement to approach their line manager for advice. The recorded call can be reviewed and any appropriate follow-up action taken. In the early days of the service, it was relatively common for nurses to ask for such advice due to a lack of confidence in themselves or the CAS. This process also led to considerable feedback on the CAS algorithms and all the systems underwent considerable readjustment. Thus risk aversion was overcome with the implementation of strong feedback loops at the local level.

At the next level, the provision of wrong advice and the incidence of 'adverse incidents' are closely monitored, often by local GP groups or policy evaluators. The major system-wide evaluations have also examined this aspect closely, the NAO study noting that 'NHS Direct has a good safety record with few adverse incidents' (NAO 2002, p. 2).

At the highest level of the system, risk was also minimised through the gradual introduction of the scheme via a series of pilots. However, once ministers had seen that it seemed to be offering a new, politically visible product, immediate roll-out of the full service was demanded, resulting in a very tight timescale for the second wave and the creation of an entire infrastructure, buildings, staff, strategy, and so on for each new site. With little time for preparation, it was difficult to identify the 'champions' who could drive the new ideas forward. It was reported that, when visiting regional GPs to inform them of the forthcoming service, many were highly negative – since they erroneously believed they were being sold a service from outside the NHS. Whether due to a lack of clear advance information from the Department of Health or a failure of this information to get through to GPs, it emphasised the need to precede an innovation with clear information.

Since ministers had embraced the idea of NHS Direct and were pressing for its rapid introduction the onus of risk shifted to the top of the political ladder, although it is clear that local Chief Executives and managers did not feel absolved from the risk of failure. This upward shift of responsibility also helped to circumvent the barrier of the high *public profile and accountability* associated with health policy decisions and actions, while the checks, balances and feedback loops introduced at the local level demonstrated that the accountability issue was being addressed by the new service.

In 1996, the Senior Medical Officer launched a *consultation* paper on 'Developing emergency services in the community'. However, the NAO evaluation (NAO 2002) noted that the consultation exercise had been curtailed due to the constraints of the timetable for roll-out. Nevertheless, strong ongoing consultative arrangements have been put in place in order to respond to the views of stakeholders. Consultation with stakeholders is also a major feature at the local level of delivery and, coupled with the strong feedback loops already described, is intended to ensure that external views and requirements are addressed. In addition, the pilot approach to some extent mitigated the absence of a full pre-launch consultation. The pilot approach and the emphasis on early evaluation of the first wave sites can be viewed as a means of overcoming the lack of clarity of the eventual outcomes, although the acceleration of the launch of the second wave sites before the full implications and impacts of the first wave had been absorbed somewhat militated against the ability to learn from the initial experience. This was partly offset, certainly in the early stages, by the system tending to be more responsive to change as a consequence of the exploratory nature of the regional systems and the absence of the need to follow specific procedural models or guidelines. In this sense, NHS Direct followed the model suggested by Abernathy and Utterback (1978) in which the innovation matured as an understanding of user (and delivery) requirements developed.

Although the *pace and scale of change* in the NHS was viewed as a barrier to innovation, NHS Direct itself represented a radical change of operation and procedures which was extended to full national coverage within an extremely tight timescale: 'Ministers decided that implementation would proceed alongside piloting and were concerned with how, rather than whether, the service would be implemented. Short lines of communication between the project team and those implementing the service at the local level enabled lessons to be learnt quickly as the projects progressed' (NAO 2002, p. 5).

Although a *lack of dedicated budgets* was found to hinder innovation in the health sector, this factor did not apply to NHS Direct, which was furnished with adequate resources.

While the *absence of a capacity for organisational learning* was identified as a barrier to innovation within the health service, in many ways NHS Direct 'broke the mould' by operating at the local level, with flexible remits (including more flexible working hours, job sharing, etc.) and the promotion of a culture of feedback and responsiveness to local needs. However, the service did operate within a guiding framework of terms and conditions and had a set of clear goals. Thus, its responsiveness to change did not lead to instability – evidence of the need for change was clearly weighed and required a strong rationale.

The barrier of *public resistance* to change in the traditional mode of healthcare delivery was not in the event realised at a general level. The NAO (2002, p. 2) report noted that 'Public satisfaction with NHS Direct was consistently very high at over 90%', and further studies endorsed this level of acceptance. However, coverage of the population is not homogeneous – while mothers and young people represent major users of the service, other groups such as the elderly, those with communication disabilities and those whose first language is not English tended to be under-represented. Thus, efforts were made to ensure that these groups are not disadvantaged, for example through the introduction of translation services and access routes for those with hearing impediments (Munro et al. 2001).

Technical barriers were not found to apply in this particular case, once the initial development and selection of the most appropriate Clinical Assessment Software had been achieved.

Drivers and facilitators

Since the service derived initially from a perceived crisis in the provision of emergency healthcare services in the UK, it could be said to have been strongly *problem-driven*.[7] The use of telephone help-lines had already been pioneered at a number of UK sites and the practice of carrying out needs assessments on emergency callers was stimulated by the US 911 emergency service. Thus, NHS Direct should be viewed as one of a collection of approaches. The somewhat radical, technology-driven approach offered by NHS Direct found resonance with New Labour thinking and hence evinced a strong *political* appeal. A concept originating from the government's Chief Medical Officer and with endorsement from politicians all the way up to the Prime Minister's office was sure to engender a strong political will to succeed, underpinned by the political need to be seen to be acting in a dynamic and positive way in an area with high public and media attention.

Elements of a *strong culture of review* permeated the development of NHS Direct, although the *ex ante* consultation was curtailed due to the need for political expediency. Nonetheless, strong consultative arrangements were put in place centrally at an early stage and subsequently reinforced as the service was rolled out and expanded. Moreover, the demand for evidence-based practice and risk avoidance ensured that local sites operated rigid quality control and review mechanisms, reinforced by strong feedback loops, which assisted in the customisation and adaptation of the service.

The *input of major resources* played a role in the development of the service and as an aid to overcoming a number of inherent barriers to innovation. Although the overall budget for the development and maintenance of NHS Direct is not known, one source noted that it had been allocated 'sufficient' (i.e. not inconsiderable) resources to ensure that it had fulfilled political desires for its success.

As a *support mechanism for innovation*, the role of the Modernisation Agency vis-à-vis the implementation of NHS Direct is hard to quantify. It is clear, however, that the local NHS Direct services were highly responsive organisations and very open to innovation. Thus, their *capacity for innovation* was generally high. The open remit of the NHS Direct sites and their senior management encouraged local problem-solving and the generation of new ideas. There are also numerous instances of NHS Direct staff having devised new applications, and several sites formed linkages with complementary NHS services. Examples of new applications include inputs to epidemiological studies: the logging of calls allowed the incidence of infectious and other diseases to be tracked more effectively. Thus, NHS Direct-generated information fed into epidemiological studies while some NHS Direct sites also assist with emergency help-lines set up in response to disease outbreaks or health scares, thereby shifting the burden from hospitals which normally deal with such services. Further developments include the use of NHS Direct to arrange GP out-of-hours cover and also more speculative investigations into how the service might assist in telemedicine applications and provide alternative ways into measuring health, and chronic disease management.

The role of *competitive drivers* is less clear in the context of NHS Direct. Certainly, the NHS operates within a framework of performance targets at various levels and there is thus a general pressure to achieve these, but their direct role on the service is difficult to quantify.

Technological factors played a major role in the development of NHS Direct, which depended on the availability of a public telephone system with a comprehensive coverage of the population. Obviously, this was in place long before the advent of the service but the rapid expansion of the use of mobile phones and the accompanying infrastructure has vastly increased the already high accessibility and flexibility of the service. More relevant, however, was the development of a suitable CAS system which could deal with the entire potential range of medical issues and problems and offer a safe yet pragmatic response to callers through the mediation of trained nursing staff. It also had to be easily modifiable and adaptable to local conditions while retaining its integrity and safety considerations. It is an interesting feature of the innovatory nature of NHS Direct that three systems were trialled during the pilot phase and that a fourth system was eventually used.

With regard to the expansion and further development of the system, the diffusion of public access to the internet was a major facilitator for the roll-out of NHS Direct Online. Likewise, technology such as touch-screen computer operating systems was a prerequisite for the NHS Direct booths. The rise in mobile phone usage and the advent of smart phone technology have also been utilised through the introduction of specific NHS Direct 'apps'.

CONCLUSIONS

It has been possible to identify a number of factors, or shared characteristics, that, at least partially, may contribute to the initiation, development and implementation of innovations in the public health sector. The following lessons are therefore not a recipe for successful innovation but only indicators of potential contributory factors.[8]

1. The presence of a *strong political pressure and support* is essential but must be combined with a complementary *dialogue with and engagement from all stakeholders* – both those that deliver the service and those that benefit from it. Much preliminary groundwork had to be undertaken to accomplish the engagement of local GPs and other healthcare workers, which appeared to pay dividends. Once the service was in operation, it was essential to ensure all stakeholders still shared the same vision, that expectations were being met and that the lessons learned were being disseminated quickly (see below). The high level of public acceptance of the service proved a positive outcome, but the extent to which the issue of patient empowerment plays a role in this is unclear.

2. Innovating organisations or key personnel must have a tendency to demonstrate *openness to ideas* and a willingness to think 'outside the box'. This can be equally important in the development of novel solutions to problems, or in the identification of solutions to previously unrecognised problems or issues. It was also an important factor in the acceptance of new ideas and new operational practices, both from the perspective of management and from the perspective of those expected to deliver or utilise the innovation. These features were strongly demonstrated from the high-level conception of the scheme through to its operation at the local level.

3. It is important to *seize opportunities* in order to implement change and to gain the acceptance of new ideas. Such opportunities could relate to the availability of resources, the need to respond to enforced change or new circumstances, and the timing of political or organisational events. The coalescence of two or more factors might also be seen as an opportunity, such as the simultaneous availability of technical solutions, a perceived crisis, and a new political philosophy and will in the case of NHS Direct.

4. The role of *'champions'* or *entrepreneurs* was clearly significant. The presence of individuals with sufficient vision and determination to both push and lead the innovation process was a characteristic offered by the leading management at the regional sites and also an ethos promulgated by the Modernisation Agency. However, such champions also had to have access to resources or influence (and ideally both) in order for them to be able to effect change and to motivate others.

5. While champions were important, they also required a supportive environment. The successful operation of NHS Direct relied on positive attitudes towards *teamwork and independent thinking* in order to take forward the innovation concept. The

service required an entirely new approach, thus the supporting team also had to be fully committed to the idea and able to deliver it in often novel, rapidly changing circumstances. The encouragement of local problem-solving and the 'open' remit of the regional sites greatly assisted in this context.

6. Innovating organisations need a *high degree of reflexivity* – an ability to demonstrate organisational learning. This behaviour was evidenced through practices such as *ex ante* appraisal (despite the curtailment of the early consultative process in the face of the rapid roll-out of the service), assessment and ongoing monitoring processes, and evaluation of the outcomes and impacts, often within very short time-frames. Coupled with such reflexivity, a high degree of responsiveness – an ability to react quickly to the outcomes of the review process – is also important. Several examples of this were evident with NHS Direct: a high level of responsiveness to local needs and conditions, with strong feedback loops in place; a strong element of safety checking and local amendment of CAS protocols; higher-level consultative arrangements; evaluation of the first wave sites; and the operation of stakeholder panels.

7. Linked to the above, *demonstration of the utility* of the implemented innovation is an important factor in terms of developing further support, either for the innovation itself or for the implementing team or organisation. This may be less critical in cases where the innovation is problem-oriented, as the success becomes self-evident. Such benefits need not be restricted to economic outcomes (such as the demonstration of a reduction in demand for GP and other emergency services): political outcomes were a major factor in the case of NHS Direct (i.e. the government was seen to be acting on a problem, with positive outcomes). Unexpected outcomes can also emerge as a consequence of the complexity of the innovation process, which underlines the need to identify and address any negative effects arising from the innovation or to capitalise on any unforeseen benefits and opportunities.

8. Closely related was the introduction of the service through a *pilot process*. This clearly minimised the risks (political and health-related) of introducing the scheme nationwide, and provided an opportunity to test the technical, operational and social aspects of the scheme and to gain some early feedback on its feasibility. The ability to pilot innovations is an option available to the public sector which is not possible in the private sector due to the risk of loss of leader advantage.

9. Linked to the previous two points is the need to *generate recognition and support* for innovation, both for the innovating organisation itself but also more widely across the public health system. This was the remit of the Modernisation Agency, which provided advice on how to undertake innovation and also encouraged the dissemination of best practice across the NHS. In the NHS Direct example, substantial financial and political support was made available.

10. *Retention of momentum.* Of particular relevance is the need for organisations and systems to exhibit flexibility and to work actively on the identification of further opportunities which may assist their particular innovation or which may benefit from them. To some extent, these features are linked to a culture of organisational learning and exploit the complex nature of innovation whereby further innovations and change may be 'spun out'. For example, several of the NHS Direct regional sites quickly identified additional innovations which could be brought in alongside the

public help-line system or where the service could complement other existing services. At the system-wide level, the opportunities for public internet access and touch-screen access points in public concourses were also quickly identified and brought into operation.

NOTES

1. The author would like to acknowledge the major contributions made by other University of Manchester colleagues in the underpinning work for this chapter, namely: Carol Grant-Pearce, Lawrence Green, John Rigby, Elvira Uyarra and, in particular, Ian Miles.
2. See: http://www.nifustep.no/English.
3. The workshops were set up so as to allow for the follow-up of novel ideas and possibilities.
4. http://www.nhsdirect.nhs.uk/en/About/History.
5. http://www.ic.nhs.uk/statistics-and-data-collections/workforce/nhs-staff-numbers/nhs-staff-2000--2010-overview.
6. In 2005 the Modernisation Agency was abolished and some of its activities were transferred to the newly created NHS Institute for Learning, Skills and Innovation.
7. Consequently non-problem-oriented drivers did not play a contributory role.
8. These share common points with the findings of other empirical studies of change management, for example J. Barnes (pers. comm.).

BIBLIOGRAPHY

Abernathy, W.J. and Utterback, J.M. (1978). Patterns of innovation in technology. *Technology Review*, 80(7), 40–47.

Department of Health (1997a). *Developing Emergency Services in the Community: The Final Report*. Series No. 97CCO128, 15 pages. Department of Health (Chair: Sir Kenneth Calman) London: NHS Executive.

Department of Health (1997b). *The New NHS: Modern, Dependable*. Health White Paper. London: Stationery Office, December.

Department of Health (1998). *Pilot Schemes Launched to Test New 24 Hours Telephone Health Advice Line – New Service to Cover the Whole Country by the End of the Year 2000*. Press release 98/107, March.

Department of Health (2005). *Staff in the NHS 2004*. Leeds: Government Statistical Service.

Department of Health, Directorate of Access and Choice (2003). *Developing NHS Direct: A Strategy Document for the Next Three Years*. London: Department of Health, April.

Fleck, J. (1993). Innofusion: feedback in the innovation process. In S.A. Stowell, D. West and J.G. Howell (eds), *Systems Science: Addressing Global Issues*. Dordrecht: Kluwer Academic/Plenum Publishers.

Geels, F.W. (2004). From sectoral systems of innovation to socio-technical systems: insights about dynamics and change from sociology and institutional theory. *Research Policy*, 33, 897–920.

Green, L., Howells, J. and Miles, I. (2001). *Services and Innovation: Dynamics of Service Innovation in the European Union*. Final Report, December, Manchester: PREST and CRIC University of Manchester.

Greenhalgh, T., Robert, G., MacFarlane, F., Bate, P. and Kyriakidou, O. (2004). Diffusion of innovations in service organizations: systematic review and recommendations. *Milbank Quarterly*, 82(4), 581–629.

Greenhalgh, T., Robert, G., Bate, P., Kyriakidou, O., Macfarlane, F. and Peacock, R. (2005). *Diffusion of Innovations in Health Service Organisations: A Systematic Literature Review*. Oxford: Blackwell.

Hanlon, G., O'Cathain, A., Luff, D., Greatbatch, D. and Strangleman, T. (2003). *NHS Direct: Patient Empowerment or Dependency?* ESRC Innovative Health Technologies Programme. Available at: http://www.york.ac.uk/res/iht/projects/l218252022.htm (accessed 5 January 2005).

Munro, J., Nicholl, J., O'Catahin, A., Knowles, E. and Morgan, A. (2001). *Evaluation of NHS Direct First Wave Sites: Final Report of the Phase 1 Research*. Sheffield: Medical Care Research Unit, University of Sheffield.

National Audit Office (2002). *NHS Direct in England*. HC-505, Session 2001–02. London: The Stationery Office January.

NHS (2001). *Primary Care, General Practice and the NHS Plan – Information for GPs, Nurses, Other Health Professionals and Staff Working in Primary Care in England*. London: Department of Health January.

Royal College of General Practitioners, Health Informatics Task Force (1999). *Electronic Patient Record Study: Team 4: Visit to NHS Direct in Milton Keynes.* London: NHS Executive.

Sabatier, P.A. and Jenkins-Smith, H.C. (eds) (1993). *Policy Change and Learning: An Advocacy Coalition Approach.* Boulder, CO: Westview Press, pp. 117–166.

Sabatier, P.A. and Jenkins-Smith, H.C. (eds) (1999). The advocacy coalition framework: an assessment. In P. Sabatier (ed.), *Theories of the Policy Process.* Boulder, CO: Westview Press.

Secretary of State for Health (2000). *The NHS Plan.* Cm 4818-I. Norwich: The Stationery Office.

Secretary of State for Health (2002). *Delivering the NHS Plan – Next Steps on Investment, Next Steps on Reform.* Norwich: HMSO, April.

33. Internal and external influences on the capacity for innovation in local government
Richard M. Walker

INTRODUCTION

Study after study has shown that innovation is within the capacity of public agencies (Borins 1998; Light 1998). New services and processes to support the delivery of public programmes are put in place on a regular basis. Innovations are developed by public organizations in response to changes in the external environment – deregulation, isomorphism, resource scarcity and customer demands – or in response to internal organizational choices – perceived performance gaps, reaching a higher level of aspiration, increasing the extent and quality of services. The evidence base on factors influencing the adoption of innovation is now longstanding (Muhr 1969) and has been growing over recent years. Given the longstanding expectations for governments to put in place new policies and organizational processes (Pollitt and Bouckeart 2004) and the necessity to respond to changes in the external context (be it through natural disasters such as tsunamis or hurricanes, or human-led acts of terrorism or fiscal collapse), it is important to take stock of what has been learned and to identify what we still need to know. To this end this chapter examines the internal and external influences on the adoption and implementation of innovation in local governments. Local governments are taken as the unit of analysis because they are responsible for the delivery of the majority of public services that people use on a daily basis, and which support many of the basic aspects of human existence: ensuring healthy environments by removing garbage and ensuring a clean supply of food and water, educating children to become future citizens, and supporting those most vulnerable through public housing programmes and social services.

This chapter commences by defining innovation and discusses innovation types, noting the importance of clear and comparable definitions of innovations to ensure that results are comparable and thus generalizable. The published empirical academic evidence on internal and external antecedents that influence the adoption of innovation is then reviewed. The review focuses upon empirical journal articles on innovation in local governments published and recorded in the Web of Science database. Lastly, conclusions are drawn on what is known and what needs to be known in order to advance the field.

INNOVATION AND INNOVATION TYPES

Innovation is a process through which new ideas, objects and practices are created, developed or reinvented, and which are new for the unit of adoption (Aiken and Hage 1968; Kimberly and Evanisko 1981; Rogers 1995). Because public organizations may innovate in search of legitimacy and not fully adopt an innovation, implementation is a critical aspect of the definition (Damanpour and Evan 1984; Boyne et al. 2005).

Prior studies have sought to address the problem of inconsistent results by distinguishing between types of innovation, such as radical and incremental innovations, as an essential aspect of understanding the adoption of innovation (Ettile et al. 1984). The debate about the need for clear and consistent definitions of innovation types is longstanding in the literature, and the lack of consistency is attributed to difficulties of generalization and limited cumulative knowledge development (Aiken and Alford 1970; Wolfe 1994). Product or service and organizational processes are most commonly distinguished. In this chapter the focus is upon product or service innovations that can be understood as *what* (e.g. what is produced, what service is delivered) and processes or *how* innovations (e.g. how a service is rendered). It is also possible to distinguish ancillary innovations, or innovations that are developed at the organization–environment boundary.

In the private sector much of the research effort is focused upon product innovation. However, the notion of the development of new products is not necessarily appropriate in public settings, because public agencies typically deliver services. Studies of public innovation typically discuss service innovations: new services offered by public organizations to meet an external user or market need that are concerned with what is produced. Service innovations occur in the operating component and affect the technical system of an organization and include the adoption of goods (which are material) and intangible services, which are often consumed at the point of production (Kimberly and Evanisko 1981; Damanpour and Evan 1984; Normann 1991).

Process innovations affect management and organization. They change relationships among organizational members and affect rules, roles, procedures, structures, communication and exchange among organizational members and between the environment and organizational members: they are concerned with *how* services are rendered (Abernathy and Utterback 1978; Damanpour and Gopalakrishnan 2001). Given these wide-ranging effects, a number of types of process innovations, including administrative, organizational and technological, are identified. Administrative process innovations are new approaches to motivate and reward organizational members, devise strategy and structure of tasks and units, and modify the organization's management processes (Daft 1978; Kimberly and Evanisko 1981; Light 1998). As such, administrative innovations are indirectly related to the organization's basic work activity and mainly affect its management systems (Damanpour and Evan 1984). They may have repercussions for the organizational and technological dimensions of an organization. They pertain to changes in the organization's structure and processes, administrative systems, knowledge used in performing the work of management, and managerial skills that enable an organization to function and succeed by using its resources effectively.

Organizational process innovations are innovations in structure and strategy (Damanpour 1987). They include improvements in an organization's practices and the introduction of new organizational structures (Borins 1998; Light 1998). Within the public sector such changes embrace methods to purchase and deliver services and generate revenue, and include the themes of contracting, externalization and market pricing of public services reflecting New Public Management (NPM).

Technological process innovations are new elements introduced into an organization's production system or service operation for rendering its services to users and citizens (Knight 1967; Abernathy and Utterback 1978; Damanpour and Gopalakrishnan 2001). The drivers of these innovations are primarily reduction in delivery time, increases in operational flexibility and lowering of production costs (Boer and During 2001), and they are typically associated with information technology in public organizations. Technological process innovations, therefore, modify the organization's operating processes and systems (Schilling 2005).

Ancillary innovations are identified by Damanpour (1987, p.678) and are differentiated from other innovations because they are 'organization–environment boundary innovations'. What distinguishes an ancillary innovation is that successful adoption is dependent on factors outside an organization's control and their successful implementation is reliant upon other actors in the organizational environment. Given that ancillary innovations involve a public organization work across their organizational boundary with others (business, users, citizens or nonprofits), they can be service and process innovations.

METHODS

Empirical literature on innovation in local governments was located in the Thompson Reuters Web of Science database. Searches of titles, abstracts and key words were made for the period 1970–2010 inclusive.[1] Search terms used were innovation AND local government, counties, cities and public (and derivatives thereof). Given the focus was on local governments, the search was restricted to the disciplinary areas of business, management, political science and public administration.[2] Careful reading of the articles led to a final sample of 20 empirical studies. Articles were excluded from the review because they were not empirical, innovation was not the dependent variable, they did not include independent variables of internal and external antecedents, case studies were presented or they were conceptual pieces.

The studies span the four decades under review, suggesting that while not a mainstream topic, innovation adoption in local government is one that scholars continue to revisit. Table 33.1 shows that studies were typically undertaken in the USA (15 of the 20 studies), with three in the UK and two in Denmark. The non-US samples focused on general purpose local governments that delivered a range of services. For example, in England the services surveyed included corporate, benefits and revenues, education, housing, land use planning, leisure and culture, social services and waste management (Walker 2006), and in Denmark education and culture, social services, technical services and city managers (Hansen 2010). The structure of government in the USA means that there are many single purpose local governments: the studies of Aiken and Alford (1970), Bingham (1978), Damanpour (1987), Teodoro (2009) and Fernández and Wise (2010) examined single purpose authorities, while the remainder examined city, municipal and county governments.

Sample sizes vary from in the 70s (Damanpour 1987; Hoyman and Weinberg 2006; Teodoro 2009; Walker 2008) to over 1,000 (Damanpour and Schneider 2006; Bhatti et al. 2010). In total the 20 studies include 26 samples and offer an average sample size of 476 (see Table 33.1). The unit of analysis is clearly organizations and the majority of

Table 33.1   Organizations and sample sizes

Study	Organizations and sample size
Aiken and Alford, 1970	646 incorporated urban places, 1930–65
Bingham, 1978	241 housing authorities, 238 school districts, 229 libraries, 213 police forces in US cities with populations over 50,000
Perry and Kraemer, 1978	112 larger municipal (50,000 plus population) and county (100,000 plus) local governments in the USA in 1975
Perry and Danziger, 1980	350 larger municipal (50,000 plus population) and county (100,000 plus) local governments in the USA in 1975
Damanpour, 1987	75 libraries serving populations from 50,000 to 500,000 in six northeast states of the USA in 1982
Brudney and Selden, 1995	297 cities in the State of Georgia, USA replying to surveys by the Department of Community Affairs in 1985 and 1990
Gainakis and McCue, 1997	180 multiservice local governments in the USA with populations over 5,000
Moon and Bretschneider, 2002	285 public, private and nonprofit organizations in Colorado, Florida and New York surveyed between 1992 and 1994
Boyne et al., 2005	79 service departments in Welsh local government surveyed in 1998, 1999 and 1999–2000
Walker, 2006	120 upper tier English local authorities surveyed in 2001
Damanpour and Schneider, 2006	1,276 cities in the USA with a population of 10,000 or taken from the 1997 International City-Managers Association (ICMA) survey
Hoyman and Weinberg, 2006	79 rural counties in North Carolina between 1970 and 2000
Walker, 2008	74 English local governments surveyed in 2001 and 2002
Teodoro, 2009	72 police departments and 67 water utilities in the USA
Damanpour and Schneider, 2009	725 local governments of populations over 10,000 in the USA which responded to two ICMA surveys in 1997
Kwon et al., 2009	731 and 726 (233 common) city governments in the USA responding to ICMA surveys in 1999 and 2004
Bhatti et al., 2010	3,931 Danish municipalities (panel 1987–2005)
Fernández and Wise, 2010	532 Texas school districts surveyed in 1999
Hansen, 2010	585 managers in 271 Danish local authorities surveyed in 2006
Morgan, 2010	271 local governments in North Carolina surveyed in 2005–06

studies surveyed one respondent from each organization, the exceptions being those in Denmark, England and Wales (Boyne et al. 2005; Walker 2006, 2008; Hansen 2010), though in the case of Hansen (2010) the analysis is undertaken on managers. The studies of Aiken and Alford (1970) and Bhatti et al. (2010) rely exclusively on secondary data.

INTERNAL AND EXTERNAL ANTECEDENTS

Innovations do not occur in a vacuum. Circumstances inside and outside an organization result in the adoption and implementation of innovations. The capacity of organizations first to respond to external stimuli and secondly to institute innovations varies across any population of organizations. Public agencies are clearly no different here and extensive work has been conducted on the diffusion of innovations, particularly in US states (see for example Berry 1994). Studies of private firms have identified a number of internal organizational characteristics that influence the adoption of innovation. Damanpour's (1991) review included administrative intensity, centralization, formalization, functional differentiation, internal and external communication, managerial attitudes towards change, professionalization, slack resources, specialization, and technical knowledge resources that were statistically associated with organizational innovation. No systematic review of external influences has been undertaken, to the author's knowledge, but influences typically include urbanization, wealth or poverty of the population, size and political context. The range of internal and external antecedents of innovation in local governments, along with the type of innovation studied, is presented in Table 33.2.

Types of Innovation Studied

The majority of the studies that examine the adoption of innovation in local governments focus upon process innovations – these are used as dependent variables on 27 occasions. Service innovations are examined on seven occasions (in four studies) and ancillary innovations 11 times. The reliance on process innovations reflects the view that public agencies primarily adopt and implement new processes into their organizations because of the limited opportunities to develop new services.

The process innovations are operationalized in a number of ways. Five studies develop an index of process innovations that combine a number of innovation types; for example Damanpour and Schneider (2009), who examine administrative and organizational innovations associated with the NPM, and Teodoro (2009), who develops two indexes, one of which includes administrative, organizational and technological innovations and a second which draws upon administrative, ancillary and organizational innovations.

Of the remaining 22 studies that use process innovations five examine administrative, seven organizational and ten technological innovations. The majority of the articles examining the antecedents of technological innovation focus on the use of computer hardware, processes and software. Many are from the 1970s and 1980s (Bingham 1978; Damanpour 1987; Perry and Danziger 1980), though also see Walker (2006). Citizen service centres (Bhatti et al. 2010), contracting and outsourcing (Hansen 2010; Walker 2006), and changes to organizational structures (Walker 2008) capture some of the organizational innovations studied. Administrative innovations have included management by objectives and quality management (Hansen 2010) and the use of visas to hire foreign skilled workers (Fernández and Wise 2010). Service innovations studied are the provision of public housing (Aiken and Alford 1970), the use of prefabricated construction (Bingham 1978), the provision of new services to existing users, new services to new users and existing services to new users (Walker 2006, 2008), and the siting of prisons (Hoyman and Weinberg 2006).

Table 33.2 *Internal and external antecedents of innovation in studies of local government*

Study	Antecedents		Innovation
	Internal	External	
Aiken and Alford, 1970		Political culture Community power Political structure Community differentiation and continuity Community integration Poverty	Service
Bingham, 1978	Organizational characteristics Size Structure Professionalism Formalization and complexity	Community environment Socioeconomic status Suburb Ethnic/ghetto Size Political culture Organizational environment Intergovernmental relations Professional relations Private sector influence Slack	Service and process for four policy areas
Perry and Kraemer, 1978	Innovation attributes Task complexity Pervasiveness Communicability Departure from current technologies Specificity of evaluation Cost relative to other agency applications	Policy interventions Locus of development Professional commitment Federal financial assistance	Index of processes

Table 33.2 (continued)

Study	Antecedents		Innovation
	Internal	External	
Perry and Danziger, 1980	Organizational domain Integration Risk Need	—	Index of processes
Damanpour, 1987	Specialization Functional differentiation Administrative intensity Organizational size Organizational slack	—	Indexes of 2 processes and ancillary
Brudney and Selden, 1995	Number of services provided Professionalism Slack resources Administrative performance Use of computers in 1985	Population	Index of process
Gainakis and McCue, 1997	Performance Seeking advice from peers Gave advice to peers Use of peers as sources of information Fund balance	—	Index of process
Moon and Bretschneider, 2002	Endogenous variables Red tape Risk-taking propensity Organizational capacity Personnel Financial Managerial	Environment Legal constraints Sector Public Nonprofit Control variables Florida	Process

Boyne et al., 2005	Organizational culture
	  Goal clarity
	  Trust
	  Ethics
	Size
	Size
	Corporate technical group
	Implementation approach
	Prior experience
	Positive attitudes towards change
	Innovation characteristics
	  Compatibility
	  Relative advantage
	  Complexity
		Urbanization
		Deprivation
			Index of process

Walker, 2006	Organizational
	  Size
	  Political leadership
	  Managerial leadership
	  Change in management from outside
	Diffusion
	  Learning
		Diffusion determinants
		  Public competition
		  Service provider competition
		  Vertical integration
		  Public coercion
		  Public pressure: external sources
		  Public pressure: user and
		    citizens
		Environmental
		  Service need
		  Diversity of service need
		  Changes in the social, political
		    and economic context
		  Political disposition
			Indexes of service,
			4 processes and
			ancillary

Damanpour and Schneider, 2006	Complexity Size Economic health Trade unions External communication	Urbanization Unemployment	Index of process

503

Table 33.2 (continued)

Study	Antecedents		Innovation
	Internal	External	

Hoyman and Weinberg, 2006	–	Motivation
		  Economic structure – poverty
		  Economic crisis – unemployment
		Resources
		  Human capital – college graduates
		  Political capital – region
		Obstacles
		  NIMBY – owner occupiers
		  NIMBY – population density
		  At risk – African-Americans
		External
		  Propinquity
			Service

Walker, 2008	Devolved management Specialization Centralization Formalization External communication Performance management Integration Slack resources Organizational size Trust	Service need Diversity of need Increase in population External political context Influence of context	Indexes of service, 2 processes and ancillary
Teodoro, 2009	Vertical promotion Diagonal promotion Professional involvement Agency size Full-time elected officials Government structure	–	Index of processes

Study			
Damanpour and Schneider, 2009	Innovation characteristics Cost Complexity Impact Organization Resources Unionization Size	Urbanization Deprivation Growth	Index of processes
Kwon et al., 2009	Structure of government Sales tax restrictions Private sector involvement Higher levels of IT Designated technology zones Dedicated economic development staff	Community wealth Community attributes	Index of ancillary (also 4 single ancillary that make up index)
Bhatti et al., 2010	Administrative professionals Public employees per capita (control) Bureaucrats per capita (control) Expenses per capita (control) Organizational size Organizational form	Regional imitation Neighbourhood imitation (control) Education level (control) Municipal wealth Share of vote	Process
Fernández and Wise, 2010	Organizational size Size of administrative component Performance Slack resources Leadership	Scarcity of human inputs Demand for specialized services Normative environment	Process
Hansen, 2010	Leadership and innovation Budget and rule control Employee–citizen relations Politics and external relations Agree public sector too large Agree private sector more efficient Disagree few advantages to outsourcing Neutral administration based on experts Political goals and visions	Urbanization Community wealth Education level Unemployment rate Politics of Mayor Size	Index of process

Table 33.2 (continued)

| Study | Antecedents | | Innovation |
	Internal	External	
Morgan, 2010	Strategic planning Incentives performance agreement Cost–benefit analysis Formal incentives policy Requirements for local hiring Clawback provision Programme evaluation Interjurisdictional competition Interjurisdictional collaboration Citizen input Role clarity Number of economic development staff Organizational participation index	Population Per capita income Poverty rate	2 indexes of ancillary

Ancillary innovations are of particular interest. Searches reveal that these types of innovation are only used in studies of public organizations. Damanpour's (1987) identification of these innovations in the early 1980s focused on a range of outreach programmes by public libraries that included community service programmes and after school supplementary education programmes. Walker (2006, 2008) extended this to include the collaboration and partnership arrangements that now typify the delivery of complex public services and the new governance. In this review the number of innovations classified as ancillary is quite high, around one quarter. This is because at the heart of Damanpour's definition was the notion of 'organization–environment boundary innovations'. It is suggested here that organization–environment boundary innovations are one of the core and defining characteristics of public service innovation because they are central to the concept of a policy innovation; that is, the adoption of a programme new to an organization rather than the invention of a programme. Morgan (2010) and Kwon et al.'s (2009) studies of local economic development capture the conception of a policy innovation as an ancillary innovation in their exploration of the antecedents of activities by local governments that seek to change the behaviour of other organizations, in these cases private businesses. Morgan's (2010, p. 687) 'alternative/demand side' economic development strategy and tools statistical factor include management training for small businesses, marketing assistance for small businesses, export development assistance, executive loan programme/mentoring and business networking, while Kwon et al. (2009, p. 984) include whether a municipality had in place strategies for economic development, retention, attraction and small businesses. These examples clearly illustrate the way in which a public organization seeks to influence the behaviour of another organization in its environment.

Innovation is measured in a number of ways. Innovation is typically a survey measure of the perception of the extent to which an innovation is adopted, but also includes survey measures of behaviour, as in the case of Perry and Kraemer (1978) and Brudney and Selden (1995), who ask about the use of information technology. Many of the articles that measure the perception of innovation adoption and implementation develop indexes, for example Damanpour (1987), Gainakis and McCue (1997), Boyne et al. (2005) and Kwon et al. (2009). The exceptions to these are Aiken and Alford (1970), who look at the adoption of housing programmes by city governments; Hoyman and Weinberg's (2006) exploration of prison siting in North Carolina; Bhatti et al.'s (2010) study of citizen service centres; and Fernández and Wise's (2010) study of the adoption of visas for skilled foreigners, who drew upon administrative datasets. These latter studies that draw upon secondary data are actually able to measure adoption and implementation. A number of the survey-based studies also sought to use this more stringent test of innovation adoption. For example, Damanpour and Schneider (2006) examined initiation (a request for funding), adoption (no funding or if funding was partial or full) and implementation (if the innovation was not, sometimes or always implemented) and Boyne et al. (2005) looked at the relationship between perceptions of the use of administrative and organizational innovations and the formal adoption of a planning mechanism.

Internal Antecedents

Internal antecedents of innovation are included in all studies bar those of Aiken and Alford (1970) and Hoyman and Weinberg (2006). The remaining 18 studies use a wide

Table 33.3   Frequently used internal antecedents of local government capacity

Internal antecedent	Expected relationship	Number of tests	Findings		
			Support	Non-significant	Negative
Administrative intensity	Positive	17	7	9	1
External communication	Positive	14	4	10	–
Slack resources	Positive	10	2	5	3
Organizational size	Uncertain	32	14	15	3

variety of internal influences on the capacity of local governments to innovate. This suggests that there are no commonly agreed or accepted concepts of internal antecedents. Given the array of variables the remainder of this section focuses on the determinants identified by Damanpour (1991) (see above) and includes organizational size.

The first point to note is that no study includes internal communication or technical knowledge. Secondly, examined once are centralization, functional differentiation and managerial attitudes towards change. Walker (2008) tests centralization against four innovation types and uncovers statistically significant negative relationships with ancillary and organizational innovations, in keeping with expectations. Damanpour (1987) does not find any associations between different innovation types and functional differentiation while Boyne et al. (2005) find that a positive managerial attitude towards change positively assists in the adoption of innovation.

Thirdly, formalization, professionalism and specialization are used as independent variables on two occasions. Formalization is expected to hurt innovation, and Walker (2008) upholds this expectation in relation to service innovations but not ancillary innovations when it assists in their adoption. Bingham (1978) undertook correlations between innovation and formalization and professionalism and typically reports statistically insignificant results. Again pertaining to computer technology, Brudney and Selden (1995) find that professionalism does not affect the adoption of computer technology in smaller local governments but it does have a positively significant correlation with the extent of adoption. In the two studies examining specialization, Damanpour (1987) finds it helpful in the adoption of technological innovations in libraries while Walker (2008) finds no relationship with any type of innovation.

Fourthly, the remaining variables of administrative intensity, external communication, slack resources and organizational size are used in at least five articles, and the findings are summarized in Table 33.3. Table 33.3 shows the total number of statistical tests undertaken, as well as the number of tests in support of the hypothesized direction, those that are not significant and the number of negative associations. The modal measure of central tendency for the relationship between these variables and innovation is non-significant in each case. Where the variables do have a statistically significant relationship they tend towards being positive, except for in the case of slack resources. While management evidence would suggest a positive relationship here, the balance is towards negative findings in the five studies that use this measure. This may be because resource constraints and annual cycles of budgeting in public organization limit the

Table 33.4   Frequently used external antecedents of local government capacity

External antecedent	Expected relationship	Number of tests	Findings		
			Support	Non-significant	Negative
Deprivation	Uncertain	42	7	30	5
Wealth	Positive	40	9	19	2
Urbanization	Positive	12	5	7	–
Size	Positive	23	11	12	–
Political context	Uncertain	29	3	21	5

ability to develop slack resources. Organizational size is used in 11 studies and is tested on 32 occasions. Size is typically measured as the number of staff, but extends to include the size of the budget and number of students enrolled in schools (Fernández and Wise 2010). The larger number of positive relationships suggests that perhaps size is an important variable and that large local governments are more likely to be able to muster the capacity for innovation. Administrative intensity was measured by the number of corporate staff (Boyne et al. 2005), and specialized professionals in economic development (Morgan 2010) and again the balance of statistically significant evidence tends towards a positive relationship.

A number of studies include measures of innovation characteristics. Perry and Kraemer (1978) only consider these factors, when controlling for policy interventions, and uncover relatively weak relationships, finding positive correlations for pervasiveness, departure from current technology and specificity of evaluation, and statistically insignificant relationships for task complexity, communicability and cost. Boyne et al. (2005) do not find any associations between characteristics (compatibility, advantage, complexity) and innovation adoption. Damanpour and Schneider (2009) note positive associations with adoption and implementation for cost and impact. The small number of studies utilizing these measures means that it is not possible to draw conclusions beyond noting the need for further research.

External Antecedents

External influences on the capacity of local governments to adopt and implement innovations are included in 16 of the 20 studies reviewed in this chapter.[3] Those studies without external antecedents are Perry and Danziger (1980), Damanpour (1987), Gainakis and McCue (1997) and Teodoro (2009). While their focus was clearly upon internal determinants, the lack of variables to control for spurious relations that might arise because of external pressures for innovation raises concerns about model specification. The 16 articles examining external antecedents once again embrace a range of concepts and variables, including community environment, policy interventions and diffusion determinants. However, the majority of articles include variables that capture the size of the local community, the affluence or level of deprivation, the degree of urbanization and the political environment. Summary findings are provided in Table 33.4 (again showing support, and non-significant and negative associations in the tests conducted).

Measures of deprivation or wealth are included in 13 articles. The arguments presented to support the impact of wealth on innovative capacity are relatively consistent: more affluent jurisdictions make innovation less demanding and can offer the possibility for co-production. Wealth is variously operationalized as the tax base of a community or as population increases, which are typically associated with the movement of more affluent households (Walker 2008). The results offer some support for arguments about the effects of poverty and affluence, but the results are not overly compelling.

The argument presented for deprivation is more complex, with some articles arguing that service need will enhance innovative capacity and others suggesting that it will hinder it. The case for enhanced innovative capacity relates to the need for public agencies to respond to the demands of their users and citizens (Bingham 1978; Fernández and Wise 2010) or innovate in the face of 'structural poverty' or 'temporary economic crisis' (Hoyman and Weinberg 2006, p. 99), and as such can be labelled a demand model. The alternative argument is one of constraints (Kwon et al. 2009). Damanpour and Schneider (2006, p. 218) clearly articulate this case when they argue that 'those whose communities have higher unemployment rates will have far fewer resources for adopting new programmes'. The summary results of the statistical relationships for deprivation presented in Table 33.4, while predominately non-significant, would suggest that argument and evidence here are not conclusive, with a relatively similar number of positive and negative associations.

Five articles include variables that capture the local political context. Results here vary widely, but with a clear modal value of non-significant. One reason for this may be the wide array of measures of political context. Aiken and Alford's (1970) measures are largely of political structure, whereas Bingham (1978), Hansen (2010) and Walker (2006) seek to measure different facets of political disposition. An alternative measure is to examine the extent to which the external political environment is uncertain, complex and changing rapidly. Walker's (2008) study of English local government adopted this approach, but again uncovered lacklustre results. It would be anticipated that the study of innovations in the public realm would seek to understand the degree to which the political environment drives or hinders innovative capacity in local government, yet only a small number of studies have examined this concept.

The results for urbanization and community size continue to present the mode of non-significant, but also offer a number of positive results. Both of these measures use population data, one as a raw measure and the other urbanization as a ratio. Taken together there are 45 tests, of which 16, or 45 per cent, are positive. This represents the clearest finding in this chapter: the size and population density of local governments matter for innovative capacity.

CONCLUSIONS

This review has sought to examine the internal and external influences on the adoption of innovation in local governments. Twenty empirical studies were identified, of which 14 used variables that measured both internal and external antecedents, while four measured internal and two external variables. These studies span the search period of 1970–2010. The first conclusion to be reached is that relatively limited attention has been paid to the phenomenon of innovation in local government (indeed many studies from the USA examine the adoption of innovation in states). When scholars have turned their attention to this important topic they have drawn upon a wide range of variables. Many of the independent variables selected have a long pedigree and have been used in studies of innovation adoption in private firms, while others, such as formalization and organizational size, are widely used in the public administration literature more generally. Though scholars have been innovative in the design of measures of antecedents, the wide range used makes the task of drawing generalizations a challenging one. It is suggested that the group of variables listed in Tables 33.3 and 33.4 be regularly used in studies of innovation in local government to assist with the generalization of results.

The strongest conclusion that can be derived from this study is that the size of a local government, whether measured as an internal or external antecedent, is a likely determinant of innovation. This finding raises interesting questions about size because it sits on both sides of the fence. Indeed internal size of local governments is sometimes operationalized by the community measure of population based on the argument that the number of employees is likely to be a function of the size of the population given the requirement to deliver key services (see Walker 2006, 2008). If populations are related to local government employees, then size should be considered as an antecedent that bridges internal and external divide in studies of local government. Competing argument is sometimes presented on the likely impact of antecedents on innovation capacity. This was very clear in relation to deprivation. While contexts clearly vary, and indeed much of the evidence presented comes from a contingency theory perspective, uncertainty in the scholarly community on the impact of key variables clearly needs to be ironed out. Having said this, the relative level of affluence or deprivation is clearly an important predictor of innovative capacity, but further conceptual and empirical work is required to clearly identify direction and impact.

Another key conclusion is that some clarity is being brought to the issue of innovation types, and authors are now much clearer about the type of innovations that they are studying. This represents important progress, but once again we must take a long pause before it will be possible to make generalizations about causal relationships or offer perceptive lessons to policy and practice because the number of studies remains very limited. One contribution briefly highlighted in this chapter is that policy innovations should be viewed as ancillary innovation in the main, yet this notion requires further conceptual and empirical elaboration.

One of the major challenges for scholars working on innovation in local government is to move towards a theory of innovation in the public sector. To date, studies draw upon a range of variables and extend prior conceptual discussions and empirical tests thereof, of a range of internal and external factors that are associated with adoption and implementation of innovation. Walker (2010) has proposed a framework from which this endeavour could commence, suggesting that future studies should include innovation characteristics and internal and external determinants, and model the way in which these variables impact on the adoption and implementation stages of innovation diffusion to move towards more comprehensive theoretical frameworks of innovation in public organizations. Developing a linear model of these relationships where characteristics and determinants in turn affect adoption and implementation may be somewhat over-simplistic (Van de Ven et al. 1999). These variables need to be located within a contingency or configurational framework that takes account of the different ways in which different types of innovations are adopted (Walker 2008). In developing empirical models of innovation, researchers need also consider the measurement of the adoption and implementation aspects in more detail (see Boyne et al. 2005 and Damanpour and Schneider 2009 for exceptions) and of differences between early, late and non-adopters (see Kwon et al. 2009 for exceptions). Others are encouraged to join this debate, bringing new perspectives, datasets and models such that over time strong research results can become the basis for normative evidence for the policy and practice of innovation in local government.

NOTES

1. This was supplemented by searches on the 'advance access' section of the websites of journals in the public administration section of the Web of Science.
2. Urban studies and town planning were not included because studies in these disciplines typically do not take an organization as the unit of analysis; rather, they focus on the city or a region as a system.
3. It should be noted that many of these variables that operationalize external influences on innovative capacity of local government are included as controls, and as such no directional relationships are specified (see Damanpour and Schneider 2009; Hanson 2010; Morgan 2010). Further research is required to understand the roles of these independent and control variables.

REFERENCES

Abernathy, W.J. and Utterback, J. (1978). Patterns of industrial innovation. *Technology Review*, June–July, 40–47.
Aiken, Michael and Alford, Robert R. (1970). Community structure and innovation: the case of public housing. *American Political Science Review*, 64(3), 843–864.
Aiken, Michael and Hage, Jerald (1968). Organizational interdependence and intra-organizational structure. *American Sociological Review*, 33(3), 912–930.
Berry, Frances S. (1994). Innovation in public management: the adoption of strategic planning. *Public Administration Review*, 54(4), 322–330.
Bhatti, Y., Olsen, A.L. and Pedersen, L.H. (2010). Administrative professionals and the diffusion of innovations: the case of citizen service centres. *Public Administration*, DOI: 10.1111/j.1467-9299.2020.01882.x.
Bingham, Richard D. (1978). Innovation, bureaucracy, and public policy: a study of innovation adoption by local government. *The Western Political Quarterly*, 31(2), 178–204.
Boer, H. and During, W.E. (2001). Innovation, what innovation? A comparison between product, process, and organizational innovation. *International Journal of Technology Management*, 22, 83–107.
Borins, Stanford (1998). *Innovating with Integrity: How Local Heroes are Transforming American Government*. Washington, DC: Georgetown University Press.
Boyne, G.A., Gould-Williams, J.S., Law, J. and Walker, R.M. (2005). Explaining the adoption of innovation: an empirical analysis of management reform. *Environment and Planning C: Government and Policy*, 23(3), 419–435.
Brudney, Jeffery L. and Selden, Sally Coleman (1995). The adoption of innovation by smaller governments: the case of computer technology. *American Review of Public Administration*, 25(1), 71–85.
Daft, R.L. (1978). A dual-core model of organizational innovation. *Academy of Management Journal*, 21, 193–210.
Damanpour, Fariborz (1987). The adoption of technological, administrative, and ancillary innovations: impact of organizational factors. *Journal of Management*, 13(4), 675–688.
Damanpour, Fariborz (1991). Organizational innovation: a meta-analysis of effects of determinants and moderators. *Academy of Management Journal*, 34(3), 555–590.
Damanpour, Fariborz and Evan, William M. (1984). Organizational innovation and performance: the problem of 'organizational lag'. *Administrative Science Quarterly*, 29(2), 392–409.

Damanpour, Fariborz and Gopalakrishnan, S. (2001). The dynamics of the adoption of product and process innovations in organizations. *Journal of Management Studies*, 38(1), 45–65.

Damanpour, Fariborz and Schneider, Marguerite (2006). Phases of the adoption of innovation in organizations: effects of environments, organization and top managers. *British Journal of Management*, 17(2), 215–236.

Damanpour, Fariborz and Schneider, Marguerite (2009). Characteristics of innovation and innovation adoption in public organizations: assessing the role of managers. *Journal of Public Administration Research and Theory*, 19(3), 495–522.

Ettile, J.E., Bridges, W.P. and O'Keefe, R.D. (1984). Organization strategy and structural differences for radical versus incremental innovation. *Management Science*, 30, 682–695.

Fernández, Sergio and Wise, Lois R. (2010). An exploration of why public organizations 'ingest' innovations. *Public Administration*, 88(4), 979–998.

Gainakis, Gerasimos A. and McCue, Clifford P. (1997). Administrative innovation among Ohio local government finance officers. *American Review of Public Administration*, 27(3), 270–286.

Hansen, Morten Balle (2010). Antecedents of organizational innovation: the diffusion of new public management into Danish local government. *Public Administration*, DOI: 10.1111/j.1467-9299.2010.01855.x.

Hoyman, Michele and Weinberg, Micah (2006). The process of policy innovation: prison siting in rural North Carolina. *Policy Studies Journal*, 34(1), 95–112.

Kimberly, J.R. and Evanisko, Michael (1981). Organizational innovation: the influence of individual, organizational, and contextual factors on hospital adoption of technological and administrative innovations. *Academy of Management Journal*, 24(4), 679–713.

Knight, K.E. (1967). A descriptive model of the intra-firm innovation process. *Journal of Business*, 40, 478–496.

Kwon, Myungjung, Berry, Frances S. and Feiock, Richard C. (2009). Understanding the adoption and timing of economic development strategies in US cities using innovation and institutional analysis. *Journal of Public Administration Research and Theory*, 19(4), 967–988.

Light, P.C. (1998). *Sustaining Innovation: Creating Nonprofit and Government Organizations that Innovate Naturally*. San Francisco, CA: Jossey-Bass.

Moon, M. Jae and Bretschneider, Stuart (2002). Does the perception of red tape constrain IT innovativeness in organizations? Unexpected results from a simultaneous equation model and implications. *Journal of Public Administration Research and Theory*, 12(2), 273–291.

Morgan, Jonathan Q. (2010). Governance, policy innovation, and local economic development in North Carolina. *Policy Studies Journal*, 38(4), 679–702.

Muhr, Lawrence B. (1969). Determinants of innovation in organizations. *American Political Science Review*, 63(2), 111–126.

Normann, R. (1991). *Service Management*. Chichester: John Wiley.

Perry, James L. and Danziger, James N. (1980). The adoptability of innovations: an empirical assessment of computer applications in local governments. *Administration and Society*, 11(4), 461–492.

Perry, James L. and Kraemer, Kenneth L. (1978). Innovation attributes, policy intervention, and the diffusion of computer applications among local governments. *Policy Sciences*, 9, 179–205.

Pollitt, Christopher and Bouckeart, Geart (2004). *Public Management Reform: A Comparative Analysis*, 2nd edn. Oxford: Oxford University Press.

Rogers, Everett M. (1995). *Diffusion of Innovations*. New York: Free Press.

Schilling, M.A. (2005). *Strategic Management of Technological Innovation*. New York: McGraw Hill.

Teodoro, Manuel P. (2009). Bureaucratic job mobility and the diffusion of innovations. *American Journal of Political Science*, 53(1), 175–189.

Tornatzky, L.G. and Fleischer, M. (1990). *The Processes of Technological Innovation*. Lexington, MA: Lexington Books.

Van de Ven, A.H., Polley, D.E., Garud, R. and Venkataraman, S. (1999). *The Innovation Journey*. Oxford: Oxford University Press.

Walker, Richard M. (2006). Innovation type and diffusion: an empirical analysis of local government. *Public Administration*, 84(2), 311–335.

Walker, Richard M. (2008). An empirical evaluation of innovation types and organizational and environmental characteristics: towards a configuration framework. *Journal of Public Administration Research and Theory*, 18(4), 591–615.

Walker, Richard M. (2010). Innovation. In Rachel Ashworth, George A. Boyne and Tom Entwistle (eds), *Public Service Improvement: Theories and Evidence*. Oxford: Oxford University Press, pp. 143–161.

Wolfe, Richard (1994). Organizational innovation: review, critique and suggested research agenda. *Journal of Management Studies*, 31(3), 405–431.

34. Innovations in structure: experience from local government in the UK

Rhys Andrews and George A. Boyne

INTRODUCTION

Structural innovation in the public sector typically involves the amalgamation of small organizations into a new bigger body, the disaggregation of large organizations into smaller units or the development of platforms for the shared delivery of services by several agencies. Such reforms have a long history as a response to both perceived weaknesses in service provision and a desire to reap gains in efficiency (March and Olson 1983). Invariably, debates on the appropriate structures for public service delivery often concentrate on the issue of scale, especially the optimum client population size in terms of its relationship with costs, effectiveness and democratic responsiveness. The impact of this issue has been especially apparent at the local level, particularly in the UK where central government has displayed a predilection for centrally mandated structural innovation in response to the perceived inefficiency of smaller local governments (John 2010).

Prior to the advent of devolution of administrative powers to Northern Ireland, Scotland and Wales, innovations in the structure of UK local government had tended to take the form of vertical consolidation and horizontal amalgamation of small units into larger ones, in an attempt to reap scale economies associated with bigger bureaucratic organizations. However, in more recent years divergent approaches to the structure of local government have emerged in England, Scotland and Wales, with greater emphasis being laid on voluntary amalgamation or the development of various forms of partnership arrangements.[1] In the coming era of fiscal austerity, it is likely that the pressure towards such innovations in local government structure in the UK will increase. It is therefore timely and pertinent to examine the recent UK experience of such structural change.

This is not only an issue of importance to the theory and practice of public administration in Britain, but is a topic of global significance. Policy-makers across the world continue to debate the merits of alternative local government structures in terms of their consequences for local service costs and performance (Council of Europe 1995; Copus et al. 2005). Indeed, in recent times central governments in several countries have enacted or contemplated structural change in local government on these grounds (see, especially, *Local Government Studies*, 36(2), 2010). In Denmark, for example, the number of local government units was reduced from 270 to 98 in 2007 in a bid to achieve scale economies. Similarly, in Australia and Canada debates have long raged about the mandatory amalgamation of local governments (Vojnovic 2000; Dollery et al. 2009). In Eastern European countries, too, municipal consolidation is now a common goal of central policy-makers (Swianiewicz and Mielczarek 2010).

At the same time, the turn to networks and collaboration in the public sector has led many central governments to urge local governments to 'join up' and make the connections with each other to increase the scale and scope of service delivery. However, in many countries policy-makers remain concerned that such voluntarism has yet to really take hold and embed itself within the culture of organizations. Invariably, where voluntary compliance is perceived to be failing, central governments may choose to turn away from 'softer' measures and draw upon legislative powers to mandate structural change. Evidence on the UK experience of 'hard' and 'soft' innovations in local government structure can therefore illustrate the challenges and opportunities that local (and central) governments are likely to confront when considering structural change.

Does the relative level of expenditure rise or fall as local governments undergo structural change? Does service performance improve or decline? Are innovating organizations better able to coordinate service delivery? And do stakeholders respond positively to structural innovations in local government? In this chapter, we seek to provide initial answers to these questions by drawing upon the experience of the UK over the past few decades. The chapter begins by providing a broad overview of innovations in the structure of UK local government since the 1970s, before elaborating on more recent development in the wake of devolution of powers over local government to Scotland and Wales in 1998. Thereafter, we theorize the potential effects of structural innovation in local government and review the available evidence on the impact of such innovation in England, Scotland and Wales. Finally, we reflect upon the future prospects for innovations in structure in English, Scottish and Welsh local government, and consider the theoretical and practical implications of the UK experience.

STRUCTURAL INNOVATION IN UK LOCAL GOVERNMENT

Four historical moments led to the foundation of distinct groups of UK local governments with territorially defined responsibilities for delivering public services (Boyne and Cole 1996). In 1888, county councils responsible for administering a range of public functions were first created across England and Wales, with further reforms sub-dividing these areas into lower-tier district councils during the 1890s. Beyond the shire county areas, 69 urban county boroughs were responsible for all local authority services. In 1965, the London county council area was replaced by a new Greater London Council area that contained 32 separate London borough councils. In 1974, almost 1400 local government units in England were consolidated into 410 units. The county boroughs were abolished and absorbed into a two-tier structure of 39 counties and 296 districts, and 36 metropolitan district councils were created to serve six large urban areas outside London. Then, in the 1990s the two-tier system in some shires was replaced by 46 new unitary authorities, based on the boundaries of several large towns and smaller cities. Thus, since the mid-nineteenth century, the pendulum of local government structure in England has swung from the creation of unitary county boroughs responsible for all local services in 1888, their replacement by a two-tier structure in 1974, and back to the re-creation of unitary authorities during the last decade. A similar decline in the number of local government units, and similar shifts between one-tier and two-tier structures, occurred between the 1880s and 1990s in Scotland and Wales (Boyne et al. 1995).

The seminal structural reforms of UK local government in the 1970s drew heavily on the idea that large authorities are more efficient (Dearlove 1979; Page and Midwinter 1980). Nevertheless, there was still recognition that smaller units could play an important role in maintaining the links between local communities and their political representatives. As a result, the two-tier system in rural areas accorded large county councils responsibility for strategic services, such as education and social services, with smaller district councils retaining control over neighbourhood services, such as housing, waste collection and parks' maintenance. Subsequent reforms in the 1990s reflected the Conservative national government's view that local governments should be 'enablers' rather than 'direct providers' of local services (Boyne 1995), and so it was deemed unnecessary for them to retain such a close link with the communities they represented. Thus, in tandem with the expanded strategic 'purchasing' role envisaged for local governments, vertical consolidation was carried out across large swathes of rural England, and all of Scotland and Wales to ensure that enabling authorities had the capacity to realize the economies of scale required for them to act as an effective contractor of local services.

Critically, the structural innovations in the 1970s and 1990s were almost uniformly mandated by central government. Although debates about scales of governance have continued unabated across the UK, with the advent of devolution in 1998 has come a marked divergence around approaches to local government structure than that which had prevailed before. During the past decade, England, Scotland and Wales have all sought to promote voluntaristic rather than mandatory structural innovation, but have each approached this from a distinctive starting-point.

England

In England, two major innovations in the structure of local government have occurred since reorganization in the 1990s. The first of these was the establishment in 2000 of Local Strategic Partnerships (LSPs) with the intention of encouraging joint working across multiple public, private and non-profit organizations in the areas served by single and upper-tier local authorities. Although the structure of LSPs was determined at the local level, resulting in some variation in the composition, structure and processes of partnerships, the basic principle has been to seek economies of scale through better collaborative working arrangements. The second major structural innovation was prompted by the invitation in the 2006 Local Government White Paper (Department of Communities and Local Government (DCLG), 2006a) to councils in two-tier shire county areas to submit proposals for structural reorganization into unitary authorities in a bid to 'enhance strategic leadership, neighbourhood empowerment, value for money and equity in public services' (DCLG 2006a, p. 20). Following consultation, proposals from five two-tier counties for consolidation proceeded, along with two-unitary options for two other areas, and on 1 April 2009 nine new unitary councils were established.

Before reflecting in more detail on the theoretical rationale for these developments and the evidence available on their relative success in the next section, we now explore the different approaches to structural innovation in local government adopted by the Scottish and Welsh governments.

Scotland

In Scotland, the devolved administration has eschewed large-scale mandatory and voluntary restructuring of local government in favour of a reliance on the partnership approach to service delivery. This was formalized in the Local Government Act Scotland (2003), which placed a duty on local authorities to initiate community planning and for partner organizations in the public, private and voluntary sectors to participate in that planning. Like LSPs in England, Scottish Community Planning Partnerships (CPPs) have been developed at the local level, and so are more or less well established depending upon the strategic leadership of local authorities. The reluctance to opt for more radical structural innovation, such as amalgamation of small units or disaggregation of large ones, is in part the product of the desire to develop a less centralist approach to relations with local government on the part of the Scottish Executive. It is also characteristic of the 'wait and see' approach to the development and application of tools for the pursuit of public service improvement that has been adopted north of the border (Cowell 2004).

Wales

Like its Scottish counterpart, the Welsh government has been reluctant to reorganize local authorities. Nevertheless, there has been a widespread perception that the small scale of many Welsh local authorities presents a problem for the efficient and effective delivery of key strategic services. Following the Beecham Review of Local Public Services in 2003, the Welsh government recommended that local authorities should intensify their joint working with other councils and public agencies to deliver cost-effective solutions to the 'wicked issues' confronting Welsh local public services (Welsh Government 2004). One particularly important outcome of this agenda was the establishment in 2008 of Local Service Boards (LSBs) comprising representatives from all the major public service providers and voluntary sector organizations within the borders of local authorities. The partnership agenda in Wales exhibits similarities with the development of LSPs in England and CPPs in Scotland, but is seen as the 'Welsh way' to do structural innovation because of the distinctiveness of the Welsh government's statutory duty to involve the public, private and voluntary sectors in public service delivery decisions.

THEORIES OF THE IMPACTS OF STRUCTURAL INNOVATION ON LOCAL GOVERNMENT

Although the putative benefits of structural innovations are often touted by policy-makers, in general very little is actually known about whether new structures ever realize these benefits and whether these outweigh any costs (Pollitt 2009). The case for unitary local government structures in England has been based on the argument that single-tier authorities have better service coordination, clearer accountability, more streamlined decision making and greater efficiency (Chisholm 2000). The case for developing partnership arrangements is based on the view that it is only through a 'multi-agency partnership response which harnesses the strengths and expertise of a variety of welfare perspectives' that today's public service delivery challenges can be met (Milbourne et al. 2003, p. 19).

Arguments about the impact of structural innovation can be examined from four key theoretical perspectives: political, competitive, technical and organizational.

Political Effects of Structural Innovation

Local government fragmentation creates particular challenges for those authorities charged with providing strategic leadership across multiple organization boundaries. Action-learning research carried out in 2003 uncovered inter-tier conflict associated with community leadership and partnership working within a sample of areas served by the two-tier structure in England (Office of the Deputy Prime Minister (ODPM) 2005a). This study found that the political priorities of county councils rarely align with all the districts within the area that they serve, and Local Strategic Partnerships in two-tier areas are frequently dominated by local politicians, sometimes to the detriment of the concerns of other public agencies and neighbourhood organizations (ODPM 2005a). This can lead both upper- and lower-tier authorities to spend excessive time and resources dealing with and coordinating responses to local issues for which they share responsibility, undermining the overall strength of strategic leadership and raising the costs of service delivery (Crampton 1996).

A fragmented local government structure and a reliance on partnership arrangements could also damage transparency and the ability of citizens to inform themselves about the operation of different government units (Snape and Raine 1999). Two tiers and multi-agency partnerships can cause confusion about who is responsible for what, and lessen the effectiveness of public scrutiny. The blurring of service responsibilities can therefore create 'accountability gaps', which disempower local communities (see ODPM 2005b). Contrary to these arguments, it is possible that the capacity of the public to influence policy makers' behaviour may be restricted if services are concentrated in a single local government tier. In a single-tier system, the public has less information about alternative packages to pressurise authorities that seek to set a fixed price for a whole line of services (Wagner and Weber 1975). Thus it is possible that a two-tier structure may facilitate additional public scrutiny and control, and thereby enhance accountability and exert downward pressure on service and administrative costs. However, it is less clear how partnership structures might elicit these benefits.

Competitive Effects of Structural Innovation

Public choice theorists claim that a multi-tier local government system is best because an absence of competition leads to inefficiency, since all organizations have a natural tendency towards laxity in the absence of market pressure (Niskanen 1971). Small local governments in a fragmented system must compete for businesses and households and seek to stave off 'fiscal migration' by potentially mobile residents, thereby placing pressure on them to drive overheads down (Tiebout 1956). In addition, Salmon (1987, p. 32) argues that in a horizontally fragmented system there is greater 'incentive to do better than local government in other jurisdictions in terms of levels and qualities of services, of levels of taxes or of more general economic and social indicators'. Thus even in the absence of fiscal migration, smaller authorities may achieve better performance because of higher and more visible levels of 'benchmark competition'; something which has characterized UK local government in the past decade or so, because of the proliferation of performance assessments and service inspections (Boyne et al. 2010).

These theoretical effects of inter-tier competition suggest that accountability will be lower and expenditure higher in a unitary system. However, in a two-tier system with dispersed service responsibilities, it is also conceivable that residents have only a limited understanding of which unit is responsible for the provision of specific services, and so have difficulty reaching an informed view on whether services provide value for money (see National Centre for Social Research 2000). At the same time, partnership arrangements too can complicate patterns of accountability as citizens are unlikely to comprehend the details of multi-agency governance within their area. In addition, the competitive benefits of single lines of responsibility may be lost when partnership structures are introduced. All of which suggests that citizens require either something akin to 'perfect information' for the positive benefits of competitive effects associated with fragmentation to be realized or that benchmarking processes must be able to accommodate the complexities of partnership performance.

Technical Effects of Structural Innovation

UK local governments are multi-functional organizations that deliver a whole variety of different public goods. They should, therefore, be particularly well placed to realize economies of scope. These occur when the cost of providing 'a diversified set of services is less than the cost of specialised firms providing those same services' (Grosskopf and Yaisawamg 1990, p. 61). The conventional source of economies of scope is via the '"sharing" of some inputs in the production of related goods or services, where these shared inputs are also often fixed' (Grosskopf and Yaisawamg 1990, p. 61). For local governments, fixed inputs which can be shared include computing facilities, central administrative staff and decentralized area offices. Joint provision of complementary services such as waste collection and waste disposal can also generate scope economies. Indeed, if all the services provided by the governments present within the same geographical area share some common overheads then full economies of scope will be attainable only in a single-tier system.

Separate governance structures entail that councils in a two-tier structure will likely have higher administrative costs than their counterparts in a single-tier structure. On the other hand, diseconomies of scope could occur in a single-tier system if different services (or governments or agencies) retain their own support functions and are unwilling to cooperate with each other (perhaps because of different professional or political traditions). Another possibility is that even though two-tier areas and partner organizations may evince divergent organizational and political goals, economies of scope could be achieved if units with overlapping boundaries agreed to share some functions. How this structural effect plays out in practice will be heavily dependent on administrative and political relationships within and between local authorities and their partners.

Organizational Effects of Structural Innovation

Of course, pursuit of the political, competitive and technical benefits of structural innovation tells one little about how the process of innovation itself might pose a significant challenge for the effectiveness of restructuring organizations. Theories of structural change, for example, suggest that any positive adaptive effects which accompany new structures may take a considerable time to emerge in the face of disruption to existing management routines and practices (Hannan and Freeman 1984).

The disruptive effects of previous reorganizations for the politics and management of UK local governments have been extensively documented in the public administration literature (see, for example, Leach and Stoker 1997; Chisholm 2002), and are believed to include:

- goal displacement as both councillors and officers are distracted from running the existing organization and instead spend their time steering the change process and jockeying for position in the new structure;
- excessive leadership turnover as some senior staff take early retirement and others, unsure of their future position in the new organization, seek employment elsewhere, thereby producing a loss of organizational memory and management expertise;
- reductions in staff morale as a result of uncertainty about roles and responsibilities;
- 'planning blight' as strategic decisions are put on hold until the new organizations are established; and
- a waste of resources as councils that are about to be abolished seek to 'lock in' expenditures that benefit their current constituents.

These arguments suggest that, in the transition period, expenditure will rise and service performance will fall. Nonetheless, the intensity with which these disruptive effects are felt is likely to vary according to the extent of structural innovation experienced by an organization.

Hannan and Freeman (1984) distinguish between changes in 'peripheral' and 'core' organizational structures, and argue that the former are less likely to be disruptive than the latter. The core of an organization comprises its identity, ownership, mission and strategy. As Lee and Alexander (1999, p. 927) argue, 'during core changes work groups are restructured, routines are revised, lines of communication are reshaped, and the mix of resources used by the organization is changed'. Peripheral characteristics are remote from the identity of the organization, and include structures that buffer it from environmental pressures or bridge it to other organizations. The voluntary amalgamations occurring in England are clearly a core change for the relevant organizations. Their identity and service mission were altered as they acquired new powers and service responsibilities. By contrast, the partnership structures that have evolved in England, Scotland and Wales represent peripheral changes at the boundaries of units of local government. Thus there is good reason to suppose that the disruptive effects of structural innovation have been felt less keenly in areas where partnership arrangements have been pursued. We now turn to the available evidence on the effects of structural innovation in the UK.

EVIDENCE ON THE EFFECTS OF STRUCTURAL INNOVATION

Although there is an abundance of anecdotal evidence on the effects of structural innovation in local government, systematic studies are much harder to come by. This reflects a wider absence of evidence on the effects of structural change in the public sector more generally. Indeed, as Pollitt (2009, p. 289) argues, 'the really hard scientific evidence is just not there. Our beliefs about the efficacy of structural reforms are more a matter of religious belief or gut feeling or rhetorical flourish.' In so far as there is an evidence base on the effects of the structural innovations wrought in UK local government, it generally exhibits several limitations. In particular, the empirical studies of innovations in local government structure that have been published typically focus upon the experiences of organizations in the aftermath of change. Much rarer is work that examines the *change* from one structure to another. Thus, in reviewing the evidence on the UK experience of the effects of structural innovation, we are restricted to a set of studies which for the most part are reliant upon a limited research design. So it is important we exhibit considerable caution when drawing any firm conclusions from the scant findings on structural change to date.

Costs

Chisholm's (2002) discussion of the costs of reorganization in the 1990s indicates that the costs of transition were greatly underestimated and that it was still unclear whether these were ever recouped through subsequent efficiency savings. Based on estimates of the costs of the potential impact of further rounds of reorganization in England, Chisholm (2004) later claimed that ongoing efficiencies are unlikely ever to exceed the initial costs of consolidation. Andrews and Boyne's (2009) analysis of administrative overheads in English local authorities in 2003 indicates that back-office costs tend to be lower in single-tier authorities. However, this study did not examine the costs of restructuring in pursuit of scale economies. By contrast, Andrews and Boyne's (2012) analysis of the transitional costs of the process of voluntary restructuring of English councils in 2009 adds further weight to the argument that amalgamations entail serious financial burdens, with the consolidating local governments witnessing a rise in costs of about 1 per cent (which translates into an absolute cost of approximately £40m). Nevertheless, further longitudinal analysis is required to provide an assessment of the extent to which the costs of this innovation might be recouped in future years.

To date, there has been precious little analysis of the costs of developing partnership structures in UK local government. The long-term evaluation of LSPs in England highlights that local governments believed that joining up had saved them money (DCLG 2011). A report on the work of Regional Centres of Excellence also furnishes examples of councils sharing services across local boundaries to generate scale economies (Office for Public Management (OPM) 2007). However, little attempt has been made to accurately estimate the costs of this species of structural innovation. In particular, as far as we are aware, researchers have yet to explore the financial impact of CPPs in Scotland. In Wales, Andrews and Entwistle (2010) find that local government services that partner more intensively with other public organizations are more efficient, but this research does not seek to analyse whether costs rise or fall when local governments enter partnership arrangements. Subsequent case research suggests that efforts to reap scale economies through partnership working have stalled in many parts of Wales (Martin et al. 2011), illustrating that much more evidence is required to underpin firm judgements about the savings attributable to sharing services.

Effectiveness

Despite widespread speculation about the likely impact on service effectiveness of the reorganization of UK local government in the 1990s, little systematic research has been carried out which explores the impact of structural innovation. Several studies assess potential scale effects on service provision in England and Wales, with some researchers uncovering statistically significant positive effects between size and performance (e.g. Travers et al. 1993), some finding significant positive and negative effects (e.g. Boyne 1996), and others little or no significant effects at all (e.g. Bailey 1991). More recently, Andrews and Boyne (2012) find that the process of voluntary restructuring of English councils led to a drop in the quality of service performance of about 5 per cent, highlighting that it is important to go beyond the simple analysis of scale effects to derive lessons about the costs and benefits of structural innovation.

To date, the effectiveness of partnership arrangements in UK local government has been much debated but little researched. Recent studies indicate that managers involved in the development of LSPs believe that they have been better able to meet the needs and demands of local people, especially in more deprived localities (DCLG 2011). However, in Scotland, Lamie and Ball's (2010) study of one community planning partnership revealed that managers and local residents were not convinced that the partnership had prompted service improvement. Andrews and Entwistle (2010) find that Welsh local government services that partner more intensively with other public organizations are more effective, but this study utilizes data that predate the implementation of the Making the Connections agenda, and so does not offer the most complete account of the successes and failures of partnership structures in Wales. Indeed, in all parts of the UK far too little is still known about the outcomes rather than the process of new forms of inter-organizational collaboration at the local level.

Capacity and Legitimacy

Craig and Manthorpe's (1998) study of social services departments in new unitary authorities in the UK suggests that they centralized decision making in response to the coordination problems they faced when seeking to (re)construct working relationships across new boundaries. Fenwick and Bailey (1999), too, find that in England the creation of unitary local authorities in the 1990s prompted some organizations to centralize decisions to enhance strategic leadership. Walters' (2001) investigation of managers' views on reorganization in 28 new English and Welsh local education authorities suggests that central control over management decisions was extended, but that this had enabled the organizations to focus on enhancing levels of community empowerment and citizen satisfaction. By contrast, Chisholm and Leach (2008) highlight that the voluntary amalgamations in England were carried out in the teeth of opposition from local residents, and so one might expect satisfaction to be correspondingly lower in the new unitary authorities. Again, longitudinal research comparing perceptions of the legitimacy of local governments before and after structural innovation is required to get a more complete picture of its impact.

In terms of the development of partnership arrangements, empirical studies point to the challenges of coordinating several separate public organizations at the local level in England, Scotland and Wales. Evidence from research on English LSPs suggests that the boards responsible for managing partnerships had developed strong planning capacity, but that implementing decisions within a multi-agency environment was extremely testing (DCLG 2011). Recent work examining the development of community planning in Scotland indicates that it is very difficult to bring together multiple actors and organizations in pursuit of shared goals if the rights and responsibilities of those different stakeholders are not (perceived to be) equivalent (Sinclair 2010). In Wales, longitudinal case study research has affirmed the importance of key personalities in building partnership capacity and legitimacy. Managerial turnover within partner organizations, in particular, can pose serious problems as new attitudes and opinions towards joining up are likely to emerge, making the attempts to build consensus increasingly complicated (Martin et al. 2011). Citizens' perceptions of the legitimacy of partnership arrangements in England, Scotland and Wales require more detailed investigation. What little evidence there is suggests that, although the potential for community engagement has been expanded, in general this has not resulted in greater satisfaction or familiarity with the new collaborative structures among local people (Lamie and Ball 2010).

FUTURE PROSPECTS FOR STRUCTURAL INNOVATION IN UK LOCAL GOVERNMENT

The Conservative–Liberal Democrat coalition government has abandoned its predecessors' proposals for further unitary authorities in England, regarding them as 'wasteful and unnecessary restructuring plans' (DCLG 2010). Nevertheless, it has been unable to resist the urge to seek out scale economies in local government through structural reform. It advocates a somewhat different form of innovation, though – the sharing by authorities of senior management teams (SMTs), which will supposedly help shield frontline services from the effects of forthcoming budget reductions (House of Commons 2011). Although these innovative practices began to emerge under the Labour government, they have quickly become the default position of the incumbent Secretary of State for Local Government, Eric Pickles, as he aims to reduce spending by 7 per cent per annum during the current parliament. By early 2011, at least 22 local governments in England had adopted or formally agreed to adopt shared SMTs (*Local Government Chronicle* 2011), with many more considering this approach. Research that seeks to evaluate the effectiveness of this latest innovation is therefore likely to contribute greatly to our understanding of the options for structural reform in local government.

In Scotland, the process of community planning has been firmed up with the introduction of Single Outcome Agreements (SOAs), which specify targeted rates of improvement on key indicators for each CPP (a similar initiative was introduced in England in 2007, but subsequently dropped by the coalition government). SOAs place an even greater responsibility on Scottish local authorities to provide strategic leadership to other partner organizations, which has added to their workload, although, according to Park and Kerley (2011), this has not problematized inter-organizational relations. Evidence from the English experience with target setting for LSPs suggests that even if SOAs lead to better outcomes their implementation requires the simplification of governance structures and high levels of specialist support (DCLG 2011). Thus, as questions are increasingly being raised about the costs of maintaining current patterns of service provision in Scottish councils, it is conceivable that more voluntarist alternatives to the present *dirigiste* approach to partnership may emerge – or indeed that proposals for full-scale reorganization are developed at either the national or local level.

In Wales, debates about the appropriate structure for local government have intensified in the wake of the financial crisis, poor international education rankings and the perceived failings of public services in some smaller councils. These debates culminated in a review of the local government system which suggested that a rationalization of the existing number of councils might be necessary (Simpson 2011). However, rather than opting for a straightforward reduction in the number of Welsh councils in order to make cost savings, politicians in Wales have plumped for the introduction of regional delivery boards for the largest strategic services (education and social services), still under the sole control of local governments. At the same time, the local government minister has repeatedly asserted, like his counterpart in England, that savings should be made by sharing senior management teams. The comparative effectiveness of regionalism and shared services in Wales will undoubtedly be under much scrutiny in the coming years as the Welsh government strives to maintain its own distinctive approach to public service delivery.

CONCLUSION

In this chapter, we have explored structural innovations in UK local government and reviewed what is known about the impact of those innovations, reflecting upon the future prospects for local government in the face of a challenging fiscal environment. Our focus on the UK experience has allowed us to examine the divergent approaches to structural innovation in England, Scotland and Wales, and to derive lessons about the efforts of central government to encourage innovations in structure through mandatory and voluntary reorganization and restructuring programmes. The evidence on the impacts of structural innovation strongly suggests that the short-term consequences of structural innovation are actually negative, leading not only to additional expenditure but also lower performance, and that these costs may not easily be recouped. In this respect, the UK experience supports theoretical arguments about the disruptive effects of structural change, and highlights that local and national policy-makers should take into account the whole process of innovation, not simply the potential benefits further down the line.

The sparseness of the current research effort in the area of structural innovation opens up several important avenues for subsequent investigations into the short- and long-term consequences of innovations in the structure of local government. First, the literature on structural innovation needs to be developed to provide better theories of the likely magnitude of adaptive and disruptive effects, and the circumstances under which the balance of these effects will be positive or negative. Theoretical arguments on the shifting balance of these effects over time also need to be developed. These theoretical advances may be achieved inductively as the number of empirical studies of the consequences of reorganization grows, but it would be useful to have more precise propositions to guide research design and data collection. If future studies also find that structural innovation has negative effects (at least in the short run), then the research agenda can move on to the reasons for differences in the size of these effects across contexts and organizations. The impact of structural innovation seems likely to be moderated by a range of organizational and managerial variables. For example, it can be hypothesized that the more intense and frequent innovations in structure are, the greater the uncertainty for the focal organizations and their network partners, and the greater the negative impact on their effectiveness. Similarly, the higher the turnover of senior staff, the higher uncertainty will be for junior staff, and in turn the greater the disruption to service provision. Tests of these potential moderators of structural innovation will require sufficiently numerous examples of the adoption of innovation to allow impacts to be teased out by statistical analysis across cases and over time.

In-depth case studies can play a critical role in building knowledge in this area by examining the enablers and barriers to structural innovation, as well as its effects on participants in the innovation journey. Such an approach could shed important light on the perceived legitimacy of the structural innovation, especially if the views of all key stakeholders (e.g. local authority officers, elected members, representatives of partner organizations and local citizens) were incorporated. Finally, there is a clear need for evidence on the effects of innovations in structure in many other local government systems, including those like the US which have a tradition of voluntary structural change and those, such as New Zealand, where central government tends to impose change upon local government. Cross-country comparative research in this area could contribute valuable evidence on what innovations in local government structure work for whom, when and why.

NOTE

1. We do not consider structural innovations in Northern Irish local government on this occasion, as the responsibilities of councils in Northern Ireland are much less extensive than those in England, Scotland and Wales.

REFERENCES

Andrews, R. and Boyne, G.A. (2009). Size, structure and administrative overheads: an empirical analysis of English Local Authorities. *Urban Studies*, 46(4), 739–759.
Andrews, R. and Boyne, G.A. (2012). Structural change and public service performance: the impact of the reorganization process in English local government. *Public Administration*, forthcoming.
Andrews, R. and Entwistle, T. (2010). Does cross-sectoral partnership deliver: an empirical exploration of public service effectiveness, efficiency and equity. *Journal of Public Administration Research and Theory*, 21(4), 679–701.
Bailey, S.J. (1991). Fiscal stress – the new system of local government finance in England. *Urban Studies*, 28(6), 889–907.
Boyne, G.A. (1995). Population size and economies of scale in local government. *Policy and Politics*, 23(3), 213–222.

Boyne, G.A. (1996). Scale, performance and the New Public Management: an empirical analysis of local authority services. *Journal of Management Studies*, 33(6), 809–826.

Boyne, G.A. and Cole, M. (1996). Fragmentation, concentration and local government structure: top tier authorities in England and Wales, 1831–1991. *Government and Policy*, 14, 501–514.

Boyne, G.A., McVicar, M. and Jordan, G. (1995). *Local Government Reform: A Review of the Process in Scotland and Wales*. York: Joseph Rowntree Foundation.

Boyne, G.A., James, O., John, P. and Petrovsky, N. (2010). What if public management reform actually works? The paradoxical success of performance management in English local government. In H. Margetts, P. 6 and C. Hood (eds), *Paradoxes of Modernisation*. Oxford: Oxford University Press, pp. 203–220.

Chisholm, M. (2000). *Structural Reform of British Local Government*. Manchester: Manchester University Press.

Chisholm, M. (2002). The cost of local government structural reorganisation in Great Britain during the 1990s. *Environment and Planning C – Government and Policy*, 20(2), 251–262.

Chisholm, M. (2004). Reorganising two-tier local government for regional assemblies. *Public Money and Management*, 24(2), 113–120.

Chisholm, M. and Leach, S. (2008). *Botched Business: The Damaging Process of Reorganising Local Government 2006–2008*. Coleford: Douglas McLean Publishing.

Copus, C., Crowe, A. and Clark, A. (2005). *Council Size: A Literature Review and Analysis: Report to the Electoral Commission*. London: Electoral Commission.

Council of Europe (1995). *The Size of Municipalities, Efficiency and Citizen Participation*. Strasbourg: Council of Europe.

Cowell, R. (2004). Community planning: fostering participation in the congested state. *Local Government Studies*, 30(4), 497–518.

Craig, G. and Manthorpe, J. (1998). Small is beautiful? Local government reorganisation and the work of social services departments. *Policy and Politics*, 26(2), 189–207.

Crampton, G. (1996). Local government structure and urban residential location. *Urban Studies*, 33(7), 1061–1076.

DCLG (2006a). *Strong and Prosperous Communities: The Local Government White Paper*. London: HMSO.

DCLG (2006b). *Invitations to Councils in England to Make Proposals for Future Unitary Structures to Pioneer as Pathfinders, New Two-Tier Models*. London: HMSO.

DCLG (2010). *Pickles Stops Unitary Councils in Exeter, Norwich and Suffolk*. Press Notice, 26 May. London: DCLG.

DCLG (2011). *Long-Term Evaluation of Local Area Agreements and Local Strategic Partnerships*. Final Report, unpublished.

Dearlove, J. (1979). *The Reorganization of British Local Government: Old Orthodoxies and a Political Perspective*. Cambridge: Cambridge University Press.

Dollery, B., Crase, L. and O'Keefe, S. (2009). Improving efficiency in Australian local government: structural reform as a catalyst for effective reform. *Geographical Research*, 47, 269–279.

Fenwick, J. and Bailey, M. (1999). Local government reorganisation in the UK: decentralisation or corporatism? *International Journal of Public Sector Management*, 12(3), 249–259.

Grosskopf, S. and Yaisawamg, S. (1990). Economies of scope in the provision of local public services. *National Tax Journal*, 43, 61–74.

Hannan, M. and Freeman, J. (1984). Structural inertia and organizational change. *American Sociological Review*, 49, 149–164.

House of Commons (2011). *Oral Evidence Taken Before the Communities and Local Government Committee: Comprehensive Spending Review*. London: House of Commons, 669–i.

John, P. (2010). Larger and larger? The endless search for efficiency in the UK. In H. Baldersheim and L.E. Rose (eds), *Territorial Choice: The Politics of Boundaries and Borders*. Houndmills: Palgrave, pp. 101–117.

Lamie, J. and Ball, R. (2010). Evaluation of partnership working within a community planning context. *Local Government Studies*, 36(1), 109–127.

Leach, S. and Stoker, G. (1997). Understanding the Local Government Review: a retrospective analysis. *Public Administration*, 75(1), 1–20.

Lee, S.D. and Alexander, J. (1999). Managing hospitals in turbulent times: do organizational changes improve hospital survival? *Health Services Research*, 34, 923–946.

Local Government Chronicle (2011). Joint management teams set to triple. 17 March.

March, J. and Olson, J. (1983). Organizing political life: what administrative reorganization tells us about government. *American Political Science Review*, 77, 281–296.

Martin, S.J., Downe, J., Entwistle, T. and Guarneros-Meza, V. (2011). *Learning to Improve: An Independent Assessment of the Welsh Government's Policy for Local Government*. Unpublished interim report.

Milbourne, L., Macrae, S. and Maguire, M. (2003). Collaborative solutions or new policy problems: exploring multi-agency partnerships in education and health work. *Journal of Education Policy*, 18(1), 19–35.

National Centre for Social Research (2000). *Revisiting Public Perceptions of Local Government: A Decade of Change*. London: Department of Environment, Transport and the Regions.

Niskanen, W. (1971). *Bureaucracy and Representative Government*. Chicago: Aldine Atherton.

ODPM (2005a). *National Evaluation of Local Strategic Partnerships: Issues Paper: Leadership in Local Strategic Partnerships*. London: ODPM.

ODPM (2005b). *National Evaluation of Local Strategic Partnerships: Issues Paper: Below the Local Strategic Partnerships*. London: ODPM.

OPM (2007). *CSR 2004 Outcomes – Strategic Study*. Report for the Regional Centres of Excellence. London: Office for Public Management.

Page, E. and Midwinter, A. (1980). Remoteness, efficiency, cost and the reorganization of Scottish local government. *Public Administration*, 58(4), 439–463.

Park, J.J. and Kerley, R. (2011). Single outcome agreements and partnership working in Scottish local government – year one. *Local Government Studies*, 37(1), 57–76.

Pollitt, C. (2009). Structural change and public service performance: international lessons. *Public Money and Management*, 29, 285–291.

Salmon, P. (1987). Decentralisation as an incentive scheme. *Oxford Review of Economic Policy*, 3(2), 24–43.

Simpson, J. (2011). *Local, Regional, National: What Services are Best Delivered Where?* Cardiff: Welsh Assembly Government.

Sinclair, S. (2010). Dilemmas of community planning: lessons from Scotland. *Public Policy and Administration*, 23, 373–390.

Snape, S. and Raine, J. (1999). The performance of new unitary councils in England. *Local Governance*, 25(3), 179–188.

Swianiewicz, P. and Mielczarek, A. (2010). Georgian local government reform: state Leviathan redraws boundaries. *Local Government Studies*, 36, 291–311.

Tiebout, C. (1956). A pure theory of local expenditure. *Journal of Political Economy*, 64(5), 416–424.

Tomkinson, R. (2007). *Shared Services in Local Government: Improving Service Delivery*. Aldershot: Gower Publishing Ltd.

Travers, T., Jones, G. and Burnham, J. (1993). *The Impact of Population Size on Local Authority Costs and Effectiveness*. York: Joseph Rowntree Foundation.

Vojnovic, I. (2000). The transitional impacts of municipal consolidations. *Journal of Urban Affairs*, 22, 385–417.

Wagner, R.E. and Weber, W.E. (1975). Competition, monopoly, and the organisation of government in metropolitan areas. *Journal of Law and Economics*, 18(3), 661–684.

Walters, B. (2001). Does size matter? Is small really beautiful? *British Journal of Special Education*, 28(1), 35–44.

Welsh Government (2004). *Making the Connections: Delivering Better Services for Wales*. Cardiff: Welsh Government.

35. Strengthening the spread of innovation in the UK's National Health Service
James Barlow

INTRODUCTION

In the next 10 years the UK will need to spend between £1.2 trillion and £1.5 trillion on health and social care just to maintain the current status quo. At current growth rates, real terms health spending in the UK will more than double to £230 billion a year by 2030 (Lansley 2011). Without innovations that help to radically reconfigure the care system, it will be hard to achieve this, let alone achieve world class standards and meet the challenges of an ageing population. This will require careful thought on the new combinations of technology, services, organisations and built infrastructure that can be designed and put in place.

So what do we know about innovation in healthcare? First, it is part of the solution to the 21st century healthcare challenges but it is also part of the problem. Unlike in other industries, where innovation tends to drive down the cost of production or final costs to the consumer, innovation in healthcare is often perceived to be expensive because it increases demand – it allows you to treat more people or identify more problems that can be treated (Cutler 1995; Cutler and McClellan 2001; Bodenheimer 2005; Skinner et al. 2006; Cutler et al. 2007; Baker 2010). It has been estimated that in the US the combined effect of demographic change, income growth, insurance costs, relative productivity growth and administrative expenses explains only half the total increase in healthcare expenditure between 1940 and 1999. The remainder is the consequence of technological change in medicine (Cutler 1995).

Secondly, innovation in healthcare is hard partly because healthcare services are a 'complex system', with all the typical attributes that have been identified by complexity theorists. These include its many interdependent constituent parts, the non-linear and often counterintuitive behaviour it displays, and its ability to adapt to changes in the environment (Plsek and Greenhalgh 2001; Bar-Yann 2004).

Thirdly, there are major problems in ensuring that innovations and recognised best practice are diffused widely across the system. Knowledge about individual pockets of excellence is not spread and pilot projects for innovations are often not sustained beyond their initial phase because of insufficient local resources to develop them further. Moreover, in the UK – and elsewhere – the overwhelming focus of policy and public support for innovation in healthcare is for the development of new technologies, with relatively little attention paid to their adoption and diffusion (Barlow and Burn 2008).

While politicians, practitioners, academics and businesses involved in healthcare all argue that innovation is essential to cope with the future, the received wisdom is that healthcare organisations often find it easier to say 'No' to innovation. They might plead lack of time, paucity of evidence, the need for a business case or just that the innovation is too complicated.

Of course, some healthcare innovations do spread easily. Initial uncertainty about the clinical value of MRI scanning was overcome by the clear superiority of its images (Grigsby et al. 2002), although the number of scanners in England and Wales is still low when compared with other countries. In the case of live polio vaccine, unambiguous evidence for its benefits and early feedback meant that it was rapidly adopted and diffused (Nelson et al. 2004).

However, the experience of many healthcare innovations is less encouraging. Even where evidence in favour of an innovation is firm, it may be adopted far more slowly than seems rational or desirable. Many advances stumble at such a multiplicity of hurdles that the UK's National Health Service (NHS) has earned a reputation for being 'anti-innovation' – it has an organisational culture that under-values innovation, staff have few financial or other incentives to engage in innovation, operational demands mean there is little time for innovation, and the constant change and reorganisation induces 'innovation fatigue'. This is all compounded by an organisational structure marked by a professional pecking order, strict demarcation, tribalism and departmental silos (Rushmer et al. 2004), and behavioural characteristics of clinicians and others that frequently inhibit innovation (Worthington 2004).

This chapter outlines the emerging research that offers some clues about what precludes the sustainable adoption of healthcare innovation in public – that is, non-profit – organisations delivering healthcare. It focuses on the NHS, the largest public sector provider of healthcare in the world.

INNOVATION IN HEALTHCARE IS NOT THE SAME AS BEST PRACTICE – BUT THEY ARE RELATED

'Innovation' is both an *outcome* and a *process* – a new method, idea or product and the action or process of innovating. It relates to the successful *exploitation* of new ideas rather than the act of invention itself. The notion of 'adoption' encompasses the processes influencing the decision to take up a specific innovation, while 'diffusion' represents the spread of an innovation through a population. The concepts have been much researched both in healthcare and in other industries.

Innovation has been categorised in a number of ways. It can be seen in terms of continuous or discontinuous innovation, either improving but preserving the current way of doing things or disrupting the status quo (Tushman and Anderson 1986; Bessant 2005; Moore 2005). Others have seen innovation as incremental – involving change at the level of individual elements of the innovation – or radical, involving change in the overall architecture of the innovation (Henderson and Clark 1990). Recently the notion of 'disruptive innovation' (Christensen et al. 2000) has been much discussed, especially in relation to healthcare. This assumes that the pace of technological progress often exceeds the wishes of most customers, so the introduction of a more affordable product or service that is simpler to use may increase market demand by engaging new customers.

How 'new' does an innovation have to be to be classed as an innovation? Some innovations, such as an improvement to an existing product or way of doing things, may have already been widely adopted within an industry and therefore simply be new to a specific firm or organisation in that industry. At the other extreme, an innovation may be wholly new both to a firm and a market, a completely new product (Cooper 2001).

This suggests that the boundaries between 'innovation' and 'best practice' can be somewhat blurred. What was once innovative may have become generally acknowledged best practice in one organisation (or industry or country), but may be new – innovative – in another. The concepts of best practice and innovation are therefore distinct but related. Best practice can be defined as the most efficient and effective way of accomplishing a task, based on repeatable procedures, which consistently shows results superior to a norm. When you visit your doctor you want to be sure that he or she is following best practice. Often, achieving this requires agreed evidence-based protocols to be followed. Depending on the clinical area, a degree of standardisation can lead to better outcomes. However, best practice should not be seen as fixed – it needs to evolve as new ideas emerge. And the reality is that in healthcare the influx of innovation means that best practice in many areas *is* constantly changing and evolving, redefining what high quality care looks like.

UNDERSTANDING THE ADOPTION AND DIFFUSION OF INNOVATION

According to standard theories, the adoption and diffusion of new ideas follows a predictable pattern. A slow initial phase, in which innovators and risk-takers adopt a new idea, is followed by take-off when its benefits have been established. This surge in uptake gradually tails off as laggards adopt what is now common practice. In the NHS, a common claim is that there is an extensive lag, colloquially known as the 'valley of death', between the early adopters and the majority take-off.

Standard explanations for the successful uptake and spread of innovations usually focus on whether or not they possess certain characteristics. Rogers (1995) emphasises the attributes of certain key factors which govern the adoption and diffusion rate for a new product:

- relative advantage (the degree to which a product is better than the product that it replaces);
- compatibility (the degree to which a product is consistent with the users' context and values);
- complexity (the degree to which a product is difficult to understand and use);
- trialability (the degree to which a product may be experimented with on a limited basis prior to launch); and
- observability (the degree to which product usage and impact are visible to others).

Other approaches to innovation adoption and diffusion include *probit models*, where potential users possessing heterogeneous preferences weigh the costs and benefits of adoption; *epidemic models*, which stress the availability of information on an innovation for potential users; and the concept of *information cascades and path dependence*, emphasising the way information eventually results in an innovation becoming legitimised and network effects ensure its widespread adoption (Geroski 2000).

HOW DOES HEALTHCARE INNOVATION TAKE PLACE? FROM CONVENTIONAL INNOVATION RESEARCH TO PROCESS STUDIES

How applicable are conventional approaches to understanding innovation adoption and diffusion in the healthcare context? Often in healthcare research – and policy-making – 'innovation' tends to be narrowly defined, focusing on new medical devices or drugs, or the processes that lead to their development. But innovation in healthcare needs to be seen as a broader concept, encompassing improvements in the technologies, the institutional and physical infrastructures, and in the clinical practices and service designs that support health services. All are related. Changes in technology are likely to have an impact on service delivery models; innovation in services may have an impact on the demand for hospital beds. The boundaries around a healthcare innovation are often opaque, with new technologies commonly requiring new practices or organisational forms for their successful introduction. A variety of different strategies to encourage the adoption of innovation and manage its implementation is therefore necessary.

Although there has been a great deal of research on the adoption and diffusion of healthcare innovations, this has suffered limitations. Until relatively recently most research has been on bounded, well-defined product innovations such as drugs and medical devices, rather than on the complex processes which underpin many innovations in health services. Adoption tends to be explained in relation to independent, individual decision-making, often in terms of correlations between the characteristics of the innovation and the adopters, and often within a single organisational unit.

The limitations of this approach have been highlighted by several major reviews of healthcare innovation research (Denis et al. 2002; Fleuren et al. 2004; Greenhalgh et al. 2004; Rye and Kimberly 2007; Robert et al. 2009). These point out that many studies focus on a small number of causal variables, so that little is known about relative effects and interactions between them and contextual influences. Moreover, while there is research on relationships between healthcare innovation and organisational characteristics, there are significant gaps, including the role of evidence and the impact of power and political dynamics on key stakeholders. Few studies focus on the sustainability of innovations beyond the initial implementation phase because research efforts are not ongoing (see Chapter 36, Greenhalgh et al.), and there is also a lack of research on disengagement from old methods and its part in poor adoption of innovation. As Rye and Kimberly (2007, p. 254) put it, 'we still do not know as much as we would like, and what we do know, we may not know for sure'.

In reality, innovation adoption and diffusion in healthcare is not as simple as conventional studies tend to suggest. Deciding whether to take up a new idea involves multiple stakeholders and is a complex, organic and untidy process. The innovation itself may be multifaceted with several objectives, for example improving service quality, productivity and safety in various degrees. Innovations may require the coordinated efforts of numerous organisations from different parts of the care system, or they may challenge existing patterns of interdependence among individuals or groups. In healthcare, where there are tightly demarcated communities of interest such as those of different health professionals, collaborative efforts can be very difficult to negotiate (Ferlie et al. 2005). The evidence for the efficacy of an innovation may also be contested by different professional groups or there may be no generally agreed criteria for judging its benefits.

Even when an innovation is relatively clear-cut, with a good evidence base and involving few stakeholders, adoption and diffusion is often ambiguous, non-linear and uneven (Edmonson et al. 2001; Fleuren et al. 2004; Nelson et al. 2004; Ferlie et al. 2005; Rye and Kimberly 2007; Robert et al. 2009). Healthcare organisations therefore should not be seen as rational decision-making machines that move an innovation through an ordered process of stages. The emerging consensus among researchers is that the interactions between the innovation itself, local actors and contextual factors are very important (Champagne et al. 1991; Denis et al. 2002; Dopson et al. 2002; Fitzgerald et al. 2002; Ferlie et al. 2005). This echoes mainstream innovation research, where it is argued that successful and sustainable implementation require compatibility between an innovation and its wider context (Rogers 1995).

There has therefore been a tendency towards 'process' studies of healthcare innovation, particularly on UK settings. According to Kimberly and Cook (2008, p. 17) this has provided 'some of the most highly visible and innovative work on the effect of organisational variables on change in healthcare organisations'.

Process research in healthcare focuses on the dynamic behaviour within organisations, especially the way organisational context, activity and actions unfold over time. It argues that far more importance needs to be placed on interactions between social or professional groups than previous, largely non-healthcare-based, research acknowledges (Fitzgerald et al. 2002). History, culture and the quality of inter-professional relationships are also very important (Ferlie et al. 2005).

Robert et al. (2009) have brought together this body of work in a major report which identifies a key component of successful innovation in health services as the way an innovation's 'outer context' and 'inner context' are related. This echoes Denis et al. (2002), who argue that a complex healthcare innovation is not something with fixed boundaries, but with a 'hard core' of well-defined irreducible elements, which have to be in place for it to succeed, and a 'periphery' of elements that are negotiable. They argue that the components and constituent parts of an innovation and its adopting context do not exist in isolation but in dynamic relation to the system as a whole and that not all the elements behave predictably. This therefore implies there may be several different routes to adoption for a given innovation.

APPLYING HEALTHCARE INNOVATION RESEARCH LESSONS TO THE NHS

Drawing this work together, what can we say about the adoption and diffusion of innovation in the NHS? Six factors are crucial to our understanding of the way innovation processes play out: complexity and the healthcare system; its costs and financing; its organisational structure; the capacity of NHS organisations for innovation; the importance of evidence-based decision-making in healthcare; and the role of communications and social networks.

Complexity and the Healthcare System

Healthcare is frequently described as a 'complex system' because of the presence of many interdependencies between its constituent parts. This means that changes in one part can trigger changes in other parts, often with counterintuitive consequences (Plsek and Greenhalgh 2001; Bar-Yann 2004). There has been interest in applying 'complexity theory' to healthcare systems, which has provided insights into the organisational and behavioural changes needed to accelerate quality improvement and the dynamics across the boundaries of different services (Barlow and Dattee 2010). A complex systems approach also implicitly permeates some government health policy and its translation into practice (Locock 2003).

It is undeniable that the health and social care systems are hugely complex, where lines of communication and spheres of responsibility are messy, power struggles and cultural silos are common, and the economics of innovation are often unpredictable and perverse. For example, caring for elderly people with long-term chronic conditions requires effective communication and collaboration between different professional teams that span the somewhat artificial divide between health and social care. Even in the absence of technological or organisational innovation in the health services for those with long-term conditions this has proved challenging. But these difficulties are multiplied when complex innovations such as telecare (the remote monitoring of patients) are involved. The costs, risks and benefits of the effort are often spread unevenly, yet every organisation must be satisfied that it is getting a good deal if a telecare innovation project is to succeed (Barlow et al. 2006; Hendy and Barlow 2011).

Costs and Financing

The effects of health system complexity on the way the costs and benefits of an innovation are distributed are compounded by financial economics. This is certainly the case in the NHS but is also common in most developed health systems. The financial apparatus of NHS health trusts (local hospital and primary care organisations) is inflexible because the control of budgets is devolved to different departments. Financial planning is restricted by the annual budgetary cycle and trusts are limited in their ability to accumulate discretionary funds or generate a financial surplus. High start-up costs for an innovation may inhibit long-term financial gains, or gains may be spread unevenly across organisations in the health system (Barlow and Burn 2008).

These factors leave very little room for investment in innovation projects that may require significant up-front expenditure or involve a contribution from different departmental budgets. The focus of management tends to be on initial costs, so expensive innovations are less likely to be adopted even if they may have significant benefits further down the line. The result is a short-term outlook and generally risk-averse behaviour, a serious barrier to the adoption of new practices. Added to this problem are the uncertainties over the future environment, in which major policy shifts are perceived as commonplace. There is a fear that the freedom to invest in innovative new business strategies and create new income streams could be withdrawn at any time.

The system of payment and reimbursement for medical procedures that operates within the NHS also causes problems for innovation. NHS providers are paid for their activity according to a tariff system, based on the average cost of a group of procedures. This is based on current practice and does not subsidise the cost of innovative, and possibly more expensive, procedures that would improve quality over time. If an innovation improves efficiency by reducing activity, a trust may be penalised because it will receive less under the tariff system. Furthermore, trusts do not have accurate costing systems giving them detailed information on what they pay per patient to provide a service. This means that trusts struggle to identify potential savings, giving them less reason to drop outdated practices and adopt new ones.

Organisational Structure

It is often argued that innovation adoption is not a one-off, all-or-nothing event but an adaptive process, and especially so in healthcare. As argued above, a typical complex healthcare innovation comprises a core of well-defined irreducible elements and a periphery of negotiable elements, allowing different routes to adoption. Successful and sustainable implementation requires compatibility between the innovation and its wider context, and possibly also the capacity to adapt features of the innovation to meet the needs of users (Robert et al. 2009).

Some healthcare innovations may lead to major modification to existing ways of working and involve collaboration across established organisational groups. In a complex healthcare system like the NHS, a degree of flexibility may therefore increase the likelihood of building coalitions that support the successful adoption of an innovation. Another important factor is how an innovation's risks and benefits are distributed across a given NHS trust and the wider organisational system of which it forms a part. The more these coincide with the interests, values and power of the various stakeholders, potentially the easier it is to build support for adoption.

Organisational Capacity for Innovation

An organisational culture that encourages innovation is influenced by strong leadership, a clear strategic vision and collective attitudes that are conducive to experimentation (Dopson et al. 2002; Ham et al. 2002). Building such a culture in the NHS has proved problematic. For more than a decade, NHS reforms have attempted to change a system dominated by top-down central control to one in which decision-making is devolved to a local level as much as possible. But changing the organisational structure of the health service does not automatically change cultures that have developed over many decades, under conditions of tight budget control and a rigid hierarchy of decision-making.

Historically managers in the NHS have not been judged by how innovative they are. Rather, they are judged by how well they stay within their budget and carry out the tasks demanded of them. According to a King's Fund (2011) report there is evidence that the NHS is over-administered as a result of extensive, overlapping and duplicating demands from regulators and performance managers. Effective leadership involves acknowledging the challenges, supporting managers and medical staff involved in innovation, and fostering learning through trial and error without the fear of penalties. But although it is recognised that leadership development needs to extend 'from the board to the ward', one of the biggest weaknesses of the NHS has been its failure to engage clinicians in management and leadership (Turnbull James 2011). The need for complicated leadership arrangements, often across NHS entities, with negotiated authority between clinicians and managers, and between clinicians from different professional backgrounds, makes it hard for individuals to be open to innovation and experimentation.

Evidence-Based Decision-Making

Innovations need to demonstrate unambiguous relative advantages over existing technologies, products or practices. The motivation to innovate partly depends on whether the organisation is rewarded for the effort it will expend on managing the change and realising the benefits. Evidence for costs and benefits is therefore important in decision-making about whether to commit resources to an innovation. However, there are particular issues relating to the collection and interpretation of evidence within healthcare. Because of the powerful position of doctors, there is a bias towards scientific fact and a positivist epistemology in the evaluation of new innovations, while epistemologies from social sciences often carry less credence (Rogers and Copeland 2004). This can lead to a view that anything short of the randomised controlled trial – the gold standard of evidence – lacks credibility. Yet healthcare innovations involving multiple interventions to modify a service are not amenable to this approach and the evidence base for such changes is therefore usually less clear-cut.

Nevertheless, since the early 1990s across healthcare there has been increasing emphasis on evidence-based clinical practice, mirroring a shift to evidence-based policy across government. The quality and rigour of health technology assessments and clinical practice guidelines from the National Institute for Health and Clinical Excellence (NICE) are widely praised around the world. But there are two problems with this approach. First, NICE recommendations are not always quickly and uniformly adopted. In part, this is due to the sheer quantity of evidence and the finite resources of the NHS available to efficiently collect, assess and disseminate it. Moreover, NICE tends to focus on new drugs rather than medical devices or evaluation of service delivery innovations.

Secondly, much evidence-based practice has been criticised because research results may be too context-specific to be generalisable (Black 2001). There is concern that too much emphasis on 'evidence' may lead to a myopia whereby only what is measurable is believed, while health policy-making requires a more pluralist and diverse approach involving compromise between competing viewpoints (Marmot 2004).

Given the potential costs and the focus on evidence creation, healthcare organisations often look more favourably on innovations that can be introduced on a trial basis before a binding decision to adopt because this reduces the risk and increases the visibility of benefits (Greenhalgh et al. 2004). However, a balance needs to be struck between trials necessary to demonstrate the impact and safety of an innovation and the excessive repetition of these trials in different localities. In the NHS, findings from a large proportion of innovation pilot projects never see the light of day. Not only does this waste resources, but it can stifle the market for a given innovation, with the developers of new medical products often facing demands for repeated trials as different local healthcare authorities wish to test the product in their own context (Barlow and Burn 2008). In the field of remote care for people with long-term conditions, the results from over 8000 trials had been reported in scientific journals by 2006, yet the evidence base still remained comparatively weak (Barlow et al. 2007).

Communication and Social Networks are Vital

The influence and membership of professional and social networks can determine how well new knowledge spreads and create normative and institutional pressures for adoption (Rogers 1995). However, rigid delineation between professional networks may limit spread if important stakeholders are excluded, so the configuration of networks is important.

Clinical reputation is an important currency in the NHS and, together with professional networks, it can form the basis of efforts to spread innovation and best practice (Locock et al. 2001). Opinion leaders in healthcare can have a strong influence on the beliefs and actions of their colleagues. These may not be the initial enthusiasts for an innovation but are the senior professionals who throw their authority and status behind it, based on their expert judgement. There are different forms of network in healthcare, with differing implications for the spread of innovation. Doctors tend to have informal horizontal networks that are effective at spreading peer influence and constructing and reframing the meaning of innovations. On the other hand, nurses tend to have formal, vertical networks that are effective at transferring codified information and passing on decisions from higher authority (West et al. 1999; Ferlie and Pettigrew 2005; Ferlie et al. 2010).

However, networking arrangements in the NHS do not function as an especially effective mechanism for communication and knowledge transfer. Innovations that require different professional groups to work together or originate outside a particular group can find it harder to win the necessary support. Communities of practice in healthcare tend to involve one profession only. The groups can be highly institutionalised, with their own rules, norms and objectives, and it takes a great effort to create functioning multi-disciplinary communities of practice.

CONCLUSIONS

The adoption of healthcare innovations can be a tortuous process, and nowhere more so than in the NHS. There are several reasons for this. First, healthcare is immensely complex – and the organisational structure and economics of the NHS are no different. It has many stakeholders, professional silos, and commissioning and provider organisations, each with their own sets of interests. Its payment and reimbursement arrangements are convoluted and there are unpredictable spillovers when it comes to the way the costs and benefits of innovation are distributed. This can inadvertently act as a disincentive to innovation, reinforcing historically risk-averse cultures.

Secondly, healthcare tends to be deeply political, so seemingly rational innovations leading to changes to services can rapidly become the subject of populist disquiet, unsettling local politicians. And, in the case of the NHS, repeated attempts by governments at organisational reforms have not only resulted in 'innovation fatigue', but have also tended to disrupt multi-disciplinary networks that are essential if professional and departmental resistance to innovation is to be overcome (Barlow and Burn 2008).

Thirdly, some of the difficulties around healthcare innovation are partly attributed to the high status of 'gold standard' empirical evidence in healthcare. When combined with inadequate institutional means for testing innovations and for advocating and implementing recommendations about adoption, this focus on evidence can slow change. The repeated trials and pilots of innovations both waste resources and often produce results which are locally specific and cannot be applied widely.

Together, these characteristics can make it easier to say 'no' to an investment in a healthcare innovation than to say 'yes' – with the typical response being 'give me a business case' or 'what's the evidence base for the benefits?' Yet the current context for healthcare – demanding higher quality and more cost-effective service delivery – requires that these issues are addressed.

Lowering the barriers to the adoption, embedding, sustaining and spreading of innovation in the NHS requires moves simultaneously on a number of fronts. In a system that increasingly places an emphasis on evidence-based policy, the institutional basis for gathering, analysing, disseminating, advocating and monitoring what works and where is weak. Improvements to the methods and institutional framework for evaluation and spread of knowledge are needed are needed. Greater transparency in information about the relative performance of healthcare organisations would highlight best practice. Changes to the financial incentives to adopt innovative technologies and processes could help to eliminate perverse behaviours. Fostering of multi-disciplinary networks and better understanding of how professional peer networks operate could overcome cultural barriers to change. Enhancement of managerial skills, capacity and leadership would make innovation smoother and less traumatic.

More broadly, attention needs to be paid to identifying the best leverage points for influencing the potential to effect change and innovation in the NHS. This will require a much better understanding of the dynamics of the system to avoid triggering counter-intuitive consequences (Forrester 1995). While 'whole system' thinking – that is, one which accounts for the structure of the entire system – has become increasingly influential in the NHS (Audit Commission 2002; Rogers and Copeland 2004; Rogers et al. 2008), the interdependencies between different health and social care subsystems, and how they inhibit innovation, are poorly understood.

The moves towards NHS system reform launched by the Coalition government in 2010 carry both challenges and opportunities. The opportunity is that devolved governance could reduce the risk aversion of a system where passivity has sometimes been the safest leadership option. The challenge is to ensure that all NHS stakeholders understand where and how best – world-class – practice is occurring and ensure that competition between healthcare providers does not reduce the communication and spread of good ideas.

ACKNOWLEDGEMENTS

This chapter draws partly on research carried out with the support of the Policy Exchange and published in Barlow and Burn (2008). The research included 80 interviews with health policy and management experts, and two roundtable discussions in the UK and US. Thanks are due to all the interviewees and to Gavin Lockhart and Jack O'Sullivan.

REFERENCES

Audit Commission (2002). *Integrated Services for Older People: Building a Whole System Approach in England*. London: Audit Commission.
Baker, L.C. (2010). Acquisition of MRI equipment by doctors drives up imaging use and spending. *Health Affairs*, 29, 2252–2259.
Bar-Yann, Y. (2004). *Multiscale Analysis of the Healthcare and Public Health System: Organizing for Achieving both Effectiveness and Efficiency*. Cambridge, MA: New England Complex Systems Institute.
Barlow, J. and Burn, J. (2008). *All Change Please: Putting the Best New Healthcare Ideas into Practice*. London: Policy Exchange.
Barlow, J. and Dattee, B. (2010). Complexity and whole-system change programmes. *Journal of Health Services Research and Policy*, 15, 19–25.
Barlow, J., Bayer, S. and Curry, R. (2006). Implementing complex innovations in fluid multi-stakeholder environments: experiences of 'telecare'. *Technovation*, 26, 396–406.
Barlow, J., Singh, D., Bayer, S. and Curry, R. (2007). A systematic review of the benefits of home telecare for frail elderly people and those with long-term conditions. *Journal of Telemedicine and Telecare*, 13, 172–179.
Bessant, J. (2005). Enabling continuous and discontinuous innovation: learning from the private sector. *Public Money and Management*, 25, 35–42.
Black, N. (2001). Evidence based policy: proceed with care. *British Medical Journal*, 323, 275–278.
Bodenheimer, T. (2005). High and rising health care costs. Part 2: technologic innovation. *Annals of Internal Medicine*, 142, 932–937.
Champagne, F., Denis, J.-L., Pineault, R. and Contandriopoulos, A.-P. (1991). Structural and political models of analysis of the introduction of an innovation in organizations: the case of the change in the method of payment of physicians in long-term care hospitals. *Health Services Management Research*, 4, 94–111.
Christensen, C., Bohmer, R. and Kenagy, J. (2000). Will disruptive innovations cure healthcare? *Harvard Business Review*, 78.
Cooper, R. (2001). *Winning at New Product Development: Accelerating the Process from Ideas to Launch*. New York: Basic Books.
Cutler, D.M. (1995). Technology, health costs, and the NIH. *National Institutes of Health Economics Roundtable on Biomedical Research*.
Cutler, D.M. and McClellan, M. (2001). Is technological change in medicine worth it? *Health Affairs*, 20, 11–29.
Cutler, D.M., Long, G., Berndt, E.R., Royer, J., Fournier, A.-A., Sasser, A. and Cremieux, P. (2007). The value of antihypertensive drugs: a perspective on medical innovation. *Health Affairs*, 26, 97–110.
Denis, J., Hebert, Y., Langley, A., Lozeau, D. and Trottier, L. (2002). Explaining diffusion patterns for complex health care innovations. *Health Care Management Review*, 27, 60–73.
Dopson, S., Fitzgerald, L., Ferlie, E., Gabbay, J. and Locock, L. (2002). No magic targets: changing clinical practice to become more evidence based. *Health Care Management Review*, 37, 35–47.
Edmonson, A., Bohmer, R. and Pisano, G. (2001). Disrupted routines: team learning and new technology implementation in hospitals. *Administrative Science Quarterly*, 46, 685–716.
Ferlie, E. and Pettigrew, A. (2005). Managing through networks: some issues and implications for the NHS. *British Journal of Management*, DOI: 10.1111/j.1467-8551.1996.tb00149.x
Ferlie, E., Fitzgerald, L., Wood, M. and Hawkins, C. (2005). The nonspread of innovations: the mediating role of professionals. *Academy of Management Journal*, 48, 117–134.
Ferlie, E., Fitzgerald, L., McGivern, G., Dopson, S. and Exworthy, M. (2010). Networks in Health Care: a comparative study of their management, impact and performance. National Institute for Health Research – Service Delivery and Organisation programme.
Fitzgerald, L., Ferlie, E., Wood, M. and Hawkins, C. (2002). Interlocking interactions: the diffusion of innovations in health care. *Human Relations*, 55, 1429–1449.
Fleuren, M., Wiefferink, K. and Paulussen, T. (2004). Determinants of innovation within health care organizations: literature review and Delphi study. *International Journal of Quality Health Care*, 16, 107–123.
Forrester, J.W. (1995). Counterintuitive Behavior of Social Systems. *The System Dynamics Road Maps*. Massachusetts Institute of Technology.
Geroski, P. (2000). Models of technology diffusion. *Research Policy*, 603–625.
Greenhalgh, T., Robert, G., Macfarlane, F., Bate, P. and Kyriakidou, O. (2004). Diffusion of innovations in service organizations: systematic review and recommendations. *The Milbank Quarterly*, 82, 581–629.

Grigsby, J., Rigby, M., Hiemstra, A., House, M., Olsson, S. and Whitten, P. (2002). The diffusion of tele-medicine. *Telemedicine Journal and E-health*, 8, 79–94.

Ham, C. et al. (2002). Capacity, Culture and Leadership: Lessons from Experience of Improving Access to Hospital Services. Birmingham: Health Services Management Centre, University of Birmingham.

Henderson, R. and Clark, K. (1990). Architectural innovation: the reconfiguration of existing product tech-nologies and the failure of established firms. *Administrative Science Quarterly*, 35, 9–30.

Hendy, J. and Barlow, J. (2011). The role of the organizational champion in achieving health system change. *Social Science and Medicine*.

Kimberly, J. and Cook, J. (2008). Organizational measurement and the implementation of innovations in mental health services. *Adm Policy Ment Health*, 35, 11–20.

King's Fund (2011). The Future of Leadership and Management in the NHS: No More Heroes. London: The King's Fund.

Lansley, A. (2011). Why the health service needs surgery. *Daily Telegraph*, 1 June.

Locock, L. (2003). Redesigning health care: new wine from old bottles? *Journal of Health Services Research and Policy*, 8, 120–122.

Locock, L., Dopson, S., Chambers, D. and Gabbay, J. (2001). Understanding the role of opinion leader in improving clinical effectiveness. *Social Science and Medicine*, 53, 745–757.

Marmot, M. (2004). Evidence based policy or policy based evidence? *British Medical Journal*, 328, 906–907.

Moore, M. (2005). Break-through innovations and continuous improvement: two different models of innova-tive processes in the public sector. *Public Money and Management*, 25, 43–50.

Nelson, R., Peterhansi, A. and Sampat, B. (2004). Why and how innovations get adopted: a tale of four models. *Industrial and Corporate Change*, 13, 679–699.

Plsek, P. and Greenhalgh, T. (2001). Complexity science: the challenge of complexity in health care. *British Medical Journal*, 323, 625–628.

Robert, G., Greenhalgh, T., Macfarlane, F. and Peacock, R. (2009). *Organisational Factors Influencing Technology Adoption and Assimilation in the NHS: A Systematic Literature Review*. London: National Institute of Health Research.

Rogers, E. (1995). *Diffusion of Innovations*. New York: The Free Press.

Rogers, H. and Copeland, J. (2004). NHS Modernisation Agency's way to improve health care. *British Medical Journal*, 328.

Rogers, H., Maher, L. and Plsek, P.E. (2008). New design rules for driving innovation in access to secondary care in the NHS. *British Medical Journal*, 337, a2321.

Rushmer, R., Kelly, D., Lough, M., Wilkinson, J. and Davies, H. (2004). Introducing the learning practice: the characteristics of learning organizations in primary care. *Journal of Evaluation in Clinical Practice*, 10, 375–386.

Rye, C. and Kimberly, J. (2007). The adoption of innovations by provider organisations in healthcare. *Medical Care Research Review*, 64, 235–278.

Skinner, J.S., Staiger, D.O. and Fisher, E.S. (2006). Is technological change in medicine always worth it? The case of acute myocardial infarction. *Health Affairs*, 25, w34–w47.

Turnbull James, K. (2011). *Leadership in Context: Lessons from New Leadership Theory and Current Leadership Development Practice* [online]. Available at: www.kingsfund.org.uk/leadershipcommission. London: The King's Fund.

Tushman, L. and Anderson, P. (1986). Technological discontinuities and organizational environments. *Administrative Science Quarterly*, 31, 439–465.

West, E., Barron, D., Dowsett, J. and Newton, J. (1999). Hierarchies and cliques in the social networks of health care professionals: implications for the design of dissemination strategies. *Social Science and Medicine*, 48, 633–646.

Worthington, F. (2004). Management, change and culture in the NHS: rhetoric and reality. *Clinician in Management*, 12, 55–67.

36. Exploring the diffusion and sustainability of service innovation in healthcare

Trisha Greenhalgh, Cathy Barton-Sweeney and Fraser Macfarlane

BACKGROUND: SERVICE-LEVEL INNOVATION IN THE NATIONAL HEALTH SERVICE

As James Barlow has described in Chapter 35, the UK National Health Service (NHS) is much exercised with the challenge of innovation. To summarise his message, healthcare is a complex field of practice; innovations which promise to lengthen life or improve its quality are alluring and (often) expensive; and for various reasons many promising innovations have limited uptake and use. The main focus of Barlow's chapter is on drugs, medical devices and technologies for diagnosing or monitoring disease. This chapter considers a somewhat more abstract form of innovation: new service models – that is, new ways of organising and delivering health services which aim to improve such things as the accessibility of care, the experience of patients and staff, and the efficiency (and hence costs) of services.

Back in 2003, the NHS Service Delivery and Organisation Programme funded our team to undertake a systematic literature review on 'Diffusion, spread and sustainability of service innovations'. The impetus for the research call was what Adler et al. had called the 'Six West problem' – that is, that a bright idea for improving service delivery on ward Six West often did not even get as far as ward Five East in the same hospital, let alone spread to other hospitals locally or nationally (Adler, Kwon and Singer 2003). The funders of our review hoped that we would identify tools or techniques which would serve to catalyse the diffusion, spread and sustainability of good ideas emerging either locally or centrally in the NHS (and ideas from outside the NHS which were relevant to its work). Our team reviewed a large and heterogeneous literature, and came to an important conclusion: not only was there no reliable 'winning formula' for spreading and sustaining service-level innovations yet, but there *never would be* such a formula because service innovation is complex and unpredictable (Greenhalgh, Robert, Macfarlane, Bate, Kyriakidou and Peacock 2004). We returned to the same literature several years later, and confirmed that, as we had predicted, the 'winning formula' was still eluding researchers and that dynamic models of adoption and assimilation (which recognised the complexity, unpredictability and contingency of these processes) were beginning to replace predictive models (which only did so in a limited and un-nuanced way) (Robert, Greenhalgh, Macfarlane and Peacock 2010). That recent update identified new theoretical perspectives on the dynamic and recursive (mutually constitutive and reinforcing) relationship between different components of the system.

Our original (somewhat schematic) multi-level model for considering the adoption of service-level innovations by individuals and their assimilation by organisations is shown in Figure 36.1. Broadly, there were seven components to this model. First, there was innovation itself, which would be more likely to be taken up if its attributes in the eyes of potential adopters included such things as relative advantage, low complexity, compatibility with values and ways of working, trialability, observability, potential for reinvention and (for technologies) usability and ease of use. Since by definition, innovations in the organisation and delivery of services are inherently complex, challenging to the status quo and difficult to trial, the odds were already stacked against the innovation process.

Second, there were potential adopters of the innovation. We found no evidence to support the widely used but stereotypical and value-laden terms 'innovators', 'early adopters', 'laggards', and so on. Rather, we found that adoption is an active and complex process in which human agency is central. As we put it at the time:

> People are not passive recipients of innovations. Rather (and to a greater or lesser extent in different persons), they seek innovations, experiment with them, evaluate them, find (or fail to find) meaning in them, develop feelings (positive or negative) about them, challenge them, worry about them, complain about them, 'work around' them, gain experience with them, modify them to fit particular tasks, and try to improve or redesign them – often through dialogue with other users. (Greenhalgh et al. 2004, p. 598)

Third, we confirmed the key role of social influence in individual adoption decisions, especially the role of opinion leaders (high-status peers or experts whom we seek to copy), champions (people who back a product and support its introduction) and boundary-spanners (people who bring ideas and examples from elsewhere).

Fourth, we noted that some organisations are inherently better set up to identify and assimilate innovations than others. Whilst some structural features (such as size and slack resources) contributed to an organisation's innovativeness, far more significant was its absorptive capacity for new knowledge (including its existing stock of knowledge and the suitability of its technical and human knowledge-sharing systems) and its receptive context for change (including good managerial relations and a risk-taking climate).

Fifth, we recognised that even when an organisation supports service-level innovation in general, its readiness for any *particular* innovation depends on the prevailing tension for change, whether supporters of the innovation outnumber its opponents and what some have called 'innovation-system fit'.

Sixth, we identified a large literature on the extra-organisational (outer) context for innovation. In particular, both the external environment (e.g. the prevailing economic and political context) and the behaviour of other organisations in the same sector (and the extent to which the index organisation is linked in with, and influenced by, these) can exert a powerful influence on the organisation-level adoption decision.

Finally, we found much evidence that the process of implementation within the organisation can be done well or badly. Devolution of decision-making to front-line teams, hands-on input from leaders and senior managers, bespoke training (especially of teams in a real-world, on-the-job setting), targeted resources, effective channels (formal and informal) for internal communication, and accurate and timely feedback on progress can all make or break an effort to introduce complex innovation even when there is broad-based support for it (and especially when there isn't).

As Figure 36.1 shows, these seven aspects of organisation-level innovation link with

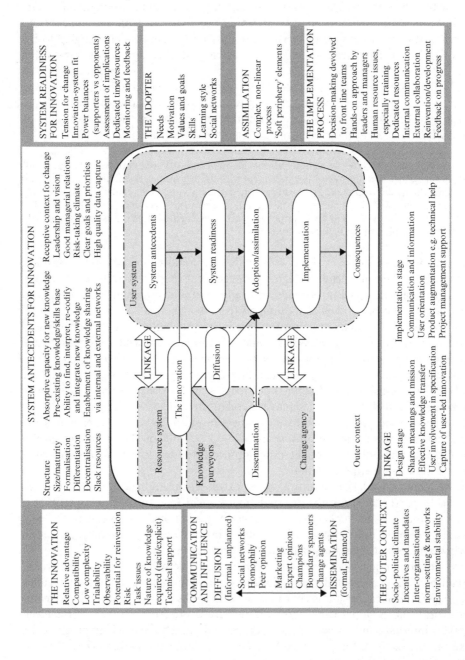

Source: Reproduced with permission from Greenhalgh et al. 2004.

Figure 36.1 Schematic summary of multiple influences on the adoption and assimilation of service-level innovations in healthcare

each other in complex and dynamic ways. Indeed, 'linkage' between the different aspects was as critical to success as any of the components. Back in 2004, we (and the authors on whose work we based our review) were somewhat hazy on what exactly this 'linkage' comprised. Revisiting our findings in retrospect, a significant aspect of the linkage relationship was developing shared perspectives and meaning-systems in relation to an innovation: to what extent do stakeholders mean the same thing when they speak of (say) 'patient-centredness', 'care pathways' or 'success'? Linkage (communication, consultation, dialogue and so on) does not lead automatically to consensus but it may lead to better orientation of one stakeholder to the other(s) and the development of a shared vocabulary with which to negotiate effectively.

Another key feature of Figure 36.1 is the absence of material on sustainability. When we undertook our review in 2003, we found so little material on this aspect of the brief that we decided not to include it in the model. In retrospect, this was partly because we failed to identify some relevant publications at the time, but it was mainly because there was a dearth of primary research on this topic until very recently. The rest of this chapter attempts to redress that deficiency. First, we offer a review of the literature on the sustainability of service-level innovations in healthcare. Secondly, we describe an empirical example from our own research, in which we returned to a field site several years after first describing a large case study of service transformation in healthcare, and considered what, if anything, of the 'innovations' which had been introduced had been sustained. Finally, we contextualise these empirical findings in the light of the literature on sustainability, and consider the implications for theory and method.

SUSTAINABILITY: A LITERATURE REVIEW

Whilst we were correct in 2004 to conclude that there was little published research on sustainability of service-level innovations in healthcare, we were incorrect to conclude that there was little in the sustainability literature from which this field might learn. Several hundred studies were available describing the persistence (or not) of 'healthcare programmes', and more has been published since. Much of this work lies outside the health and medicine literature, partly because programme evaluation as a field of scholarship has emerged more in education, development studies and social policy than health. In addition to the somewhat sparse literature on sustainability of organisational change (especially the diffusion of innovations work described above), health-related studies of persistence/endurance (i.e. sustainability) of programmes come from two areas of research: (a) health promotion and public health programmes in low- and middle-income countries (and deprived regions within high-income countries); and (b) health dividends of community development (Shediac-Rizkallah and Bone 1998; Greenhalgh et al. 2004; Gruen, Elliott, Nolan, Lawton, Parkhill, McLaren and Lavis 2008).

This literature consists mostly of small, parochial and methodologically questionable studies which have been critiqued by others (see reviews cited above). We therefore restricted this current overview to two types of study: (a) systematic reviews; and (b) conceptual models produced as part of a systematic or other scholarly review. We identified these via a keyword search (institutionalisation, routinisation, sustainability) of

Medline and the Social Science Citation Index, followed by citation-tracking of selected papers in Google Scholar.

An early review of health promotion research by Shediac-Rizkallah and Bone (1998) identified three categories of indicators for sustainability of programmes: maintenance of health benefits; institutionalisation or routinisation within an organisation; and capacity-building in the recipient community. These authors also proposed a parallel taxonomy of influences on sustainability: (a) project design and implementation factors; (b) organisational factors; and (c) community and environmental factors. This triad of factors has formed the basis of a number of subsequent reviews. One recent overview, for example, reviewed over 500 studies of programme implementation and added detail to Shediac-Rizkallah and Bone's original triad as well as identifying additional factors, notably the support system for programme activities (i.e. training and technical assistance) (Durlak and DuPre 2008).

Many early reviews talked about steps, stages or phases. For example, Johnson et al.'s 2004 systematic review of 105 disease prevention programmes produced a five-step sustainability planning model (assess, plan, implement, evaluate, reassess/modify), along with attention to building the capacity of the wider system to support sustainable programmes (structures and formal linkages, champion roles and leadership, strategies for acquiring resources, policies and procedures, expertise) and to demonstrating and documenting benefits. In an article entitled 'Is sustainability possible?', Sheirer considered five phases of health programmes: initiation, development, implementation, sustainability (i.e. local continuation) and dissemination (more widespread replication) (Sheirer 2005).

Such 'phase models' have lost favour in the more recent literature, since they tend to imply a linear and predictable sequence (the 'logic model'), and also assume that programmes will be implemented and continued more or less as originally planned. Pluye et al. have declared phase models conceptually misleading, since (they argue) sustainability needs to be built into a programme from the outset (Pluye, Potvin, Denis, Pelletier and Mannoni 2005). They offer evidence that key activities to build sustainability should be commenced at an early stage in the programme, including resource stabilisation (anticipating where ongoing funding might come from and taking steps to mobilise this); risk-taking (encouraging organisational members to try out different ways of routinising tasks and processes, thereby building creativity and confidence); incentives (e.g. rewards or accolades for those who continue programme activities); adaptation (modifying activities to achieve closer fit with local client needs); objectives-matching (modifying either the programme or the context, or both, to achieve closer match with the organisation's objectives and mission); and open communication (measures and structures to enable stakeholders to share ideas, build trust and negotiate interpretations of the programme).

Sustainability is both a process (i.e. a set of activities oriented to maintaining services beyond the original funding period) and an outcome (the actual maintenance of those services), a fact which can lead to confusion between dependent and independent variables (Pluye, Potvin and Denis 2004). Scheirer, Hartling and Hagerman (2008, p. 345) warn against 'using this word [sustainability] as an umbrella term for the complexity of all the prior processes that may be related to the continuation of varying outcomes'.

In terms of institutionalisation, Goodman et al.'s psychometrically validated (but lengthy and little-used) 'Level of Institutionalisation' questionnaire considers: (a) passage (does the innovation feature in formal documentation such as strategic plans?); (b) cycles

(does this happen year-on-year, for example recurring budget line?); and (c) niche saturation (is the innovation integrated in all subsystems in the organisation?) (Goodman,
Mcleroy, Steckler and Hoyle 1993). This instrument reflects these authors' focus on organisational research; hence their central interest in routinisation (incorporation of a particular programme into an organisation's business-as-usual) rather than the more organic
notion of sustainability (meeting the continuing needs of a target population or group).

The landmark work of Shediac-Rizkallah and Bone in 1998 had highlighted the
paradox that if a programme is sustained as originally planned, the system will stop
evolving and adapting. They recommended that rigid definitions (in terms of maintaining
the original goals of the programme) should be rejected in favour of a more organic
notion of continuing, ongoing change in a positive direction. Some aspects of any programme must be abandoned with time, while others must expand and spread. Thus,
evaluating sustainability requires complex judgements about the evolving programme-
in-context.

In 2008, the Lancet published a systematic review of conceptual models and empirical
studies of health programme sustainability (Gruen et al. 2008). They noted a shift in the
literature from somewhat static models focused on 'factors' towards more dynamic
models which explored the evolving relationships and interdependencies in a complex
system. The narrative and holistic definitions of sustainability which they offered (e.g.
'The ability of a project to function effectively, for the foreseeable future, with high treatment coverage, integrated into available health care services, with strong community
ownership using resources mobilised by the community and government' – p. 1580) arguably offer greater analytical potential than the lists of individual variables linked in linear
sequence preferred by most earlier publications.

Gruen et al. identified three domains to be considered in a dynamic analysis of sustainability: health status of the population; programme drivers, both positive and negative
(especially whether alignments between stakeholders such as sponsors, project managers,
policymakers and community leaders are supportive); and programme components and
infrastructure. They also identified four levels at which interventions might be targeted
to promote sustainability: individual (e.g. education and training), organisational (e.g.
policies and practices), community (e.g. social action to create new partnerships and
redistribute resources) and system (e.g. social advocacy for legislative change). Their
dynamic model for considering programme sustainability is reproduced (slightly adapted)
in Figure 36.2.

If we take a dynamic view, the primary focus for a study of sustainability is not the
hexagons in Figure 36.1 but the double-headed arrows. Problem definition is how different stakeholders define and interpret the health concern – and the extent to which there
is consensus (or at least, accommodation – that is, acknowledgement of and some adaptation to others' positions) on the nature and priority of the problems to be addressed.
The quality cycle is the link between the programme and the health concern; it includes
issues such as the validity of metrics chosen, the consistency and rigour with which they
are applied, the robustness of the plan–do–study–act cycle and the tightness of feedback
loops (formal and informal) intended to monitor the programme. Political economy is
how stakeholders interact with the programme and vice versa. It includes the various
ways in which the programme is interpreted and framed; struggles over competing values
or priorities; the micro-politics of integrating the programme into established structures

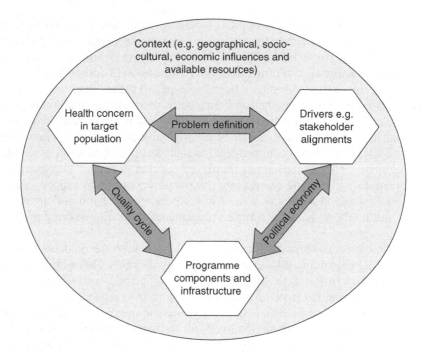

Source: Adapted from Gruen et al. 2008.

Figure 36.2   Dynamic model of health programme sustainability

and systems; and how efforts to strengthen key institutions (e.g. local communities, third-sector partners) play out on the ground.

Whereas the quality cycle is a relatively 'hard' construct oriented to metrics and measurement, both problem definition and political economy are somewhat 'soft' constructs – that is, they are, to a large extent, what the programme's various stakeholders say or perceive they are. It follows that, in addition to a robust quality cycle, sustainability of a programme requires attention to the way it is framed and the profile it has within the local health economy and community. These 'soft' dimensions may be particularly significant when the programme's goals are abstract (e.g. 'promote patient-centred services') and hard to capture in simple metrics.

In relation to a women's health programme with dozens of component projects, for example, Rogers et al. proposed an organic definition of sustainability ('Michigan model') with a view to producing 'a solid, sustainable infrastructure that allows the program to grow into new areas, expand existing initiatives, and continue to meet the needs of the community and the goals of the faculty without heavy reliance on outside funding and support' (Rogers, Johnson, Warner, Thorson, and Punch 2007, p. 920). Their three-pronged approach comprised institutional championing (named individuals in strategic positions making a case for the programme within key decision-making bodies); unified vision (a compelling, over-arching narrative of what is being done and why, told and re-told in both formal and informal spaces); and demonstrated value (measures and metrics of 'hard' benefits).

Researchers who have embraced the shift from static to dynamic conceptualisations of sustainability have mostly considered this challenge in ecological terms (i.e. in terms of the programme's organic growth, adaptation and embedding in the local health economy) or in terms of narrative and sense-making. Some, however, have drawn on more radical theories and conceptual models. One such approach, actor-network theory, considers people and technologies as linked in ever-changing and inherently unstable socio-technical networks (Bisset and Potvin 2007). A programme is sustained when a critical alignment of people and technologies becomes stabilised – and this tends to happen when the 'soft', human elements of the programme (e.g. stakeholders' differing interpretations, their feelings about the programme and the power distribution between them) align with 'hard', technical and procedural elements (components of the programme and impact metrics).

Others have argued, again from an actor-network theory perspective, that the litera-ture on sustainability exhibits a strong bias towards analysing continuity and change in the technical aspects of a programme at the expense of a systematic analysis of the human components of the socio-technical network (Bisset and Potvin 2007). They describe health programmes as 'negotiated spaces' and point out that the contestations and (some-times) conflicts between stakeholders have been inadequately researched. To redress this balance, they propose the study of 'Program genealogy [which] would reveal those inter-ests and negotiation bouts that critically oriented program implementation.' An actor-network analysis of programme genealogy would draw out the tensions between (on the one hand) dialectically changing human interests and power balances and (on the other hand) the structural and technical components of the programme.

In sum, the dynamic models reviewed briefly above suggest that the first task in analys-ing the sustainability of a programme would be to: (a) outline the health concern, the stakeholder alignments and the programme components (i.e. the hexagons in Figure 36.1); (b) consider the dynamic issues of problem definition (i.e. how stakeholders define the health concern), quality cycle (i.e. how closely the programme components match the health concern) and political economy (i.e. how stakeholder alignments play out in rela-tion to the programme) and how all these dynamic influences change over time; and (c) assess the level of stability (but, importantly, not of stasis) in the ever-changing socio-technical network which links problem definition, quality cycle and political economy. Below, we describe an empirical study and present a selection of key findings analysed through this multi-level analytical lens.

CASE STUDY: THE MODERNISATION INITIATIVE 2003–07 AND 2010–11

Back in 2003, we were awarded a contract to evaluate a four-year transformational change effort in London, UK. The Modernisation Initiative, as it was called, covered three diverse programmes of work in stroke, kidney and sexual health services. It involved both primary and secondary care providers in the local NHS as well as third-sector part-ners, and occurred in the context of a multi-ethnic, inner-city population with high turnover and multiple health and social care needs. In late 2010, we were approached by the funder of that initiative (Guys and St Thomas' Charity) and invited to bid for a unique opportunity – to return to the case and see what (if anything) had been sustained. Our brief was to advise the Charity on whether the investment of £15 million for the change effort (and some £400,000 for the original evaluation) had been worthwhile.

At the time of the initial evaluation, the Modernisation Initiative was seen by our team and by the academic community more widely as an important example of a large-scale service transformation effort from which transferable lessons about innovation and change in public-sector healthcare might be learnt. The Charity's desire to assess whether the gains had been sustained was matched by a question being asked by academics and evaluation scholars: 'Given the inherent tension between innovation (discontinuous change from previous practice) and sustainability (persistence of previous practice), what exactly do we mean by the "sustainability" of a complex service innovation – and how might we measure this?'

In our final report submitted in 2008 to the Charity's trustees on the Modernisation Initiative, we had concluded that it had been a complex and ambitious collaborative effort which appeared to have led to an impressive range of local impacts, though some stakeholders said these would have happened anyway (Greenhalgh, Humphrey, Hughes, Macfarlane, Butler, Connell and Pawson 2008). Over the lifetime of the Modernisation Initiative, various projects and sub-projects had developed, fed into one another and evolved over time, such that plans set out in early strategy documents had morphed, merged and sometimes been abandoned altogether. New initiatives had taken the programme in directions not initially foreseen or planned for. Performance metrics had been difficult to apply because of the programme's organic nature and the dynamic context of structural and policy changes in the NHS.

When we wrote up our initial evaluation for an academic audience, we identified six broad change mechanisms which had underpinned the transformational change effort: (1) integrating services across providers; (2) finding and using evidence (including research evidence, routinely collected data such as audits, and surveys of the patient experience); (3) involving service users in the transformational change process (e.g. on project steering groups, as teachers and peer supporters, and as 'mystery shoppers'); (4) supporting self care in both acute and chronic illness; (5) developing the workforce; and (6) extending the range of services (Greenhalgh, Humphrey, Hughes, Macfarlane, Butler, and Pawson 2009; Macfarlane, Greenhalgh, Humphrey, Hughes, Butler, and Pawson 2011). Involvement of service users was a particularly prominent mechanism of change, and one with which the Charity and other stakeholders had sought to 'brand' the programme. More than anything else, the Modernisation Initiative had been *about* involving service users (i.e. patients and carers) in the transformation process; changing the hearts and minds of managers and front-line staff so as to place the user at the centre of the service model; and measuring success in terms of what mattered most to the user (Greenhalgh 2009; Greenhalgh, Humphrey and Woodard 2010).

The nine-month study reported here was a follow-up to the original evaluation, commissioned by competitive tender and conducted between September 2010 and May 2011. It aimed to assess the 'lasting impact' of the Modernisation Initiative. Specifically, we sought to: (a) review gains in relation to original policies and business plans; (b) explore the tension between sustaining achievements of past projects and continuing evolution of services; (c) identify unintended consequences, both positive and negative; and (d) make recommendations to the Charity for future investments.

The study design was mixed-method organisational case study, following Stake's 'naturalistic' approach (Stake 2005). TG and FM had been part of the original evaluation team; CB-S was a new member whose 'naïve' perspective helped balance the other researchers' long familiarity with the programme and staff. The evaluation had a lay chair, JH (see Acknowledgements), a service user who had originally been recruited to chair one of the project management groups of the Modernisation Initiative. We built the case study from four data sources: (a) in-depth semi-structured interviews with 50 key stakeholders across acute and community services (four Charity, five third-sector, five directors and senior programme managers of the Modernisation Initiative, seven middle managers, 10 doctors, six nurses, three physiotherapists, six service users, two commissioners and two other); (b) documents (business plans, strategies, internal evaluations, audits, commissioning plans before and after the change period, financial reports and one independent report by a management consultancy); (c) ethnographic observation in six visits to the services; and (d) a questionnaire survey to 48 service users.

The data we collected were mostly qualitative (free text) and supplemented by descriptive statistics already produced by others (e.g. in audits and annual reports). Free text data were analysed using the framework approach to thematic analysis (Ritchie and Spencer 1994), informed by the theoretical model of sustainability derived from the literature described above. We used narrative to synthesise qualitative and quantitative findings into a coherent, reflexive account which teased out and sought to explain ambiguities, inconsistencies and unforeseen consequences. All interviewees were offered a draft copy of the final report to comment on, highlighting their own contributions to it, and the report modified in response to feedback. Thirty-three of the 50 took us up on this offer, added factual details and/or made minor changes of emphasis in quotes attributed to them.

Main Findings

In this follow-on evaluation, we found a number of service models and practices which had begun under the Modernisation Initiative in 2004–08 and which were still part of mainstream business-as-usual three years after the funding period had ended; examples of these are described in detail in a separate report (Greenhalgh, Macfarlane, Barton-Sweeney and Hope 2011). They included radically streamlined patient pathways in all services; a 'holistic' approach to service provision (e.g. in sexual health, contraception and sexually transmitted infections managed in a one-stop shop); a community focus (e.g. strengthened early supported discharge for stroke patients along with 'in-reach' of community support teams to the acute service); and more patient-centred services (e.g. self-management on haemodialysis units, an active living kidney donor programme, and end-of-life care for those choosing to withdraw from dialysis). Many though not all these changes were underpinned by new business models such as revised financial flows and mainstreamed staff posts. But it was impossible confidently to assign particular hard patient outcomes to the programme of transformational change that had been so generously funded several years earlier.

Indeed, given the prevailing economic downturn, the high local population turnover (hence, changes in demographics and patterns of health need), the turbulent policy context which characterised the UK NHS in 2003–11, the multiple sub-projects in the original Modernisation Initiative and the extent to which their goals and direction changed even before the funding period had ended, it would have been possible to construct a set of metrics which demonstrated either 'success' or 'failure' of the initiative depending on how the story was framed. As other researchers had found before us, large-scale service innovation initiatives in the real world rarely, if ever, have direct, causal links with particular outcome metrics years later (Johnson et al. 2004; Bisset and Potvin 2007; Rogers et al. 2007; Sheirer, Hartling and Hagerman 2008). As the theoretical literature reviewed above suggests, searching for linear links between resource inputs and sustained service models or patient outcomes would have been an impoverished way of analysing this complex initiative.

The first question we asked our 50 stakeholders was 'What was the Modernisation Initiative?' Not a single one responded by naming specific projects or service models or by referring to outcome metrics. Nor did they equate the initiative with the 'modernisation toolkit' which had been widely used in the original work (such as the plan–do–study–act cycle and statistical techniques for analysing demand and capacity in real time), or with the new-blood service improvement facilitators who had been skilled in using these tools and training others to use them. Rather, they recalled the initiative in abstract and strongly value-driven terms, as a coming-together of people and resources in a way that built relationships, developed a common sense of purpose and resulted in worthwhile, patient-relevant changes to services. One, for example, described the Modernisation Initiative as 'an opportunity to bring together people with power, authority and money in a way that would make a difference' (Primary Care Trust manager, 14); another as 'reform, redesign, fresh thinking, with a focus on quality' (Primary Care Trust commissioner, 40).

That is not to say that stakeholders had forgotten the numerous projects which had been funded under this major programme of work – but that the specific projects were seen as secondary to the development of an ongoing culture of improvement and a corresponding skill base across the local health system. Indeed, some respondents recalled a shift away from specific, concrete projects towards a more abstract change in attitudes and ways of working as the Modernisation Initiative unfolded:

> It wasn't ultimately about having money to build a snazzy new research facility. The original proposal was a Kidney Research Institute with a glass front on the South Bank and we moved away from that to understand that we could do more by involving our service users in improving the service we currently had. (Programme manager, 10).

Importantly, the idea of transformational, patient-centred change was viewed by our respondents not as an official mission statement or objective but as a collective undertaking that was linked to personal identity and shared sense of purpose, not dissimilar from a social movement (Bate Robert and Bevan 2004). Several described having 'thrown' themselves into the work ('It was five years of my life' – programme manager, 05) and as having been changed both personally and professionally by the experience.

In the light of this finding (which initially surprised us), it is worth revisiting one widely cited definition of an innovation: 'an idea, practice or object which is perceived as new in the minds of potential adopters' (Rogers 2003, p. 12). Three years after the funding period had ended, it was the enacted *idea* of transformational change which was recalled by stakeholders as the defining feature of the Modernisation Initiative. If innovation is defined in this abstract and radical way, it follows that its sustainability would be demonstrated if such things as 'reform', 'redesign' and 'fresh thinking' were still part of the culture of the health system and being enacted and driven by staff and service users. If this were the case, we should be less concerned to report that service model or patient pathway X was still in existence than that the *process* of improvement, and a broad-based commitment to that improvement, was still business-as-usual.

Bearing in mind that a generous but time-limited funding stream had now ended and a deep economic recession was occurring, there was evidence that the attitudes, commitments and ways of working which had been introduced as the Modernisation Initiative had persisted, sometimes in attenuated form:

> We have databases, we use them all the time. Run charts for the purposes of service improvement, we look at those every week but [we now take] less of a wider overview. In the MI [Modernisation Initiative] there was a system to do it for you and you had paid time to do it, the impetus to do it was built into the system, but we did know we had to continue doing it, even though we haven't got lots of money and protected time. (Clinical champion, sexual health, 11)

The governance structure of the Modernisation Initiative (the Modernisation Board and various project management groups) had been disbanded when the funding period ended, though some members from these formal groups were subsequently accommodated in other cross-organisational governance structures such as commissioning boards. But when we asked participants what they felt had been sustained, few spoke of this formal infrastructure. Rather, the commonest response to our question was in terms of interpersonal relationships ('I think I and my colleagues have the best working relationships, across providers and organisations in London' – clinical champion in sexual health, 30, in response to question 'What has been sustained?'). They described themselves as being on 'first-name terms' and able to 'pick up the phone' to colleagues in other organisations. They also spoke of having a shared sense of what the health problems in the local health economy were – and as continuing to get together periodically to make sense of new problems as they arose.

Interestingly, bringing staff and service users together across organisations (including two hospital trusts with a history of poor relationships) to plan services and spearhead improvements had been viewed at the time as a luxury only affordable because of the dedicated funding. However, the sustained efficiency gains from whole-pathway streamlining of services were considered to be so great that 'bringing people together' was now seen as a sound investment in its own right: 'The interesting thing is that back then it [working together across organisations] was seen as very nice and that it helped patients, but it has now become a business need' (director, Modernisation Initiative, 06).

The story of ongoing patient-centred improvement driven by warm relationships, a shared sense of purpose and an ongoing process of collective sense-making was not, however, universally told – and herein lie many of the most significant insights of this study. An important source of data in qualitative research is 'disconfirming cases' – individuals or teams who give different viewpoints or which do not fit the model. A handful of dissenters viewed the Modernisation Initiative very differently from the preceding descriptions. Some of these were interviewed directly; others were unavailable for interview and their perspective was gained indirectly from documentary sources such as correspondence and minutes of meetings. These dissenters did not mention the sense of energy and shared purpose described so enthusiastically by others in our sample; they did not view the orientation to the user perspective as an unproblematic driver of positive change; and they felt that the early relationship-building groundwork which others had identified as essential to the programme's long-term success had been a cosmetic exercise which had borne little fruit.

Most dissenters self-identified as not having bought into the Modernisation Initiative's values or goals and were identified by some others as 'difficult to work with'. All who commented attributed these challenges mainly to differences in personalities and/or working styles. Our own analysis affirmed these interpretations but also identified three other key issues which map broadly to the double-headed arrows in Figure 36.1: (a) differences in how stakeholders perceived the health need; (b) differences in how they perceived the quality cycle; and (c) political economy – that is, conflicts in stakeholder values and the micro-politics of their involvement with the programme (in particular, what each stood to gain or lose). Below, we offer two examples of these conflicting perspectives.

In the stroke programme, all stakeholders were broadly agreed on the need for rapid, evidence-based care in acute stroke (such as brain scanning and thrombolysis) to maximise physiological preconditions for recovery, followed by intensive rehabilitation with ongoing support for the patient and their family in the home and community. Co-ordination between acute and community stroke services, prompt handovers and seamless transfer of care were agreed to be key. But stakeholders did not agree, either at the time of the funded programme or in retrospect, on how this challenge should be addressed. Some prominent dissenters in our sample considered that high-quality evidence had already been available in the form of research findings and that this could have been identified and put into practice: 'the MI [Modernisation Initiative stroke] team were not aware of the existing evidence and so chose to use a non-evidence based model or to try and create their own model' (dissenting senior doctor, source code withheld).

In contrast, those who were positive about the Modernisation Initiative highlighted the regular 'sharing the learning' events (informal, facilitated discussions about what was happening) which had linked acute and community staff; they also emphasised the value of local audits and surveys of staff and patient opinion. One example mentioned by several of our interviewees was that, in the early stages of the programme, analysis had revealed the 'fact' (presumably derived from a local audit) that only 12 per cent of speech therapist time was actually spent in patient-facing activities. This had been seen as shocking at the time and was recalled as a powerful motivator for change. No external (research) evidence or benchmark was considered necessary.

This example reveals fundamental differences within the stroke programme in stakeholders' perceptions about the nature of knowledge and the value placed on different types of evidence. The dissenters considered knowledge to be objective, context-free, value-neutral and existing independently of the knower – what has been called 'Mode 1 knowledge' (Gibbons, Limoges, Nowotny and Schwartzman 1994). They found it difficult to view 'evidence' as anything other than the kind of systematically collected, before-and-after data which might form the basis of a research paper. Most stakeholders, however, saw the most useful knowledge about the programme as at least partly subjective, context-specific, value-laden and (most importantly perhaps) socially shared – what has been called 'Mode 2 knowledge' (Gibbons et al. 1994). These people talked of 'evidence' as something that had been locally generated, based on local data, and which was repeatedly circulated and discussed amongst key participants within the stroke project.

Most stakeholders in the stroke programme depicted quality improvement and service transformation as linked to personal identity and achieved via 'soft' activities such as building relationships, gaining understanding of others' perspectives and reflecting on values. Dissenters, in contrast, portrayed this process in technical and managerial terms as 'models' to be 'implemented'. They saw the infrastructure needed for change as structural, procedural and readily transferable: 'what the Charity should fund is an infrastructure generically to modernise any service that comes along with an idea' (dissenting senior doctor, source code withheld).

It is also worth examining the political economy of knowledge claims in the stroke programme. The stroke programme manager and many of the community staff were experienced NHS employees whose main strengths were their extensive experience and contacts and their intuitive knowledge of local ways of working. The dissenters included three senior staff on academic contracts (both clinical and non-clinical) who had published widely in the academic literature and sat on national steering groups for evidence-based practice in stroke care. Their units attracted considerable research income for randomised trials, cohort studies and qualitative studies of the user experience, all of which were oriented to producing generalisable lessons intended for an international (and predominantly academic) audience. Their bids to the Modernisation Initiative Board for funding from the £5 million allocated for stroke care had included a number of work packages framed explicitly as research. Another dissenter, who represented a third-sector charity, had resigned from the programme back in 2005 because of the 'politics' (specifically, because substantial amounts of the funding were said to be being channelled into research projects within the NHS acute sector).

All this made for what Bisset and Potvin (2007) would call an unstable actor-network in the stroke programme. Not only were there deep schisms in the alignments of human interests and values, but there were also (at least in the perception of some of the people we interviewed) differences in these stakeholders' power to mobilise resources. Whilst a great deal was achieved in the stroke programme and one or two new service models appear to have been sustained, we cautiously conclude that the instability of the network may be limiting the capacity for ongoing, whole-system innovation in this complex service area.

Another example of an unstable network for sustainability was the sexual health programme. In its early days (2003–04), stakeholders – who included general practice, community-based family planning and sexually transmitted infection clinics, hospital-based genito-urinary medicine (GUM) specialists and a wide range of third-sector organisations including women's rights groups, sexual minorities and faith groups – struggled to gain alignment on what the key health concerns were. Some hospital consultants (who, as it turned out, became the minority dissenters in this programme) had articulated the problem in terms of a disease model, and sought a conventional 'referral pyramid' with general practitioners and nurses dealing with 'mild cases' and referring 'complex cases' to secondary care, all supported by a common guideline. Some of these consultants argued for funding to be put into a specialist institute oriented to sexually transmitted infections and considered 'family planning' to be a different specialty.

But community staff and many third-sector groups had viewed the problem very differently – in what they called 'holistic' terms. They had rejected the term 'genito-urinary medicine' as non-holistic and took the position that 'sexual health services' (addressing illness, risk behaviour *and* contraception) should be provided by a single care provider in a way that minimised the number of contacts the patient needed to make with the healthcare system. They had emphasised, from a critical and feminist perspective, that women seeking sexual health services may be in coercive relationships and/or socially excluded. They had felt that 're-branding' (i.e. de-stigmatisation) of the service and reducing waiting times were key to increasing its accessibility to vulnerable groups such as teenagers and minority ethnic groups. They had also proposed creating an infrastructure for supporting 'self-management' of acute sexual health problems (e.g. taking and labelling one's own specimens without involvement of a doctor or nurse) so as to encourage vulnerable groups to attend clinics in the knowledge that they would not need to be questioned or examined by clinicians in white coats.

Between 2004 and 2008, the sexual health programme undertook radical restructuring of services, introduced new staff roles (such as healthcare assistants in a 'meeting and greeting' role), developed new 'holistic' training and qualifications (covering family planning and sexually transmitted infections), trained and incentivised GPs and pharmacists to offer sexually transmitted infection testing, and invested heavily in redesign of community sexual health clinics. Our follow-up evaluation showed that the rebranded (and considerably more streamlined) service was indeed very popular with younger people and that the under-18 pregnancy rate (which had been the worst in the country before the initiative began) remained low, though the very popularity of the service meant that waiting times were as bad as ever (and in some cases had got worse). However, the 'self-management' options were little used, especially by those clients considered most vulnerable ('The clients invariably label things incorrectly and then the labs, who understandably are extremely strict, can't test the sample. And do you really want a 16-year-old going out unsupported after having a positive pregnancy test?' – service manager, community sexual health, 45).

We also learnt that the dissenting GUM consultants, whose early vote of no confidence in the community-based sexual health team had been rejected by the Modernisation Initiative Board, had been preparing their own separate bid to a different funder for an 'HIV institute' based in the community. This would be disease-focused, consultant-led and run along traditional lines with a referral pyramid and a biomedical research agenda. It would redress what some of them felt was an over-emphasis on the socio-emotional problems of women and bring the physical/medical problems of a mostly male cohort of HIV positive patients back into the frame. Whilst some felt that this initiative was complementary to rather than conflicting with the efforts to establish community-based acute sexual health services, others framed it as symptomatic of continuing deep schisms across the service.

The follow-up of the sexual health Modernisation Initiative thus suggests another unstable actor-network characterised by fundamental differences in interests and values amongst key human stakeholders. At the time of the original Modernisation Initiative, one group (this time the community-based team driven by an emphasis on the social determinants of health and a feminist agenda) had been able to exert power over rival groups in defining the health need and mobilising resources. However, despite impressive short-term progress and popular new service models, the long-term sustainability of the innovative approach introduced in 2004–08 is by no means secure. As one interviewee put it: 'You can't expect people to help design a system that will do them out of a job' (community clinician, 46).

In both the above examples, the instability of the socio-technical network around the 'modernised' service may have been exacerbated by the limited availability of reliable and agreed data on key aspects of performance of the service. Absence of a fixed denominator (because of a mobile population and rapidly changing patterns of health need over time), lack of granularity (i.e. performance of subunits could not be teased out from a wider picture) and missing data (because staff charged with collecting it or assuring its quality were not in post) meant that the meaning and significance of particular measures and metrics remained highly contested both during and after the funding period. This can be explained theoretically from an actor-network perspective in that components of the network which are durable (such as established and agreed performance metrics) can add significant stability over and above the softer components such as opinions, perceptions and relationships.

Another aspect of 'durable' components of the network is contracts and commissioning plans. In the Modernisation Initiative, a significant contributor to instability of the network was the ambiguous position of commissioners and the commissioning process. This finding initially emerged as another discrepancy in our interview data, with some participants considering that commissioners had had early and extensive input whilst others considered their input to have been late and limited. It is worth unpacking these conflicting perspectives.

Because of its external funding and innovative ethos, the Modernisation Initiative had a somewhat 'offshore' status within which much creative work to create new service models was made possible. The original vision from the Charity was that commissioners would later adopt those models which were shown to be more efficient, effective and appropriate than current practice. This framing – and the root of the ambiguity – implied that 'service models' were readily separable from the context of their development and could be unproblematically mainstreamed in future commissioning rounds. Participants who had worked for the Modernisation Initiative recalled that work with commissioners was begun at a relatively early stage to set such a chain of events in motion:

> In terms of sustainability, we did a phenomenal amount of work. Eighteen months after the onset, I asked the Programme Managers to go through every project in their portfolio and ascertain if, where and how successful they were. Projects were then categorised, for instance those projects that had achieved the tipping point, those that required further work, internal and system projects, those that required money and those which we needed to stop. Then I identified where money might need shifting within the pathway and worked to convince commissioners that savings should be invested to do something else in the pathway. In some cases they could get half the outcome again within the same financial envelope. (Modernisation Initiative director, 06)

But the commissioners themselves did not share this framing – and indeed they viewed it as somewhat naïve. Services, they said, had been wrongly treated as a 'package' that could be 'picked up' by providers. They felt that new service models would have been more sustainable had commissioners been more actively involved right from the planning stage, because commissioning is a highly skilled and embedded process involving the building-in of financial levers and incentives in a way that has to be *co-designed* alongside the service models themselves. A good example of this is the difference between a service which is deemed (in general terms) 'cost-effective' and one which generates cost savings in a particular commissioning context:

> The MI needed to be based on service redesign, change management and financial incentives. The last of these came in very late – in phase 3 – and wasn't really addressed. . . . Understanding the difference between a cost and a price has been a massive difficulty. So from an academic point of view, often people are looking at a cost–benefit analysis in regards to cost, but the incentive is about *price*. . . . There's a difference between a cost–benefit analysis and understanding the market we're in. And I still don't think we've really grasped the difference. So something can make absolute sense on a 'cost' basis, but make no sense in the way we manage the system. (Primary Care Trust commissioner, 27)

In other words, commissioners felt that there was an over-emphasis on 'change management', which they felt had happened at the expense of a nuanced understanding of the (sometimes complex) financial levers and incentives that would need to be built into the services to ensure that the models made local business sense. By the time commissioners became actively involved (as opposed to just having a seat on the project management group), it was too late for many of these ideas to be successfully incorporated. This was perhaps best illustrated by a description by an ex-Modernisation Initiative manager of their new job in a different locality:

> I'm now doing a similar piece of work (at X Primary Care Trust), it's more embedded in contracts, in a way that the MI [Modernisation Initiative] wasn't. The MI was like, we're doing this because we've got an external source of funding. In the one I'm doing now, the contracts have changed, the service specifications have all been agreed, commissioning is more the driver in terms of what's wanted. . . . The patient experience *is* in there, but it's balanced across a range of things. The user experience really has to fit too with the commissioning process, with financial flows, with estates, with care outside hospital, with what it's possible to provide. To be honest the work seems more embedded here in the organisation's goals. The MI was allowed to step outside the organisation's goals, but when we tried to step back in, it was difficult. (Modernisation Initiative programme manager, 13)

The embeddedness of service models – specifically, their intricate dependence on particular framings of the health need, particular relationships and ways of working, and particular service agreements and financial flows – explains why spread of these models beyond the Modernisation Initiative was sometimes but not always problematic. On the one hand, many of the flagship projects within the Modernisation Initiative acquired a kind of unofficial 'Beacon' status, attracting teams from elsewhere who were actively seeking to make similar innovations in their own service and who successfully replicated the models (sometimes with adaptation) in new settings. For example, active involvement of patients in service evaluation and redesign in kidney services attracted much interest and was adopted in many other centres within and beyond the UK. On the other hand, some service models proved extremely resistant to spread even at a local level. For example, a third-sector-led peer support programme which had been worked up and refined in one borough ran into problems when efforts were made to extend it to an adjacent borough:

Working in [borough X] was particularly difficult and I feel it never really succeeded. I had no contacts within the borough and so had to develop all the relationships afresh. I hadn't worked with the purchasers before, and relationships with the [Primary Care Trust] are *still* non-existent. I hadn't anticipated how difficult it would be to work across the two boroughs. (Third-sector partner which took over a peer support service spanning two boroughs, only one of which the organisation had worked with previously, 18)

Note that the speaker expresses the difficulty mainly in terms of the impossibility of introducing a cross-sector service model in the absence of warm relationships and historical patterns of working. The apparent paradox that teams sometimes came from distant settings and adopted the model more readily than the adjacent borough may be explained by the fact that the warm relationships were already present – an explanation which resonates with previous research into the Beacon scheme (Rashman and Hartley 2002).

DISCUSSION

In this chapter, we have described a three-year follow-up of a complex transformational change effort and explored the issue of sustainability from both theoretical and empirical perspectives. We have noted the inherent tension between innovation (discontinuous change from previous practice) and sustainability (persistence of previous practice). Our findings support a number of conclusions.

First, in the context of a large-scale healthcare transformation initiative taking place at a time of high environmental turbulence, rapid population turnover (hence, changing demographics and patterns of need), multiple external policy initiatives and a complex and changing service infrastructure, all of which militate against the long-term continuation or relevance of any particular innovation, a 'logic model' becomes absurd. To define success in terms of persistence of projects or service models commenced many years previously would be to create an oxymoron in which innovation is necessarily couched in the past tense. In such circumstances, the focus must shift from innovation as noun (referring to a specific project) to innovation as verb (referring to a culture and practice of innovativeness). Sustainability can then be productively reframed as: (a) persistence of the *idea* of continuous, patient-relevant service improvement; (b) endurance of the values, practical techniques, interpersonal and intersectoral relationships, and resource streams underpinning this idea; and (c) ongoing efforts to realise that goal.

Second, we have affirmed work by previous scholars who argued that much analytical purchase is gained by going beyond a static conceptualisation of sustainability in terms of 'project/programme factors', 'organisational factors' and 'environmental factors', or in terms of 'phases' in the institutionalisation of a particular innovation, and instead considering the *dynamic* interplay of multiple interdependent influences which evolve over time. In particular, the programme components, targeted health concerns and stakeholder alignments of a complex change effort must be analysed in terms of the continuously changing ways in which they link with and influence one another. Three questions must be asked, repeatedly over time as the programme evolves: (a) how do stakeholders define the health concern and what are the key points of consensus and contestation among them?; (b) to what extent do the programme components and infrastructure remain aligned to the priority health concerns in a tight quality cycle?; and (c) whose interests are served by the programme and how are the micro-politics of resource allocation playing out?

Third, our findings have illustrated the well-documented paradox in the literature between innovation and sustainability: the 'offshore' nature of the Modernisation Initiative (which made it easier to introduce and test new service models across organisations and sectors) also made it *more* difficult to embed those models in the business-as-usual of the NHS. Despite a relatively high level of awareness of the danger of focusing on the former at the expense of the latter, all stakeholders (including the Charity, the Modernisation Board and the project teams) were swept up in the short-term task of developing new service models, experimenting with what 'worked' and achieving change. To some extent, we were also guilty of pro-innovation bias in our initial evaluation and academic analysis, which used a realist framework to identify six 'mechanisms of change'. We did at the time tentatively identify some stakeholder alignments which we felt would be necessary to sustain the change, but we did not explore these in detail (or publish them).

Fourth, this study appears to confirm that only limited insights can be gained from analysing the 'hard' components of a programme such as artefacts (business plans, commissioning plans, contracts and so on) and governance arrangements (boards, committees) in isolation from the historical, economic, socio-cultural and interpersonal influences which gave rise to them and within which they acquire local meaning and significance. Furthermore, whilst many of these hard elements of the socio-technical network are crucial to its stability, and hence to sustainability of innovations (and, more importantly, of innovativeness), it may be difficult or impossible to build in such elements unless they are negotiated and renegotiated in real time as the programme takes shape. For this reason, calls by stakeholders trained in the tradition of evidence-based medicine for 'transferable models' and a 'generic infrastructure for implementation' will be difficult if not impossible to operationalise.

Fifth, the knowledge needed to sustain complex service innovations which span multiple organisations and sectors appears to a large extent to be tied to individuals, embedded in relationships and strongly value-laden. That key individuals remain in the health economy (even if their roles and job titles have changed) and that interpersonal relationships remain 'warm' means not only that the informal wheels are oiled for further innovation and adaptation (because, for example, a shared sense of priorities, needs and potential solutions is continually being negotiated), but also that, despite the complexities of the health economy, new governance arrangements and business plans which cut across organisational and sectoral boundaries can be initiated or reassembled relatively swiftly when the need arises.

In conclusion, our team has covered a great deal of ground since 2003 when we embarked on two studies – an empirical study of large-scale transformational change and a systematic review of diffusion, spread and sustainability of service-level innovation. Our early work (both primary and secondary) focused primarily on the process of innovation and the extent to which change was achieved, but was hazy about how 'sustainability' should be defined, measured or promoted. More recently, we have revisited both our empirical case study and our literature review. We have begun to make sense of the empirical and theoretical literature on sustainability, to extract sophisticated insights from this literature and to apply these to our own empirical findings. We have found it helpful to focus less on factors, components and prediction than on relationships, interactions and explanations – and how the latter change over time.

Our findings suggest that the research agenda on sustainability needs to rise above the deterministic questions, bounded focus and implicit logic models that can give a research proposal the appearance of robustness. A few teams have already gone beyond researching the 'factors' that predict sustainability of service-level innovations and sought to develop ways of studying the dynamic interactions, interdependencies and socio-technical complexities that account for the unfolding fortunes of healthcare programmes (Pluye, Potvin and Denis 2004; Pluye et al. 2005; Scheirer 2005; Bisset and Potvin 2007; Gruen et al. 2008). But this emerging paradigm, at whose heart is a challenge both ontological (what is the nature of reality?) and epistemological (how might we know that reality?), is in its infancy and faces considerable resistance from the rationalist mindset which dominates much (though not all) health services research. This paradigm needs to be nurtured and extended.

ACKNOWLEDGEMENTS

We are grateful to Guys and St Thomas' Charity for research funding. We thank Jonathon Hope who chaired the steering group for this study and students David Hill, Fatima Atif and Rob Macfarlane who assisted with data collection.

REFERENCES

Adler, P.S., Kwon, S.-W. and Singer, J.M.K. (2003). *The 'Six West' Problem: Professionals and the Intraorganizational Diffusion of Innovations, with Particular Reference to the Case of Hospitals.* Working Paper 3-15. Marshall School of Business, University of Southern California.

Bate, S.P., Robert, G. and Bevan, H. (2004). The next phase of healthcare improvement: what can we learn from social movements? *Quality and Safety in Health Care,* 13, 62–66.

Bisset, S. and Potvin, L. (2007). Expanding our conceptualization of program implementation: lessons from the genealogy of a school-based nutrition program. *Health Education Res.,* 22(5), 737–746.

Durlak, J.A. and DuPre, E.P. (2008). Implementation matters: a review of research on the influence of implementation on program outcomes and the factors affecting implementation. *American Journal of Community Psychology,* 41(3–4), 327–350.

Gibbons, M., Limoges, C., Nowotny, H. and Schwartzman, S. (1994). *The New Production of Knowledge: The Dynamics of Science and Research in Contemporary Societies.* London: Sage.

Goodman, R.M., Mcleroy, K.R., Steckler, A.B. and Hoyle, R.H. (1993). Development of level of institutionalization scales for health promotion programs. *Health Education Quarterly,* 20(2), 161–178.

Greenhalgh, T. (2009). Patient and public involvement in chronic illness: beyond the expert patient. *British Medical Journal,* 338, b49.

Greenhalgh, T., Humphrey, C. and Woodard, F. (2010). *User Involvement in Healthcare.* Oxford: John Wiley and Son.

Greenhalgh, T., Macfarlane, F., Barton-Sweeney, C. and Hope, J. (2011). *The First Modernisation Initiative: A Follow-Up Evaluation.* London: Barts and the London School of Medicine and Dentistry.

Greenhalgh, T., Humphrey, C., Hughes, J., Macfarlane, F., Butler, C. and Pawson, R. (2009). How do you modernize a health service? A realist evaluation of whole-scale transformation in London. *Milbank Quarterly,* 87(2), 391–416.

Greenhalgh, T., Robert, G., Macfarlane, F., Bate, P., Kyriakidou, O. and Peacock, R. (2004). Diffusion of innovations in service organisations: systematic literature review and recommendations for future research. *Milbank Quarterly,* 82, 581–629.

Greenhalgh, T., Humphrey, C., Hughes, J., Macfarlane, F., Butler, C., Connell, P. and Pawson, R. (2008). *The Modernisation Initiative Independent Evaluation: Final Report*. London: University College London. Available from the authors.

Gruen, R.L., Elliott, J.H., Nolan, M.L., Lawton, P.D., Parkhill, A., McLaren, C.J. and Lavis, J.N. (2008). Sustainability science: an integrated approach for health-programme planning. *Lancet*, 372(9649), 1579–1589.

Johnson, K., Hays, C., Center, H. and Daley, C. (2004). Building capacity and sustainable prevention innovations: a sustainability planning model. *Evaluation and Program Planning*, 27, 135–149.

Macfarlane, F., Greenhalgh, T., Humphrey, C., Hughes, J., Butler, C. and Pawson, R. (2011). A new workforce in the making? A case study of strategic human resource management in a whole-system change effort in healthcare. *Journal of Health Organization and Management*, 25(1), 55–72.

Pluye, P., Potvin, L. and Denis, J.-L. (2004). Making health programs last: conceptualizing sustainability. *Evaluation and Program Planning*, 27, 121–133.

Pluye, P., Potvin, L., Denis, J.-L., Pelletier, J. and Mannoni, C. (2005). Program sustainability begins with first events. *Evaluation and Program Planning*, 28, 123–137.

Rashman, L. and Hartley, J. (2002). Leading and learning? Knowledge transfer in the Beacon Council Scheme. *Public Administration*, 80(3), 523–542.

Ritchie, J. and Spencer, L. (1994). Qualitative data analysis for applied policy research. In A. Bryman and R.G. Burgess (eds), *Analysing Qualitative Data*. London: Taylor and Francis, pp. 173–194.

Robert, G., Greenhalgh, T., Macfarlane, F. and Peacock, R. (2010). Adopting and assimilating new non-pharmaceutical technologies into health care: a systematic review. *Journal of Health Services Research and Policy* 009137: 1–8.

Rogers, E.M. (2005). *Diffusion of Innovations*, 4th edn. New York: Free Press.

Rogers, J.L., Johnson, T.R., Warner, P., Thorson, J.A. and Punch, M.R. (2007). Building a sustainable comprehensive Women's Health Program: the Michigan model. *Journal of Womens Health (Larchmt.)*, 16(6), 919–925.

Shediac-Rizkallah, M.C. and Bone, L.R. (1998). Planning for the sustainability of community-based health programs: conceptual frameworks and future directions for research, practice and policy. *Health Education Research*, 13, 87–108.

Sheirer, M.A. (2005). Is sustainability possible? A review and commentary on empirical studies of program sustainability. *American Journal of Evaluation*, 26, 320–347.

Sheirer, M.A., Hartling, G. and Hagerman, D. (2008). Defining sustainability outcomes of health programs: illustrations from an on-line survey. *American Journal of Evaluation*, 31, 335–346.

Stake, R.E. (2005). Qualitative case studies. In N.K. Denzin and Y.S. Lincoln (eds), *The Sage Handbook of Qualitative Research*. London: Sage, pp. 443–466.

PART VII

CONCLUSIONS

37. Innovation in public services: old and new directions for knowledge
Louise Brown and Stephen P. Osborne

The Handbook aims to cover the key areas of the innovation process and to help us to better understand the issues that arise in managing innovation in a public services context. The chapters identify specific issues, such as ethics, stakeholders and risk, which we clearly need to be mindful of when implementing innovation. The examples cover the range of different innovations, including service, process, organisational, policy and system innovation. The Handbook usefully aims to put some of these in context, by providing examples of innovations from specific sectors, such as health and local government. Combined it offers an up-to-date overview of our knowledge about the key issues involved in the process of innovating in a public service context. The book demonstrates through the range of topics covered just how far the knowledge base has developed in recent decades from an early starting point of trying to transfer the learning and lessons from the private sector. Both Miles and Osborne remind us how much of the research was dominated by the manufacturing industry and how in relation to understanding innovation in service organisations, there are some important similarities and lessons – but also differences in the process. The chapter by Hartley nicely summarises how our learning has moved on to a point where the public sector is now building its own knowledge base. It is clear that whilst innovation theory relating to the public sector remains underdeveloped, progress is being made through contributions such as those published here. Although there are distinctive elements about the purpose, role and external environment of public sector organisations the managerial processes are close enough for us to still learn from examples in the private sector.

Whilst the innovation process is often described as creative, sexy and fun, the contributions here also demonstrate how public sector innovation is complex, costly and hard work, often with little visible reward. Colville and Carter, amongst others, highlight how effective innovation and change require skilful ability. The chapters demonstrate how various compass points now exist from which we can learn to move forward. The innovation process, although portrayed at times as somewhat linear, is much more likely to be cyclical, eventful and requiring repetition of certain stages of the process. Even when an idea has moved from invention through development and is heading towards implementation it can be knocked off course, put in reverse or simply stopped in its tracks. We are just beginning to understand more about the factors or barriers that cause these stages to often lurch forward as opposed to run smoothly. The chapter by Roberts and Longley nicely demonstrates how easily an idea can be forced backwards, highlighting the importance of resources to the process. Brown and Katz urge entrepreneurs to 'embrace the mess' and allow 'complexity to exist' (2009, pp. 85–86). This message is one that is repeatedly recounted in the literature relating to tales of innovating in public sector services.

We know that a number of factors impact upon the success of the adoption, diffusion and sustainability of innovations. The chapter by Radnor et al. shows how a number of these factors are interrelated. We know from the private sector literature of the importance of entrepreneurs or champions in driving forward innovative ideas. This is the same for the public sector. However, we also know that champions can become isolated and that, by themselves, their presence may not be enough – they can be left 'holding the baby' as it were. The local government case study described in the chapter by Radnor et al. links two important factors, namely the association between successful entrepreneurs and the ability to take risks. The notion of risk is further explored by Osborne and Brown. The importance of engaging with risk is highlighted amidst a literature that to a large extent has so far ignored the concept. In the same way that Bryson and Crosby argue for a process involving the negotiation of stakeholders, Osborne and Brown strongly advocate that stakeholders adopt a negotiated approach towards managing (not minimising) risk. The importance of stakeholders is identified in a number of chapters (Bryson and Crosby, for example) and the usefulness of stakeholder analysis is strongly felt. Not only does the chapter by Bryson and Crosby highlight the importance of stakeholder analysis, but it also identifies the importance within this analysis of 'direction setting'. This aspect of the innovation process, often referred to as goal setting or the presence of a shared vision, is also known to be significant. Torfing advances our understanding with an analysis of multi-actor collaboration calling upon aspects of governance network theory to help further our understanding of this process.

A number of the chapters consider the functioning of, and role of, different types of networks as sources of inter-organisational learning and knowledge sharing. In themselves they constitute a resource and are home to leaders and champions. In terms of what we currently know about the process, leadership (and its influence) is often identified as a crucial component of a successful innovating process. Mandell and Keast link networks and leadership, arguing for greater understanding of how different types of networks require a different type of leadership. Lewis, Alexander and Considine highlight the importance of the interplay between informal networks, entrepreneurs and policy support in driving innovation forward. Alongside the importance of networks and managing stakeholders almost all studies identify the importance of adequate resources in a successful innovation process. By resources we mean financial resources as well as staff (Baginsky et al. 2011). Organisational conditions such as a stable staff group and a culture of communication through informal networks are acknowledged as positive factors.

One area of the literature that remains underdeveloped and yet critical to the understanding of the innovation process is the part played by evidence. The role of evidence in assisting with the implementation of innovation remains contested. There are examples of innovative models which have been adopted despite a lack of evidence that they 'work' (e.g. Sure Start) and models which have failed to scale up or reach mainstream practice despite evidence of their effectiveness (Nurse Family Partnerships). Despite the vast number of pilots, projects are notoriously poor at detailing the implementation process in such a way that other practitioners or policy makers can take the learning and transfer it to the same or different fields. The chapters by Brian Head and Gill Harvey help to explain this phenomenon and the difficulties associated with developing a robust evidence-base.

A number of chapters are timely and rightfully focus upon and explore the role of service users in the innovation process. Moving beyond the rather simplistic concept of 'consumerism', co-production, user-centred innovation, open innovation, citizen involvement and co-creation all refer to the interaction between organisations and the users of their services – albeit with different emphases. Based upon the assumption that it will lead to an improvement or greater satisfaction of services the literature leaves a number of unanswered questions at this time, such as: how best to involve service users, who to involve, the degree of involvement that is appropriate and the form this should take. We know that policy fit leading to policy support is essential in innovating and therefore this must present a particular challenge to citizen-led projects that are not based within existing organisations. This collection of chapters suggests that such activity will need to be facilitated, perhaps through 'open space' initiatives – with ICT playing a potentially central role. This theme is picked up further in the collection of chapters on this theme.

Whilst the literature on diffusion is growing and is drawn from a range of disciplines, such as health and development studies, it remains very varied, from adequate sanitation facilities (Smits et al. 2005) to mental health services in low resource countries (Patel et al. 2009). It is probably the stage of the innovation process or journey that we know least about in terms of different contexts and fields. With an emphasis still upon patents as the mechanism for scaling up innovations, we cannot say which other mechanisms work best for which types of innovation in particular contexts. The most documented processes tend to examine top-down mechanisms, such as experimentation leading to subsidiary projects or a mandate through legislation. Further work is required to understand the role that accreditation or licensing can play in helping to roll out good ideas. Work is emerging in this arena to develop more systematic management models that can assist with scaling up; for example, the use of Normalisation Process Theory (Murray et al. 2010) and the AIDED Model based upon a systematic review of the literature of health innovation in low income countries (Yale Global Health Leadership Institute 2011). However, although offering great potential they remain relatively untested at this stage.

It is fair to say that of the range of public services this book aims to cover, the field that has attempted to tackle the innovation process most has been health. Particularly in the UK, a raft of government initiatives has been established to help facilitate and support the development and adoption of innovative ideas (products and services). Compared with other areas, a great deal of attention has been paid to the role that procurement can play in influencing innovation in this field. The chapter by Edler and Uyarra adds to the growing body of literature on this topic. It is clear that public procurement offers great potential to support the initiation and subsequent development and diffusion of innovation. Amidst the climate of austerity in public services, where commissioning from a range of organisations, including the third sector, is of growing importance, this could represent a significant area for potential learning in terms of facilitating innovation. Thus it is of growing importance that we better understand the relationship between third sector organisations and innovation. As indicated in the chapter by Osborne et al., this relationship is changing and whilst once argued as the defining feature of the voluntary and non-profit sector, innovation is now being squeezed from there and is no longer seen as the preserve of non-statutory organisations. The picture is becoming more complicated as services are now being delivered through a complex network of public, private and third sector organisations (highlighted in the chapter by Windrum). Such relationships are again characterised by key individuals and trust.

To conclude, this Handbook is testament to the fact that the public sector, with its range of organisations, actors, stakeholders and users, is more innovative than its reputation for being slow unwieldy, bureaucratic and lacking in R&D capacity would have us believe. In response to continuous pressure from the top down to be creative, innovative and to do more for less, the public sector has responded with a positive, if somewhat uncoordinated approach, across all sectors. As Torfing points out in his chapter, 'the solution of the increasing numbers of "wicked problems", which cannot be solved by standard solutions or by spending more money, calls for innovative solutions'. What we know so far is that the public sector can initiate and generate ideas which it is able to translate into innovative models, structures, products or services. In so doing the process of innovating, involving a series of stages, is at times more cyclical than linear, messy and complicated. Certain factors play an important part in helping to facilitate and support innovations to move through the stages. These include adequate resources, the presence of champions, a clear vision or set of goals, strong leadership and a well-managed network of stakeholders to collaborate with and help manage the risks. Whilst these factors appear to be significant, our detailed knowledge as to how they operate, interact or impact upon the process in relation to different types of innovation or different contexts remains weak. Hence, despite the burgeoning literature on innovation in public services, there remain significant gaps in our knowledge, theory and subsequent skill-set. In particular these gaps, which constitute a research agenda for the future, include amongst others the role that evidence plays in the process of adoption and diffusion, the appropriate type and level of service user involvement, and effective mechanisms for diffusion and scaling up. As McDonald et al. (2006, p. 16) state: we 'do not expect that cookie-cutter solutions will be sufficient to adequately address the challenges posed by various, dynamic environments with unique and changing target populations'. Hence, as we continue to research and understand the life-cycle of different innovations in different areas of public service, the Handbook should be seen as placing a marker in the sand as to the journey travelled so far and signposts for the future.

REFERENCES

Baginsky, M., Teague, C., Emsley, L., Price, C., Sames, K. and Truong, Y. (2011). *A Summative Report on the Qualitative Evaluation on the Eleven Remodelling Social Work Pilots 2008–2011*. London: Children's Workforce Development Council.

Brown, T. and Katz, T. (2009). *Change by Design: How Design Thinking Transforms Organizations and Inspires Innovation*. New York: Harper Collins.

McDonald, S.K., Keesler, V.A., Kauffman, N.J. and Schneider, B. (2006). Scaling-up exemplary interventions. *Educational Researcher*, 35, 15–24.

Murray, E., Treweek, S., Pope, C., MacFarlane, A., Ballini, L., Dowrick, C., Finch, T., Kennedy, A., Mair, F., O'Donnell, C., Nio ONg, B., Rapley, T. and Rogers, A. (2010). Normalisation process theory: a framework for developing, evaluating and implementing complex interventions. *BMC Medicine*, 8, 63–73.

Patel, V., Singh Goel, D. and Desai, R. (2009). Scaling up services for mental and neurological disorders in low resource settings. *International Health*, 1, 37–44.

Smits, S., Fonseca, C. and Pels, J. (2005). *Proceedings of the Symposium on Learning Alliances for Scaling-Up Innovative Approaches in the Water and Sanitation Sector Held in Delft, Netherlands, June 2005*. The Netherlands: IRC International Water and Sanitation Centre.

Yale Global Health Leadership Institute (2011). *Dissemination, Diffusion, and Scale Up of Family Health Innovations in Low-Income Countries*. Bill and Melinda Gates Foundation, Foundation's Family Health Division. Global Health Leadership Institute, New Haven, CT 06510.

Index

Abernathy, W.J. 74
accountability
  ethics of innovation, and 243
  innovation implementation 53–4
  inter-organisational innovation, in 324
  public sector entrepreneurship, and 163
  risk management, and 158
Ackermann, F. 124–7, 132
adoption, of innovation *see* diffusion
African American Men Project, Minnesota
  135–6
Aiken, M. 499, 501, 507
Albury, D. 4
Alexander, J. 520
Alford, R. 499, 501, 507
Alliance for Innovation 206
Allison, G. 45–6, 61
ancillary innovation 340, 446, 498, 507
Andrews, R. 317, 522
Apple 244
architectural innovation 5
Arnstein, S.A. 377
artisanal innovation model 83–4
Ashworth, R. 108, 110, 112
asylum seekers, innovation through co-
    production case study
  challenges 382–3
  co-management and co-governenace 385–7
  enhanced co-production 383–5
  networks, role of 385
  participative co-production 382–3
  regulatory background 381–2
  service customization 384
  study method 382
  third sector organisations, role of 377–8,
    383–4, 386–7
Australia
  collaborative network model case study 355–6
  policy networks case study (Kilbourne)
    362–70
  public sector change management strategies
    113–15
Austria
  innovation networks case study 409–12

Backoff, R.W. 110, 132–3
Bailey, M. 522
Baird, L.S. 163

Baldock, J. 6
Ball, R. 522
Bardach, E. 319–20
Barras, R. 77
Barzelay, M. 30
bases of power interest diagrams 125–7
Bason, C. 47, 447
Baumol, W. 38, 324
Beer, S. 321
Behn, R. 37, 324
benchmarking 18
Beresford, P. 447
Berger, P.L. 377–8
Berry, F.S. 210–11, 218
Bertschneider, S. 499, 502–3
Bessant, J. 92–3, 97, 421
Better Regulation Executive (UK) 114–15
Bevir, M. 311–12
Bhatti, Y. 499, 505
Bingham, L. 111
Bingham, R. 499, 501, 508
Birkinshaw, J.M. 103–4
Bisset, S. 553
Bone, L.R. 544–5
Borins, S. 6, 49, 307, 390
bottom-up innovation
  attention, management of 188
  challenges 176, 190
  collective entrepreneurship, role in 186, 189
  conditions necessary for 185–7
  conflict and resistance, management of
    188–90
  ideas champions 186
  ideas management 186–8
  incubators of innovation, and 186–7
  models 37
  network management 189–90
  organisational interface, management of 189
  problem-solvers, and 185–6
  retrenchment 190
  start-up resources, importance of 186
  studies, generally 176
  see also Lighthouse (US military innovation)
    case study
Bouckaert, G. 16, 30–31
bounded rationality
  deliberative rationality 21–2, 26
  New Public Administration, and 20–25